LIFE IN EARLY
MEDIEVAL WALES

The period *c*. AD 300–1050, spanning the collapse of Roman rule to the coming of the Normans, was formative in the development of Wales. *Life in Early Medieval Wales* considers how people lived in late Roman and early medieval Wales, and how their lives and communities changed over the course of this period. It uses a multidisciplinary approach, focusing on the growing body of archaeological evidence set alongside the early medieval written sources together with place names and personal names. It begins by analysing earlier research and the range of sources, the significance of the environment and climate change, and ways of calculating time. Discussion of the fourth, fifth, and sixth centuries focuses on the disintegration of the Roman market economy, fragmentation of power, and the emergence of new kingdoms and elites alongside evidence for changing identities, as well as important threads of continuity, notably Latin literacy, Christianity, and the continuation of small-scale farming communities. Early medieval Wales was an entirely rural society. Analysis of the settlement archaeology includes key sites such as hillforts, including Dinas Powys, the royal crannog at Llangorse, and the Viking Age and earlier estate centre at Llanbedrgoch, alongside the development, from the seventh century onwards, of new farming and other rural settlements. Consideration is given to changes in the mixed farming economy reflecting climate deterioration and a need for food security, as well as craftworking and the roles of exchange, display, and trade reflecting changing outside contacts. At the same time cemeteries and inscribed stones, stone sculpture and early church sites chart the course of conversion to Christianity, the rise of monasticism, and the increasing power of the Church. Finally, discussion of power and authority analyses emerging evidence for sites of assembly, the rise of Mercia, and increasing English infiltration, together with the significance of Offa's and Wat's Dykes, and the Viking impact. Throughout, the evidence is placed within a wider context, enabling comparison with other parts of Britain and Ireland and, where appropriate, with other parts of Europe to see broader trends, including the impacts of climate, and economic and religious change.

MEDIEVAL HISTORY
AND ARCHAEOLOGY

General Editors

John Blair   Helena Hamerow

The volumes in this series bring together archaeological, historical, and visual methods to offer new approaches to aspects of medieval society, economy, and material culture. The series seeks to present and interpret archaeological evidence in ways readily accessible to historians, while providing a historical perspective and context for the material culture of the period.

Life in Early Medieval Wales

NANCY EDWARDS

OXFORD
UNIVERSITY PRESS

Great Clarendon Street, Oxford, OX2 6DP,
United Kingdom

Oxford University Press is a department of the University of Oxford.
It furthers the University's objective of excellence in research, scholarship,
and education by publishing worldwide. Oxford is a registered trade mark of
Oxford University Press in the UK and in certain other countries

© Nancy Edwards 2023

The moral rights of the author have been asserted

All rights reserved. No part of this publication may be reproduced, stored in
a retrieval system, or transmitted, in any form or by any means, without the
prior permission in writing of Oxford University Press, or as expressly permitted
by law, by licence or under terms agreed with the appropriate reprographics
rights organization. Enquiries concerning reproduction outside the scope of the
above should be sent to the Rights Department, Oxford University Press, at the
address above

You must not circulate this work in any other form
and you must impose this same condition on any acquirer

Published in the United States of America by Oxford University Press
198 Madison Avenue, New York, NY 10016, United States of America

British Library Cataloguing in Publication Data
Data available

Library of Congress Control Number: 2023900660

ISBN 978–0–19–873321–8

DOI: 10.1093/oso/9780198733218.001.0001

Printed and bound by
CPI Group (UK) Ltd, Croydon, CR0 4YY

Links to third party websites are provided by Oxford in good faith and
for information only. Oxford disclaims any responsibility for the materials
contained in any third party website referenced in this work.

LEVERHULME

TRUST ─────────

Research for and the writing of this book was funded by the award of
a Leverhulme Trust Major Research Fellowship.

I Iestyn

PREFACE AND ACKNOWLEDGEMENTS

I have long wanted to write a book about early medieval Wales. My interest was sparked by my move to Wales in 1979 and further encouraged by Wendy Davies, whose book *Wales in the Early Middle Ages* (1982) used archaeological evidence alongside the written sources and defined the subject for a generation. It also made it possible for me to teach the archaeology of early medieval Wales within a wider context to many cohorts of students who helped me to think through the evidence and ask the right questions. At the same time the meetings of the Early Medieval Wales Archaeology Research Group with their opportunities to hear about new research and the help and friendship of those, too many to name, who have attended over the years have been central to the development of the subject and the evolution of my ideas. It is hoped that this book will not only be of interest to a wide readership but will also encourage further research and archaeological excavation in the future.

The opportunity to write this book was made possible by the Leverhulme Trust, who generously granted me a Major Research Fellowship (2015–18) for which I am immensely grateful. This gave me the time and space to devote to the project, including delving into the 'grey literature' which was not always easy to come by. I would also like to thank Professor Robin Fleming at Boston College for welcoming me as a Visiting Scholar during my stay in Cambridge, Massachusetts, in Spring 2017 and Professor Catherine McKenna, Department of Celtic Languages and Literatures at Harvard University, for facilitating my application as an Associate, giving me access to study space and the amazing resources of the Widener Library. I also greatly benefited from the opportunity to attend an event on early medieval climate change and the Justinian plague organized by Professor Michael McCormick. Thanks also to the staff of the Sackler and Bodleian Libraries, University of Oxford, where I conducted the early stages of my research.

Research for this book would not have been possible without the help of many organizations and individuals. The Historic Environment Record staff of the four Welsh Archaeological Trusts have been unfailingly helpful in providing lists of early medieval sites, copies of grey-literature reports, and answering many other queries. I would also particularly like to thank Andrew Davidson, Jane Kenney, and Dave Hopewell of Gwynedd Archaeological Trust, who made it possible for me to take students to excavate at Rhuddgaer, helping me to think about settlement change at first hand. I am also very grateful to Ken Murphy and Marion Shiner of Dyfed Archaeological Trust, who facilitated my visits to the excavations at St Patrick's Chapel and provided me with a variety of other information. Other archaeological units, including Cotswold Archaeology and Brython Archaeology, have also provided material. It should be noted that throughout the book I have used the pre-1974

viii PREFACE AND ACKNOWLEDGEMENTS

historic counties rather than the present unitary authorities. There are two reasons for this. First, the historic counties, which were in use for over 400 years, are relatively consistent in size, giving a much better idea of location. Second, when I began research for this book, there were plans afoot for Welsh Government to change the local authority structure for the third time since 1974, though this has not been carried through.

At Amgueddfa Cymru–National Museum Wales I would like to thank the staff of Archaeology and Numismatics, especially Mark Redknap, Evan Chapman, Sian Isles, Mark Lodwick (Portable Antiquities Scheme), and Jodie Deacon. Steve Burrow also kindly gave me access to his list of radiocarbon dates from Wales. All radiocarbon dates in the book are shown at 2 sigma (95 per cent probability) and have been rounded outwards to the beginning or end of the decade in accordance with Mook 1986. Where possible I have recalibrated radiocarbon dates using Ox-cal. 4.3. Richard Brewer kindly discussed his excavations at Caerwent with me, and Edward Besley shared his expertise on numismatics. I would also like to thank Emma Williams (Swansea Museum) and Harriet Eaton (Neath Port Talbot, Libraries and Museums) for facilitating my visits to their early medieval collections, and Peter Reavill, the Portable Antiquities Scheme, Finds Liaison Officer for Shropshire and Herefordshire.

There are many others who have helped in specific ways. I would like to thank Gary Robinson (Bangor University) and Howard Williams (University of Chester) for helping me to organize the excavations at the Pillar of Eliseg which were instrumental in making me think about early medieval places of assembly. I am also grateful to Wendy Carruthers for sharing her expertise in plant and charred cereal remains, Tim Young for discussing the evidence of archaeometallurgy, especially ironworking, Kate Waddington for discussing various aspects of the settlement archaeology of Gwynedd with me, Rachel Pope for discussing the functions of Late Prehistoric hillforts, Peter Guest for giving me access to grey-literature reports of his excavations at Caerleon, Niall Sharples and Oliver Davis for those relating to Caerau, and David Austin for that relating to Carew. Thanks too to Thomas Charles-Edwards for discussing various written sources and providing hospitality on visits to Oxford. I would also like to thank Alan Lane, Andy Seaman, Ewan Campbell, Rhiannon Comeau, Tudur Davies, Julie Edwards, Mark Hall, Katie Hemer, and Heather James for help in various ways and for responding to my many queries.

This book has taken longer to write than it should have done. My University of Wales O'Donnell lecture in 2017 (Edwards 2017b) provided the foundations for Chapter 4, and the J. E. Lloyd Memorial Lecture at Bangor University in 2018 was based on the second half of Chapter 2. Later chapters were written after the outbreak of the Covid-19 pandemic early in 2020, and I am grateful to the staff of Bangor University library for their efficient operation of a 'click and collect' system once restrictions eased and to Sarah Semple, who facilitated my appointment as an Honorary

Professor at the University of Durham, greatly increasing my access to electronic resources.

I am particularly grateful to Jackie Chadwick (J Chadwick Illustrator Ltd), who has drawn all the maps and plans for this book, unless otherwise indicated. Her skill in transforming my often rough-and-ready instructions into the finished product is much appreciated as well as her patience in waiting for their final publication. Thanks also to Charles Green and Penny Icke of the Royal Commission on the Ancient and Historical Monuments of Wales for illustrations and help with sourcing pictures. I am indebted to Jeff Davies for reading and commenting on an earlier draft of Chapter 3 and also to the series editors, John Blair and Helena Hamerow, and the anonymous referee for their helpful comments on the final draft of the book. Finally, as ever, I am immensely grateful to Huw Pryce, who has discussed so many aspects of this book with me and read and commented on the entire text.

Nancy Edwards

September 2022

CONTENTS

List of Illustrations   xiii

1. Rediscovering the Early Medieval Past in Wales:
   Approaches and Sources   1
   Antiquarians and the Archaeology of Early Medieval Wales   3
   The Later Nineteenth and First Half of the Twentieth Centuries   7
   Modern Approaches   13
   Approaching the Written Sources   20

2. Space and Time   35
   Land and Sea   35
   Climate Change and its Impact   46
   Reconstructing the Early Medieval Landscape   49
   Time and Memory   53

3. Continuity and Collapse   64
   Problems with Dating and Chronology   66
   From Roman to Post-Roman Wales: A Regional View   69
   Crossing the Divide   96

4. The Legacy of Rome, Irish Settlement, and Changing Identities   105
   The Roman Legacy and its Reinvention   105
   Inscribed Memorial Stones   114
   Other Evidence for Irish Settlement and its Impact   129
   Conclusion   132

5. Hearth and Home   134
   In Search of Settlements   134
   Hillforts, Promontory Forts, and Related High-Status Sites   142
   Other High-Status Settlements   152
   Farmsteads   159
   Buildings and the Use of Space   172
   Conclusion   179

6. Food, Farming, and the Agricultural Economy   183
   The Farming Landscape: Fields and Estates   184
   Cereals and Other Crops   192
   Animal Husbandry   204
   Hunting, Fishing, and Gathering   208
   Diet and Health   213
   Conclusion   217

xii CONTENTS

7.	Craft, Display, and Trade	221
	Materials, Craftworking, and Technology	222
	Display, Identity, Social Interaction, and Belonging	239
	Trade and Exchange	250
	Conclusion	265
8.	Christianity: Identifying the Evidence	269
	Church Buildings	271
	Inscribed Stones and Stone Sculpture	273
	Burials and Cemeteries	278
	Enclosures	282
	Holy Wells and Trees	284
	Relics, Reliquaries, and Other Christian Metalwork	285
	Written Sources	286
	Place Names and Church Dedications	287
	Conclusion	289
9.	Conversion, Commemoration, and Burial	290
	Pre-Christian Religions	290
	The Origins of Christianity	294
	Commemoration	296
	Burial	302
	Conclusion	310
10.	Christian Sites and Christian Landscapes	313
	Major Monasteries, Mother Churches, and *Clasau*	313
	Island Monasteries, Hermitages, and Female Religious Sites	326
	Lesser Churches, Chapels, and Cemeteries	330
	Christianity and the Wider Landscape	339
	Conclusion	345
11.	Ritual and Belief	349
	Saints' Cults, Relics, and Pilgrimage	350
	Death and Commemoration	364
	Conclusion	373
12.	Power and Authority	374
	Assembly Sites and Other Meeting Places	378
	Building Borders and Frontiers: Changing Relations with Anglo-Saxon England	387
	The Viking Impact	398
13.	Conclusion	412

References	429
Index	491

LIST OF ILLUSTRATIONS

1.1.	The inscribed stone at Llangadwaladr, Anglesey, commemorating King Catamanus (Cadfan) of Gwynedd.	5
1.2.	Llangorse crannog, Breconshire, excavated in 1869.	11
1.3.	The Lichfield Gospels, the end of St Matthew's Gospel.	26
1.4.	The opening page of the Martyrology in the Psalter of Rhygyfarch.	31
2.1.	Wales: physical features.	36
2.2.	Wales, showing the locations of pre-Roman peoples, early medieval kingdoms, and other regions.	39
2.3.	Latin-inscribed stone commemorating Dervacus son of Iustus standing beside the Roman road, Ystradfellte, Breconshire.	45
2.4.	Llangynfelyn trackway, Cors Fochno, Cardiganshire.	46
2.5.	Wentlooge Level, Monmouthshire, showing a reconstruction of the evolution of the landscape between the Roman period and the eleventh century.	52
2.6.	Sundial, Clynnog Fawr, Caernarfonshire.	59
3.1.	Major events noted in the written sources relevant to the ending of Roman control in Britain.	66
3.2.	Later Roman Wales: principal fourth-century sites and others mentioned in the text.	70
3.3.	The walls of the *civitas* capital at Caerwent, with an additional mid-fourth-century bastion.	73
3.4.	Roman-period rural settlements: comparative plans.	77
3.5.	Late finds from the auxiliary fort at Caernarfon.	86
4.1.	The auxiliary fort at Caernarfon, showing its spatial relationship.	106
4.2.	The Roman legionary fortress of Caerleon and the Roman town of Caerwent, with later sites and other features.	108
4.3.	Distribution of fifth- to seventh-century roman-letter- and ogham-inscribed stones.	115
4.4.	Fifth- and sixth-century roman-letter and ogham inscriptions.	119
4.5.	Later sixth-century, Latin-inscribed stone from Margam Mountain.	121
5.1.	Early medieval settlement sites and some other possible sites.	136
5.2.	Glanfred, aerial photograph.	138
5.3.	The twin summits of Degannwy.	143
5.4.	Comparative plans of hillforts and promontory forts.	145
5.5.	Llanbedrgoch, plan of the enclosed settlement.	153
5.6.	Llangorse crannog.	156
5.7.	Farmsteads with evidence of early medieval occupation.	162
5.8.	Geophysical survey of the open settlement at Rhuddgaer, Anglesey.	164
5.9.	Excavated remains of an open settlement at South Hook.	167
5.10.	Building plans.	168
5.11.	Diagram of the promontory fort at Dinas Powys, showing internal use of space.	178

xiv LIST OF ILLUSTRATIONS

6.1.	Early medieval estates donated to the Church recorded in charters in the Book of Llandaf: Llan-gors and Penally.	191
6.2.	Figure-of-eight-shaped corn-dryer of fifth- or sixth-century date, Parc Cybi.	199
6.3.	Later seventh- or eighth-century fish-trap, Oldbury flats.	211
7.1.	Bone and antler combs.	227
7.2.	South Hook, iron-smelting workshop.	229
7.3.	Dinas Powys, fine-metalworking evidence.	232
7.4.	Portrait of an armed man on the cross-slab at Llandyfaelog Fach.	240
7.5.	Parts of the fragmentary Llangorse embroidered garment.	241
7.6.	Penannular brooches.	242
7.7.	Sites with imported pottery, glass, and other exotic finds in Wales and the borders, mid-fifth to early eighth centuries.	253
7.8.	Discoveries of coins and silver/coin hoards in Wales dating from the late seventh to mid-eleventh centuries.	256
7.9.	Balance weights from Llanbedrgoch.	259
7.10.	The Llandwrog Hoard.	260
7.11.	The Hywel Dda penny.	262
8.1.	Early medieval ecclesiastical sites.	270
8.2.	Distribution of early medieval cross-carved stones and stone sculpture.	274
8.3.	Distribution of early medieval cemetery sites.	279
8.4.	Llanmerewig Church, with its curvilinear embanked enclosure.	283
9.1.	Votive offerings from Llys Awel, near Pen-y-Corddyn Mawr hillfort.	291
9.2.	Rhuddgaer lead coffin.	297
9.3.	The Llantrisant inscribed stone.	300
9.4.	Early medieval 'undeveloped' cemeteries.	305
10.1.	Llandough, showing the site of the modern church, the early medieval cemetery, and the Roman villa, with other burials nearby.	317
10.2.	Bangor, showing the Cathedral and associated buildings, the probable line of the monastic enclosure, and other early medieval remains.	318
10.3.	St Patrick's Chapel, showing the eleventh- or twelfth-century building, with the rectangular burial enclosure beneath.	334
10.4.	St Patrick's Chapel, showing the eighth-century *leacht* during excavation in 2021.	334
10.5.	Capel Maelog, showing evidence for the earlier settlement, the cemetery, the enclosure, and the late twelfth- or early thirteenth-century chapel.	336
11.1.	Llaniestyn, early medieval cemetery and mortuary enclosure, and Pennant Melangell Church, with its eastern apse and the grave later associated with St Melangell.	354
11.2.	The reliquary known as *Arch Gwenfrewi*, recorded by Edward Lhuyd at Gwytherin.	357
11.3.	An iron bell from Llangenau and a copper-alloy bell from Llangwnnadl.	359
11.4.	Tywyn cross-carved stone, with commemorative inscriptions in Old Welsh.	371
11.5.	Disc-headed cross, Margam.	372

12.1.	The Pillar of Eliseg.	381
12.2.	*Maen Achwyfan,* with the figure of an armed warrior on the cross-shaft.	383
12.3.	The polyfocal landscape of Bayvil in the *cantref* of Cemais.	385
12.4.	Offa's Dyke from the air.	388
12.5.	Map showing Offa's and Wat's Dykes with other short dykes.	390
12.6.	Evidence for the Viking impact on north-west Wales.	400
12.7.	Evidence for Viking settlements in the vicinity of the Dee and Mersey estuaries.	404
12.8.	Evidence for the Viking impact on south Wales.	406

ONE

Rediscovering the Early Medieval Past in Wales: Approaches and Sources

How did people live in early medieval Wales and how did their lives change over time? The period *c.* AD 300–1050, spanning the collapse of Roman rule to the coming of the Normans, was formative in the development of Wales as an entity. At the end of the Roman period the colonial infrastructure based on military occupation, taxation, and a monetized market economy with mass-produced goods disintegrated and authority fragmented. Nevertheless, elements of Roman culture, including Latin literacy and Christianity, survived, and Latin- and ogham-inscribed stones testify to the rise of new elites, amongst them settlers from Ireland, and the establishment of small kingdoms. Although Roman settlements, such as forts, were largely abandoned, there is also increasing evidence for the continuation of long-established native ways of living. Hillforts and other high-status sites identifiable through craftworking and luxury imports became the homes of elites, who largely controlled the dissemination of wealth. However, the post-Roman centuries were also a period of climate deterioration leading to population decline and the need for agricultural adaptation. At the same time cemeteries and inscribed stones, later stone sculpture, and early church sites chart the course of conversion to Christianity, the rise of monasticism, and the increasing power of the Church. From the later seventh century onwards changes in both elite and farming settlements as well as the growing visibility of estates suggest societal change with indications of an expanding agricultural economy. However, the increasing wealth and power of Anglo-Saxon kingdoms, particularly Mercia, led to the loss of British lands to the east, and by the end of the eighth century the borders of Wales were being defined by the construction of Offa's Dyke. Nevertheless, Anglo-Saxon pressure continued, especially in the north-east, and from the mid-ninth century onwards limited Hiberno-Scandinavian settlement was also taking place. Whilst raiding was undoubtedly destructive, external contacts also brought new opportunities for wider international trade and limited access to silver bullion and occasionally coin as means of exchange. Nonetheless, the economy remained underdeveloped compared with that of Ireland, England, and the Continent. At the same time continuing internal conflict is apparent and some kingdoms, notably Gwynedd in the north-west,

Life in Early Medieval Wales. Nancy Edwards, Oxford University Press. © Nancy Edwards 2023.
DOI: 10.1093/oso/9780198733218.003.0001

became more powerful, with the consequent need for mechanisms of control facilitated, for example, by places of assembly. Indeed, shortly before the advent of the Norman incursions, Wales was briefly united under the rulership of Gruffudd ap Llywelyn of Gwynedd.

Even though the early Middle Ages are seen as seminal in the evolution of Wales and the Welsh, there has been comparatively little analysis of the spectrum of archaeological evidence, and earlier studies have largely focused on a historical perspective.[1] Apart from a brief period of attention in the 1960s and 1970s in the context of broader archaeological and historical studies of western and northern Britain, early medieval Wales has too often been an object of neglect. As far as the archaeology is concerned, this has arisen for a variety of reasons. The most important is the comparative lack of wealth in the material record and difficulties in locating early medieval sites in Wales, particularly in comparison with the archaeology of southern and eastern Anglo-Saxon England. This has tended to deflect attention elsewhere, even though the resource and the ways in which we can interrogate it continue to expand. Indeed, in Wales itself the focus has often been on the more visible remains from prehistory, the Roman period, and the later Middle Ages. More generally, the virtual purging by archaeologists of the Celts from the Iron Age and the ongoing debate about the origins of Celtic languages[2] may have served to shift attention away from western and northern Britain in the early Middle Ages, in parts of which such languages continue to be spoken to this day. At the same time, the rise of World Archaeology as part of a broader global turn in the humanities, prompted by an emphasis on widespread developments and interconnections, may lead to the perception that the early medieval archaeology of Wales is at best regional, at worst an adjunct to that of Anglo-Saxon England, rather than part of a wider and more diverse Britain.[3]

The emphasis here is on using the archaeological evidence to try and reconstruct how people lived in the early Middle Ages in the land that became Wales, thereby enabling a better understanding of the factors that drove societal change over a period of more than seven hundred years. But although analysis of the material evidence has shaped my discussion, this is used as part of a multidisciplinary approach that also considers aspects of the written record and, where appropriate, linguistic evidence in the form of place names and personal names. By so doing, the aim is to enhance our understanding of a period for which the sources, archaeological and written, are frequently very patchy and challenging to interpret. Although historical figures, principally rulers such as Catamanus (Cadfan) of Gwynedd or Hywel Dda

---

[1] The most important studies focusing on early medieval Wales are Lloyd 1911, Davies, W. 1982a, and Charles-Edwards 2013. All three, but particularly Davies, include some analysis of archaeological evidence. The only primarily archaeological general study is Arnold and Davies 2000.

[2] For a key discussion of the 'Celtic' debate from an archaeological perspective, see Collis 2003, and, on linguistic research, see Sims-Williams 2020.

[3] For recent consideration of Wales within a wider British context, see Fleming, R. 2010; Carver 2019.

(Hywel 'the Good'), but also saints such as David, whose life has come down to us in the form of much later hagiography, are mentioned, my principal concern is with how the archaeological record and other sources can cast light on society more generally, ordinary people as well as the elite. It is also the intention as far as possible to place the evidence within a wider context, enabling comparison with other parts of Britain and Ireland and, where appropriate, with other parts of Europe in order to see broader trends, including the impacts of climatic, economic, and religious change.

This introductory chapter has two objectives. The first, focusing primarily on the material evidence, is to examine both earlier and more modern approaches to the study of the early medieval past in Wales. My aim is to introduce the evidence, the ways it has been studied, and the impact of these on how our understanding of it has developed over time. Discussion begins with antiquarian notices of Offa's Dyke and the recording of inscribed stones and stone sculpture beginning in the sixteenth century, subjects that have continued to be major objects of interest until the present day. It ends with consideration of the growing archaeological resource resulting from both modern research and developer-led investigations and the increasing impact of scientific and other archaeological techniques at our disposal allowing a much broader and chronologically better-defined interpretation of the evidence to emerge. The second aim is to introduce the written sources concerned with early medieval Wales that are considered alongside the archaeological evidence elsewhere in this book. This includes an assessment of what has survived, before a chronological discussion of the main genres and some of the difficulties associated with using them. I also include consideration of some sources written beyond Wales that have relevant material and a number of later medieval sources that, if judiciously used, can shed some light on the early Middle Ages. I end with a brief assessment of research on place names.

ANTIQUARIANS AND THE ARCHAEOLOGY OF EARLY MEDIEVAL WALES

That Offa's Dyke was the first early medieval monument in Wales to receive antiquarian attention is hardly surprising given its early mention in Asser's *Life of King Alfred*[4] and the scale of the earthworks that still survive today. The earliest antiquarian description is by John Leland (*c.*1503–52), who visited Wales in the late 1530s and had clearly observed stretches of the dyke, which he termed a *limes* or fortified boundary.[5] A century later his work undoubtedly influenced the polymath John Aubrey (1626–97),

---

[4] Stevenson 1959, 12, ch. 14; Keynes and Lapidge 1983, 71.
[5] Toulmin Smith 1906, viii–ix, 40; Ray and Bapty 2016, 57–8.

who had also seen the dyke and later wrote a short account of it in his unpublished *Monumenta Britannica*.[6]

From the later sixteenth until well into the twentieth century, however, the study of the material remains of early medieval Wales was concentrated on the recording of stone monuments. These comprise memorial stones with commemorative Latin inscriptions and sometimes inscriptions in Primitive or Old Irish oghams, broadly datable between the fifth and mid-seventh centuries, and a range of Christian sculpture, notably large free-standing crosses with complex ornament and occasionally iconography as well as sometimes Latin inscriptions mainly datable to between the ninth and eleventh centuries. There are two main reasons for this. Firstly, the fact that these were substantial stone monuments gave them durability and meant that, when they were first noted, many still survived in the landscape or were rediscovered during nineteenth-century church restorations. Secondly, those with inscriptions drew the attention of those seeking a way to understand their own national history, and their recording began as a small part of a much wider interest in the humanist recovery of the past centred in Italy, which was largely focused on classical remains, including sculpture and inscriptions.[7] In Britain, however, it was also precipitated by the Reformation and dissolution of the monasteries, which placed many of these monuments in danger, a threat which increased during the mid-seventeenth century as a result of the destruction of the Civil War and subsequent neglect. This focused antiquarian efforts on recording what remained before even more was lost.[8]

The earliest references to the inscribed stones and stone crosses were made by both antiquaries with an interest in Wales who were based in London and by members of the local gentry. For example, William Camden (1551–1623),[9] the famous chorographer and author of *Britannia*, visited Wales in 1590 and noted the Latin inscription on the stone at Clocaenog, Denbighshire,[10] while George Owen of Henllys in north Pembrokeshire (*c*.1552–1613) was the first to mention the cross at Nevern.[11] However, the earliest major advances in our knowledge and understanding of these monuments were made a century later by the Welsh antiquary, linguist, and natural scientist Edward Lhuyd (*c*.1660–1709), who became the second keeper of the Ashmolean Museum in Oxford.[12] He knew Aubrey and became part of an intellectual circle at the vanguard of Anglo-Saxon studies,[13] as a result of which he contributed the important Welsh additions to the new edition of Camden's *Britannia* published

---

[6] Scurr 2015, 184; Fowles and Legg 1980–2, iii, 884–5; Ray and Bapty 2016, 58.

[7] Weiss 1969, which includes discussion of the study of classical inscriptions, 145–66; Barkan 1999, 17–18, 26–8; for the roots of nationalist history in the Renaissance, see Díaz-Andreu 2007, 31–4.

[8] Parry 1995, 14.   [9] Herendeen 2007.

[10] Camden 1594, 519; Edwards 2013, 19, no. D1; for further early records of inscribed stones, see Redknap and Lewis 2007, 7.

[11] Charles 1948, 270; Edwards 2007a, 12, no. P73; for further early records of sculpture, see Edwards 2013, 19.

[12] Roberts 2022.   [13] Edwards 2007b, 168.

Fig. 1.1. The inscribed stone at Llangadwaladr, Anglesey, commemorating King Catamanus (Cadfan) of Gwynedd (d. c.625), first recorded by Edward Lhuyd in 1699 (Crown copyright: Royal Commission on the Ancient and Historical Monuments of Wales).

in 1695.[14] Lhuyd carried out an immense amount of fieldwork in Wales and subsequently in other Celtic-speaking countries as well as having a wide range of correspondents. This enabled him to record a considerable number of archaeological sites and monuments of all periods, including nearly ninety early medieval inscribed and sculptured stones in Wales, which he often noted with remarkable accuracy.[15] Equally, as a Welsh speaker, he developed a pioneering interest in Celtic philology, and the early medieval inscriptions with their British and Irish names were therefore clearly of interest to him. He recognized, for example, that the inscribed stone at Llangadwaladr, Anglesey, commemorating 'Catamanus, wisest and most illustrious of all kings' could be identified as King Cadfan of Gwynedd, who had died c.625 (Fig. 1.1).[16]

During the later eighteenth and early nineteenth centuries at the height of European Romanticism,[17] Wales became a fashionable destination for travellers seeking to

---

[14] Camden 1695, cols 583–678, with Lhuyd's additions at the end of each county; Parry 1995, 347–54; Edwards 2007b, 180–1.

[15] Edwards 2007b; 2010.

[16] Edwards 2013, 21, no. AN26. The inscription reads *Catamanus rex sapientisimus opinatisimus omnium regum*.

[17] For the impact of Romanticism on the development of medieval archaeology, see Gerrard 2003, 23–9.

6 LIFE IN EARLY MEDIEVAL WALES

explore its picturesque scenery.[18] As a result, tours of Wales were published drawing attention to early medieval stone monuments and other antiquities worthy of notice. The most influential was *A Tour in Wales* by Thomas Pennant (1726–98), the popular Flintshire travel writer and naturalist.[19] For example, drawing on Lhuyd, he described and illustrated the ninth-century Pillar of Eliseg, Denbighshire, and mentioned the opening of the burial cairn on which it had once stood and its recent re-erection.[20] He also visited other early medieval sites, such as the hillfort at Dinas Emrys and the monastery on Ynys Enlli (Bardsey Island), Caernarfonshire, giving lively accounts of the stories associated with them.[21] Other tours include that of Pembrokeshire by Richard Fenton (1747–1821), who came from St Davids. He noted several carved stone monuments in the south-west, as well as 'stone coffins' at St Non's Chapel, which are almost certainly early medieval graves.[22] The artist and naturalist Edward Donovan (1768–1837) also toured south Wales and made fine illustrations of crosses at Llantwit Major and Margam, sometimes setting them within romantic landscapes.[23]

The next major breakthroughs in our understanding of early medieval Wales, its inscribed stones, and stone sculpture were fostered by the foundation of the journal *Archaeologia Cambrensis* in 1846 and, in the following year, the Cambrian Archaeological Association, which gradually placed the study of material remains in Wales on a more scientific footing.[24] This should be seen as the Welsh expression of a similar expansion of interest in antiquarian societies in England and Ireland at this time alongside an increasing concern to preserve medieval remains from destruction.[25] Members of the Association, some of whom had international contacts and included a number who lived outside Wales, met annually in different parts of the country. These meetings provided important opportunities to visit sites and monuments in a particular area and debate their significance as well as to deliver papers, many of which were published in the journal. During the mid- and later nineteenth century, four members stand out for their research on the early medieval inscribed and sculptured stones. Harry Longueville Jones (1806–70), co-founder of the Association and its journal, described and illustrated a considerable number of monuments, especially on Anglesey during the 1840s.[26] Secondly, in 1846, J. O. Westwood (1805–93), later Hope Professor of Zoology at Oxford University and a scholar of early medieval Insular art, recognized for the first time the significance of the ogham inscription on the stone at Eglwys Nynnid, Glamorgan.[27] He went on to compile *Lapidarium*

---

[18] Andrews 1989, 39–66, 85–151. [19] Evans, R. P. 1991; Withers 2007; Edwards 2013, 21–2.
[20] Pennant 1778–83, i, 399–401, pl. XXVI; Edwards 2013, no. D3.
[21] Pennant 1778–83, ii, 182–4, 205–8.
[22] Fenton 1903, 63, pl. opp. p. 353; Edwards 2007a, 13, 450.
[23] Donovan 1805, i, 332–49, ii, 4–7, 24–7; Redknap and Lewis 2007, 13–15, figs 8–11.
[24] Thomas 1978; Moore, D. 1998, 3–16; Edwards and Gould 2013, 144–9, 161–3.
[25] Gerrard 2003, 30–55. [26] Edwards 2013, 22–4.
[27] Ibid., 24–5; Westwood 1846; Redknap and Lewis, 2007, 16.

Walliae, the earliest illustrated catalogue of inscribed stones and stone sculpture in Wales, which included over 200 early medieval examples.[28] Thirdly, from the 1870s, there was a revival of interest in Celtic philology led by John Rhys (1840–1915), an outstanding Welsh scholar with an international reputation, who in 1877 became the first Professor of Celtic at Jesus College, Oxford. Much of his research in Wales was focused on the early inscribed stones, especially those with oghams, and the forms of the personal names on them, though he also understood the importance of recording their contexts.[29] Finally, the art historian and archaeologist J. Romilly Allen (1847–1907), now best known as the co-author of *The Early Christian Monuments of Scotland*,[30] also had connections with Pembrokeshire and was the first to analyse the form and ornament of the early medieval crosses in Wales.[31]

THE LATER NINETEENTH AND FIRST HALF OF THE TWENTIETH CENTURIES

The later nineteenth and first half of the twentieth centuries saw archaeology in Britain and Ireland gaining in significance as a discipline, and it is during this period that we can also identify several important developments in Wales which were to have a significant impact on our understanding of the early medieval period. These were set in motion by what has been termed a 'National Awakening', which focused above all on efforts to foster Welsh culture and education.[32] The founding of the University of Wales in 1893 allowed the professional study of history in Wales for the first time, and in 1911 J. E. Lloyd (1861–1947), Professor of History at the University College of North Wales, Bangor, published *A History of Wales from the Earliest Times to the Edwardian Conquest*.[33] This was a landmark since it sought to dispel the myths of the past and set the medieval history of Wales on a more scientific footing. Interestingly, in the book Lloyd not only demonstrates a deep knowledge of the Welsh landscape and its interaction with society but also tries to break down the barriers between historical and archaeological evidence,[34] as, for example, in his discussion of the ogham-inscribed stones as proof of Irish settlement during the fifth century.[35]

In Wales, however, there was no equivalent of the Victoria County History, established in England in 1899, or the English Place-Name Society founded in 1923.[36]

---

[28] Westwood 1876–9; Redknap and Lewis 2007, 15–18; Edwards 2007a, 14.

[29] Morris-Jones 1925; Sims-Williams 2019b; Edwards 2007a, 14–15.

[30] Allen and Anderson 1903; Henderson 2004; Redknap and Lewis 2007, 21, fig. 16; Edwards 2013, 25.

[31] Allen 1899.   [32] Morgan 1981, 90–122; Pryce 2011, 4–6.

[33] Lloyd 1911.   [34] Pryce 2011, 95–113, 131–4.   [35] Lloyd 1911, 111–21.

[36] Gerrard 2003, 78–9. The first county history in Wales was Carmarthenshire, sponsored by the London Carmarthenshire Society, Lloyd 1935–9. Publication continues on a piecemeal basis. Cymdeithas Enwau Lleoedd Cymru (Welsh Place-Name Society) was founded in 2010.

Nevertheless, the foundation of three other Welsh institutions at this time undoubtedly championed the recording and preservation of the Welsh past and aided the development of archaeology in Wales, not least that of the early medieval period. The National Museum, centred in Cardiff, was finally set up after over half a century of struggle in 1907,[37] and two exceptional archaeologists were early directors, Mortimer Wheeler (1924–6) and Cyril Fox (1926–48).[38] The Museum provided an important focus for research and excavation as well as a repository for artefacts. The Royal Commission on the Ancient and Historical Monuments of Wales was likewise established in 1908 to compile inventories of monuments county by county,[39] and the University of Wales Board of Celtic Studies, which acted as a significant catalyst through initiating, funding, and publishing research within its remit, including archaeology, was inaugurated in 1919.[40]

The early volumes of the Royal Commission,[41] apart from occasional speculation on possible early medieval sites, continued to record the only identifiable monuments known at that time: Offa's and Wat's Dykes,[42] together with the inscribed stones and stone sculpture. However, they also emphasized the lack of knowledge of what was considered a formative period of Welsh history[43] and the archaeology associated with it:

> Perhaps the most difficult period that the Welsh antiquary has to deal with is that which lies between the departure of the Romans and the arrival of the Normans. From the archaeologists' point of view this period extends for at least 700 years, and is in Wales the most barren of remains that may with fair assurance be attributed to it.[44]

Up to 1925 the volumes had been largely antiquarian compilations of earlier work and contained little original archaeological recording. However, when *Pembrokeshire* was published, it was roundly criticized and this resulted in new guidelines being adopted, proposed by Cyril Fox, which included the necessity for on-site survey and recording in the future and the need to employ professional archaeological staff.[45] As a result, the *Anglesey* volume was of a very different standard. C. A. Ralegh Radford (1900–98), who was employed as Inspector of Ancient Monuments in Wales and

---

[37] Morgan 2007; Mason, R. 2007, 23–9.

[38] Hawkes 1982, 83–102; Carr 2012, 88–123; Scott-Fox 2002, 61–180.

[39] Browne and Griffiths 2008, 19–24. Royal Commissions were established in England and Scotland the same year, Gerrard 2003, 79.

[40] Pryce 2011, 73–6.

[41] RCAHMW 1911–25, vols I–VII, covering Montgomeryshire, Flintshire, Radnorshire, Denbighshire, Carmarthenshire, Merionethshire, and Pembrokeshire.

[42] RCAHMW 1912, xix. Wat's Dyke was assumed to be the later and was mistakenly seen as a boundary between the English and the Danes.

[43] RCAHMW 1921, xviii.   [44] RCAHMW 1917, xxi.

[45] Phillips 1987, 41; Browne 2007, 33–7.

Monmouthshire (1929–34)[46] and then became a Commissioner, was responsible for the introduction to the early medieval period. He drew upon both written sources and archaeological evidence and showed a particular interest in the sites of what he termed the 'Celtic Church', suggesting, for example, that the remains on the island of Ynys Seiriol (Priestholm) were those of an early Christian hermitage. He also considered a small number of secular sites ascribed to the period, as well as cemeteries with stone-lined graves, finds, such as the Viking silver arm-rings from Dinorben quarry, and the full range of inscribed stones and stone sculpture. Where possible, he also attempted to place the monuments within a wider archaeological context, for example, for the first time, drawing attention to comparisons between some of the fifth- to seventh-century inscriptions and those in Gaul.[47]

Two other important projects were undertaken by the National Museum at this time, the second in partnership with the Board of Celtic Studies. In 1925 Cyril Fox (1882–1967) embarked upon his truly pioneering survey of the length of Offa's Dyke together with Wat's Dyke and the short dykes, completed in 1934, the foundation of all research since. To establish a detailed record of their extent, features, and condition, he systematically walked the dykes describing the remains and annotating the 6-inch Ordnance Survey map, as well as drawing profiles and taking photographs. Fieldwork was published annually and the results subsequently analysed, being finally brought together in 1955.[48] Secondly, during the 1930s V. E. Nash-Williams (1897–1955), Keeper of Archaeology at the National Museum, embarked on research to catalogue and classify the inscribed stones and stone sculpture, which by now comprised over 400 monuments, though its highly influential publication was not achieved until after the Second World War.[49]

In England, pagan and conversion-period Anglo-Saxon graves had long attracted antiquarian attention, including excavation, because of the presence of mounds, cremation urns, and often rich grave goods, and their early medieval date was first recognized in the late eighteenth century.[50] The first Anglo-Saxon settlements, notably Sutton Courtenay, Oxfordshire, were identified in the early twentieth century, though similar remains at the time were long interpreted to indicate miserable living conditions.[51] By contrast, in Wales there were almost no excavations of sites ascribed to the early medieval period during the later nineteenth and first half of the twentieth centuries. This was because a lack of diagnostic artefacts made them almost impossible to identify unless they were mentioned in the written sources. Nonetheless, Llangorse crannog, Breconshire, provides an interesting early exception. Its discovery by Edgar

---

[46] Gilchrist 2013, 343.   [47] Radford 1937; Edwards 2007a, 25–6.

[48] Fox, C. 1955; Ray and Bapty 2016, 68–77.

[49] Nash-Williams 1950; Randall 1956; Redknap and Lewis 2007, 22–3; Edwards 2013, 26–8.

[50] Kendrick and Hawkes 1932, 307–20; Lucy 2000, 5–14; Williams, Howard 2006, 5–6.

[51] Kendrick and Hawkes 1932, 320–4; Hamerow 2012, 7–8.

10 LIFE IN EARLY MEDIEVAL WALES

and Henry Dumbleton in 1867 led to some excavation with, for the time, careful recording of the structural remains (Fig. 1.2), and even if there was no attempt at dating them, their archaeological significance was immediately recognized by comparison with similar lake dwellings then coming to light, not only in Switzerland but also in Ireland and Scotland.[52]

Instead, during the second half of the nineteenth and first half of the twentieth centuries, at the height of the British Empire, there was, as in England, an emphasis on the excavation of Roman sites.[53] For example, the first large excavations at the Roman town of Caerwent (*Venta Silurum*), first noted at an early date because of its extensive remains, were conducted in 1855. These were followed by a major programme led by Thomas Ashby and Alfred Hudd between 1899 and 1913. By this date almost two-thirds of the town had been uncovered, though the trenching methods used were only successful in recording the plans of late Roman buildings.[54] Even so the excavators were aware that, according to the twelfth-century *Life* of St Tatheus, the saint had founded an early monastery on the site.[55] They dug up large numbers of early medieval graves west of the church and, in 1910, outside the east gate in the vicarage orchard.[56] Furthermore, as part of a High Anglican reinvention of an Early Christian Celtic past, one long-cist burial from the latter was claimed to be that of the saint, and the remains were translated with considerable ceremony to be reinterred under a Latin plaque in the south aisle of the church.[57] Early medieval artefacts also came to light from time to time, but their potential significance has only gradually been recognized.[58] Later, during the 1920s, particular interest was shown in the conquest and military occupation of Wales and included Mortimer and Tessa Wheeler's much more scientific excavations at the Roman auxiliary forts at Caernarfon (*Segontium*) and Brecon Gaer, both of which were argued to have early medieval activity.[59]

From the early twentieth century onwards in Britain, it is also possible to trace a growing interest in the exploration of native settlements in a bid to understand how people had lived in the past. In Wales attention was directed to the well-preserved hillforts and hut groups, especially in the north, which were presumed to date to the Iron Age and Roman periods, a pattern also evident in south-west Britain.[60] In Scotland the early medieval occupation of hillforts at both the Mote of Mark and Dunadd was also identified at this time.[61] Some cursory excavations were carried out

[52] Dumbleton 1870 and frontispiece; Lane and Redknap 2019, 11–17.
[53] Hingley 2008, 278–325.
[54] For a summary of antiquarian interest from Leland onwards and early excavations, see Brewer 2006, 3–5.
[55] Wade-Evans 1944, 274–7, 286–7, chs 6, 9, 17; Knight 1970–1.
[56] Ashby et al. 1911, 434–5, 444–5; Campbell and MacDonald 1993.
[57] Baring-Gould and Fisher 1907–13, iv, 214; Wood 1912, 3, 11–12; Boon 1981–2.
[58] Fox 1946, 108; Knight 1996.   [59] Wheeler 1923, 93–4; 1926, 11–16.
[60] Kendrick and Hawkes 1932, 177–82; Wheeler 1925, 259–68.
[61] Curle 1913–14; Craw 1929–30, 111–27.

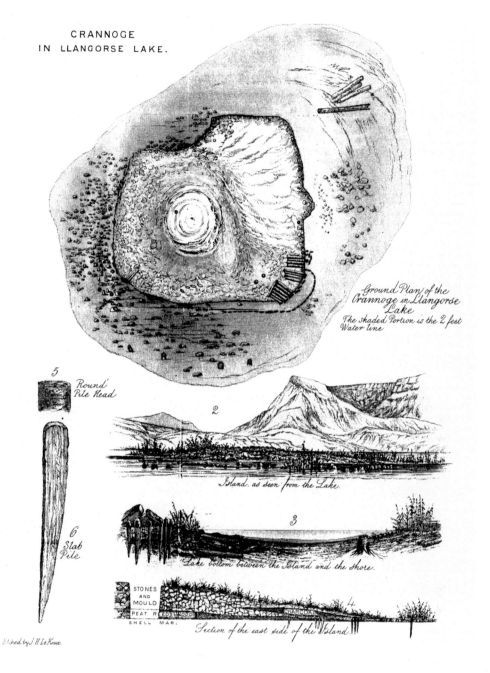

Fig. 1.2. Llangorse crannog, Breconshire, excavated in 1869, showing a plan, a view of the island from the lake, two cross-sections—one showing the lake bottom between the island and the shore, the second the east side of the crannog—and drawings of the wooden piles (by permission of the Cambrian Archaeological Association).

at Dinas Emrys in 1910, most likely because of the early medieval legends associated with the hillfort.[62] Equally, at Dinorben, Denbighshire, it was thought, as a result of sectioning the defences, that occupation might extend beyond the Roman period.[63] It was also argued that conjoined subrectangular structures excavated on Gateholm Island, Pembrokeshire, one of which was associated with a ringed pin, indicated an early medieval date.[64] The most important excavation was, however, of the enclosed hut group at Pant-y-Saer, Anglesey, directed and very promptly published by C. W. Phillips (1901–85).[65] A penannular brooch was found in a rectangular stone structure adjoining one of the round huts and, as a result, the Roman material from the site was declared 'mere flotsam' and the settlement was dated to between the fourth and sixth centuries AD.[66] Sherds of what became known as 'Very Coarse Pottery' also found on the site were wrongly identified as 'Dark Age', suggesting that other hillforts and hut groups with this material were also of this date. Indeed, the failure to recognize this as briquetage from Iron Age salt containers meant the misconception lasted well into the 1960s.[67]

From the second quarter of the twentieth century the impact of geographical approaches is also apparent on the archaeology of early medieval Wales as well as more widely.[68] We can see this in the work of Cyril Fox, E. G. Bowen (1900–83), and Glanville R. J. Jones (1923–96). In *The Personality of Britain*, first published in 1932, Fox made a compelling argument for the impact of physical geography, landscape, and ecology on the development of Britain and introduced three highly influential concepts: the Highland Zone encompassing northern and western Britain, including Wales, where he perceived a greater continuity of cultural character; the Lowland Zone of southern and eastern Britain, which was more open to external impact and economic growth; and the Irish Sea as a 'culture province' (Chapter 2).[69] His argument clearly reflected the contemporary theoretical outlook by emphasizing a culture-historical approach and environmental determinism.[70] Bowen, Professor of Geography and Anthropology at Aberystwyth, focused on the 'Age of the Saints' by mapping the distribution of church dedications in Wales to chart the course of conversion, the growth of Celtic saints' cults, and interchange along the western seaways, thereby contributing to the long-held, romantic view of the 'Celtic Church'.[71] During the 1960s Jones, who also received his education as a historical geographer at Aberystwyth, developed his controversial 'Multiple Estate' model as a way of understanding how

---

[62] Breese 1930; Edwards and Lane 1988, 54–7.   [63] Gardner and Savory 1964, 98–9.

[64] Lethbridge and David 1930; Kendrick and Hawkes 1932, 324–5; Edwards and Lane 1988, 72–5.

[65] Phillips 1934; 1987, 42–4; Edwards and Lane 1988, 1, 99–101; Waddington 2013, 155–7.

[66] Phillips 1934, 33–4.

[67] Ibid., 28; Edwards and Lane 1988, 1–2; Gelling and Stanford 1967; Morris 1985, fig. 10.

[68] Gerrard 2003, 83–4.   [69] Fox 1943, 28–44.   [70] Rippon 2009, 228–9.

[71] Bowen 1954; 1969. For critiques of both these outmoded concepts, see Davies, J. R. 2002, 361–5; Edwards 2016a, 98–100, and below.

the landscape was managed and exploited. Though the model was derived from twelfth- and thirteenth-century Welsh legal texts, he argued that it could be projected backwards through the early Middle Ages into prehistory and was, indeed, still detectable on the ground, not only in Wales but in England as well.[72]

MODERN APPROACHES

From the 1950s onwards there has been a rapid expansion in knowledge and understanding of early medieval archaeology across Europe, making it possible to ask much more complex questions about how people lived and why major changes occurred during this period. In southern and eastern England in particular Anglo-Saxon and Viking Age archaeology has been transformed by modern research and increasingly rescue excavations that have revealed not just cemeteries but also a range of rural, urban, and ecclesiastical settlements and the religious, economic, and social structures that underpinned them.[73] There has been a similar revolution in our understanding of early medieval Ireland as a result of the rapid rise in data available for analysis largely from rescue excavations associated with massive infrastructure projects driven by the 'Celtic Tiger' economy (1997–2007).[74] In Scotland, even though there has been less development-led rescue excavation, other investigations have led to significant advances in our understanding of the period. The Picts are no longer considered the enigma they once were, and there is better recognition of regional difference and chronological change.[75] In contrast, advances in western and south-west England have been more limited. This is not only because of fewer development-led rescue excavations compared with the south and east but also because the archaeological evidence, especially for early medieval settlements, has proved harder to identify, particularly in areas with no native ceramics.[76] This is equally true of Wales.

Nonetheless, the research excavation (1954–8) of a small promontory fort in the Vale of Glamorgan by Leslie Alcock (1925–2006), then a lecturer at University College Cardiff,[77] opened an important new era in the early medieval archaeology of Wales and more widely in western and northern Britain. Indeed, Dinas Powys remains

---

[72] The evidence is brought together in Jones, G. R. J. 1972. See also recent critiques: Roberts with Barnwell 2011b; Seaman 2012.

[73] Cramp 2009; Hamerow et al. 2011.   [74] O'Sullivan et al. 2014, 19–33.

[75] Wainwright 1955; Foster 2004; Driscoll et al. 2011.

[76] For discussion of the comparative lack of evidence for rural settlements in these areas, see Blair 2013, including fig. 2. See also Thomas 2012 for discussion of our understanding of early medieval rural settlement and society and how it changed across Britain and Ireland in this period. This highlights regional diversity and differences in evidence survival, including a 'black hole' in Wales.

[77] Alcock 1963, 8. The project was funded by the Board of Celtic Studies.

14 LIFE IN EARLY MEDIEVAL WALES

an iconic site to this day.[78] The defended settlement was identified by Alcock as the 'seat of a princely household' occupied during the fifth to seventh centuries AD on account of the rich artefactual assemblage, which included a fragment from a die for a penannular brooch with Irish parallels and a range of imported pottery from both the Mediterranean and western France.[79] Although such pottery had been known from the 1930s as a result of excavations by Radford at Tintagel, Cornwall, and also from sites, such as Garranes, in Ireland, its true significance was only more widely recognized as excavations at Dinas Powys were underway.[80] Imported pottery was similarly identified in north-west Wales at the hillfort of Dinas Emrys, partially excavated in 1954–6 by H. N. Savory (1911–2001) of the National Museum.[81] The recognition of elite strongholds with imported pottery and other diagnostic artefacts, particularly Dinas Powys, precipitated greater optimism and a growing interest in the 'Dark Ages' in Celtic Britain.[82] This led to further research excavations on post-Roman hillforts including Degannwy in north Wales, South Cadbury and Cadbury Congresbury in Somerset, and Dundurn, the Mote of Mark, and Dunadd in Scotland, largely chosen because they featured in early medieval written sources.[83] Moreover, in a romantic reflection of contemporary culture,[84] the fifth to seventh centuries were dubbed 'Arthur's Britain', though Alcock's popular book of that name, which drew on both archaeological and written evidence, was the first to provide a detailed synthesis of how the Britons in this period had lived.[85]

This burgeoning interest in the archaeology of early medieval Celtic Britain also resulted in research excavations of ecclesiastical sites and cemeteries, leading to a more critical assessment of the evidence for Christianity, conversion, and the growth of monasticism. This was led by Charles Thomas (1928–2016), who finally dismissed the widely held view, espoused by Radford and followed by Nash-Williams and Bowen, that Christianity had been reintroduced into western Britain from southern Gaul in the late fifth and sixth centuries alongside the early inscribed stones.[86] He argued

---

[78] For recent work, see Seaman 2013; Seaman and Lane 2019.   [79] Alcock 1963, 59–61.

[80] Radford 1935, 415, n. 4; 1956; Ó Ríordáin 1942, 125–34; Thomas 1959.

[81] Ibid., 107–8. Thomas noted imported pottery on two other Welsh sites—Longbury Bank, Pembs., and Cae'r Mynydd, Caerns.—but the sherd from the latter is now regarded as Roman, Edwards and Lane 1988, 125; see also Savory 1960, 60–3, fig. 7; Alcock 1958.

[82] Davies, W. 1983, 69. The 1960s and early 1970s have been described as a 'Golden Age' for Dark Age archaeology, Rahtz et al. 1992, 2.

[83] Alcock 1967, 198; 1972; 1995; Rahtz et al. 1992; Alcock et al. 1989; Laing and Longley 2006; Lane and Campbell 2000.

[84] The musical *Camelot* (1960) that defined the Kennedy era in the United States was based on T. H. White's series of novels *The Once and Future King* (1958); it was made into a film in 1967. One of the novels, *The Sword in the Stone*, was also adapted as a Walt Disney cartoon (1963).

[85] Alcock 1971, 197–252. It has become a classic and remains in print.

[86] Radford 1937, xciv; Nash-Williams 1950, 1, 55; Bowen 1954, 14–17; for further discussion, see Edwards 2016a, 98–9.

instead for its continuity from the Roman period onwards.[87] Interestingly, however, there were no excavations on major ecclesiastical sites in Wales identifiable in early medieval written sources, most likely because these continued in use. Nevertheless, the possible remains of an early medieval hermitage on the tidal islet of Burry Holms off the Gower peninsula were excavated,[88] as were two important cemeteries, Arfryn and Capel Eithin, on Anglesey.[89]

This upsurge in activity was not confined to archaeology but can also be seen in a more critical assessment of the surviving early medieval written sources, including those concerned with Wales, and new editions of works such as Gildas's *De Excidio Britanniae*,[90] which did much to make this material more widely accessible. Most of this research was conducted in academic institutions outside Wales, particularly in the Department of Anglo-Saxon, Norse and Celtic in Cambridge. For example, Nora Chadwick (1891–1972) studied culture and learning in the early medieval Church in Wales,[91] while Kathleen Hughes (1926–77) unravelled the complexities of the Welsh Latin chronicles.[92] In a strong but on the whole justifiable attack, David Dumville also turned on the uncritical use of later sources, such as the early ninth-century *Historia Brittonum*, to try and reconstruct the earlier political history of the so-called 'Age of Arthur' in the fifth and sixth centuries.[93]

Nonetheless, Wendy Davies's important research on the early twelfth-century Book of Llandaf took a very different historical approach. She argued that the charters within this, though extant in edited form, derived from earlier material datable by reference to their witness lists, thereby opening a new window on the development of the early medieval Church in south Wales, social organization, landholding, and the rural economy.[94] She was also rightly critical of the long-held concept of a 'Celtic Church' that had assumed uniformity of practice and belief in much of Britain and Ireland during the fifth to seventh centuries.[95] Moreover, in her subsequent ground-breaking study of *Wales in the Early Middle Ages*, although she focused on the reconstruction of early medieval society through an analysis of the written evidence, she also readily engaged with the landscape and environment as well as the increasing amounts of archaeological data.[96]

By the mid-1970s, however, the destruction of Britain's past during the course of infrastructure projects and redevelopment had led to the recognition that proper provisions were needed for rescue archaeology, resulting in greatly increased government

---

[87] Thomas 1971, 10–27; 1981.

[88] Burry Holms was never published, but see Hague 1974, 29–33; RCAHMW 1976b, 14–15.

[89] White 1971–2; Hedges 2016; White and Smith 1999.

[90] Winterbottom 1978.   [91] Chadwick 1958a; 1958b.   [92] Hughes 1973.

[93] Dumville 1977. The attack was primarily levelled at John Morris's *The Age of Arthur* (1973) but also at Leslie Alcock's use of written sources in *Arthur's Britain* (1971).

[94] Davies, W. 1978; 1979a. See below.

[95] Davies, W. 1974–5; see also Davies, W. 1992.   [96] Davies, W. 1982a.

16 LIFE IN EARLY MEDIEVAL WALES

funding and the establishment of professional archaeological units.[97] In Wales four regional archaeological trusts were initiated by staff in the Ministry of Public Building and Works based in Cardiff and have had a considerable impact on archaeology in Wales ever since.[98] Still substantially funded by the now devolved Welsh Government via Cadw, they continue to focus on identification and management of the archaeological resource as well as rescue excavation, especially since the advent of developer funding in 1990 leading to a number of significant early medieval investigations. More recently, the regularly updated Welsh Archaeological Research Frameworks have also helped to identify early medieval priorities.[99] So, what approaches have been taken and what advances made in our knowledge and understanding of early medieval archaeology in Wales over the last half-century?

The optimism engendered by the discovery of Dinas Powys and a handful of other high-status hillforts with imported pottery and ornamental metalwork in Wales gradually eroded. By the end of the 1980s, because of a lack of characteristic site types and diagnostic artefacts, only a very small number of new early medieval settlements had come to light, in marked contrast to most other parts of Britain and Ireland, where identification was becoming easier. Moreover, at this stage, although radiocarbon dating was sometimes being used, the very small number of dates and their large margins of error frequently made definite early medieval identifications difficult and the recognition of changes during the period impossible.[100]

This inability to identify settlements has had major consequences, with a natural tendency to concentrate available resources on expanding understanding of periods with diagnostic sites and artefactual assemblages. From the mid-1990s Cadw commissioned pan-Wales surveys on specific themes, such as the uplands and deserted rural settlements, to assess the resource and identify well-preserved sites for protection.[101] Aerial photography, now carried out by the Royal Commission, became an increasingly important tool in site recognition, but remains need to be visible in order to record them and visits could only be followed up by geophysics and trial excavation in a small number of instances. Therefore, in many cases periods have been assigned to sites on the basis of what is already known, so, for example, hillforts are characteristically regarded as later prehistoric, hut groups as later prehistoric or Roman, and rectangular buildings as later medieval. A few early medieval cemeteries have, however, been identified from the air, mainly because they include square-ditched grave enclosures.[102] Nevertheless, some advances are evident. For example, the survey of

---

[97] Rahtz 1974; Gerrard 2003, 133, 164–72.

[98] Musson 1984; Welsh Archaeological Trusts 2016, 1–17.

[99] Edwards et al. 2005; 2010; 2016.   [100] Edwards and Lane 1988, 2–4.

[101] Welsh Archaeological Trusts 2016, 42–8; Browne and Hughes 2003; Roberts 2006a.

[102] E.g. cemeteries at Druid, Corwen, Mer.; Meusydd, Llanrhaeadr-ym-Mochnant, Denbs.; and Llanbeblig (Tyddyn Pandy), Caerns., all subsequently excavated. See St Joseph 1980, 51, fig. 5; Driver 2006, 143, 147; Jones, N. W. et al. 2013b; Kenney and Parry 2012.

early medieval ecclesiastical sites was particularly successful because many were still in use as parish churches and, together with other abandoned sites, could be identified using a range of written and material evidence, especially stone sculpture.[103]

Over the past half-century, although levels of development and rescue archaeology have been much lower in Wales than in most parts of England and Ireland, there has nonetheless been significant progress in the recognition and investigation of early medieval sites and their associated activities. Indeed, at Graeanog, Caernarfonshire, rescue excavations in advance of gravel extraction have continued intermittently throughout the period, revealing a multiperiod landscape, including evidence of early medieval occupation.[104] Prior to the introduction of developer-funded excavation in 1990, there were occasional rescue excavations of early medieval sites, such as the church and cemetery at Capel Maelog, Llandrindod Wells, Radnorshire.[105] There were also important early but limited developer-funded excavations: for example at Hen Gastell (Briton Ferry), where the remains of a hillfort were investigated during construction of the M4 motorway, and at Llandough, Glamorgan, where a major cemetery was uncovered in the course of building a housing estate.[106] More recently infrastructure projects have become increasingly important. For example, the extension of the A55 Expressway across Anglesey (1999–2001) offered a significant opportunity, revealing a cemetery at Tŷ Mawr, Holyhead, as well as early medieval activity at several other earlier sites.[107] Coastal erosion has likewise resulted in the excavation of a number of cemeteries, including Tywyn-y-Capel, Anglesey, and St Patrick's Chapel near St Davids, Pembrokeshire.[108]

The difficulty in identifying early medieval sites has also resulted in the fact that remarkably few have undergone research excavation. During the 1980s there were occasional such excavations by the Welsh Archaeological Trusts (funded by the Manpower Services Commission to create jobs), for example the cemetery at Tandderwen, Denbighshire.[109] Since then, however, university funding, including from the Board of Celtic Studies, and funding by the National Museum have supported three significant projects. At Longbury Bank, Pembrokeshire, the presence of imported pottery and glass enabled identification of an unenclosed settlement on a low-lying promontory.[110] Secondly, recognition of the significance of the mid-nineteenth century account of Llangorse crannog resulted in a series of investigations that linked the site with the rulers of Brycheiniog. The fragility of the archaeology led

---

[103] Edwards 2009a, 6–7; Davidson 2009a; Silvester and Evans 2009; Ludlow 2009; Evans, E. M. 2009; Longley 2009.

[104] Fasham et al. 1998, xvi–xix.   [105] Britnell 1990.

[106] Wilkinson 1995, 1–2; Holbrook and Thomas 2005, 1–3.   [107] Cuttler et al. 2012.

[108] Davidson 2009b, 167–73; Murphy et al. 2014, 2–3; excavations at St Patrick's Chapel have continued in 2015, 2016, 2019, and 2021, see Murphy and Hemer 2022.

[109] Musson 1984, 7; Welsh Archaeological Trusts 2016, 26; Brassil et al. 1991.

[110] Campbell and Lane 1993.

to limited excavation of waterlogged deposits on the island and recording of structural remains in the surrounding water that were dated by dendrochronology to the late ninth century.[111] Thirdly, metal-detector finds reported to the National Museum precipitated extensive, long-term excavation of a high-status early medieval settlement with later Viking occupation at Llanbedrgoch, Anglesey.[112] In addition, long-running multiperiod research and recording on the Gwent Levels has been a rare example of such work in Wales, enabling a much better understanding of the changing landscape and human exploitation of this wetland environment during the early Middle Ages.[113]

The foundation of the Portable Antiquities Scheme (PAS) for England and Wales in the wake of the 1996 Treasure Act has resulted in the recording of large numbers of early medieval metal-detector finds—mainly ornamental metalwork and coins—in eastern and southern England but fewer in the west and north. Using the data has also enabled new research, for example on Viking identities in the Danelaw.[114] In Wales, while the numbers of early medieval finds recorded remain very low compared with England, they nonetheless represent a significant increase on what was known before, again allowing analysis of the data within a broader context, notably for Hiberno-Scandinavian contact and settlement in different parts of Wales.[115] However, it should be noted that the distributions of finds are affected not only by patterns of loss and environmental factors, notably their survival rate in the acid soils prevalent in Wales, but also by the locations and intensity of metal-detecting activity in a particular locality and the ease and standard of reporting discoveries, all of which can lead to bias in the results.[116]

Many of the most important recent breakthroughs in our knowledge and understanding of early medieval archaeology in Wales and elsewhere have been the result of new and improving scientific techniques. The most significant of these are developments from the mid-1980s onwards in the accuracy of radiocarbon dating brought about, first by the introduction of calibration and then by the instigation of accelerator mass spectrometry (AMS), which requires smaller samples, thereby allowing short-lived material, such as a single cereal grain, to be dated.[117] In addition to improving calibration, Bayesian statistical modelling of multiple dates in relation to stratigraphic information is now beginning to facilitate the construction and refinement of both site and period chronologies, allowing more fundamental archaeological questions to be addressed about how people lived in the past.[118] These advances have enabled radiocarbon dating to be applied much more successfully to the historic

---

[111] Campbell and Lane 1989; Redknap and Lane 1994; Redknap 2004c; Lane and Redknap 2019.

[112] Redknap 1994; 2004a, 164–73; 2016.

[113] Rippon 1996, 25–38, 61; Brown et al. 2010.   [114] PAS; Kershaw 2013.

[115] On the PAS in Wales, see Lodwick 2009, 107–11; Redknap 2022, 73–7, 103–5.

[116] Kershaw 2013, 13–19.

[117] For the impact of these on Anglo-Saxon cemetery archaeology, see Bayliss et al. 2013, 35–8.

[118] Bayliss et al. 2007.

period, and in Wales this has resulted in increased recognition of a range of early medieval sites and their closer dating, which can now be used to aid identification of wider changes during the period. However, plateaus in the radiocarbon calibration curve, notably at the beginning of the period *c.* AD 425–550, continue to make study of the fundamental transition between Roman and post-Roman more difficult.[119] The importance of multiple radiocarbon dates from short-lived samples and sealed stratigraphic contexts has also only comparatively recently been recognized for the identification of early medieval activity in Wales, especially in the case of rescue excavations. Similarly, though Bayesian modelling has been successfully applied to the chronology of Anglo-Saxon cemeteries,[120] it has yet to be employed to any extent in Wales on early medieval sites.[121]

The better recovery and increasingly sophisticated analysis of a range of more closely dated environmental data in Wales are also of significance.[122] For example, the number of pollen diagrams relevant to the early medieval period is slowly expanding,[123] and study of plant remains is now able to shed light on changes in the early medieval landscape and food production.[124] There has, however, been little scientific analysis of technology and its impact on the economy apart from the examination of craftworking debris, notably ironworking,[125] or artefacts from individual sites. Equally, an increasing array of techniques associated with palaeopathology and bioarchaeology is now at hand to facilitate the study of early medieval human remains, where these survive in Wales, revealing evidence about health and mortality. The application of isotope analysis has also demonstrated clear potential for illuminating the mobility of people and aspects of diet.[126] However, there has been remarkably little analysis of animal bone assemblages because they so seldom survive.[127]

Therefore, over the past half-century the amount of archaeological data of relevance to the early medieval period in Wales has steadily increased, and dating and other scientific methods have improved significantly. However, because of the frequently scattered and fragmentary nature of the archaeological evidence, largely derived from rescue excavations, many of which are very small-scale, there has been comparatively little wider analysis of its significance.[128] As a result, there has also been little consideration of its place within the broader context of the early medieval archaeology

---

[119] Bayliss et al. 2013, 35–7.   [120] Ibid., 554.

[121] For its early use on the multiperiod site at Parc Bryn Cegin, Llandygái, Caerns., which includes an early medieval smithing site, see Marshall and Kenney 2008, 131–2.

[122] Expansion in the data and opportunities for its interpretation can be gauged to some extent by comparing Caseldine 1990, 94–111, and Caseldine 2015.

[123] Davies, T. L. 2019.   [124] E.g. Carruthers 2010; Ciarialdi 2012.   [125] E.g. Young, T. P. 2010.

[126] E.g. Loe and Robson-Brown 2005; Adlam and Wysocki 2009; Hemer et al. 2013; 2017.

[127] The Dinas Powys assemblage was the first to be analysed; see Alcock 1963, 192–4; Gilchrist 1988.

[128] For a general discussion, see Arnold and Davies 2000, 148–97; for the Roman/post-Roman transition, White 2007; for the Vikings, Redknap 2000; for the Church, Petts 2009; for aspects of the farming economy, Comeau and Seaman 2019.

20 LIFE IN EARLY MEDIEVAL WALES

of Britain and Ireland and, indeed, other parts of Europe. In contrast, Thomas Charles-Edwards's recent critical appraisal of the written and linguistic evidence for the evolution of early medieval Wales within the wider British context is a significant milestone.[129] Furthermore, the application of a theoretical perspective to the archaeological evidence in Wales has been very largely lacking, though this is surely at least partially because of the continuing comparative scarcity of the data. Instead, in some ways it may appear that research on the archaeology of early medieval Wales has turned full circle since, in recent years, the inscribed stones and stone sculpture, as well as Offa's Dyke and Llangorse crannog, have all returned to the spotlight.[130]

APPROACHING THE WRITTEN SOURCES

Surviving written sources dating to the early medieval period in Wales may be divided into two principal categories: manuscripts written on parchment and inscriptions carved on stone. Wooden tablets, either waxed for use with a stylus or written on in ink, were doubtless another important medium for more everyday writing, but in Wales the only examples that have come down to us are Roman.[131] There are, however, other hints of their existence, notably the depiction of a pair of inscribed tablets joined by leather thongs, together with an open book, on the probably early tenth-century cross-shaft from Llantwit Major, Glamorgan, thereby emphasizing the power of the written word.[132] A possibly post-Roman stylus is also known from New Pieces, Montgomeryshire.[133] Pieces of slate and mudstone could also be used for writing, indicated by the recent discovery of graffiti at St Patrick's Chapel, Pembrokeshire.[134] These may be compared with similar examples of graffiti and writing found elsewhere, in a secular context at Tintagel in Cornwall and on monastic sites in both Scotland and Ireland.[135]

In a society that was largely illiterate, surviving evidence for writing in early medieval Wales is almost exclusively in Latin, a direct inheritance from the Roman past which, once British Latin ceased to be spoken by around 700, became a learnt language

---

[129] Charles-Edwards 2013.

[130] Redknap and Lewis 2007; Edwards 2007a; 2013; Ray and Bapty 2016; Lane and Redknap 2019.

[131] Frere et al. 1986, 450–1; Tomlin 2001. Early medieval examples of waxed tablets include those from Springmount Bog, Co. Antrim, and Blythburgh, Suffolk, Webster and Backhouse 1991, 80–1.

[132] Redknap and Lewis 2007, no. G66, 386–7; Edwards 2015, 2–3.

[133] O'Neil 1937, 121, fig. 8 no. 2; Campbell 1991, 125. A possible stylus from Dinas Powys is too fragmentary to identify, Alcock 1963, 119, no. 44.

[134] Found in 2021, see Murphy and Hemer 2022, 182–205.

[135] For an inscribed slate from Tintagel, see Thomas 2007, with a second discovery in 2018, Jacky Nowakowski (pers. comm.). See also examples from Inchmarnock in the Clyde estuary, Forsyth and Tedeschi in Lowe 2008, 128–75, and Nendrum, Co. Down, Lawlor 1925, 144–6, pl. XII; Bourke 2007, fig. 13.26.

centred on the Church.[136] In contrast, native British, which had evolved into Old Welsh by around 800, seems to have remained predominantly oral, though there are some indications of a vernacular writing tradition as well.[137] Nevertheless, Old Welsh is first clearly evidenced during the ninth century, and may be exemplified by the only known early medieval inscription in the vernacular at Tywyn, Merioneth, and marginalia added to the Lichfield Gospels, then at Llandeilo Fawr, Carmarthenshire.[138] In addition, memorial inscriptions carved in ogham and, to a lesser extent those with Irish names, indicate the presence of Primitive Old Irish speakers in parts of the north-west and south-west as well as in Brycheiniog until *c*.600.[139]

Fewer than twenty surviving manuscripts can be associated with Wales and Cornwall before the twelfth century, and none can be attributed to Scotland with any certainty. All of these have been preserved because they moved, usually to England, at an early date. This poor survival rate contrasts sharply with the hundreds extant from Anglo-Saxon England and more than fifty known from Ireland[140] and may reflect not only destruction but also the availability of materials for production. Therefore, almost all the written sources relevant to early medieval Wales have come down to us in later manuscripts, sometimes in several differing copies, and sometimes in a much altered form, making it all the more difficult to discern early medieval content from later changes and accretions. In other instances we are dealing with sources that certainly post-date the earliest Norman incursions into Wales in the 1070s, sometimes by a couple of centuries, and yet, judiciously used, still have the potential to cast some light on the early Middle Ages. Furthermore, the comparative lack of early medieval sources makes those written elsewhere, in Anglo-Saxon England, Ireland, and Brittany, which make mention of people, events, and places in Wales, all the more significant.

The small number of extant sources relevant to Wales before *c*.800 are almost exclusively concerned with Britain. This is certainly true for the fourth and fifth centuries, as the Roman province of *Britannia* slowly slipped beyond the purview of writers on the European mainland and in Constantinople.[141] The only item of potential consequence is in the *Notitia Dignitatum*, probably compiled *c*.395 but with later additions. This relates to the administration of the empire and lists the *Seguntienses*, formerly stationed at *Segontium* (Caernarfon), but now in Illyricum in the eastern Mediterranean.[142]

Gildas's *De Excidio Britanniae* ('The Ruin of Britain'), now thought most likely to have been written *c*.530 × 545,[143] is of seminal importance despite its inherent difficulties

---

[136] Charles-Edwards 2012, 392.   [137] Sims-Williams 1991, 20–30, 72–5, 78–9.

[138] Ibid., 21–4; Edwards 2013, no. MR25; Jenkins and Owen 1983, 50–61.

[139] Sims-Williams 2002, 22–31; Charles-Edwards 2013, 112–14.

[140] McKee 2012, 167.

[141] Mattingly 2006, 231–2, table 6; Millett 1990, 229, table 9.2.

[142] Mann 1976, 5, 8; Burnham and Davies 2010, 63–4.

[143] Charles-Edwards 2013, 215–18. Some have regarded it as earlier, notably Wood 1984, 22–3.

22 LIFE IN EARLY MEDIEVAL WALES

of style and interpretation. Gildas was a deacon and teacher in the British Church and the purpose of his work was to denounce the sins of the Britons, especially those of their rulers and ecclesiastics, and urge repentance. He writes in the manner of an Old Testament prophet and the text is peppered with biblical quotes, but it is equally clear that he had received a classical rhetorical education with its roots in the Roman past.[144] His dramatic description of the end of Roman Britain and subsequent events, which once shaped archaeological interpretation, is now rightly regarded as misleading,[145] but it is the nearest to a contemporary account that we have. Likewise, when a Latin- and ogham-inscribed stone was found in 1895 at Castell Dwyran, Carmarthenshire, reading in Latin *Memoria Voteporigis protictoris* ('The memorial/tomb of Voteporix the Protector'), it was immediately identified as commemorating one of the 'tyrants' named by Gildas, Vortipor of the Demetae, a misapprehension only recently refuted on linguistic grounds.[146] Nonetheless, *De Excidio Britanniae* remains of considerable value for the light it can shed on society in Gildas's own day; it was also highly influential on later writers, such as Bede.[147]

A small number of other works are also informative about the early British Church, including the fragmentary penitential attributed to Gildas and, a century earlier, St Patrick's *Confessio*, as well as Constantius of Lyon's *Life* of St Germanus of Auxerre, written around 480.[148] In contrast to Ireland and Anglo-Saxon England, there is very little surviving hagiography relevant to Wales before the end of the eleventh century. There are two significant exceptions. The first, the *Life* of St Samson of Dol, who lived in the mid-sixth century, was written by a Breton, almost certainly in the late seventh. However, it draws on earlier material and the author had visited places in Britain associated with the saint, including the monasteries at Llantwit Major and on Caldey Island (Ynys Bŷr).[149] The second consists of episodes from a different *Life* of St Germanus incorporated into the early ninth-century *Historia Brittonum* indicating his continuing influence in the kingdom of Powys at this time.[150]

Inscriptions are of particular importance to our understanding of the post-Roman centuries in western and northern Britain. Over 150 inscribed memorial stones are now known from Wales and the borders, mostly in the north-west and south-west with smaller numbers further east, particularly in Glamorgan and Breconshire.

---

[144] Charles-Edwards 2013, 202–19; Lapidge 1984.

[145] Winterbottom 1978, chs 2–26; Esmonde Cleary 1989, 166–8.

[146] Edwards 2007a, no. CM3; Laws 1895; Rhys 1895; Winterbottom 1978, ch. 31; Sims-Williams 1990b, 226.

[147] Miller 1975; Pryce 2022, 18, 19–22.

[148] Winterbottom 1978, 83–6, 146–7; Hood 1978, 23–34, 41–54; Thompson 1984; Charles-Edwards 2013, 49–51.

[149] Taylor 1991; Flobert 1997, 111, has dated it later, *c.*750; for recent discussion, see Olson 2017, 1–11, 15–16.

[150] See below. Morris 1980, chs 32–5, 39, 47–9; Lewis 2016, 448–52. The saint is also mentioned in the inscription on the Pillar of Eliseg, Denbs., Edwards 2013, no. D3.

These monuments primarily functioned as elite grave-markers and, though very few now survive *in situ*, it is often still possible to say something about their broader archaeological contexts. The majority are incised in Latin with terse commemorative inscriptions which include the name of the deceased, but there are also nine similar inscriptions in Primitive Old Irish ogham and a further twenty-five monuments with both ogham and Latin inscriptions naming the same person. The two most common commemorative Latin formulae are the Christian *hic iacit* ('here lies') and the religiously neutral *X fili Y* ('X son of Y'), a variation of the Irish *X maqi Y* characteristically found on the ogham inscriptions, though women were also sometimes commemorated, usually as daughters, wives, or mothers.[151] Only one example, from Llangadwaladr, Anglesey, naming King Catamanus of Gwynedd, who died *c*.625, commemorates a known individual. Another from Penmachno, Caernarfonshire, has been argued to include a consular date of 540 or slightly later. Such inscribed stones are otherwise broadly datable from the fifth to mid-seventh centuries, though most can be assigned a narrower relative date range based on a combination of language, formulae, and epigraphy, with the letter forms in the Latin inscriptions evolving directly from those in late Roman Britain.[152] Overall these inscribed stones are of considerable significance in attempting to reconstruct important aspects of post-Roman society concerning Irish settlement, changing identities, wider cultural contacts, and the consolidation of Christianity. The memorial stones in Wales are, however, part of a much wider Irish Sea phenomenon. In Britain there are similar monuments in the south-west, where some also have both Latin and ogham inscriptions, and in the north around Carlisle and between Hadrian's Wall and the Forth, though none of these have oghams, bringing the total number to around 225. There is likewise a small cluster on the Isle of Man comprising five ogham and two Latin inscriptions,[153] and over 360 ogham stones have so far been recorded in Ireland, the majority of which are from Munster, but here the number of Latin-inscribed stones is extremely small.[154] There is also a handful of early Latin-inscribed stones from Brittany.[155]

From the later eighth century onwards the meagre surviving evidence argues for an increasing interest in historical writing, both in recovering the post-Roman past and reworking it to suit contemporary political and ecclesiastical circumstances, as well as recording events. The most important examples of this survive in British Library MS Harleian 3859, which, though it dates to *c*.1100, was copied, probably in St Davids, from an exemplar dating to between 954 and 988. The manuscript contains the

[151] Redknap and Lewis 2007; Edwards 2007a, 30–48; 2013, 41–67.

[152] Edwards 2013, nos AN26, CN37, 121–6.

[153] Okasha 1993; Tedeschi 2005, 225–302; Forsyth 2005; Preston-Jones and Okasha 2013, 253–6; Charles-Edwards 2013, 139–52.

[154] Moore, F. 1998, 23, fig. 4.1; Ogham in 3D; Macalister 1945, ix, 1–305, including Latin inscriptions nos 1, 19, 186, see also McManus 1991, 61; Swift 1997, 57–8.

[155] E.g. Davies, W. et al. 2000, nos F5, C1–2, M3; Charles-Edwards 2013, 169–73.

Historia Brittonum ('History of the Britons') written in Gwynedd in 829/30, quite possibly by a learned ecclesiastic named Nennius, and, inserted into it, is the text of a chronicle now known as the Harleian Chronicle (formerly the A text of the *Annales Cambriae*, 'The Annals of Wales'), which ends in 954, together with a set of royal genealogies which, it has been argued, began as a collection focused on Gwynedd to which other material was added.[156] The Harleian Chronicle, which began to be kept contemporaneously at St Davids in the late eighth century, contains earlier material derived from Ireland and north Britain, but some entries also indicate the incorporation of records compiled in north Wales, very possibly at Abergele. Although it terminates in 954, two later copies (*Annales Cambriae* B and C) indicate that the chronicle continued to be compiled in St Davids up until the beginning of the twelfth century. Though the entries are often laconic, they do nonetheless mention people, places, and events, such as Viking raids, not just in Wales but further afield, thereby helping to provide some kind of chronological framework for the period concerned.[157]

The most remarkable of the three is, however, the *Historia Brittonum*, which aims to provide a history of the Britons from their origins, through the Roman period, and up to the late seventh century. This is achieved through attempting to synchronize a range of disparate sources including myths, origin legends, hagiography, genealogy, computistics, folk tales, wonders, and poetry in a manner also found in Ireland at this time. It is therefore unreliable as history but is particularly interesting in providing evidence for intellectual, cultural, and antiquarian activity in both Latin and the vernacular in early ninth-century Gwynedd that articulates a strong sense of ethnic self-identification as Britons at a time of an emerging national consciousness in Wales.[158] For example, it demonstrates a lively interest in stories associated with places in the landscape, such as Caernarfon, the hillforts of Dinas Emrys and Moel Fenlli, and the Severn estuary,[159] and such onomastic lore played an important role as a mnemonic in understanding and reworking the past. It is also the first source to mention the poets Aneirin and Taliesin,[160] though the earliest manuscripts containing the poetry associated with them date to the thirteenth and fourteenth centuries.[161] Likewise, the story of Arthur hunting the magic boar, *Twrch Trywyth*, later appears in the Welsh tale of 'How Culhwch won Olwen', which survives in fourteenth-century manuscripts but

---

[156] Guy 2015; 2020, 39–40, 53–79, table 2.2, 334–7.

[157] Morris 1980, 45–9, 85–91; Dumville 2002; Guy 2015, 25–45; for the later textual history, see Hughes 1973; Pryce 2020, 7–8.

[158] Morris 1980; Dumville 1986; Hanning 1966, 94–5; Thomas 2022a, 2–3, 10–14.

[159] Morris 1980, chs 25, 32–5, 40–2, 67–9.

[160] They are placed chronologically immediately before Maelgwn of Gwynedd, one of the 'tyrants' castigated by Gildas, whose obit is recorded as 547 in the Harleian Chronicle; ibid., ch. 62, 45, 85.

[161] For wider discussion of the content and dating of poetry in these manuscripts, see Charles-Edwards 2013, 364–80, 659–78.

may have been composed in its present form sometime during the late eleventh or first half of the twelfth century.[162]

There has been considerable debate on the extent to which the early medieval Welsh were writing in the vernacular, since so little has come down to us.[163] The earliest written Welsh is found in the form of marginalia and glosses added to two manuscripts during the ninth and early tenth centuries, though in both cases these appear alongside Latin and are sometimes mixed with it, demonstrating the interplay of Latin and vernacular scholarship in ecclesiastical circles in Wales at this time. In the case of the Lichfield Gospels, the marginalia were added during the ninth century while the manuscript was at the monastery of Llandeilo Fawr and include an account in Latin of how it was acquired by Gelhi for the price of a horse (Fig. 1.3). Other marginalia are, however, of particular significance since they make up the earliest surviving evidence in Wales for legal writing. They comprise the manumission of a slave written in Latin, the resolution of a land dispute, written mainly in Welsh, and Latin charters with some Welsh insertions recording donations of land to the Church.[164] The charters are of considerable interest because they provide valuable information about working agricultural estates and are particularly important since they survive as contemporary examples. There are also 159 charters included amongst other works in the *Liber Landavensis* ('Book of Llandaf') compiled in the 1120s for Urban (d.1134), the first Norman bishop, in pursuit of claims concerning the extent of his diocese. These, however, have only come down to us in a form which has been edited, added to, and then reworked in pursuit of Urban's claims. They are therefore potentially much more difficult to use as evidence for the early Middle Ages than those in the Lichfield Gospels. Nevertheless, Wendy Davies demonstrated that it was possible to recover the original cores of many of these charters relating to estates largely in south and south-east Wales and south-west Herefordshire, and to provide a broad chronology anchored to otherwise identifiable historical figures who appear in the witness lists. Prior to the mid-ninth century, however, close dating is problematic. The earliest may have their origins as early as the mid-sixth century, but more probably in the seventh, and the latest can be dated to the end of the eleventh century. Nevertheless, judiciously used, these charters can cast valuable light on the landscape, changing practices of landholding, and the nature of the economy, as well as the early medieval Church.[165]

---

[162] Morris 1980, ch. 73; Bromwich and Evans 1992, lxiv–lxx; Davies, S. 2007, 198, 257, 270. On problems of dating, see Charles-Edwards 2013, 653–5.

[163] For discussion of the parameters and what is known about the uses of the written vernacular, see Sims-Williams 1998.

[164] Evans, J. G., and Rhys 1893, xliii–xlvii; Jenkins and Owen 1983; 1984.

[165] Davies, W. 1978; 1979a. For recent discussion supporting Wendy Davies's original interpretation with some modifications, see Davies, J. R. 2003, 3–5, who also analyses the early twelfth-century context of *Liber Landavensis*, Charles-Edwards 2013, 245–67, and Sims-Williams 2019a, which includes consideration of the problems with dating and the chronological sequence, 50–9.

Fig. 1.3. The Lichfield Gospels, the end of St Matthew's Gospel (p. 141). At the top of the page two ninth-century Latin and Welsh marginalia have been added recording its donation to Llandeilo Fawr, followed by the *surrexit* memorandum resolving a land dispute (copyright Lichfield Cathedral).

The second manuscript is the Cambridge Juvencus, a copy of the gospel story composed in Latin verse by the fourth-century poet Juvencus that was used as a scholarly text. It dates to the second half of the ninth century and may have been written in south-east Wales, possibly at Llantwit Major or Llancarfan. It contains large numbers of marginalia and glosses in Latin, Welsh, and Old Irish, the most significant of which are two groups of Welsh verses, the earliest examples of three-line verses known as *englynion* to have survived, one secular, the other in praise of God, which seem to have been added *c*.900 or slightly later.[166]

Oral performance of Welsh poetry was clearly important, but it is also argued that some poems in Welsh that have come down to us, predominantly in twelfth-, thirteenth-, and fourteenth-century manuscripts, may have their written origins during the latter half of the early Middle Ages. For example, two poems of three-line *englynion*, a dialogue between the old man Llywarch and his son Gwên and Llywarch's lament after his death defending a ford called Rhyd Forlas, form the earliest parts of the poem cycle *Canu Llywarch* ('The Song of Llywarch'). These survive in manuscripts of the thirteenth century and later but are now thought to have been composed between the late eighth and mid-ninth century,[167] though they depict the contemporary concerns of frontier life in the heroic past. It has also been shown, using place name evidence in a variety of sources demonstrating the importance of landscape lore, that the Llywarch cycle is associated with Brycheiniog and was very likely composed at Llangorse. Here there was both the royal crannog and an adjacent monastery offering opportunities for composition, performance, and preservation of the poems.[168]

Other poems are of interest to archaeologists because they refer to ancient monuments, such as prehistoric cairns and standing stones.[169] Verses known as *Englynion y Beddau* ('Stanzas of the Graves') enumerate the graves, mainly of mythical heroes, in different parts of Wales, a genre also found in early medieval Ireland. These have largely come down to us in a manuscript dated to the mid-thirteenth century, though most are thought to be earlier and have been attributed to the ninth or tenth. It is also proposed that these verses not only relate to stories rooted in local landscapes, some of which are traceable on the ground, but also indicate a desire to harness the ancient monuments within them as part of a heroic past that was also relevant to present concerns.[170] Similarly, a poem known as *Etmyg Dinbych* ('The Praise of Tenby'), the earliest copy of which belongs to the first half of the fourteenth century, has been dated to the ninth. It was composed in praise of the hillfort overlooking Tenby harbour in Pembrokeshire and its former lord, once the poet's patron.[171] Lastly, *Armes Prydein Vawr* ('The Great Prophecy of Britain'), in the same manuscript, was very possibly written at St Davids in the years leading up to King Æthelstan's victory at the Battle of Brunanburh in 937. It draws us into the complex politics of the time, calling

---

[166] McKee 2000; Williams, I. 1980, 90, 101–2.

[167] The most recent edition is Rowland 1990, 7–72, 386–9, 404–8, 468–70; see also Charles-Edwards 2013, 668–74.

[168] Sims-Williams 1993; see also Seaman 2019c.

[169] E.g. Petts 2007, 163–7, 170–1; Longley 2009, 105.

[170] Jones, T. 1967; Bollard and Griffiths 2015. On the role of prehistoric monuments in Anglo-Saxon England, see Semple 2013.

[171] Williams, I. 1980, 155–72; Gruffydd 2005; Charles-Edwards 2013, 659–65.

28 LIFE IN EARLY MEDIEVAL WALES

on the Welsh to resist harsh payments of tribute to the 'great king'. Instead, it predicts that the Welsh, with their allies, including the Irish, the 'heathens of Dublin', and the men of Strathclyde, with St David as their leader, will finally expel the English from Britain.[172]

In addition to simple cross-carved stones that mostly functioned as grave-markers, we also see, from the late eighth century onwards, more ambitious stone sculpture, mainly in the form of crosses and cross-slabs decorated with interlace and other ornament, and occasionally iconography.[173] These monuments are now very largely, but not exclusively, concentrated on church sites, with the grander examples often associated with the more important foundations. A significant number of these have sometimes lengthy inscriptions, though there are considerably more examples in the south than in the north. Almost all are in Latin, with the Old Welsh inscription at Tywyn and a personal name in runes on the cross-shaft at Corwen, Merioneth, the only exceptions.[174] Most are commemorative and sometimes include blessings or request prayers for the soul, and a few name historic figures, thereby helping to build a chronology. For example, one at Llantwit Major, Glamorgan, names Hywel ap Rhys, king of Glywysing (d.886), as the patron who set up the cross in memory of his father.[175] The latest datable monument, which is from St Davids, memorializes the sons of Bishop Abraham, who was killed by the Vikings in 1080.[176] However, a small number of inscribed monuments fulfilled other functions, notably as records of the donation and ownership of land.[177] In the case of the Pillar of Eliseg, Denbighshire, erected by Cyngen, the ruler of Powys (d.854) in memory of his great-grandfather, it also served as a form of propaganda, using the past to establish a legal right to the kingdom both in the present and in the future.[178]

There are, of course, several well-known outside sources that touch on Wales. In Ireland various sets of annals, such as the Annals of Ulster, are thought to be based on a lost Chronicle of Ireland. This was initiated at Iona in Dalriada in the later sixth century and then continued, probably in the eastern kingdom of Brega, from *c.*740 to 911, after which the main chronicle was compiled at Clonmacnoise.[179] The annals contain occasional entries relating to Wales and also follow the course of Hiberno-Scandinavian settlements in the Irish Sea region. Another example is the eighth-century

---

[172] Williams, I. 1972; Isaac 2007; Charles-Edwards 2013, 519–35.

[173] Edwards 2015; the inscription on Llantwit Major 3 suggests a late eighth-century date, Redknap and Lewis 2007, no. G65.

[174] Edwards 2013, nos MR25, MR4.

[175] Redknap and Lewis 2007, no. G63. The inscription reads: *[I]n inomine D(e)i Patris et [S]peretus Santdi (h)anc [cr]ucem Houelt prope[a]bit pro anima Res pa[tr]es e(i)us*, 'In the name of God the Father and the Holy Spirit, Houelt prepared this cross for the soul of his father Res'.

[176] Edwards 2007a, no. P98.

[177] See, for example. Llanfihangel Ystrad 1, Edwards 2007a, no. CD20, and St Brides Major and Wick 1, Redknap and Lewis 2007, no. G117.

[178] Edwards 2013, no. D3, 334.   [179] Charles-Edwards, T. M. 2006, 7–15.

origin legend known as *The Expulsion of the Déisi* that recalls Irish settlement in Dyfed in the post-Roman period and includes a genealogy comparable with that of the rulers of Dyfed in Harleian MS 3859.[180] Continuing ecclesiastical links across the Irish Sea were also important, as indicated by the spread of Welsh saints' cults, such as those of David and Deiniol, to Ireland, as evidenced in early ninth-century Irish martyrologies, and similar connections are also apparent with Brittany.[181]

Sources written in Anglo-Saxon England are particularly relevant to the development of the border region and changing relationships between Welsh and English kingdoms, as well as the Viking incursions. Bede's *Ecclesiastical History of the English Church and People* (*c.*731) charts the gradual contraction of British-controlled areas of England during the seventh century as well the ambitions of rulers such as Cadwallon of Gwynedd (d.634), Edwin of Deira (d.633), who claimed control of Anglesey, and Oswald of Northumbria, who was killed in the borderlands at *Maserfelth* (in Welsh sources *Cogwy*) near Oswestry in 642.[182] Later the Anglo-Saxon Chronicles, which commenced contemporaneously in the 890s during the reign of Alfred but continued in various interlinked strands beyond the Norman Conquest, record the role of Anglo-Saxon kings in cross-border relations,[183] for example, the raid on *Brecenanmere* in Brycheiniog, where Llangorse crannog was situated, on the orders of Alfred's daughter Æthelflæd in 916.[184] The *Life of King Alfred* is likewise of considerable interest since it was written by a Welshman, Asser of St Davids (d. *c.*909), who after 885 also spent extensive periods at Alfred's court, and though comparatively little of the work is directly concerned with Wales, it seems nonetheless to have been partly aimed at a Welsh audience.[185] In contrast, the *Ordinance concerning the Dunsæte*, which has recently been tentatively dated to the late tenth or early eleventh century rather than earlier during the reign of Æthelstan, is the record of an agreement between the Welsh and English on either side of a river, identified as the Wye in Archenfield (in Welsh, Ergyng) south of Hereford. It therefore focuses, not on kings, but on local cross-border relations and the pursuit of stolen cattle.[186]

Parts of Domesday Book, commissioned in late 1085 by William I to survey the economic resources of England and their value, also take in the borders of Wales, since the Normans were by then beginning to make inroads here as well, though the

---

[180] Ó Cathasaigh 1984; Rance 2001, 252–4.

[181] Stokes 1905, 80, 86; Best and Lawlor 1931, 20, 71; Ó Riain 1990; for Brittany, see Davies, W. 1982a, 215–16.

[182] Colgrave and Mynors 1969, ii.5, ii.9. iii.9; Stancliffe 1995; Charles-Edwards 2013, 391–2.

[183] For recent discussion of the relationship between the various Anglo-Saxon Chronicle texts, see Brooks 2010.

[184] Whitelock 1979, 916 (*s.a.* 919). The entry is in the Mercian Register or 'Annals of Æthelflæd', see Stafford 2008. On *Brecenanmere* and Llangorse crannog, see Lane and Redknap 2019, 3–4, 413–14.

[185] Keynes and Lapidge 1983, 56–7, chs 79–81.

[186] Molyneaux 2011; for a translation of the text, see Noble 1983, 103–9.

30 LIFE IN EARLY MEDIEVAL WALES

entries are less detailed, suggesting varying degrees of control. In the north-east the Cheshire survey includes the borderlands of *Exestan* and *Atiscros* hundreds between the Dee and the Clwyd, as well as Rhos and Rhufoniog between the Clwyd and the Conwy, and mention is also made of lands further west which had been invaded by Robert of Rhuddlan. Welsh borderlands now coming under Norman control are likewise included under Shropshire, and in Herefordshire the regions of Archenfield and Ewias centred on the Golden Valley, with parts of Gwent coming under Gloucestershire.[187]

The advent of the Norman incursions into Wales during the 1070s seems to have acted as an important catalyst for an upsurge in intellectual activity mainly centred in important ecclesiastical centres, both those that remained in native hands and those which had been taken over. As such, this reflects not only the end of an era with the need to save what might be lost but also an accommodation to the changing circumstances that inspired new works which might equally incorporate material adapted and reworked from the past. During the later eleventh and first half of the twelfth century there was an outstanding centre of native learning focused on Sulien (1011–91) and his sons Rhygyfarch (d.1099), Ieuan (d.1137), and Daniel (d.1127), at Llanbadarn Fawr in Ceredigion. However, the family also had an important link with St Davids, where Sulien became bishop 1073–8, returning for a further five years in 1080 after the murder of Bishop Abraham. A small number of manuscripts have survived associated with Llanbadarn Fawr, notably an illuminated psalter and martyrology (Fig. 1.4), as well as an important collection of Latin poetry, which includes Rhygyfarch's lament on the Norman invasion of Ceredigion in 1093.[188] Composition in Welsh is likewise suggested by an *englyn* to St Padarn copied by Ieuan into his manuscript of St Augustine's *De Trinitate*,[189] and David Stephenson has proposed that Rhygyfarch and Daniel were both involved in Latin chronicle writing at this time.[190] However, the most substantial work to have come down to us is Rhygyfarch's *Life* of St David (*Vita Sancti David*), which John Reuben Davies has argued, was written immediately after Sulien's death in 1091 × 1093.[191] This clearly sought to promote David's cult, thereby reflecting contemporary concerns, but it also shows a lively interest in the sacred landscape and claims to incorporate material 'found scattered in the most ancient writings of our country', including evidence for an earlier ascetic rule.[192]

A similar concern to recapture the lives of the early Welsh saints through writing hagiography is demonstrated in other sources of the period. *Liber Landavensis*, compiled in the 1120s for Urban, the first Norman bishop of the see, contained

[187] Williams, A., and Martin 2002; Darby 1987, 1–15; for Welsh communities living in English-controlled areas before the conquest noted in Domesday Book, see Lewis 2007.

[188] Lloyd 1941; Edwards 1995; Lapidge 1973–4.

[189] Russell 2012.   [190] Stephenson 2016, 25–8.

[191] Sharpe and Davies 2007; Davies, J. R. 2007a, 159–60; Dumville 2001, 12–15; Pryce 2022, 40–3.

[192] Sharpe and Davies 2007, chs 21–31, 54, n. 102, 66.

REDISCOVERING THE EARLY MEDIEVAL PAST IN WALES 31

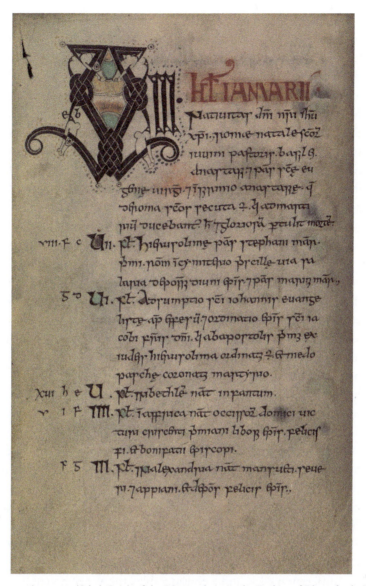

Fig. 1.4. The opening page (8 kal. Ian.) of the Martyrology in the Psalter of Rhygyfarch, Trinity College Dublin MS 50, fol. 5v (copyright the Board of Trinity College Dublin).

(in addition to the charter material already discussed) a series of saint's lives, including those of Dyfrig, Teilo, and Euddogwy, who were adopted as founding saints and whose former spheres of influence Llandaf now claimed. A second important collection of Welsh and two Irish saints' lives is contained in BL Cotton Vespasian A.XIV, which was probably copied in either Brecon or Monmouth Priory *c.*1200. This has the earliest version of Rhygyfarch's *Life* of St David as well as that of St Cadog of Llancarfan (*Vita Sancti Cadoci*), written by Lifris, a resident of that community and

32 LIFE IN EARLY MEDIEVAL WALES

the son of Bishop Herewald of Llandaf (d.1104), who was Urban's predecessor. This *Life* is more secular in tone than that of St David; the emphasis is on upholding the interests of Llancarfan and it includes an interesting account of the landed estates in possession of the various members of the community.[193]

A further development around this time was the emergence of written prose tales in Welsh. The earliest of these are the interlinked stories known as *Pedeir Keinc y Mabinogi* ('The Four Branches of the Mabinogi'). These demonstrate a long tradition of oral storytelling and performance. However, it is thought that they were first committed to writing, most likely by a single author, between *c.*1060 and 1120, though the two main manuscripts in which they are found date to the second half of the fourteenth and early fifteenth centuries. They are of interest here because they do not show any signs of Norman influence. Indeed, though there are traces of Christianity, they claim to depict a pre-Roman world of myths, heroes, shape-shifters, and Celtic deities, such as Rhiannon, who seems to be derived from the Celtic horse goddess Epona.[194] Therefore, although these lively tales cast a fascinating light on the mindset of the period in which they were written down, they are of little use as evidence for how most people lived, though they may reflect some aspects of courtly life. Nevertheless, the stories which make up these tales are deeply rooted in the landscapes of Wales and can, again, inform us about attitudes to archaeological monuments and the places where they stood.

The Welsh laws have been of considerable interest to those trying to reconstruct aspects of life in early medieval Wales, including archaeologists, because they contain evidence for the regulation of society and the economy.[195] However, they are extremely difficult to use for several reasons. They survive in three different redactions in Welsh—Cyfnerth (the earliest), Iorwerth, and Blegywryd—in over forty manuscripts dating from the early thirteenth to early sixteenth centuries; there are also five Latin versions. According to the prologues, they were compiled at the behest of the Welsh king Hywel Dda (d.950). However, it is more likely this was a later attribution, though this does not preclude his having been a lawgiver. At any rate, they now exist as law books put together in the later twelfth and early thirteenth centuries comprising tractates on different topics, and a considerable amount of material relates to that period rather than any earlier; other parts may have been updated or added at that time. Nevertheless, because some parts have parallels in early Irish laws committed to writing in the seventh and eighth centuries, it is generally believed that there is a core

---

[193] Pryce 2022, 38–44; Davies. J. R. 2003, 76–97; Davies, W. 1981, 519–30; Wade-Evans 1944, *Vita Sancti Cadoci*, chs 48–52; Charles-Edwards 2013, 604–7. On Herewald, see Sims-Williams 2019a, 18–21.

[194] Williams, I. 1951; Davies, S. 2007; Charles-Edwards 2013, 653–5.

[195] See in particular wider discussion of economic aspects of the hillfort at Dinas Powys in the light of the Welsh laws in Alcock 1987, 34, 39–40, 70, 73, 78–9, 85–6. G. R. J. Jones also took the laws as a starting point to project his 'multiple estate' model back through the early Middle Ages and even earlier. For a critique of this model, see Seaman 2012.

of early material within the Welsh laws as well.[196] Thomas Charles-Edwards has usefully listed what he believes to be the approximate date of the various tractates. For example, the tractate on Joint Ploughing seems to be early because of similarities with early Irish law, whilst the Laws of Court appear to have been written or rewritten during the tenth century.[197] However, much of the material which is potentially of most interest to archaeologists, such as the tractates on the Value of Wild and Tame, Corn Damage, and the Value of Houses, Trees, and Equipment, contains nothing which suggests they are of great antiquity. Such evidence may therefore touch on the lives of people in Wales at the end of the early Middle Ages, but these tractates may equally be responding to changes in Welsh society during the twelfth and early thirteenth centuries.

The three extant Middle Welsh chronicles known as *Brut y Tywysogion* ('The History of the Princes'),[198] which cover the period from 682 to shortly before the death of Llywelyn ap Gruffudd in 1282 and survive in manuscripts from the fourteenth century onwards, should also be considered here. They are most likely translations of a succession of earlier Latin chronicles, initially compiled at St Davids, then in the early twelfth century at Llanbadarn Fawr, very possibly by Daniel ap Sulien, and subsequently at the Cistercian house of Strata Florida.[199] The St Davids material is important here since it provides a chronological framework for the tenth and eleventh centuries and records events concerning various Welsh rulers, as well as relations with England and Ireland, including Hiberno-Scandinavian and other raids.

Three further sources are also significant, even though they were all written well after the advent of the Normans in Wales. The first is the Latin *Life* of Gruffudd ap Cynan, the ruler of Gwynedd, written sometime during the generation after his death in 1137. The work, which concentrates on Gruffudd's protracted struggle to gain the kingdom, is particularly illuminating on links across the Irish Sea, especially with Dublin, since his mother was Hiberno-Scandinavian and he had been brought up in Swords.[200] The other two were both written by Gerald of Wales (*c*.1146–*c*.1223). The *Itinerarium Kambriae* describes his journey round Wales in the spring of 1188 with Archbishop Baldwin of Canterbury to preach the Third Crusade, and the first redaction was written shortly afterwards. The aim of the *Descriptio Kambriae*, the earliest version of which was completed in 1193 or early 1194, is to describe Wales and its people, their good and bad points. Despite the fact that the first in particular depicts the world of native princes and marcher lords, what is relevant here, though sometimes

---

[196] Jenkins 1986, xi–xxxvii; Charles-Edwards 2013, 267–72. On the association with Hywel Dda, see Pryce 1986.

[197] Charles-Edwards 2013, 270–2.

[198] Peniarth MS 20 and the Red Book of Hergest are the main versions, but *Brenhinedd y Saesson* is also closely related; see Jones, T. 1952; 1955; 1971.

[199] Jones, O. W. and Pryce 2019, 214–18; Pryce 2020, 11–15.

[200] Russell 2005, 46–7, chs 2–6.

34 LIFE IN EARLY MEDIEVAL WALES

idealized, is Gerald's deep knowledge of his native country and its landscapes and his interest in local stories, in long-held customs, and, more generally, in how people lived.[201]

Finally, place names can potentially provide a valuable resource for the study of the early Middle Ages, particularly in conjunction with other forms of evidence. However, place names in Wales have yet to receive the scholarly attention afforded to those in English historic counties as a result of a century of research by the English Place-Name Society.[202] County and other place name surveys are also ongoing in Scotland, but in Wales Pembrokeshire and Cardiganshire are the only counties to have received detailed attention,[203] though parts of others have also been published as well as general and more popular county surveys.[204] In addition there are two significant online resources: firstly, place name forms collected from dated sources by Melville Richards, a pioneering scholar in the field, and now *The List of Historic Place Names of Wales* database with hundreds of thousands of place names derived from historic maps and other sources.[205] Nevertheless, only a very small number of place names in Wales were recorded before the later Middle Ages, making it more difficult to determine whether or not they were in use earlier. Indeed, some of the earliest noted are located in the Welsh borderlands contained in the Domesday survey.

Therefore, the number of surviving early medieval manuscripts associated with Wales is extremely small, and very few works relevant to Wales written before *c*.800, other than inscriptions, have come down to us. Nevertheless, from the early ninth century onwards, there is a gradual increase in the amount and variety of material, both in Latin and Welsh, including poetry, which has survived, and there is also a range of sources in England, Ireland, and Brittany which touch on Wales. However, the real upsurge in native written sources in Wales coincides with the advent of the Normans, who were an important catalyst, both inspiring new works and acting as a spur to save what might otherwise have been lost. These, and a small number of later medieval written sources, are also informative providing they are handled judiciously. Thus, when critically used in conjunction with the archaeology, the written evidence can indeed help to provide a fuller picture of how people lived in early medieval Wales.

[201] Thorpe 1978.   [202] Survey of English Place-Names.
[203] Charles 1992; Wmffre 2004.
[204] E.g. Jones, G. T. and Roberts 1996; Pierce 2002; Owen and Gruffydd 2017.
[205] Archif Melville Richards.

TWO

Space and Time

To understand how early medieval people lived, we need to consider the relationship between Wales as a geographical entity and the wider world, including both the Irish Sea region and the borderlands with England. We should also be aware of potential influences that the distinctive geography of Wales had on people's lives, how communities interacted with and shaped their physical surroundings, and how the changing climate and environment affected productivity. In addition, it is relevant to consider ideas about time and how early medieval people perceived it, including their response to earlier monuments in the landscape and how these were harnessed to meet contemporary concerns. My aim in this chapter is to introduce some more general concepts before returning to some aspects in more detail later on.

LAND AND SEA

The landscape of Wales is dominated by its central mountainous massif, but it also has, at 2,120 kilometres, a very long coastline (Fig. 2.1). Early medieval settlement, as today, would have been concentrated in the more fertile coastal areas and river valleys, leading to distinctive regional landscapes and identities. Nonetheless, in approaching the extent to which their geographical surroundings affected people's lives, we need to recognize the continuing impact of ideas brought to the fore by Cyril Fox in *The Personality of Britain* (Chapter 1).[1] Whilst his views on environmental determinism and the lack of human agency are clearly outmoded, we should acknowledge that the choices and innovations people made were in part the result of coming to terms with their physical surroundings and the opportunities and limitations these presented.[2]

Gildas describes the island of Britain as lying 'virtually at the end of the world'.[3] Even so, western Britain and Ireland were not cut off, as they are located on the

---

[1] Fox 1943.

[2] For discussion with reference to early medieval England, see Williamson 2013, 2–5; for the west, see Cunliffe 2001, 19.

[3] *Brittannia insula in extremo ferme orbis*, Winterbottom 1978, ch. 3. For discussion of the perceived location of Britain at this time with Jerusalem as the centre of the known world, see O'Loughlin 1997.

Life in Early Medieval Wales. Nancy Edwards, Oxford University Press. © Nancy Edwards 2023.
DOI: 10.1093/oso/9780198733218.003.0002

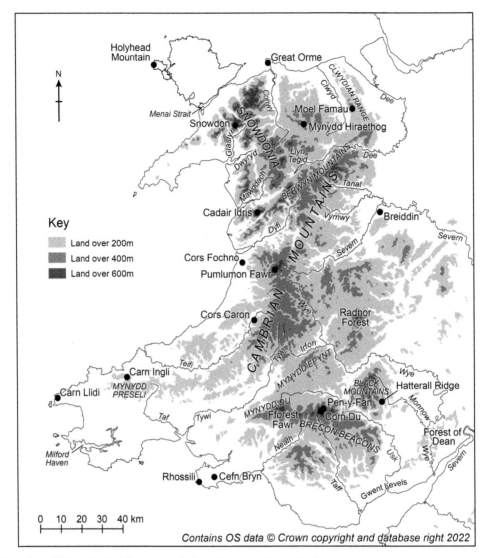

Fig. 2.1. Wales: physical features, including places mentioned in the text.

Atlantic seaways, of which the Irish Sea is a part, and it has long been argued that, from prehistory onwards, this maritime environment has helped to shape people's lives.[4] During the Roman period and up to around 700, contacts via long-distance routes through the Irish Sea were largely concentrated southwards towards Brittany, western France, Iberia, and ultimately the Mediterranean. However, from the mid-seventh century, though some contact along the Atlantic seaways probably persisted, the focus moves to the east with the rise of North Sea and cross-Channel routes

[4] Cunliffe 2001, 16–18.

between England, the Continent, and Scandinavia. And from the ninth century onwards, there is a further shift north towards Scandinavia as the Irish Sea region was drawn into the ambit of the Viking world.[5] We need to view early medieval Wales within these changing networks and recognize the significance of the Irish Sea as a routeway rather than a barrier. For example, on a clear day, from Holyhead Mountain (Mynydd Cybi) on Anglesey, it is possible to glimpse both the Isle of Man and the Wicklow mountains of Ireland. The latter are similarly visible from Carn Llidi in Pembrokeshire. Coastal maritime contacts would also have been important. For instance, from the Great Orme a very wide seascape is visible—to the west Anglesey, the island of Ynys Seiriol, and the approach to the Menai Strait, and to the east as far as the Dee estuary and Wirral. It is also only a short hop across the Severn estuary to Somerset. In the case of St Martin's Haven, Pembrokeshire, a cross-carved stone found near the beach may have functioned as a prayer station marking an embarkation point for pilgrims travelling across St Bride's Bay to St Davids.[6]

Of course those traversing the Irish Sea needed to be cognizant of the often hazardous winds and tides outside the summer months, as well as coastal rocks and reefs.[7] That Mediterranean ships were reaching the Irish Sea as early as the second or first century BC is demonstrated by a lead anchor stock discovered in a rocky cove near the tip of the Llŷn peninsula, Caernarfonshire.[8] Later, evidence for coastal and riverine trade around the Severn estuary is highlighted by the Barland's Farm boat, a plank-built, flat-bottomed sailing vessel originally about 11.4 metres long, which was found on the edge of the Caldicot Level and dated to the late third or early fourth century AD. Such 'Romano-Celtic' boats were capable of travelling considerable distances, but there is no indication how long they remained in use beyond the Roman period.[9] Equally, there is no archaeological evidence of Mediterranean vessels in northern waters at this time.[10] However, the early medieval Irish, timber-framed, hide *currach*, propelled by oars or sail, could undoubtedly have crossed the Irish Sea and may have reached Brittany or even further.[11] Whether similar craft were also used in Britain is less clear, though Gildas refers to *curuci* in the hands of the Picts.[12]

[5] Loveluck 2013, 14–20; Cunliffe 2001, figs 2.18, 11.2, 11.7; Charles-Edwards 2013, 469, map 22.

[6] Edwards 2007a, no. P59.

[7] Cunliffe 2001, 36–9, 59. On maritime conditions in the Severn estuary and Bristol Channel, see Nayling and McGrail 2004, 212–15.

[8] Boon 1977.   [9] Nayling and McGrail 2004, 208–9, 216, 227–9.

[10] Cunliffe 2001, 68–71; Nayling and McGrail 2004; Kingsley 2009.

[11] McGrail 1998, 173–91; MacCarthaigh 2008. A recent *currach* voyage using oars from Dublin to Anglesey took seventeen hours; Darina Tully (pers. comm.). For a modern, long-distance voyage using sail, see Severin 1978.

[12] Winterbottom 1978, ch. 19; the Latin ablative *curucis* (a unique word) has been translated as 'coracles', but these would have been too small for sea voyages. Williams, Hugh 1899–1901, i, 44, suggests the boats must have had sails. Gerald of Wales refers to a *currach* in *The History and Topography of Ireland*, contrasting it with a Welsh coracle, detailed in *The Description of Wales*; O'Meara 1982, 111; Thorpe 1978, ch. 17.

38 LIFE IN EARLY MEDIEVAL WALES

By the early seventh century, Bede's references to Edwin of Deira's claims over the Isle of Man and Anglesey suggest that clinker-built, plank boats of Anglo-Saxon type were reaching the Irish Sea.[13] However, from the end of the eighth century, the advent of Viking sailing ships had a more lasting impact. The unearthing of clench nails in a tenth-century midden at Llanbedrgoch, Anglesey, demonstrates the use of such craft in north Wales,[14] and a century later the Welsh ruler Gruffudd ap Llywelyn had his own fleet on the Clwyd, destroyed in a surprise attack on Rhuddlan in 1063.[15] In addition, the importance of long-distance contacts between the Irish Sea region and Scandinavia has been highlighted by the discovery of Skuldelev 2 at Roskilde in Denmark. Dendrochronology has shown that this warship had been built *c.*1042, probably in Dublin, and adds to the significant number of timbers from both large and small Hiberno-Scandinavian vessels found in the town.[16] However, the recovery of a Hiberno-Scandinavian, Urnes-style, sword pommel dating to the early twelfth century from the Smalls Reef off Pembrokeshire is indicative of a wreck site that underlines the perils of the sea.[17]

Early medieval maritime communications and the mobility of people around and across the Irish Sea, as well as potentially further afield, are also being revealed as a result of rapid developments in strontium and oxygen isotope analysis of teeth and bone from individuals in Wales, Ireland, and the Isle of Man, suggesting that some were not locally born. For example, investigation of individuals whose remains have been radiocarbon-dated to the pre-Viking period from cemeteries in the Isle of Man has indicated that, while the majority were local, some seem to have arrived on the island from coastal areas of Britain (including Wales), Ireland, and the Atlantic sea-board. There is also the possibility that one young woman could have come from southern Iberia or the Mediterranean, though other dietary factors might be at play. Even so, the notion of such long-distance travel is supported by well-evidenced trade in imported ceramics and glass from the Mediterranean and south-west France reaching the Irish Sea region at this time.[18]

Geographically, west Wales looks primarily towards the Irish Sea, However, in the eastern part communication is easier with the north-west, West Midlands, and south-west of England since the uplands, with their older geology, give way to the newer rocks in the lowlands to the east. For example, the panorama from the Breiddin hill-fort, sited on a dramatic dolerite hill east of the Severn, takes in, to the west, the

[13] Colgrave and Mynors 1969, ii.5, ii.9; Maddicott 2000, 39–40; Gifford and Gifford 1999.

[14] Redknap 2000, 57, fig. 72. Although part of a clinker-built ship, found near the mouth of the Usk in 1878, was originally identified as of Viking type, radiocarbon dating of heartwood (cal. AD 880–1220) was inconclusive and a later medieval date is more likely; see Morgan 1882; Hutchinson 1984; Redknap 2000, 15, 60; Redknap et al. 2019, 95.

[15] Douglas and Greenaway 1981; Davies, M. 2002, 231–2, 240.

[16] Wallace 2016, 182–8.   [17] Redknap 2000, 55, 58–60, 91; Redknap et al. 2019, 98–9.

[18] Hemer et al. 2014; Campbell 2007a; Duggan 2018.

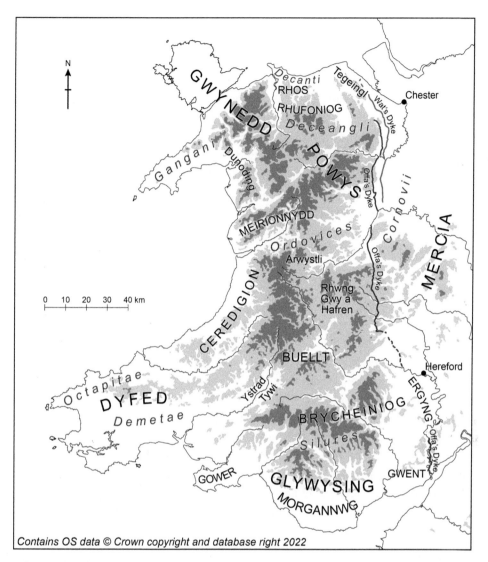

Fig. 2.2. Wales, showing the locations of pre-Roman peoples (in italics), early medieval kingdoms (in capitals), and other regions (in upper/lower case) (after W. Davies 1982a, figs 32, 38, with alterations and additions).

Berwyn Mountains and, to the east and north-east, the lowland expanse of the Shropshire and Cheshire plains.[19] From the seventh century onwards the formative change was the gradual evolution of these borderlands resulting from the rise of Mercia with the consequent loss of British territory to the east (Fig. 2.2). However, further south, Ergyng (Archenfield in English)—situated west of the Wye but

---

[19] In Fox's terminology this is the border between the highland and lowland zones. Milward and Robinson 1978, 20–1, fig. 1; Musson 1991, 173–93.

probably originally stretching eastwards to include the small Roman town of *Ariconium* (Weston-under-Penyard), from which it takes its name—continued to have a Welsh identity into the eleventh century.[20] The process of defining a border between Wales and England commenced in the later eighth and early ninth centuries with the construction of Offa's and Wat's Dykes; therefore the concept of a frontier region, later known as the Welsh Marches, was already beginning to evolve.[21]

The central mountainous massif of Wales dominates the landscape in almost every part of the country. From Anglesey, Gerald of Wales comments on the spectacular views of northern Snowdonia (Eryri), the mountains seeming 'to rear their lofty summits right up to the clouds',[22] with Snowdon (Yr Wyddfa) rising to 1,085 metres. The fifth-century inscribed stone from Llanaber, Merioneth, commemorates *Caelexti Monedorigi* and his second name—literally 'mountain king'—similarly draws attention to the terrain in which he had lived.[23] Cadair Idris commands the dramatic scenery to the south. To the east of the Conwy, the bleak undulating moorland of Mynydd Hiraethog stretches to the Clwyd and, to the east again, is the Clwydian Range, with its rolling hills crowned by Moel Famau.[24] South of the Dee, the Berwyn Mountains rise steeply, with the central ridge towering over the Dee valley. Mid Wales south of the Dyfi is dominated by the north-east/south-west spine of the Cambrian Mountains, the highest peak of which is Pumlumon Fawr, while to the east are the hills, high moorland plateaus, and steep-sided, narrow valleys of Radnor Forest. The south and south-east of Wales also have considerable areas of upland. Mynydd Epynt is a desolate expanse pierced by rivers flowing into the Usk,[25] whilst south of the Wye are the Black Mountains, stretching eastwards into the borders as far as Hatterall Ridge, the slopes of which are broken by cliffs with narrow valleys below. To the west are the Brecon Beacons with the twin 'tabletop' summits of Pen-y-Fan and Corn Du, the smaller peaks and ridges of Fforest Fawr and Mynydd Du, and, to the south, the plateau is broken up by numerous valleys.[26] In the far south-west Mynydd Preseli extends into northern Pembrokeshire.

In his *Description of Wales*, Gerald lists the principal rivers and their courses.[27] The most important is the Severn, which rises in the mountains of Pumlumon before flowing out into the Severn Sea (Bristol Channel). Gildas compares it with the Thames as two 'arms of the sea along which luxuries from overseas used to be brought by ship', a route which may already have been important in later prehistory.[28] The river also had

[20] Charles-Edwards 2013, 381–436; Lieberman 2008, 79–80; Molyneaux 2011; Copplestone-Crow 2009, 11–15; Burnham and Davies 2010, 309–10.

[21] Lieberman 2008, 75–82; Ray and Bapty 2016, 254–97, 344–62; Malim and Hayes 2008.

[22] Browne and Hughes 2003, 9–10; Thorpe 1978, 194.   [23] Edwards 2013, no. MR1.

[24] Brown 2004, 3–12.   [25] Browne and Hughes 2003, 81–3, 87–8.

[26] Brereton 1990, 9–10, 24–6.   [27] Thorpe 1978, 224–30.

[28] *brachiis, per quae eidem olim transmarinae deliciae ratibus vehebantur*, Winterbottom 1978, ch. 3. On the river's significance in later prehistory, see Sherratt 1996, 214, 216.

a sacred dimension, a vestige of which may still be apparent in the *Historia Brittonum*, which includes no fewer than three 'Wonders of Britain' associated with the estuary and its dramatic tidal bore.[29] However, though it was navigable in the later Middle Ages as far as Pool Quay in Montgomeryshire,[30] with the loss of British territory to the east much of its course fell into English hands, potentially creating a barrier rather than a conduit. This is also true of the Wye, which flows south through Hereford and the borderlands of Ergyng to join the Severn estuary. Similarly, the Dee, the name of which also has sacred connotations,[31] rises near Llyn Tegid, flowing eastwards into England and then northwards through Chester, its wide estuary separating Wirral from the lowlands of north-east Wales.

Fords were noted places of confrontation in border warfare, made clear in the poetry of Llywarch Hen, whose son Gwên dies defending Rhyd Forlas, and also in the long-term strategic significance of the crossing point at Rhydwhyman on the Severn in Montgomeryshire. As with rivers and streams, fords are commonly mentioned on estate boundaries in the Llandaf charters, but only occasionally bridges.[32] Coracles and log-boats would have provided suitable transport on rivers and lakes. The former, small, rounded boats with wooden frames covered in hide are mentioned by Gerald,[33] and a well-preserved example of the latter was found close to the shore of Llangorse Lake near the late ninth-century royal crannog and is of a broadly similar date.[34]

When Gerald journeyed through Wales in 1188, he travelled clockwise from Hereford round the perimeter through the borderlands and coastal lowlands. The central mountainous massif and river valleys divide these up into four distinct regions. The south-east, from the Wye to the Neath, broadly speaking by the Roman period embraced the territory of the Silures, later the early medieval kingdoms of Brycheiniog, Ergyng, Gwent, and Glywysing (Fig. 2.2).[35] In landscape terms Brycheiniog was centred on the fertile valley of the Usk, extending eastwards to Llangorse Lake, while, as we have seen, Ergyng originally straddled the Wye, taking in the undulating farmlands of southern Herefordshire. To the south again, between the Wye and Severn, the landscape later known as the Forest of Dean was rich in iron ore.[36] West of the Wye, Gwent took its name from the Roman town of *Venta Silurum* (Caerwent), the *civitas* capital of the Silures, though it was later subsumed into Glywysing (later Morgannwg),

[29] Ross 1967, 47–8; Rivet and Smith 1979, 450–1; Morris 1980, chs 68–9, 72. On *Mirabilia*, 'Wonders', see Roberts 1991, 88–90. On the sacred nature of estuaries, see Nicolaisen 1997.

[30] Silvester 1992, 152.   [31] Rivet and Smith 1979, 336–7.

[32] Rowland 1990, 404–8, 468–70; Barker and Higham 1982, 1–4; Davies, W. 1978, 26, 30.

[33] Thorpe 1978, 252, i.17; on construction and more modern coracle use, see Jenkins 2006.

[34] Lane and Redknap 2019, 341–6.

[35] For pre-Roman tribal territories, see Jarrett and Mann 1968; Burnham and Davies 2010, 19–22; for early medieval kingdoms, see Davies, W. 1982a, 90–102, figs 32, 38.

[36] Darby 1954, 23, 29–32, 52–3.

42 LIFE IN EARLY MEDIEVAL WALES

the focus of which extended westwards across the coastal wetlands of the Gwent Levels and the rich lowlands of the Usk and Vale of Glamorgan.[37]

Having traversed the south-east, Gerald crossed the River Neath by boat, after his horse had almost succumbed to the treacherous quicksands, and into the south-west.[38] By the Roman period this region comprised the territory of the Demetae with their probable *civitas* capital at *Moridunum* (Carmarthen) on the Tywi, and a likely sub-group, the Octapitae, to the north.[39] By the mid-sixth century the lands of the Demetae had evolved into the early medieval kingdom of Dyfed, but there is also evidence for the one-time existence of further kingdoms: Gower, which may also have included Ystrad Tywi, and Ceredigion.[40] Geographically, the Gower peninsula has a distinctive limestone landscape with coastal cliffs and caves dominated by the hills of Cefn Bryn and Rhossili. To the west is the broad, lush valley of the Tywi and, west again, the long, ragged coastline of Pembrokeshire, pierced by the creeks and mudflats of Milford Haven. However, in the north the landscape is rockier and less productive, whilst the slopes of Mynydd Preseli, crowned by moorland and the rock-strewn summit of Carn Ingli, drop sharply onto the narrow coastal plain. Ieuan ap Sulien praises Ceredigion, which stretches north from the Teifi to the Dyfi, in a poem (1085 × 1091) to his father. He extols his native region with its rich pastures in the uplands of Pumlumon and fertile coastal lowlands[41] broken up by east–west flowing rivers, with the distinctive raised bogs of Cors Caron and Cors Fochno.

Gerald then took a boat across the Dyfi into the northern half of the country. It is argued that, by the beginning of the Roman period, the lands of the Ordovices were centred on mid Wales with other territories along the north Wales coast: the Gangani on the Llŷn, the Decanti east of the Conwy estuary and possibly on Anglesey, and the Deceangli roughly between the Clwyd and the Dee.[42] In the early medieval period, Anglesey seems to have been the core of the kingdom of Gwynedd, which had emerged by the mid-sixth century and was focused on the north-west but later expanded eastwards. There is also evidence for the existence of the kingdom of Meirionnydd and possibly Dunoding, which may have been subject to it.[43]

---

[37] Davies, W. 1982a, 93–4; Rippon 1996, 2–5.   [38] Thorpe 1978, 130–1.

[39] Jarrett and Mann 1968, 166–7.

[40] Vortipor is 'tyrant of the Demetae' in *De Excidio Britanniae*; see Winterbottom 1978, ch. 31. See also Davies, W. 1982a, 93; Edwards 2007a, 5.

[41] Lapidge 1973–4, 81–5, ll. 56–66.

[42] Jarrett and Mann 1968, 165–6, 167–70; Arnold and Davies 2000, fig. 9.2b. The name of the Decanti survives in *Arx Decantorum*, the hillfort of Degannwy, noted in the Harleian Chronicle in 812 and 822 (Morris 1980, 88–9), but may also be referenced in the Irish personal name *Maccvdecceti* on the early to mid-sixth-century inscribed stone from Penrhosllugwy, Anglesey; Edwards 2007a, no. AN56, 239.

[43] See Gildas's reference to Maglocunus (Maelgwn) of Gwynedd as *insularis draco* ('dragon of the island'), Winterbottom 1978, ch. 33, 102. King Catamanus (d. *c*.625) was commemorated at Llangadwaladr, near Aberffraw, Anglesey, and for *Venedotis* ('Gwynedd') see the inscription on Ffestiniog 1, Edwards 2013, 8, nos AN26, MR8. See also Davies, W. 1982a, 92, 98–9; Charles-Edwards 2013, 476.

Geographically, the north-west, which extends as far as the Conwy, is dominated by Snowdonia, but also takes in the narrow coastal strip of Meirionnydd, the wide river estuaries of the Glaslyn and the Dwyryd, and the more productive soils of the Llŷn peninsula with its isolated hills and dramatic coastal scenery with Bardsey Island (Ynys Enlli) at its tip. The narrow coastal strip continues north into Arfon, forming the eastern side of the Menai Strait, with the large, relatively low-lying island of Anglesey across the water. Despite its rocky landscape, which he compared with that around St Davids, Gerald also emphasized the island's suitability for grain, giving it the Welsh epithet *Môn mam Cymru* ('Anglesey the mother of Wales'), a productivity similarly alluded to by Bede.[44]

North-east Wales stretches from the Conwy valley, with its rich rolling farmlands, to the Dee and then south as far as of the upper reaches of the Severn. In the early Middle Ages lands east of the Conwy included the shadowy kingdoms of Rhos and Rhufoniog, which may have been subject to Gwynedd, and the contested borderlands east of the Dee, later known as Tegeingl, a name derived from the Deceangli.[45] However, the major kingdom in this region was Powys, the origins of which are obscure. In the earlier ninth century it may have been centred on the Vale of Llangollen but also extended southwards and may once have stretched much further east into the former territory of the Cornovii, whose *civitas* capital had been at *Viroconium* (Wroxeter), and northwards to the Roman legionary fortress of *Deva* (Chester).[46] In landscape terms, though there are substantial areas of upland, the region takes in both the coastal lowlands extending into the Cheshire plain and fertile river valleys, notably the Clwyd with—to the west—its characteristic limestone scenery and the east–west corridor of the Dee with the undulating hills of the Vale of Llangollen.[47] South again, facing the Shropshire plain, is a landscape of rolling hills and river valleys, including the Tanat and Vyrnwy, tributaries of the Severn. Very little is known about possible early medieval kingdoms or territories in this region or further south between the Severn and the Wye (Rhwng Gwy a Hafren), though a ruler of Buellt and Gwerthrynion is mentioned in the *Historia Brittonum*.[48]

Gerald noted that it took eight days to cross the country from Porth Wygir on Anglesey to Portskewett in Gwent, a distance of about 320 kilometres.[49] Pieces of decorated equine equipment, mainly dating to the tenth and eleventh centuries, testify to the importance of horses as a means of transport amongst the elite, who may regularly have journeyed long distances, and this is also supported by the written

---

[44] Thorpe 1978, 187; Colgrave and Mynors 1969, ii.9.

[45] Morris 1980, 48, 89, AD816; Davies, W. 1982a, 98–9; Owen and Gruffydd 2017, 184.

[46] Ibid., 94; Charles-Edwards 2013, 14–17. The location of the Pillar of Eliseg suggests the Vale of Llangollen was a core territory; see Edwards 2013, 8–9, 13, no. D3.

[47] Clwyd-Powys Archaeological Trust.

[48] Morris 1980, ch. 49; Charles-Edwards 2013, 16–17.   [49] Thorpe 1978, 220.

sources.[50] For example, Asser travelled by horse from King Alfred's court to St Davids, and Hywel Dda, one of several rulers to attend the court of King Æthelstan, also undertook a pilgrimage to Rome.[51] However, most people would probably have travelled on foot and, although oxygen and strontium isotope analysis suggests that some moved considerable distances, it remains impossible to tell how common this may have been.

Roman roads and, in some instances, older prehistoric trackways remained important routes of communication in early medieval Wales, as they did in England.[52] A significant number of fifth- and sixth-century inscribed stones found in the uplands of the north-west, Breconshire, and Glamorgan were sited with reference to Roman roads so that they would have been visible to passers-by and thereby remained important waymarkers in the landscape. A particularly good example is the monument commemorating Devacus son of Iustus at Ystradfellte, Breconshire, which still stands in moorland beside the Roman road running between the forts of Brecon Gaer and Coelbren (Fig. 2.3). An exploratory excavation prior to its re-erection suggested that the stone had originally been set into the side of the road, indicating that by this time the edge was overgrown.[53] Continuing burial beside Roman roads is likewise indicated by the siting of cemeteries, such as that at Druid, Denbighshire.[54] A cross of likely seventh- to ninth-century date incised on the living rock marks the line of the only routeway west from the Conwy through the upland pass at Bwlch y Ddeufaen. This had its origins in the Neolithic but was later followed by the Roman road heading for the fort at *Segontium* (Caernarfon).[55] It has also been argued that a cross-incised stone sited close to the modern road signals the path taken by pilgrims travelling westwards across northern Pembrokeshire since it marks where they first glimpsed the *cantref* of Pebidiog, where St Davids was located.[56]

Even though a significant number of boundary clauses in the Llandaf charters mention both upland and lowland roads in the south-east, identifying them on the ground is far from easy.[57] Equally, fords and their associated routeways may have continued in use over many centuries as, for example, a hollow way approaching the Monnow near Clodock, Herefordshire, but dating is very difficult.[58] Andrew Fleming has also proposed that long-distance horse routes were an essential instrument of elite power, but the earliest dating indications are later medieval.[59] There is nonetheless some evidence for the construction of new roads and tracks in Wales towards the end of the early

---

[50] Redknap 2013.

[51] Keynes and Lapidge 1983, 94, ch. 79; Whitelock 1979, AD 926; Morris 1980, 49, 91, AD 928.

[52] Reynolds and Langlands 2011, 412–17.

[53] Fox, A. 1939; Fox, C. 1940a; Redknap and Lewis 2007, no. B50. See also Edwards 2007a, Castell Dwyran 1, no. CM3; 2013, 46–7.

[54] Jones, N. W. et al. 2013b, 85–90.   [55] Edwards 2013, Caerhun 1, no. CN13.

[56] Edwards 2007a, Fishguard South 1, no. P16.   [57] Davies, W. 1978, 30–1.

[58] Bick 2004, 103.   [59] Fleming 2010.

Fig. 2.3. The sixth-century, Latin-inscribed stone commemorating Dervacus son of Iustus standing beside the Roman road, Ystradfellte, Breconshire (from the collections of the National Monuments Record of Wales © Paul R. Davis).

medieval period. The most significant archaeological discovery is a wooden trackway on the fringes of Cors Fochno, where a length of some 800 metres has been traced approaching the church at Llangynfelyn (Fig. 2.4). Its construction has been dated by radiocarbon and dendrochronology to the early to mid-eleventh century, though repairs continued into the twelfth. In wetter areas a foundation had been laid consisting of driven stakes, large irregular stones, and sometimes gravel, and at one point bundles of small rods had been placed on the side of the track, probably to facilitate drainage. The superstructure of side rails supporting mainly cross timbers largely consisted of alder, but hazel, oak, willow, and ash were also represented, all readily available in the vicinity.[60] In other cases dating is inconclusive. Investigation of a site on Newton Moor in the Vale of Glamorgan after the discovery of a penannular brooch revealed undated pieces of oak, alder, and hazel, suggesting a possible trackway.[61] A fragmentary timber path forming a crude bridge made of alder, ash, and willow also came to light on the foreshore at Llanaber, Merioneth, but the radiocarbon dates may be later medieval.[62] Rare examples of early medieval wooden trackways known in

---

[60] Page et al. 2012.   [61] Redknap 1992.

[62] Musson et al. 1989. Radiocarbon dates from three timbers span the early eleventh to later thirteenth centuries: HAR 742, 890±80, cal. AD 1010–1280; HAR 743, 850±70, cal. AD 1030–1280; HAR 741, 840±70, cal. AD 1040–1280.

Fig. 2.4. Llangynfelyn trackway, Cors Fochno, Cardiganshire (photograph: Dyfed Archaeological Trust).

England appear earlier, for example a causeway and bridgehead associated with the monastery at Glastonbury. This is also true in Ireland, where discoveries are more common as, for example, the trackways at Bloomhill and Lemanaghan, Co. Offaly, where the stimulus for construction may likewise have arisen from the organization of monastic estates.[63] Similarly, Rhygyfarch, in his *Life* of St David (1091 × 1093), depicts the brethren digging a road near the monastery boundary to facilitate the delivery of goods, though this story may also reflect the influence of Irish hagiography.[64]

CLIMATE CHANGE AND ITS IMPACT

The climate of Wales is shaped by both the central mountainous massif and exposure to the prevailing, rain-bearing winds and gales coming in from the Atlantic. However, the effects of the latter are often ameliorated by the relatively sheltered position of Wales in relation to the Irish Sea. The climate today is therefore wet and windy but often quite mild, though the temperature depends on proximity to the coast. The amount of cloud and rainfall rapidly increases in the uplands, rising in

---

[63] Brunning 2010; Breen 1988; O'Carroll 2001, 16–18; Bhreathnach 2014, 118–19.
[64] Sharpe and Davies 2007, ch. 41, 137, n. 80.

parts of Snowdonia to over 4,000 millimetres a year, with snow on the mountaintops in winter. Prior to the more serious effects of climate change we are now experiencing, the average temperature in December and January could be as high as 5°C, whilst that in July and August only reached 15°C. Nevertheless, regional differences lead to significant variations in the climate and the length of the growing season as well as the dates of first and last frosts which, together with height above sea level and soil fertility, have important implications for food production. Anglesey, Llŷn, and lowland Pembrokeshire, though windy, are relatively mild with comparatively low rainfall and a long growing season with only occasional frosts between November and early April. Rainfall on the north-east coast is also low but the growing season is shorter, and this is also true in the Vale of Glamorgan, though here the rainfall is higher. However, inland lowland valleys in the eastern half of Wales, while having relatively restricted rainfall, also suffer from low night-time temperatures with frosts from early October to the middle of May.[65]

Unusual weather events were occasionally recorded in the chronicles. For instance, 'The rain turned to blood...', noted in 689, refers to red dust blown up from the Sahara, whilst the 'parched summer' of 721 was clearly exceptional. By contrast, in 1047 snow lay from the beginning of January to the feast of St Patrick (17 March). Rain causing swollen rivers and high tides could also be a real danger: for example, the *Life* of St Illtud notes that floods frequently threatened to inundate the cemetery at Llantwit Major.[66]

While the main characteristics of the climate in the later Roman period and early Middle Ages would have been broadly similar to the present, there were also important differences. These have been identified over the last thirty years through major advances in our understanding of first-millennium AD climate change in the northern hemisphere. This has been achieved through the establishment of long dendrochronological sequences in which annual tree-ring widths reflect weather events and summer temperatures alongside the study of well-dated Greenland ice cores which preserve indications of volcanic eruptions, as well as other environmental evidence, such as the advance and retreat of glaciers and lake, bog, and marine sediments. There is a consensus that during the Roman period the climate in Britain and Ireland was warmer and drier than previously. However, this trend was then reversed, and it has been argued that, beginning in 536, there was a serious climatic downturn across the northern hemisphere lasting until *c*.550, with a longer-term impact partly caused by a decline in solar output until *c*.660. What is now known as the 'Late Antique Little Ice Age' was precipitated by a series of major volcanic eruptions centred on North and Central America with the first in 536 causing a dust veil followed by further episodes in 539/40 and probably 547. These brought about abrupt summer cooling prolonged

---

[65] Sumner 1977, 55–9, fig. 13; 1997.

[66] Morris 1980, 46–7, 87; Jones, T. 1952, 14; Wade-Evans 1944, 210–13, ch. 13. See also Grigg 2013.

48 LIFE IN EARLY MEDIEVAL WALES

by other environmental factors.[67] The Irish tree-ring chronology clearly reflects the first two of these volcanic events followed by wetter conditions, and these are also found in northern Britain,[68] thereby signalling their potential relevance to Wales. Even so, not all would accept that these events had any significant impact in Britain.[69] From *c*.800, however, it has been suggested that in the northern hemisphere the climate warmed until around 900, before cooling somewhat *c*.900–50, with renewed warming until around 1100, though some harsh winters were also recorded which likewise reflect volcanic activity.[70]

It is also argued that, following 536, the consequent disruption to food resources leading to weakened populations was an important factor in the devastation caused by the Justinian bubonic plague pandemic, which broke out in Egypt in 541 but subsequently swept through much of Europe; it only seems to have finally died out in the mid-eighth century. Its impact is still widely debated, but the archaeological presence of bubonic plague in cemetery populations has now been identified at Edix Hill in eastern England, as well as in southern Spain, southern France, and Bavaria.[71] It is also the most likely contender for the deadly disease recorded in the Irish annals in 544, probably brought from Gaul via the Atlantic seaways, though a further epidemic noted in the early 550s may have had other causes.[72] This may also be relevant to Wales, since there are terse, retrospective references in the Harleian Chronicle to *mortalitas* in Britain in 537, presumably from famine following severe weather as a result of the volcanic eruption in 536, with a second *mortalitas magna*, possibly the Justinian plague, in 547 in which King Maelgwn of Gwynedd perished.[73] There were also outbreaks of bubonic plague in England and Ireland in 664–*c*.666 and *c*.684–*c*.687, the first of which, Bede mentions, followed a very hot summer.[74] The second broadly tallies with entries in the Harleian Chronicle recording 'A great death in Britain in which Cadwaladr [ruler of Gwynedd] son of Cadwallon dies' in 682 and 'Death in Ireland' the following year.[75]

---

[67] Dark, P. 2000, 19–28; Sigl et al. 2015, 547–8; Büntgen et al. 2016; Dull et al. 2019, indicating the impact of the Ilopango eruption in El Salvador 539/40. For a more general discussion, including accounts of the 536 dust veil, see Harper 2017, 249–55.

[68] Baillie 1995, 93–8; see also Coyle McClung and Plunkett 2020, 13–18.

[69] Rippon et al. 2015, 336–7; Rippon 2018.

[70] Dark, P. 2000, 28; McCormick et al. 2007.

[71] On a link between climatic disruption and the Justinian plague, see Büntgen et al. 2016, 234. On the debate around the spread and impact of the Justinian plague, see Little 2007b; Sallares 2007; Meier 2016; Harper 2017, 207–44. Mordechai and Eisenberg 2019 take a minimalist view. However, the plague pathogen, *Yersinia pestis*, has now been traced in the aDNA of well-dated skeletons; see Keller et al. 2019.

[72] Dooley 2007; Grace 2018.   [73] Morris 1980, 45, 85; Grigg 2013, 11, 15–16, 31–5.

[74] Maddicott 1997 discusses symptoms, notably buboes (the swellings associated with bubonic plague) mentioned by Bede.

[75] Morris 1980, 46, 87.

Therefore, although the temperate climate of Britain and Ireland would have mitigated the impact of the 'Late Antique Little Ice Age', evidence points to at least a short-term impact on food production that would have been more marked in agriculturally marginal areas, particularly those with colder winters and shorter growing seasons evident in some parts of Wales. Weakened populations would have been more susceptible to disease, and therefore the spread of the Justinian plague to Britain and Ireland as well as other epidemics could have had a significant effect on mortality, leading to population decline. Further research is therefore needed to trace the plague pathogen in cemetery populations in Wales as well as other parts of Britain and Ireland. Equally, the impact of climate variation on life in early medieval Wales cannot be seen in isolation but, rather, within the broader context of economic and social change.[76]

RECONSTRUCTING THE EARLY MEDIEVAL LANDSCAPE

Although the physical geography of Wales is helpful in providing a framework for how people interacted with their environments, it is less easy to reconstruct a more detailed picture of the early medieval landscape and how it evolved over time. Much of our current understanding is based on the analysis of a slowly increasing number of pollen cores and a growing body of other environmental evidence, notably charcoal and charred and waterlogged plant remains.[77] Nevertheless, each study can only provide a 'snapshot' of a particular place and its landscape context, though where there are well-dated pollen sequences, it is possible to gain insight into changes in the landscape and how it was exploited over prolonged periods of time, offering valuable opportunities for comparison with similar evidence from elsewhere. However, the number of relevant pollen cores is still comparatively small, as many have insufficient radiocarbon dates to be informative concerning changes in the late Roman and early medieval periods. Most also relate to upland environments rather than the more fertile lowlands where most people undoubtedly lived, and there have been very few studies in some regions including, until recently, in the south-east. This makes it all the more difficult to approach some of the larger questions concerning the impact of climate change on the landscape of Wales, how the land was exploited during the later Roman period and throughout the early Middle Ages, and how this may have affected people's lives. My aim here is to give some examples that illuminate our understanding of different elements in the early medieval landscape. A more detailed consideration of the changing patterns of landscape exploitation will be undertaken in discussing farming and the agricultural economy (Chapter 6).

[76] Rippon 2019, 20–2. For Ireland see Coyle McClung and Plunkett 2020.

[77] For overviews focusing on Wales, see Davies, W. 2001; Caseldine 2015; Davies, T. L. 2015, 42–75, 206–41; 2019. For upland and lowland Wales within a wider regional British context, see Rippon et al. 2015, 295–304.

The pollen core from Moel Llys y Coed in the Clwydian Hills provides a valuable 'snapshot' of changes in an upland landscape. Between the end of the Iron Age and the mid-first millennium AD, there was some evidence of woodland and scrub regeneration and a decline in cattle grazing indicated by a rise in bracken. Wetter conditions at the end of this period, which coincide with the climatic downturn, may have favoured alder, and damp meadow habitats are signalled by the presence of great burnet, St John's wort, tufted vetch, and valerian that went unchecked by grazing. However, some cereal pollen suggests continuing cultivation in the area. Then, in the mid-seventh to early ninth century, heather growth exploded, though there is subsequent evidence for burning, possibly to reclaim land for grazing as the climate improved around the end of the early medieval period.[78]

Palaeoenvironmental analyses in the western Brecon Beacons demonstrate the complexity of vegetation change in a comparatively small upland region, reflecting the influence of both topography and local microclimates. Here it is suggested that a major expansion in peat growth resulted from the climatic downturn during the mid-sixth to mid-seventh centuries. However, on the lower slopes at Pen Rhiw-wen, from c.850 woodland was being cleared to facilitate cereal cultivation, whilst at Mynydd Myddfai there was a marked growth in heather and grassland associated with grazing during the early Middle Ages, with a shrinkage of peat signalling the climatic upturn at the end of the period.[79]

By contrast, in the Anglesey lowlands at Llanfechell there is evidence of a more open agricultural landscape. A pollen sample and charred plant remains from a context radiocarbon dated to cal. AD 720–970 suggested that the surrounding area was dominated by heath grasses providing pasture, together with herbs such as chamomile, dandelion, ribwort plantain, and thistle, as well as sedges indicative of boggy areas. Cereals were being cultivated nearby associated with weeds such as corn marigold, sheep's sorrel, docks, and stitchworts. Hazel scrub, together with some oak and alder woodland, was also growing in the vicinity.[80] Equally, at Conkland Hill, Wiston, Pembrokeshire, charred plant remains from deposits, together spanning the mid-seventh to early eleventh century, indicate the cultivation of grain, particularly oats and barley, together with weeds such as wild radish, fat hen, sheep's sorrel, and scentless mayweed. Charcoal from small branches of hazel, oak, and cherry indicates coppicing on a relatively short rotation, possibly from hedges, while both seasoned hazel, probably infested with long-horned beetles, and gorse had been exploited for fuel. Gorse and a crowberry seed, which grow in similar habitats to heather, also point to heathland and rough grazing with moors or bogs in the neighbourhood.[81]

Early medieval waterlogged and wetland sites, though rare, are of particular significance, as organic and environmental evidence is unusually well preserved and can

---

[78] Grant 2008, 11–12.   [79] Leighton 2012, 27–35.

[80] Smith, G. H. 2013, 65–73.   [81] Hart 2014, 26–57.

be closely dated. The most important is the late ninth- and early tenth-century royal crannog at Llangorse, Breconshire, where waterlogged remains have given significant insights into the management and exploitation of woodlands in the surrounding landscape (Chapter 7).[82] However, at Llangynfelyn, on the edge of Cors Fochno, radiocarbon-dated pollen sequences, waterlogged wood dated by dendrochronology, and other environmental evidence together provide a detailed picture of the changing landscape and exploitation of this wetland and its environs from the Late Iron Age to the end of the early Middle Ages. The sequence clearly reflects economic as well as climatic change. During the Roman period lead mining and smelting impacted on both alder growing at the margins of the bog and oak further away. Nonetheless, pastoral farming is demonstrated by ribwort plantain and other herbs as well as fungal spores indicating dung, though some grain was also being grown. Alder persisted but, around the end of the Roman period, industrial activity ceased, with some regeneration of birch on the dry land followed by an increase in oak woodland and a consequent decline in grazing. This was, however, reversed, beginning between the later seventh and later ninth century, and by the time the trackway was constructed in the eleventh, the landscape was largely open with evidence for both pastoral farming and some cereal cultivation. The immediate environment of the trackway included wetland grasses, reeds, sedges, heather, and cotton grass as well as bog myrtle nearby.[83]

Turning to the salt marshes of the Gwent Levels, a multidisciplinary approach, including landscape regression analysis and examination of the written sources, as well as environmental sampling and targeted archaeological investigation, has enabled a reconstruction of the changing coastal landscape over time (Fig. 2.5). It has been persuasively argued that the Wentlooge Level, stretching between the Rhymney and Ebbw rivers, was drained, probably by the Roman military in the second century AD. This was achieved through construction of a putative sea wall, behind which were a series of drainage ditches, known as 'reens', creating a pattern of long, narrow, rectilinear fields. At this time the landscape, which may have been subject to occasional inundations during spring tides or storms, was open, damp pasture with some arable weed seeds indicative of cultivation as well. However, in the post-Roman period, perhaps partly as a result of the worsening climate, only the central part of this reclaimed area centred on Peterstone remained, whilst the land to either side was inundated, returning it to tidal salt marsh. The resulting deposition of alluvium buried the Roman-period landscape, and it is suggested that early medieval sites were located on the fen edge. The later, irregular, field patterns in Rumney and St Brides are therefore the product of renewed reclamation during the eleventh century, most likely in the wake of the Norman Conquest, though it may have commenced slightly earlier.[84]

[82] Lane and Redknap 2019, 110–49.   [83] Page et al. 2012, 288–91, 295, 313–49.
[84] Fulford et al. 1994; Rippon 1996, 25–38, 61–8; Davies, W. 2001, 9.

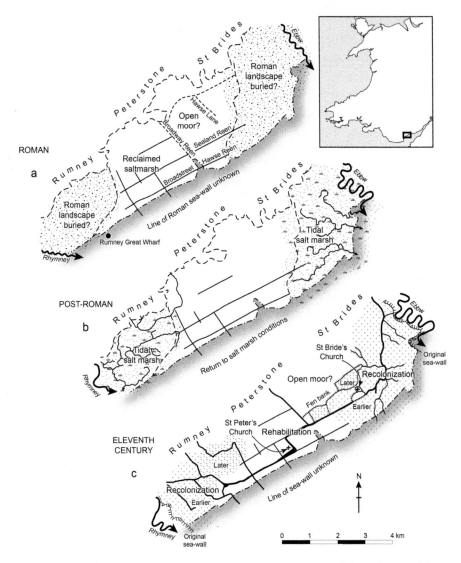

Fig. 2.5. Wentlooge Level, Monmouthshire, showing a reconstruction of the evolution of the landscape between the Roman period and the eleventh century (after Rippon 1996, figs 34–5).

It is more difficult to reconstruct the early medieval Welsh landscape from written sources alone. Poetry, notably *Claf Abercuawg*, which may date to the later ninth century, demonstrates a keen sense of the natural world, but it is used as a backdrop to mood.[85] Hagiography, by its very nature, is charged with enhancing the cult of a particular saint and the rights of associated foundations. Therefore, the late eleventh- and twelfth-century Welsh saints' lives are more concerned with sacred and idealized

---

[85] Rowland 1990, 190–228, 389, 448–52, 497–9.

landscapes, and the language is often laced with biblical quotes. For example, while Rhygyfarch's *Vita* shows an appreciation of the rocky coastal landscape around St Davids, the purpose of this is to form a backdrop for episodes in the saint's life and to inform pilgrims about where these had occurred.[86] The description of Llantwit Major in the *Life* of St Illtud as in a 'most fertile open plain' with 'a very thick wood, planted with diverse trees' and 'a very pleasing river' appears highly idealized.[87] However, ninth-century charters added to the Lichfield Gospels and the probably tenth- and eleventh-century boundary clauses relating to estates in the Llandaf charters are, potentially, more useful since they incorporate a range of landscape features such as hills, woodland, rivers, and streams, which can sometimes be located with reference to the modern landscape (Chapter 6).[88]

Overall, the evidence suggests a landscape which, though clearly recognizable today, also appears wilder and less managed. Whilst the lowlands demonstrate evidence of cereal cultivation, there were also large tracts of rougher grazing with scrub and probably considerable areas of managed woodland, also used as wood pasture, as well as some forest, and more marginal habitats, such as pools, bogs, and coastal salt marshes. Where available, communities would have made use of a range of environmental zones, for example fertile valley floors and lower slopes, woodlands on steep valley sides, and grazing on the higher slopes, though large stretches of the uplands consisted of wild moorland with peat bogs. The pollen cores also suggest that, in some cases but not all, it is possible to discern the impact of climatic deterioration on the landscape in the post-Roman period as well as improving conditions at the end of the early Middle Ages.

TIME AND MEMORY

Concepts of time and memory are fundamental to our daily human lives. It is therefore important to explore the different ways in which the inhabitants of early medieval Wales experienced and manipulated these concepts. In so doing, both material evidence—monuments in the landscape and archaeological artefacts—as well as the written sources can be used to reveal different and sometimes competing ways of experiencing and measuring time and articulating memory, as well as changing attitudes to these. During the early Middle Ages we are dealing not only with different forms of natural time and social and cultural constructions of these but also with major changes in the ways in which time was ordered and measured. The demise of

[86] Sharpe and Davies 2007, e.g. ch. 6, on the site of his birth, 114–17. For discussion of the archaeology of this sacred landscape, see James 1993.

[87] Wade-Evans 1944, 202–3, ch. 6.

[88] Jenkins and Owen 1983, 52–5, but only Chad 6 has a boundary clause; Davies, W. 1978, 27–32.

Roman imperial control and the rise of new secular and Christian authorities brought consequent transformations in how these power structures sought to manipulate aspects of both natural time and memory.[89]

Natural time is experienced through the repetition of habitual action within the daily and seasonal round and the relationship of this to life cycles and generations. This relationship is not fixed, however, but is subject to constant social and cultural adaptation and reworking. At the simplest level, the shifting seasons, together with the changing lengths of hours of daylight and the varying weather conditions they brought, were central to the daily lives of farming communities in early medieval Wales. These were propelled by astronomical time, notably the solar and lunar cycles. Our understanding of the framework underpinning the months and seasons and how these shaped the farming year is largely based on the later medieval law texts, but for linguistic reasons this is thought to be much older. There were four seasons, each of three months, with winter beginning on 1 November, spring on 1 February, summer on 1 May, and autumn on 1 August. The Welsh names of the three summer months of May, June, and July are *Cyntefin* (*Mai*) ('Beginning of summer' or 'First month'), *Mehefin* ('Middle month'), and *Gorffennaf* ('End of summer'). *Cyntefin* and *Mehefin* both correspond to their Old Irish equivalents (*Cétemain*, *Mithem*), and early medieval Ireland likewise had three-month seasons. Similar three-month seasons are also evident in Anglo-Saxon England.[90]

Where skeletal material survives in early medieval cemeteries, osteoarchaeologists can study people's natural life cycles, including age of death and patterns of infant mortality. However, the life cycle was also manipulated both socially and culturally, and evidence for this is present in both the archaeological and the written record.[91] For example, infants seem to be under-represented in most early medieval cemeteries in Wales. Initially this probably reflects Roman period burial practices, but subsequently, as the numbers appear to rise, customs are likely to have been increasingly influenced by the dictates of the Church, which, from the sixth century onwards, permitted baptized babies to be interred in consecrated ground.[92] Thomas Charles-Edwards has noted the continuation in early medieval Wales of Roman rituals of first hair and beard cutting associated with rites of passage for both infants and pubescent young men,[93] while the fifth-century Christian inscribed stone from Llanerfyl, Montgomeryshire, commemorates R(u)stece the daughter of Paterninus, a girl of 13 years. This rare recording of age also follows pagan Roman practice, but it is relevant to note that R(u)stece was similarly on the cusp of puberty and was yet to leave her family to marry. Other women commemorated on the inscribed stones are likewise

---

[89] My thinking has been influenced by Gosden 1994 and Gilchrist 2012.

[90] Comeau 2020, 73–8, 205–14. I am grateful to Thomas Charles-Edwards for discussing the linguistic evidence with me.

[91] Gilchrist 2012, 1–31.   [92] Page 2011, 106–8.   [93] Charles-Edwards 2013, 300–3.

almost always found in conjunction with the names of male kin, most frequently as wives or, in one instance on the monument from Spittal, Pembrokeshire, as a mother named alongside her son, perhaps because she was a widow.[94] Occasionally, names in inscriptions also indicate old age, as, for example, Senacus meaning 'old' on Aberdaron 2, Caernarfonshire, dating to the first half of the sixth century, and Hiroidil meaning 'of long life' on the ninth-century cross-carved stone from Llanwnnws, Cardiganshire.[95] This suggests that in some cases personal names might change, reflecting a later stage in the life cycle. The poems *Gwên and Llywarch* and *Marwnad Gwên* focus on the frailties of old age.[96]

Time expressed in generations (thereby linking it to kinship) was important in Wales throughout the early Middle Ages, not least because of the connections it had with status and inheritance, including that of land where co-heirs came to consist of those who shared the same agnatic great-grandfather.[97] At the beginning of the period, the early inscribed stones, particularly in south-west Wales, usually record the patronym together with that of the deceased, a practice initiated in the ogham inscriptions introduced by Irish settlers, but found in the Latin inscriptions as well. For example, the bilingual inscription on St Dogmaels 1, Pembrokeshire, commemorates 'Sagragnus son of Cunatamus'—in ogham *Sagragni maqi Cunatami* and in Latin *Sagrani fili Cvnotami*. However, Bivadus is noted as the 'grandson' or 'descendant' (*avus*) of Bodibeve on a bilingual monument from Llanwinio, Carmarthenshire, and Bodvocus as the son of Catotigirnus and 'great-grandson' (*pronepos*) of Eternalis Vedomavus on the Latin stone from Margam Mountain, Glamorgan. The lost Latin-inscribed stone from Llanymawddwy, Merioneth, is unusual as it commemorates three women, indicating a more complex set of family relationships bound by ties of blood and marriage spanning three generations.[98]

From the seventh century onwards, however, recording patronyms and generations in this way largely ceases on the stone sculpture, though there are exceptions, mainly in the south-west.[99] Nevertheless, the most significant example of generational time is found in the lengthy Latin inscription on the Pillar of Eliseg, formerly a cross, which is datable to the first half of the ninth century. The inscription opens with a four-generation genealogy, beginning with Concenn (Welsh: Cyngen, d.854), the last early medieval ruler of the kingdom of Powys who set up the monument, and going back to his great-grandfather, Eliseg, a contemporary of King Offa of Mercia (d.796). The inscription, a piece of royal propaganda, demonstrates the manipulation of time at the behest of a secular ruler. Its purpose was partly to commemorate

[94] Edwards 2013, 54, no. MT4; 2007a, no. P136.
[95] Edwards 2013, no. CN2; 2007a, no. CD27.
[96] Rowland 1990, 404–8, 468–70; Charles-Edwards 2013, 668–74.
[97] Ibid., 293–313, discusses the complexities of early medieval Welsh kinship and status in the written sources.
[98] Edwards 2007a, 36, nos P110, CM34; 2013, 54, no. MR20; Redknap and Lewis 2007, no. G77.
[99] See Edwards 2007a, nos CD9, CD20, CD27, P97; 2013, nos AN5, D7.

56 LIFE IN EARLY MEDIEVAL WALES

Eliseg's success against the English. However, it also invokes a much longer time span, most likely going back to what were perceived as the origins of the kingdom of Powys since it names the late fourth-century imperial usurper, Magnus Maximus, and the shadowy sub-Roman ruler Vortigern, who likewise figures in Gildas's *De Excidio*, Bede's *Historia Ecclesiastica*, and the *Historia Brittonum*. The inscription ends by looking forwards, probably to the Day of Judgement, thereby making an important link with Christian time. Furthermore, as with the earlier inscribed stones, the permanence of the monument means that it was intended to preserve the memory of those named for future generations to read and their links with the kingdom of Powys and therefore the land on which the cross stood.[100] The harnessing of genealogy and time here coincides with an upsurge of interest in the recording and compilation of royal genealogies, some headed by Roman emperors or biblical or mythical ancestors, as seen in the *Historia Brittonum* and the Harleian genealogies which were later appended to it.[101]

The Roman occupation of Britain had imposed complex systems of calendars and timekeeping, although the impact of these on people's everyday lives would have varied considerably depending on the degree of contact with the imperial administration. The Romans used the Julian calendar alongside other mechanisms for predicting astronomical and meteorological events and the *fasti*, which noted civil cycles and those of the official religion. Commemoration of anniversaries was also important, and, from the fourth century, elements of Christian time began to be incorporated as well. Years were recorded with reference to the names of the two consuls in Rome, the regnal years (of tribunician power) of the Emperor, and in 312 a system of indiction years was introduced, each indiction being fifteen years. It has been demonstrated, partly as a result of the Vindolanda excavations on Hadrian's Wall, that the military conformed closely to Roman time systems, and discoveries include a fragment of a water clock with a calendrical device around the rim.[102] Legionaries at *Isca* (Caerleon) and auxiliaries at *Segontium* (Caernarfon), for example, would have done likewise, and there is also evidence for knowledge of Roman calendars in the town of Caerwent.[103] In the countryside, official monuments in the form of milestones recording the name of the Emperor and sometimes the year of his reign were set up beside the Roman roads, and one example from Margam, Glamorgan, was reused with an additional commemorative inscription in the first half of the sixth century.[104]

---

[100] Edwards 2009c; 2013, no. D3; Winterbottom 1978, ch. 23.1; Colgrave and Mynors 1969, i.14–i.15; Morris 1980, chs 31–49.

[101] Ibid., chs 31, 48–9, 57–8, 63; Guy 2020, 61, 334–7. Guy also discusses the Insular origins of royal genealogies in Ireland, England, and Wales; see 16–19, 39–40.

[102] Hannah 2005, 112–46; Deliyannis 2001, 6–7; Mattingly 2006, 204; Birth 2014; Meyer 2019.

[103] For relevant inscriptions from Caerleon, see Collingwood and Wright 1995, nos 327, 330, and Caerwent, no. 309.

[104] Ibid., nos 2251–67; Tomlin et al. 2009, nos 3522–3; Redknap and Lewis 2007, no. G92; see also Edwards 2013, no. CN1.

The extent to which elements of Roman timekeeping impinged on the lives of those outside Roman enclaves is likely to have been limited, and there would have been little reason to maintain methods of Roman timekeeping once day-to-day imperial administration had been run down. It is notable that by the mid-sixth century Gildas does not include any dates at all in *De Excidio*.[105] Some knowledge may, however, have persisted or been subsequently reintroduced from Gaul. A Latin-inscribed stone from Penmachno, Caernarfonshire, commemorating the son of Avitorius, also bears the fragmentary *in te(m)po(re) Ivst...con...* ('in the time of Just(inus) the consul...*or* consulship...'), which has been interpreted as a consular or post-consular date. Although the practice of appointing consuls ceased in Rome in 540, this dating system continued to a certain extent on the Continent, and especially in the kingdom of Burgundy, where it was commonly used in epitaphs *c.*480–580. The Penmachno inscription is most likely to date to 540 or slightly later.[106] Interestingly, as late as the early ninth century the author of the *Historia Brittonum* was using a source for the fifth century that included consular dates.[107]

The increasing significance of Christian time, especially for the correct calculation of Easter involving both lunar cycles and biblical exegesis, is first evident in a north Wales entry in the Harleian Chronicle in 768. This records the change to the 'Roman' calculation of Easter by the Britons at the instigation of Elfoddw over a century after the change was made at the Synod of Whitby in Northumbria.[108] There is also a concern with the recording of celestial events, some retrospectively, in the Welsh chronicles more generally as, for example, the solar eclipse of 807, the lunar eclipses of 810 and 831, and the presence of a comet in 676. However, in contrast to such events in the Irish annals, there is insufficient evidence to argue for a link with predicting the Apocalypse rather than a more general interest in computistics and the calculation of Easter.[109] The earliest definitely Welsh book, the *Liber Commonei*, includes a lunar table and an Easter table for the years 817–35, whilst the earliest surviving treatise in Welsh is in a *computus* fragment dating to the late ninth or early tenth century, which discusses methods of recording the lunar cycle. Both are derived from Bede's highly influential *De Temporum Ratione* ('On the Reckoning of Time'), the latter with later additions.[110] There is also a complex series of tables in the late eleventh-century *Psalter of Rhygyfarch*.[111] The *Historia Brittonum*, as a syncretic history, makes use of further

---

[105] Deliyannis 2001, 15.

[106] Handley 2003, 129–35; Edwards 2013, no. CN37; Charles-Edwards 2013, 235–8.

[107] Morris 1980, chs. 31, 66; Miller 1980.

[108] Morris 1980, *s.a.* 665, 768; Colgrave and Mynors 1969, iii.25–26; Guy 2015, 38–42. The change is from the eighty-four-year cycle of Sulpicius Severus to the Dionysian nineteen-year cycle: for the background, see Charles-Edwards 2000, 391–415.

[109] Morris 1980, 46–8, 87–9; Grigg 2013, 11–14, 18, 21–4, 28; Flechner 2013, 440–9.

[110] McKee 2012, 168–9; Hunt 1961, fol. 20r–fol. 21r; Lindsay 1912, 18–19, 53; Williams, I. 1927, 256–7. On Bede and the reckoning of time, see Wallis 2010, 119–25.

[111] Lawlor 1914, i, 112–20; ii, fols 25v–28v, pls xlviii–liv.

methods of calculating Christian time, from the years of Christ's Incarnation and Passion, and it is notable that the work commences with the Six Ages from the Beginning of the World to the Day of Judgement.[112]

The monastic life required adherence to the demands of Christian time, which controlled both the daily round and the liturgical year, though their severity is likely to have varied. The earlier ascetic rule incorporated into Rhygyfarch's *Life* of St David (*c.*1091 × 1093) demonstrates a strict ordering of the day according to manual labour, reading, writing, praying, and worship. Material evidence for the division of the day into segments comes in the form of two eighth- or ninth-century carved stone sundials (comparable with Irish examples), associated with the monasteries at Clynnog, Caernarfonshire (Fig. 2.6), and Tywyn, Merioneth, with a further likely sundial from the probable hermitage on Ramsey Island associated with St Davids. The four equal segments on the dial of the first represent natural time in the form of 'temporal hours' made up of 'three-hour' spans, the lengths of which would have varied according to the seasons, and the separating lines may denote the times of liturgical offices—Prime, Terce, Sext (noon), Nones, and Vespers.[113] The rule further indicates that bells were used to call the monks to church, and this may have been the original function of the two iron and five copper-alloy quadrangular handbells that still survive from Wales and west Herefordshire. They are, however, more commonly found in Ireland, where evidence for the making of brazed iron bells has been dated to the late seventh or eighth century (Chapter 11).[114] The *Psalter of Rhygyfarch* also has a martyrology indicating the importance of celebrating saints' feast days, including that of St Padarn of Llanbadarn Fawr where Rhygyfarch lived. His *Life* of St David ends with the saint's genealogy, which recalls those of Christ in the Gospels, as well as those in the secular sphere.[115]

The ordering of Christian time would most clearly have impacted on other people's lives through control of aspects of the life-course and the introduction of rituals together with a range of feasts and festivals tied to the Christian calendar and linked with the seasons and the agricultural year.[116] Although we know comparatively little about pastoral care in early medieval Wales, this would have been key to its implementation.[117] For example, the sacrament of baptism, whether adult or infant, marked the first step on the Christian life-course. The fifth-century inscribed stone from Trawsfynydd, Merioneth, proclaiming Porius as 'a Christian man'

---

[112] Morris 1980, chs 1–6; Guy 2015, 40–4.

[113] Sharpe and Davies 2007, chs 21–7; Edwards 2013, nos CN14; MR27; Edwards 2007a, no. P99. For the use of 'temporal hours' associated with Roman sundials and water clocks, see Birth 2014, 408; Meyer 2019, 193. See also biblical accounts of the Crucifixion, e.g. Matt. 27:45–6.

[114] Sharpe and Davies 2007, chs 23, 25; Borst 1993, 42; Bourke 2020, 60, 381–3, 422–6.

[115] Lawlor 1914, i, xxxiv, 72–3; Sharpe and Davies 2007, ch. 68; Matt. 1:1–17; Luke 3:23–38; for the genealogy of St Cadog, see also Wade-Evans 1944, 118–19, ch. 46. For more general discussion see Guy 2020, 20, 42.

[116] Gilchrist 2012, 14.   [117] Pryce 1992.

Fig. 2.6. Sundial, Clynnog Fawr, Caernarfonshire (Crown copyright: Royal Commission on the Ancient and Historical Monuments of Wales).

(*homo [x]p(ist)ianvs*), implies he was baptized.[118] However, fonts are not generally known in Wales or other parts of Britain and Ireland before the end of the early Middle Ages,[119] and the hagiography suggests that baptisms were conducted in streams, springs, and holy wells. According to Rhygyfarch, for example, David was

---

[118] Ibid., 42–3; Edwards 2013, 74–6, no. MR23.
[119] Ibid., 74–6, with one possibly earlier exception, a fragment from Llanrhaeadr-ym-Mochnant, Denbs., no. D8.

60 LIFE IN EARLY MEDIEVAL WALES

baptized at a spring, now the holy well adjacent to St Non's Chapel where there is a seventh- to ninth-century cross-carved stone. Another cross-carved stone with a fish associated with a well near Llandeilo Llwydarth, Pembrokeshire, may mark a similar site.[120]

As the period progresses, there is increasing evidence for Christian control of burial alongside extension of the life-course into the future through belief in purgatory and resurrection of the body on the Day of Judgement.[121] Archaeologically, there is the potential to examine this more closely in the cemetery evidence and, from the late eighth century onwards, there are other indications of the increasing importance of the concepts of purgatory and the afterlife. For example, names added in the margins of the Lichfield Gospels suggest it acted as a *liber vitae* ('book of life') recording those, living or dead, regularly remembered in the prayers of the community at Llandelio Fawr.[122] Inscriptions on sculpture refer more specifically to the erection of monuments for the soul of a named person; for example, the cross-carved stone from the monastic site on Caldey Island, Pembrokeshire, requests all those who pass by to 'pray for the soul of Catuoconus'. Moreover, a unique ninth-century inscription from Llanlleonfel, Breconshire, points to a sense of apocalyptic imminence since it reads, 'Silent in the shroud, Iorwert and Ruallaun in their graves await in peace the dreadful coming of the judgement'.[123]

Christianity sought to provide a structure for time stretching from the creation of the world to the Last Judgement. However, it is equally clear that other conceptions of deep time were also important during this period which similarly resulted in the manipulation of the past to support contemporary needs, not only in Wales but also elsewhere in early medieval Britain and Ireland and more widely in other parts of Europe.[124] We have already noted that written sources in Wales from the ninth century onwards, including the *Historia Brittonum*, *Englynion y Beddau* ('Stanzas of the Graves'), and early Welsh prose tales, demonstrate a lively interest in stories and other lore associated with places in the landscape and a heroic past. These incorporate references to natural features and phenomena, such as the Severn bore, as well as a range of archaeological monuments, particularly Neolithic and Bronze Age burial monuments and standing stones viewed as the graves of heroic ancestors, but also hillforts and more recent Roman sites. Therefore the landscapes in which people lived, often over many generations, were perceived as mnemonic triggers, and as such were seen in cultural (rather than purely economic) terms as palimpsests of the past.

---

[120] Whitfield 2007; Sharpe and Davies 2007, ch. 7; Edwards 2007a, nos P23, P100.

[121] Gilchrist 2012, 19–20; Paxton 1990, 66–8; Effros 2002, 169–204.

[122] Maddern 2013, 206–11; Charles-Edwards, G., and McKee 2008, 83, 87. See also a charter in the *Life of St Cadog*, Wade-Evans 1944, 116–17, ch. 56.

[123] Edwards 2007a, 93–6, no. P6: *Et singno crucis illam fingsi rogo omnibus ammulantibus ibi exorent pro animae Catuoconi*; Redknap and Lewis 2007, no. B34: *[In s]indone muti Ioruert Ruallaunq(ue) sepulc(h)ris + Iudicii adventum specta(n)t i(n) pace trem(en)dum.*

[124] Bradley 1987; Williams, Howard 1998; Semple 2013, 1–12.

We can gain some idea of the archaeological complexity of these landscapes by examining the site of Parc Cybi, Holyhead, Anglesey, where an area of over 41 hectares comprising rough pastureland with rocky outcrops and marshy hollows was investigated. Today the Neolithic chambered tomb of Trefignath and a late Neolithic or early Bronze Age standing stone remain clearly visible in this landscape, but excavation of over 20 hectares also revealed a range of other prehistoric sites and monuments indicating domestic occupation as well as farming and ritual activities. These included a small Bronze Age burial complex made up of a round barrow with multiple stone cists, a ring ditch, and other features. During the third and fourth centuries AD there is also evidence of Roman craftworking, and fifth- and sixth-century corn-drying ovens in the vicinity indicate the continuing proximity of a farming community nearby. However, the location of a small, late Roman, long-cist cemetery on a rounded hillock is also significant since it resembles a Bronze Age barrow and is sited between the chambered tomb and the standing stone. To the north-east, a further Bronze Age ring ditch became the focus of a second, probably early medieval, long-cist cemetery.[125] Their siting in both instances signals a conscious link with the past, most likely associated with the ownership of land. During the first half of the ninth century, the placing of the Pillar of Eliseg on top of an early Bronze Age burial cairn makes a more explicit statement concerning memory, since it demonstrates how the graves of the powerful dead might be harnessed with the inscription to project the authority of the rulers of Powys back into the distant past (Chapter 12).[126]

The *Englynion y Beddau* ('Stanzas of the Graves'), thought to be ninth or tenth century but with some later accretions, offer valuable insights into how prehistoric monuments were perceived in the early Middle Ages and their connection with mythical and heroic figures of the distant past. The stories attached to specific examples are, however, often lost to us, and the sites are frequently difficult to identify on the ground. Nevertheless, 'the three graves on Cefn Celfi' of Cynon, Cynfael, and Cynfeli may refer to three standing stones, the remains of two of which still survive on the farm of that name at Rhos, near Pontardawe, Glamorgan, and 'the grave of Hennin Old-head' may be a largely destroyed chambered tomb near Dinorben hillfort, Denbighshire.[127] As ancient landmarks, such monuments also feature in charter boundaries, notably a late Neolithic or early Bronze Age standing stone, *Hirfaen Gwyddog*, mentioned in one of the additions to the Lichfield Gospels. At 4.8 metres tall, it remains a prominent marker on the modern border between Carmarthenshire and Ceredigion.[128]

---

[125] Kenney et al. 2020; Kenney and Longley 2012.

[126] Edwards 2013, no. D3, 328; Edwards et al. 2015.

[127] Jones, T. 1967, 112–14, stanzas i.65, i.71; 1936; Bollard and Griffiths 2015, 47, 97; Archwilio GGAT prn. 00516w; Davies, E. 1929, 398; Archwilio CPAT prn 101985.

[128] SN 6245 4645; Evans, J. G., and Rhys 1893. xlv; Jones, G. R. J. 1972, 313–14; for examples in the Llandaf charters, see Davies, W. 1978, 31–2.

Archaeological monuments also make frequent appearances in the *Mabinogi*, as the tales relate to magical beings in the distant past. For example, the Fourth Branch is primarily located in Gwynedd, particularly in the coastal landscape of Arfon around the monastic site of Clynnog, where the stories may well have been brought together sometime during the second half of the eleventh or early twelfth century. This landscape is associated with the family of Dôn, a pre-Roman goddess. Her brother Math lives in *Caer Dathyl*, possibly the hillfort of Tre'r Ceiri, whilst her grandson, Lleu Llaw Gyffes, is raised in the hillfort of Dinas Dinlle, where recent excavations have revealed settlement during the Roman period. In *Englynion y Beddau* the grave of Dôn's son, Gwydion, is also located on the shore nearby. Roman sites are similarly reinvented in the tale. The fort at Tomen-y-Mur in the Vale of Ffestiniog becomes the home of Lleu Llaw Gyffes and his wife, Blodeuedd, and the final episodes in the story leading up to the killing of her lover Gronw are played out in the adjoining landscape along the line of the Roman road to the north.[129]

The concept of deep time and memory evident in the landscape and its monuments was also harnessed by the Church and employed in hagiography to demonstrate the power of the saint and to establish the rights of the ecclesiastical community. A story in the probably later seventh-century *Life* of St Samson of Dol tells how a standing stone in Cornwall worshipped by the local people as an idol to celebrate 'the magical arts of their ancestors' was converted by the saint who incised it with a cross.[130] Equally, a tale associated with St Germanus in the *Historia Brittonum* describes how he destroyed the fortress of the tyrant Benlli, the multivallate hillfort of Moel Fenlli, Denbighshire, where there is also evidence of third- and fourth-century Roman activity.[131]

Sometimes evidence of a saint's cult survives in the landscape in the naming of natural features and prehistoric sites. A good example of this is the wider landscape around the church of Llanhamlach, Breconshire, which is dedicated to St Illtud. Monuments associated with the saint include Tŷ Illtud, a Neolithic chambered tomb, as well as Maen Illtud, a lost standing stone, and a holy well. However, it is impossible to say when these were renamed, and the incised graffiti crosses added to the stones of the tomb are more likely antiquarian than early medieval.[132]

In farming communities, therefore, concepts of natural time based on the seasons and the changing weather, alongside the landscapes in which they lived, remained fundamental in the decisions they made concerning the rearing of livestock, the cultivation of crops, and the exploitation of natural resources. The very nature of such seasonal time creates a sense of the *longue durée*, whilst the life cycle marks important transitions in the lives of individuals and communities, and generational time indicates

---

[129] Sims-Williams 2001; Ford 1977, 89; Jones, T. 1967, stanza iii.3; Davies, S. 2007, 59–64; Bollard 2009, 44–5, 49–51. On the Dinas Dinlle excavations, see Archwilio, GAT prn 46240.

[130] *...mathematicam eorum parentum...*, see Taylor 1991 and Flobert 1997, ch. 48.

[131] Morris 1980, chs 32–4; Archwilio CPAT prn 102310.   [132] Grinsell 1981.

the significance of kin, inheritance, and ownership. The imposition of elements of Roman timekeeping on these natural cycles gave way to the authority of Christian time, which stretched from the creation to beyond the grave. In early medieval Wales, such imposed methods of timekeeping are associated with secular and ecclesiastical elites and are much easier to identify in the written sources and in inscriptions than in the archaeological record. Nevertheless, Christian festivals and feast days became part of the seasonal cycle of farming communities, just as baptism and Christian burial came to shape the life-course. Other senses of deep time incorporating and manipulating prehistoric and later monuments and the heroic stories that evolved to explain them were also important and provided a different sense of the *longue durée*. Therefore, the landscapes of early medieval Wales and its wider location on the Atlantic seaways and how people shaped and interacted with these should be viewed not just in economic terms but culturally as well.

THREE

Continuity and Collapse

An examination of the archaeological and written evidence for the fourth, fifth, and sixth centuries demonstrates a major transition. Roman Britain, with its colonial military and civilian administration, tax collection, large agricultural surpluses, significant numbers of masonry structures, industrial production of many artefacts, partially coin-based market economy, and complex networks of trade, gave way to a patchwork of kingdoms, some ruled by the descendants of Germanic or other incomers, frequently hard-to-identify settlements with very different artefactual assemblages, and the disintegration of a complex economy. Over the last thirty years or more the processes that lay behind this transition have gradually escaped the former straitjacket of recorded events[1] and become the subject of intense debate driven largely by an expanding and increasingly complex body of archaeological data, together with improved scientific and theoretical techniques for its analysis.[2]

The Emperor Honorius's letter to British towns in 410 telling them to look to their own defence has traditionally been viewed as the chronological divide between Roman and post-Roman.[3] As a result there has been a tendency to see the ending of Roman Britain *either* from the Roman period looking forwards *or* from the early medieval looking backwards, leading to the development of quite different trajectories. Setting Roman Britain, a province on the north-west periphery, within the context of the barbarian incursions and the fate of the Western Empire, the former would tend to favour a comparatively rapid political and economic collapse by around 430.[4] The latter, influenced by models developed for the broader study of Late Antiquity, would

---

[1] For classic discussions focusing on the historical framework, see Salway 1981, 374–501; Frere 1987, 353–77. Esmonde Cleary's influential 1989 book, with its much greater emphasis on archaeology, was the first to break this mould.

[2] The most recent significant discussions of the archaeological evidence are Gerrard 2013 and Fleming 2021.

[3] Noted by the early sixth-century Greek historian, Zosimus; see Ridley 1982, VI.x.2. Frere 1987, 358–9, 376, n. 16, suggests Gildas had knowledge of the letter; see Winterbottom 1978, ch. 18, though the wording is inconclusive. The letter has sometimes been thought to deal with the southern tip of Italy, not Britain; see Salway 1981, 442–5. For recent scepticism, see Mattingly 2006, 530, who regards 409 as the divide.

[4] Esmonde Cleary 1989; Faulkner 2000; Ward-Perkins 2005, who also considers the historiography, 1–10, as does Gerrard 2013, 2–7.

Life in Early Medieval Wales. Nancy Edwards, Oxford University Press. © Nancy Edwards 2023.
DOI: 10.1093/oso/9780198733218.003.0003

see it as a much longer and more gradual process of change beginning in the later Roman period and continuing through the fifth and into the sixth century, particularly in western Britain.[5] More recently, James Gerrard, focusing on the archaeological evidence, has argued that the notions of catastrophe and the collapse of a complex society are misleading. Rather, he emphasizes a longer process of adjustment stressing the significance of regionality, considerable continuity in rural production despite declining outputs, and the rise of militarized elites with personal retinues and differing modes of display.[6] Robin Fleming has, however, focused on the impact of the collapse of the complex interlocking networks of the Roman 'political economy' by around AD 430, as seen through the material evidence suggesting that this swift decline was most significant for the soldiers, administrators, villa estate owners, and industrial workers and their families who most depended on it, whilst rural farming populations lower down the scale could more easily adapt and therefore demonstrate much more continuity.[7]

With the exception of K. R. Dark and Roger White, who have traced the transition of the province of *Britannia Prima* (of which Wales was a part) into a number of successor kingdoms,[8] there has been comparatively little consideration of the evidence for the ending of Roman Wales and the impact of this on how people lived. By contrast, some other parts of Roman Britain, notably Wroxeter and its hinterland (just beyond the modern borders of Wales) and the northern frontier, have received considerably more notice.[9] Equally, in contrast to southern and eastern England where furnished burials provide a rich array of evidence, less attention has been paid to the impact of incomers and how identities changed and were reinvented during this period, as well as the legacy of around 350 years of Roman occupation and rule. In Wales 410 has too often continued to be viewed as an academic as well as a period divide, with a resulting tendency for studies to be somewhat inward-looking, and, if the period of transition is considered at all, it has largely concentrated on the process of military withdrawal rather than the significance of the broader picture.[10]

Therefore, to try and understand how people lived in early medieval Wales, it is first necessary to consider the late Roman period and the nature of the transition. I shall begin with a brief discussion of the fragmentary record of events that has come down to us in the written sources and the problems caused by the virtual demise of archaeological dating evidence. I shall then consider the archaeological evidence for people's varying experiences of Romanization in the regions identified in the previous chapter and how their lives changed over the course of the fourth century and

---

[5] Dark, K. R. 1994a, 172–216; 2000.   [6] Gerrard 2013, 243–4, 274–6.

[7] Fleming 2021, 10–33, 181–6.   [8] Dark, K. R. 1994a; 2000; White 2007.

[9] E.g. Barker et al. 1997; White and Barker 1998, 102–36; Lane 2014; Collins and Allason-Jones 2010; Collins 2012.

[10] For discussion of the same problem in England, see Fitzpatrick-Matthews and Fleming 2016, 23–4.

66 LIFE IN EARLY MEDIEVAL WALES

into the fifth, before analysing the broader processes of continuity and collapse that lie behind the transition from Roman to early medieval Wales and the reasons that may have caused them.

PROBLEMS WITH DATING AND CHRONOLOGY

The main course of events noted in the written sources relating to Britain during the later fourth and first decade of the fifth centuries is well known (see Fig. 3.1).[11] These are mainly recorded, first by Ammianus Marcellinus writing contemporaneously in Gaul, but when his account ceases in 378, the dependability of what sources there are declines. Zosimus, who lived in the Eastern Empire in the early sixth century, now becomes the chief source, though he also drew on the work of the early fifth-century author Olympiodorus.[12] The documented events highlight serious attacks from

Date	Events	Source(s)
360	The Irish and the Picts break their treaty with Roman authorities and attack Britain	Ammianus, *Res Gestae*, xx. 1.1
364	Continued attacks by the Picts, Saxons, and Irish (including the *Attacotti*)	Ammianus, *Res Gestae*, xxvi. 4.5
367–8	The 'Great Barbarian Conspiracy' resulting in a serious combined attack on Britain and restoration of control by Count Theodosius	Ammianus, *Res Gestae*, xxvii. 8.5, xxviii. 3.2
381–3	Usurpation of Magnus Maximus in Britain; success against Pictish and Irish incursions; crosses to Gaul with a large army and kills the Emperor Gratian	The Gallic Chronicle of 452 Zosimus, *Historia Nova*, iv, 4.35
396–8	Stilicho (or another) campaigns in Britain against the Picts and Irish	Gildas, *De Excidio*, chs 13–14 Claudian, Stilicho II, 247–55
401–2	Stilicho withdraws some troops from Britain to defend Italy	Claudian, *De Bello Gothico*, 416–18
406–7	Usurpation of Marcus in Britain Vandals, Suevi, and Alans cross the frozen Rhine into Gaul Usurpation of Gratian in Britain, replacing Marcus After four months, usurpation of Constantine III who leaves Britain for the Continent	Zosimus, *Historia Nova*, v (1–2), vi.3(1) Prosper of Aquitaine, i, 465 (1230, 1232) Orosius, vii. 40.4
410	Letter of Honorius to the cities in Britain telling them to look to their own defence	Zosimus, *Historia Nova*, vi.10(2) ? Gildas, *De Excidio*, ch. 18

FIG. 3.1. Major events noted in the written sources relevant to the ending of Roman control in Britain.

[11] Salway 1981, 374–437; for recent discussion with reference to Wales, see Charles-Edwards 2013, 31–56.

[12] Rolfe 1950; Ridley 1982. For the Gallic Chronicle of 452, see Burgess 2012, 67–8. Other relevant sources are Orosius (Fear 2010), the poet Claudian (Platnauer 1922), and the chronicle of Prosper of Aquitaine (Mommsen 1892).

beyond the empire, notably by the Irish since these would have focused on western Britain, a series of usurpers, and the steady withdrawal of troops. Internal unrest probably also played a role. The only other major account is in Gildas's *De Excidio*, written *c*.530 × 545. While this has the great advantage of being geographically close to events and spans the entire period,[13] the vagueness, dramatic tone, and purpose of the work makes it unreliable, dates are absent, and the chronology suspect. The only other relevant source, the *Notitia Dignitatum*, compiled *c*.395 with some later additions, makes no mention of military units in Wales, only the *Seguntienses*, an infantry unit whose name links them with the fort at *Segontium* (Caernarfon), who were by then stationed in Illyricum.[14] Therefore, though the meagre written sources give some indication of the nature and overall chronology of events leading up to the demise of Roman control in Britain and the aftermath, we are entirely dependent on the archaeological record to provide a broader approach and more nuanced view of the complex processes and regional differences that lie behind them.

Archaeological dating during the Roman period in Britain is generally reliant on coins and, to a lesser extent, ceramics, together with datable inscriptions, though the number of inscriptions declines significantly during the second half of the third century, and fourth-century examples are rare.[15] Artefacts, such as brooches and other items of personal adornment, though less precisely datable, also have a role to play.[16] Nevertheless, as soon as the Roman authorities ceased dispatching coins to Britain at the beginning of the fifth century—there are very few after 402—dating sites becomes much harder and the problem of how long some coins remained in use for monetary purposes is a matter of considerable debate.[17] Therefore it becomes all the more important to understand the contexts of these coins: whether they were deposited in hoards, or were accidentally or even deliberately discarded, as well as whether they are from sealed contexts, or contexts where they can only provide a *terminus post quem*, and where they are residual.[18] Because of frequent continuing dependence on coins for dating, it is, however, more difficult to establish when individual Roman pottery industries and their distribution networks ceased in Britain and the extent to which some pottery, notably shell-tempered wares which become more common in the later fourth century, continued production at a local level, albeit increasingly with much simpler technology.[19] Equally, though fashions in personal adornment and other artefacts changed during the course of the fourth century, chronological nuances are lacking, and bridging the divide between the Roman and early medieval periods

---

[13] Winterbottom 1978, chs 13–26.   [14] Mann 1976, 5, 8; Burnham and Davies 2010, 63–4.

[15] Hope 2016, 286–9.   [16] Cool 2000; Allason-Jones 2010.

[17] For a recent review of the evidence, see Walton and Moorhead 2016. For further discussion and alternative views, see Moorhead 2006; Abdy 2006; Williams, Gareth 2010.

[18] For more detailed discussion in relation to late Roman Britain, see Lockyer 2012.

[19] Tyers 1996, 77–80, 192–3; Gerrard 2013, 10, 80, 91–3, 106; Fitzpatrick-Matthews and Fleming 2016, 1–4.

68 LIFE IN EARLY MEDIEVAL WALES

continues to be problematic, though manufacture of belt fittings, which alongside crossbow brooches are now recognized as signs of late Roman, military, or civic status, continued well into the fifth century.[20] It is also now recognized that recycling played a significant role in the Roman economy and into the early medieval period. Roman pottery and some other artefacts either remained in use or were scavenged and redeployed, sometimes for a different purpose, whilst metals were more systematically melted down to make new objects.[21] Again, dating is often very difficult and particular attention needs to be paid to the contexts in which this evidence is found. Furthermore, in most parts of western and northern Britain, the cessation of the production and distribution of Roman ceramics and other goods did not lead to their replacement with a range of other diagnostic early medieval artefacts. Indeed, pottery was not made again in Wales until the coming of the Normans, and distinctive datable artefactual assemblages, which include ornamental metalwork and imported glass and ceramics, are almost entirely confined to a small number of elite sites, making the identification and dating of others all the more difficult.

Scientific dating is, however, now beginning to offer some important opportunities. Accelerator mass spectrometry (AMS) of multiple short-lived samples, continuing refinement of the calibration curve, and Bayesian statistical analysis have enabled more accurate radiocarbon dating, but the plateau in the curve c. AD 425–550 remains a significant obstacle to understanding the chronology of the late Roman to early medieval transition more precisely.[22] This may be a reason why dating on what are perceived to be later Roman excavated sites has continued, all too often, to depend exclusively on coins and ceramics, while the valuable extra dimension that would have been provided by radiocarbon dating of suitable short-lived samples from closed contexts, thereby facilitating the recognition of any post-Roman activity, has failed to be recognized.

Finally, it has to be admitted that, although some older excavations, for example at Caerwent where modern investigations have also taken place, can still yield valuable insights into the processes behind the Roman to early medieval transition, the lack of understanding of dating and stratigraphy at the time they were dug presents obstacles which threaten to challenge any chronological interpretation. Equally, many modern Roman and post-Roman excavations on sites in Wales have only sampled very limited areas, making a fuller picture of the dating and chronology of a site more difficult to discern.

Therefore, although the written sources provide a brief chronological framework for events in Britain during the second half of the fourth century and first decade of

[20] Cool 2000; Allason-Jones 2010; Collins 2010; Swift 2020, 433.

[21] Swift 2012; Fleming 2012; 2021, 51–157. For more general discussion of recycling in the Roman empire, see Duckworth and Wilson 2020.

[22] Bayliss et al. 2013, 35–7.

the fifth, they can only indirectly contribute to our understanding of the ending of Roman Wales. Consequently, we are almost entirely dependent on the expanding archaeological record. Despite continuing problems with dating and chronology, this not only provides a broad, if somewhat patchy, picture of the demise of Roman control and the collapse of the associated colonial market economy in Wales but also highlights significant underlying continuities.

FROM ROMAN TO POST-ROMAN WALES: A REGIONAL VIEW

In the early fourth century under Diocletian south-west Britain became part of the new administrative province of *Britannia Prima* stretching from Chester right down to Cornwall, with Cirencester as its capital.[23] The concepts of Romanization and what it might have meant by this time to be Roman in such a provincial setting on the edge of the empire have been widely debated[24] and have continuing relevance beyond the Roman period.[25] In this context we need to recognize the significance of different social groupings and the likelihood of switching between multiple ethnic and cultural identities—indigenous, Roman, and other—according to the differing circumstances of the lives people led, whether in the military, in an urban setting, or in the countryside. People's experiences of Romanization in terms of authority, economic impact, and material culture would have varied greatly, not only as a result of their attitudes and standing in society, but also according to the region in which they lived and how it was exploited, even within the province itself. Indeed, in Wales the archaeological evidence suggests considerable regional differences between, for example, the south-east, with its wider adoption of Roman architectural forms and ways of living, and the north-west, where this was largely limited to military installations, suggesting greater indigenous resistance to Romanization.[26]

The South-East

Though economic development in Wales was much less advanced, the Roman experience in the south-east is best understood as an extension of that in areas of *Britannia Prima* centred on Cirencester, Gloucester, and Bath. Indeed, the large number of coins from the foreshore at Black Rock, Portskewett, half of them fourth-century ending with the House of Valentinian (364–78), testifies to the importance of the

---

[23] Mattingly 2006, 227–9, fig. 9; White 2007, 31–42.

[24] E.g. Millett 1990; Mattingly 2006; for a more theoretical approach see Revell 2016; Gardner 2016.

[25] For a wide-ranging historiographical discussion of changing perceptions of 'Romanness' in the Roman and post-Roman world, see Pohl 2018.

[26] On landscapes of opportunity (mainly south-east Britain) and resistance, see Mattingly 2006, 369, 522–3.

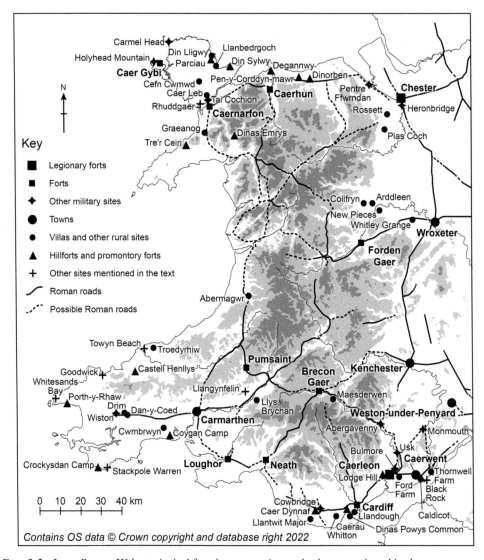

Fig. 3.2. Later Roman Wales: principal fourth-century sites and others mentioned in the text.

ferry across the Severn estuary linking the two regions and suggests military control of the crossing (Fig. 3.2).[27]

By the fourth century army recruitment had become more local and increasingly hereditary, bolstered by troops from beyond the empire, but the decline in inscriptions means little is known about Britain.[28] Most units were becoming more static, with the result that soldiers and their families were simply one element in a more local provincial society, and it is likely that, as the century progressed, decisions were

---

[27] Hudson 1970–8; Arnold and Davies 2000, 10, 35; Guest and Wells 2007, 59–60, no. 126.
[28] Mattingly 2006, 247–50.

CONTINUITY AND COLLAPSE 71

increasingly made at this level.[29] Even so, our broader understanding of the archaeo-logical evidence for the continuing role of the military in south-east Wales remains patchy and is difficult to interpret.

The most important military site in the region was Caerleon (*Isca*), the fortress of the II Augustan legion, strategically located on the tidal part of the Usk, which has been extensively excavated from the mid-nineteenth century onwards. During the late third or early fourth century key structures, such as the baths and *basilica principio-rum*, had been partially demolished, suggesting substantial troop reduction that probably included withdrawal of the legion, but there is also clear evidence of con-tinuing fourth-century occupation of a military kind. This includes road resurfacing, notably the *via principalis* twice, the first no earlier than the mid-fourth century, rub-bish deposition in abandoned areas, and the rebuilding of barrack blocks north of the east gate (*Insula XVII*) post 350.[30] Fragments of belt fittings and bracelets from the barrack blocks, the latter characteristic of female attire though occasionally also worn by men, suggest that families were now living in the fort. A small number of Theodosian coins (388–402) and South Midlands shell-tempered jars point to late fourth-century or even later occupation.[31] In this context, results from the recent excavation of a warehouse in the south-west quadrant (*Insula IV*) are particularly interesting. The warehouse remained in use until at least the mid-fourth century and was superseded by several unmortared stone walls, which included *spolia*, with rubble spreads indica-tive of later buildings erected within the shell. This is part of a pattern found else-where in Britain, suggesting that building supplies and know-how were no longer available. In this case radiocarbon dates from deposits associated with a stone-lined hearth, including grain, indicate that these structures were in use during the fifth and sixth centuries, thereby pointing to intensive post-Roman activity in this area of the fort.[32] Indeed, some activity continued, at least sporadically, within the fort through-out the early Middle Ages (Chapter 4).

In contrast, we know almost nothing about the later phases of the late Roman fort at Cardiff or its relationship to Caerleon. Probably constructed post 260, its roughly square plan with walls originally around 5 metres tall with projecting polygonal bas-tions, as well as its location near the mouth of the Taff, demonstrate an affinity with the later forts of the Saxon shore, notably Portchester. It would therefore have oper-ated together with a fleet to protect the Severn estuary and Bristol Channel from Irish incursions. Although the interior is poorly preserved, small interventions on the

[29] Gardner 2007, 247, 249.

[30] Gardner 1999, 405–8; Evans, D. R., and Metcalf 1992, 74–5; Burnham and Davies 2010, 166–7.

[31] Seaman 2010a, 44; Burnham and Davies 2010, 167; Evans, D. R., and Metcalf 1992, 129–31, 144–6; Allason-Jones 2010, 83; Guest and Wells 2007, 87, 102, nos 203, 233.

[32] Gardner and Guest 2010, 4–5, figs 4, 9–11; 2011, 20–2, 27–8; Peter Guest (pers. comm.). On the break-down of Roman building supplies and the loss of know-how associated with the construction of Roman build-ings, see Fleming 2021, 94–109.

western side have revealed an important collection of late ceramics, some associated with dark earth deposits indicative of the abandonment of the fort. They include South Midlands shell-tempered jars and another fabric also found in late contexts in the forum at Caerwent and at Gloucester. The latest coins are, however, Valentinianic (364–78).[33]

The only other military site in the region with evidence of fourth-century occupation is the auxiliary fort at Brecon Gaer, which is located north of the Brecon Beacons at the confluence of the Usk and Yscir, thereby controlling land routes to the east, west, and south. The comparatively few fourth-century coins from the site, the latest of which are again Valentinianic (364–78), suggest only limited activity. Despite some recent work in the *vicus*, our understanding of the later occupation is still dependent upon Wheeler's 1920s excavations in the interior. The final phase of the defences consisted of a substantial revetment of reused unmortared masonry to the rear of the earlier perimeter wall, the intervening space being filled with earth, rubble, and other building material. This extended round the eastern half of the fort, blocking the south and east gates. Wheeler argued this phase was post-Roman since it was built when the earlier defences were ruinous and because of the manner of construction. However, there is no dating evidence whatsoever and extensive metal detecting discoveries recorded by the Portable Antiquities Scheme in the eastern *vicus* have not revealed any early medieval finds.[34] Further work is therefore required to resolve this, but the construction technique, though unmortared, might fit better into a fourth-century horizon than later.

The later Roman economy in south-east Wales was boosted not only by continuing occupation of these forts but also by the town of Caerwent (*Venta Silurum*), the *civitas* capital of the Silures.[35] Prominently placed in the landscape, it is today still largely a greenfield site with remarkably well-preserved defences enclosing an area of 18 hectares, making it one of the smallest *civitas* capitals in Britain. Nonetheless, as elsewhere, its impressive town walls, by the end of the fourth century neglected public buildings and elite town houses, some with agricultural structures, all point to shifts in the use of space and the ways civic power operated. A sharply declining urban economy and recycling are also evident.[36] A stone wall had been added to existing earthwork defences at Caerwent in the late third century. In the mid-fourth this was

---

[33] Pearson 2002, 63; Webster 2002; Evans, P. 2004; Guest and Wells 2007, 126–7, no. 320; Burnham and Davies 2010, 230–3.

[34] Ibid., 201–4; Guest and Wells 2007, 258–9, no. 790; Lewis 2015; Wheeler 1926, 11–16, figs 1, 4–5, 8–9, 107. It was also suggested that the revetment might relate to the Norman Conquest; there is a motte south-west of the fort.

[35] For evidence that Caerwent was a *civitas* capital, see Collingwood and Wright 1995, no. 311; Brewer 1993, 61; 2004, 220–1.

[36] Mattingly 2006, 325–50.

Fig. 3.3. The walls on the south side of the *civitas* capital at Caerwent, showing an additional mid-fourth-century bastion (© Amgueddfa Cymru–National Museum Wales).

strengthened by the addition of polygonal stone bastions projecting at intervals along the north and south sides (Fig. 3.3). Excavation of the north-west bastion revealed a sealed coin hoard dating to 349–50 on a temporary floor surface, thereby providing a precise date of construction. Although these towers suggest an increasing need for defence, they also imply continuing civic confidence and imperial investment, as well as some form of garrison. Both the north and south gateways into the town were also blocked with masonry, but the date at which this occurred is unknown. It has been suggested that the blocking in the north gateway, which includes recycled carved stones, occurred as late as the fifth century, but in fact such *spolia* were being

74   LIFE IN EARLY MEDIEVAL WALES

incorporated into town walls in London and elsewhere from the later third century onwards.[37] Nevertheless, two late Roman lead-weighted javelin heads (*plumbatae*) and the exceptionally large number of Theodosian bronze coins—in the region of 6,000, including later types dated *c*.395–402—are indicative of both a military presence and a basic market economy within the town into the first decade of the fifth century.[38] However, the discovery of a later bronze *nummus* (421–35) is more unusual, though it is doubtful how much longer such base-metal coins continued as currency.[39] The presence of shell-tempered pottery similarly points to occupation during the later fourth and into the fifth century.[40] Late Roman belt fittings, one example of which came to light in antiquarian spoil during re-excavation of the basilica, were probably worn by both soldiers and civic dignitaries.[41]

Although large areas of Caerwent were excavated between 1899 and 1913, revealing the later Roman town layout and building plans, this has largely destroyed any subsequent evidence. Even where modern excavations have taken place, for example on the sites of the Romano-Celtic temple and courtyard house I.28N, any early medieval archaeology there may have been has not survived later activity.[42] Nevertheless, it is possible to trace the histories of some buildings, thereby demonstrating civic stability as well as the wealth and Romanized lifestyle of some of the inhabitants, very likely local dignitaries, during the first half of the fourth century. However, an accelerating decline thereafter points to falling living standards and changing attitudes to buildings and their functions. The forum-basilica on the main street represented the heart of commercial and civic life, including tax collection. Re-excavation by Richard Brewer of parts of this complex has demonstrated that the basilica, including the *curia* (council chamber), originally built in the early second century, was still functioning as an administrative centre in the 330s. Indeed, continuing civic confidence is demonstrated by its partial reconstruction which, on coin evidence, was completed around 350. By around the end of the century, however, metalworking hearths appear in the great hall which were used for recycling and the manufacture of iron nails, perhaps for reroofing the ranges. Shortly afterwards the roof of the basilica hall became unsafe, leading to the systematic demolition of this part of the building, leaving an open space. Even so, some other rooms continued in use and a hypocaust was constructed in the *tribunal*, where legal cases were heard, as late as the end of the century, though how long

[37] Manning 2003; Casey 1983, 54, 57–62, 76; Speed 2014, 108–10; Barker et al. 2018, 337–42.

[38] Knight 1996, 43–4, 46; Walton and Moorhead 2016, 3.3; Casey 1989, 325–6. Several large Theodosian hoards and concentrations of coins were noted from old excavations; see Nash-Williams 1923, 92–4; Robertson et al. 2000, 401–2; Guest and Wells 2007, 24–43; Brewer 2004, 232.

[39] Other examples are known from Wroxeter, Richborough, St Albans, and Dunstable; Moorhead 2006, 102–3.

[40] Jeff Davies (pers. comm.).   [41] Knight 1996, 37–42, 46–7.

[42] Richard Brewer (pers. comm.). For a plan of the town showing excavated areas and Roman buildings, see Guest 2022, fig. 2.

afterwards they remained in use is unclear.[43] Nevertheless, it is likely that, in the wake of a sharply contracting economy, the mechanisms of power, which had formerly required such public buildings, were already in the process of change. At least part of the forum colonnade was also dismantled and a path of recycled roof tiles was laid over it and out into the piazza sealing a Theodosian coin (388–*c*.395). Adjacent shops may, however, have continued to operate.[44]

Next to the forum-basilica, the Romano-Celtic temple was erected as late as *c*.330. That it continued in use after the 341 edict banning temples within towns and was maintained at least to the 370s (since a coin of Valentinian was sealed beneath repairs), demonstrates the continuing importance of paganism to the late Roman inhabitants, which is also seen at rural temples across the Severn estuary, such as Lydney (Chapter 9). It may nonetheless be significant that in Caerwent a statuette of a seated mother goddess was deposited in a pit near the temple and no votives were found in the interior, which might indicate deliberate closure and systematic clearance.[45] There were, however, also Christian inhabitants, evidenced by the careful deposition of pottery of later fourth-century date and other artefacts which included a pewter bowl with a chi-R graffito, possibly part of a Christian feasting set, in courtyard house IX.7N east of the basilica (Chapter 9).[46]

Excavation of two other courtyard houses in the north-west quadrant of the town demonstrates the status, wealth, and Romanized lifestyle of those who lived in them during the first half of the fourth century, but also subsequent decay and collapse. House I.28N was rebuilt in the early fourth century with hypocausts, mosaics, and wall plaster, but the inclusion of a large storeroom and a corn-dryer suggests that agricultural produce was being collected and processed within the town, and adjacent buildings may have been barns and byres, indicating that it also functioned as a farm. Nevertheless, it was abandoned in the mid-fourth century. However, at around this time, House VII.27N, which was joined to a functioning blacksmith's, was rebuilt with mosaics, but the hypocaust was never completed. It has been argued that this house continued in use into the fifth century, but hearths in two former living rooms demonstrate that they were now used for industrial purposes, and a dispersed hoard of Theodosian bronze coins found in rubbish overlying a mosaic floor may originally have been hidden in the roof which then collapsed.[47] Therefore, by around 425 Caerwent had been in decline for around seventy-five years. Although there are some indications of an operating civic authority into the fifth century,

[43] Ibid. For discussion of metalworking in and more general remodelling of the forum-basilica elsewhere, e.g. Cirencester, where metalworking began *c*.350, see Speed 2014, 110–13.

[44] Guest 2022.

[45] Mattingly 2006, 348; Brewer 1993, 58–60; 2004, 224–6; 2006, 44–6. For the sequence at Lydney, see Woodward and Leach 1993, 317.

[46] Ashby 1907, 459–60; Boon 1992, 16–18.   [47] Brewer 2006, 46–53; 2004, 231–2.

the market economy had collapsed and the population contracted, but as we shall see, occupation continued at some level throughout the early Middle Ages, though the former town now functioned in a very different way (Chapter 4).

Our limited understanding of other Roman-period settlements in the fertile lowlands of Gwent and the Vale of Glamorgan has gradually increased through aerial photography and field walking, indicating a potentially well-populated landscape consisting almost entirely of dispersed farms that demonstrate considerable continuity from the later prehistoric period onwards.[48] However, remarkably few sites have been substantially excavated using modern techniques. This makes it more difficult to determine the nature of these settlements and the changes they underwent during the fourth century and later as well as their relationship to the changing economy and supply chain.

Settlement types vary greatly in their degree of Romanization and a hierarchy is clearly apparent. At the upper end of the scale are the small number of ribbon settlements, a characteristic type in the south and east of England. Located on Roman roads, they grew up as a result of the military and carried out industrial activities. They include Bulmore, whose fortunes reflect those of Caerleon, and Cowbridge (probably *Bovium*) in the Vale where agricultural activity continued nearby well into the later fourth century with quite a number of fourth-century coins, the latest of which is Valentinianic (364–78). To the east there are signs of similar nucleated settlements persisting into the fourth century at Abergavenny, Monmouth (*Blestium*), and Usk (*Burrium*).[49] Around twenty villas have also been identified, demonstrating the Romanized aspirations of a largely indigenous elite, as well as some military veterans, with landed estates and workforces producing significant agricultural surpluses. As might be expected, there is a cluster around Caerwent, but there is also a group south of Cowbridge in the Vale of Glamorgan, with outliers on Gower and at Maesderwen in the Usk valley.[50] They are characterized by distinctive rectilinear plans, masonry walls, and other Romanized features such as mosaics, painted wall plaster, hypocausts, and baths. However, their histories are poorly understood, and even where there has been more investigation, the date of abandonment has rested on the evidence of coins, pottery, and other small finds. For example, excavations at Cae'r Mead, Llantwit Major, recovered the plan of an unusually large courtyard villa (Fig. 3.4) comparable with those in the Cotswolds. The phasing cannot be entirely resolved, but it seems to have reached its apogee with the insertion of a new mosaic in the mid-fourth century but declined thereafter since there is undated ironworking in the furnace room of the

---

[48] For reviews of the evidence, see Arnold and Davies 2000, 80–7; Evans, E. M. 2018.

[49] Burnham and Davies 2010, 132, 170–1, 192, 264, 304; Brewer 2004, 211–12; Burnham and Wacher 1990, 296–300; Parkhouse and Evans 1996, 233; Guest and Wells 2007, 163–9. On the Roman place names, see Rivet and Smith 1979, 269, 273–4, 285.

[50] RCAHMW 1976a, 110–19; 1986, 179–82; Brewer 2004, 234–5; Davies, J. L., and Driver 2018, 206–10.

CONTINUITY AND COLLAPSE 77

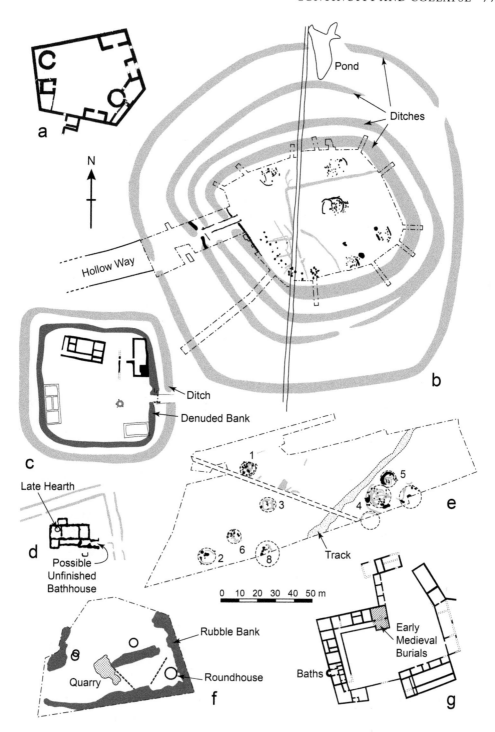

FIG. 3.4. Roman period rural settlements: comparative plans. a. Din Lligwy; b. Collfryn; c. Whitton villa; d. Abermagwr villa; e. Cefn Cwmwd; f. Thornwell Farm; g. Cae'r Mead (Llantwit Major) villa (after Waddington 2013, fig. 6.16; Britnell 1989, fig. 24; Arnold and Davies 2000, fig. 7.5F; Davies, J. L., and Driver 2018, fig. 4; Waddington 2013, fig. 6.60; Hughes 1996, fig. 47; Arnold and Davies 2000, fig. 7.4G).

78 LIFE IN EARLY MEDIEVAL WALES

baths. The latest coin is of Constantius II (337–61). The villas at Maesderwen, an antiquarian discovery, and Ford Farm, Langstone, investigated following Portable Antiquities Scheme finds, both revealed evidence of bath suites. The latest reported coin at the latter was also of Constantius II, while that at the former was of Valentinian (364–75).[51]

Some other villas were, however, much more modest, notably Whitton, which has been totally excavated with particularly interesting results. It was essentially a native farmstead with Roman pretensions and was probably inhabited by the same extended family over many generations. It had evolved from a first-century, subsquare, enclosed settlement with timber roundhouses of late prehistoric kind to, by the mid-third, a denuded enclosure with ranges of rectangular buildings on masonry footings, one with unfinished hypocausts. The final-phase buildings may have been confined to the northern half and the latest dating evidence, consisting of ceramics and two Constantinian coins, has led to the suggestion that it was abandoned *c*.340, though a fragment of later fourth-century belt fitting and two post-Roman glass beads, all unstratified, were also found on the site.[52] Nearby graves included the prone burial of a probably local, adult male whose grave goods included a silver crossbow brooch, a sword, and hobnailed boots, suggesting an official role.[53]

In contrast, as in northern and south-west England, some lower-status farmsteads of the Roman period continued to use indigenous, late prehistoric building forms, notably wood and clay-walled roundhouses, throughout their existence and are more difficult to locate as a result. In other cases, systems of quadrangular paddocks and small fields have been identified, as at Dinas Powys Common, where a square enclosure contained at least two rectangular wooden houses, with occupation continuing during the fourth century. Generally, however, there are few signs of domestic structures, though in some instances evidence, such as roof tiles, indicates more substantial buildings nearby, and rubble spreads and banks are also sometimes found.[54] The presence of ceramics and occasional coins as well as other artefacts demonstrates contact with the Roman market economy, but to varying degrees. As with the villas, the virtual demise of pottery and coins around the mid-fourth century has led to the persistent belief that such farmsteads were consistently abandoned around this time.[55]

Nevertheless, there are some scraps of evidence to suggest that this may not necessarily have been the case. For example, Thornwell Farm, on the edge of the Gwent Levels, is a small roundhouse settlement with late prehistoric origins. The final recorded phase has been dated to the third and first half of the fourth centuries and

---

[51] Nash-Williams 1953, 116–18, 156; Hogg 1974, 236–42, 248–50; RCAHMW 1986, 181; Macdonald 2001.

[52] Jarrett and Wrathmell 1981, 82–101, 162, nos 18–19, 178–9, no. 37.

[53] Vale of Glamorgan Council, site 16.

[54] Arnold and Davies 2000, 76–80; Evans, E. M. 2018; on roundhouses in England, see Taylor 2007, 31.

[55] E.g. Webster 1984, 300; Brewer 2004, 237. For an alternative view see Evans, E. M. 2001, 30, 43.

consisted of roundhouses partially surrounded by rubble banks overlying earlier stone walls. The banks included differentiated accumulations of Roman pottery, animal bone, and earlier material, which may indicate deliberate sorting and structured deposition that might therefore suggest a later aceramic phase of activity on the site. A few pots had been repaired using rivets, indicating problems with the supply chain and the need to conserve.[56] Nearby, the settlement at Caldicot has been interpreted as possibly having rectangular timber buildings with stone roofing slabs in the later stages, as well as walls and field boundaries pointing to probably extensive agricultural activity, while the Roman artefactual assemblage demonstrates considerable prosperity. The latest coin is Valentinianic, suggesting occupation at least until the 370s. However, such coins are generally very rare on rural sites in south-east Wales, which contrasts with both Gloucestershire and Somerset where Theodosian coins (388–402) are also relatively common. Nevertheless, the lack of such coins merely indicates that in south-east Wales the market economy had already contracted substantially and therefore their demise does not necessarily indicate abandonment of the settlements themselves, which may have continued alongside agricultural production for some time.[57] There is currently insufficient information to determine the extent of flooding on the Caldicot Level in the post-Roman period, though a radiocarbon date from Goldcliff indicated the renewal of marine transgression between the late fourth and mid-sixth century. However, the lack of inundation in the Peterstone part of the Wentlooge Level to the west is suggestive of the continuation of grazing, though very likely on a reduced scale.[58]

Relatively few hillforts of later prehistoric type have been excavated in south-east Wales, but more than twenty have produced evidence of Roman period activity, mainly in the form of pottery. In the case of Caer Dynnaf near Cowbridge, there seems to have been a change in settlement type, with perhaps two large farmsteads set within the hillfort and pottery spanning the first to fourth centuries. Equally, at the imposing site of Lodge Hill Camp overlooking the fort at Caerleon (and therefore in a militarized zone), a small oval enclosure within the hillfort was associated with abraded pottery sherds of third- and fourth-century date. Although it was suggested that this might indicate renewed occupation, perhaps in the post-Roman period, the lack of radiocarbon dates makes this impossible to verify.[59] Caerau is, however, a particularly interesting large, multivallate hillfort west of Cardiff close to the villa at Ely. Here recent excavations have found evidence of a substantial secondary inner rampart containing Roman pottery on both the north and south sides of the hillfort, suggesting

[56] Hughes 1996, 89–97.
[57] Arnold and Davies 2000, 78; Vyner and Allen 1988; Seaman 2010a, 46–7.
[58] Rippon 1996, 35; Roberts 1999, Beta-12089: cal. AD 380–560.
[59] RCAHMW 1976a, 40–1; Coflein, NPRN 93053; Davies, J. L. 1967; Pollard et al. 2006, 58–61.

80　LIFE IN EARLY MEDIEVAL WALES

a remodelling of the enclosure, most likely in the early medieval period, though again there is as yet no conclusive dating evidence to prove this.[60]

Therefore, in south-east Wales the real period of change seems to begin in the mid-fourth century, with construction of the bastions at Caerwent the final evidence of substantial military intervention as well as civic pride. Afterwards there are increasing signs of changes in how power was exercised, which likely included the mechanisms for tax collection with the consequent impact on the need for production of agricultural surpluses. Alongside this, although there was probably the continuation of some more limited, local defence suggested by the late phases at Caerleon, this left the population vulnerable to the threat of Irish raids and more general unrest. There were clearly mounting pressures on the maintenance of a coin-based market economy and supply chains both in Caerwent and on other Romanized sites, notably villas, as well as lower-status farms, many of which had continued with little change, sometimes over many centuries. However, conclusive evidence for the abandonment of these sites is frequently lacking and agricultural activities may well have continued, though likely at a reduced level.[61] Instead, we are seeing a major change in how people lived involving a culture of recycling and continuing use of what was available, together with a dearth of other diagnostic artefacts or radiocarbon dates which might aid recognition of later fourth- and fifth-century activity.

The South-West

We have much less understanding of what Romanization and the continuing impact of Roman control might have meant to the lives of the population in the region of the Demetae and how this changed during the course of the fourth century. In contrast to the south-east, there is remarkably little evidence of a late Roman military presence—indeed of a military presence at all beyond the mid-second century. However, at the fort of Pumsaint, Carmarthenshire, a timber building which burnt down has been dated to the later third or early fourth century and was most likely connected with activity at the nearby gold mines at Dolaucothi.[62] On the evidence of pottery, occupation also continued, until the mid-fourth century, in a large agricultural village outside the abandoned fort at Wiston, Pembrokeshire, which has been compared with the more Romanized settlement at Tai Cochion, Anglesey.[63] There are further indications of occupation in the forts at Neath (*Nidum*) and Loughor (*Leucarum*) around this time. The latest coin from Loughor is of Constantine II (*c*.324–30) with no firm evidence after this, but the discovery close by of a fragmentary fifth- or sixth-century

---

[60] Davis and Sharples 2015; Davis et al. 2015; Niall Sharples (pers. comm.).

[61] For likely continuity of a proportion of Roman period field systems into the early Middle Ages in south-east Wales, see Rippon 2019, 23–30.

[62] Burnham and Davies 2010, 279–80.　　　[63] Meek 2017, 208–9.

ogham inscription is surely significant. A likely personal name had been added to a Roman altar and this points to later Irish activity in the vicinity of the fort, which is located strategically at the lowest crossing over the river.[64] In the later third and earlier fourth centuries Neath and Loughor were probably part of a coastal defence system stretching from Cardiff westwards to the Roman town of Carmarthen on the north bank of the Tywi, which could have provided a port of call for naval as well as trading vessels in the Bristol Channel. A small number of post-348 coins have also been recorded in other coastal locations including Stackpole Warren, Traeth Mawr (Whitesands Bay), Goodwick Harbour, and Towyn Beach, and it has been suggested that these might have a military connection.[65] Locations such as these may denote the regulation of traffic across the Irish Sea and possibly the presence of Irish mercenaries in the late Roman army.

Carmarthen (*Moridunum*), usually identified as the *civitas* capital of the Demetae, was the seat of the Roman administration, whose functions included tax collection, but its easterly location probably meant it had little directly associated territory, thereby limiting its wider influence on the economy and life in the region.[66] It was also very small—only 13.2 hectares. Despite several modern excavations, our understanding of the settlement during the fourth century is extremely limited and nothing is known of its subsequent history for several centuries. A stone wall was added to the existing clay bank defences, probably in the mid- to late third century, but there are no signs of later bastions as at Caerwent.[67] The forum-basilica has not been investigated, though a continuation of some civic authority is indicated by street resurfacing well into the second half of the fourth century. At Priory Street in the northern corner of the town, the streets were maintained even after most of the buildings, only one of which had stone footings, had been demolished and other activities, including iron smithing, had virtually ceased. The latest coins from beside these streets were a securely stratified *siliqua* of Constantine II (360–3) and a coin of Honorius minted in Constantinople (393–5), which, because of its exotic origin, has sometimes been regarded as a later loss. There are, however, no known Theodosian copper *nummi*, which were so common in Caerwent. Equally, there are surprisingly few Constantinian coins, suggesting that a limited monetary economy was already faltering in the earlier fourth century.[68] Other discoveries pointing to continuing official and perhaps military interest include a commemorative pillar with a rare inscription of a type current

---

[64] Rivet and Smith 1979, 388–9, 425; Burnham and Davies 2010, 262–4, 266; Marvell and Owen-John 1997, 216–17, 227–8; Redknap and Lewis 2007, no. G76.

[65] James 2016a, 330–2; 2003, 288. Remarkably, a gold coin of Arcadius (395–400) was found at Pencarreg, Carmarthenshire, on the surface of the Roman road running from Carmarthen to Llanfair Clydogau; see Guest and Wells 2007, 220, no. 652.

[66] Rivet and Smith 1979, 422; James 2003, 10, 21–2.

[67] Ibid., 182–96.   [68] Ibid., 74–80, 87, 286–7.

from the early fourth century, a crossbow brooch dated *c.*340–80 found in a roadside drain in Priory Street, and an unstratified belt stiffener from the same site.[69]

Our knowledge of the pattern of rural settlement in south-west Wales has greatly increased since the 1980s as a result of aerial photography, a handful of major excavations, notably at Llawhaden and Castell Henllys, Pembrokeshire, as well as more limited interventions elsewhere. However, much of the emphasis has been on understanding the late prehistoric to Roman transition, which demonstrates considerable continuity, rather than the Roman to early medieval one.[70] Nevertheless it is clear that, although there was some activity in hillforts and promontory forts in the later Roman period, the rural population mainly lived in enclosed farmsteads with roundhouses most likely associated with extended family units, a very common native settlement form which became the most characteristic in the region in the second and first centuries BC. There is also slight evidence for unenclosed roundhouses at this time. Although the occupants of the enclosed farmsteads and other sites had some access to Roman pottery, this was probably intermittent and coins are generally rare,[71] together indicating only limited engagement with the Roman market economy.

At the top of the scale occupation and reoccupation of some hillforts and promontory forts undoubtedly persisted during the later Roman period, with some indications of continuing activity in the fifth and sixth centuries. The most convincing example of this is Coygan Camp, which was partially excavated prior to destruction by quarrying in the early 1960s. This Late Iron Age promontory fort was very prominently sited on a rock overlooking Carmarthen Bay west of the Taf and Tywi estuaries. The rich Roman period artefactual assemblage demonstrates occupation from the late second century onwards by a farming and craftworking community who were able to take advantage of coastal trade. Although the latest coins from the site are Constantinian, there is also a sherd of late fourth-century shell-tempered ware, suggesting continuing activity, together with sherds of eastern Mediterranean imported pottery indicative of elite occupation during the later fifth and earlier sixth centuries.[72] Other coastal promontory forts also have fourth-century Roman pottery, for example Porth-y-Rhaw and Crockysdan Camp, but no evidence of later activity has been identified.[73] There has been little investigation of inland sites apart from Castell Henllys, which is located in the Duad valley, a tributary of the Nevern. Extensive excavations demonstrated that in the Late Iron Age occupation shifted from the promontory fort into the northern annexe and consisted of two farmsteads with roundhouses,

[69] Ibid., 310–12, 315–16, nos 36, 50; Collingwood and Wright 1995, no. 412.

[70] Williams and Mytum 1998; Mytum 2013. For general reviews of the evidence, see Murphy and Mytum 2011; Murphy 2016, 227–64; James 2016a, 315–26.

[71] James 2003, 287–8.

[72] Wainwright 1967; Guest and Wells 2007, 209–10; Edwards and Lane 1988, 44–6.

[73] Crane and Murphy 2010a, 76–7, 89–94; Grimes 1931.

four-post storage structures, and a stockyard together with artefacts indicating continuing elite status despite the change in settlement form. Roman ceramics, particularly Black-burnished ware, show that occupation continued into the fourth century. Furthermore, based on the stratigraphy, it has been argued that there was a short-lived refurbishment of the severely denuded hillfort defences, including the gateway, in the late Roman or post-Roman period, possibly in response to well-evidenced Irish settlement in the area in the form of ogham-inscribed stones. However, without scientific or artefactual dating, this is very difficult to substantiate.[74]

Equally, it may be argued that some later Roman enclosed farmsteads continued in use or were reoccupied in the early Middle Ages, including two of the intensively investigated Llawhaden group, though precise dating remains consistently elusive. A later phase at Dan-y-Coed, probably after a period of abandonment, included construction of a subsquare, partially paved structure within the enclosure, but the Roman pottery was residual and the radiocarbon dates from beneath it inconclusive. Similarly, at Drim slight remains of a possible roundhouse may represent a late phase of either more-or-less continuous occupation from the Late Iron Age onwards or reoccupation of the earlier severely decayed enclosure. Finds include fourth-century pottery and an unusual, post-Roman, Type G penannular brooch. A post-hole associated with the possible roundhouse was radiocarbon-dated to the mid-seventh to later ninth century AD.[75] At Troedyrhiw, south Cardiganshire, investigation of a subsquare enclosure defined by a bank and ditch with a rectangular annexe revealed pottery suggesting occupation throughout the Roman period until the mid-fourth century. Although it may have been abandoned at this time, it is also possible that occupation continued, but there was no longer any access to Roman goods, the only dating evidence.[76]

Only a small number of the inhabitants in this region seem to have chosen a more Romanized lifestyle demonstrable in the construction of a handful of villas with larger rectangular dwellings on stone footings and other Roman features, often within earlier enclosed sites. However, they are small-scale and demonstrate few signs of luxury. Even so, evidence for a hypocaust, wall plaster, and tesserae were found at Llys Brychan in the Tywi valley, and Cwmbrwyn had a bath suite, but an understanding of their overall chronology and abandonment is lacking.[77] The only modern excavation is at Abermagwr, an isolated example in the Ystwyth valley, indicative of a prosperous farming estate, possibly focused on stock-rearing. The rectangular, winged corridor building was constructed of stone with pentagonal shale roofing slates and a later room with a likely unfinished hypocaust, possibly intended as a bathhouse. The

---

[74] Mytum 2013, 12–19, 275–91, 308–9; James 2016a, 322–3; Thomas 1994, 71–2, fig. 6.3.
[75] James 2016a, 319–21; Williams and Mytum 1998, 12–14, 50–2, 62–4, 88–9, 99; CAR-473, cal. AD 630–880.
[76] Murphy and Mytum 2013.
[77] Arnold and Davies 2000, 86–7; James 2016a, 315–18; Davies, J. L., and Driver 2018, 206–7; Jarrett 1962; Ward 1907.

occupation of the villa has been dated to *c*.230–330/40 since no later fourth-century pottery or coins were found. Particularly interesting, however, is evidence for the abandonment of the building. This followed a catastrophic fire in the western and central rooms, ultimately causing the roof to collapse. Subsequently, large post-holes were dug through the floors of the central and northern rooms, suggesting the erection of some kind of structure, and in the western room a hearth was made from the fallen slates. Further hearths with evidence of lead working indicating systematic recycling may also date to this phase, and in the possible bathhouse a large pit filled with domestic rubbish and dumped building material was also part of the abandonment process. Nevertheless, it is impossible to determine the events that led up to the fire, whether accidental or the result of conflict.[78]

Therefore, the pattern of rural settlement in this region was clearly part of a much longer continuum seen from the later prehistoric onwards, which persisted through the Roman period and in some cases beyond. Nonetheless, it would be wrong to regard it as unchanging since some sites were abandoned and later reoccupied or the focus of settlement moved. Rather, it responded to the changing needs and aspirations of local communities and their power structures as well as to the rural economy they sustained. Though these communities demonstrate some engagement with more Romanized ways of living through the acquisition of pottery, and in a few cases the construction of modest villas, their access to a market economy, which had always been limited, seems rare by the mid-fourth century. By that time, the only clear evidence of continuing Roman authority was confined to Carmarthen.

The North-West

In this region people's experience of Romanization was shaped by military rather than civil authority, and the auxiliary fort at Caernarfon (*Segontium*) remained the main base throughout the fourth century. The fort is located on a ridge overlooking the Seiont, thereby commanding the western end of the Menai Strait. There have been periodic excavations on the site since the mid-nineteenth century, most importantly those of Wheeler (1921–3) investigating large areas north-east of the *Via Principalis*, and those of Casey and Davies (1975–9) in the south-east quadrant. Both revealed extensive fourth-century occupation, though Wheeler's phasing and conclusions have now been revised.[79] The volume of coins and ceramics demonstrates increased density in the occupation of the fort from the late third century and well into the fourth,[80] most likely reflecting reorganization following the establishment of *Britannia Prima*

---

[78] Davies, J. L., and Driver 2018. Robin Fleming (2021, 109–13) would see wells in particular with similar deposits on Roman sites elsewhere as part of a ritual closing of the site, and in this instance the location within the possible bathhouse might also be significant.

[79] Wheeler 1923; Casey and Davies 1993, 1–9.   [80] Ibid., 15, 124, 128–9.

under Diocletian, as well as military need in a region subject to escalating Irish attacks. The eastern wall of the fort in the south-east quadrant was rebuilt around the mid-fourth century, probably contemporaneously with the digging of two external ditches investigated outside the north-east gate. This was one of three gateways excavated by Wheeler that were probably likewise modified at this time. He also argued that at least two new barrack blocks were constructed and the headquarters building (*principia*) substantially altered, with a coin of 364–75 sealed beneath the floor of a later structure partially overlying the filled-in cellar in the shrine. The commander's house (*praetorium*) was also largely rebuilt, with a coin of 348–50 providing a *terminus post quem*. However, Wheeler's firm dating of this phase as beginning 'in or shortly after the middle of the fourth century' is too confident; it probably covers much of that century.[81] In the south-east quadrant in the early to mid-fourth century, the only identifiable building was a post-built cook- or bakehouse, but industrial activity, including metalworking, continued and there were also rubbish pits containing sherds of late East Midlands shell-tempered jars. The last major feature was a large, timber-lined drain, which may have taken the overflow from a water tank or fountain associated with the aqueduct that was later filled with rubbish, including artefacts of late fourth-century or even later date.[82]

The finds assemblage from the latest phases in the south-east quadrant is of considerable interest not only because it sheds light on the occupants but also because it has been argued that some of these items are characteristic of probable fifth-century levels on other Roman sites, mainly in northern England.[83] The assemblage (Fig. 3.5) includes late Roman military equipment, notably three lead-weighted javelin heads (*plumbatae*) and several crossbow brooches in addition to a prestigious gold example discovered in the early nineteenth century, which must have belonged to a man of rank.[84] Other items of personal adornment include Type E penannular brooches and one Type F with zoomorphic terminals. By this time elaborate women's Roman hairstyles held up with pins had gone out of fashion and been replaced by plain strip copper-alloy and bone bracelets indicating that, by the later fourth century, women were also living inside the fort. The recycling of earlier Samian pottery to make spindle whorls is also noteworthy, and the predominance of jars suggests family rather than communal cooking.[85] Casey argued on the basis of the considerable number of Valentinianic coins (364–78) but only a small number of Theodosian ones (388–402), including a clipped *siliqua*, that the *Seguntienses* were finally withdrawn in the early 390s, possibly when Britain was under the control of the Continental usurper

---

[81] Ibid., 6, 15–16, 65–6; Casey 1974a; Wheeler 1923, 73–89, quote on p. 89.

[82] Casey and Davies 1993, 15–17, 65–74.   [83] Cool 2000.

[84] Casey and Davies 1993, 166–7, nos 8–12, 187–9 nos 275–7; Hemp 1918; Wheeler 1923, 130.

[85] Casey and Davies 1993, 168–73 nos 16–20 and 39–48, 204 no. 461, 209 no. 500, 309; Wheeler 1923, 136–7, no. 6; Cool 2000.

86 LIFE IN EARLY MEDIEVAL WALES

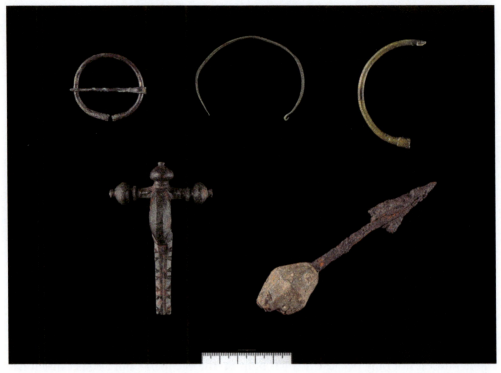

FIG. 3.5. Late finds from the auxiliary fort at Caernarfon: a Type F penannular brooch, two bracelets, a copper-alloy crossbow brooch, and a lead-weighted javelin (*plumbata*) (© Amgueddfa Cymru–National Museum Wales; photograph: Robin Maggs).

Eugenius.[86] Nevertheless, this may be too prescriptive. Although coinage ceased to arrive on the site, suggesting the ending of official control, the assemblage above may indicate a continuing, perhaps unofficial, garrison into the fifth century. In the future radiocarbon dating of animal bones preserved from sealed late contexts would almost certainly help to refine the chronology and, as we shall see, some activity continued in the vicinity of the fort for some time after this (Chapter 4).

There has been little exploration of the extensive *vicus*, mostly now built over, apart from the temple of Mithras which, it has been argued, was first deserted, then desecrated sometime after 350. Overlooking the Seiont are the still impressive remains of Hen Waliau, a presumed rectangular, stone-walled enclosure with distinctive herringbone masonry that guarded the harbour and may have acted as a storage compound. It was probably constructed at the same time as the refurbishment of

---

[86] Casey and Davies 1993, 129–31, 158–61; in total seven Theodosian coins (388–402) have been recorded, Guest and Wells 2007, 333–40.

the fort defences in the mid-fourth century, or even later, as two sherds of southern shell-tempered pottery were found in the layer beneath.[87] The Seiont was probably the embarkation point for a ferry to south-west Anglesey. Here, at Tai Cochion, Llanidan, geophysical survey revealed a large Romanized settlement, comparable with Cowbridge, strung out along a road stretching westwards from the shore. On either side was a complex pattern of rectangular buildings with rectilinear yards and enclosures. Small-scale excavations indicated an industrial, agricultural, and trading economy with a pottery sequence similar to the life of the fort, with an upswing during the first half of the fourth century. However, the latest coin is from the 350s and the lack of later shell-tempered wares has led to the view that in the areas excavated occupation ceased shortly afterwards.[88]

The only other significant evidence of a late Roman military presence in this region is the small fort at Caer Gybi (Holyhead) in north-west Anglesey, which, with its fine harbour, would have functioned as a naval base linked to both Caernarfon and the legionary fortress at Chester (*Deva*). Its construction would likewise have demonstrated the continuing presence of Roman authority and, in conjunction with two coastal watchtowers that were presumably part of a wider network of signal stations, it operated to counter Irish raiders. The fort overlooking the harbour now consists of three sides of a rectangle with the remains of round corner towers. There has been little archaeological investigation and dating remains problematic as no Roman artefacts have been found and subsequent reuse as the site of an early medieval church foundation has likely destroyed much of the evidence. However, the herringbone masonry is comparable with Hen Waliau, suggesting that Caer Gybi is of a similar mid-fourth-century or possibly later date, and parallels have also been made with fortifications along the Rhine–Danube frontier.[89]

The watchtowers, one on top of Holyhead Mountain, the other near Carmel Head in the north-west corner of the island, would have provided wide views across the Irish Sea. They may be broadly compared with late Roman examples on the Yorkshire coast and also have parallels with towers on the Rhine and Danube. The former, situated inside the large hillfort of Caer y Tŵr, has been excavated to reveal the stone footings of a small square tower, and a Constantinian coin incorporated into the masonry indicates construction after *c*.340.[90] The coin sequence, which includes a

---

[87] Burnham and Davies 2010, 223; Boon 1960; Boyle 1991; Symonds 2015, 49–53, 59.

[88] Hopewell 2016; 2018, 313–18.

[89] RCAHMW 1937, 31–4; Griffiths 1954; Davies, J. L. 2012a, 374; Boyle 1991, 210–11; Symonds 2015, 49–52, 59.

[90] Gerrard 2013, 40–1; Davies, J. L. 2012a, 374–6; Crew 1980; Boon 1986a, 432; Burnham and Davies 2010, 64, 301; Hopewell 2013; 2018, 320–1. The suggested watchtower at Capel Eithin, Gaerwen, can now be discounted, see White and Smith 1999, 116–24; Longley 2009, 120.

88 LIFE IN EARLY MEDIEVAL WALES

likely hoard from beneath the collapse of the tower, ends with Theodosian copper *nummi* and a clipped silver *siliqua* (388–402), thereby suggesting, as with Caernarfon, activity into the last decade of the fourth century or even later. An unusual hoard of Constantinian gold *solidi* (330–41) is also known from the eastern slope and is possibly a votive deposit, as the mountain itself may have been considered sacred.[91] Otherwise there is slight evidence from the fort at Caerhun (*Canovium*), located on the west bank of the Conwy, pointing to reoccupation during the third and fourth centuries. The nature of this activity is, however, poorly understood, though the coin sequence spans the fourth century, ending with four Theodosian *nummi*; other late coins formerly associated with the site may now be discounted.[92]

Since there was no town or *civitas* administration in the region, the *vicus* at Caernarfon would have continued to provide the most important nexus for interaction between the military and the rural population, thereby creating opportunities for requisition, supply, and trade.[93] Archaeological investigation of late prehistoric and Roman period rural sites in this region has focused on Anglesey and Arfon with little work on either Llŷn or in Merioneth, areas which, once garrisons were withdrawn from conquest period forts in the mid-second century, are likely to have experienced much less contact with Roman authority. As a result of more recent excavations, some with radiocarbon dates, our understanding of the chronology of rural settlements has improved. It is now clear that, as in the south-west, late prehistoric settlement types, mainly in the form of a variety of enclosed and, less commonly, unenclosed hut groups, as well as some hillforts, continued to be inhabited during the Roman period, though some sites were abandoned and others constructed, altered, or reoccupied according to social and economic need. Though still comparatively slight, there is also more evidence from this region than any other that a proportion of these settlements which were occupied in the later Roman period persisted into the fifth and sixth centuries or were reused at a later date.[94] In other cases evidence for such continuity may be lacking, but a continuing sense of place was undoubtedly significant. In the rare instances where more extensive archaeological landscapes associated with fertile soils have been investigated, as, for example, the Graeanog Ridge, it has been shown that, though direct continuity of late prehistoric and Roman farmsteads into the early Middle Ages remains unproven, there is other evidence of early medieval farming and ironworking that indicates continuing exploitation of the land and occupation in the immediate vicinity that persisted into the later Middle Ages.[95] Equally, a hut group with a scatter

---

[91] Boon 1986a, 434–5; Guest and Wells 2007, 355 no. 1110; Casey 1989; Stumpe 2014, 62–4.

[92] Burnham and Davies 2010, 219; Guest and Wells 2007, 292–3, nos 899–900; Nash-Williams 1969, 59; Casey 1989, 323.

[93] For discussion of the pottery demonstrating that the *vicus* was supplying rural sites, see Longley et al. 1998, 210–13.

[94] For the most recent study, see Waddington 2013; on chronology, see 88–116, fig. 4.1.

[95] Ibid., 34–5, 223–30; Fasham et al. 1998; Kenney 2001; Young 2015a; Kelly 1982.

of Roman pottery, coins, including a clipped *siliqua* of 388–402, and other artefacts has been found close to the elite early medieval settlement at Llanbedrgoch, as well as a few earlier features on the site itself.[96]

No villas have been securely identified,[97] and in the later Roman period enclosed hut groups, often of drystone construction, are the most characteristic type of settlement. Some of these also indicate Roman architectural influence, with the introduction of polygonal enclosures and rectangular structures alongside round-houses. Others show the continuation of native forms without Roman influence. Curvilinear and sometimes earlier eroded embanked enclosures with timber and clay-walled roundhouses which were increasingly replaced with stone, also persisted into the fourth century alongside unenclosed settlements, which by this time were less common.[98] Artefactual assemblages include Roman pottery and other items demonstrating considerable economic contact, but these are often also the only form of dating evidence, making the establishment of complete site chronologies all the more difficult. Nevertheless, on a small number of sites there are signs of likely occupation into the fifth century (Chapter 5).

Firstly, this is suggested by the identification, as at Caernarfon, of shell-tempered ware on some rural sites, such as Din Lligwy, Anglesey, which, though excavated in the early twentieth century, remains an important site demonstrating considerable prosperity which may have been linked to the exploitation of copper at nearby Parys Mountain. The main, Roman-period, stone-built settlement (Fig. 3.4, a) consists of a pentagonal enclosure with two roundhouses, but also several rectangular buildings, with evidence for both farming and metalworking. The coin sequence spans the later third and first half of the fourth centuries and, in addition to shell-tempered vessels, some Black-burnished 1 kitchenware had been mended with iron clamps, signifying lack of supply and a potentially long life cycle. Fragments of Roman tile, including ridge and box tiles, had also been brought onto the site, thereby indicating recycling, but when exactly this was taking place is unknown.[99] Shell-tempered ware has likewise been identified on Anglesey at Caer Leb, a square embanked enclosure with both a roundhouse and rectangular structures.[100]

---

[96] Redknap 1996; 1999, 56–7; 2001, 133; 2004b, 156–7; Waddington 2013, 151–2; Guest and Wells 2007, 357–8.

[97] The only possible example at Tremadog, which included a bathhouse, was associated with agriculture and possibly iron extraction. Alternatively, it could have been a *mansio* associated with the crossing of Traeth Mawr. Activity probably continued during the first half of the fourth century; Parry and Kenney 2013.

[98] Waddington 2013, 40–51, 106–7.

[99] Baynes 1908; 1930; Waddington 2013, 149–51; Guest and Wells 2007, 353–4 nos 1102–4; Davies, J. L. 2012a, 380, 383–4. Clamping vessels is quite common in north-west Wales and occurs at higher levels than generally; Longley et al. 1998, 215–16; Cuttler et al. 2012, 195.

[100] RCAHMW 1937, 103–4; Williams, W. W., and Prichard 1866; Caer Leb also has a Type D penannular brooch.

90 LIFE IN EARLY MEDIEVAL WALES

Continuity may be suggested more securely by the discovery of diagnostic early medieval artefacts on some earlier sites as at Cefn Cwmwd, Anglesey, where excavations uncovered a complex sequence of activity (Fig. 3.4, e). During the Iron Age and Roman periods the unenclosed settlement, which was located beside a track, included several phases of timber, then clay-walled roundhouses made up of curvilinear gullies, clay floors, drains, hearths, pits, and post-holes. Later Roman pottery (but no shell-tempered ware) was associated with roundhouses 5 and 6, where a small, disturbed coin hoard (*c.*273–85) was found, and there is an unusually high number of vessels with rivets. Parts of the settlement were subsequently overlain by rubble spreads containing residual Iron Age briquetage and Roman ceramics as well as three, probably sixth-century, artefacts: a Type G1 penannular brooch, a sherd of imported pottery from south-west Gaul, and a Byzantine intaglio. This suggests the accumulation of structured abandonment deposits after the dwellings went out of use and early medieval high-status occupation in the immediate vicinity.[101]

Late prehistoric, mostly stone-walled, hillforts and promontory forts are likewise a characteristic element in the landscape. As elsewhere, most probably ceased occupation in the Late Iron Age, but the discovery of Roman ceramics on a growing number of sites demonstrates renewed activity, with sometimes more intensive occupation demonstrated by third- and fourth-century artefacts indicating a resurgence of interest in sites which had a prehistoric past.[102] Continuity from the later Roman period through the fifth and sixth centuries is clearly evident at Dinas Emrys, a rocky outcrop in the Nant Gwynant valley, an important route through Snowdonia. Although the excavations have proved difficult to interpret and it is unclear whether the hillfort originated during the Iron Age, there is activity in the early Roman period. This continues with ceramics, including sherds of late fourth-century shell-tempered pots, and glass vessel fragments, indicating significant later Roman occupation. Sherds of post-Roman imported amphora and a disc cut from a sherd of south-west Gaulish pottery point to continuing high-status activity (Chapter 5).[103]

In some other instances, although no early medieval evidence has been found, the presence of Roman artefacts may suggest occupation beyond the fourth century. Din Sylwy, for example, is a very prominent, naturally defended, flat hilltop in south-east Anglesey near the eastern approach to the Menai Strait with commanding sea views along the north Wales coast. The place name suggests it was the 'Fort of the Silwy tribe'. The site has never been excavated but, in addition to Iron Age artefacts, there is a large assemblage of later Roman finds, including fourth-century coins—the latest is Valentinianic (364–78)—and a shell-tempered jar. Equally, box-flue tiles from

[101] Cuttler et al. 2012, 30–65, 154–60, 195–9; Davies, J. L. 2012a, 382–3; Waddington 2013, 160–2.
[102] Ibid., 106, 108; Smith, G. H. 2005, 38–9; 2006, 34.
[103] Savory 1960; Edwards and Lane 1988, 54–7.

the inland promontory fort at Parciau, Anglesey, suggest the recycling of Roman materials.[104]

On the mainland, Tre'r Ceiri provides a particularly interesting example of extensive Roman occupation that could have continued into the early Middle Ages. This large and complex hillfort with associated animal pens is located on the eastern peak of Yr Eifl, which rises to 485 metres, thereby dominating approaches to the Llŷn peninsula. Such a position suggests seasonal use for ceremonies and gatherings rather than year-round settlement, as well as a continuing need to assert authority over the surrounding landscape. There are around 150 stone structures in the interior, many of which were excavated in the early twentieth century. Roundhouses were superseded by D-shaped structures and later, sub-rectangular cellular buildings indicative of Roman influence. Although the D-shaped structures were frequently associated with Roman pottery, this was comparatively rare in the roundhouses and sub-rectangular buildings suggesting that the latter date to a later, largely aceramic phase which might extend into the early medieval period.[105]

Therefore, in the north-west, although there was an important military base at Caernarfon which remained in occupation to the end of the fourth century and possibly later, an official Roman presence was otherwise focused on north-west Anglesey. The emphasis would have been on maintaining a visible centre of Roman authority as well as keeping coastal supply routes, notably that to the legionary fort at Chester, free from Irish attack. The settlement evidence indicates that for the rural population there was considerable continuity in ways of living and social organization, the origins of which may be seen in Late Prehistory. In the later Roman period, apart from the limited adoption of rectangular structures adapted to local building styles and varying access to Roman goods, the impact of Romanization appears to have been very limited. Although well-dated chronologies are lacking, increasing evidence also hints at the continuation of some sites into the fifth and sixth centuries. Contact with the Roman market economy, seen principally in the presence of later Roman ceramics on rural sites, at least in the fertile areas of Anglesey and Arfon, argues for their continuing supply of the Roman military, though there is also some evidence of curation and recycling, suggesting attempts to maintain elements of the convenience of a more Romanized lifestyle once this role had come to an end and supplies had ceased.

The North-East

For those who lived between the Conwy and the Dee, the territory of the Deceangli, and in the upper reaches of the Severn, probably on the eastern edge of that of the

---

[104] Lynch 1991, 258–62, 273–6; Davies, J. L. 2012a, 379; Guest and Wells 2007, 351–2, nos 1096–8.

[105] Waddington 2013, 110, 220–3; a fragmentary, single-sided, composite bone or antler comb with ring-and-dot ornament has also been recorded from a rectangular building (23) on the site and may be of Viking Age date; see Baring-Gould and Burnard 1904, 10, fig. 7; Hughes 1907, 55.

92 LIFE IN EARLY MEDIEVAL WALES

Ordovices, experience of Roman authority, culture, and the market economy almost entirely emanated from two foci beyond the region: the legionary fortress at Chester (*Deva*) and Wroxeter (*Viroconium*), the *civitas* capital of the Cornovii. Chester is located on the east bank of the Dee, where it may be assumed there were mooring facilities for vessels sailing along the north Welsh coast; the road to Caernarfon also served as an important link. During the second half of the third century Chester, like Caerleon, had suffered a period of neglect and the legion, the XX Valeria Victrix, is last specifically mentioned on the coinage of the usurper Carausius (286–93). Nevertheless, as at Caernarfon, there is evidence of major renovation during the fourth century, with occupation continuing at least into the 390s. There has been considerable debate concerning the date of the extensive rebuilding of the northern defences incorporating over 100 gravestones of legionaries and their families as *spolia*, the latest of which are early third-century. Although LeQuesne argued that this was associated with the *burh* established by Æthelflæd of Mercia in 907, Mason and Clay have made a very good case for it taking place during the earlier fourth century (though this does not rule out further rebuilding in the tenth).[106] City walls incorporating *spolia*, including tombstones, are found widely across the empire from the mid-third century onwards as, for example, in London,[107] and at Chester the rebuilding of the walls also fits with other repairs and alterations made within the fortress throughout the fourth century. Several barrack blocks also remained in use. Modifications were made to the headquarters and its adjacent probable storage building, as well as to the main baths, and there were also late alterations to the enigmatic elliptical building and its baths, the latter dated by Valentinianic coins (364–78). Gold-working crucibles, possibly used for melting down coins, have also been found nearby. The latest coins from the fortress are Theodosian (388–402), but very little is known about its subsequent history.[108]

The only evidence of a later fourth-century military presence within the region is at Forden Gaer (*Levobrinta*?), an auxiliary fort on the east bank of the Severn sited near the strategic ford of Rhydwhyman, the crossing of which allowed access westwards by road and probably marked the bounds of Ordovician territory. The fort and its later history are poorly understood, as what little excavation there has been, focused on the defences, took place in the 1920s. Nevertheless, it may be suggested that, after a long period of abandonment, activity recommenced in the earlier fourth century with Valentinianic coins (364–78) possibly signalling more intensive occupation, but these are the latest known from the site. Its reoccupation at this time suggests the presence of a garrison to secure the river crossing, but nothing is known about the nature of contacts with the surrounding population.[109]

---

[106] LeQuesne 1999, 114–21, 138–48; Mason 2001, 199–204; Clay 2004.   [107] Barker et al. 2018.

[108] Mason 2001, 196–9, 210–11; Clay 2004, 12; Burnham and Davies 2010, 98; Casey 1989, 326.

[109] Rivet and Smith 1979, 391; Burnham and Davies 2010, 243–5; Davies, J. L. 2012b, 54; Guest and Wells 2007, 272, no. 834.

Wroxeter has become an iconic site in debates concerning the fate of Roman towns in Britain. It was argued, following extensive excavations at the baths-basilica, that there was some continuity of urban life, together with signs of a post-Roman authority, well into the sixth century. This included a range of Roman-style buildings constructed on rubble platforms in the final phase (Z).[110] However, aspects of the original interpretation, notably the existence of a large timber building originally thought to be that of a post-Roman ruler or bishop, and the long chronology have now been called into question, making it more difficult to unravel the true significance of what was found. Moreover, the almost total lack of post-Roman artefacts, particularly Mediterranean and Gaulish imported pottery and glass, which began to arrive in Britain in the later fifth century and might therefore be expected to have reached Wroxeter, makes continuation of major high-status occupation into the sixth century much less likely. The few radiocarbon and archaeomagnetic dates have proved of little use in establishing an absolute chronology.[111] Instead, the excavators argued that the inhabitants continued to pursue a Roman lifestyle as late as Phase Z by conserving and reusing late Roman artefacts such as glass and ceramics, including a substantial amount of shell-tempered ware, and some Black-burnished vessels mended with rivets. There were also later Roman crossbow and penannular brooches that may have continued in use into the fifth century, but no early medieval examples of the latter have been found. Coins ceased to arrive on the site in the 390s and a possible late coin of Theodosius III (*c*.430–5) found in the mid-nineteenth century is no longer extant.[112] Overall, assuming one accepts what limited evidence there is for Roman-style timber buildings constructed on rubble platforms which were then dismantled leaving few traces, it is very difficult to ascertain how long this occupation continued, and a more truncated chronology seems preferable. That some elite activity continued in the vicinity is, however, supported by an inscription, probably on a fragmentary reused Roman tombstone, found within the defences but close to the eastern cemetery. This commemorates *Cvnorix macvs Ma(q)viColine* ('Cunorix son of MaqqosColine'), presumably a man of some standing to be remembered in this way. The use of both *macvs* instead of the Latin *fili* and the patronymic indicate an Irish connection, and the inscription is linguistically more likely to date to the first half of the sixth century than earlier.[113]

Though linked by road, Wroxeter lay on the Shropshire plain more than 40 kilometres east of Forden Gaer, and its cultural and economic reach into the upper Severn valley appear slight. For those living between the Dee and the Conwy contacts with the Roman administration in Chester, as well as economic activity in the adjacent

---

[110] Barker et al. 1997.

[111] Lane 2014. A new campaign of radiocarbon dating with Bayesian analysis by Roger White and Alex Bayliss is underway to enable reassessment of the chronology.

[112] Barker et al. 1997, 192–220; Casey 1974b.   [113] Redknap and Lewis 2007, no. S2, 538–9.

canabae, would have been much more significant. Though settlements of a more Romanized type are found in the vicinities of both Chester and Wroxeter, it has recently been argued that their hinterlands developed quite differently.[114] Military-related sites west of the Dee include two industrial strip settlements: Heronbridge, which continued well into the second half of the fourth century, whilst the latest pottery from Pentre Ffwrndan, which was associated with lead processing, is somewhat earlier.[115] Nevertheless, villas have proved very difficult to find apart from the recent discovery near Rossett of a winged-corridor building with evidence of occupation into the early fourth century. Plas Coch may be a further example.[116]

In contrast, several villas are known in the vicinity of Wroxeter, notably Whitley Grange, which may have been a hunting lodge. Excavation revealed parts of a court-yard villa, including a room with a later fourth-century mosaic and an earlier bath-house, the hypocaust of which was last fired between 420 and 520. The villa was then demolished. Significantly, however, settlement continued; at least three ephemeral buildings were constructed on rubble platforms and one of the villa rooms was extensively reused. As at Wroxeter, finds included riveted Black-burnished ware but no identifiable early medieval artefacts, and it has been suggested that this phase is probably fifth-century.[117]

Our understanding of later prehistoric and Roman-period, indigenous farming settlements in north-east Wales and the borders is very variable indeed. West of the Dee numbers known are still comparatively small, but in the upper reaches of the Severn aerial photography has revealed a well-populated landscape of rectilinear and some curvilinear enclosed farmsteads, some with multiple ditches, preserved as earth-works on hillslopes and crop-marks in the river valley. Similar enclosed settlements are also characteristic of the Cheshire and Shropshire plain and as far south as Radnorshire and Herefordshire, where fewer are known. To date the focus has been on their distribution and morphology, and remarkably little excavation has taken place to cast light on their full complexity, not least their dating and chronology. Nevertheless, considerable continuity in settlement forms is suggested in the upper Severn area and there are some indications of continuing activity or reoccupation into the early Middle Ages.[118] For example, excavation of the multi-ditched curvilinear enclosure at Collfryn (Fig. 3.4, b) revealed occupation beginning in the Iron Age, with roundhouses and four-post storage structures. After some remodelling of the enclosure in the late Iron Age, occupation continued, consisting mainly of four-post structures and a later rectangular ditched enclosure in the interior. Small amounts of first- to fourth-century

---

[114] Smith, A. et al. 2016, 300–6.

[115] Burnham and Davies 2010, 182–3; Smith, A. et al. 2016, 287–8; Jones, N. W. 2020.

[116] Anon. 2021; Jones, N. W. 2011, 106–8.

[117] Gaffney and White 2007, 95–142; White 2007, fig. 51.

[118] Arnold and Davies 2000, 70–3; Wigley 2007; Silvester 2011; Ray 2015, 124–7, 172–6; Smith, A. et al. 2016, 291–2, 371–3; Britnell and Silvester 2018.

Roman pottery signal intermittent, low-level contact with the Roman market economy. The latest identifiable building, a rectangular post-hole structure with a small corn-dryer, was late Roman, but possible post-Roman activity has also been mooted based on the discovery of at least one glass bead.[119] Nearby at Arddleen, a similar enclosed farmstead with a small assemblage of Roman pottery, including riveted coarseware and a single later third-century coin, has indisputable evidence of post-Roman occupation or reoccupation (Chapter 5),[120] as has the high-status, D-shaped enclosed settlement of New Pieces, situated beneath the Breiddin hillfort. Here there was a rich array of Roman artefacts, including pottery spanning the late second or early third and fourth centuries, but also sherds of eastern Mediterranean red slipware and south-west Gaulish imported pottery and glass, pointing to occupation during the later fifth to seventh centuries. The Breiddin itself was probably utilized for agricultural activity in the later Roman period and finds include later fourth-century shell-tempered jars.[121]

Several other later prehistoric hillforts, which are often very prominent sites in the landscape across the region, demonstrate renewed activity in the later Roman period.[122] Dinorben, which once commanded the coastal flatlands west of the Clwyd, is the most significant of these, as it was extensively excavated prior to destruction by quarrying, though interpretation of the results, some as yet unpublished, remains a challenge.[123] The interior was intensively occupied, with evidence of building platforms with both roundhouses and four-post structures. Some activity continued during the first and second centuries AD, but a significant rise in the amount of Roman pottery from a variety of sources as well as coins from the later third century is suggestive of wealth and engagement with the Roman market economy. The latest are Valentinian (364–78) and the pottery also indicates occupation well into the second half of the fourth century, though no late forms of South Midlands shell-tempered ware have been found.[124] There is evidence of metalworking and other artefacts include high-status metalwork, notably a pine-cone shaped top for a wand or staff. Indeed, it is likely that Dinorben re-emerged as a local gathering place, perhaps with an additional religious function, and there are hints of its continuing significance into the post-Roman period. These include a rubble spread containing second- to fourth-century pottery overlying bank 1, animal bones from the upper fills of ditch 3 with radiocarbon dates

[119] Britnell 1989, 119–29, figs 22–4. For bead see fig. 31, no. 2; no. 3 may also be post-Roman, in litt. Margaret Guido to Bill Britnell, 10 Aug. 1991.

[120] Grant 2004.

[121] O'Neil 1937; Edwards and Lane 1988, 97–8; Musson 1991, 128, 192–4; Arnold and Huggett 1997; 2000; Campbell n.d.

[122] Arnold and Davies 2000, 88–9.

[123] Guilbert 2018. For the main excavations, see Gardner and Savory 1964; Savory 1971; Savory's interpretation of late Roman and possibly sub-Roman structures (1964, 66–74) is no longer regarded as tenable.

[124] Guest and Wells 2007, 295–7, nos 908–13; Webster 2011, 67–71.

96 LIFE IN EARLY MEDIEVAL WALES

together spanning the later third to mid-seventh century AD, possibly indicative of occupation outside the hillfort,[125] and a likely post-Roman glass bead and fragment of copper-alloy rim binding, as well as part of a strap-end with Anglo-Saxon Style 1 ornament.[126] The hillfort at Degannwy overlooking the Conwy also shows signs of continuity since it has both late Roman finds, including shell-tempered pottery and sherds of early medieval imported amphorae and glass.[127]

Thus, during the fourth century in the north-east and the borders of Wales the population's experience of Roman authority through a continuing military presence, taxation, and supply, as well as access to Roman goods and a developed market economy, was largely dependent on contacts outside the immediate region with the legionary fortress at Chester and the town of Wroxeter, though there were also a small number of other more Romanized sites in their immediate hinterlands. Although the evidence from the baths-basilica at Wroxeter remains key to understanding how long Roman lifestyles may have persisted beyond the Roman period both in this region and more widely, survival of urban functions as late as the sixth century is now highly questionable, and a shorter chronology is preferred here. Nevertheless, as in the north-west and south-west, enclosed farming settlements indicate considerable continuity both in site types and ways of living from Late Prehistory across the Roman centuries, but there are also indications of continuing occupation into the post-Roman period and some hillforts remained significant nodes in the landscape.

CROSSING THE DIVIDE

The preceding discussion has drawn attention to the few documented events relevant to the ending of Roman control in Britain and the fact that, though Irish attacks are specifically mentioned, nothing explicit is said about Wales. The continuing problems of archaeological dating have also been noted, particularly our reliance on Roman coins and pottery, and the consequent difficulties encountered in establishing chronological markers for crossing the divide between the fourth and fifth centuries. The archaeological evidence from a range of sites in different regions of Wales has indicated people's differing experiences of Roman control, their contacts with the Roman market economy and ways of living, and how these changed over the course of the fourth century and beyond. The aim here is to analyse the evidence thematically to determine what it can and cannot currently tell us about the ending of Roman

---

[125] Guilbert 1979a; 1979b; 1980. The radiocarbon dates are CAR-130: cal AD 420–660; CAR-203: cal AD 250–610; CAR-204: cal AD 390–620.

[126] Edwards and Lane 1988, 64–6; Seaman 2016, 39. The radiocarbon dates are CAR-130: cal AD 420–660; CAR-203: cal AD 250–610; CAR-204: cal AD 390–620.

[127] Edwards and Lane 1988, 50–3; Campbell 1991, 114–15.

authority and its consequences, economic and otherwise, in this western part of *Britannia Prima*.

Around the turn of the fourth century the late Roman army underwent substantial reorganization into static units of frontier troops, known as *limitanei* and *ripenses*, together with more prestigious, mobile, field-army units, known as *comitatenses*. However, developments in different parts of the empire doubtless responded in different ways to local conditions, and in Britain our knowledge of late army structures is largely derived from the *Notitia Dignitatum* and, as we have seen, this makes no direct mention of Wales. We know almost nothing about the late Roman fleet.[128] Archaeological evidence indicates, however, that during the fourth century the Roman military presence in Wales and the borders was limited to a small number of sites located largely on the north and south coasts and river estuaries, indicating a need to safeguard the seaways and provide defence against Irish attack. In contrast, much of the west coast had long been unprotected. Inland the continued occupation of Brecon Gaer and reoccupation of Forden Gaer suggest the need to police important routes and, as a result, may point to local unrest.

In the south, though considerably reduced, some activity continued at Caerleon throughout the fourth century and at least intermittently beyond this. However, the later third-century fort at Cardiff was probably the more significant installation, testifying to the need to protect communities in this wealthier and more Romanized region along the Severn estuary. Both the walls and bastions at Caerwent, together with large numbers of Theodosian bronze coins, which would have entered the system via the state and as an element of military pay, suggest some kind of garrison, at least until the beginning of the fifth century. However, there is no such evidence at Carmarthen, where no bastions have been identified, and there are few fourth-century coins. Therefore, in the south, if the coin evidence can be relied upon to any extent, with the exception of Caerwent, there appears to have been virtually no official military presence beyond the Valentinianic period (364–78). However, to what extent this might be linked to the aftermath of the 'Barbarian Conspiracy' or, indeed, to the usurpation of Magnus Maximus in 383 and his removal of troops to the Continent is unknown.

By contrast, in the north there is evidence of a resurgence of military activity demonstrated by fourth-century refurbishments at both Caernarfon and Chester. Furthermore, despite the lack of a firm date for the new fort at Caer Gybi, this would seem, together with the adjacent watchtowers, to fit most comfortably into a mid-fourth-century horizon, and could be as late as Count Theodosius's reported restoration of control in 367–8 following the 'Barbarian Conspiracy'. The discovery of some Theodosian coins at Caernarfon, the watchtower at Caer y Tŵr, Caerhun, and

[128] Southern and Dixon 1996, 23–38; Mattingly 2006, 238–41.

Chester suggests an official military presence, at least into the 390s. Nevertheless, the lack of coins of Honorius, which must have first reached Britain *c*.395, led Casey to argue that their cessation at this time might be connected with a disruption of supply caused by the usurpation of Eugenius on the Continent in 392–4.[129] However, it might equally be related to the more general demise of coins being struck after *c*.402 in Trier, Lyon, and Arles, which meant that they were no longer officially reaching Britain. At any rate, the cessation of coins does not necessarily argue for complete military withdrawal, as payment in bullion and other goods had become increasingly important.

It has also been argued that during the fourth century, since most units were static, the military became less clearly aligned with the structures of the Roman state and instead developed closer ties with their local communities.[130] It is possible that this ultimately resulted in the breakdown of command structures and fragmentation.[131] Indeed, one might envisage, with the demise of taxation and military pay, not only deserters but also the emergence of local militias who operated on the edges of or outside what was left of the Roman state, and ultimately the evolution of some of these into the retinues of post-Roman warlords and rulers—the 'tyrants' of Gildas. Archaeologically, evidence such as crossbow brooches, belt fittings (which certainly continued into the fifth century), bracelets, and ceramic jars associated with barrack blocks at Caerleon and rubbish deposits at Caernarfon indicates that in the second half of the fourth century and probably later soldiers were living alongside their families within the fort, and abandoned areas signal increasingly reduced numbers of troops. This scenario is comparable with communities on military sites on the northern frontier and more widely, suggesting important changes in military society at this time.[132]

Though evidence is slender, it is likewise important to consider the potential significance of Irish recruits within late Roman army units in Wales and the influence this may have had on subsequent Irish settlements, particularly in the south-west. The *Scotti* and the *Attacotti*, who are also thought to have been an Irish confederation, are first mentioned as raiders in the 360s, and the latter are also attested in units on the Continent in the *Notitia Dignitatum*.[133] That Irishmen were already serving in Britain is suggested by an inscription on a third-century building stone from a barrack block at Housesteads fort on Hadrian's Wall reading *Cvnaris*, a man with an Irish name, as well as the fact that a small number of Latin military loanwords passed into Old Irish.[134] The silver hoards found at Balline, Co. Limerick, and Ballinrees, Co. Derry,

---

[129] Casey and Davies 1993, 131–2.   [130] Gardner 2007, 19, 55–6.

[131] For discussion of the likely change from a frontier army to highly regionalized units on the northern frontier, see Collins 2012, 106–10.

[132] See above; Cool 2000; Collins 2010.

[133] Charles-Edwards 2000, 158–60; Rance 2001, 243–51.

[134] Sims-Williams 2002, 25; McManus 1983, 42–3, n. 50.

though considerably later, have traditionally been seen as booty from raids on Britain, and this certainly remains possible. The latter contains fragmentary plate, but also parts of three rare, gilded, military-style dress fittings, and a variety of ingots, some with official stamps. In addition, there are 1,701 *siliquae*, many of which are clipped, and the latest coin of Honorius dating to 419–23 provides a *terminus post quem* for the deposition of the hoard. Its make-up strengthens the argument for alternative interpretations as a donative or diplomatic gift, or simply payment made to an Irish mercenary commander and his men.[135]

In Wales itself there is intriguing evidence of a possible Irish military presence in the form of an incomplete lead coffin lined with plaster unearthed at Rhuddgaer in south-west Anglesey in the 1870s. The two long sides have reverse inscriptions, both originally reading *Camvloris hoi* ('Camuloris here'), with *hoi* being the equivalent of Primitive Old Irish *xoi*, found in some ogham inscriptions in Ireland. Most lead coffins of this type elsewhere in Britain are dated to the fourth century, though *xoi* is not found in Ireland before the fifth (Chapter 9). The discovery is significant because it is a Roman form of burial, but the inscriptions indicate Irish influence and the site is not far from the Romanized satellite settlement at Tai Cochion. The burial might therefore be linked to an Irish presence in the fort at Caernarfon around the end of the Roman period.[136]

The ogham- and roman-letter-inscribed stone from Castell Dwyran, Carmarthenshire, is also relevant here, since the Latin commemorates Voteporix the Protector. Although the monument has been dated to the late fifth or early sixth century, Voteporix was a man with an Irish name but who also had a Roman military title originally used by members of the imperial bodyguard. If the title is regarded as hereditary rather than purely an expression of continuing or adopted *romanitas*, it indicates that his forbear had been in the Roman military and might have belonged to a unit accompanying a Roman emperor, usurper, or possibly some other commander. The Cunorix inscription at Wroxeter might be interpreted in a similar way.[137] If we can accept that there were Irishmen in the late Roman military in Wales, their presence may have acted as one catalyst for the subsequent settlements. However, the notion that Irish federates were settled in south-west Wales, perhaps by Magnus Maximus, in return for military service and their recognition of Roman authority[138] must be set aside since there is no evidence to support it. Indeed, it is impossible to say exactly when these settlements took place because the ogham-inscribed stones in Wales, which are generally regarded as commencing sometime in the fifth century rather than earlier, provide the only

[135] Bateson 1973, 63–4. 73–4; 1976, 171–2; Edwards 1990, 4, illus. 2; Marzinzik 2013; Cahill Wilson 2014, 35–7, 43, figs 2.21, 2.26.

[136] Edwards 2016b, 183–5; Sims-Williams 2003, 27.

[137] Edwards 2007a, no. CM3; Redknap and Lewis 2007, no. S2.   [138] Rance 2001, 255–8.

100 LIFE IN EARLY MEDIEVAL WALES

contemporary evidence; the relevant written sources are much later, dating to the eighth, ninth, and tenth centuries.

The only towns in Wales, the *civitas* capitals of Caerwent and Carmarthen, were in the south, with the result that urban life had a very limited impact on the population as a whole. Both were small compared with most other Roman towns in Britain and had not been founded until the Hadrianic period. During the first half of the fourth century, however, Caerwent appears as a confident urban settlement with wealthy town houses indicative of a small, Romanized elite who presumably held positions of influence, and a range of public buildings, including a still functioning forum-basilica denoting continuing civic authority.[139] Indeed, the impressive town walls with their bastions added in the mid-fourth century combined defence with a display of civic pride. Nevertheless, this confidence appears short-lived. Subsequently, the townscape changed rapidly with the abandonment and sometimes systematic demolition of buildings, including parts of the basilica, suggesting shifting priorities and changes in civic authority. At the same time, there was an acceleration in the culture of make do and mend and recycling, both official and *ad hoc*, indicating a sharp decline in the operation of a market economy and supply chain as well as in the availability of raw materials, including metals.[140] However, a blacksmith's workshop, probably engaged in recycling, continued industrial activity into the earlier fifth century. Although large numbers of Theodosian bronze *nummi* from this house (which may have been destined for the melting pot) and elsewhere in the town indicate that low-level monetary transactions continued for a time, the lack of Theodosian silver *siliquae* suggests they were being melted down as bullion.[141] Increasingly limited access to transported, manufactured goods associated with a Romanized lifestyle was also matched by a shortage of skills that would have enabled their fabrication on a more limited local scale. Changes in civil authority—perhaps even its disintegration—imply that a declining ability to collect taxes and bring agricultural goods to market would have been further factors heralding the end of urban life, though some activity and occupation continued, at least intermittently, throughout the early Middle Ages, indicating continuity of place and its past significance, though its role had changed (Chapter 4). We know much less about Carmarthen, but the comparative lack of coins during the first half of the fourth century suggests the market economy was already struggling, and by this time any military presence was probably transitory. Though there are some signs of continuing civic maintenance after this, parts of the settlement were already

[139] In some other Romano-British towns, notably London and Wroxeter, the forum-basilica had already been largely demolished, but that at Exeter was still operational at this time; see Mattingly 2006, 336–7; Gerrard 2013, 132–3; Speed 2014, 110–13.

[140] For discussion of the rapid decline in availability of iron and other minerals, as well as evidence for iron-smelting, leading to the necessity of iron recycling, see Fleming 2012; 2021, 119–31.

[141] For a catalogue of coin finds in Caerwent indicating the large numbers of bronze *nummi* from the town, see Guest and Wells 2007, 24–43.

abandoned, implying that town life, which may always have been limited, was now a thing of the past.

Mineral extraction was undoubtedly important in Wales and the borders during the Roman period. This included iron in the Forest of Dean and southern Herefordshire, copper at Parys Mountain, Anglesey, and Llanymynech Hill, Montgomeryshire, lead and silver, concentrated in the north-east, and gold at Dolaucothi, Cardiganshire. Such activity was primarily under the control of the Roman military and peaked during the later first and second centuries.[142] However, we know much less about the later Roman period and to what extent the decline contributed to economic contraction more generally. Copper and gold extraction likely continued into the fourth century under the auspices of the forts at Caernarfon and Pumsaint respectively. West of the Dee lead and silver exploitation also continued at this time, probably under the control of Chester, and at Llangynfelyn, Cardiganshire, it had ceased by cal. AD 340–540. Iron extraction, however, probably continued much more widely in the late Roman period, driven by everyday need, since the properties of recycled iron make it less effective for making blades. This is suggested not only by a concentration of evidence in the Forest of Dean with its rich iron deposits but also by smelting debris at Dinorben hillfort, demonstrating the continuation of iron ore processing in a native setting.[143] Even so, recycling of metals, including iron, became increasingly common, and it has been suggested, for example, that the small town of Weston under Penyard (*Ariconium*), Herefordshire, which had long-standing evidence of ironworking, sharply declined after the mid-fourth century, perhaps as a result of the reorganization of supplies to the Roman military.[144]

Rural settlement in late Roman Britain and the pastoral and agricultural economy on which such communities depended show more signs of continuity. It has persistently been argued that rural sites in the more Romanized south-east of Wales were abandoned around the middle of the fourth century because of the cessation of ceramics and, more significantly, coins, the latest of which date to the Valentinianic period (364–78) or slightly earlier.[145] This broadly coincides with their demise on military sites and the decline of Caerwent. A similar equation has sometimes been made for other parts of Wales as well. Limited evidence in the south-east suggests that the conspicuous display of *romanitas* inherent in the small number of more luxurious villas likewise disintegrated around this time as access to Romanized building materials and specialized craft skills declined, and, notably at Cae'r Mead, Llantwit Major, demolition and recycling activities are also evident, as well as ironworking in the furnace room of the baths. However, it is very difficult to ascertain how long occupation may have continued at a

---

[142] Arnold and Davies 2000, 96–105.

[143] Casey and Davies 1993. 13–14; Burnham and Davies 2010, 279–80; Page et al. 2012, 330; Allen et al. 2017, 182–3; Gardner and Savory 1964, 108–9.

[144] Fleming 2021, 122–4.   [145] E.g. Webster 1984, 300; Brewer 2004, 237.

102 LIFE IN EARLY MEDIEVAL WALES

severely reduced economic level on some of these sites, as exemplified by the ephemeral post-Roman structures found at Whitley Grange near Wroxeter.

More generally, our increasing archaeological understanding of the full range of rural settlements in the more fertile lowlands of Wales and the borders indicates the duration of late prehistoric forms dominated by a range of dispersed enclosed farmsteads with regional variations which persisted throughout the Roman period and in some cases into the fifth and sixth centuries. Such settlements included wooden and clay-walled roundhouses, or stone-walled roundhouses in the north-west, as well as the continuation on some sites of four-post storage structures. We can also see the influence of Roman architectural forms in the advent of rectilinear buildings, both in timber and drystone construction. Nonetheless, it would be a mistake to see such settlement patterns as static, and it is clear that farmsteads on fertile soils were abandoned and others built according to the needs of families and their kin and the changing demands of the economy. Whilst in many cases the inhabitants had limited access to the products of a Roman market economy, most clearly visible in the form of ceramics, these largely ceased around the middle of the fourth century, though the supply of shell-tempered wares to some sites may have continued for some time after this. Efforts were also made to curate and recycle pottery, and in some cases—as, for example, at Thornwell Farm, Monmouthshire, and Cefn Cwmwd, Anglesey—deposits may have been systematically structured and sorted, suggesting continuing occupation once the pottery supply had ceased.[146] However, pottery and other Romanized goods are often only found in small quantities and could therefore be dispensed with since there was an underlying set of essential craft skills that persisted in such rural communities, mainly at a domestic level, throughout the Roman period and beyond. These included a variety of woodworking skills and the more specialized craft of blacksmithing, as well as the making of agricultural tools such as querns, and for women in particular the production of textiles, all of which were fundamental to daily living.

Occupation or reoccupation of late prehistoric hillforts in the late Roman period has also been noted on some sites in all regions of Wales, and in certain cases the presence of early medieval high-status artefacts, notably imported pottery, indicates continuing elite activity during the later fifth and sixth centuries. In some cases, especially in the south-east, many hillforts became the locations of small farmsteads during the Roman period. However, elsewhere some of the larger hillforts, such as Dinorben and Tre'r Ceiri, and possibly Caerau in the south-east, may have re-emerged or continued to function as ritual nodes and seasonal gathering places for the rural population and may have been places where stock and other goods were traded. This is indicative of the maintenance or reinvention of local tribal identities and a social hierarchy with its own leaders, whether or not they had taken on a more Romanized lifestyle, who with

---

[146] Hughes 1996, 89–97; Cuttler et al. 2012, 193.

their retinues may also have played a significant role in the advent of post-Roman kingdoms in Wales.

It is now generally accepted that from around the mid-fourth century onwards a decline in the ability to collect taxes and a rapidly contracting Romanized market economy would have resulted in more limited food production leading to a consequent drop in surpluses.[147] It may also be contended that subsequently the climatic downturn that peaked during the 'Late Antique Little Ice Age' evident in the northern hemisphere between *c.*536 and the 660s resulted in cooler temperatures and more precipitation, leading to a shorter growing season and reduced yields, thereby accelerating the process, especially in the more marginal areas of Wales (Chapter 2). Tudur Davies has demonstrated that, although radiocarbon dates have proved rather imprecise, the majority of available pollen diagrams (which are predominantly from the uplands) indicate declining production around the fifth and sixth centuries, though it should be stressed that this trend is not universal since some continuity in farming practices is also evident. Furthermore, both heath and woodland regeneration were taking place across Wales, though in the north there are some instances of deforestation. Wetland indicators were also by and large increasing whilst, apart from a couple of exceptions, arable and pastoral indicators either decreased or remained the same (Chapter 6).[148] In the south-east, part of the Caldicot Level was inundated cal. AD 380–560 but not the Wentlooge Level around Peterstone, which suggests that farming continued with an emphasis on grazing but at a reduced level.

Without radiocarbon dates the demise of Roman artefacts and often poor preservation because of acidic soils can make any subsequent occupation of sites virtually invisible, particularly those of low status, a problem which persists throughout the early medieval period. The fifth century remains particularly difficult to bridge because of this. At the beginning Roman artefacts, including some ceramics and diagnostic metalwork such as crossbow brooches, certain types of bracelet, and belt fittings, appear to have remained in use for some time. Other Roman artefacts and building materials continued to be scavenged, recycled, and curated. As the century progresses, penannular brooches evolve from Fowler Types D7 and E to the more robust Types F and G1, both of which first appear as clusters around the Lower Severn valley and emerge as elite badges of post-Roman native identity. Though not common in Britain, Type F, with its zoomorphic terminals occasionally ornamented with red enamel, was also adopted by the Irish and is of considerable interest since it may span the very late fourth and fifth centuries. Five examples are now known from Wales and these are found on both Roman sites, Caerwent and Caernarfon, and native ones, Porth Dafarch, Anglesey, and Minchin Hole cave, Gower, as well as a metal-detector find from Mathry, Pembrokeshire. In addition, a fragmentary lead die, doubtless destined

[147] Mattingly 2006, 530–1; Gerrard 2013, 96–101.   [148] Davies, T. L. 2015, 218–22; 2019, 174–84.

for recycling, came to light on the hillfort at Dinas Powys.[149] Type G1, a small penannular with faceted terminals with lozenge shapes, is more common and was probably current during the later fifth and sixth centuries since examples are found in Anglo-Saxon graves and only very rarely on Roman sites. There are a handful from Wales, including one from the Roman fort at Castell Collen abandoned in the late third century, an unstratified brooch from the post-Roman East Gate cemetery at Caerwent, and another in a female grave at Llangefni, Anglesey (where Roman finds have also been recorded). There are further examples from settlement sites at Cefn Cwmwd and the early medieval hillfort of Hen Gastell (Briton Ferry).[150] On the other hand, it is unclear exactly when the erection of inscribed memorial stones begins, though sometime during the first half of the fifth century seems likely,[151] and imported Mediterranean pottery spans the later fifth to mid-sixth centuries.[152] The unusually large finds assemblage from the hillfort at Dinas Powys includes not only imported pottery and glass but also recycled Samian ware spindle whorls and other sherds of Roman pottery, suggesting that useful material was still being scavenged from Roman sites, a situation paralleled on some other elite sites, such as Hen Gastell (Briton Ferry).[153]

What we are seeing, therefore, is firstly the fragmentation of Roman authority, military and civil, but also the probable continuation or re-emergence of native power structures and the settling of Irish emigrants, some of whom were probably originally attached to the Roman army. Others may simply have taken the opportunity afforded by this fragmentation to seize power. By the mid-sixth century, however, as Gildas's *De Excidio* makes clear, kingdoms had emerged ruled by 'tyrants' such as Maelgwn in Gwynedd and Vortipor in Dyfed. Secondly, the Roman market economy declined rapidly during the second half of the fourth century, leading to the end of a Romanized lifestyle, though communities continued to scavenge, curate, and recycle Roman artefacts, but a limited range of identifiable early medieval artefacts take some decades to evolve. Thirdly, though political fragmentation and the rapid economic downturn undoubtedly affected the rural population, a proportion of farmsteads and the rural economy associated with them persisted at a reduced level through the fifth century. However, such communities are also likely to have been further buffeted by climatic deterioration, particularly between the second quarter of the sixth and mid-seventh centuries. During this time the drop in average temperatures would have resulted in a shorter growing season and lower yields, which are likely to have impacted further on an already weak economy (Chapter 6).

[149] Fowler 1963, 101–7; Ó Floinn 2001; Youngs 2007; Redknap 2007a, 30, 70, nos 1–3; Wheeler 1923, 136–9, figs 58.6, 59; Savory 1956, pl. Vb; PAS no. NMGW-EBFCB6; Alcock 1963, 120–2. There is also one from near Hereford, and another from Wem probably used to secure a bag containing a fifth-century hacksilver hoard; see White 2020.

[150] Dickinson 1982; Redknap 2007a, 32–3, 70–1, nos 4–8; PAS no. NMGWPA 2006.187; Burnham and Davies 2010, 236. For the Llangefni brooch, see Parry and Parry 2016; Edwards forthcoming.

[151] Edwards 2007a, 113; 2013, 122–4.   [152] Campbell 2007a, 138–9.

[153] Alcock 1963, 148–9, nos 1–3; Campbell 1991, 429; Wilkinson 1995, 17.

FOUR

The Legacy of Rome, Irish Settlement, and Changing Identities

Identities in the post-Roman period were complex and overlapping.[1] In Wales the Roman legacy continued to be influential, playing a significant role in memory and reinvention of the past, whilst Irish settlement and integration also had a lasting impact. At the same time British (and thus later Welsh) identity, which drew on a native past stretching back into prehistory, was being reasserted, even though large swathes of what had been Roman Britain were gradually lost to Anglo-Saxon control. I shall first examine aspects of the continuing impact of Roman sites and material culture during the early Middle Ages in Wales and how the Roman legacy was reshaped to serve new ends. Secondly, the fifth- to mid-seventh-century inscribed memorial stones provide a rich seam of evidence, enabling an examination of changing identities, including the impact of Irish settlement and integration. Finally, I shall consider the value of other relevant evidence with reference to Irish settlement and its longer-term impact, including ornamental metalwork and place names, as well as the written sources.

THE ROMAN LEGACY AND ITS REINVENTION

The centuries of Roman control resulted in two lasting impacts on the lives of people in early medieval Wales: Christianity and Latin literacy. However, the Romans also had a major effect on the landscape through construction of the road system linking a network of forts and other installations, only a small number of which continued in military use until the end of the Roman period. In the south there was also the impact of the towns together with the villas and their estates. What use was made of these

---

[1] Much more research has been done on the interaction of indigenous and migrant identities in southern and eastern England than on changing identities in Wales. See, for example, Hills 2011; on Anglo-Saxon burial and identity, see Lucy 2000, 173–86. Some of my ideas here were first formulated in Edwards 2017b.

Life in Early Medieval Wales. Nancy Edwards, Oxford University Press. © Nancy Edwards 2023.
DOI: 10.1093/oso/9780198733218.003.0004

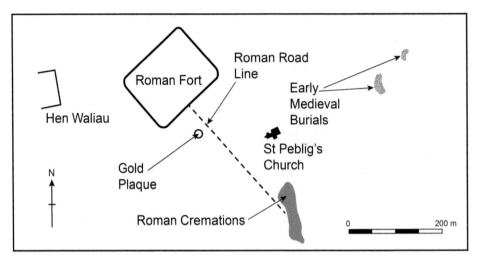

Fig. 4.1. The auxiliary fort at Caernarfon, showing its spatial relationship to the Roman road heading south-east, its associated cremation cemetery, a post-Roman inhumation cemetery, and the church of St Peblig (Publicius) (after Pollock 2006, map 13, with alterations and additions).

increasingly ruinous sites and structures, how were they perceived, and what new roles did they play? Equally, despite the loss of Roman technology, some Roman artefacts were recycled, whilst others continued to be valued without alteration. What was the significance of such objects? The following discussion will consider a small number of examples in order to explore these questions.

It would be wrong to think that all Roman forts were completely abandoned during the early medieval centuries. In the north-west it has already been suggested that some occupation may have lingered into the fifth century within the fort at Caernarfon and continued subsequently either there or nearby. However, although the exterior walls of the fort still survive to some height in places, any post-Roman levels within are no longer extant. Wheeler tentatively identified a rough wall in the *praetorium* and a clay-walled structure incorporating *spolia* within the south-east guardroom of the south-west gateway as early medieval, but there is no evidence to support this. Nor is there any dating for wattle-and-daub structures overlying the fort ditches.[2] Wheeler also noted a Type F penannular brooch (Fig. 3.5), but only two definite early medieval finds have been recorded. A *styca* of Eanred of Northumbria (810–41) was found close to the clay-walled structure in the south-west gateway but was not associated with it, and there is a penny of Cnut (1016–35) from the fill of the fourth-century ditch.[3] Nevertheless, the recent excavation of an inhumation cemetery with sixth- to seventh-century radiocarbon dates located 300 metres east of the fort strengthens the idea that some occupation continued in the vicinity (Fig. 4.1). To the west St Peblig's

---

[2] Wheeler 1923, 93–4, figs 19–20, 35; Edwards and Lane 1988, 115–16.
[3] Wheeler 1923, 94, 136–9, fig. 58.6; Casey 1974a, 71; Besly 2006, 716–17, nos 1, 23.

THE LEGACY OF ROME, IRISH SETTLEMENT, AND CHANGING IDENTITIES   107

Church, the dedication of which is derived from the Latin name Publicius, probably overlies the Roman cemetery, which might also suggest the revival of an early Christian cult.[4] By the early ninth century there was clearly also antiquarian interest in the site and legends associated with it. The author of the *Historia Brittonum* notes a tomb with an inscription thought to be that of the Roman emperor Constantine II, the son of Constantine the Great.[5]

In the south-east research and extensive excavations at the former legionary fortress of Caerleon indicate the extent to which the Roman layout and structures survived as well as evidence of at least intermittent occupation (Fig. 4.2). The modern street plan of Caerleon still reflects that of the fortress, particularly in the vicinity of the four gates, which may have remained standing for some time. Indeed, substantial parts of the fortress survived throughout the early Middle Ages, providing a powerful reminder of the Roman past. For example, the tetrapylon, a massive four-way triumphal arch, which stood as a landmark in the centre of the fortress at the junction of the *via prin-cipalis* and the *via praetoria*, and the *frigidarium* in the fortress bath complex were only demolished in the early thirteenth century.[6] Recently, the Roman warehouse excavation in Priory Field revealed several stretches of later drystone walling which included a building with three rooms, inside one of which was a stone-lined storage pit containing charred cereals which, on the basis of radiocarbon dates, are thought to date to *c.* AD 400–600, thereby suggesting continuing activity on the site.[7] Earlier excavations in the north-east quadrant overlying one of the barrack blocks also uncovered a small round-ended building of posts and unmortared walling set amongst the rubble, with another overlying the street nearby, both tentatively interpreted as early medieval. There was likewise some structural evidence in the rubble overlying Roman buildings outside the fortress in the eastern *canabae*. Isolated early medieval burials were also found in both these areas. That in the north-east quadrant, which was cut through the barrack-block wall, was radiocarbon-dated to between the mid-seventh and late ninth centuries, whilst that in the *canabae* seems somewhat earlier.[8] However, the only early medieval finds are a probable penannular brooch pin from the amphitheatre and a penny of Burgred of Mercia (852–74) discovered in a garden.[9]

The remains of the fortress and its environs also provided the setting for two significant Christian sites. Firstly, Gildas's *De Excidio* mentions the martyrdoms of Julius and Aaron at Caerleon. A Llandaf charter, the core of which is datable to the mid-ninth century, records the donation of the *territorium* associated with the *merthyr* of Julius and Aaron, suggesting either the continuation or revival of this

[4] Kenney and Parry 2012, 261–70, fig. 2; Edwards 2016b, 182–3.
[5] Morris 1980, ch. 25.   [6] Howells 2012, 12–14.
[7] Gardner and Guest 2011, 11–12, 20–2, 25, 27–8, 58, 64; Peter Guest (pers. comm.).
[8] Evans, D. R., and Metcalf 1992, 54–6, CAR-395, cal. AD 659–940; Evans, E. M. 2000, 170–3, 486; Howells 2012, 12.
[9] Redknap 1991, 32, NMW acc. no. 35.119; Besly 2006, 716, no. 6.

108 LIFE IN EARLY MEDIEVAL WALES

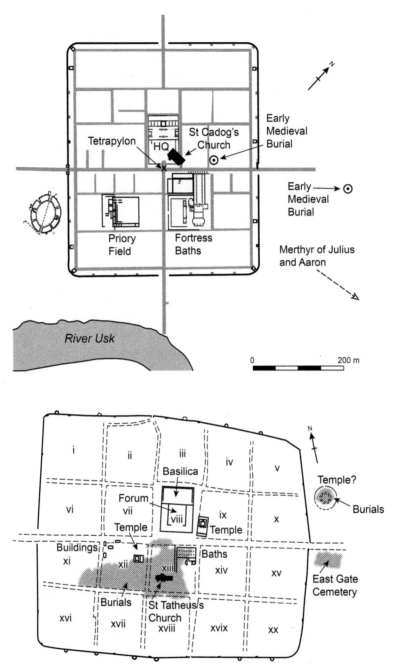

FIG. 4.2. The Roman legionary fortress of Caerleon and the Roman town of Caerwent (divided into *insulae*) (after Knight 1996, fig. 1), both also showing later sites and other features mentioned in the text.

Romano-Christian cult.[10] The site is thought to have been located on a hill east of Caerleon (Chapter 9).[11] Secondly, at some point the centre of the fortress partly overlying the *principia* was transformed by the foundation of St Cadog's Church, the earliest evidence of which is a fragmentary tenth- or early eleventh-century cross-slab found in the churchyard. Later a charter recording the donation of land to St Cadog at Caerleon is also included in Lifris's *Life* of the saint.[12]

The most substantial evidence for sustained early medieval activity associated with a major Roman site is from Caerwent, but though the town walls remain impressive, the loss of levels overlying much of the late Roman interior means that any early medieval structures are no longer likely to survive. Although it has been suggested that four subrectangular buildings with drystone footings excavated in 1909 overlying House XVIS in Insula XII might be early medieval, there is nothing to date them.[13] Nevertheless, two cemeteries provide the most compelling evidence. The first, following Roman custom, was located outside the East Gate. Well over a hundred graves have been excavated south of the road, including a few in stone cists, with a further smaller group of burials to the north overlying a possible late Roman temple. Radiocarbon dates from the former centre on the sixth and seventh centuries, but burial may have commenced in the late Roman period.[14] The second intramural cemetery, investigated intermittently since the mid-nineteenth century, covers an extensive area south of the main east–west street around the parish church. More recent observation of a pipe-trench along the street revealed several more graves on the edge of this cemetery, two of which provided radiocarbon dates centring on the seventh and eighth centuries.[15] In addition, V. E. Nash-Williams excavated nearby a small east–west apsidal building north of the baths, which he tentatively identified as a sub-Roman church, but again there is no dating evidence and nothing to prove that it functioned in this way.[16]

There is a small but significant number of early medieval artefacts from Caerwent. Early ornamental metalwork comprises two penannular brooches: a Type F1, and an unstratified Type G1 found in the East Gate cemetery. There are also a handful of pins, two spiral-headed, broadly datable to the mid-seventh to mid-ninth centuries, as well as a later knobbed Hiberno-Scandinavian ringed pin.[17] Nevertheless, there is no fifth- to seventh-century imported pottery or glass, and the discovery of four Byzantine

---

[10] Evans, J. G., and Rhys 1893, 225–6; Davies, W. 1979a, 121, no. 225; Winterbottom 1978, ch. 10.

[11] Seaman 2015, 201–9; 2018.

[12] Howell 2012, 13–14; Redknap and Lewis 2007, no. MN1; Wade-Evans 1944, 128–9, ch. 60.

[13] Ashby et al. 1911, 433–4, plan opp. 420; Knight 1996, 60–1, fig. 1.

[14] Campbell and MacDonald 1993; Pollock 2006, 67–8; Hudd 1913, 447–52.

[15] Campbell and MacDonald 1993, 90–1; Knight 1996, 56–8, fig. 1; Farley 1984, 229–30, HAR-5110 cal. AD 430–770; HAR-5152 cal. AD 610–890.

[16] Nash-Williams 1930, 235–6.

[17] Redknap 2007a, 70, nos 2, 6, pl. III; Knight 1996, 50–4, 56, fig. 7.

110 LIFE IN EARLY MEDIEVAL WALES

copper coins of sixth- and seventh-century date remains controversial because not everyone would accept they are ancient losses, though more recent discoveries of Byzantine coins elsewhere in Wales and England strengthen the view that they may be contemporary deposits (Chapter 7).[18] However, there is no such doubt about an early Anglo-Saxon penny (*sceat*) dated *c.*690–720, probably minted in Dorestad, from outside the walls, one of only four known from Wales, and there are also three late Anglo-Saxon pennies: one of Eadmund (939–46), one of Æthelræd II (978–1016), and one of Harthacnut (1040–2).[19]

What does all this amount to? Although evidence of fifth- to seventh-century activity is mainly confined to the large East Gate cemetery, its location is certainly indicative of continuity and suggests a population with continuing ties to the town, though to what extent they were still living in the ruins is impossible to say. By the early ninth century *Venta Silurum* ('The Market of the Silures'), the name of the *civitas* capital, had become Cair Guent. *Venta* was also retained in the name of the early medieval kingdom of Gwent, evidenced in the later seventh-century *Life* of St Samson of Dol, pointing to an element of political continuity.[20] Nor is it known how long the extramural cemetery continued in use, but the discovery of most likely seventh- or eighth-century burials, which were clearly part of a much larger cemetery in the vicinity of the church, indicates a change of focus. It would be reasonable to equate this with the foundation of an ecclesiastical site, presumably the monastery later associated with the Irish saint Tatheus where Asser stayed during his illness in *c.*885–6. In addition, according to a Llandaf charter, the core of which is datable to *c.*955, King Nowy met a bishop at Caerwent in order to settle a dispute.[21] There is also a tenth- or eleventh-century cross-head from the churchyard.[22] The pins may represent trade and the small number of coins also suggest commercial activity. Therefore, even though it had ceased to function as a town, the Roman ruins of Caerwent continued to provide an important backdrop for activity throughout the early Middle Ages, but from around the seventh or eighth centuries the former *civitas* capital was reinvented as a monastic *urbs* of some importance where assemblies and markets might also have been held.[23]

---

[18] These are *folles* of Justin I (518–27), mint: Constantinople; Justin II and Sophia (565–78), mint: Cyzicus; Heraclius (610–41), mint: Constantinople 629–30 overstruck on a *follis* of Nicomedia; Constans II (641–68) Syracuse; Abdy and Williams 2006, 34, 36–8, nos 79, 98, 104, 111. Boon 1958 was, however, adamant they were not contemporary depositions because of their lack of provenance and discovery history.

[19] PAS no. NMGW-9A4808; Dykes 1976, 28, nos 4, 7, 9; Besly 2006, 716–17, nos 11, 19, 24; that of Eadmund is an imitation.

[20] Rivet and Smith 1979, 262–5, 493; Morris 1980, *Historia Brittonum*, ch. 66a; Taylor 1991 and Flobert 1997, i, ch. 1.

[21] Keynes and Lapidge 1983, 27, 94, 261, n. 175; Evans, J. G., and Rhys 1893, 218–21; Davies, W. 1979a, 120, no. 218. For mentions of abbots and priests from Caerwent see Davies, W. 1978, 136. For the twelfth-century saint's life, see Wade-Evans 1944, 270–87; Knight 1970–1.

[22] Redknap and Lewis 2007, no. MN2.

[23] Caerwent is termed a *civitas* by Asser (Keynes and Lapidge 1983, 261 n. 175), and an *urbs* in the Llandaf charters (Davies, W. 1978, 61–2).

The post-Roman histories of the villas at Cae'r Mead (Llantwit Major) and Llandough in the Vale of Glamorgan likewise indicate a continuing interest in Romanized rural sites in this part of Wales. At the former around fifty burials have been excavated, mostly in the late nineteenth century, focused on Rooms 8 and 9 in the north range (Fig. 3.4, g). The graves, some of which included tiles reused to form cists, had been cut through the Roman floors and walls when the villa was in ruins. Radiocarbon dates from two burials suggest the cemetery was in use for some time between the late sixth and late tenth centuries. That the villa had purposely been reused for burial seems certain since it was clearly difficult to dig through the Roman levels, with the result that some skeletons were flexed rather than extended.[24] At Llandough, St Dochdwy's Church is located only 100 metres north of a villa (Fig. 10.1). A very large early medieval cemetery has been excavated north of the church, with a few further graves to the south in the vicinity of the villa. It was suggested that the villa had been abandoned during the earlier fourth century, but residual shell-tempered ware, as well as sherds of later fifth- to mid-sixth century imported amphorae found in the cemetery, hint at later activity nearby. It is, however, unclear whether the cemetery originated in the Roman period which would suggest continuity. The earliest radiocarbon-dated burial is sometime between the mid-fourth and earlier seventh centuries.[25] Perhaps the most likely scenario is the foundation of a monastery during the later fifth or earlier sixth century on the villa estate. However, the obit of 'Doccus, abbot of the Britons', noted as 473 in the *Annals of Ulster*, is not a contemporary record and no church is mentioned. Nonetheless, clergy associated with the foundation are named as witnesses in more than thirty Llandaf charters from around the mid-seventh century onwards.[26]

These examples, mostly from the south-east, all emphasize the links between the legacy of Rome and the rise of Christianity. Evidence of continuing occupation in the ruins of these Roman sites is limited and currently very poorly dated. Nevertheless, at Caernarfon and Caerwent we see the persistence of extra-mural burial and the possibility of the continuation or reinvention of Roman Christian cults at Caernarfon and Caerleon. Later we also see the establishment of new ecclesiastical sites within Caerleon and Caerwent. These were set in the midst of the Roman ruins, thereby highlighting Christian continuity with the Roman past in this part of Britain and the authority of those who had founded them. In Anglo-Saxon England the establishment of important ecclesiastical foundations by kings and churchmen in Roman towns is well evidenced from the late sixth century at Canterbury, but also, for example, during the seventh at Winchester, Lincoln, and York. Forts, such as Bradwell-on-Sea, Reculver,

---

[24] Nash-Williams 1953, 93, 102–3, fig. 1, pls V–VI; Hogg 1974, 240–2; Redknap and Lewis 2007, 575; Beta-2001 49: 1380±40BP, cal. AD 580–770; Beta-2001 50: 1140±40BP, cal. AD 770–990.

[25] Owen-John 1988, 143–7, fig. 58; Holbrook and Thomas 2005, 86–91; Beta-76,463: 1570±70BP, cal. AD 340–630.

[26] Knight 2005; CELT, *The Annals of Ulster*, U473.2; Davies, W. 1978, 124.

112 LIFE IN EARLY MEDIEVAL WALES

and probably Burgh Castle, were similarly reused.[27] However, it is well known that the transformation of earlier Roman urban landscapes into new Christian ones is a more widespread phenomenon found, not just in Rome, but across much of Western Europe at this time. It is possible therefore that these influences were also reaching south-east Wales directly from the Continent.[28] The foundation of a monastic site near the villa at Llandough and later reuse of that at Cae'r Mead (Llantwit Major) for burial similarly point to a Christian transformation of the Roman past. The reuse of villas in this way is quite rare in England but is found in adjacent parts of *Britannia Prima* stretching from the Cotswolds down to Exeter, with further examples of early Anglo-Saxon cemeteries further east, some with Roman tiles reused as grave covers. Nevertheless, the reuse of villas for burial is more common in Spain and Gaul, and this may likewise suggest Continental links.[29]

Attention has already been drawn to the importance of recycling in the later Roman period, a practice which continued during the early Middle Ages. It has also been argued that some artefacts were curated and may therefore have remained in use for a century or more, while other 'found objects' were again utilized in a new context or modified to fulfil a new purpose.[30] As Roberta Gilchrist has shown, some objects may have been valued because they were perceived to have symbolic or protective qualities, whilst others may have been treasured heirlooms passed down through generations.[31] Yet others were valued as materials which could be recycled and used in a different way. It is possible to identify the curation and recycling of Roman artefacts in both burial and settlement contexts in early medieval Wales.

Though grave goods are generally rare, Roman objects of personal adornment are occasionally found on the body or within the grave fill. An elderly woman buried in a corn-dryer at Biglis, Vale of Glamorgan, was wearing a gilded copper-alloy bracelet on each wrist, and sherds from two late third- or fourth-century vessels were included in the grave fill. The burial was radiocarbon-dated to cal. AD 400–650, suggesting the possibility that the bracelets were heirlooms.[32] At Caerwent, however, a young woman buried on the line of the east–west road on the edge of the intramural cemetery was thought to have been wearing a late Roman copper-alloy strip bracelet, and a counterfeit coin of Dalmatius Caesar (*c.*335–48) was found between her toes. The burial, which lay on a mortar layer beneath paving, was radiocarbon-dated to between the mid-sixth and later eighth century, so in this case the objects seem more likely to have been found than inherited. Two other fragmentary undated burials nearby had finger

[27] Blair 2005, 66–9, 188–9, 271–5.

[28] See Esmonde Cleary 2013, 170–80, on Iberia and Gaul; on Luxeuil in France, see Bully and Picard 2017; on Rome, see Pohl 2014, 216.

[29] Eckhardt and Williams 2003, 157, 163; Blair 2005, 189–90; Knight 2005, 94–9; Semple 2013, 132–3; Esmonde Cleary 2013, 181–8.

[30] Fleming 2012; Swift 2012.   [31] Gilchrist 2012, 216–18, 237–51.

[32] Parkhouse 1988, 16, fig. 21 nos 11–12, CAR-270.

THE LEGACY OF ROME, IRISH SETTLEMENT, AND CHANGING IDENTITIES   113

rings, which may also have been late Roman, and a late Iron Age or early Roman glass bead was found with them, but not directly associated.[33]

The cemetery at Llandough is of particular interest because a significant number of the 850 or so excavated graves had Roman artefacts. These were concentrated in the southernmost part of the cemetery, but interpretation has proved difficult because many of the graves were disturbed, truncated, or intercut. Much of this material, particularly the sherds of Roman pottery, was regarded as residual, but not necessarily all. In a few instances the individual was buried wearing a Roman bead at the neck, which may have functioned as an amulet, and in one case a turquoise melon bead is thought to date to the first or second century, indicating that it was of considerable age at the time of burial.[34] It was also suggested that a first-century Roman brooch, surely a 'found object', had been reused to secure a shroud. Several fourth-century coins, one of which might have been placed over the left eye or in the mouth, may also have been deliberately deposited as talismans. Small numbers of hobnails in the grave fill were surprisingly common; in one case they were found in the area of the feet and it was thought that a shoe might have been deliberately deposited with the backfill. This grave was radiocarbon-dated to probably between the later seventh and late tenth centuries, so, unless there was some unexplained revival of a token version of the Roman practice of placing hobnailed boots in the grave for the journey to the afterlife, they seem more likely to have been residual. There is, however, some evidence to suggest the practice may have continued into the post-Roman centuries, notably at the Roman roadside settlement of Shepton Mallet, Somerset, where a grave with hobnails found at the feet was radiocarbon-dated to between the mid-fifth and later seventh centuries AD.[35] Beyond the south-east there is very little evidence for Roman artefacts in early medieval graves. For example, a fragmentary first- or second-century Roman brooch found in Llanychlwydog churchyard, Pembrokeshire, may be associated with a grave, but not conclusively so, whilst Roman coins and abraded sherds of pottery, including Samian, found in the cemetery at Coed y Meirw, Llangefni, Anglesey, were regarded as residual.[36]

Roman artefacts were also scavenged and brought onto early medieval settlement sites. Pottery sherds were found at the hillforts of Dinas Powys and Hen Gastell (Briton Ferry), Glamorgan, as well as at lower-status sites such as Capel Maelog, Radnorshire. It is unclear whether whole pots were being collected, but the recycling of sherds is suggested since spindle-whorls made from Roman pottery were

[33] Farley 1984, 229, 247, fig. 17.2, HAR-5110, cal. AD 430–770; Nash-Williams 1930, 230.

[34] Holbrook and Thomas 2005, 29–3, 35, 67–8.

[35] Ibid., 29, 32–5, 67, fig. 35.1, 70–1, burials 796, 93, 87, Wk-6936, 1140±50BP, cal. AD 770–1012; Philpott 1991, 165–75; Leech and Evans 2001, 45.

[36] Murphy 1987, 80–1, 93, fig. 4, section 92; Llangefni: Iwan Parry (pers. comm.).

114 LIFE IN EARLY MEDIEVAL WALES

also discovered on these sites.[37] Such spindle-whorls were likewise recovered at the late ninth-century royal crannog at Llangorse, as well as two gaming pieces, one recycled from Roman pottery, the other a smooth black glass counter, which may or may not have been recognized as Roman but was valued for its aesthetic qualities nonetheless.[38]

Although evidence for the curation and recycling of Roman artefacts in early medieval Wales is scrappy, a couple of general points emerge. Despite the fact that only a few such artefacts can be demonstrated as conclusively worn on the body or deposited in the grave, a small number were clearly valued as heirlooms or *objets trouvés* which were probably perceived to have symbolic or amuletic powers. This may be compared with the much larger numbers of Roman artefacts and other curios found in early Anglo-Saxon furnished graves, some of which were functional but in many cases may be regarded as amulets that gave protection after death as well as in life and in the construction of social memory.[39] A few of the Roman artefacts found on settlement sites may also have functioned in this way. In contrast, the Roman pottery sherds indicate collection and recycling with a utilitarian purpose, and this is probably 'the tip of the iceberg'. Indeed, as Robin Fleming has argued, because of economic dislocation, a wide range of materials, such as metals and glass, were being systematically salvaged from Roman sites for recycling, perhaps repeatedly, over several centuries.[40]

INSCRIBED MEMORIAL STONES

The fifth- to mid-seventh-century memorial stones from Wales and the borders, inscribed in Latin or primitive Old Irish in the form of oghams, or both, are the most prolific material evidence we have for this period. An examination of their contexts and inscriptions, including the names, together with other evidence, allows us to glimpse not just the survival of elements of a Roman identity but also the growing significance of a British identity and the impact of Irish settlers, as well as something of how identities changed over time. The persistence of tribal signifiers and the emergence of new ones associated with kingdoms are also important. These monuments can likewise illuminate the spread of Christianity and the increasing power of the Church, which, as already indicated, were significant factors affecting the evolution of identities at this time (Chapter 9).

---

[37] Alcock 1963, 148–9; Campbell 1991, 429; Wilkinson 1995, 16–18; Britnell 1990, 33, 58–9; Swift 2012, 104–5.

[38] Lane and Redknap 2019, 205–6, 336–8. See also a fragmentary Roman glass gaming piece from Dinas Powys, Amgueddfa Cymru–National Museum Wales acc. no. NMW 62.203/G211.

[39] Eckhardt and Williams 2003. See also Meaney 1981, 222–31; White 1990.

[40] Fleming 2012; 2021, 71–117.

THE LEGACY OF ROME, IRISH SETTLEMENT, AND CHANGING IDENTITIES 115

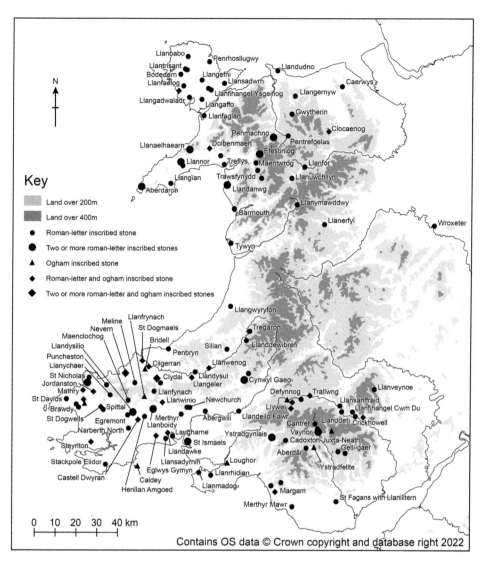

FIG. 4.3. The distribution of fifth- to seventh-century roman-letter- and ogham-inscribed stones.

The distribution of inscribed memorial stones (Fig. 4.3) in Wales indicates concentrations in the north-west and south-west, with further clusters strung out along the edges of the uplands in the south-east and an isolated example from Wroxeter. This broadly reflects the regions where there was Irish settlement, demonstrated most clearly by the distribution of ogham inscriptions and monuments commemorating individuals with Irish names, though these do not necessarily indicate that they were of Irish ethnicity. Since the monuments in Wales are part of a wider Irish Sea phenomenon, it may be proposed that they were being erected not only as grave-markers and expressions of identity but also as part of a wider struggle for land and authority which was taking place at this time. Indeed, in Ireland the function of ogham stones as

116 LIFE IN EARLY MEDIEVAL WALES

markers of landownership as well as burial is demonstrated in the early legal texts and it is likely that similar attitudes prevailed in Wales.[41] At Arfryn, Bodedern, Anglesey, for example, it has been argued that the monument commemorating Ercagnus, a man with an Irish name, may have been a 'founder's grave', and its hilltop location gave access to wide views across the surrounding countryside. The associated cemetery was sited within a Bronze Age curvilinear settlement enclosure which, by the time it was reused, resembled an early Irish *fert*, or prehistoric burial monument.[42] It has been demonstrated that in Ireland *ferta* were reused for burial, mainly in the fourth, fifth, and sixth centuries, to assert claims to land ownership by harnessing the power of the 'ancestors' and myths associated with them.[43] This is part of a much wider practice of reusing sites, such as early Bronze Age cairns and barrows, for early medieval burial found across Britain and Ireland at this time. In north Wales almost a quarter of the inscribed stones are either sited in association with prehistoric monuments or, like Llanfaelog 1, Anglesey, reused them more directly. This large prehistoric standing stone, which unusually remains *in situ*, was later incised with a Latin inscription commemorating Cunogusus, also an Irish name, preserved in that of the medieval township meaning 'the land of Conisiog'.[44] Such associations were equally important for those with British and Latin names. For example, at Llannor, Caernarfonshire, two monuments, one commemorating Vendesetl, the other Iovenalis son of Eternus, were discovered in the vicinity of two prominent prehistoric standing stones sited in a natural amphitheatre with impressive views of the mountains around.[45]

In considering the continuation of Roman identities, it is surely significant that there are fewer inscribed stones known from the eastern half of Wales and the borders, even though the fertile lowlands of the south-east were the most Romanized parts of Wales. Presumably, in these areas it was thought largely unnecessary to erect such monuments and express identities in this way, and inscriptions on stone are rare in later Roman Britain more generally.[46] However, Roman milestones—with more than a hundred now known from Britain including around twenty from Wales[47]—remained significant markers in the landscape and were clearly influential on the development of early medieval inscribed memorial stones. That from Port Talbot reused an early fourth-century milestone upended to receive the secondary inscription.[48] This link is further supported by the fact that this and a significant number of other stones, mainly located in the uplands of Breconshire and Glamorgan

---

[41] Charles-Edwards 1976; Swift 1997, 43–4.   [42] Edwards 2013, no. AN1; Hedges 2016, 155–61.

[43] O'Brien and Bhreathnach 2011.   [44] Edwards 2001, 18–23; 2013, no. AN12.

[45] Ibid., nos CN30–1.

[46] For a handful of likely late Roman Christian inscriptions from northern Britain, see Petts 2003, 150–5.

[47] Collingwood and Wright 1995, nos 2251–67; Tomlin et al. 2009, nos 3522–3.

[48] Collingwood and Wright 1995, no. 2254; Redknap and Lewis 2007, no. G92. For a further possible example from Aber, Caernarfonshire, see Edwards 2013, no. CN1.

THE LEGACY OF ROME, IRISH SETTLEMENT, AND CHANGING IDENTITIES 117

as well as Caernarfonshire and Merioneth, were originally prominently sited along Roman roads, thereby continuing the practice of roadside burial, a direct inheritance from the Roman past. There is a particularly interesting group to the north and south of the fort at Tomen-y-Mur, which is thought to have been abandoned *c*.130. They include a unique example dated to the fifth century from the fort itself which perpetuates the use of the common Roman commemorative formula *D(is) M(anibus)* ('to the shades of the dead') followed by British names. This and other examples indicate a continuing or renewed interest in Roman forts as strategic sites with a powerful presence in the landscape and suggests their erection at these locations and on roadsides was intended to reinforce claims to authority and the Roman past as well as to the surrounding land.[49]

More generally, a considerable number of inscribed memorial stones are associated with early medieval cemeteries, a proportion of which went on to become the sites of monasteries and later parish churches, demonstrating the increasing significance of Christianity and the growing authority of the Church. Indeed, approximately 36 per cent of the inscribed stones may be associated with later church sites in the south-east, almost 40 per cent in the north, but this rises to almost 70 per cent in the south-west.[50]

The usually terse inscriptions on these monuments demonstrate the use of two different alphabets—roman-letter and ogham—and three different languages—Latin, British, which was evolving into Old Welsh, and primitive Old Irish, which was inscribed in oghams. Of the 151 monuments known from Wales and the borders, 77.4 per cent have inscriptions in the roman-letter alphabet, 6 per cent use oghams, and 16.6 per cent have both ogham and roman-letter inscriptions. Except for a small number of reused Roman *spolia*,[51] the inscriptions are carved on natural pillars, slabs, and boulders of local stone, and their appearance is affected by the characteristics of the geology. The letters are punched or incised, usually with a hand-pick and/or chisel, though occasionally they are scratched with a knife.[52] Though no evidence has survived, they may then have been painted in the manner of Roman inscriptions to make the letters stand out.

The ogham alphabet was primarily used in Ireland but could equally have originated in later Roman Britain as a result of Irish immigrants coming into contact with

---

[49] Edwards 2001, 23–9. The inscription on Maentwrog 1 (now lost) read *D(is) M(anibus) Barrect[i] Caran[te]i*; Edwards 2013, 46–8, no. MR21. See also other monuments sited with reference to Roman forts and roads: nos MR 8–9, MR18–19, MR22–3, CN18; 2007a, no. CM3; Redknap and Lewis 2007, nos B21, B50, G7, G27, G76, G86. On MR19 one name incorporates *Bvr[g]*-meaning 'rampart' or 'watchtower', making a clear link with the fort where it was found.

[50] Edwards 2013, 45; 2007a, 33.   [51] Redknap and Lewis 2007, nos G76, G92, S2.

[52] For examples demonstrating carving techniques, see ibid. no. G77; Edwards 2007a, no. CD22; 2013, 59, nos CN35, MR8, MR12.

118 LIFE IN EARLY MEDIEVAL WALES

both Latin and literacy.[53] Ogham inscriptions, which are made up of horizontal and diagonal strokes representing the consonants and notches representing the vowels, were normally set out vertically on the angle of the stone, as on Bridell 1, Pembrokeshire (Fig. 4.4, b),[54] and are consequently often prone to damage, especially the vowel notches, which can make them difficult to decipher. They are read from bottom to top, though in the case of bilingual monuments the inscriptions are sometimes set out so as to indicate that they are translations of the roman-letter inscription, as on Eglwys Gymyn 1, Carmarthenshire, commemorating 'Avitoria daughter of Cunignus' (Fig. 4.4, c).[55]

Apart from many of the personal names, the roman-letter inscriptions are in Latin, and the gradual breakdown in grammar and case endings indicates that this was still evolving as a living language up until *c.*700 as well as continuing to influence British.[56] The majority of inscriptions are vertical, running in one or more lines from top to bottom of the stone, and it is thought that this was affected by the layout of oghams, though the shapes of many of these monuments would also have made the longer vertical lines more aesthetically pleasing and easier to read. Horizontal inscriptions, which follow Roman practice, are much rarer than vertical ones, a feature paralleled elsewhere in western Britain. In north Wales, however, horizontal inscriptions form nearly 20 per cent of the total, and those from Llangefni, Anglesey, and Llanfaglan, near the Roman fort at Caernarfon, are also framed in the manner of many Roman inscriptions, suggesting more direct influence.[57] Some were elegantly set out, but the layout of others can appear haphazard. Nevertheless, the letter forms were likewise an inheritance of Roman practice and it has been argued that they show characteristics of more workaday scripts. Indeed, some epitaphs may originally have been composed on wax tablets and then copied onto the stone.[58] The words are hardly ever separated, and the use of ligatures and conjoined letters, as seen, for example, on the stone from Aberdaron (Fig. 4.4, d),[59] is a distinctive feature also found on Romano-British inscriptions, as are some of the letter forms, notably R, as well as angular S, and reversed and turned letters such as D and I on the stone commemorating Cantiorix from Ffestiniog, Merioneth (Fig. 4.4, a).[60] But over the course of the fifth to mid-seventh

---

[53] McManus 1991, 1–41; Johnston 2013, 11–12; 2017. Though a second-century origin for oghams has been proposed (see Harvey 2017, 57–60), the earliest-known ogham inscription in Ireland dates to the first half of the fourth century (see Charles-Edwards 2013, 119, n. 10). There is also a likely fourth- or early fifth-century ogham stone from the Roman town of Silchester (Fulford et al. 2000).

[54] Edwards 2013, 56–7; 2007a 34–41, no. P5.

[55] Ibid., no. CM7, Latin: *Avitoria filia Cvnigni*, ogham: *Avittoriges inigena Cunigni.*

[56] Charles-Edwards 2013, 76–88, 96–112.   [57] Edwards 2013, 57–8, nos AN39, CN24.

[58] Charles-Edwards, G. 2002, 31, 39; 2006, 29–52; Redknap and Lewis 2007, 77–80.

[59] Edwards 2013, no. CN3, reads *Senacvs pr(e)sb(yter) hic iacit cvm mvltitvdinem fratrvm* ('Senacus the priest lies here with the multitude of the brethren').

[60] Ibid., no. MR8, reads *Cantiori hic iacit Venedotis cive fvit [c]onsobrino Ma[g]li magistrati* ('Cantiorix [*or* Of Cantiorius], here he lies. He was a citizen of Gwynedd, cousin of Maglus the magistrate').

THE LEGACY OF ROME, IRISH SETTLEMENT, AND CHANGING IDENTITIES 119

FIG. 4.4. Fifth- and sixth-century roman-letter and ogham inscriptions: a. Ffestiniog; b. Bridell, with a later cross; c. Eglwys Gymyn; d. Aberdaron, with a secondary inscription, PRESBITER ('priest'), an explanatory gloss on the P̄R̄S̄B abbreviation above (Crown copyright: Royal Commission on the Ancient and Historical Monuments of Wales).

120 LIFE IN EARLY MEDIEVAL WALES

centuries the letter forms also changed and increasingly inscriptions were composed of mixed alphabets with both capitals and lower-case letters, as seen on the inscribed stone commemorating King Catamanus of Gwynedd datable to *c.*625 (Fig. 1.1), by which time the process was almost complete.[61]

The most common epitaph on roman-letter-inscribed stones in the north-west consisted of the name of the person commemorated alongside the Christian, vulgar Latin formula *hic iacit* ('here lies'), which is sometimes elaborated in a variety of ways. However, this formula is much rarer in other parts of western Britain and the Isle of Man. It may therefore be suggested that the elite in this region were perpetuating elements of a Roman identity alongside an overtly Christian one. The formula originated in Rome in the earlier fourth century, spreading throughout the Western Empire, and probably reached western Britain from Gaul in the earlier fifth. It may have been introduced via contact with Trier, the second most important imperial city, or along the Atlantic seaways, either from Lyon and Vienne in the Rhône valley, or from the west coast around Bordeaux or the mouth of the Loire.[62] By contrast, the most important roman-letter formula in the south-west and Brycheiniog, where the vast majority of ogham and bilingual inscriptions are found, as well as in Devon and Cornwall, is the Latin *X fili Y*. This means 'of X son of Y' and it is usually thought that a word, such as 'stone', 'monument', or 'grave', of the person commemorated is understood. Although *X fili Y* is most common, other family relationships are sometimes given and, interestingly, women are more commonly commemorated in north Wales, where they form almost 20 per cent of the total.[63] The inscribed stone from Margam Mountain, Glamorgan, dated to the second half of the sixth century, commemorates Bodvocus son of Catotigirnus and great-grandson of Eternalis Vedomavus, thereby underlining the importance of inheritance and descent, the public display of which may have been particularly significant where rights to land might be contested (Fig. 4.5).[64]

The use of *X fili Y* is the equivalent of the most common formula found in ogham inscriptions in Ireland, *X maqi Y*, from which it was probably derived, and in southwest Wales this relationship may be exemplified by the bilingual monument from Nevern, Pembrokeshire, which commemorates *Maglicunas maqi Clutar...*('of Maglicu son of Clutar...') in oghams and in roman letters *Maglocvn* (or *Maglocvvi*) *fili Clvtori* ('Maglacu son of Clutorius'). However, during the course of the sixth century, as ogham inscriptions slowly died out, the *hic iacit* formula in roman-letter inscriptions is used increasingly alongside *X fili Y*, as, for example, on the Margam

---

[61] Tedeschi 2001; 2005, i, 43–81; Charles-Edwards, G. 2006, 78–100; Redknap and Lewis 2007, 77–87; Edwards 2007a, 43–7; 2013, 60–5, 121–6, no. AN26.

[62] Edwards 2013, 49, 122–3.   [63] Ibid., 54, n. 3; 2007a, 42; see also Edwards 2016c, 187–91.

[64] Redknap and Lewis 2007, no. G77, *Bodvoci hic iacit filivs Catotigirni pronepvs Eternali Vedomavi.*

THE LEGACY OF ROME, IRISH SETTLEMENT, AND CHANGING IDENTITIES

FIG. 4.5. Later sixth-century, Latin-inscribed stone from Margam Mountain, with the stem of a cross incised on the top of the stone (Wikimedia Creative Commons Attribution-Share Alike 3.0 Unported).

Mountain stone, which also has a cross on the top demonstrating the growing importance of also expressing a Christian identity.[65]

Where identifiable, names on the inscribed stones were Latin, British, or Irish, and sometimes Celtic rather than specifically British or Irish. Forms and spellings may show the influence of more than one language and especially that of Latin upon British. This reflects the fact that during the fifth and sixth centuries a proportion of the population of Wales would have been bilingual or even trilingual, though by about 600 the use of ogham and spoken Irish had died out, with Latin following as a normal spoken rather than written language about a century later. From around 600 British was also evolving into Welsh.[66] During the Roman period Latin as well as native names are recorded in a wide variety of texts in different media, but as Patrick Sims-Williams has noted, the latter often seem to refer to people of lower status. In contrast, the names on the inscribed stones indicate that, though Latin names continued, there was a resurgence in the use of Celtic names amongst the elite, and by

[65] Edwards 2007a, 41, no. P70; 2013, 123. [66] Charles-Edwards 2013, 75–115.

122 LIFE IN EARLY MEDIEVAL WALES

around the mid-sixth century these were increasingly the norm.[67] Therefore the names on the inscribed stones can with other evidence shed important light on changing identities.

As there are fewer inscribed stones in the south-east, many examples of the continuing use of Latin names come from parts of Wales where there had previously been less evidence of *romanitas*. They are frequently found alongside British names and a considerable number were eventually transferred into Welsh.[68] The horizontal Latin inscription from Llanerfyl, Montgomeryshire, provides an early example of an extended Christian epitaph with Latin names; unusually, the various words and phrases are separated by stops known as *punctus*. It reads *Hic [in] tvm[v]lo iacit · R[.]stece · filia · Paternini · an(n)i(s) XIII · in pa(ce)* ('Here in the tomb she lies, of R[.]stece, the daughter of Paterninus, 13 years (old), in peace'). The daughter's name is derived from the Latin *Rustica*.[69] Latin names are also found on a small number of bilingual, ogham, and roman-letter inscribed stones in the south-west, as, for example, Clydai 2, Pembrokeshire, which may be dated to the late fifth or first half of the sixth century and commemorates Etternus son of Victor, thereby demonstrating a more complex identity and the need to communicate with more than one linguistic audience.[70] In the north-west the continuation of Latin names is more common, with an interesting cluster of three monuments from the church at Llandanwg, Merioneth, indicating the perpetuation of exclusively Latin names into the second half of the sixth century. The inscriptions read *Ingenvi Barbi (h)ic iacit* ('of Ingenus Barbius, here he lies'), *Eqvestri nomine* ('of Equester by name'), and *Geronti hic iacit fili Spectati* ('of Gerontius, here he lies, son of Spectatus (*or* Spectatius)').[71] Latin names also seem to have been favoured in the commemoration of some whose Christian identity is also emphasized, as, for example, at Llanerfyl. Other examples include Llansadwrn, Anglesey, and Cynwyl Gaeo 2, Carmarthenshire. The latter reads *Servatvr fidaei patrieq(ve) semper amator hic Pavlinvs iacit cvltor pientisimvs aeqvi* ('Preserver of the faith and always lover of his homeland, here lies Paulinus the most devout supporter of righteousness'). This elaborate phraseology, which emphasizes a sense of place, may indicate the survival of a tradition of Latin panegyric poetry in post-Roman Britain, as it did in Gaul.[72]

The persistence of Roman identities is also indicated by the continuation of Roman titles and other terminology. The significance of *protictoris* ('protector') as a title that originally referred to a member of the imperial bodyguard on the roman-letter- and ogham-inscribed stone from Castell Dwyran, Carmarthenshire, has already been

---

[67] Sims-Williams 2002, 14–16.   [68] For lists of Latin names found on inscribed stones, see ibid., 17–18.

[69] Edwards 2013, no. MT4.   [70] Edwards 2007a, no. P14; see also nos P71, P138.

[71] Edwards 2013, nos MR10–12.

[72] Ibid., nos MT4, AN45; 2007a, no. CM5; Sims-Williams 1984, 170–1; Brown 2013, 503–4. See also Llantrisant 1, Edwards 2013, no. AN46, see Chapter 9 below.

THE LEGACY OF ROME, IRISH SETTLEMENT, AND CHANGING IDENTITIES **123**

noted (Chapter 3).[73] In addition, *civis*, meaning a citizen in the Roman secular sense, and *magistratus*, a Roman magistrate or office holder, are both found on Ffestiniog 1, Merioneth.[74] The likely continuation of occupations within families is also suggested by the inscription from Llangïan, commemorating Melus the doctor, who might have been the descendant of a military physician based at the fort of Caernarfon.[75] Likewise, Llannor 1, Caernarfonshire, which may date to as late as the early seventh century, commemorates Figulinus, son of Loculitus. The first name, which is Latin, refers to a potter and the British patronym means 'dusty' or 'earthy', which also seems apposite in this context. However, since there is no evidence for the continuation of ceramic production in post-Roman Wales, nor for pottery-making at Caernarfon, one must conclude that this reflects hereditary naming practices, and it is conceivable that the family had moved into the area.[76]

The use of British names on inscribed stones is also more common in the north. However, monuments with exclusively British names—as, for example, the Latin inscriptions from Gwytherin, Denbighshire, commemorating *Vinnemagli fili Senemagli* ('of Vinnemaglus son of Senemaglus') or *Velvor...filia Broho...* ('Velvor(ia?) daughter of Broho(maglus?)') from Llandysul, Cardiganshire—are relatively rare.[77] They are more often found alongside Latin names in the north and Irish names in the south-west, demonstrating mixed identities. Nevertheless, the small number of late Latin inscribed stones, all with unusual wording, show a high incidence of British names. Llangadwaladr commemorating King Catamanus (Welsh: Cadfan) may be dated to *c*.625, while the names on Llangaffo 12 nearby, which is broadly contemporary, are Gurgnin, Cuuris, and Cini. However, the late sixth- or early seventh-century stone from Llanboidy, Carmarthenshire, has a British name, Mavohenus, with a Latin patronym, Lunaris.[78]

Patrick Sims-Williams has demonstrated that Irish names are surprisingly common on the inscribed stones and are not confined to those with ogham or bilingual inscriptions.[79] This therefore indicates more generally the importance of expressing an Irish identity through commemoration in this way. In Pembrokeshire, for example, where the thirty-five monuments are concentrated in the northern and central parts of the county, there are four with ogham only and twelve with ogham and roman-letter inscriptions, but a larger number also have at least one Irish name. There is likewise a significant number of monuments west of the Tywi demonstrating an Irish connection, but there is only very limited evidence of this north of the Teifi. This overall area became the early medieval kingdom of Dyfed. Further east in Breconshire and Glamorgan, there is also significant evidence of an Irish connection since there are

---

[73] Edwards 2007a, no. CM3.   [74] Edwards 2013, 54–5, no. MR8; see below.

[75] Ibid. no. CN 25: *Meli medici fili Martini iacit.*   [76] Ibid., no. CN29.

[77] Ibid., no. D2; Edwards 2007a, no. CD14.

[78] Edwards 2013, nos AN26, AN38; 2007a, no. CM13.   [79] Sims-Williams 2002, 27–31, map 4.

124 LIFE IN EARLY MEDIEVAL WALES

four ogham-only monuments and five with ogham and roman-letter inscriptions, but again the large number of Irish names indicates the significance of an Irish identity focused on the area of the later kingdom of Brycheiniog. In the north there are only three, widely scattered, bilingual inscribed stones—Llanfaelog 2, Anglesey; Dolbenmaen 2, Caernarfonshire; and Clocaenog 1, Denbighshire—with a further Latin outlier from Wroxeter which reads *Cvnorix macvs Ma(q)viColine* ('Cunorix son of MaqqosColine'), a Latinized form of the ogham *X maqi Y* formula.[80] On Anglesey, however, there are also at least four monuments with Irish names, demonstrating that the Irish connection on the island was more widespread. In contrast, Irish names in the rest of north and central Wales are rare.

In essence, this distribution of ogham and bilingual inscribed stones, together with the concentrations of Irish names, provides by far the most significant evidence we have for Irish settlement in Wales. The significance of Irish raids and a likely Irish presence in the military in the later Roman period, which may have acted as a catalyst for subsequent settlement, has already been discussed (Chapter 3). Nevertheless, in the absence of other contemporary archaeological evidence, it remains very difficult to estimate the numbers of settlers since the stone monuments only represent the elite families who erected them. It is, however, possible in the south-west to trace both the gradual demise of ogham and, through an examination of the names, the gradual reduction in the significance of an Irish identity. For example, the ogham-only inscribed stone from Bridell just south of the Teifi (Fig. 4.4, b) commemorates *Nettasagri maqi mucoi Briaci* ('of Nettasagri son of the kindred of Briaci'). This is the only example in Wales of the *maqi mucoi* formula commonly found in Ireland, where *mucoi* refers to the ruling kindred. The first name is Irish, the second probably so, and the cross is a later addition. The only other monument in Britain to use this formula is from the Roman town of Silchester. The combination of an ogham-only inscription with *maqi mucoi* indicates that both are early in the series.[81] The introduction of stones with bilingual inscriptions, which may date to the later fifth and earlier sixth centuries, together with the names, signals the beginnings of the integration of Irish incomers into the native population, which led to the development of a mixed identity. For instance, the bilingual stone from St Dogmaels on the Teifi estuary uses the 'X son of Y' formula and commemorates *Sagrani fili Cvnotami* in Latin and *Sagragni maqi Cunatami* in ogham; interestingly, the father's name is British but his son's is Irish.[82] Equally, some bilingual inscriptions also show evidence for conversion to Christianity by combining the *X fili Y* and *hic iacit* formulae in the Latin, but the ogham inscription never includes the latter and may be confined to the name of the deceased. The monument from Llanwenog is a good example. It has a roman-letter inscription reading *Trenacatvs (h)ic iacit filivs Maglagni* ('Trenacatus, here he lies,

---

[80] Edwards 2013, nos AN12, CN18, D1; Redknap and Lewis 2007, no. S2.
[81] Edwards 2007a, no. P5; Fulford et al. 2000, 10–15. [82] Edwards 2007a, 113, no. P110.

THE LEGACY OF ROME, IRISH SETTLEMENT, AND CHANGING IDENTITIES   125

the son of Maglagnus'), but the ogham simply reads *Trenaccatlo*, though both names are Irish.[83] The final stage, broadly datable to the sixth century, may be represented by three inscribed stones which almost certainly commemorate two generations of the same family, all with Irish names. The two from the church site at Llandeilo, Pembrokeshire, commemorate brothers. The first is bilingual, the Latin reading *Andagelli iacit fili Caveti* ('of Andagellus, (here) he lies, son of Cavetus'), while the ogham includes a late form of the *X maqi Y* formula, *Andagelli macu Caveti* ('of Andagellus son of Cavetus'). However, the second has no ogham inscription and the Latin simply reads *Coimagni fili Caveti* ('of Coimagnus son of Cavetus'). The third monument from Maenclochog nearby likewise only has a Latin inscription which commemorates *Cvrcagni fili Andagelli* ('of Curcagnus, son of Andagellus').[84] In addition, the horizontal Latin inscription on St Nicholas 1, Pembrokeshire, dated to the sixth century, may provide evidence of intermarriage. It commemorates *Tvnccetace vxsor Daari hic iacit* ('of Tunccetaca, wife of Daarus, here she lies'). The wife's name is British but her husband's is almost certainly Irish.[85]

It is possible to detect similar processes at work in Brycheiniog. There is, for example, an interesting cluster of monuments in the upper Usk valley, including those from the parish of Llywel. The first of these is an ogham-only inscription with the personal name *Taricor[o]*. It is notable that this overlies and partially obliterates an unrelated horizontal Latin inscription of probable sub-Roman date. This could indicate the simple reuse of a monument, but it might also suggest a claim was being made to land formerly owned by someone else. The second is bilingual and commemorates *Maccvtreni Salicidvni* in Latin, *Maqitreni Saliciduni* in ogham. The first name is Irish and the second may be a British place name meaning 'Willow Fort', perhaps a settlement site associated with the deceased,[86] but, if so, we do not know where this was. The last monument is lost and the ogham reading unknown, but the Latin may read *Canntiani et pa(t)er illi[vs] M(a)ccvtreni hic iac[ivnt]* ('of Canntianus and his father Maccutreni, they lie here').[87] Canntianus is a British name indicative of integration but the father's is the same as that on the previous stone, possibly denoting the same man (though he cannot have been buried in more than one place), but more likely another member of the same elite family with Irish roots in this small area.

In contrast, on Anglesey, of the fourteen inscribed stones only one, Llanfaelog 2, commemorating *Mailisi* and *Ma[ili]su* in ogham, is bilingual. This, and three or four other monuments, have Irish names[88] and are all located in the north-western half of the island, thereby suggesting an area of likely Irish settlement. The rarity of ogham

---

[83] Ibid., no. CD26.   [84] Ibid., nos P21–2, P58.

[85] Ibid., no. P133; Sims-Williams 2002, 31.   [86] Redknap and Lewis 2007, nos B40, B42.

[87] Ibid., no. B41. The reading is dependent on a sketch by Edward Lhuyd. For further stones with a British commemorand and an Irish patronym, see Sims-Williams 2002, 30.

[88] Edwards 2013, nos AN1, AN9, AN12–13, AN58.

should not be seen as evidence to the contrary since ogham stones in Ireland are concentrated in the southern half of Munster with few from the eastern coastal areas closest to Anglesey.[89] Bodedern 1 and Llanfaelog 1 have already been mentioned, and the latter, together with Llanfaelog 2 and Penrhosllugwy 1, also have evidence of a Christian identity. The last, dated early to mid-sixth century, reads *Hic iacit Maccvdecceti* ('of Maccudecceti, here he lies') and, as Patrick Sims-Williams has demonstrated, this is an Irish name which refers to the protective divinity of the Decanti. This may therefore suggest a claim to territory associated with this native people and/or the taking on of a mixed identity. The name also survives as *arx Decantorum* in the *Historia Brittonum*, identifiable as the early medieval hillfort of Degannwy at the mouth of the Conwy.[90]

The *maqi mucoi* formula in the Bridell inscription followed by *Briaci* is thought to refer to a ruling kindred associated in fifth- and sixth-century Ireland with a people or small kingdom, known as a *túath*, and there has been a fierce debate concerning to what extent we are dealing with a tribal society in Ireland at this time.[91] The Irish who settled in Wales and south-west Britain were integrating and adapting to local circumstances and society in a period of flux, and a small number of inscribed stones can also shed important light on this process. That from Penbryn, Cardiganshire, stands on the remains of a cairn that once contained a Roman cremation burial, though this may in turn have reused an earlier Bronze Age monument. In its location, therefore, a clear link was being made with the past, and from here also there are wide views over the surrounding landscape and westwards across the Irish Sea. The Latin inscription reads *Corbalengi iacit Ordovs* ('of Corbalengus, (here) he lies, an Ordovician'). Corbalengus is an Irish name but the epitaph also proclaims his identity as a member of the Ordovices, the pre-Roman people whose territory was located some way to the north.[92] In an area of Wales where there was less Roman intervention this would seem to indicate the continuity of an older native regional identity, but it may also be argued that this was reinvigorated and actively promoted in the period of political fragmentation and kingdom formation that followed the ending of Roman control. On this monument such an identity is surely indicative of integration but might also have been attractive to Irish settlers and their descendants, who had been separated from similar societal systems in their homeland. The Penbryn inscription may also be compared with a bilingual stone from Buckland Monachorum, Devon. The ogham may give the father's name, *Enabarr*, which is Irish, but the roman-letter inscription commemorates his son, a blacksmith named *Dobunni*, the same as that of the Iron Age people, the Roman *civitas* capital of which was established at Cirencester (*Corinium Dobunnorum*).[93]

---

[89] Moore, F. 1998, 23–4, fig. 4.1.   [90] Edwards 2013, no. AN58; Morris 1980, 88–9, *s.a.* [812, 822].
[91] Charles-Edwards 1993, 143–65; 2000, 96–100; Bhreathnach 2014, 42–4.
[92] Edwards 2007a, no. CD28.   [93] Macalister 1945, no. 488; Sims-Williams 2002, 26.

The roman-letter- and ogham-inscribed stone from St Dogwells, Pembrokeshire, provides a further example. The Latin reads *Hogti[.]is fili Demeti* meaning 'of Hogtivis (*or* Hogtinis) son of Demetus (*or* Demetius)', though the ogham is confined to the name *Ogten[as]*. This is Irish but the patronym is derived from the pre-Roman people, the Demetae, and both the continuity and evolution of this regional identity may be assumed if Carmarthen was their *civitas* capital. *Demetia* is the old name for the early medieval kingdom of Dyfed, and this continued to be used in Latin texts.[94] Vortipor, the 'tyrant of the Demetae', who was berated by Gildas,[95] likewise had an Irish name, indicating the continuing significance of an Irish identity and quite possibly the authority of a family of Irish descent over the kingdom during the second quarter of the sixth century. However, he cannot be equated with the man commemorated with a Christian epitaph on a probably slightly earlier monument from Castell Dwyran, Carmarthenshire, which reads *Memoria Voteporigis protictoris* ('The memorial/tomb of Voteporix the Protector'), with simply the name *Votecorigas* ('Votecorix') in ogham, but it is possible that they were related.[96]

In the north inscribed stones are also important for understanding the processes of changing identities in relation to kingdom formation. The massive, bilingual, inscribed pillar from Clocaenog, Denbighshire, dated to the later fifth or early sixth century, formerly stood in a commanding location on high open moorland with wide views across the Clwydian hills to the east. The inscriptions commemorate Similin(i)us Tovisacos, a man with a Latin name, but Tovisacos is an earlier form of *tywysog* in Welsh and *taoiseach* in Irish, meaning a leader, though it is unclear in this context whether a title or name is intended. Whichever, the inscriptions proclaim the commemorand's complex identity and the need to communicate with different audiences as well as a claim to authority over the surrounding landscape.[97]

Secondly, three monuments from the vicinity of Llyn Tegid point towards the existence of a ruling family and possibly a small proto-kingdom in this area in the fifth and sixth centuries. Their locations and naming patterns indicate the significance of both Roman and British identities. The first, now lost, was found at the Roman fort of Caer Gai at the south-western end of the lake. The inscription probably read *(h)ic iacit Salvianvs Bvr[g]ocavi filivs Cvpitiani*, though whether this was commemorating one or two men is now unclear and *Bvr[g]ocavi* may be a territorial epithet referring to the fort. A second lost stone was found 12 kilometres to the south near the church at Llanymawddwy but was sited with reference to an important routeway running south from Caer Gai, up through the pass at Bwlch y Groes, and then down to the Dyfi estuary. This monument seems to have commemorated three women, one of whom was the daughter of Salvianus, in all probability the man remembered at Caer Gai. The last, from the north-east end of Llyn Tegid, was found at the church near the

---

[94] Edwards 2007a, no. P119. [95] Winterbottom 1978, ch. 31, *Demetarum tyranne Vortipori.*
[96] Edwards 2007a, no. CM3; Sims-Williams 1990b, 226. [97] Edwards 2013, no. D1.

128 LIFE IN EARLY MEDIEVAL WALES

Roman fort at Llanfor. The fragmentary inscription names '…Cavosenus Argius…' and incorporates the same name element, *Cavo-*, as in *Bvr[g]ocavi* at Caer Gai, suggesting a further link with the same elite family commemorated on the other two. The core of such a proto-kingdom might therefore be indicated by the area enclosed by the three monuments, around 3,300 hectares, which comprises a range of different landscapes.[98]

Thirdly, the monument from Beddau Gwŷr Ardudwy, Merioneth (Fig. 4.4, a), probably datable to the first half of the sixth century, is of great significance because it provides the earliest evidence for the existence of Gwynedd (*Venedos*), a very much larger kingdom that probably expanded to embrace a number of smaller entities and eventually came to dominate the whole of north Wales.[99] Gildas is also referring to it indirectly in his harangue of the tyrant Maglocunus, *insularis draco* ('dragon of the island [Anglesey]'), later identified as Maelgwn, King of Gwynedd, who died *c*.547.[100] The Latin inscription reads *Cantiori hic iacit Venedotis cive fvit [c]onsobrino Ma[g]li magistrati*, 'Cantiorix (*or* of Cantiorius), here he lies, he was a citizen of Gwynedd, cousin of Maglus the magistrate'.[101] Both personal names are indicative of a British identity,[102] but the terms *civis* ('citizen') and *magistratus* ('magistrate/office holder') also demonstrate a continuing (or renewed) sense of Roman identity, which has sometimes been used to imply that an ordered government survived in the north-west centred on Caernarfon which eventually evolved into the kingdom of Gwynedd.[103] However (as with *protictor* on Castell Dwyran 1), we do not know the precise meanings of these terms by the time the stone was erected: they may have been either hereditary or reinvented, but their use was drawing on a conscious link with the past. As with Penbryn, commemorating an Ordovician, it is important to note that the 'citizen of Gwynedd' was interred beyond the main orbit of the kingdom, which, as Gildas indicates, was at this time centred on Anglesey and probably the adjacent mainland.[104] In the absence of clear boundaries, the concept of a kingdom might also have been related to those who identified with it. The original location of the stone also reiterates the significance of British and Roman identities by drawing attention to links with the past. Beddau Gwŷr Ardudwy ('The Graves of the Men of Ardudwy') refers to prehistoric burial monuments destroyed during the nineteenth century, but

---

[98] Edwards 2012, 391–6; 2013, nos MR18–20.   [99] Davies, W. 1982a, 92, 98–9, 101–12.

[100] Winterbottom 1978, chs 34–6; Morris 1980, 45, 85.   [101] Edwards 2013, no. MR8.

[102] It is misleading to equate the second name with Maelgwn Gwynedd, as Gruffydd 1989–90, 9, attempted to do; see Edwards 2013, 388.

[103] Nash-Williams 1950, no. 103.

[104] See also Llanaelhaearn 2 commemorating *Aliortvs Elmetiaco hic iacet* ('Aliortus from Elmet lies here'). His Latin-derived British nickname means 'Stranger'. He very probably came from the British kingdom of Elmet centred on Leeds, Edwards 2013, no. CN20.

it was also situated close to the late Iron Age hillfort of Bryn-y-Castell as well as beside the Roman road running north from the fort at Tomen-y-Mur.[105]

The Latin-inscribed stone from Llangadwaladr, Anglesey, which has an incised cross, commemorates *Catamanus rex sapientisimus opinatisimus omnium regum* ('King Catamanus, the wisest, most illustrious of all kings'), the ruler of Gwynedd whose *floruit* was *c.*616–*c.*625 (Fig. 1.1). This monument indicates a later stage in the evolution of Gwynedd as a dominant Christian kingdom. The superlative adjectives relating to the character of Catamanus reflect the ideals of Old Testament kingship, demonstrating the growing influence of the Church, and the final phrase may denote the concept of overlordship. On the Continent inscriptions likewise include superlative character adjectives when recording the works of rulers, such as the Ostrogothic King Theodoric (d.526) or the Visigothic King Chindasuinth (d.653).[106] It is therefore possible that the epitaph was also a form of propaganda asserting the wider ambitions of the royal dynasty of Gwynedd at a time when his son Cadwallon (d.634) had newly inherited the throne. He is much better known than his father because of his alliance with Penda of Mercia, which led to the death, in 633, of Edwin of Northumbria, who had previously besieged Cadwallon on the island of Ynys Seiriol off Anglesey.[107]

OTHER EVIDENCE FOR IRISH SETTLEMENT AND ITS IMPACT

The inscribed memorial stones are the only definite contemporary evidence for Irish settlement in both Wales and south-west England. It is not possible to identify any fifth- or sixth-century ornamental metalwork or other artefacts found on this side of the Irish Sea as Irish, since the increasing contacts between Britain and Ireland towards the end of the Roman period, which included British speakers settling in eastern parts of Ireland, clearly influenced the material culture of the latter.[108] For example, Type F1 zoomorphic penannular brooches with red enamel originated in the lower Severn valley but were introduced into Ireland around the end of the Roman period, and subsequently distinctive forms developed there.[109] Therefore, although a scrap lead die for a Type F1 penannular brooch from Dinas Powys was originally identified as of Irish type, it might equally be British.[110]

Nor can we recognize sites associated with Irish settlement. This is because we still know comparatively little about settlements in Ireland in the early centuries AD, and

---

[105] Ibid., no. MR8.   [106] Ibid., no. AN26.

[107] Charles-Edwards 2004. Cadwallon figures in Bede's *Historia Ecclesiastica*, Colgrave and Mynors 1969, ii.20, iii.1; see also the Harleian Chronicle, Morris 1980 *s.a.* [629–31]. For an early Welsh praise poem, *Moliant Cadwallon*, see Gruffydd 1978, 27–34.

[108] Bateson 1973; 1976; Laing 1985; Johnston 2017, 32–6.

[109] Ó Floinn 2001, 7–8.   [110] Alcock 1963, 120–2; Redknap 2007a, 45–9.

the enclosed homesteads, including raths and cashels, which were beginning to emerge during the fifth century appear quite similar to those, also sometimes known as raths, which had been common from the later prehistoric period onwards in south-west Wales (Chapter 3).[111] Although in the past similar settlements in the north-west were frequently known as *cytiau('r) Gwyddelod* ('Irishmen's huts'), this is a misleading antiquarian term first noted in the late sixteenth century.[112]

Place-name elements have also played a significant role in attempting to estimate the extent of Irish settlement in Wales. Melville Richards used Ordnance Survey maps to locate Welsh place names with *cnwc* (*cnwch*), meaning 'hillock', which may be derived from the Irish *cnoc*, and demonstrated that these were mainly found in northern Pembrokeshire, stretching northwards up the Cardiganshire coast and along the Teifi and Tywi valleys, with a small group on Anglesey. He also examined *meidr* (*moydir*), meaning 'lane', which has a smaller distribution focused on north Pembrokeshire with concentrations around Fishguard Bay and St Davids.[113] While these distributions are broadly similar to that of the Irish-influenced inscribed stones, apart from north of the Teifi, recent research has urged considerable caution in accepting the place names as contemporary evidence. If *meidr* is an Irish loanword, then it probably does reflect Irish settlement at an early date, but *cnwc* is much later and may not necessarily be derived from Irish.[114] In the north-west only a very small number of place names have been suggested as Irish. These include the Llŷn (Lleyn) peninsula and Dinllaen, a multiphase promontory fort on its northern coast, the names of both of which are thought to be derived from the Laigin, the Leinstermen of south-east Ireland.[115]

In addition, strontium and oxygen isotope analysis of teeth and other skeletal material is beginning to have an important impact on our perceptions of mobility in the early Middle Ages, since this can identify individuals who had spent their early years elsewhere, though their precise origins are currently much more difficult to determine.[116] For example, a study that sampled four early medieval cemeteries in south Wales found four individuals with results that suggested they came either from the extreme west coast of Britain or the south-west coast of Ireland, but further refinement is not currently possible.[117]

Even though our understanding of the contemporary impact of Irish settlement is currently restricted to the evidence of the inscribed stones, the longer-term impact

---

[111] O'Sullivan et al. 2014, 64–6.   [112] Wmffre 2007, 46–8.

[113] Richards 1962; 1960, 147–61.

[114] Davies, W. 1982a, fig. 31; Thomas 1994, fig. 6.3; Wmffre 2007, 50–9.

[115] Charles-Edwards 2013, 176; Koch 2006, iii, 1079. The banks and ditches of the fort were recently sectioned, revealing more than one phase, but no samples were radiocarbon-dated; see Parry et al. 2012.

[116] See, for example, Speed and Walton Rogers 2004, 61–3; Richards and Montgomery 2012, 721–2; Symonds et al. 2014.

[117] Hemer et al. 2013, 2256; analysis has also been carried out on individuals of fourth- to sixth-century date in Ireland, a few of whom could have come from Britain; see Cahill Wilson et al. 2014.

THE LEGACY OF ROME, IRISH SETTLEMENT, AND CHANGING IDENTITIES   131

was considerable. As we have seen, Christianity and literacy were key legacies of the Roman experience in early medieval Wales, but this is equally true in Ireland. As well as literacy, the rite of extended inhumation was introduced into Ireland from Roman Britain around the early fourth century, though these developments cannot initially be equated with Christian belief.[118] The Romano-British Patrician contribution to the conversion of the Irish is well known, but what we need to emphasize here is that Christian contacts between Ireland and western Britain, including Wales, remained important long after the integration of Irish settlers. Archaeologically, this is evident, for example, in the distribution, from around 600 onwards, on either side of the Irish Sea of simple cross-carved stones, which mainly functioned as grave-markers, and later in the development of the cult of relics (Chapters 8 and 11). Such links would also have provided a context for wider contacts, including small-scale trade and exchange.

Apart from the dramatic references of Gildas to Irish attacks,[119] it is only from the eighth century onwards that we have any written evidence for Irish settlement in Wales. The sources—largely origin tales and genealogies—are of dubious historicity and were subject to manipulation and change over time, but they do give some indication of where those who came may have come from. The *Expulsion of the Déisi*, which has been dated to the eighth century, provides the earliest mention of Irish settlement in Dyfed. This origin tale is primarily concerned with how the Déisi came to live in what is now Co. Waterford and south Co. Tipperary. However, it also describes how one branch headed by 'Eochaid, son of Artchorp, went over the sea with his descendants into the territory of Demed [Dyfed], and there his sons and grandsons died', and this is followed by a genealogy which claims that they had founded the ruling dynasty of Dyfed.[120] Some names in the genealogy are the same as those in the Dyfed genealogy dating to the third quarter of the tenth century in Harleian MS 3859. These include Guortepir, generally identified as Vortipor, 'tyrant of the Demetae', in Gildas, but in the latter Helen, the mother of the emperor Constantine, heads the genealogy, thereby emphasizing Christian Roman continuity rather than Irish intervention.[121] Secondly, the *Historia Brittonum*, written in Gwynedd in 829/30, mentions the 'sons of Liathan' who held Dyfed, Gower, and Kidwelly. These were the Uí Liatháin, neighbours of the Déisi, in east Co. Cork. It goes on to claim that Cunedda and his sons, who came from Manaw Gododdin (the region around Edinburgh) and founded the royal dynasty of Gwynedd, expelled the Irish from Britain, a tale repeated amongst the genealogies in Harleian MS 3859.[122] This story is now usually regarded as a later invention, possibly a product of political

[118] O'Brien 2009, 138.   [119] Winterbottom 1978, chs 14, 19.
[120] Meyer 1900, 112–13, ch. 11; Ó Cathasaigh 1984.
[121] Bartrum 1966, 9–10, no. 2; Guy 2020, 334, no. 2.
[122] Morris 1980, chs 14, 62; Bartrum 1966, 13, no. 32; Guy 2020, 337, no. 32.

132 LIFE IN EARLY MEDIEVAL WALES

circumstances in Gwynedd in the early ninth century.[123] However, it also reflects the very limited evidence of the Irish-influenced inscribed stones in Gwynedd, which are largely concentrated in north-west Anglesey.

Later still, in the kingdom of Brycheiniog, there is an important revival of interest in the Irish past, triggered, perhaps, in part by the survival of ogham-inscribed stones in the landscape, as well as a rich oral tradition. The most important evidence for this is the royal crannog in Llangorse Lake constructed in the late ninth century (Chapter 5). Since this site is currently unique in Wales, it may be argued that it was modelled on an Irish crannog. Such settlements, which are sometimes identifiable as royal sites, are common in the northern half of Ireland between the later sixth and eleventh centuries.[124] Such emulation would have drawn direct attention to the perceived Irish origins of the rulers of Brycheiniog at this time. A distant folk memory of these is also preserved in an origin tale known as *De Situ Brecheiniauc*, probably datable to the late eleventh or early twelfth century. This tells how the king's daughter went to Ireland to marry and returned with her son, the eponymously named Brachan, some of whose progeny are associated with the saints and churches of Brycheiniog.[125]

In the foregoing discussion it has been suggested that Irish settlement in Wales may have stemmed from Irish recruits in the late Roman army as well as being the end result of raiding which sought to take advantage of both the wealth of Roman Britain and the ensuing fragmentation of power at the beginning of the fifth century. The evidence of the inscribed stones and later written sources supports the notion that settlement emanating from Munster in the region of modern Co. Waterford and east Co. Cork was focused on Dyfed and may have been sufficiently influential to achieve political dominance. However, those in Gwynedd, where settlement may have been largely confined to north-west Anglesey, probably came from Leinster, but their influence was considerably less. A further group established themselves in Brycheiniog. The evidence of the inscribed stones indicates integration by around the end of the sixth century, but the impact of Irish settlement lasted much longer and is evident in continuing Christian contacts across the Irish Sea.

CONCLUSION

This chapter has focused on aspects of the archaeological evidence for the legacy of Rome and how this was primarily reinvented in Christian terms. It has also considered how the early inscribed stones can cast light on changing identities during the fifth to earlier seventh centuries. This indicated the survival of elements of a Roman identity sometimes clearly linked to a Christian one, the significance of Irish settlement and

---

[123] Dumville 1977, 181–2; 1986, 23; Charles-Edwards 2013, 190, 328, 359–62.
[124] O'Sullivan et al. 2014, 68–9.   [125] Wade-Evans 1906; Bartrum 1966, 14–16; Guy 2020, 130–6.

integration, and, alongside kingdom formation, the growing importance of a British identity, which drew on both an ancient and a Roman past while acknowledging the increasing power of the Church. In addition, the inscribed stones provide the only contemporary evidence of Irish settlement around the end of the Roman period, though some later written sources can provide an insight into how this period was later perceived.

Indeed, by the early ninth century in Gwynedd, where the *Historia Brittonum* was written, a British (and therefore Welsh) identity was seen as all-important. Using both written and oral sources, the author traces the first inhabitants of Britain back to Brutus (*or* Britto), who is cast as having both classical descent from Aeneas and biblical descent from the sons of Noah, thereby looking back to the Roman past whilst also embracing a Christian one. He also emphasizes the ancient origins of the British, who were deemed to have arrived in Britain before either the Picts or the Irish, let alone the Romans and the Saxons. In this context, both memory and reinvention were clearly important, and this might also go some way to explain the continuing interest in prehistoric monuments, particularly Bronze Age cairns and barrows, which were equated with the graves of ancestral heroes. However, the author also placed Britto alongside all the other peoples of early medieval Europe including the Burgundians, Franks, Goths, Lombards, and Vandals, thereby indicating the equal standing of the Britons with them.[126]

---

[126] Morris 1980, chs 7–18; Jones, T. 1967. For a recent detailed consideration, see Thomas 2022a, 89–120.

FIVE

Hearth and Home

Secular settlements were entirely rural and closely related to the land on which the day-to-day lives of the vast majority of the population depended. Investigation of such settlement sites is key to our understanding of how people lived in early medieval Wales but also raises some very fundamental questions. Where did people live, what types of settlement did they live in, and what did their houses look like? How did settlement types and settlement patterns change over time and what are the underlying reasons for this? How do the various settlement forms, ranging from the dwellings of the poorest to those of the elite, reflect what we know of early medieval society in Wales and the economy and changes in these over time? Such questions are not, however, easy to answer. This is because only a very small number of settlements in Wales and the borders can currently be identified as securely datable to the period *c*.400–1050. Even though the number is slowly increasing as a result of modern archaeological methods and radiocarbon dating, in many cases the evidence remains fragmentary and therefore difficult to interpret. Nevertheless, it will be argued some broader trends are apparent that may be set in a wider context and, where possible, compared with the development of settlements elsewhere in early medieval Britain and Ireland.

I shall first examine various problems associated with the identification of early medieval settlements in Wales and the reasons underlying them. I shall then analyse the evidence for various settlement forms and their chronological development, beginning with those of the elite followed by those of the lower-status farming population in different parts of Wales. Lastly, I shall consider the limited evidence for houses and the internal use of space as well as the wider use of space within settlements where sites have been more extensively investigated.

IN SEARCH OF SETTLEMENTS

Calculations of population are extremely difficult, but it has been estimated that that of Roman Britain in the first half of the fourth century could have been as high as 3.7 million, around 3.4 million of whom lived in the countryside, though some more

Life in Early Medieval Wales. Nancy Edwards, Oxford University Press. © Nancy Edwards 2023.
DOI: 10.1093/oso/9780198733218.003.0005

recent estimates have centred on somewhere between 2 million and 3 million.[1] It has been calculated using Domesday Book that in the later eleventh century the population of England was likely somewhat lower, between around 1.5 million and 2.2 million, though the Welsh borders had a much lower density than parts of eastern England, probably reflecting a similar difference over a much longer timescale.[2] Indeed, the population of Wales in the early Middle Ages has been regarded as 'exceptionally small' and may only have reached somewhere between 150,000 and 300,000 by the thirteenth century.[3] One reason for this view is the lack of identifiable early medieval settlements and associated material culture. Nonetheless, as we have seen, evidence for later prehistoric and Roman rural settlements in Wales is growing steadily and in some areas it is now possible to discern well-populated archaeological landscapes (Chapter 3). However, we face much greater difficulty in identifying early medieval sites. Indeed, to date only around thirty-five settlements can definitely be dated to the early medieval period, with a similar number less conclusively so (Fig. 5.1). It is therefore important to establish both how early medieval settlements have been identified and the reasons that lie behind this failure to locate further examples. This problem of identification is not, however, confined to Wales. It is almost equally acute in northern and western England, since the distribution pattern of Anglo-Saxon settlements is concentrated in the east and south.[4] In Scotland, although the ability to recognize early medieval settlements has improved significantly, these are much better represented in some regions than in others. By contrast, in Ireland the evidence is exceptionally rich.[5]

In Wales, early medieval settlements continue to be identified almost entirely by chance. One major reason for this is the lack of native ceramic production throughout the period. Had pottery been produced, this would undoubtedly have made site recognition easier, since sherds can survive, even in very acidic soils. The elite defended settlement at Dinas Powys, Glamorgan, was identified as broadly dating to between the later fifth and seventh centuries because of its unusually rich artefactual assemblage. This included both imported pottery and glass from the Mediterranean and south-west France, as well as a range of ornamental metalwork, together with other objects such as bone combs (Chapter 1).[6] In the case of non-elite sites, however, there are commonly few if any surviving artefacts. For example, the identifiable early medieval artefactual assemblage from the ironworking and crop-processing settlement

---

[1] Millett 1990, 183–5. More recent figures are summarized in Fleming 2021 11, n. 1.

[2] Darby 1977, 87–94; Rippon et al. 2015, 4–5, 323–4.

[3] Davies, W. 1982a, 41; 2004, 214–15.

[4] For discussion of this distribution, see Blair 2013, 5–13; 2018, 24–33. See also Hamerow 2012, 2–6; Philpott 2015.

[5] Foster 2004, 39–61; Driscoll 2011, 257–66; O'Sullivan et al. 2014, 47–138.

[6] Alcock 1963.

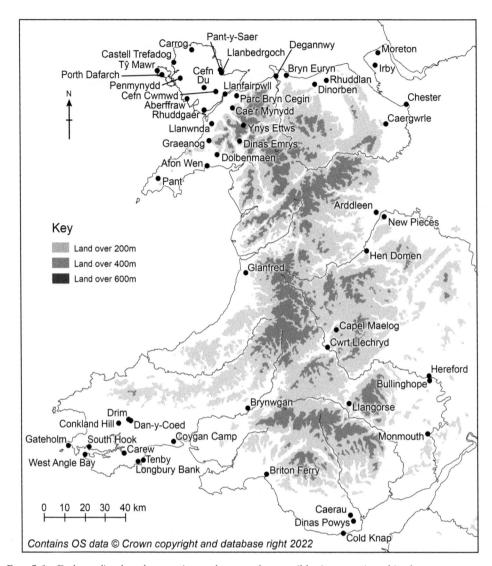

Fig. 5.1. Early medieval settlement sites and some other possible sites mentioned in the text.

at South Hook, Pembrokeshire, was confined to hones and a few rotary quernstones.[7] This lack of diagnostic artefacts, particularly native ceramics, means that, in contrast to eastern and southern England, field walking is unproductive and metal-detecting has only led to the discovery of one elite site at Llanbedrgoch, Anglesey, in the early 1990s. It is also notable that aerial photography has failed to recognize potential early medieval settlement sites which might then be followed up by geophysics and excavation, as has happened in England.[8]

[7] Crane and Murphy 2010b, 152–7.   [8] Redknap 1994, 58; Hamerow 2012, 3.

Only a handful of settlements, all of them elite, have been identified, directly or indirectly, because they are mentioned in the written sources. For example, the hillfort at Degannwy, Caernarfonshire, is noted in the early ninth century in the Harleian Chronicle, first when it was struck by lightning and subsequently when it was destroyed by the Saxons.[9] Later, in the Anglo-Saxon Chronicles, the raid instigated by Æthelflæd of Mercia on *Brecenanmere* in 916 has been equated with the site of Llangorse crannog, Breconshire,[10] while the establishment of a fortified base (*burh*) at *Cledemutha* in 921 by King Edward the Elder has been identified at Rhuddlan, Flintshire.[11] Equally, some sites noted in the written sources, such as Castle Hill, Tenby, Pembrokeshire, the subject of the probably ninth-century poem *Etmyg Dinbych* ('The Praise of Tenby'),[12] and Bryn Euryn, Denbighshire, which could be the site of Dineirth alluded to by Gildas in *De Excidio*,[13] have yet to yield any definite evidence of early medieval occupation. In the south, although the Lichfield and Llandaf charters note donations of landed estates to the Church, the farming settlements on these have proved extremely difficult to pinpoint, though the ecclesiastical sites are frequently still identifiable on the ground (Chapter 6).[14]

Over the past twenty-five years, however, recognition of sites has improved because of the application of scientific dating techniques, and this has now accelerated as a result of the introduction of AMS radiocarbon dating (Chapter 1). However, many sites investigated in developer-led excavations, such as Conkland Hill, Wiston, Pembrokeshire, were only recognized as early medieval when the radiocarbon dates were returned.[15] So far Llangorse crannog is the only early medieval site in Wales to have been dated by dendrochronology because of its unique and substantial waterlogged remains: oak planks from the palisades were felled between *c.*889 and 893.[16]

Since only a very small number of sites can be examined by excavation, morphology and typology continue to be important tools in assigning those with upstanding remains to particular periods of use. However, because early medieval settlements have proved so difficult to identify, these have rarely been applied, since characteristics that might aid recognition have so far remained very difficult to detect. Notably, Ken Dark suggested models that might be used to identify early medieval hillforts and included a list of sites that might be investigated, but this has failed to result in successful

---

[9] This is termed *arx Decantorum, s.a.* [812, 822], Morris 1980, 47–8, 88–9; Alcock 1967, 190.

[10] Whitelock 1979, *s.a.* 916. Lane and Redknap 2019, 3–4, 413–14.

[11] Wainwright 1950; Manley 1987; Quinnell and Blockley 1994, 208–13.

[12] Williams, I. 1980, 155–72; Gruffydd 2005; Charles-Edwards 2013, 659–65; Redknap 1991, 15. The only upstanding evidence is the later medieval castle (Soulsby 1983, 250), but two gold *solidi* of Justinian (527–65) and Tiberius III (698–705) minted in Constantinople have been found nearby (Bland and Loriot 2010, 329–30, no. 851).

[13] Longley and Laing 1997; Winterbottom 1978, 31, 101, ch. 32.1.

[14] Davies, W. 1978, 30–2, 121–4.   [15] Hart 2014, 8, 11–12, 53–4.

[16] Lane and Redknap 2019, 102–7.

Fig. 5.2. Glanfred, aerial photograph revealing the parch marks of the ditches of a pear-shaped promontory enclosure (Crown copyright: Royal Commission on the Ancient and Historical Monuments of Wales).

identification elsewhere.[17] It has also been proposed that small 'citadel' enclosures built within the larger, later prehistoric, stone hillforts in Caernarfonshire might be early medieval, but when the 'citadel' at Caer Lleion, Conwy, was reinvestigated radiocarbon dates suggested it was constructed during the fourth or third century BC.[18]

On the other hand, a wide range of hillforts, promontory forts, and enclosed farmsteads, as well as some open settlements, many of which have been recorded as a result of aerial photography, have been assigned a later prehistoric date, though sometimes Roman activity in the form of pottery and other artefacts is also noted. This is, however, misleading since it does not allow for the proposition that an unknown proportion of these sites continued in occupation, were reoccupied, or constructed in the early Middle Ages.[19] That some have been wrongly assigned may be exemplified by the site at Glanfred, Llandre, Cardiganshire (Fig. 5.2). This pear-shaped enclosure, sited on a natural promontory, was revealed by aerial photography and was regarded as typically Iron Age until trial excavation found food waste deposits in the lower part

---

[17] Dark, K. R. 1994b; excavations by Dark at Brawdy Castle, Pembrokeshire, Archwilio DAT prn 2820, a site with later prehistoric and Roman evidence where early medieval activity has also been claimed, remain unpublished; see Dark, K. R. 1990; 2000, 185. Radiocarbon dates are, however, Iron Age; Murphy 2016, 238, 278, 280.

[18] The site is also known as Caer Seion; Longley 1997, 48–51; Smith, G. H. 2012a, 72–7, figs 3–6.

[19] See, for example, Murphy and Mytum 2011; Silvester 2011.

of the inner ditch that were radiocarbon-dated to between the fifth and mid-sixth century AD, with further late seventh- to ninth-century AD ironworking activity in the interior.[20]

Equally, though the problems of building a chronological framework have been recognized, there is a misleading perception that subrectangular buildings represented by drystone footings or the platforms on which they once stood, either isolated or in small clusters, are probably later medieval or post-medieval in date.[21] This perception is underlined by the fact that the majority of such sites have been recorded in the Welsh uplands, where a significant number have been associated with transhumance. However, such sites do sometimes survive in the more fertile lowlands as well. Only a very small number have been excavated, including the iconic lowland farmstead at Graeanog, Caernarfonshire, dated to the twelfth and thirteenth centuries, and Ynys Ettws, Nant Peris, Caernarfonshire, which may have been constructed as early as the mid-eleventh century.[22] Nonetheless, it should now be acknowledged that some sites with subrectangular buildings (which have their origins as early as the Roman period), are definitely of early medieval date, since a number of sites have been recognized using radiocarbon dating. These may be exemplified by a cluster of subrectangular structures with drystone footings set amongst fields at Rhuddgaer, Anglesey. Unusually, these were recognized beneath blown sand as a result of geophysical survey, but only one structure was partially excavated. Radiocarbon dating suggests it was in use during the second half of the seventh or the eighth century AD.[23]

It is logical to expect that, as at Rhuddgaer, early medieval settlements would have been concentrated on good agricultural land with access to a range of other resources such as pasture, woodland, and water. However, this is also the land which is most likely to have been intensively cultivated, thereby destroying the archaeological evidence. This is particularly true in the case of unenclosed settlements and buildings constructed of more ephemeral materials such as wood, turf, and cob rather than stone.[24] In some instances, where early medieval settlement features have come to light, as at Longbury Bank, Pembrokeshire, the plough-soil directly overlaid the bedrock in most areas, thereby destroying the stratigraphy, and at South Hook features were truncated and, as a result, only the most robust evidence, such as hollows, iron-smelting furnaces, corn-dryers, and stone paving, has survived.[25] It is also possible that some sites lie under present-day farms, though this would imply an enormous level of continuity rather than settlements which moved within agricultural landscapes

---

[20] Driver 2016, figs 1.8, 1.18; Jones, I. et al. 2018. The radiocarbon dates are cal. AD 410–560 from the ditch fill (UBA-30455) and cal. AD 680–890 from the interior (UBA-24080).

[21] Roberts 2006b, 1–2; Silvester 2006; Longley 2006.

[22] Kelly 1982; Smith, G. H., and Thompson 2006, 114–17.

[23] Hopewell and Edwards 2017, 230–1.   [24] Blair 2018, 51–70.

[25] Campbell and Lane 1993, 22; Crane and Murphy 2010b, 186.

as a response to human instigation and social, economic, or environmental change. A good example of this is the Graeanog Ridge, Caernarfonshire, with its relatively fertile soils. Excavations over many years in advance of gravel extraction have uncovered a complex archaeological landscape with its origins in prehistory. During the Roman period the number of enclosed farmsteads increased and one of these, Cefn Graeanog 2, might have continued into the post-Roman period. Definite early medieval occupation of an earlier site is, however, indicated 500 metres north-east at Graeanog East, and evidence of early medieval ironworking and further probable buildings have also been found nearby. The latest excavated farmstead was occupied during the twelfth and thirteenth centuries.[26]

In recent years geographic information systems (GIS) have also been used to identify likely areas of early medieval settlement on fertile soils, but these techniques have yet to lead to the recognition of specific sites on the ground. Andy Seaman examined Dinas Powys hundred in the eastern Vale of Glamorgan and built a predictive model relating environmental zones and the sites of Roman and later medieval settlements to recognize 'core settlement zones' where early medieval settlements are most likely to have been located. As an adjunct, he also studied field names on the mid-nineteenth-century tithe maps, but it has proved impossible to project the evidence backwards to any significant extent. Rhiannon Comeau has similarly used GIS alongside archaeology, documents, and place names to reveal the evolution of the historic landscape in the *cantref* of Cemais in northern Pembrokeshire, leading her to emphasize the significance of the *longue durée*.[27]

Compared with England and Ireland,[28] there have been notably fewer developer-funded rescue excavations in Wales, and these have also played a less significant role in the discovery of early medieval settlements. This may be partially because methods of assessment, notably trial trenching prior to full-scale excavation, are likely to miss ephemeral evidence of buildings, especially since there are so seldom any associated diagnostic artefacts. South Hook was, however, identified in this way because obvious features, including evidence of ironworking, were subsequently radiocarbon-dated to the early Middle Ages.[29] More generally, such techniques have been successful in recognizing evidence of crop-processing, particularly corn-dryers, as well as ironworking residues, but, since indications of buildings, for example post-holes, may be limited or non-existent, there has been an understandable tendency to think that settlement peripheries were being investigated rather than the settlements themselves, though this is certainly not the case at South Hook. Instead, we need to recognize a more

---

[26] Fasham et al. 1998, 9–12, 28–9, 117–38; Young 2015a, 1; Kelly 1982.

[27] Seaman 2010b; 2017; Comeau 2020, 92–116.

[28] Blair 2013, 4–9, fig. 2; 2018, 15–17, 24–35, on the mapping of early medieval settlements in England using data from developer-funded excavation; O'Sullivan et al. 2014, 21–6.

[29] Crane and Murphy 2010b, 119.

nuanced picture. Some buildings had complex life cycles which seem to suggest construction for habitation with sometimes several phases, and in some cases use or reuse for other purposes as the structure deteriorated. Developer-funded excavations have also identified early medieval settlements because they reuse earlier sites with more visible archaeology. For example, the building at Conkland Hill was recognized because it partially overlay probable roundhouses located between two substantial ditches, part of a multivallate hilltop enclosure of Late Iron Age or early Roman date. However, frequently the evidence is more uncertain. At Cefn Du, Anglesey, the main settlement was Late Iron Age and Roman. However, it was suggested that ephemeral remains might be early medieval since they preceded a corn-dryer which was radiocarbon dated to between the eleventh and late thirteenth centuries.[30]

Generally, cemeteries of early medieval date have proved much easier to identify during developer-funded evaluations and are also sometimes visible on aerial photographs. However, to date very little has been done to examine the wider landscape to see where those who were buried might have lived, and there has certainly been nothing on the scale of Anglo-Saxon excavations such as Mucking, Essex, which explored the settlement alongside the associated cemeteries.[31] There are, however, sometimes hints. For example, at West Angle Bay, Pembrokeshire, very limited excavation revealed a substantial rectangular ditched enclosure with a later annexe. The basal fill of the ditch was radiocarbon-dated to between the mid-sixth and mid-seventh centuries AD, and it has been suggested that this was the site of both a settlement, since a corn-dryer or hearth was also located, and an adjacent cemetery. Burial subsequently changed focus to within a small curvilinear enclosure, probably with a later chapel of unknown date. Evidence of crop-processing dumped in this ditch was radiocarbon-dated to between the mid-seventh and later eighth century AD. There are also the remains of an undated promontory fort nearby. This site clearly had a complex history and has tentatively been compared with what have been termed 'cemetery settlements', now recognized as a characteristic early medieval site type in Ireland where other activities, such as crop-processing, were also carried out.[32]

Therefore, though more evidence of early medieval settlements is now coming to light in Wales, mainly as a result of AMS radiocarbon dating, it is still virtually impossible to identify such sites without excavation, which is often very limited in extent, making what are probably complex sequences very difficult to unravel. The lack of diagnostic finds assemblages, other than on elite sites, also remains a serious obstacle to recognition. The use of written evidence has led to the identification of only a very small number of elite sites. Morphological analysis continues to be a relevant but

---

[30] Hart 2014; Cuttler et al. 2012, 25–6, fig. 2.22; Waddington 2013, 163–5, no. AN65.

[31] Hamerow 2012, 6.

[32] Groom et al. 2011, 193–4; Ó Carragáin 2010b, 335–48. For further discussion of this site and others and the relationship between the living and the dead, see Shiner 2021.

142 LIFE IN EARLY MEDIEVAL WALES

difficult tool to use since it can result in early medieval settlements being wrongly assigned either to later prehistory or to the later Middle Ages. GIS landscape analysis is likewise useful, but only to identify likely areas of settlement, not to locate the settlements themselves.

HILLFORTS, PROMONTORY FORTS, AND RELATED HIGH-STATUS SITES

The reoccupation of hillforts is a widespread phenomenon in different parts of Europe in the early Middle Ages. In western and northern Britain also, a variety of hillforts and promontory forts were an important characteristic of the settlement pattern, and their evidence of high-status occupation is often connected with kingdom formation.[33] A proportion of these sites, some of which were initially constructed in later prehistory, also retained a significance long after their early medieval use and some became the locations of later medieval castles. In Wales, only a handful can conclusively be identified as datable to the post-Roman centuries. Of these, Dinas Powys, Hen Gastell (Briton Ferry), Coygan Camp, Carew, Degannwy (Fig. 5.3), and Dinas Emrys[34] were recognized because of the discovery of imported pottery from the Mediterranean and south-west France, sometimes alongside imported glass and ornamental metalwork, but the extensive early medieval artefactual assemblage from Dinas Powys is still unique. Mediterranean and Continental imports have also been found at Longbury Bank, which, though not strictly an inland promontory fort since it only has natural defences, has much in common with these sites.[35] The recognition of imported pottery, glass, and ornamental metalwork is regarded as indicative of high status, and this is equally true of similar sites in Scotland and south-west England. Their distribution in Wales is focused on the south and north-west, even though hillforts and promontory forts dominate much of the wider landscape, suggesting that many more examples await discovery. In the north-east, although two sites with early medieval activity have been identified, neither is typical. New Pieces, a substantial D-shaped enclosure below the Breiddin hillfort, has both imported pottery and glass.[36] However, neither of

[33] For recent research on early medieval hillforts in Europe, see Christie and Herold 2016, xxvii, and other articles in that volume. On Scotland, see Noble et al. 2013, Noble 2016; on Wales, Seaman 2016. There is no recent synthesis of sites in south-west England, but see, for example, South Cadbury, Alcock 1995; Cadbury Congresbury, Rahtz et al. 1992, and Tintagel, Thomas 1993; Barrowman et al. 2007. In north-west England early medieval activity has also been recognized at Shoulthwaite Crag, Cumbria, Paterson et al. 2014, 21; Steve Dickinson (pers. comm.).

[34] Alcock 1963; 1987, 5–150; Campbell 2007a, 83–101; Seaman 2013; Seaman and Lane 2019; Wilkinson 1995; Gerrard 1987; Austin 1995; Savory 1960; Edwards and Lane 1988, 44–6, 50–7. Degannwy and Dinas Emrys also have documentary evidence; see above.

[35] Campbell and Lane 1993.   [36] O'Neil 1937; Arnold and Huggett 2000; Campbell n.d.

Fig. 5.3. The twin summits of Degannwy from the north. Evidence of early medieval activity comes from the larger (© Gwynedd Archaeological Trust).

these has been found at Dinorben.[37] Gateholm, Pembrokeshire, with a small number of early medieval artefacts, may also be added to the list.[38] Caerau, a large Iron Age and Roman multivallate hillfort in the Vale of Glamorgan, is also a probable site supported by the stratigraphy and radiocarbon dating. A midden with Roman pottery of second- to fourth-century date was found underlying the secondary inner enclosure bank on the southern side, thereby providing a *terminus post quem* for its construction. A radiocarbon date of cal. AD 775–960 from cereal grains overlying hill-wash above the bank on the northern side provided a *terminus ante quem*, and a corn-dryer was also radiocarbon-dated to cal. AD 420–640.[39]

Therefore, our understanding of these sites and their distribution in Wales has largely been conditioned by those identifiable because they had access to early medieval imports. In all likelihood, continued occupation, reoccupation, and construction of hillforts, promontory forts, and related sites *c.* AD 400–700 were much more

---

[37] Edwards and Lane 1988, 64–6.

[38] Cantrill 1910; Gordon-Williams 1926; Lethbridge and David 1930; Davies, J. L. et al. 1971; Edwards and Lane 1988, 72–5; Redknap 2008; Davis 2011; see Anon. 2012 for exploratory excavations by Time Team. The stratigraphy has been disturbed by rabbits and structures are now obscured by fescue grass.

[39] Davis and Sharples 2014, 34, 55; 2015, 73–4; Davis et al. 2014, 36, 41–2; 2015; Oliver Davis (pers. comm.); Comeau and Burrow 2021a, 141, no. 68.

widespread, as now recognized in Scotland, where fortified sites show considerable regional variety.[40] However, without modern excavation and radiocarbon dating, as at Glanfred,[41] such sites cannot be identified. It may also be misleading to regard all such sites as high-status. Nevertheless, construction or substantial refurbishment of the enclosure required investment in both time and labour, in itself a demonstration of status and power; reuse of earlier sites may also have served to underline such aspirations.

The early medieval hillforts and promontory forts that have been recognized are overwhelmingly coastal. Degannwy, Hen Gastell (Briton Ferry), and Coygan Camp were prominent sites close to navigable river estuaries, making them visible from both sea and land as well as emphasizing their strategic importance. Prior to their destruction, Hen Gastell overlooked the west bank of the Neath close to the historic ferry crossing, while Coygan Camp surveyed the confluence of the Taf and Tywi estuaries. Degannwy still dominates the east bank of the Conwy estuary, clearly visible for some distance to the west. Tenby may also be comparable, since the promontory overlooks the harbour near the mouth of the Ritec. However, Longbury Bank, situated only 2 kilometres upstream, appears less conspicuous, as does Carew, which is sited on a low promontory at the head of the Carew estuary flowing out into Milford Haven. Glanfred lies near the Afon Leri close to Cardigan Bay. It may be argued that Gateholm, a steep-sided tidal island at the western end of Marloes Bay, was originally a dramatic promontory projecting out into the sea. Caerau is sited on a broad ridge south of the Ely, and nearby Dinas Powys is on two natural routeways at the nearest defensible point inland overlooking the valley of the Cadoxton.[42] Dinorben, now destroyed by quarrying, rose from the coastal plain and, though Dinas Emrys is strategically sited in the Nant Gwynant valley in Snowdonia, it too is close to the Afon Glaslyn, providing access to the sea. All these sites are comparatively low-lying, with Dinorben the highest, at 168 metres above sea level. In contrast, New Pieces, at 322 metres OD, is much higher, with the Breiddin dominating the landscape for miles around.

As already indicated, it would be wrong to think of these sites as a homogeneous group since they demonstrate considerable variety, only partly explained by their topography and geology. The dramatic twin basalt summits at Degannwy, for example, are the product of intense volcanic activity, and the precipitous rock on which Dinas Emrys is located is an igneous intrusion of Ordovician rhyolite, but Dinas Powys is sited on a limestone whaleback hill. In contrast to many later prehistoric hillforts, particularly in north Wales and the borders, a significant number of which also have Roman activity, sites with early medieval activity are mostly very small, the enclosed area ranging from over 2 hectares at Dinorben to under 0.1 hectares at Dinas Powys (Fig. 5.4).[43]

---

[40] Noble 2016.   [41] Jones, I. et al. 2018.
[42] Seaman and Sucharyna Thomas 2020, 555–9.
[43] Seaman 2016, 41.

HEARTH AND HOME 145

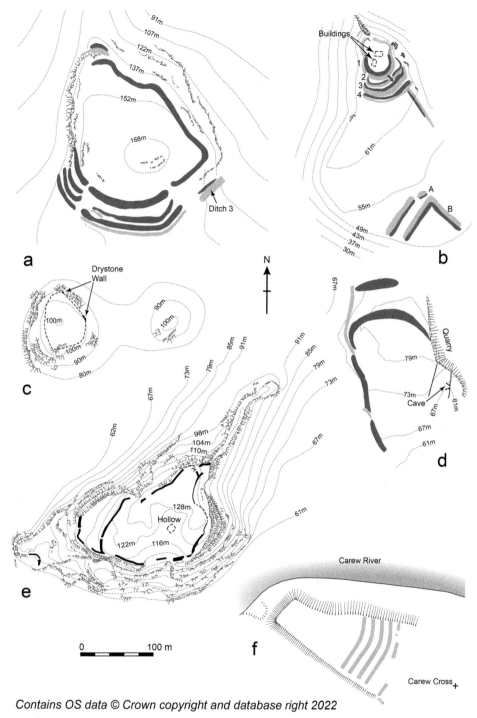

Contains OS data © Crown copyright and database right 2022

FIG. 5.4. Comparative plans of hillforts and promontory forts: a. Dinorben; b. Dinas Powys; c. Degannwy; d. Coygan Camp; e. Dinas Emrys; f. Carew (after Guilbert 1979a; Alcock 1963, fig. 1.2, with additions; Edwards and Lane 1988, fig. 9; Wainwright 1967, fig. 2; RCAHMW 1960, fig. 30; Austin 1995, fig. 4).

If the secondary bank at Caerau is post-Roman, the site, at 5.1 hectares, appears more comparable with those in south-west England, such as South Cadbury, which is 7.2 hectares, whilst Gateholm is even larger at nearly 8 hectares.

The enclosures at Dinorben are later prehistoric, but radiocarbon-dated animal bones in the upper fill of ditch 3 on the southern side suggest post-Roman occupation in the vicinity. Coygan Camp, a promontory fort, was likewise constructed in later prehistory with occupation also in the later Roman period. It is, however, doubtful whether there was any late prehistoric phase at Dinas Emrys, where Roman pottery and glass demonstrate both late first- and early second-century AD activity and a significant phase of later Roman occupation. The inner and middle drystone ramparts overlie a layer containing late fourth-century pottery and glass, thereby indicating a probable post-Roman date for their construction. The earliest evidence at Degannwy is also Roman, but a small stretch of drystone walling excavated by Leslie Alcock, which is thought to represent an enclosure encircling the western hill, remains undated.[44] At Carew, where there are at least five rock-cut ditches cutting off the promontory, the picture is more complex. Second- and third-century pottery was found in one ditch, suggesting Roman-period construction, with imported E ware sherds in another indicating that the ditches were probably of more than one phase. Another had been recut, with radiocarbon dates suggesting the first phase was probably Roman, the second early medieval.[45] The remains at Gateholm, though poorly understood, include considerable artefactual evidence of later Roman occupation. The low rampart across the landward approach is undated, though mortar near the entrance points to a later medieval phase, also suggested by eleventh- to thirteenth-century pottery.[46] At Hen Gastell (Briton Ferry) and Dinas Powys, however, later Roman pottery was probably brought onto the early medieval settlement, and this is also true at Longbury Bank.[47]

In truth the multivallate promontory fort of Dinas Powys remains the only site where we have a more detailed understanding of the early medieval sequence of banks and ditches and their chronology, though evidence originally advanced by Alcock suggesting refortification as a late eleventh- or early twelfth-century ringwork[48] can now be set aside. The earliest phase, a small-scale bank of dump construction with a V-shaped ditch (2), is not securely dated but, as Ewan Campbell has argued, it is most likely fifth-century (Fig. 5.4, b). He also established that the more substantial rubble bank and ditch (1) subsequently constructed on the inner side dated to around the

---

[44] Guilbert 1979b, 14; 1980, 338, CAR 203, cal. AD 250–610; CAR 204, cal. AD 390–620; CAR 130, cal. AD 420–660; Edwards and Lane 1988, 44–6, 50–7; Campbell 1991, 111–18.

[45] Gerrard 1987; Campbell 1991, 111; Austin 1995, 2A, fig. 4.

[46] Cantrill 1910, 274; Davies, J. L. et al. 1971, 103, n. 5; Edwards and Lane 1988, 74; Coflein, NPRN 102906.

[47] Wilkinson 1995, 16–18; Alcock 1963, 25; Campbell and Lane 1993, 17–20.

[48] Alcock 1963, 27, 73–82, 90–1, figs 13–16.

later sixth century because Mediterranean imported pottery was found beneath it and later Continental imports overlying it. This is supported by two recent radiocarbon dates, one from beneath the bank, cal. AD 560–650, and one from the bank itself, cal. AD 550–650. Two further massive banks and ditches (3 and 4) were added sometime during the seventh century, though the site was abandoned shortly afterwards.[49] Radiocarbon dates from the ditch of southern bank A suggest construction around the end of this sequence, while southern bank B is Late Iron Age.[50] The overall effect of the banks and ditches demarcating the promontory remains impressive, indicating defensive need as well as status.

Equally, the Dinas Powys excavations continue to shape our understanding of interior structures, but the evidence is sparse. The earliest (IA), perhaps a rectilinear wooden building, is suggested by a few rock-cut post-holes most likely contemporary with the earliest bank and ditch. In the next phase broadly contemporary with bank 1, this was replaced by two buildings set at right angles, thereby providing a sheltered yard between them. The only remains, however, consisted of stretches of substantial eaves-drip gullies cut into the rock and filled with stones, suggesting the presence of two subrectangular buildings (IB, II), but there were no other indications of what they may have looked like or the materials from which they were made.[51]

How typical these buildings may have been is unclear, since we also know very little about early medieval structures on other sites. At Longbury Bank a sunken, rock-cut, subrectangular building was excavated on the south-eastern periphery and a sample from one of the post-holes was radiocarbon-dated to cal. AD 420–650.[52] At Dinorben, Hubert Savory claimed to have found the post-holes of a post-Roman, rectangular, aisled building and a roundhouse in the north-western part of the hillfort. However, the stratigraphy was complex, with the former more plausibly representing four-post storage structures, and only late prehistoric and Roman artefacts were found.[53] Savory also excavated in the sheltered hollow below the summit of Dinas Emrys, revealing various structures including a later medieval cistern, as well as early medieval imported pottery, but the area was heavily disturbed, both in the later Middle Ages and by antiquarian digging. As a result, his phasing and interpretation are no longer tenable.[54] Nor are there any identifiable early medieval structures at Degannwy or Carew, both sites of later castles, and almost nothing of the interior at Glanfred was excavated. Buildings of probable later Roman date were found on the northern periphery of the enclosure at Coygan Camp, but imported pottery came from the topsoil above and

---

[49] Campbell 1991, 85–109; 2007a, 96–7; Seaman 2013, 5–7.   [50] Seaman and Lane 2019.

[51] Alcock 1963, 28–32, figs 6, 18, reassessed by Campbell 1991, 100–6.

[52] Campbell and Lane 1993, 21–9 (Beta-52349) 1510±60 BP.

[53] Gardner and Savory 1964, 70–4, 106–7, figs 3, 14; Edwards and Lane 1988, 65–6.

[54] Savory 1960, 28–48, 51–2; Edwards and Lane 1988, 55, 57; Campbell 1991, 116–17.

148 LIFE IN EARLY MEDIEVAL WALES

layers overlying the rampart tumble.[55] At Hen Gastell (Briton Ferry) early medieval occupation was probably concentrated on the summit, though by the time of the excavation almost all of this had been quarried away. Nevertheless, post-holes connected with a timber building together with an area of burning and a stone-lined hearth were found near the southern lip of the quarry. Archaeomagnetic dates suggested this phase was broadly later ninth-century, though an *in situ* deposit further down the slope contained sherds of sixth- or seventh-century imported glass, signalling two different phases of early medieval occupation.[56]

The remains on Gateholm present particular problems of interpretation. Well over a hundred, mainly subrectangular, buildings have been recorded, most of which are conjoined in groups, either around yards or strung out on either side of a central pathway. Excavation in 1930 of a subrectangular building with turf and drystone footings and opposing entrances in the long walls, together with part of an adjacent structure, demonstrated more than one phase of occupation. The later Roman pottery was seen as residual, and three early medieval finds—a baluster-headed ringed pin, a perforated whetstone, and a shale finger ring—were seen as dating the occupation of the structure. Recent keyhole investigation of structures in a different part of the site uncovered a possible floor surface with late Roman pottery, and an unstratified early medieval amber bead was found elsewhere.[57] What evidence there is indicates that the subrectangular structures are third- or fourth-century or later. Superficially, the steep-sided promontory has much in common with Tintagel, which is also covered with groups of conjoined rectangular buildings of more than one phase, some of which had turf and stone footings, whilst others were of stone. Earlier buildings are associated with large amounts of Mediterranean pottery dated *c.*450–550, though there is also evidence suggesting late Roman occupation on the site.[58] At Gateholm, however, there are no imports, and we may be seeing intensive later Roman occupation followed by renewed activity around the tenth century, though continuing occupation into the post-Roman centuries cannot be ruled out.

There is also evidence of renewed interest in promontory forts during the second half of the eleventh and twelfth centuries. Radiocarbon dates indicate that both Hen Gastell (Llanwnda), Caernarfonshire, and Castell Trefadog, on the north-west Anglesey coast, were constructed and occupied around this time. Their impressive

---

[55] Wainwright 1967, 45–56; Edwards and Lane 1988, 45–6; Campbell 1991, 111–13.

[56] Wilkinson 1995, 6–11, 34–5.

[57] Lethbridge and David 1930; Redknap 2008; Anon. 2012, 5, 15, figs 5, 13. The early medieval finds are comparable with examples from Viking Dublin (ringed pin) (Fanning 1994, 22–5) and Woodstown (shale finger ring, amber bead) (Russell and Hurley 2014, 286–7, 323). See also two unstratified shale finger rings from Llangorse crannog with wider discussion in Lane and Redknap 2019, 245–7. The whetstone is also of Viking Age type.

[58] Thomas 1993, pl. 4; Barrowman et al. 2007, 313, 320; Duggan 2018, 69–70.

ramparts and ditches testify to the need for defence as well as the display of status.[59] It has been argued that Castell Trefadog is comparable with the Viking Age occupation of coastal promontory forts on the Isle of Man and this is certainly possible, but they might also be regarded as a more traditional, native response to castle building first evidenced in Gwynedd in the mid-1070s as a result of Norman incursions.[60]

The foregoing discussion makes it clear that the dating, phasing, and chronology of hillforts, promontory forts, and related sites are complex since, in addition to their early medieval occupation, some have their origins in the later prehistoric or Roman periods, whilst others were still being constructed in the later Middle Ages, with some earlier sites being reused at this time. The fact that so far only Dinas Powys and Glanfred have any AMS radiocarbon dates means that understanding their early medieval chronology still largely depends upon the analysis of artefacts, particularly imported pottery and glass. This has tended to suggest that early medieval occupation was broadly focused on the later fifth to later seventh centuries, though at Dinas Powys, where both Mediterranean and Continental imports were found, the radiocarbon dates may indicate abandonment somewhat earlier. There is a similar range of imports at Hen Gastell (Briton Ferry) and Longbury Bank. The picture is, nonetheless, more complex. At Coygan Camp, Degannwy, and Dinas Emrys late Roman artefacts and Mediterranean imports may well reflect continuing activity throughout the fifth century, though the only evidence of Continental imports is a reworked DSPA sherd from Dinas Emrys. At Carew, however, though there is a significant amount of Roman pottery, only Continental E ware, broadly datable to the later sixth and seventh century, has been found, and it is therefore unclear whether this indicates a break in occupation or lack of access to earlier Mediterranean imports. The evidence is, however, sufficient to indicate that, as elsewhere in northern and western Britain, hillforts and promontory forts continued as characteristic settlement types during the fifth to seventh centuries, somewhat later in Scotland, whether they were constructed *de novo* or occupied earlier sites.

It is also clear that some of these sites had significant afterlives, reflecting both their strategic locations in the landscape and the continuity of memory and its reinvention to serve new ends. References in the Harleian Chronicle to the lightning strike that burnt Degannwy in 812 and its destruction by Saxons in 822 provide testimony of its continuing strategic and symbolic importance,[61] but whether the site was still occupied, or had been reoccupied, is impossible to determine, and no archaeological evidence of ninth-century activity has been found. The tale of Emrys in the *Historia Brittonum* demonstrates that, by the earlier ninth century, Dinas Emrys had acquired a mythic status, suggesting its true significance lay in the past, though it maintained

---

[59] Kenney 2014; 2016; Longley 1991.
[60] Ibid., 82–3; Lewis 1996, 67.   [61] Morris 1980, 47–8, 88–9.

150   LIFE IN EARLY MEDIEVAL WALES

an important mnemonic role nonetheless.[62] In contrast, the discovery of a broadly later ninth-century structure at Hen Gastell (Briton Ferry), as well as a perforated amber disc and glass 'string bead' suggesting a Hiberno-Scandinavian connection,[63] clearly supports a later phase of activity associated with surveillance of the Neath estuary and the continuing significance of this strategic site. Was it, as the later artefacts might suggest, at least briefly in Viking hands, as recorded in 870 at Dumbarton Rock in Strathclyde?[64] Or, since the objects are not martial, does it simply denote renewed access to the products of international trade? Similarly, the Hiberno-Scandinavian artefacts from Gateholm indicate a Viking Age phase and the place name is regarded as Scandinavian as well.[65] The erection of a tall stone cross of later tenth- or early eleventh-century date outside the enclosure at Carew is also significant. It denotes not only continuing interest in the site, but in all likelihood its appropriation and reinvention guided by *Margiteut Recett* ('Maredudd the Generous'?), named in an inscription on the monument.[66] Later still Carew, Degannwy, and Hen Gastell (Briton Ferry) all became the sites of castles, and a stone tower was also erected at Dinas Emrys, suggesting that the continuing power of these places in the landscape was as important as their strategic role, a situation paralleled elsewhere in northern Britain, and at Tintagel its mythic status was also key.[67] The locations of later medieval castles may therefore be useful markers aiding identification of other early medieval sites as, for example, at Caerau and Tenby, and at Caergwrle Castle, Flintshire, it has been suggested that the outer drystone enclosure encircling the hilltop is post-Roman since there are later Roman radiocarbon dates from beneath the bank.[68]

The functions of hillforts, promontory forts, and related sites during their early medieval phases of use were complex and subject to change over time, and in some instances the past may also have been influential in this respect. The small enclosed area at Dinas Powys, as well as the structures and artefacts, indicate that it was the defended home of a single extended household who were the patrons of different craftworkers practising on the site. They also had access to and probable control of a range of raw materials and luxury imports, the latter, with the animal bone assemblage, indicating the significance of food preparation and feasting. This all points to an elite lifestyle commensurate with the operation of Dinas Powys as an estate centre and a stronghold, in all likelihood inhabited by rulers of a small post-Roman kingdom.

---

[62] Ibid., chs 40–2.

[63] Wilkinson 1995, 22–3, 35; see also 'string beads' from Kilmainham, Dublin, Harrison and Ó Floinn 2014, 146, ill. 77.

[64] There is also a similar finds sequence from this site; see Alcock 1975–6.

[65] Charles 1992, ii, 611.   [66] Edwards 2007a, no. P9, 303–10.

[67] For northern Britain, see, for example, Dumbarton Rock, Alcock 1975–6; Canmore ID 43376; Dunollie, Argyll, Alcock and Alcock 1987, 119–27; Dunottar, Aberdeenshire, Canmore ID 36992; the Bernician royal site of Bamburgh Castle, Northumberland, Kirton and Young 2017. On Tintagel, see Thomas 1993, 13–28, 87.

[68] Manley 1994, 109–110, GrN-16520 cal. AD 230–280, GrN-16521 cal. AD 250–420, fig.3.

The same link between such elite sites and kingdom formation has been made persuasively for hillforts and promontory sites in both northern Britain and at Tintagel in the south-west.[69] At Coygan Camp, however, the range of ceramics already demonstrates elite occupation in the Roman period, with an unusually high incidence of late Roman fine wares, as well as the discovery of Mediterranean imports indicative of elements of continuity into the fifth and sixth centuries,[70] a situation clearly comparable with Dinas Emrys. This strongly implies the continuation of some native power structures as well. At Dinas Emrys, however, the location makes anything more than seasonal occupation unlikely. Here the tale of Emrys creates a further link with kingdom formation, but in addition emphasizes the magical powers of both boy and place. This may indicate the memory of a possible pre-Christian cult centre, a role already hinted at for some other larger hillforts with late Roman activity in north Wales. A similar argument has been made for some hillforts and promontory forts in northern Britain, such as Burghead, and there are also several later prehistoric hillforts, including Lydney and probably South Cadbury, with late Roman shrines or temples in the south-west (Chapter 9).[71] Nevertheless, it has also been argued that not all hillforts and promontory forts, for example Glanfred, were necessarily high-status sites, so may rather have functioned as prosperous farmsteads, the enclosures giving a measure of status and providing defence from sudden attack. In the early ninth century, the strategic siting, status, and symbolism of Degannwy made it the object of Saxon attack, and sieges are also noted in northern Britain. Equally, artefacts from Hen Gastell and Gateholm suggest they may have functioned as strongholds associated with Hiberno-Scandinavian activity, or possibly places of trade and exchange. The later erection of the cross at Carew signals a change in function associated with elite performance and display, pointing to a place of assembly (Chapter 12).

Therefore, although hillforts and promontory forts were characteristic early medieval sites in Wales, as they were in northern and south-west Britain, particularly in the fifth to seventh centuries, their habitation, in some cases probably temporary, seasonal, or intermittent, together with other activities, was often part of a much longer continuum. However, our limited understanding of the chronology and functions of these sites in the early Middle Ages remains dependent on only a very small number of examples, mostly excavated half a century or more ago. Dinas Powys is still the only site with extensive early medieval structural and other archaeological evidence of habitation enabling us to understand its development, chronology, and functions more clearly. Although other sites suggest longer and more complex histories and a wider

[69] Seaman 2013, 12–15; 2016, 41–2; Noble 2016, 32; Thomas 1993, 87–8.
[70] Wainwright 1967, 134–60; Arnold and Davies 2000, 112.
[71] Edwards 2017a, 394–5; Wheeler and Wheeler 1932, 60–3; Casey and Hoffmann 1999; Barrett et al. 2000, 176–8.

152   LIFE IN EARLY MEDIEVAL WALES

range of functions, these will only be elucidated as a result of better dating and more extensive archaeological investigation as other early medieval examples are identified.

OTHER HIGH-STATUS SETTLEMENTS

Apart from hillforts and promontory forts, we know remarkably little about other early medieval high-status settlements in Wales, especially those in the latter half of the period. Indeed, it remains impossible to identify any other characteristic site types. Although the discovery of a sherd of Continental imported pottery, a Byzantine intaglio, and a Type G1 penannular brooch at Cefn Cwmwd, Anglesey, suggests an alternative form of post-Roman, high-status site on farmland in the vicinity of an earlier settlement, nothing more is known (Chapter 3). The most significant of the later sites are Llanbedrgoch, Llangorse crannog, and Rhuddlan, all of which appear unique. The first two, which have undergone extensive recent archaeological investigations, are of immense significance for what they can reveal about the homes and lifestyles of their inhabitants in the second half of the ninth and first half of the tenth centuries, though Llanbedrgoch also has evidence of elite occupation at an earlier date. At Rhuddlan, however, with excavations in the late 1960s and early 1970s, the complex stratigraphy and nature of the remains, some of which, it will be argued, are associated with the tenth-century Anglo-Saxon *burh*, make interpretation much more difficult. Although high-status sites have also been claimed in other places, notably Monmouth, Aberffraw, Anglesey, and Cwrt Llechryd, Radnorshire, definitive evidence has proved elusive.[72]

The enclosed settlement at Llanbedrgoch[73] (Fig. 5.5) is centred on a spring on a gentle, south-facing slope in fertile farmland west of Traeth Coch (Red Wharf Bay), an excellent natural landing place. In early phases there is evidence of prehistoric activity, and later the presence of a small Roman period farmstead, including fourth-century coins.[74] The nature of the transition between the Roman and early medieval phases remains uncertain, but by the mid-seventh century occupation was focused on

---

[72] Despite a lack of supporting evidence, it has been suggested that Monmouth might also be an Anglo-Saxon *burh*. An estate centre seems more likely, and a few sherds of Late Saxon pottery have been found; Courtney 1994, 111; Crawford 2011. For a summary of possible early medieval evidence, see Clarke 2008, 190–5, and for a useful critique, see Seaman 2010a, 257–8. On Aberffraw, a royal site associated with the rulers of Gwynedd, see Edwards and Lane 1988, 18–21; White and Longley 1995; Burnham and Davies 2012, 310. On the moated site at Cwrt Llechryd, see Musson and Spurgeon 1988. The radiocarbon date of cal. AD 720–1030 (CAR-672) from beneath the bank only provides a *terminus post quem* (Seaman 2016, 48), and excavations in the immediate vicinity since have produced nothing; Williams, D., and Marvell 1995; Barber 2008.

[73] The final report is in preparation and Mark Redknap has kindly provided me with his latest interpretation of the phasing based on approx. 90 radiocarbon dates and the artefactual assemblage. The main interim discussions include Redknap 2000, 67–83; 2004a; 2006; 2016.

[74] Redknap 1995b, 50; 1996, 72; 1997, 95; 2000, illus. 109; 2001, 120, 133; 2004b, 149, 155–6.

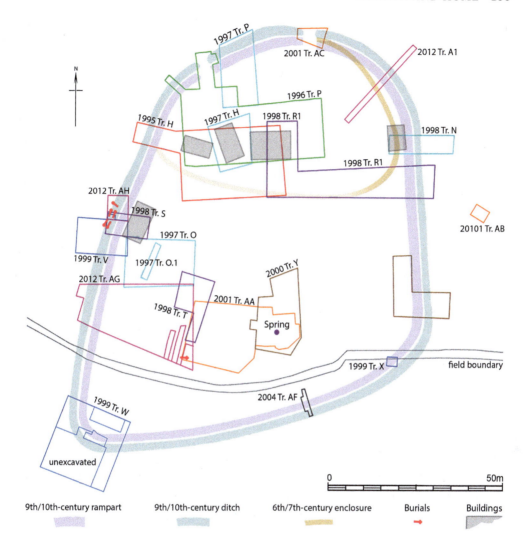

Fig. 5.5. Llanbedrgoch, plan of the enclosed settlement, showing the excavation trenches, main phases, and principal archaeological features (© Amgueddfa Cymru–National Museum Wales).

a comparatively small, curvilinear enclosure around 80 metres in diameter with a rock-cut ditch and northern entrance. Subsequently, this was enlarged to around 1 hectare so that it now included the spring to the south. This D-shaped enclosure was made up of a small bank with a stone revetment on the inner face and a ditch 1.7–2 metres wide and up to 1.4 metres deep, with two causewayed entrances at the northern end. A seventh-century penannular brooch with bird-head terminals was found in the ditch fill. Two interior structures have been linked to this phase: at the northern end of the enclosure a possible aisled building, indicated by two rows of substantial post-holes, and a curved gully with stake-holes, possibly related to a roundhouse. Further features interpreted as part of this phase were found near the spring with its stone-lined pool.[75] The sizable enclosure with a large timber building with earth-fast posts, perhaps a hall, as well as the finds assemblage, all point to a wealthy, high-status site with outside contacts, but the lack of imported E ware from here and elsewhere in north Wales suggests that these were not with the Atlantic seaways. Instead, a plain silver, pyramidal scabbard fitting of Anglo-Saxon type and a fragment of deep brown vessel glass with off-white, marvered decoration found in a midden probably belonging to this phase, like the bird-headed penannular brooch, are indicative of contacts with England.[76] The earliest coin, a penny of Queen Cynethryth, the wife of Offa of Mercia (757–96), may also suggest this, but is not from the site itself but close by.[77]

In the final early medieval phase spanning the ninth and tenth centuries the ditch was recut and the enclosure rebuilt as a much more imposing structure with a massive wall up to 2.3 metres wide with drystone facings and an earth-and-rubble core. In the northern part of the interior three rectangular buildings (1–3) were found, with further buildings close to the wall of the enclosure. An archaeomagnetic date for the final use of the hearth in the earlier phase of Building 1 gave a date of AD 890–970, and a sample from charcoal overlying the floor of Building 2 was radiocarbon-dated to cal. AD 855–1000. West of the spring there was also a sunken-floored structure with an oven and a paved path headed northwards towards the other buildings. This phase is unusually rich in finds, mainly of Hiberno-Scandinavian character, and contexts associated with Buildings 1–3 have produced tenth-century artefacts, including a copper-alloy strap-end with Borre ring-chain ornament. Other finds included hacksilver and lead weights indicative of commercial activity, and a fragment of a lead trial piece for a broad-band arm-ring of Hiberno-Scandinavian type, as well as evidence for craft-working and food preparation (Chapters 6 and 7).[78] Six punishment burials found in the upper fill of the ditch are also broadly datable to this phase, with a further burial in the interior (Chapter 12).[79] Although it is not known precisely when habitation ceased, the latest coins are Anglo-Saxon pennies of Edmund (939–46) and Eadred or Eadwig (955–9), suggesting abandonment shortly afterwards.[80]

Final elucidation of the phasing and chronology must await completion of post-excavation analysis and final publication. Nevertheless, two quite different interpretations of this final phase have emerged. Mark Redknap has consistently argued that during the eighth and ninth centuries Llanbedrgoch was a high-status local estate centre which was transformed into a more important regional one. As part of this

[75] Redknap 1997, 95; 2001, 145; 2004a, 147–50, with details of the radiocarbon dates; 2016, fig. 2.

[76] Seaman 2016, 46; Campbell 2007a, figs 17, 34, 85, 63–4; Cuttler et al. 2012, 198–9; Mark Redknap (pers. comm.).

[77] Redknap 1994, 58; 2006, 18, fig. 6.

[78] Redknap 2000, 75–84; 2004a, 150–3, 156–64; 2006, 20–33. For the wider distribution of Borre-style strap-ends, which focuses on the Danelaw, see Thomas 2012, fig. 4.8.

[79] Redknap 2000, 72–3; 2007b, 67–8; 2016, 161–3.

[80] Besly 2006, 716–17, nos 12, 14; Redknap 2004a, 155.

transformation, sometime in the ninth century the enclosure was strengthened as both a native response to the Viking threat and a sign of the increasing social, economic, and political significance of the site. He has also proposed that by the late ninth or early tenth century the number of inhabitants had risen, with the distinctive Viking artefacts demonstrating the introduction of a Hiberno-Scandinavian element amongst the population with a mixed cultural identity becoming evident as a result.[81] This interpretation has, however, been questioned by Andy Seaman, who has contended that the remodelling of the enclosure, together with the advent and range of the Hiberno-Scandinavian artefacts, should be regarded as contemporary. Indeed, it should be seen in terms of a Viking takeover, a situation which would chime with the known fluidity of the political situation on Anglesey from the mid-ninth century onwards (Chapter 12).[82]

In contrast to Llanbedrgoch, of which there is no mention in the written sources, Llangorse crannog is clearly identifiable as a royal site associated with the rulers of Brycheiniog. This lake dwelling (Fig. 5.6) is located in shallow water close to the northern shore of Llangorse Lake (Llyn Safaddan) and, as Gerald of Wales indicates, this was rich in wildlife, both waterbirds and fish.[83] The site itself is on a natural rise in the lakebed, which has been artificially extended and built up to form an island, now around 40 metres across. It was first investigated in 1869, but by the 1980s when it was rediscovered, erosion and fluctuating water levels severely threatened the waterlogged archaeology.[84] The visible remains in the water and along the shoreline were therefore recorded, and subsequently limited excavations were carried out on the island and into the water (Trenches A–D) alongside a systematic underwater survey around much of the southern and western sides and between the northern perimeter and the shore (1989–93).[85] There were also further investigations in 2004 prior to the construction of a protective bund around much of the island.[86] The artefact and ecofact assemblages are particularly rich, but it is important to note that the majority of finds were unstratified since they were recovered from disturbed underwater contexts, though a midden deposit containing food remains was also found.[87]

Although no buildings or occupation levels survived on the crannog, excavations revealed how it had been constructed. This would have been a major undertaking requiring substantial resources, particularly wood, as well as skill and a considerable labour force. It also needed to be carried out during the summer months when water levels were lower. First, lengths of post-and-wattle fencing, mainly of hazel with some alder and willow, were driven into the peat and shell marl of the lakebed to demarcate

[81] Ibid., 164–9.
[82] Seaman 2016, 46–7. On the wider context, see Davies, W. 1990, 51–5; Edwards 2011, 82–7.
[83] Thorpe 1978, 93–6.   [84] Campbell and Lane 1989; Lane and Redknap 2019, 19–20.
[85] Redknap and Lane 1994; 1999; Lane and Redknap 2019, 22–9.
[86] Redknap 2004c; Lane and Redknap 2019, 398–402.   [87] Ibid., 67.

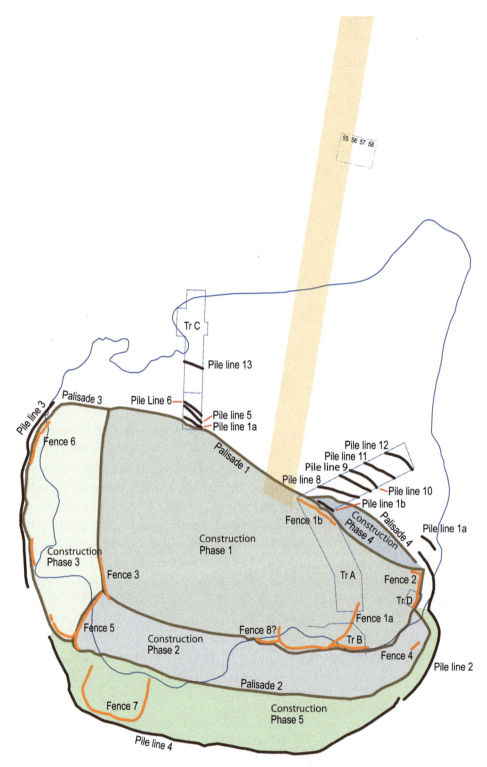

Fig. 5.6. Llangorse crannog, diagram showing the various phases of crannog construction and excavation trenches A–D. The line of the walkway is shown in yellow (© Amgueddfa Cymru–National Museum Wales).

an approximately D-shaped area and contain the crannog make-up. This consisted of bundles of roundwood branches laid down to form a substantial raft held in position from above by horizontal oak beams secured with pegs. To stabilize the structure, a palisade of oak planks was driven into the peat immediately outside the enclosure and the gap between filled with stones, clay, and soil. The crannog was then topped off with a layer of carefully laid sandstone boulders to provide a level building platform. Extensions to the original enclosure were constructed in a similar way in subsequent seasons to increase the size of the structure, and rows of piles, mainly of ash and alder with some oak, were also driven into the lakebed beyond to strengthen the shoreline and protect it from erosion. Even so, the crannog structure would have quickly compacted, making it inherently unstable with the need for regular maintenance and repair. Further piles marked the line of a wooden walkway stretching northwards towards the shore. This would have aided construction of the crannog but also provided an impressive approach to the artificial island, which may have been enhanced by the height of the outer palisade timbers and piles acting as a barrier and deterrent against attack.[88]

The short lifespan of this site is unusually well understood. Dendrochronological dates from planks in the palisades have established that timbers for the earliest palisade had been felled during the summer months of 889 and 890, indicating that the D-shaped enclosure was built shortly afterwards. Timbers from palisades 2 and 3 were felled in 892 and 893. However, occupation came to an abrupt end on 19 June 916 when Æthelflæd of Mercia, probably in an act of revenge after the murder of Abbot Ecgberht three days before, 'sent an army into Wales and destroyed *Brecenanmere* and captured the king's wife and thirty-three other persons'.[89] The excavations revealed evidence of a destruction horizon with charred structural remains and burnt artefacts including the remnants of a fine embroidered textile found in the water.[90] The crannog may therefore be identified as a royal site built in the time of Elise ap Tewdwr, the ruler of Brycheiniog who had, according to Asser, submitted to King Alfred in 886 in the face of the rising power of Gwynedd. Occupation ceased either later in his reign or that of his son, Tewdwr ab Elise, who was probably a witness to a charter of Æthelstan in 934.[91]

That Llangorse is the only known crannog in Wales is surprising and, although some other suitable lake environments and various possible sites have been investigated, nothing has so far been found.[92] This seems unexpected because crannogs are characteristic of the early Middle Ages in parts of both Scotland and Ireland where

---

[88] Ibid., 30–101.   [89] Whitelock 1979, *s.a.* 916; Lane and Redknap 2019, 412–14.

[90] Ibid., 35, 276–8.

[91] Keynes and Lapidge 1983, 96, ch. 80; Charles-Edwards 2013, 489–90, 516; Lane and Redknap 2019, 412–13.

[92] Roberts and Peterson 1989.

158 LIFE IN EARLY MEDIEVAL WALES

they are part of a much longer sequence of lake settlement stretching back into prehistory and sometimes forwards into the later medieval or early modern periods as well.[93] In Ireland, dendrochronological dating has revealed an upsurge in crannog building during the later sixth and early seventh centuries, also apparent to a lesser extent in Scotland. In Ireland, some construction continued, with Ballinderry 1, Co. Westmeath, for example, being built and occupied during the tenth and eleventh centuries. Such sites demonstrate considerable variety, in part dependent upon available materials, but typically their locations and construction methods have much in common with Llangorse. As the term crannog (from the Irish *crann*, 'tree') indicates, their make-up often includes large amounts of timber and brushwood, though stones are also sometimes used, contained within sturdy post palisades or later, as at Llangorse, plank palisades with exterior piles. High-status artefacts and associated craftworking indicate that many but not all of these crannogs were high-status and, like Llangorse, some Irish examples are documented royal sites. These include Lagore, Co. Meath, rebuilt at various times between the seventh and tenth centuries, and Cró Inis, Co. Westmeath, initially constructed in the mid-ninth century with further occupation in the eleventh and early twelfth.[94]

Why was Llangorse crannog constructed in the late ninth century and how did it function? If the site is, indeed, unique, it may be argued that a political strategy lay behind it to enhance the status of the rulers of Brycheiniog. As a region of Irish settlement indicated by fifth- and sixth-century ogham-inscribed stones, it seems that elements of this identity were later revived (Chapter 4). As part of this, the construction of Llangorse crannog was emulating the continuing significance of such royal sites in Ireland, implying the importance of royal contacts across the Irish Sea. Indeed, one might speculate that the skills of an Irish crannog builder were imported to achieve it. The crannog was also part of a wider early medieval estate focused on the monastery of Llan-gors on the mainland nearby. As such it was probably one of several royal residences, in this case occupied most likely during the summer months to exploit its wider resources for hunting, feasting, and the patronage of craftworkers, as well as to provide a base for administrative functions. Its watery location would also have acted as a means of defence (Chapters 6, 7, and 12).

Rhuddlan is sited on a low bluff on the east bank of the Clwyd at its highest tidal and lowest fording points.[95] This highly strategic position, commanding both land and sea routes further west, is reflected in its complex and well-documented history as part of the contested border area of Tegeingl, which passed at intervals between Welsh and English control prior to the establishment of the castle and borough by

---

[93] On chronology: for Scotland, see Crone 1993; Barber and Crone 1993, and for excavated early medieval examples at Buiston, Ayrshire, see Crone 2000, and at Loch Glashan, Argyll, Crone and Campbell 2005. For Irish crannogs, see Edwards 1990, 34–41; O'Sullivan 1998, 101–50.

[94] Ibid., 113–15, 130–1, 136; Farrell 1991.   [95] Quinnell and Blockley 1994, 1.

Edward I in 1277. First mentioned in the Harleian Chronicle in 796 as the site of a battle, it may be identified as the *burh* of *Cledemutha* ('Clwydmouth'), founded in 921 by the English king Edward the Elder as part of a strategy to both stabilize north-west Mercia in the face of Hiberno-Scandinavian attack and establish a strategic foothold in north-east Wales.[96] However, by 1063 when it was burnt by Harold Godwinson, Rhuddlan was an important residence of Gruffudd ap Llywelyn of Gwynedd.[97] Evidence of early medieval habitation has been found north of the motte-and-bailey castle within the area of the Norman borough established in 1073. This includes part of a rectilinear structure defined by trenches with stake-holes in them, dated to before 900, and three sunken-floored buildings with artefacts of broadly tenth-century date. These were located just within the line of the Norman borough ditch. Although the phases of this are not closely datable, it has been argued that the earliest, which is aceramic, may relate to the *burh* and enclosed a comparatively small, curvilinear area west of the ford.[98] There is therefore no reason to think that the *burh* established by Edward the Elder in 921 was conceived as a planned military and economic centre on the scale of Cricklade or Wallingford in Wessex or that set up by Æthelflæd of Mercia in the ruins of Roman Chester.[99] Rather, it was a smaller fortified settlement guarding the river crossing in the manner of the *burh* at Runcorn,[100] and it may not have been occupied for long. Once back in Welsh control, it developed into a major *llys* ('court') associated with the rulers of Gwynedd.

Llanbedrgoch, Llangorse crannog, and Rhuddlan are therefore all elite settlements of great significance, but their uniqueness, as well as a failure to identify other examples and characteristic site types, continue to impede our understanding of wider changes in the pattern of settlement, economy, and society, both in the seventh century, as hillforts and promontory forts gave way to other forms of high-status site, and later.

FARMSTEADS

The problems associated with the identification and dating of the homes of the early medieval farming population should not detract from the significance of a slowly increasing number of radiocarbon-dated sites enabling us to begin to construct more

---

[96] Morris 1980, 47, 88, *s.a.* [797]; Whitelock 1979, *s.a.* 921, Mercian Register; Wainwright 1950.

[97] Douglas and Greenaway 1981, *s.a.* 1063; Davies, M. 2002, 230–4, 239–40.

[98] Quinnell and Blockley 1994, 10–16, 33–8, 59–65, 208–13.

[99] Following sections across the impressive 'Town Ditch' at Rhuddlan enclosing a roughly rectangular area of around 30 hectares with the river forming the western side, this was originally equated with the line of the *burh* defences (see Manley 1987), but this interpretation is no longer tenable (see Quinnell and Blockley 1994, 212–16).

[100] Griffiths 2010, 42–3.

160 LIFE IN EARLY MEDIEVAL WALES

accurate chronologies and reassess older excavations, making it more possible to discern characteristic forms and changes over time. There are, however, major differences in the amount of evidence from different regions of Wales. In the north-west, and to a lesser extent in the south-west, the still fragmentary evidence suggests a broader view of settlement change nonetheless. In the north-east and the borderlands, however, there is even less evidence, and in the south-east it remains almost non-existent, making it all the more difficult to detect wider regional similarities and differences over time.

In the north-west the *longue durée*, stretching from later prehistory through to the early Middle Ages, has been emphasized for both settlement forms and their locations.[101] It has also been argued that there is more evidence pointing to settlement continuity from the later Roman into the post-Roman period than in any other part of Wales (Chapter 3). A range of open and enclosed farming settlements has been recorded, with roundhouses dating from the later Bronze Age onwards and sometimes, from the Roman period, also with subrectangular buildings. Where excavation has taken place, there is evidence of timber- and clay-walled structures, with stone-built examples becoming more common over time. These settlements are concentrated in the more fertile coastal lowlands and the edges of the uplands of Snowdonia, with the majority below the 350-metre contour. The most recent study of their morphology indicates that open settlements are the most common and, from the Iron Age onwards, these become more nucleated. Most settlements have curvilinear enclosures and date to the Late Iron Age and Roman periods, but settlements with rectangular and polygonal enclosures also evolve as a result of the influence of Roman building traditions, though rectangular embanked enclosures, such as Bryn Eryr, Anglesey, are first found in the Middle to Late Iron Age.[102] Evidence of early medieval settlement has been identified across these categories but is mostly associated with earlier sites, thereby emphasizing the continuity of a sense of place within the wider farming landscape.

Settlements with early medieval evidence are concentrated in the more fertile lowlands of Anglesey and Caernarfonshire. Their absence in coastal Merioneth largely reflects the lack of developer-funded archaeology in this area. Although data remains very limited for the post-Roman centuries and the problems of chronology are exacerbated by the radiocarbon plateau at this time, some evidence is now emerging to suggest continuity in both settlement sites and structures. Nonetheless, in the absence of radiocarbon dates from older excavations, it remains difficult to determine to what extent open and enclosed farmsteads with late Roman ceramics, including shell-tempered ware, as at Din Lligwy and Caer Leb, Anglesey, continued into the post-Roman period and for how long. Equally, other artefacts are rare, though a Type F

[101] Waddington 2013, 10.   [102] Ibid., 40–51, fig. 3.2, pls 3.5–3.6.

penannular brooch was found at Porth Dafarch, Anglesey (Chapter 3).[103] However, it has also been plausibly suggested that, where there is an aceramic phase after the supply of Roman pottery ceased, as at Cae'r Mynydd and Cefn Graeanog 2, Caernarfonshire, this also signals continuing occupation into the post-Roman period, but without radiocarbon dates this remains impossible to resolve.[104]

Nevertheless, recent excavations at Dolbenmaen, Caernarfonshire, caught the edge of a settlement, revealing the gully of a wooden roundhouse alongside a four-post storage structure radiocarbon-dated to cal. AD 380–540, with a corn-dryer of similar date nearby. The combination of a roundhouse and a four-post structure, characteristic Iron Age forms that continued in Wales during the Roman period, is particularly interesting since it suggests that such structures were still being built into the post-Roman centuries.[105] At Tŷ Mawr, Anglesey, up to fifty roundhouses have been recorded on the lower, south-facing slopes below the hillfort on Holyhead Mountain. Some were excavated in the 1860s, others subsequently, and it has been argued that they represent a series of homesteads together spanning the Iron Age to the post-Roman period. Modern re-excavation of a multiphase, stone-built, curvilinear enclosure with two roundhouses and a square, post-built storage structure (Fig. 5.7, c) revealed the main period of occupation as Middle to Late Iron Age, but a radiocarbon date from charred plant remains on the floor of the smaller roundhouse (T1) also suggested early medieval activity on the site. This was confirmed by the excavation of two early medieval stone structures close by—a small, somewhat angular, roundhouse (T3) and part of a subrectangular building (T4), both of which were associated with an earlier field boundary. Radiocarbon dates together indicate occupation sometime during the fifth to ninth centuries AD but are broadly focused on the sixth.[106]

Other evidence for this period appears even more ephemeral and the sites concerned have been identified as a result of radiocarbon-dated metalworking and crop-processing evidence, mainly associated with earlier settlement sites. At Pant on the Llŷn peninsula, for example, at least three timber- and clay-walled roundhouses were dated to the Late Iron Age and Roman period. However, one of these demonstrated a late phase of copper-working, probably when the structure was falling into ruin, and this was radiocarbon-dated to the sixth or seventh centuries AD. In light of this, the adjacent roundhouse could also be early medieval, since the only dating evidence from it is an abraded sherd of Samian pottery.[107] Much larger-scale excavations on a fertile ridge overlooking the Menai Strait at Llandygái, Caernarfonshire, revealed a multiperiod settlement and ritual landscape stretching back into the Neolithic, and on

---

[103] Ibid., 172–4.   [104] Edwards and Lane 1988, 31; Fasham et al. 1998, 9–12, 28–9, 33.

[105] Kenney and McNicol 2017, 59–61; McNicol et al. 2017, 379, 381 (SUERC 68324, 68,325, 70,637, 70,638).

[106] Smith, C. 1985; 1987; Waddington 2013, 158–60.

[107] Ward and Smith 2001, 55–74; Waddington 2013, 238–9.

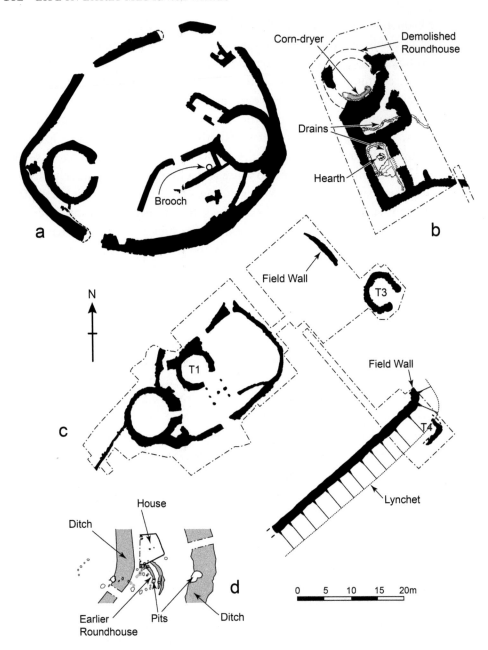

Fig. 5.7. Farmsteads with evidence of early medieval occupation: a. Pant-y-Saer; b. Graeanog East; c. Tŷ Mawr; d. Conkland Hill (after Waddington 2013, figs 6.18, 6.53, 6.19; Hart 2014).

the eastern side those at Parc Bryn Cegin included both open and enclosed wooden roundhouse settlements, together spanning the Iron Age and Roman periods. However, there is also early medieval activity in the form of iron-smithing and charred plant remains overlying and adjacent to an isolated Early Iron Age roundhouse.

Features included post-holes indicative of a structure, and this phase was radiocarbon-dated to between the later sixth and later seventh century AD. Even if this was not the homestead itself, there would certainly have been habitation in the immediate vicinity, since there was also at least one early medieval cemetery nearby.[108] In addition, isolated hearths and hearth pits which may be all that is left of domestic activity are also sometimes found, as at Afon Wen, Caernarfonshire, which was radiocarbon-dated to cal. AD 390–650, and Penmynydd, Anglesey, similarly dated to cal. AD 340–630.[109]

From around the later seventh century onwards, however, there is slowly accumulating evidence from sites with scientific dating that roundhouses and four-post storage structures were no longer being constructed and subrectangular buildings with stone footings or of post-hole construction were becoming the norm. Many of these were still closely associated with earlier sites, but new open settlements of scattered subrectangular buildings were also being established with associated field systems.

Rhuddgaer (Fig. 5.8) is key to this argument as it provides an excellent example in this region of the creation of a new open farming settlement with no apparent evidence of earlier occupation, since the Roman-period habitation was focused on a subrectangular earthen enclosure some 600 metres north-east. The settlement overlooks the Menai Strait close to the mouth of the Braint with wide views across the mountains of Snowdonia beyond. Geophysics revealed a succession of field systems. The earliest was clearly associated with eight subrectangular buildings of similar size, each about 14 metres long by 7 metres wide, including a central group and one contained within a rectangular yard. Excavation of one of these revealed the sturdily built stone footings of a subrectangular building, presumably a dwelling, measuring externally 12.2 metres long by 7.4 metres wide (Fig. 5.10, b) with opposed doorways in the two long walls. The south-west corner was conjoined with a field boundary. The floor level did not survive except in the south-eastern doorway which had subsequently been blocked, and a grain deposit on this floor produced a radiocarbon date of cal. AD 660–770. There was, however, also evidence for a less substantial, earlier phase visible in the south-east corner, where it partially underlies the building.[110] The discovery of this settlement, though so far unique, nevertheless offers the prospect of identification of others in the fertile lowlands of this region.

Others remained closely associated with earlier settlements as, for example, on the Graeanog ridge, but precise dating can still be a problem. At Graeanog East, after Mid to Late Iron Age and Roman-period occupation, there was at least one phase of early medieval use (Fig. 5.7, b). An earlier roundhouse was demolished, but the associated subrectangular annexe was retained, with a larger rectangular dwelling built onto it.

---

[108] Kenney 2008, 106–8, 131–2, figs 3, 21, 34, and the dates have been the subject of Bayesian analysis. For the cemeteries, see Lynch and Musson 2001, 106–15; Driver 2006, 147.

[109] Berks et al. 2007, 7, fig. 2; Cuttler et al. 2012, 100, 102, fig. 5.3.

[110] Hopewell and Edwards 2017. The Rhuddgaer lead coffin was also found nearby (Chapter 4).

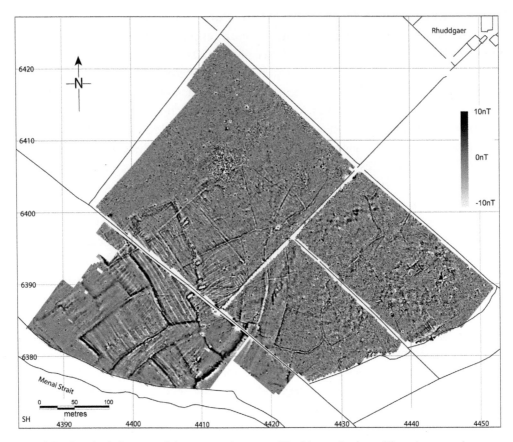

Fig. 5.8. Geophysical survey of the open settlement at Rhuddgaer, Anglesey. The subrectangular structures are associated with fields, and the excavated building is just to the left of the modern field boundary (© Gwynedd Archaeological Trust).

The Roman pottery in this phase was regarded as residual and an archaeomagnetic sample for the last firing of the hearth was dated to cal. AD 500–900. A corn-dryer was later set into the remains of the earlier roundhouse, probably towards the end of the early Middle Ages, and some other minor alterations were made.[111] Recent excavations nearby have also revealed what may be a new settlement with complexes of features, probably buildings, associated with ironworking radiocarbon-dated to between the late seventh and late ninth century AD.[112]

Graeanog East may be compared with Cefn Du, where a nucleated roundhouse group of Mid Iron Age and Roman date also has early medieval occupation. A charcoal-rich layer produced evidence of malting radiocarbon-dated to cal. AD 390–720, associated with a length of stone walling and a stone spread, most likely all that is left

---

[111] Fasham et al. 1998, 120–48. For an alternative view of the dating of Phase III, see Waddington 2013, 228–30.

[112] Young 2015a.

of a rectilinear building. A rotary quern was found on the floor but there is no other dating evidence. This phase may also be associated with the deliberate infilling of one of the earlier roundhouses with stones and stone artefacts, including further quern-stones. Finally, a corn-dryer was constructed utilizing part of the wall of the earlier structure. This was radiocarbon-dated to cal. AD 1000–1280.[113]

In other instances, the lack of radiocarbon dates means that we are forced to rely on rare discoveries of early medieval artefacts likewise associated with open and enclosed settlements that were undoubtedly occupied at an earlier date. While such finds could be interpreted as later casual losses, if we accept that there were frequently several phases of occupation and rebuilding on such sites, this may well have extended into the post-Roman period. Pant-y-Saer, Anglesey, excavated in the 1930s, provides a good example (Fig. 5.7, a). This stone-walled, curvilinear, enclosed settlement has two roundhouses, one with two later rectangular conjoined annexes and other stray walls, indicating multiple phases of rebuilding. Briquetage from salt containers and abraded sherds of pottery demonstrate settlement in the later Iron Age and Roman period respectively. A phase of early medieval occupation may also be suggested since a probably seventh-century penannular brooch was discovered in fill close to the wall inside the larger rectangular annexe—a substantial structure which, at around 11 metres × 3.5 metres, would have been large enough to function as a dwelling.[114]

Other buildings were more ephemeral. On a hilltop at Carrog, Anglesey, the site of a Late Bronze or Early Iron Age curvilinear, enclosed settlement was also reused in the early Middle Ages. The enclosure was partly demolished and the exterior ditch infilled to create a platform on which to build a rectangular house with fragmentary stone wall footings, though only one corner was revealed in the excavation (Fig. 5.10, e). This was radiocarbon-dated to cal. AD 760–900 and associated artefacts included a rotary quernstone, a possible stone loom weight, and a yellow glass bead.[115]

At the very end of the early Middle Ages, however, there is some evidence of a return to the construction of enclosed settlements, suggesting an increased need for defence, though it is also likely to have been a mark of status. Close to the Menai Strait at Llanfairpwll, Anglesey, aerial photography and geophysical survey revealed a subcircular enclosure 40 metres in diameter. No bank survived but exploratory exca-vations indicated that the external ditch was up to 5.2 metres wide and 1.8 metres deep with post-holes and a beam-slot in the entrance showing the existence of a hefty wooden gate. Unfortunately, the interior was not investigated, though some domestic refuse was found in the ditch. Radiocarbon dating indicated that the settlement was built and occupied *c.* AD 1025–1170. As a result, it has been compared with the

---

[113] Cuttler et al. 2012, 19–20, 25–6, fig. 2.22, 228–31; Waddington 2013, 108–10, 163–5 (Wk-9273, 9275).

[114] Phillips 1934, figs 3, 4, 7; Waddington 2013, 155–6; Edwards 2008, 154–5.

[115] Smith, G. H. 2014.

166 LIFE IN EARLY MEDIEVAL WALES

broadly contemporary habitation of promontory forts elsewhere in the region at Castell Trefadog and Hen Gastell (Llanwnda) (see below).[116]

Our understanding of settlement forms in the post-Roman centuries in south-west Wales remains poor, improving somewhat from around the eighth century onwards. In other cases we are seeing evidence of crop-processing rather than the discovery of the settlements themselves. In this region, although a few open settlements are now being recognized, small enclosed farmsteads upwards of 30 metres in diameter became characteristic during the Late Iron Age and, it has been argued, these persisted into the post-Roman period. These lowland settlements were concentrated on hilltops and valley sides and, in contrast to the north-west where building in stone was common, the enclosures mostly have earthen banks with exterior ditches. They are largely curvilinear with some later rectilinear examples and have both wooden roundhouses and rectangular four- and six-post storage structures, though some stone buildings are also apparent.[117]

To date evidence of early medieval settlements in this region is focused almost entirely on the lowlands of Pembrokeshire, with only occasional discoveries elsewhere. The radiocarbon dating of corn-dryers and associated crop-processing evidence occasionally hints at occupation in the post-Roman centuries. For example, at Brynwgan, Carmarthenshire, where an undated probable enclosed settlement was located, a nearby corn-dryer had radiocarbon dates focusing on the fifth and sixth centuries AD.[118] Otherwise, as already indicated (Chapter 3), Late Iron Age and Roman curvilinear enclosed farmsteads, as at Dan-y-Coed and Drim near Llawhaden, Pembrokeshire, probably also had early medieval occupation, but the evidence is fragmentary and the radiocarbon dating insecure. The most significant evidence at Dan-y-Coed was the remains of a late subsquare, stone-walled building with a stone floor and possible hearth located in a slight hollow in the north-eastern part of the enclosure. Roman pottery from beneath the structure was regarded as residual.[119] At Drim, a probably sixth-century Type G penannular brooch was found, and a post-hole at one end of a slot has been radiocarbon-dated to cal. AD 630–880 and interpreted as part of the wall of a wattle roundhouse.[120] This raises the possibility that the construction of roundhouses continued longer in this region than in the north-west. Indeed, at Maenclochog, Pembrokeshire, trial excavations revealed the arc of a double-walled wattle roundhouse which could be associated with a bank and ditch enclosure located underneath the twelfth-century castle. A radiocarbon sample from the likely central hearth in the structure gave a remarkably late date of cal. AD 980–1160, with a second date from under the bank of cal. AD 880–1020.[121]

---

[116] Smith, G. H. 2012b, SUERC 37186–37188.

[117] For general discussions, see Murphy and Mytum 2011; Murphy 2016, 227–64.

[118] Brannlund 2013.   [119] Williams, George, and Mytum 1998, 50–2, structure VIII.

[120] Ibid., 62–3, 88–9, fig. 51 (CAR-473).

[121] Schlee 2007; 2008 (Beta-24028, Beta-24029); Seaman 2016, 48.

There are also hints of post-Roman coastal settlements in this region as, for example, at Linney Burrows, Pembrokeshire, where a Type G penannular brooch was found together with a sherd of imported E ware pottery and a comb.[122] Similarly, at Twlc Point, Llangennith, Gower, an area of blown sand with a buried land surface and shell middens, both Roman artefacts and a Type G1 penannular brooch came to light.[123]

As with Rhuddgaer in the north-west, there is now evidence in this region for the establishment of open farming settlements during the second half of the period. The primary example is South Hook, sited on a south-facing slope overlooking the shore of Milford Haven. The truncated archaeological remains (Fig. 5.9) consisted of complexes of features, including hollows, several of which indicated slightly sunken-floored structures. One of these (6) was better preserved (Fig. 5.10, d) revealing a

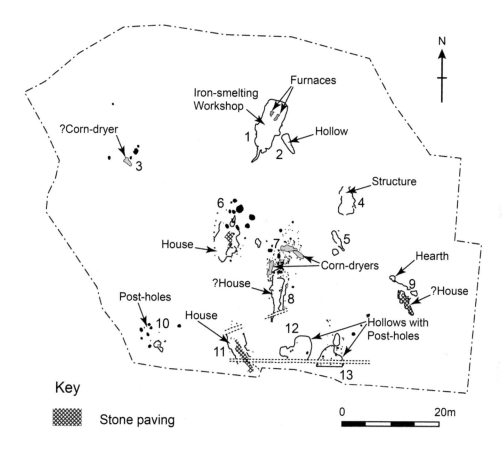

FIG. 5.9. Excavated remains of an open settlement at South Hook, showing houses, corn-dryers, and an iron-smelting workshop (after Crane and Murphy 2010b, fig. 2).

---

[122] Campbell and Lane 1993, 33; Redknap 1995a, 64.
[123] Penniman 1936; Edwards and Lane 1988, 117; see also penannular brooches from similar locations at Llanmadog, Gower, and Kenfig, Glamorgan; Redknap 1995a, 64; 2007a, 70–1, nos 4, 10.

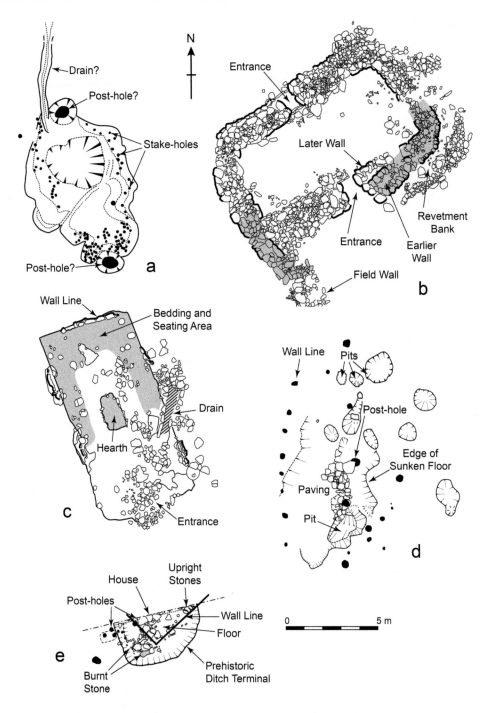

Fig. 5.10. Building plans: a. Rhuddlan; b. Rhuddgaer; c. Llanbedrgoch; d. South Hook; e. Carrog (after Quinnell and Blockley 1994, fig. 3.1; Hopewell and Edwards 2017, fig. 6; Redknap 2000, illus. 108; Crane and Murphy 2010b, fig. 3; Smith, G. H. 2014, fig. 2.5).

slightly bow-sided, post-and-wattle house around 9 metres long by 5 metres wide with a stone-paved floor. It may have been of more than one phase. A charcoal rich layer associated with the paving was radiocarbon-dated to cal. AD 720–960. Further complexes of hollows, pits, and post-holes were also recognizable as dwellings. The economic mainstays of the settlement were both iron-smelting and agriculture, since both furnaces and corn-dryers, as well as rotary quernstones, were found, but no associated fields survived. Overall, the radiocarbon dates show that the settlement was established around the late eighth century with a *floruit* in the ninth to eleventh.[124]

At South Hook there is some evidence of prehistoric activity, but other farming settlements involved in ironworking were clearly constructed on top of older sites, as at Conkland Hill, Wiston (Fig. 5.7, d), which is comparable with Carrog on Anglesey. Here aerial photography revealed a complex series of enclosures on the south-west-facing slope. Limited excavation in advance of a pipeline uncovered two concentric ditches relating to an enclosed settlement and a timber-built circular structure of Late Iron Age and early Roman date. Evidence for early medieval reoccupation consisted of the partial remains of a subrectangular, sunken-floored building, together with a variety of pits and post-holes. The building was radiocarbon-dated to cal. AD 810–1010, though other pits with crop-processing debris indicate slightly earlier activity as well.[125] Whether this was a single farmstead or part of a larger settlement, as at South Hook, is not, however, known. Elsewhere, structures of some kind have been located but are too ephemeral to attempt further interpretation, as, for example, at Castell Cadw, Felindre Farchog, Pembrokeshire, where a few post-holes were found together with a pit radiocarbon-dated to cal. AD 890–1020. The continuing discovery of corn-dryers, as at Newton, Llanstadwell, Pembrokeshire, one of which was radiocarbon-dated to cal. AD 690–970, also points to settlement nearby.[126]

In the north-east and central borderlands of Wales evidence of early medieval farming settlements is extremely limited, and this is equally true in Shropshire, though the number in Cheshire is now growing.[127] In this region of Wales the lack of early medieval settlements in part reflects the fact that so little archaeological investigation has taken place on what are presumed to be later prehistoric and Roman-period rural sites except in the upper Severn valley. As we have seen, in this area such settlements are characterized by curvilinear (or sometimes rectilinear) enclosures, with one or more banks and ditches, and, as indicated by excavations at Collfryn, Montgomeryshire, these contained timber- and clay-walled roundhouses and four-post storage structures. This type of settlement also extends eastwards across the Cheshire and Shropshire plains (Chapter 3). Nevertheless, examples of the early medieval use or reuse of such

---

[124] Crane and Murphy 2010b (Beta-222360).
[125] Hart 2014 (Beta-249349); Murphy 2016, 239–41; Darvill et al. 2020, 111–13, figs 7.6–7.7.
[126] Crane 2008a (Beta-239950); 2008b; 2004; Comeau and Burrow 2021a, 136, no. 10 (Beta-182946).
[127] On Shropshire, see White in press; on the lowlands of north-west England, see Philpott 2015, 110–16.

170   LIFE IN EARLY MEDIEVAL WALES

sites and the identification of other characteristic settlement types have proved elusive, with the result that chronological markers are very difficult to discern.

Arddleen, however, is one example of the early medieval reuse of a late prehistoric and Roman-period enclosed settlement. The site, which overlooks the floodplain of the Severn, was located by aerial photography, which recorded the crop-marks of a curvilinear, double-ditched enclosure around 100 metres in diameter. Although the site was heavily damaged by ploughing, partial excavation revealed a roundhouse and a possible four-post structure indicating occupation similar to Collfryn nearby. Early medieval reuse was demonstrated by two recuts to the outer ditch, the earliest of which was radiocarbon-dated to between the mid-seventh and mid-ninth century AD, but no contemporary interior structures were recognized.[128] This may also have happened elsewhere in the region as in the north-west and south-west, and use and reuse of earlier sites are also a feature of early medieval settlements in lowland north-west England, as at Irby on Wirral.[129] The only other settlement evidence from this region is also from the upper Severn valley, from underneath the rampart of the motte-and-bailey castle at Hen Domen. In the northern half of the bailey two post-built rectilinear structures partially underlay the rampart, one of which was interpreted as a domestic structure, most likely of early medieval date.[130]

The picture is equally unclear in the southern borderlands of Radnorshire and Herefordshire, though continuity of place would also seem to be important. Capel Maelog, Radnorshire (Fig. 10.5), provides an interesting example of intermittent or continuous settlement and agricultural activities spanning the late Roman and post-Roman centuries on a site later used as a cemetery, though the exact nature of the occupation is now difficult to deduce. The earliest evidence from the site, which is on a hillslope overlooking a stream, consisted of a subrectangular ditched enclosure around 18 metres in diameter with later Roman pottery and a radiocarbon date of cal. AD 330–600 from the primary fill, but no bank or internal structures survived. To the east was a curvilinear ditch with radiocarbon dates suggesting sixth- and seventh-century activity, and to the west curvilinear gullies indicated timber- and clay-walled roundhouses, one of which was radiocarbon-dated to cal. AD 390–650, and another to cal. AD 600–780, pointing to the continuation of earlier settlement forms.[131] Only two early medieval settlements have so far been noted in Herefordshire, both south of the Wye and therefore probably originally in Ergyng. Rotherwas consisted of at least one ditched enclosure with seventh-century radiocarbon dates, whilst nearby Bullinghope was made up of a cluster of pits, ditches, and other features dated to the

---

[128] Grant 2004.   [129] Philpott 2015, 110–13.

[130] Barker and Higham 1982, 26–9; Higham and Barker 2000, 25–34. Nearby timber buildings outside Forden Gaer Roman fort and at Dyffryn Lane, Berriw, were originally thought to be early medieval on analogy with timber halls in England. Radiocarbon dates have now identified the former as Roman; Blockley 1990; Archwilio CPAT prn 4086; Kevin Blockley (pers. comm.); the latter is probably Neolithic, Gibson 1995, 54–6.

[131] Britnell 1990, 32–4 (CAR-1080, CAR-1974, CAR-1077).

eighth or ninth centuries on the strength of the artefactual assemblage which included a bun-shaped loom weight and a linen smoother.[132]

The problems of identifying early medieval settlements in south-east Wales have already been noted. Nevertheless, it is likely that, as elsewhere, occupation of some rural settlements persisted into the post-Roman period, with early medieval farmsteads focused on areas with fertile, free-draining soils, including the Vale of Glamorgan and the coastal lowlands of Gwent. In the former, Andy Seaman's study of Dinas Powys hundred has demonstrated that both Roman and later medieval settlements were concentrated on free-draining soils suitable for crops but also with easy access to less productive land for pasture. Moreover, it is only in the later Middle Ages that there is evidence of rural settlement on more marginal land. Therefore, early medieval farmsteads were also most likely concentrated in areas of Roman and later medieval settlement and this is where we need to look for them, even though these are the areas of heaviest later cultivation leading to the destruction of ephemeral settlement evidence. There is, however, no evidence of when the expansion onto less free-draining soils began—either during the long eighth century as a result of increasing agricultural production or, more likely, towards the end of the period when, as the climate improved, there is evidence for increasing utilization of more marginal uplands as well.[133]

The only lower-status settlement so far identified in the whole of this region is overlooking the sea at Cold Knap, Barry, where the ruins of a probable late third-century Roman *mansio* were later reoccupied. According to the excavators, sherds of shell-tempered jars and other late Roman pottery indicated the final demolition of the building in the later fourth century. However, rubble spreads filled large areas of the building, with reoccupation indicated by alterations to the remains of the original structure, drystone walling, and rough stone paving, though no early medieval artefacts were recognized. Dating evidence is sparse, but in one room in the west range animal bone was radiocarbon-dated to the seventh to ninth centuries AD, while in the courtyard bone from rubble associated with a small, subrectangular, drystone structure had a radiocarbon date focused on the mid-ninth to mid-eleventh centuries AD.[134]

Therefore, although our understanding of early medieval farmsteads is gradually improving, largely as a result of more accurate radiocarbon dating, we still have a very long way to go. In the north-west the investigation of stone-walled buildings has certainly enabled a more detailed picture to emerge, and this is complemented by more fragmentary evidence from the south-west, where wooden buildings were more common. In both regions there are growing indications of the continuity of use of lowland landscapes with fertile soils from later prehistory through the Roman period and on through the early Middle Ages. It is also evident that early medieval

---

[132] Blair 2018, 163, 292, n. 46; Mann and Vaughan 2008; Shoesmith 2008, 123.
[133] Seaman 2010b.   [134] Evans, E. M. et al. 1985; Edwards and Lane 1988, 76–8.

172   LIFE IN EARLY MEDIEVAL WALES

settlements continued to use or reuse earlier farmsteads or shifted only a short distance, as on the free-draining soils of the Graeanog ridge. However, with the extensive excavations at South Hook and more limited explorations at Rhuddgaer, we can also propose a new development from around the late seventh century onwards, which suggests that new open farming settlements with clusters of subrectangular buildings were also being established. However, in the eastern half of Wales and the borderlands of England, although there are some hints of similar processes at work, we currently have insufficient archaeological evidence to be sure.[135] Therefore, to confirm the trend suggested here and make more breakthroughs in our understanding, once potential early medieval farmsteads are recognized, more extensive archaeological investigations with sufficient radiocarbon dates are required to recover the often ephemeral remains and to produce well-dated sequences in all regions of Wales to enable comparison of settlement morphologies and chronological developments more fully.

BUILDINGS AND THE USE OF SPACE

The excavation of a range of early medieval settlement sites, both high- and low-status, also enables some consideration of building types and construction materials, as well as internal and external use of space. As already indicated, in later prehistory roundhouses were the norm and persisted as dwellings during the Roman period when rectilinear buildings were also introduced and had varying amounts of influence on the architecture of native farmsteads (Chapter 3). It has also been argued that the construction of roundhouses continued into the early Middle Ages and may have endured as an architectural form in some instances into the eighth century, as at Capel Maelog, or possibly even later if the radiocarbon date from Maenclochog has been correctly attributed to the structure concerned. During the sixth and seventh centuries, however, subrectangular buildings were being used as elite dwellings, as indicated by those at Dinas Powys, as well as for other purposes, as at Longbury Bank. Later they become increasingly common, as, for example, at South Hook, Rhuddgaer, and Llanbedrgoch. A change from round to rectangular buildings is evident in Ireland from around the ninth century and has recently been linked to agricultural expansion; a more general trend has likewise been noted in Scotland, particularly on elite sites, but also the seventh- to ninth-century, subrectangular, byre-houses at Pitcarmick, Perthshire.[136] In England, there are also hints of this process in the seventh century as far east as Quarrington, Lincolnshire, where roundhouses were replaced with rectangular

---

[135] On the ephemeral evidence for similar farming settlements in parts of northern and western England, including the west Midlands, see Blair 2018, 156–63.

[136] Edwards 1990, 26–7; Jones, I. 2013; O'Sullivan et al. 2014, 92–3; Foster 2004, 56; Carver 2019, 212–13.

buildings. Whilst some continuity of Roman-period rural architectural forms is likely, especially in the west and north, in the south and east rectangular buildings with earth-fast posts may have incorporated features of both native and wider north-west European traditions. John Blair has also shown that in the east from the seventh century onwards the latter become more significant, whilst elsewhere the continuation and reassertion of more ephemeral native traditions seem more apparent.[137]

Most buildings in Wales were of wood and other perishable materials, leaving behind only complexes of features such as post-holes, stake-holes, pits, and gullies, making it difficult to recover plans, and more than one phase of building is sometimes evident. It is only in the north-west where environmental factors led to the construction of buildings with stone footings giving them increased longevity that more evidence has survived. Floor levels are likewise seldom preserved, making it harder to determine how buildings were used and in some instances how their functions changed over time.

If the post-Roman roundhouse (T3) at Tŷ Mawr, Holyhead Mountain (Fig. 5.7, c), is anything to go by, such buildings were small. It was internally about 4 metres in diameter with stone footings over a metre thick made up of drystone facings and a rubble core, a characteristic form of construction in north-west Wales over a long period. The superstructure is more difficult to determine, but the broad stone footings make low turf walls more likely. The wooden roof supports probably rested on the tops of these and it is likely that the roof was thatched with reeds or straw. In the interior, part of a stone-edged hearth was excavated, not in the centre but on the southern periphery, possibly indicating secondary use. As is most common with roundhouses, the entrance faced south-east to make the best of the daylight within, but the unusually large width may indicate either collapse or change of use, possibly from a dwelling to a workshop, as the structure deteriorated. It may have been in use contemporaneously with the nearby fragmentary subrectangular building with similar stone footings and a succession of hearths near the centre of the interior suggesting domestic occupation.[138]

Where likely early medieval wood- and clay-walled roundhouses have been identified, the remains amount to little more than a fragmentary wall gully, as at Dolbenmaen and Capel Maelog. However, if the dating is correct, Maenclochog is an important exception, since here the arc of a double-walled roundhouse was found with posts set into a gully on the outside and stakes on the inside, together with a central hearth; further stake-holes suggest bedding areas against the wall. Roundhouses of broadly this type are found in Wales from the Iron Age but are also characteristic of early

[137] Blair 2018, 35–51. Hamerow 2012, 18–24, has, however, emphasized the influence of the north-west European building tradition from the outset in the east and south.

[138] Smith, C. 1985, 36–41. For more general discussion of roundhouse size, construction materials, and entrance orientation, see Waddington 2013, 56–60.

174 LIFE IN EARLY MEDIEVAL WALES

medieval Ireland. Waterlogged examples of eighth-century date at Deer Park Farms, Co. Antrim, have preserved double walls of woven hazel with an insulation layer of organic material between them, and in some instances clay weatherproofing to the exterior. It has also been suggested that the uprights were bent and brought together to form a conical roof which could then be thatched.[139]

Domestic buildings in Wales continued to be modest throughout the period, even on high-status sites, and the use of substantial earth-fast posts is rare. This contrasts not only with the later fifth- or sixth-century large timber hall at South Cadbury, Somerset, but also with traditions of wooden buildings with earth-fast posts exemplified by the 'great hall complexes' found in Atcham, Shropshire, and other parts of northern, central, and south-eastern England in the seventh century.[140] Indeed, Llanbedrgoch provides the only possible evidence so far for a post-built, aisled, timber hall in Wales in the pre-Viking period or later,[141] though there is probably a smaller post-built structure (IA) around 8 metres × 10 metres in the earliest phase at Dinas Powys. Instead, subrectangular buildings constructed in other ways became the characteristic form. At Dinas Powys, although only the slightly curving eaves-drip gullies survived from structures of later sixth- or seventh-century date, this was enough to suggest the existence of two subrectangular buildings (IB, II) set at right-angles to each other with dimensions of around 8 metres × 15 metres and 7 metres × 12 metres respectively, and artefact distributions suggest domestic functions for them both.[142] Indeed, their superstructures, as well as furnishings and fittings, may have been considerably more sophisticated than the surviving structural evidence suggests.[143]

During the second half of the period subrectangular, slightly sunken-floored, post-and-wattle buildings that may also have incorporated other perishable materials such as turf and cob are identifiable as a distinct form in the south-west at South Hook, Conkland Hill, and probably Dan-y-Coed. At South Hook four complexes of features may be interpreted as dwellings, sometimes of more than one phase, though it is possible that others were later utilized as workshops for iron-smelting or for crop-processing as they fell into decay. Building 6, radiocarbon-dated to between the early eighth and mid-tenth century AD, was the best preserved (Fig. 5.10, d). Small post-holes delineated the uprights of the wattle walls of a slightly bow-shaped building measuring around 11 metres north–south by 6 metres east–west, with the entrance most likely at the southern end. The interior was hollowed to a maximum depth of 0.3 metres and at one stage in its use was partially paved with evidence of overlying occupation debris. It was suggested that larger post-holes underlying the paving might have been supports for a ridge pole, which, in an earlier phase, had held up the

[139] Schlee 2008, 6–7, 9–10, fig. 4, pls 11, 16; Lynn and McDowell 2011, 119–86, 433–46, 593–602.
[140] Alcock 1995, 30–41, 120; Blair 2018, 114–25.   [141] Redknap 2000, illus. 109; 2004a, 148.
[142] Campbell 1991, 101; 2007a, 99.
[143] For discussion in connection with Anglo-Saxon wooden buildings, see Blair 2018, 51–67.

roof which otherwise rested directly on the walls. In Buildings 9 and 11 stone flooring was the most obvious feature, with a paved entrance passage to the south-east. In both buildings a reused quernstone had been embedded in the paving, with possible plough pebbles likewise reused in Buildings 8 and 11.[144] This could signal ritual deposition, linking the home to the annual cycle of cultivation and harvest; similar practices have also been noted in early medieval houses in Ireland.[145]

It is not easy to tell whether the three subrectangular, sunken-floored buildings at Rhuddlan are a form that might be expected more widely in the north-east or are a product of Anglo-Saxon occupation. However, the largest and best preserved (S1) (Fig. 5.10, a) has more in common with those at South Hook than with the rectangular, post-built, cellared buildings found in tenth- and eleventh-century Chester and other towns in England.[146] It consisted of an irregular hollow around 10 metres × 5.5 metres and up to 1.2 metres deep, with traces of clay and a large number of stake-holes indicating wattle walls. A rounded depression at either end of the structure was thought to have held a post supporting the ridge pole holding up the roof. Artefacts indicated a tenth-century date and pieces of antler suggest that it functioned as a workshop, and this may also be true of the other smaller, less sunken examples since one contained a loom weight.[147]

In the north-west subrectangular buildings with stone footings or with some stone in the foundations seem characteristic, though surviving examples demonstrate considerable variety. The house at Graeanog East (Fig. 5.7, b), which measured 10 metres × 4 metres internally, was built onto a subrectangular roundhouse annexe, indicating its roots in an earlier, Roman-period building tradition. The walls, up to 2 metres thick and 0.7 metres high, had drystone facings with a rubble core and may originally have been higher so as to support the roof timbers resting directly on top of them. The wide entrance in the centre of the long wall faced broadly east onto a farmyard and was probably the only source of daylight within, while in the interior a peripheral stone-capped drain exited through a culvert in the opposite wall. The northern end had a central stone hearth, the last firing of which was archaeomagnetically dated between the sixth and ninth centuries AD. This surely acted as the focus for

[144] Crane and Murphy 2010b, 122–45.

[145] Quernstones were also incorporated into corn-dryers; Waddington 2013, 111. On Ireland, see O'Sullivan et al. 2014, 98–100. In England placed deposits are associated, not with dwellings, but with sunken-floored buildings, some of which were used for storage, making a connection with the fertility of the soil; Hamerow 2012, 139–40.

[146] Griffiths 2010, 131; Mason, D. J. P. 2007, 100–10; 1985, 6–7; Ward, S. W. 1994, 38–40, 61–3. The Rhuddlan buildings appear somewhat closer to Early and Middle Saxon *Grubenhäuser*, an example of which has been found at Moreton, Cheshire, than to Late Saxon sunken-floored buildings; Philpott 2015, 114–15. On the differences between the two, see Tipper 2004, 12–14.

[147] Quinnell and Blockley 1994, 12–14, 34–6, fig. 4.2.

176 LIFE IN EARLY MEDIEVAL WALES

cooking and domestic life, while the stone floor surface in the southern part suggests a different purpose, possibly storage.[148]

The building at Rhuddgaer (Fig. 5.10, b), which had at least two phases and was radiocarbon-dated to between the later seventh and later eighth centuries AD, was also remarkably sturdy and of a similar size. However, here the stone walls with their earth and rubble core were interpreted as the footings for walls in another medium, most likely turf, thereby keeping rising damp at bay. Again, the roof timbers probably rested on the walls but, as no clear floor levels survived, no post-holes or post-pads were found to indicate further supports, essential if the roof was of turf rather than of reeds or straw. Interestingly, this building has quite narrow entrances in both long walls so the doors could be opened or closed according to the direction of the wind. Such opposing entrances would also have made the best use of daylight within, while the discovery of a probable stone oil lamp suggests how it was lit at night. The comparatively small interior and lack of drains indicate that the cross-passage is unlikely to have separated the human living space from a byre in the manner of a longhouse, and it is more likely that one end acted as a store. In the final phase, however, the south-east entrance was blocked and, after the roof collapsed, was probably used as an animal shelter.[149]

At least five late ninth- or tenth-century rectangular buildings are known from Llanbedrgoch, but their more ephemeral remains point to a different building tradition. The best-preserved was the first phase of a house (Building 1) measuring internally about 10.5 metres × 5 metres with the entrance at the southern end (Fig. 5.10, c). A fragmentary line of stones survived, delineating the perimeter of the building, and these provided the foundations for the walls which, it was suggested, were of sill-beam construction, thereby demonstrating increasing sophistication,[150] but this seems unlikely as it is a later medieval construction technique[151] and the form of the superstructure is unknown. The floor was slightly sunken and partially paved, with considerable evidence of occupation debris. In the centre was a slightly bowed, subrectangular, stone-kerbed hearth with bedding and sitting areas set against the walls towards the northern end.[152] The method of construction may be similar to the fragmentary building at Carrog (Fig. 5.10, e) suggesting a local building tradition. However, the form of the hearth and the associated bedding and sitting areas are characteristic, for example, of waterlogged houses of this size in Hiberno-Scandinavian Dublin, but these are of post-and-wattle construction. Indeed, only one building more similar to that at Llanbedrgoch is known from Dublin and is dated to the mid or late eleventh century.[153] Thus, it seems likely that the buildings at

---

[148] Fasham et al. 1998, 127–9.   [149] Hopewell and Edwards 2017, 220–9, 232–3.

[150] Redknap 2004a, 151–2. Low drystone footings are more evident for some of the other buildings.

[151] John Blair (pers. comm.).   [152] Redknap 2004a, 151–3.

[153] Smith, G. H. 2014, 60–1; Wallace 2016, 79–89; Murray 1983, 94–7.

Llanbedrgoch were of a local type with possible internal adaptations to Hiberno-Scandinavian ways of living.

The waterlogged conditions at Llangorse crannog have meant that, uniquely in Wales, timbers have survived with the potential to cast significant light on the construction of buildings in the late ninth and early tenth centuries here and on other sites with access to substantial amounts of timber (Chapter 7). Amongst reused planks in the palisade were some with notches, enabling them to be slotted together at the corners to form interlocking laftwork structures. This form of walling, which requires almost nothing in the way of foundations, was traditionally very common in Scandinavia from the Viking period onwards and in Eastern Europe but is also evident in the final, tenth-century phase of the royal crannog at Lagore in Ireland, suggesting that the technique may have been widely used at this time.[154]

The rectangular house at Castell Trefadog probably dates to a century or so later and demonstrates definite improvements in construction techniques, which were clearly necessary for the exposed position of the promontory fort in which it was located. Though of a similar size to earlier buildings, the stone wall facings were now bonded with clay, which was likewise used to fill the cavity between them. Clay floors also survived in part of the building together with a round stone hearth and an elaborate system of drains to keep the dwelling warm and dry.[155]

Therefore, our understanding of some regional building types and wider changes over time is gradually increasing. We can now identify individual houses and analyse their life cycles and internal use of space, but there is still much that we do not understand concerning the wider use of space within the settlement. This is because only a very small number of settlements have been more extensively excavated, with the emphasis on high-status sites. At Dinas Powys (Fig. 5.11), Ewan Campbell's analysis of artefact distributions demonstrated that both buildings (IB, II) were dwellings as they were associated with eating and drinking, but in 1B 'clean' crafts—spinning and weaving—were also being carried out, pointing to a more specifically feminine space. Whilst the area between the buildings was kept clear of debris, more toxic crafts, such as metal- and glass-working, were located towards the periphery or up against the bank. Middens were also on the south-eastern periphery, but after construction of bank 1 halving the internal space from 1650 square metres to 850 square metres, rubbish was also disposed of beyond the bank or over the cliff to the north.[156] A similar use of space is suggested at Longbury Bank, with metalworking towards the periphery. The rock-cut, subrectangular building on the southern edge was interpreted as a storage structure to keep food cool, with rubbish thrown over the cliff onto the northern slope downwind from the main area of occupation.[157] At Llangorse crannog

---

[154] Lane and Redknap 2019, 134–7; Blair 2018, 52–3; Edwards 1990, 40–1.
[155] Longley 1991, 70–2.   [156] Campbell 2007a, 98–9.
[157] Campbell and Lane 1993, 21–9.

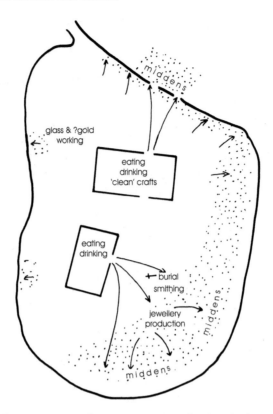

Fig. 5.11. Diagram of the promontory fort at Dinas Powys, showing the internal use of space suggested by artefact distributions (© Ewan Campbell).

it was being thrown into the lake.[158] Conspicuous consumption and the build-up of middens is equally evident at Llanbedrgoch. Here the two enclosure entrances in both main phases were on the northern side, providing access to the main buildings, though the door of central house (1) faced south across an open yard towards the spring and a sunken-floored outhouse with an oven beside it. The two rectangular buildings (4–5) on the eastern and western peripheries of the enclosure may have functioned as storehouses or workshops, though no firm evidence has survived. From an early stage, rubbish was dumped downslope on the western side in the vicinity of Building 5, first beneath, then up against the perimeter wall, with the burials in the ditch beyond.[159]

For lower-status farmsteads the picture is much less clear, a problem exacerbated by lack of artefacts and middens; presumably as much waste as possible was recycled or spread on the fields as manure. At Dolbenmaen the roundhouse and four-post storage structure were adjacent to each other, while the corn-dryer was some 80 metres away

---

[158] Lane and Redknap 2019, 67.   [159] Redknap 2004a, 148–55; 2016, fig. 3.

from the settlement.[160] However, at South Hook, though the structures may not all be contemporary, there is no sense of the core and periphery model outlined above. Instead, the dwellings and other structures with evidence of ironworking and crop-processing were grouped together, with some houses probably later repurposed for such use, but the wider environment was not investigated.[161] By contrast, the settlement at Rhuddgaer has a distinctly linear arrangement, which appears directly linked to the field system associated with it.[162]

CONCLUSION

Although our knowledge of early medieval secular settlements in Wales is slowly improving, there is still much that remains unclear. Only more, and more extensive, excavations will enable a better understanding of their characteristic morphology, dating, and chronology, as well as the hierarchy of settlements, the range of structures, what they were made of, and the use of space allowing wider trends to be more clearly articulated. Since diagnostic artefacts are largely focused on elite sites, the recognition of other, often ephemeral, structures and settlements rests almost entirely on scientific dating. Therefore, where any early medieval settlement is suspected, further investigation to enable AMS radiocarbon dating of multiple short-lived samples and Bayesian analysis should be seen as a priority.

It is now clear that settlement forms in the post-Roman centuries were rooted in what had gone before. Whilst villas were either abandoned or may only have survived at a basic level, indicating economic contraction and societal change, native forms of open and enclosed farmsteads with their origins in later prehistory continued as settlement forms with some regional variations. There is also significant evidence pointing to a continuity of landscape use focusing on fertile free-draining soils. At the same time, hillforts and promontory forts may be identified as characteristic elite settlements during the fifth to seventh centuries, though some have much longer and more complex histories. Some like Dinas Powys functioned as the defended homes of high-status families where they entertained their retinues and were the patrons of craftworkers. These were also estate centres allowing wider control of farming communities, produce, and other resources, and some were the focus of small kingdoms. However, as suggested by Glanfred, not all such sites were necessarily those of the elite, and we may be seeing the settlements of some more prosperous farming families as well. The functions of others, such as Dinas Emrys, appear more complex, with a possible ritual element that may also have been harnessed in the forging of identities and kingdom

---

[160] Kenney and McNicol 2017, 59–60, fig. 1.   [161] Crane and Murphy 2010b, 120–45.
[162] Hopewell and Edwards 2017, 217.

180 LIFE IN EARLY MEDIEVAL WALES

formation. Although there are also some hints of other types of elite post-Roman settlement, as at Cefn Cwmwd, their forms remain as yet unrecognized.

By the later seventh century there are signs of major changes in settlement forms taking place. Hillforts and promontory forts go out of use as elite settlements, though they continued as important nodes in the landscape and were sometimes—at least temporarily—reoccupied at a later date. What replaced them is still unclear since so few later elite sites have been identified. Llanbedrgoch, an enclosed settlement with later evidence of Hiberno-Scandinavian occupation, a summer residence of the rulers of Brycheiniog at Llangorse crannog, and the fortified Anglo-Saxon *burh* at Rhuddlan are all unique, though all had varying degrees of defence. At the other end of the scale, whilst some earlier farmsteads continued or were reoccupied, in the west new open settlements were also being established with subrectangular buildings and adjoining field systems, as at Rhuddgaer and probably originally at South Hook. As farming was dependent upon cooperation between kin and neighbours, these may have been the homes of extended families, perhaps of free farmers or, more likely, hereditary tenants on estates that were subject to the collection of food renders.

A combination of factors may lie behind these changes, some of which will be considered in the next chapter. The impact of climate deterioration and the likely onset of the 'Late Antique Little Ice Age' after 536 leading to crop failures, as well as human and animal disease, would probably have put additional pressures on food production, leading to a declining population and fewer occupied settlements, with a more serious impact in parts of Wales subject to high rainfall or where the growing season is shorter. The establishment of new open farming settlements may also coincide with increased arable indicators in the pollen evidence between the seventh and ninth centuries, suggesting a possible reverse in the decline. However, the abandonment of hillforts and promontory forts and the emergence of new settlement forms also imply societal change. Some kingdoms, such as Gwynedd, were expanding at the expense of smaller polities, and the power of the Church was increasing, leading to the accrual of landed estates. In the south the Llandaf charters also indicate significant changes in landholding during the eighth century: the size of estates donated to the Church became much smaller, and they were given by laymen rather than kings. From around this time onwards the charters also reveal more about the different levels of society, ranging from kings to the landowning aristocracy and hereditary tenants who did not necessarily farm the land themselves, as well as those who did, with slaves at the very bottom.[163] However, it is almost impossible to equate such social strata with settlements on the ground.

The smaller estates in the charters were termed *uillae* in Latin, *trefi* in Welsh. A *tref* means a dwelling, farmstead, hamlet, or estate and is also found in Cornish and

---

[163] Davies, W. 1978, 43–7, 110–16.

Breton, as well as in north-west England and southern Scotland, indicating that the term is early.[164] Its earliest written occurrence in Wales is in a ninth-century charter added to the Lichfield Gospels recording the donation of *tref guidauc* in the vicinity of Llan-y-Crwys, Carmarthenshire, to Llandeilo Fawr.[165] It is therefore likely that the farms and newly established hamlets of the later seventh century onwards, such as Rhuddgaer and South Hook, were the *trefi* of the written record. Nevertheless, though *tref* remains a very common place-name element in Wales, this does not necessarily aid the location of early medieval farming settlements since the element remained active in the formulation of place names well into the later Middle Ages.[166]

There are pointers to further change towards the end of the early Middle Ages. In the north-west there is a renewed interest in promontory forts, possibly a native response to the introduction of castle building. There are also signs of new curvilinear enclosed farmsteads as well as expansion into more marginal areas, such as Nant Peris in Snowdonia, aided by the climatic upturn beginning in the tenth century.

Various comparisons have been noted with settlement forms and their chronologies elsewhere in Britain and Ireland, notably continuing or renewed occupation or the construction of hillforts and promontory forts characteristic of much of western and northern Britain in the post-Roman centuries. We also see the phasing out of round-houses and the increasing use of subrectangular buildings, currently most clearly demonstrated in Ireland, but there are hints elsewhere. In addition, some interesting parallels may be drawn with Cornwall and some other parts of the south-west where, like much of Wales, the imprint of Romanization on settlement forms and the land-scape was significantly less than further east. In Cornwall it has also been suggested that the late seventh century was a pivotal moment marking societal change. Here the distribution of imported pottery is more widespread than in Wales, and local ceramic traditions continued to some extent, though identification of settlement sites after the seventh century has proved difficult.[167] Before this the promontory fort at Tintagel with its concentration of Mediterranean imported pottery was the most significant elite settlement with a *floruit* suggested between *c*.450 and 550. Below this, some 'rounds', later prehistoric and Roman-period curvilinear enclosed homesteads with roundhouses, such as Trethurgy, continued to function as prosperous farms through the fifth and sixth centuries and possibly into the seventh.[168] However, the only later settlement so far extensively excavated is Mawgan Porth, with its subrectangular stone buildings with byres at one end dated to the tenth or eleventh century. The use of the term *tref* in both Cornwall and Devon suggests it came into use before the Anglo-Saxon takeover. As in Wales, the term is similarly attested over a long period, though no identifiable examples have so far been excavated. There is also continuing debate

---

[164] Pierce 1968, 347–8; Padel 1985, 223–8.
[165] Evans and Rhys, J. G. 1893, xlv; Jenkins and Owen 1983, 53; Jones, G. R. J. 1972, fig. 44; Charles 1992, xxx.
[166] Ibid., xxx–xxxi.   [167] Preston-Jones and Okasha 2013, 44.   [168] Quinnell 2004, 238–44.

182   LIFE IN EARLY MEDIEVAL WALES

as to whether *trefi* indicate the migration of settlements and their establishment in new locations once rounds had gone out of use or whether there was more continuity in settlement landscapes. Most likely it was a combination of the two.[169] This scenario is also relevant to Wales, since in both areas *trefi* remain important elements in the dispersed settlement pattern still so characteristic today.

[169] Preston-Jones and Rose 1986, 140–6; Preston-Jones and Okasha 2013, 44. On the south-west more generally, see Rippon 2008, 132.

SIX

Food, Farming, and the Agricultural Economy

The rapid expansion in our understanding of the changing economy of north-west Europe over the course of the early Middle Ages has been driven in large part by increasing archaeological evidence. This embraces trade, the establishment of markets, and new urban centres with their concentrations of craft and industry, but also developments in the agricultural economy, production of surpluses, and the role of elites in economic exploitation.[1] This is also reflected in research on the changing economy in early medieval Wales, a society that was, by contrast, entirely rural in character, thereby signalling a comparative lack of economic development.[2] Even though problems remain with the recognition of settlements and dearth of excavations on major ecclesiastical sites, archaeological evidence for the early medieval economy is now growing and can be used alongside the limited written record to gain an understanding of underlying change.

The cultivation of crops, livestock farming, and, to a lesser extent, exploitation of natural sources of food, as well as the processes of food production would have dominated the vast majority of people's lives and the economy throughout the period in question. Everyday domestic crafts, such as woodworking and the fabrication of textiles, were also key, as were some more specialized crafts, notably the manufacture of iron, for which there is increasing archaeological evidence. These activities helped to shape the wider landscape in which people lived. While many may have existed at little more than a subsistence level, secular and increasingly ecclesiastical elites with landed estates would have demanded renders, creating the need for agricultural surpluses enabling the accrual of wealth and the patronage of specialized craftworkers and others who benefited from the redistribution of goods via social mechanisms, such as gift-giving or donating alms as well as payments of tribute. However, archaeological evidence illuminating systems of trade and exchange remains sparse with the exception of exotic goods indicative of long-distance contacts.

---

[1] See, for example, Hodges 1982; Wickham 2005; Loveluck 2013.

[2] On the agricultural economy, see Comeau and Seaman 2019.

Life in Early Medieval Wales. Nancy Edwards, Oxford University Press. © Nancy Edwards 2023.
DOI: 10.1093/oso/9780198733218.003.0006

184 LIFE IN EARLY MEDIEVAL WALES

This chapter will focus on the land, its exploitation for food, and the farming economy. I shall first examine the agricultural landscape and how it and the wider countryside were managed. I shall then consider the mixed-farming economy of crop growing and livestock rearing, as well as the significance of other food resources. Finally, I shall discuss what is known about diet and the preparation of food and drink. The aim is to identify changes in the farming economy in Wales over time and analyse possible underlying reasons for these.

THE FARMING LANDSCAPE: FIELDS AND ESTATES

As previously indicated, evidence for settlement and food production in early medieval Wales was concentrated on free-draining soils in the more fertile lowlands, such as Anglesey and coastal Pembrokeshire, but doubtless included other similar regions, such as the Vale of Glamorgan, and river valleys, such as the Wye and Tywy, where evidence is sparse (Chapter 5). Limited well-dated pollen samples, mainly from the uplands, broadly suggest a deteriorating climate in the post-Roman centuries. At this time, with some exceptions in the north-west and lowland south-east, there are signs of woodland regeneration and an increase in heath and wetland habitats generally matched by a decline in pastoral and arable indicators, suggesting widespread contraction in food production. This may be linked to the wider collapse of the Roman market economy as Roman authority declined but also very likely to climate deterioration and the more localized impact of the 'Late Antique Little Ice Age' in the century or so after 536. Increased rainfall in the west and cooler temperatures in the inland valleys of eastern Wales and the borders would have made harvests less reliable and the growing season shorter (Chapter 2).[3] During the seventh and eighth centuries, though climate indicators in Wales are less clear, the earlier decline in pastoral and arable indicators is reversed, with evidence of decreasing woodland and heath pollen suggesting that more land was being cleared and an increase in cereal cultivation.[4] Although a climatic upturn is detectable in the northern hemisphere from around 950, the limited pollen record in Wales currently demonstrates no overall pattern of environmental change, though there is some evidence for an increase in pastoral indicators in the north-west.[5]

We might envisage a lowland landscape of scattered farms and small agricultural settlements surrounded by fields, but the inhabitants also exploited and to some extent managed the wider environment, including a variety of rough grazing depending on the topography, ranging from lowland river margins, heaths, bogs, and saltmarshes to

---

[3] Büntgen et al. 2016; Davies, T. L. 2019, 180–5, figs 10.2a–b.   [4] Ibid., 2019, 185, figs 10.3a–b.

[5] Ibid., 189–92, figs 10.4a–b. For more general discussion of such environmental indicators, see Rippon et al. 2015, 295–304.

woodland and upland pastures (Chapter 2). Nevertheless, we still know remarkably little about early medieval field systems in Wales. Archaeological work on field systems more generally has tended to concentrate on upland landscapes, especially in the north-west where, because a combination of earthwork and drystone field boundaries were favoured, such evidence is more likely to survive, rather than in the more heavily agriculturally exploited lowlands where banks and ditches, as well as hedges and fences that could be easily removed or rearranged, were probably much more common. It has been argued that from the Bronze Age onwards the uplands in the north-west were characterized by curvilinear enclosures for corralling animals and small fields associated with roundhouses indicative of different periods of transhumance and at least seasonal upland settlement. By the later Middle Ages, however, subrectangular buildings and house platforms, sometimes inserted into what appear to be much earlier field systems with few visible alterations except the addition of occasional ridge and furrow, likewise denote transhumance and upland settlement that initially focused on cattle but later on sheep. By contrast, in the lowlands below 300 metres small, rectangular, terraced fields with lynchets, where they survive, are the norm and are frequently associated with Iron Age and Roman-period enclosed settlements, though their origins may lie somewhat earlier. Again, such terraced fields sometimes continued with comparatively little modification apart from the addition of undated subrectangular buildings, as at Muriau Gwyddelod, Merioneth, and Caerau, Caernarfonshire, or ridge and furrow that are also presumed to be later medieval.[6] Elsewhere the remnants of later medieval open fields or 'sharelands' (*rhandiroedd*) with strips and furlongs are first attested in the late twelfth- and thirteenth-century Welsh lawbooks. Smaller than their English counterparts, these sometimes still survive or are still visible on nineteenth-century maps as, for example, those adjacent to the thirteenth-century royal *llys* at Rhosyr, Anglesey, and in the *cantref* of Cemais, Pembrokeshire.[7] Therefore, as with identifying early medieval settlements, the problem lies in bridging the chronological gap between the later prehistoric and Roman on the one hand and the later medieval on the other. Allied to this is the difficulty of dating field boundaries and evolving field systems scientifically rather than through association or landscape regression analysis.

We have seen that in the north-west what evidence there is for early medieval settlements, together with corn-dryers and ironworking debris, is often identified during investigation of lowland sites and landscapes with more visible earlier and later remains, as at Graeanog, Llandygái, and Parc Cybi, indicating that the land continued to be occupied and exploited, though not at the same intensity. It may therefore be argued that some terraced field systems continued in use as, for example, at Tŷ Mawr

---

[6] Waddington 2013, 69–71; Smith, G. H. et al. 2011, 21–9; RCAHMW 1960, nos 826–34; Kenney 2015, 9–10, 13, 17–18, fig. 20; Silvester and Hankinson 2013, 10–14.

[7] Ibid., 6–8, 10, fig. 5; Comeau 2019, 130–8; 2020, 108–16.

below Holyhead Mountain, where the remains with still substantial lynchets stretch over 16 hectares. Excavation of part of one of these fields established that it predated a post-Roman roundhouse and subrectangular building but remained in use for some time after their construction, with the collapse of its downslope drystone boundary and associated lynchet eventually destroying the latter (Fig. 5.7, c.).[8]

During the seventh and eighth centuries, the rise in arable indicators evident in the pollen record appears to coincide with evidence for settlement reorganization (Chapter 5) alongside changes in the farmed landscape. During the latter half of the early Middle Ages in the north-west new field systems were being laid out which also suggest an expanding agricultural economy with land being brought back into production. For example, at Melin y Plas, Anglesey, clearance of blackthorn, gorse, and hazel in the vicinity of a Late Iron Age and Roman-period roundhouse cluster was associated with the establishment of a long, narrow, ditched field. This was linked with crop-processing debris, radiocarbon-dated between the seventh and eleventh centuries AD, dumped in two of the structures.[9] However, entirely new settlements with their own field systems were also being established with no evidence of landscape continuity, notably at Rhuddgaer near the mouth of the Braint. Here geophysics revealed field systems covering more than 10.5 hectares that were subsequently fossilized by sand inundation that began in the first half of the twelfth century (Fig. 5.8). The earliest consisted of small rectangular fields with slightly curved boundaries associated with subrectangular structures, one of which was dated to between the later seventh and later eighth centuries AD. This was conjoined with one of the field boundaries, which was constructed of edge-set stones. The eastern half of the field system is less clear, which may suggest that it was additional or managed differently, though it may equally have been truncated or buried more deeply beneath the sand. It may be part of an infield–outfield system where crops were primarily grown in the western half whilst the eastern half was only periodically brought into cultivation.[10] Animals would have been penned to prevent them damaging the crop and only brought into cultivated areas after harvest to eat the stubble and manure the land. Otherwise, they grazed the surrounding rough pasture on the margins of the Braint with its saltmarsh estuary and the shores of the Menai Strait. In the final phase sometime after the building became ruinous but before the sand blow commenced in the earlier twelfth century, there is a further change to what is more clearly an open field system with ridge and furrow indicative of the introduction of a mouldboard plough.[11] At Rhuddgaer,

---

[8] Smith, C. 1985, 42–6.

[9] Cuttler et al. 2012, 90, 94–5, 238–40, fig. 4.18; Waddington 2013, 166–8.

[10] Silvester 2019, 99. On the later use of this system in south-west Wales, see Comeau 2020, 8–9, 83–6.

[11] Hopewell and Edwards 2017, 216 –29, 236–7; Sarah Davies (pers. comm.). A field system at Goetre Isaf, Bangor, has also been tentatively identified as early medieval following a radiocarbon date from an associated pit; Bradley 2013, 38–40, cal. AD 870–1000 (SUERC-45099).

therefore, we may be detecting in the late seventh and eighth centuries the origins of a system of small, open fields, part of an infield–outfield system that later came to characterize a settlement pattern of dispersed farmsteads. However, more work is needed to test this hypothesis.

Beyond the north-west there has been very little archaeological work to identify early medieval field systems, and even those of Roman date are rare, making their fate more difficult to determine.[12] However, occasionally some continuity of land divisions can be detected. For example, a field ditch near Rhuddlan, Denbighshire, a sample from the base of which was radiocarbon dated to cal. AD 420–570, was one of several on the same alignment as the modern field boundaries.[13] What little evidence there is from the lowlands of the south-east also indicates some continuity between Romano-British landscapes and medieval field boundaries, as at Trowbridge on the edge of the Wentlooge Level. This had been drained in the Roman period and seems to have remained in use for pasture throughout the early Middle Ages, unlike the adjacent Caldicot Level, which was abandoned at this time. Nevertheless, detectable continuity appears much less than in what became Anglo-Saxon England and may be more similar to Devon and Cornwall where the pollen evidence suggests major changes in the layout of the landscape were taking place during the eighth century.[14]

GIS and landscape regression analysis may offer a way forward. Rhiannon Comeau's study of the landscape of the *cantref* of Cemais in northern Pembrokeshire identified focal lowland zones of settlement and agriculture linked to areas of rough grazing and upland pasture. In these zones, for example in Bayvil, there are the remains of systems of small open fields still visible on nineteenth-century maps as part of the dispersed settlement pattern. She has argued that these were part of an infield–outfield system described in the area in the sixteenth century and indicated in the later twelfth- and thirteenth-century Welsh law texts. Without archaeological evidence, however, their origins, as well as their longevity, remain very difficult to determine, though they could also lie in the period of settlement change suggested during the long eighth century.[15]

Otherwise debate has tended to focus on the development of large open field systems of the type characteristic of the 'central zone' of England, where the dating of their inception has been hotly contested. Their origins probably lie in the mid-Saxon period or a little later, though elements of earlier field systems appear to be incorporated into them.[16] However, they are also found on the Welsh borders where they are regarded as indicative of English infiltration, though they later spread alongside nucleated villages to parts of Wales, such as the eastern Caldicot Levels and southern

---

[12] Smith, A. et al. 2016, 379–80; Rippon et al. 2015, 295.   [13] Weigel 2015, 33–4 (Beta-396128).

[14] Rippon 2019, 26–30. On south-west England, see Rippon 2008, 108–36. On the varying survival, according to region, of late prehistoric and Romano-British field systems more generally in England and Wales, see Rippon et al. 2015, especially 221–46; 295–342.

[15] Comeau 2020, 73–116.   [16] Silvester 2019, 94–9; Rippon et al. 2015, 35–44, 97–9, 329–31.

188 LIFE IN EARLY MEDIEVAL WALES

Pembrokeshire, under Anglo-Norman control.[17] At Hen Domen, Montgomeryshire, a large open field system with ridge and furrow was in existence prior to the erection of the motte-and-bailey castle *c.*1071–86, though how much earlier is unclear. Ridge and furrow has also been closely examined in relationship to Offa's Dyke at Dudston near Chirbury, Shropshire, where it was originally regarded as earlier than the dyke, but this is no longer thought to be the case.[18]

Therefore, much more archaeological work is necessary in order to identify early medieval fields and field systems in Wales and to understand both continuity and change in their evolution from later prehistoric and Roman systems until the emergence of Welsh 'sharelands' and English open fields, though there are some hints that the origins of small open fields linked to an infield–outfield system of exploitation could lie during the long eighth century. Research has instead concentrated on larger early medieval land units in the form of estates. The study of these has focused on two different approaches. Firstly, Glanville Jones's concept of the 'multiple estate' has proved highly influential in both Wales and England.[19] In this regard, whilst the notion of encompassing access to different environmental zones within an estate allowing exploitation of a range of resources remains valid, as does the idea that many farmed landscapes were the product of management over the *longue durée*, the model is otherwise highly problematic for understanding how landholding was organized in early medieval Wales. This is because it is founded on the highly schematized systems of land organization and terminology set out in the Welsh lawbooks of the late twelfth and thirteenth centuries which are then projected backwards through the early Middle Ages and sometimes even earlier.[20] This would argue for systems of landholding remaining largely unchanged over many centuries, when other evidence, written, environmental, and archaeological, suggests that this was not in fact the case.

Aspects of the organization of early medieval estates, and how these changed over time, are, however, revealed in the charter material recording their donation to the Church as working concerns requiring the payment of renders. Although charters may originally have been written on single sheets of vellum, the earliest surviving original charters in Wales are the ninth-century additions to the Lichfield Gospels, then at Llandeilo Fawr, a practice also seen from the ninth century onwards elsewhere in Britain and Ireland.[21] However, the much more extensive Llandaf charter collection, though only reaching its final form in the early twelfth century, can also cast valuable light on estates in the south, including Ergyng, with a further small group of charters

---

[17] Rippon 2008, 201–48.   [18] Barker and Lawson 1971; Everson 1991.

[19] For Wales, see particularly Jones, G. R. J. 1972; for a compilation of many of Jones's studies of multiple estates, see Roberts and Barnwell 2011a.

[20] For major critiques, see Gregson 1985 (answered in Jones, G. R. J. 1985); Roberts with Barnwell 2011b; Seaman 2012.

[21] Chad 3, 4, and 6, Evans, J. G. and Rhys 1893, xlv, xlvii; Jenkins and Owen 1983, 53–5; Sims-Williams 2019a, 10–16.

attached to the *Life* of St Cadog *c.*1100 relating to estates held by Llancarfan.[22] Wendy Davies has argued that the form and language of the charters in Wales were part of a wider early medieval Latin charter-writing tradition in Celtic-speaking regions also found in Ireland, Scotland, south-west Britain, and Brittany.[23] In the case of the Llandaf charters, she has proposed that those containing material regarded as datable prior to the eighth century demonstrate royal donations of very large estates, typically up to 800 hectares and often on the best agricultural land. These are termed *agri* and are measured in *unciae*, and it is argued that they were the direct successors of Roman systems of landholding. However, during the course of the eighth century there was a major change. The estates in the charters, increasingly granted by laymen, became much smaller, mostly around 50 hectares, and were now measured in *modii* and termed *uillae*, the equivalent of *trefi* in Welsh, the primary meaning of which is a settlement but which also takes on the concept of the land associated with it.[24] These smaller estates are easier to trace on the ground and one wonders to what extent such reorganization was accompanied by the establishment of new settlements and field systems in the manner of Rhuddgaer in the north-west, where no charter evidence has survived. Since many of the estates granted in the Welsh charters include boundary clauses, albeit in most cases only relating to comparatively late in the period, their landscapes and soils can be examined alongside archaeological evidence and their settlement history to try to reconstruct them and determine how they were exploited.

For example, one of the charters added to the Lichfield Gospels (Chad 6) records the donation of *mainaur med diminih* (*maenor* Meddyfnych), centred on a farm in the parish of Llandybïe, Carmarthenshire, to Llandeilo Fawr. The farm concerned is still identifiable and the *maenor* would have included several *trefi*, and the bounds of the estate, given in Welsh reflecting daily speech, can also be located on the ground. They demonstrate the significance of the many rivers, streams, springs, confluences, and fords in the area in demarcating the land, as, for example, *pennant ircaru* ('source of the brook frequented by deer') followed by *boit bahne* ('the wood of the summits'?), which together suggest terrain for hunting. Other boundary points include *guoum hen lan* ('meadow of the old enclosure or church'), rough upland pasture still identifiable in modern field and farm names, and *hitir melin* ('yellow cornlands'), indicating its agricultural use as well as *toldar* ('a boled oak'), a haven for wild bees and therefore a source of honey. The inclusion of a *bir main* ('short stone'), a now prostrate prehistoric standing stone, amongst the bounds also signals that much earlier monuments continued to have a territorial resonance in the landscape.[25]

[22] Evans, J. G., and Rhys 1893; Davies, W. 1978; 1979a; Wade-Evans 1944, 124–37, chs 55–68.
[23] Davies, W. 1982b.
[24] Davies, W. 1979b. For a critique of this hypothesis, see Sims-Williams 2019a, 104–16.
[25] Evans, J. G., and Rhys 1893, xlvii; Jones, G. R. J. 1972, 308–10; James 1998; James and Thorne 2020.

190   LIFE IN EARLY MEDIEVAL WALES

Similarly, analysis of the Llandaf charters has enabled the location of many early medieval estates and a number of these can be plotted on the ground. For instance, three charters (146, 167, 237b), the core of the earliest of which (146) has been dated to *c.*720 naming King Awst of Brycheiniog and his sons as patrons, records the donations of two adjoining estates to the monastery at Llan-gors (Fig. 6.1, a). The boundary clauses are likely to be considerably later but pre-Norman nonetheless. The first estate (146), on either side of the Afon Llynfi, is large at around 1200 hectares. The second, *Lann Mihacghgel Tref Ceriau* (167), which has been plausibly identified as the church of Llanfihangel Tal-y-Llyn to the south-west, is around 240 hectares and was granted slightly later but reconfirmed *c.*935 (237b). The boundary clause of 146, in which the monastery was located, commenced at the mouth of a spring dedicated to the twelve saints (*Finnaun y Doudec Seint*) on the eastern side of Llangorse Lake (*Linn Syuadon*) with its royal crannog occupied in the late ninth and early tenth centuries. This was at around 150 metres OD, but the boundary then followed the brook (*guver*) climbing to over 300 metres on the lower slopes of the upland to the east. Therefore, the estate took in a variety of environmental zones including both fertile agricultural lowland and rough grazing. Interestingly, according to the boundary clause, the limits of the upland were marked by Llywarch Hen's Dyke (*Claud Lyuarch Hen*), still traceable as a hollow-way and field bank that is in part on the line of the parish boundary. It then followed the Llynfi as far as *Brynn Eitel* before descending to the source of the Nant Tawel and then south along the Lynfi to the lake.[26] Such donations to the Church were not, however, restricted to the most productive land. Another very large estate (154), around 2500 hectares, also originally granted by King Awst and his sons, probably to the church of Llandeilo'r-fân at its heart, had little agricultural potential beyond the river valley with its wooded slopes. Rather, it was located to take advantage of the upland horse and cattle pastures of the Epynt and included *Brinn Bucelid* ('Hill of the Herders') on its bounds.[27] Further Llandaf charter material incorporating a list of Teilo churches dating to *c.*1025 relates to a group of estates bounded by tributaries along the River Ritec in Pembrokeshire, originally donated to the nearby monastery of St Teilo at Penally (Fig. 6.1, b). Those along the south bank, one of which included the settlement at Longbury Bank, were each around three *modii* (50 hectares) in size and encompassed three ecological zones: marshland and grazing along the river margins, arable and pasture on the low-lying, highly fertile, free-draining soils, with rough pasture and scrubland on the rising

[26] Evans, J. G., and Rhys 1893, nos 146, 167, 237b; Davies, W. 1979a, 98, 106, 124. For discussion of the boundary clauses and place names, see Coe 2001, 110, 180–1, 286–7, 443–4, 975–6, 985; for mapping and further discussion, see Seaman 2019a, 161–6; Seaman in Lane and Redknap 2019, 415–21.

[27] Evans, J. G., and Rhys 1893, 154; Davies 1978, 101; Seaman 2019a, 166–9; Coe 2001, 96–7, 977–8.

FOOD, FARMING, AND THE AGRICULTURAL ECONOMY 191

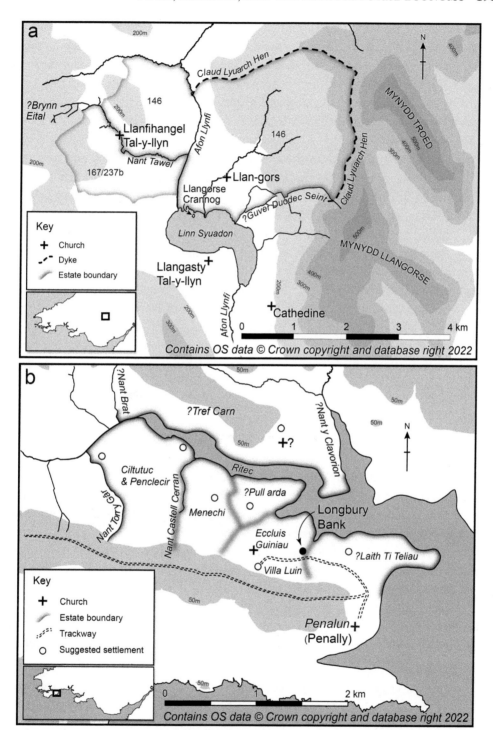

FIG. 6.1. Early medieval estates donated to the Church recorded in charters in the Book of Llandaf: a. Llan-gors (after Campbell and Lane 1989, fig. 1, and Seaman 2019, fig. 9.3, with alterations); b. Penally (after Campbell and Lane 1993, fig. 9).

192 LIFE IN EARLY MEDIEVAL WALES

ground above.[28] The next step should be to investigate archaeologically any evidence for early medieval settlements and associated field systems on estates such as these, which may or may not be on the same sites as later medieval farms, alongside more detailed examination of the wider landscape and how it was exploited over time.

Finally, who was farming the land and living in the settlements on estates such as these? The charter material demonstrates that estates were being donated to the Church by kings and later by more wealthy laymen. The unfree, hereditary tenant farmers who lived in the *trefi* on these estates were transferred as well and now paid food render to their new landlords, presumably reflecting the situation when land was sold or passed into the hands of a new secular owner.[29] As kinship was key in early medieval Welsh society, we can envisage that the farms and hamlets on these estates were occupied by families linked by ties of kinship and marriage facilitating cooperation in some farming activities. Ploughing, for example, required oxen, their harness, and the plough itself—a considerable investment—and there are indications that joint ploughing may have been an early medieval practice in Wales, as it was in Ireland.[30] There were also undoubtedly slaves—the manumission of Bleiddudd and his progeny is the subject of one of the Lichfield marginalia (Chad 5)—but because of their lowly position they are seldom mentioned and have left no mark on the archaeological record. Therefore we do not know to what extent farming as well as other aspects of the economy were dependent upon their labour.[31]

CEREALS AND OTHER CROPS

Cereals would have been the dietary mainstay, consumed as bread, porridge, gruel, and ale. In contrast to livestock farming, our understanding of cereal cultivation during the early Middle Ages in Wales has grown significantly over the last twenty years as the result of an increase in radiocarbon-dated archaeobotanical samples derived from excavations, such as those along the A55 expressway on Anglesey and the gas pipeline across south Wales.[32] The archaeobotanical evidence is in the form of charred cereal grains, often associated with corn-dryers, and as a result other indications of cultivated crops that do not need to be processed in this way, as well as weed seeds that might give an indication of the environment, are less likely to survive. The only site with some waterlogged evidence is Llangorse crannog.[33] Though little overall

[28] Evans, J. G., and Rhys 1893, 125b, 127a, 253; Davies, W. 1978, 96, 126; Campbell and Lane 1993, 55–9; Coe 2001, 587–8, 629–30, 818–19; Soilscapes.

[29] Davies, W. 1978, 44.   [30] Charles-Edwards 1993, 453.

[31] Evans, J. G., and Rhys 1893, xlvii; Davies, W. 1982a, 64–7. For a broad historiographical discussion of early medieval slavery focusing on Britain and Ireland, see Wyatt 2009, 1–60.

[32] Caseldine 2015, 8; Cuttler et al. 2012; Darvill et al. 2020, 108–25, 167–73.

[33] Caseldine and Griffiths 2019.

analysis has taken place, examination of the plant remains alongside limited structural and artefactual evidence reveals some significant trends. However, there is currently insufficient data to enable identification of chronological changes with any precision or to confirm possible regional differences dependent on climate and soils as well as human preference that without doubt once existed. Furthermore, most of the evidence so far recovered is from the western half of Wales and, though some comparisons can be made, it is far less than that from southern and eastern England or many parts of Ireland at this time.[34]

This comparative lack of evidence is also true for the Roman period in Wales. Nevertheless, the archaeobotanical remains indicate that, as elsewhere in Roman Britain, spelt wheat became the main crop, largely replacing emmer, but cultivation of six-row hulled barley was also important. During the mid-Roman period the cultivation of spelt and barley drove an expansion in cereal production for the market, and in some parts of Wales it has been argued that this enabled local supply of the military as, for example, at Caernarfon, though there was a probable reduction from around the mid-fourth century once the economy began to falter. There is also some evidence for the cultivation of free-threshing wheat, rye, and oats, but these were not significant crops.[35] During the early Middle Ages, however, it is possible to detect significant changes in the cereals grown. Whilst barley continued as a major crop, the production of oats became increasingly important and, in addition to common oats, the bristle variety has been identified, which is well suited to upland environments and has been found on several early medieval sites in south-west Wales.[36] Though some cultivation of spelt probably continued, at least initially, free-threshing wheat replaced it but is only found in small quantities on production sites. This, like barley and oats, is easier to process for consumption than spelt and emmer, which are glume wheats, but it does better on heavier, more fertile soils and requires more labour to produce.[37] It is also less well suited than barley and oats to the often wet and windy weather in the west and the shorter growing season in the east. Sometimes small amounts of rye have also been recorded and these may have been grown with wheat as a maslin crop to reduce the risk of failure.

The course of these changes and the reasons behind them are currently less easy to establish. The post-Roman downturn in the climate indicated by the pollen evidence that created a need to minimize risk is probably a significant factor in the emphasis on barley and increasingly oats, but it is also likely that the collapse of the Roman market economy is relevant in the decline of spelt. Free-threshing cereals also required less

[34] See, for example, Banham and Faith 2014, 19–74; McKerracher 2018; McClatchie 2014; O'Sullivan et al. 2014, 194–209.

[35] Allen et al. 2017, 11–21, 31–2; Davies, J. L. 2002; Burnham and Davies 2010, 154–5; Darvill et al. 2020, 165, 167.

[36] Carruthers, in Crane and Murphy 2010b, 178–81; Caseldine 2015, 8; Darvill et al. 2020, 169–71.

[37] McClatchie 2014, 48; McKerracher 2018, 84–7.

194 LIFE IN EARLY MEDIEVAL WALES

effort to process, which may have been a factor in a period of declining population. Samples of plant remains from the post-Roman period demonstrate that these changes were already underway. In the north-west barley dominated in a group of fifth- or sixth-century corn-dryers at Parc Cybi, with some oats and wheat. A broadly contemporary oven at Dolbenmaen contained mainly two-row barley with a significant amount of oats, suggesting they may have been grown together as a dredge crop, though there was also a small amount of free-threshing wheat. In another sample of this period from Glanfred, Cardiganshire, it was, however, oats that dominated, followed by six-row hulled barley, with only a single grain of free-threshing wheat.[38] Elsewhere, there is some evidence that cultivation of glume wheats continued, as at West Angle, Pembrokeshire, since these dominated a sample dating to cal. AD 540–650, whilst free-threshing bread wheat was found later.[39]

By the eighth century, however, samples demonstrate the increasing dominance of oats followed by six-row hulled barley across Wales, particularly in the south-west. This may be linked to an increase in cereal cultivation broadly indicated by the pollen. At South Hook, for example, a settlement occupied between the late eighth and twelfth centuries, large quantities of charred grain were found. It was noted here that where oats were dominant these were of bristle type and were found in conjunction with stinking chamomile, indicating the heavier, nutrient-poor soils on which they had grown. In contrast, where barley was dominant, it was found alongside common oats, indicating the two were grown together as dredge, thereby minimizing the risk of crop failure. Again, free-threshing wheat was only present in small quantities throughout the period of occupation, but it was suggested that whilst club wheat, which is comparatively robust and well suited to the wet and windy climate, was found in the eighth and ninth centuries, bread wheat was subsequently preferred. Perhaps there were only the resources for a small crop to be grown or better care was taken to avoid waste.[40] Bearing this in mind, it is possible that free-threshing wheat was being grown largely as food render since it produced a more luxurious loaf. In support of this, large samples of charred and a little waterlogged cereal were recovered from the 916 destruction horizon of the royal crannog at Llangorse, probably associated with a grain store. This had been processed apart from some contaminant weed seeds removed prior to grinding. Interestingly, here free-threshing, mainly bread wheat predominated, but there were also large amounts of hulled barley and oats, both common and bristle, as well as some rye. These and the surviving weed seeds indicate the cultivation of both light sandy soils and heavier ground,[41] and overall the evidence

[38] Kenney et al. 2020, i, 212–13; Kenney and McNicol 2017, 59–60; McNicol et al. 2017, 358–60; Jones. I. et al. 2018, 230–3.

[39] Groom et al. 2011, 177–81.

[40] Caseldine and Griffiths 2019, 173; Carruthers, in Crane and Murphy 2010b, 178–81.

[41] Caseldine and Griffiths 2019, 169–70.

suggests that cereals were being brought to Llangorse as food render. Indeed, bread is standard amongst such items listed as render in the Welsh charter material.[42] For example, in the ninth-century charter in the Lichfield Gospels donating Trefwyddog in Ystrad Tywi to Llandeilo Fawr (Chad 3), the main render for both summer and winter was forty loaves. It is, however, difficult to imagine for practical reasons that the loaves themselves were rendered, unless they were consumed in a feast, so it may have been the grain, which could be stored to produce them.[43] Although no indication of ingredients is given, a variety of cereals may have been acceptable, as indicated in a Llancarfan charter dated to the seventh-century that allows for the substitution of ale with wheat.[44]

Trends identified above may be closely compared with those in early medieval Ireland, where the climate is broadly similar. Here, it has been argued that cereal cultivation increased from the seventh century onwards and, like Wales, barley and oats were dominant, with more barley in the earlier part of the period and more oats later on. Wheat is also present but in the later period it was usually part of a mixed assemblage. It may likewise have been favoured for food render as it has been found in quantity on some elite sites, such as the monastery at Clonfad, Co. Westmeath, and the royal crannog at Lagore, Co. Meath. Rye is, however, rare.[45] In Anglo-Saxon England it has been shown that, as in Wales, the cultivation of barley continued to be important in the post-Roman period, sometimes alongside spelt, but free-threshing wheat was also beginning to replace the latter. From the seventh century onwards, however, an expansion in cereal production is more clearly evident, with barley and free-threshing bread wheat dominant, with the written sources likewise indicating the importance of the latter as food render. Spelt, however, continued to be grown as a niche crop and there are increasing indications of rye. The cultivation of oats also increased and this was a significant crop in the west Midlands as, for example, in Stafford, but overall it fails to show the same dominance evident in Wales and Ireland.[46]

We know very little about crops other than cereals. Samples of crop-processing waste dating to the latter part of the period from outside Rhuddlan revealed both field beans and peas for human consumption alongside wild vetches that may have been grown for fodder. However, very little evidence for the cultivation of legumes has come to light in more recent, better dated samples, though peas have recently been identified at Conkland Hill in the eighth to eleventh centuries, and legumes at

---

[42] Charles-Edwards 2013, 280–2.

[43] Evans, J. G., and Rhys 1893, xlv. Sources indicate that in early medieval Ireland loaves were standard sizes; see Sexton 1998, 79–81. For England, the laws of Ine of Wessex (688–726), for example, list renders argued to have been consumed in feasting, though a charter of Offa of Mercia (793 × 796) also suggests food for storage; see Lambert and Leggett 2022.

[44] Wade-Evans 1944, ch. 64, 132–3; Charles-Edwards 2013, 278.

[45] McClatchie 2014, 43–6; McClatchie et al. 2019, 71; Edwards 1990, 60.

[46] McKerracher 2018, 88–110, 119–20; Banham and Faith 2014, 19–33; Hamerow et al. 2020, 591.

Steynton, Pembrokeshire, in the seventh to ninth.[47] This suggests that they were grown but, as in both Ireland and Anglo-Saxon England, the archaeological evidence is sparse.[48] From time to time flax seeds have also been identified in Wales. Flax was, of course, used to make linen, but the context in which the seeds were found at South Hook points to the extraction of linseed oil for human consumption, though this has not been attested elsewhere.[49] Vegetables and fruit would also have been grown in gardens and orchards, but the rarity of waterlogged early medieval sites means that evidence is very hard to find. However, plum stones have been identified at both Longbury Bank and Llangorse crannog, suggesting orchards nearby.[50]

Our understanding of developments in agricultural technology in early medieval Wales, as well as how cereals were cultivated, processed, and stored, is extremely patchy. Manuring was clearly important for growing cereals and therefore animals would have grazed the stubble in the fields after harvest. However, the lack of early medieval pottery in Wales means there is no evidence for the spreading of farmyard and domestic waste. Middens are also rare on excavated sites other than high-status settlements, such as Dinas Powys and Llanbedrgoch, suggesting that this may normally have been the case. The identification of weed seeds, such as fat hen and wild radish, in corn-dryers, as at Bayvil and South Hook, also suggests manuring was taking place, and in coastal areas of Pembrokeshire, for example, seaweed may well have been utilized as a fertilizer.[51] There is, however, no clear evidence of lime spreading to counter soil acidity.[52]

Ploughing took place in the late winter and early spring prior to sowing barley and oats.[53] It is also likely that free-threshing wheat was spring-sown, even though autumn sowing provided a longer growing season. During the Roman period, the wooden ard, probably drawn by two oxen and sometimes with an iron share, as, for example, that from Coygan Camp, continued as the usual method of breaking up the ground, making cross-ploughing essential. However, the Romans also introduced a plough with a heavier iron share and coulter that may also have had a mouldboard. It is therefore interesting that a winged iron share that dispersed the earth but did not turn a furrow, for which a mouldboard would have been necessary, has been found in a late Roman context at Dinorben hillfort, indicating the availability of this technology in

---

[47] Manley et al. 1985, 111–13; Hart 2014, 54; Barber et al. 2014, 8, 27–8. The single field bean from Llangorse crannog is not from a secure early medieval context; Caseldine and Griffiths 2019, 173.

[48] McClatchie 2014, 48–9; Banham and Faith 2014, 33–6; McKerracher 2018, 115.

[49] Carruthers, in Crane and Murphy 2010b, 175; Banham and Faith 2014, 38.

[50] Campbell and Lane 1993, 54; Caseldine and Griffiths 2019, 169.

[51] Comeau 2021, 65; Carruthers, in Crane and Murphy 2010b, 176; Groom et al. 2011, 183; Hemer et al. 2017, 434–8.

[52] Material from a stone-built, keyhole-shaped lime-kiln at Betws-yn-Rhos, Denbighshire, has been dated to cal. AD 890–1160 (Beta-241246) but is likely associated with a later medieval building project; Grant 2007, 20, 20–2, 25–6.

[53] Also indicated by weed seeds, such as fat hen and wild radish, in corn-dryers; Comeau 2021, 65.

native elite contexts in Wales.[54] However, to what extent this more advanced technology persisted in Britain into the post-Roman period is unclear, as is its impact in Ireland.[55] Plough technology is still a matter of debate and archaeological remains in early medieval Britain and Ireland are rare. It has generally been thought that ards continued as the usual method of tillage in both Britain and Ireland prior to the tenth century.[56] In England, however, the discovery of an iron coulter from a heavy swivel plough with a mouldboard at Lyminge, Kent, now demonstrates at least some localized innovation, probably the result of elite contacts with the Continent around the turn of the seventh century.[57] In Ireland coulters were definitely in use by the tenth century and possibly earlier.[58] By contrast, in Wales no early medieval iron shares or coulters have been found. Indeed, the only evidence is in the form of two plough pebbles identified at South Hook, though the type of plough with which these were associated is unknown. Nevertheless, the presence of stinking chamomile in samples alongside the bristle oats indicates that it was being grown on heavy clay soils, possibly indicating new land was being brought into production in the latter part of the early Middle Ages that may have been aided by technological improvements in the plough. Such pebbles were set into the wooden sole of the plough, terminating in the share, thereby giving it some protection as it was propelled through the ground. Comparable examples are also known from early medieval contexts at Whithorn and Portmahomack in Scotland, but whether they were associated with a heavy mouldboard plough is contested.[59] Though oxen were normally used for traction, Rhygyfarch's *Life* of St David states in the earlier rule that the monks themselves took the yoke as a mark of asceticism, making this a possibility, primarily in a religious context.[60] The date of the wider adoption of a heavy, usually wheeled, plough drawn by six or eight oxen with an iron share and coulter together with a wooden mouldboard to turn the furrow, thereby doing away with the need for cross-ploughing, therefore remains a matter of contention frequently linked to the origins of ridge and furrow. A later tenth-century Anglo-Saxon riddle and eleventh-century manuscript illustrations only demonstrate that this type of plough was becoming more common in England by this time. Indeed, the ridge and furrow already noted under the motte-and-bailey castle at Hen Domen is still the only evidence suggesting the impact of this technology in the Welsh borderlands by the

[54] Allen et al. 2017, 41–3 (wooden shares have been found in Wales at Usk and Walesland Rath); Rees 1979, 215, fig. 55b–c; Gardner and Savory 1964, 158–9, fig. 24(11).

[55] McKerracher 2018, 119. Rynne 2018, 64–5, has argued for the impact of Roman agricultural technology in early medieval Ireland.

[56] Fowler 2002, 203–4; Brady 2016, 146–9.   [57] Thomas et al. 2016.

[58] Brady 2016, 147–9, though Rynne 2018, 44–7, 56, has argued for an earlier introduction.

[59] Crane and Murphy 2010b, 158, 178–9; Davies, T. L. 2015, 226; Brady 2016, 149–50; Hill 1997, 464–6; Carver et al. 2016, 96–7.

[60] Sharpe and Davies 2007, 126–7, ch. 22, n. 61. For later use of the breast plough in Pembrokeshire, see Comeau 2019, 132.

198   LIFE IN EARLY MEDIEVAL WALES

end of the early Middle Ages.[61] In the north the ridge and furrow at Rhuddgaer is only datable to the earlier twelfth century or before (see above), and in parts of south Wales and south-west England a lighter plough with a minimal or absent mouldboard drawn by four to six oxen was still in use into the early modern period.[62]

The cereal harvest began in August. The grain was cut with a sickle quite low on the stalk, as indicated at Brynwgan, Carmarthenshire, so the straw could be used for other purposes, including fodder and thatch.[63] It then had to be processed to remove the chaff and to preserve it prior to storage, grinding, and consumption. The change to free-threshing cereals meant processing was simpler, but it can also result in fewer surviving archaeobotanical remains. It is likely that the grain was initially gathered into sheaves so it could dry in the field prior to processing, though the need to dry damp grain to prevent it spoiling or oats harvested before they were ripe meant that it was sometimes dried in a corn-dryer before rather than after threshing and winnowing took place. Lifris's *Life* of St Cadog *c*.1100 situates an episode on the site of a threshing floor where winnowing and the drying of oats were also being carried out.[64] Archaeological evidence of such floors is difficult to identify, but possible examples were found at Felindre, Glamorgan, associated with a fifth- or sixth-century corn-dryer, and at Coed y Meirw, Llangefni, Anglesey, where a stone surface contained several quernstones with a likely corn-dryer nearby.[65]

Corn-dryers are now the main source of evidence for early medieval crop-processing in Wales and are being recognized in increasing numbers as a result of radiocarbon-dating the charred grain associated with them. During the later Roman period often elaborate, stone-built, T-shaped ovens were used to dry glume wheats prior to processing and to malt barley, but these are rare in Wales. Others were, however, much simpler, with archaeological remains consisting only of a pit, sometimes lined with stones and clay as at Tai Cochion, Anglesey, which functioned as the oven, with a stoke-hole connected to it by a short flue so as to avoid burning the grain.[66] It is versions of these that persisted throughout the early Middle Ages in Wales with the introduction of more efficient stone-lined, comma- and keyhole-shaped corn-dryers with much longer flues around the end of the period.[67]

It is generally thought that corn-dryers were located in the fields but, if so, this cannot have been far from the settlements themselves. A variety of such simple pit

---

[61] Allen et al. 2017, 47; Banham and Faith 2014, 46–50; Comeau 2019, 132–3.

[62] Comeau 2020, 86.

[63] Banham and Faith 2014, 61; Rackham 2013, 20; Caseldine and Griffiths 2019, 170. A sickle blade or billhook was found at Dinas Powys; Alcock 1963, 115(9), fig. 21.

[64] Wade-Evans 1944, 36–41, ch. 7.

[65] Leonard 2013, 20–1; James, in Darvill et al. 2020, 124, fig. 7.12; Joyce 2019, 16–17.

[66] Allen et al. 2017, 55–61; Comeau and Burrow 2021a, 124–5; Hopewell 2016, 44–5, 101–2.

[67] For discussion of typology and chronology, see Comeau and Burrow 2021a, 125–5, 132–4, figs 6–8; for the gazetteer with plans, see Comeau and Burrow 2021b.

Fig. 6.2. Figure-of-eight-shaped corn-dryer of fifth- or sixth-century date, Parc Cybi (© Gwynedd Archaeological Trust).

ovens, including pear-shaped, figure-of-eight, and subcircular examples, some with flues and other features, have been recognized. In the north-west an important group, all radiocarbon-dated to the fifth or sixth centuries AD, has been excavated at Parc Cybi (Fig. 6.2). Two of these were located in the lea of buildings in an abandoned Roman-period settlement, whilst the rest were sited on an adjacent hillock close to a small cemetery. Most were of figure-of-eight type consisting of an oven and adjacent stoke-hole, sometimes with traces of a flue, and were wholly or partly lined with stones, with heat cracking indicating the location of the fire. In some instances different fills also show that they had been fired more than once. At Dolbenmaen, where there is a corn-dryer of similar date, stones may also have been placed between the higher stoke-hole and the lower oven to act as a baffle, preventing sparks from the stoke-hole reaching the oven, with the drying grain on the wicker rack above.[68] To what extent they may have had superstructures is unclear. A group of mainly pear-shaped corn-dryers from Sarn-y-bryn-caled, Montgomeryshire, include two with adjacent post-holes and one with a beam-slot indicative of an associated structure or

---

[68] Kenney et al. 2020, i, 208–13, 359–61; Kenney and McNicol 2017, 39–41; Monk and Kelleher 2005, 82.

windbreak, and these have been radiocarbon-dated to the fifth or sixth and sixth or seventh centuries AD respectively. Further fifth- or sixth-century examples have been found at Buttington Cross, Montgomeryshire, and also in the south-west at Bayvil, Pembrokeshire, and Brynwgan, Carmarthenshire.[69] However, in contrast to the rest of Wales, a small number of sites in this region could indicate an increasing use of corn-dryers from around the turn of the eighth century, which, alongside the pollen evidence, might signal an expansion in cereal farming at this time. At South Hook, for example, a cluster of elongated pits identified as corn-dryers (Fig. 5.9) were found within the settlement rather than in the fields and the charred grain had been threshed, winnowed, and cleaned to remove the chaff and weeds prior to drying. One of these was associated with a peripheral arc of post-holes, again suggesting an associated structure. In the case of Love Lodge Farm, Ffairfach, a multiperiod site near the Roman fort at Dinefwr, Carmarthenshire, two corn-dryers were identified. The first, radiocarbon-dated to cal. AD 660–780, had a large number of stake-holes within the elongated oval pit that had probably supported a succession of wicker grain-drying racks, while peripheral stake-holes also suggest some kind of superstructure. The fuel used was mainly hazel with some alder and oak. The second, radiocarbon-dated to cal. AD 1020–1190, indicates the continuation of these simple corn-dryers at least to the end of the period.[70] However, by that time new, better-built, and more efficient comma-type ovens were being introduced in the north-west. That at Llandygái was earth-dug with a bulbous oven and a very long flue, whilst a well-preserved, stone-lined example at Graeanog East (Fig. 5.7, b) had a curving flue terminating in a round chamber; the stone-lined flue at Cefn Du was also roofed with lintels.[71] Elsewhere those of keyhole type appear more common.[72]

Early medieval corn-dryers in Wales may be closely compared with those in Ireland, with its similarly damp climate and emphasis on the cultivation of barley and oats. Here earth-dug, often figure-of-eight, pits were likewise replaced with keyhole-shaped ovens around the end of the period, though some earlier examples have also been identified. It has been argued that in Ireland there was a steep rise in the use of corn-dryers, particularly in Leinster, in the fifth to seventh centuries, with a steady decline thereafter, picking up again at the end of the period. Although there are far fewer examples, this seems broadly comparable with Wales. Climate deterioration was probably a significant factor in the post-Roman-period rise and this is also supported by the emphasis on barley and increasingly on oats. The reasons behind the

[69] Blockley and Taverner 2002, 46–57; Mann and Hurst 2014, 138, fig. 8; Comeau 2021, 63–5; Brannlund 2013, 17–19, fig. 3.

[70] Crane and Murphy 2010b, 132–6; Hourihan et al. 2015, 51, 55, figs 28a, 39, pls 9, 14; Shiner 2016, 13; Comeau and Burrow 2021a, 136–7, no. 18 (UBA-27754, UBA-27747).

[71] Kenney 2008, 108–11, 132; Fasham et al. 1998, 132–3; Cuttler et al. 2012, 25–6, fig. 2.22.

[72] Comeau and Burrow 2021b.

subsequent decline when other indicators suggest modest expansion in cereal production are less clear, though in some cases a change of location from fields to settlements, such as South Hook, might be a factor.[73] By contrast, corn-dryers are generally rare in early Anglo-Saxon England, suggesting cereals were dried over the domestic hearth. Nevertheless, with the expansion of cereal growing during the long eighth century, later examples have been identified, some very similar to those in Wales, whilst others are significantly larger and sometimes found in urban contexts or alongside mills, indicating that considerable quantities of grain were being processed.[74] Proximity to mills is also true of some later examples in Ireland, such as Raystown, Co. Meath,[75] but to date no mills have been discovered in Wales.

Grain needed to be stored to protect it from damp, weevils, and vermin. This was undoubtedly a problem at South Hook, where the barley had signs of insect damage and some barley and oats had accidentally sprouted owing to inadequate drying or damp storage conditions.[76] Sheaves could be built into ricks prior to processing but once this had taken place storage within houses or other structures was necessary. In north-west Wales four-post, above-ground storage structures of Iron Age type persisted into the post-Roman period, as at Dolbenmaen, but more Romanized stone buildings may have done likewise, as at the enclosed hut group Cefn Graeanog 2, where the entrance building, which had a cross-passage, was partly used as a sheaf store, with the other half as a byre.[77] In the seventh or eighth century the house at Rhuddgaer also had a cross-passage (Fig. 5.10, b) and it seems likely that the lower part was used for storage.[78] However, on high-status sites, both secular and ecclesiastical, that functioned as estate centres the collection of food render and potentially more mouths to feed would have made larger-scale storage essential. Buildings 4 and 5 on the periphery of the enclosure at Llanbedrgoch (Fig. 5.5) could have functioned in this way, and it has been suggested that a dedicated store burnt down in the 916 attack was the source of the grain excavated at Llangorse crannog.[79] Grain-storage structures have proved equally difficult to identify in both Ireland and England, though there are hints of the early medieval use of four-post and related above-ground structures in both. It has also been suggested that in England barns become a feature of estate centres from around the eighth century onwards, sometimes with threshing floors as in the monastic phase at Lyminge, but clearly nothing on this scale is known from Wales.[80]

Prior to human consumption the processed grain needed to be ground into flour or meal for making bread, bannocks, and oatcakes. Done by hand, this would have

[73] Monk and Power 2012; Comeau and Burrow 2021a, 132–3.
[74] Hamerow 2012, 151–2; McKerracher 2018, 77–9. [75] Seaver 2016, 87–104, 126–7.
[76] Carruthers, in Crane and Murphy 2010b, 164.
[77] Kenney and McNicol 2017, 59, fig. 2; Fasham et al. 1998, 48, 71.
[78] Hopewell and Edwards 2017, 232–3. [79] Redknap 2004a, 153; Caseldine and Griffiths 2019, 170.
[80] O'Sullivan et al. 2014, 199; McKerracher 2018, 72–6; Thomas 2016, 361–3.

been a laborious task commonly carried out at a domestic level by women. Stones, often fragmentary, from hand-operated rotary querns are a comparatively frequent find on early medieval sites in Wales, both high-status and otherwise. It has been shown that the larger, flatter, and more efficient disc-type rotary querns introduced by the Romans began to replace the 'beehive' form on native sites during the third and fourth centuries[81] and then remained in use throughout the early Middle Ages. The querns are usually made of local sandstones, some so coarse, as, for example, those found in cist-graves at Coed-y-Meirw, Llangefni, Anglesey, that the grit remaining in the bread had caused serious wear to the teeth of those interred.[82] Some of these and others, such as the fragmentary lower stone from Dinas Powys, are incised with radial grooves on the grinding surface to help spread the grain more evenly, showing the continuation of a characteristically Roman form also found around three centuries later at Llangorse crannog.[83] Most are, however, plain, as indicated by examples from a number of sites in the south-west including a rather roughly executed stone from Newton, Llanstadwell, Pembrokeshire, found in the upper fill of a corn-dryer radiocarbon-dated to cal. AD 720–960. Those from around the same time at South Hook were severely worn, with one showing signs of reconditioning, demonstrating that they were items of considerable investment used over an extended period of time. One may originally have had a rynd, an iron fitting supporting the upper stone, which was attached to the underside, whilst another from Brownslade had a slot which may have been for a handle to turn the stone.[84] Most from Wales are between 300 and 450 millimetres in diameter, but there are several larger stones from Llanbedrgoch, where nearly forty have been found. Two are more than 800 millimetres in diameter and, as a result, would have been very difficult to manipulate by hand. On analogy with Roman examples, these might be millstones, since a watermill would have been an appropriate piece of equipment in the vicinity of this wealthy estate centre. A sunken-floored building with what has been interpreted as a bread oven has also been excavated on the site.[85]

Therefore, though no early medieval mill structures or evidence for the water management systems associated with them have so far been found in Wales, their former existence, most likely on land owned by elites, seems almost certain, especially when considered in a broader context. Roman mills have mostly been identified in southern and eastern England, though to what extent they continued to operate beyond the

[81] Cuttler et al. 2012, 165, 169–70; Allen et al. 2017, 71–2.

[82] Parry and Parry 2016, 7–9; Parry 2017, 5.

[83] Alcock 1963, 166–8; Lane and Redknap 2019, 248–50. See also an example from Phase 1 of Llanelen ecclesiastical site, Gower; Schlesinger and Walls 1996, 135–6.

[84] Crane 2004, 14–15 (Beta-182946); Crane and Murphy 2010b, 152–6; Groom et al. 2011, 155–7, no. 4.

[85] Crane and Murphy 2010b, 153, table 1; Redknap 2000, pl. 115; 2001, 144–7; 2004a, 165; Allen et al. 2017. Roman millstones have been identified in a villa context at Whitton and probably Llancarfan, Glamorgan; Jarrett and Wrathmell 1981, 222–3, 225.

Roman period is unknown. In Ireland, however, nearly seventy have been dated by dendrochronology indicating the introduction of mainly horizontal watermills, probably from the Continent, in the early seventh century, as at the monastic site of Nendrum, Co. Down.[86] In Anglo-Saxon England watermills are extant from the late seventh century onwards, largely associated with monasteries and secular estate centres, though the context of the most westerly examples, two horizontal mills of late seventh- and early eighth-century date from Wellington Quarry, near Hereford, is unclear.[87] Interestingly, even by the time of Domesday Book, mills still seem to have been comparatively rare in both Cheshire and Herefordshire, suggesting that hand-milling remained common. Equally, few mills are noted west of the Dee and in the valleys of the Wye, Team, and Dore in western Herefordshire, both areas of English settlement before the Norman conquest, and only six are mentioned west of the Wye in Gloucestershire.[88]

Therefore, although the amount of well-dated grain samples from Wales remains small and associated evidence for cultivation, processing, and storage is largely confined to corn-dryers and rotary querns, some trends may be suggested. Firstly, as in Ireland, whilst barley remained an important crop, oats rapidly gained in significance during the early Middle Ages. This was most likely a response to climate deterioration in the post-Roman period as indicated by the pollen evidence and Irish dendrochronological data as well as an increasing number of ovens to dry the grain prior to storage. Concentration on barley and increasingly oats, as in Ireland, would have given the greatest chance of food security whilst requiring less processing than glume wheats at a time of population decline. Spelt was already being replaced by bread wheat at the end of the Roman period, though, as in Ireland, but in contrast to Anglo-Saxon England the latter was never a major crop since it was more difficult to cultivate in Wales as the climate and soils were less suitable, and it required more labour to grow successfully. As a luxury crop, it may largely have been produced as food render and primarily for consumption on high-status sites. Although there are some indications, as at South Hook, of an increase in cereal farming in the south-west from around the eighth century, there is certainly nothing in Wales on the scale of that noted in both Ireland and southern and eastern England at this time, and there is currently little evidence of technological change and innovation. Whilst secular and ecclesiastical estates and the development of payments of food render are evident in the written sources in Wales from the seventh century onwards, it is still impossible to discern to what extent either rural communities could produce or elites obtain sufficient surpluses to facilitate the development of other mechanisms of local exchange and trade.

[86] O'Sullivan et al. 2014, 203–9; Rynne 2018, 56–60; McErlean and Crothers 2007, 434–5.
[87] Hamerow 2012, 152–4; McKerracher 2018, 79–80; Watts 2017, 177–8.
[88] Terrett 1962, 376, 385; Atkin 1954, 98–100; Darby 1954, 53–4.

ANIMAL HUSBANDRY

Our understanding of livestock farming in early medieval Wales is severely hampered by the continuing lack of archaeological evidence owing to the predominantly acidic soils with the result that bone seldom survives. Where it does, as, for example, at Longbury Bank and Cold Knap, samples are often very small, making anything other than species identification almost impossible.[89] There are, however, three much larger and more important assemblages, all from elite sites. Of these Dinas Powys is the only site dating to the earlier part of the period, but, as it was excavated in the late 1950s, apart from a small sample only selected bones were kept, meaning that, despite reassessment, it is difficult to draw more than basic conclusions.[90] Therefore, since the assemblage from Llanbedrgoch awaits publication, that from Llangorse crannog, dating to the late ninth and early tenth centuries, provides the only modern study, making any wider comparison extremely difficult.[91] Although some evidence on the significance of livestock husbandry can be gleaned from other, mainly written, sources, this is clearly inadequate when attempting to reconstruct a fuller picture of the role of animals in the early medieval farming economy in Wales. In the past, pastoralism has been overemphasized,[92] but we now risk downplaying its significance in early medieval Welsh society because the evidence for cereal cultivation is more plentiful in the archaeological record.

At Rhuddgaer, crops were grown in the fields surrounding the settlement, while livestock would have grazed the autumn stubble and were otherwise confined, probably by pens or temporary fences, especially at night, to prevent them from damaging the crops. More generally, herders would have driven cattle and sheep to graze meadows, saltmarshes, and other rough pasture in the neighbourhood of settlements, and in the autumn pigs would have been taken to woodlands to be fattened on acorns and other mast. We have already seen examples of early medieval estates encompassing a range of environmental zones—arable, woodland, and a variety of seasonally exploited rough pasture, including moorland (*ffridd*)—during the summer months. In mainland north-west Wales an increasing number of pollen diagrams indicate an expansion in pastoral farming during the ninth to eleventh centuries, pointing to increasing exploitation of the uplands for grazing livestock, particularly cattle. Heather burning may also have been practised to improve the pasture, as at Moel Llys y Coed in the Clwydian hills.[93]

---

[89] Campbell and Lane 1993, 53; Evans, E. M. et al. 1985, 122.

[90] Alcock 1963, 34–40, 192–3; 1987, 67–82; Gilchrist 1988.   [91] Mulville et al. 2019.

[92] For a demolition of earlier twentieth-century interpretations emphasizing nomadic pastoralism, see Jones, G. R. J. 1961.

[93] Davies, T. L. 2015, 71, 232; 2019, 189–92; Grant 2008, 11–12.

Exploitation of the uplands in this way raises the important question as to what extent transhumance—the moving of livestock to the uplands to graze for an extended period during the summer months—was practised in early medieval Wales. This would have made the best use of available resources, thus helping to manage risk in more marginal environments, and during the climatic optimum, a period of expanding population from *c.*1100 until the early fourteenth century, seasonal grazing associated with dairying often evolved into more permanent upland settlement. However, pollen evidence suggests that this phase of transhumance may have begun somewhat earlier, during the ninth and tenth centuries, but to what extent it was practised before this is currently unknown, though the more general fall in pastoral indicators during the post-Roman period might suggest a decline that was later reversed. Nevertheless, in the absence of archaeological evidence, place names may also provide a clue to the existence of transhumance, since it has been argued that the Welsh *hendre* ('home farm') and *hafod* ('summer dwelling') elements are also found in Cornish (*hendre* and *havos*). This suggests that their use in both areas predates the expansion of Wessex into Devon and Cornwall beginning in the later seventh and earlier eighth century.[94] Equally, charters and other pre-Conquest sources confirm that transhumance, particularly the exploitation of wood pasture, was practised in the west Midlands, though it appears to have diminished by the time of the Domesday survey as more permanent settlements were established.[95]

Animal bone assemblages of later Roman date in Britain demonstrate the increasing significance of cattle farming on rural sites and for the market as, for example, in the vicinity of Caerleon and Caerwent, where the Gwent Levels provided rich pastures, and at Caernarfon. Beef was the main food product, with dairying playing only a minor role.[96] At the same time cattle were increasingly seen as a means of displaying wealth amongst native elites.[97] By contrast, the written sources in early medieval Wales clearly demonstrate the significance of cows, showing milk and other dairy products, most likely prepared by women, as an important source of protein in the diet. This indicates, as in Ireland, that a major change of emphasis had taken place that may also have been a way to manage risk because of the collapse in the Roman market economy, climate deterioration, and population decline, since the raising of beef cattle is more labour-intensive and needs more resources.[98] Factors such as these may have led elites to measure wealth in terms of numbers of cattle, thereby encouraging dairying rather than beef production. A small group of Llandaf and Llancarfan charters show that by the early eighth century the value of purchased land in the south-east was measured in cows, a unit of value that remained in use, though gradually replaced by

[94] Davies, T. L. 2019; Ward 1997; Herring 2012, 89–92; Padel 1985, 127, 129.
[95] Hooke 2019, 38–41.   [96] Allen et al. 2017, 85, 91–4, 110–14; Casey and Davies 1993, 97, 100.
[97] Gerrard 2013, 102–3.   [98] Gilchrist 1988, 59.

silver, up to the twelfth century.[99] Cattle and other livestock were also the object of cross-border raids indicated in Ergyng in the tenth- or early eleventh-century *Ordinance concerning the Dunsæte*, which includes the value of a plough ox at thirty pence.[100]

Cattle and other animal bones from Llangorse crannog demonstrate that the inhabitants were consuming meat brought onto the site, probably in the form of food render. Interestingly, cattle formed only around a quarter of the assemblage and were secondary to pigs. This is broadly comparable with Dinas Powys in the fifth to seventh centuries. The cattle at Llangorse were quite small compared with the size range of early medieval cattle in Britain as a whole, but the age-of-slaughter pattern indicates that they were largely mature females, suggesting the consumption of older cows and oxen past their prime, which would be consistent with a dairying economy. The comparative lack of cattle heads and the higher number of hindlimbs compared with forelimbs indicates that they were slaughtered off-site but then delivered as almost complete carcasses.[101]

Pigs—prolific breeders—are reared for their meat, which can also be salted and smoked for preservation. Pig bones are rarely more than 10–15 per cent of the total assemblage in Roman contexts, but they are more commonly found on military sites, in towns, such as Caerwent, and at villas, where there is some evidence for suckling pig, regarded as a delicacy, suggesting elite consumption. It has been argued that this is also evident on some Roman sites, such as Wroxeter, occupied in the fifth century.[102] An association with high status and feasting is more marked both in Anglo-Saxon England and Francia,[103] and the unusually high proportion of pig bones found at both Dinas Powys and Llangorse crannog indicates that this was also true in Wales. At Llangorse pigs, mainly sows, were slaughtered often in their third year, though some younger animals (which predominated at Dinas Powys) would have provided the best meat. The animals varied considerably in size, some being unusually large, perhaps showing that they were bred for food render on different farms. Equally, heads and forelimbs were more common than hindquarters, which were regarded as the prime cuts, and extremities, suggesting that only certain parts of the animals were rendered.[104] The value of sows for breeding is also recognized in the *Ordinance*

[99] Davies, W. 1978, 51–4, 60; Charles-Edwards 2013, 286–8. Milch cows were likewise the basic unit of value in the eighth-century Irish law texts, also gradually replaced by silver; see Kelly 1997, 58. Their importance in Ireland is also evident in bone assemblages, with cattle consistently dominating the livestock economy until around 800; see O'Sullivan et al. 2014, 209–11.

[100] Noble 1983, 108–9.

[101] Mulville et al. 2019; Gilchrist 1988, 56, also hints at a sex and slaughter pattern suggesting a dairying economy at Dinas Powys.

[102] Allen et al. 2017, 89, 118–19; Maltby 2016, 797–8; Gerrard 2013, 162.

[103] Banham and Faith 2014, 97–9, 115–16; Loveluck 2013, 116–17.

[104] Mulville et al. 2019; Gilchrist 1988, 57.

FOOD, FARMING, AND THE AGRICULTURAL ECONOMY 207

concerning the Dunsæte where they are worth twenty-four pence, whereas a pig was worth only eight.

The bones of sheep and goats are often difficult to distinguish in the archaeological record, though in the *Ordinance concerning the Dunsæte* the former, valued at a shilling, were clearly more important than the latter at two pence.[105] The comparatively low value is reflected at both Llangorse crannog, where sheep and goat bones make up less than 20 per cent of the total, and at Dinas Powys, where the percentage appears similar. Sheep and goats may be kept for meat and dairy products, particularly cheese, as well as for their wool and hair. At Llangorse there were very few young animals and the proportions of male and female are similar. Most were slaughtered between two and four years, but some were older, and they were probably brought to the site as whole carcasses or sides. This suggests the significance of both mutton and wool production.[106]

Horses were highly valued amongst the elite in early medieval Welsh society for riding, hunting, and warfare, but were also used as beasts of burden. Most were probably no larger than ponies, but interbreeding with imported horses during the Roman period may have increased the size and value of some. The early Irish law texts specifically refer to the import of mares, indicating a market for horses from Britain.[107] In Wales horses figure in payments for both goods and land. An early ninth-century addition to the Lichfield Gospels records how Gelli son of Arthudd bought the gospel book with a 'best horse' (*equm optimum*) before placing it on the altar of St Teilo at Llandeilo Fawr. Equally, amongst the Llandaf charters dated to the eighth century horses used in payments for land later donated to the Church are valued in terms of cows ranging from 'a best horse' worth twelve cows to others worth only three. The former purchase price also included a hawk and a hunting dog, demonstrating that horses used in the chase were particularly prized.[108] Furthermore, huntsmen on horses are depicted on two crosses at Margam and Penmon,[109] indicating how their patrons wished to be portrayed—a widespread practice more commonly found on sculpture in Ireland, Pictland, and to a lesser extent some Scandinavian-settled parts of the Danelaw. Indeed, by the eleventh century horses for riding are evident amongst a greater range of society in England, partly as a result of Scandinavian influence, and this is seen in the discovery of large numbers of pieces of decorated equine metalwork, though the number from Wales remains small.[110] By this time we can also see the considerable value of horses in terms of silver. In the *Ordinance concerning the Dunsæte* a horse was worth thirty shillings, a mare and a year-old stallion twenty.[111] By contrast,

[105] Noble 1983, 109.   [106] Gilchrist 1988, 57; Mulville et al. 2019, 177–9, 184.

[107] Allen et al. 2017, 124–30; Banham and Faith 2014, 79–82; Kelly 1997, 88–91.

[108] Jenkins and Owen 1983, 50; Davies, W. 1978, 53–4; Evans, J. G., and Rhys 1893, xliii, 201, 203b.

[109] Redknap and Lewis 2007, no. G79; Edwards 2013, 99–100, no. AN51.

[110] Naylor and Geake 2011, 290; Kershaw 2013, 177; Webley 2014; Redknap 2013.

[111] Noble 1983, 109.

archaeozoological evidence remains negligible. Only a small number of horse bones were found at both Dinas Powys and Llangorse, making it very difficult to say anything further about either breeding or husbandry.[112]

Chickens may have been introduced into Britain during the Iron Age, but in the course of the Roman period they began to be reared for their meat and eggs and the number of bones gradually increases, especially in towns, but, though few in number, they also become more widespread on rural sites.[113] Equally, chicken bones, the fragility of which means that they are less likely to survive in the archaeological record, are generally only found in small numbers on both early medieval Irish and Anglo-Saxon sites and this is also true at Llangorse crannog, the only site in Wales where they have so far been identified.[114]

Therefore our understanding of livestock husbandry in early medieval Wales is still largely based on the meagre written record because so little animal bone evidence normally survives and what has come to light is concentrated on elite sites, notably Llangorse crannog. Nevertheless, it is possible to discern the significance of cattle, at least in the earlier part of the period, and the change to a dairying economy, as in Ireland, most likely as a response to risk since milk products are high in protein. The elite consumption of pork and preserved meats is clearly demonstrated at both Dinas Powys and Llangorse, and this is also found on elite sites in England. The rearing of horses also supported an elite lifestyle, though in Wales equine equipment remains rare compared with England where it becomes increasingly common towards the end of the period. Sheep, goats, and chickens were much less important.

HUNTING, FISHING, AND GATHERING

Wild animals, birds, and fish, as well as fruits, nuts, and other edible plants, were potentially significant adjuncts to the diet, especially in times of need, but to what extent these resources were exploited by different levels of early medieval society in Wales remains very difficult to gauge because of the limitations of the evidence. Hunting was an important high-status male pursuit and this is corroborated by a range of evidence. The main animals hunted were red and roe deer, the bones of which have been found in small numbers at the elite sites of Dinas Powys and Longbury Bank, both dating to the earlier part of the period.[115] However, by the late ninth century a different picture emerges at Llangorse crannog, where red and roe deer bones, at 9 per cent of the total assemblage, were unusually common, clearly demonstrating the significance of hunting for game and the consumption of venison

---

[112] Mulville et al. 2019, 175, table 8.1.1; Alcock 1963, 192–3.   [113] Allen et al. 2017, 134–6.

[114] McCormick and Murray 2007, 71–5; Mulville et al. 2019, 182.

[115] Alcock 1963, 192; Campbell and Lane 1993, 53.

as part of the diet on this royal site. Indeed, the emphasis on large red deer may show the particular pursuit of mature stags in woodland on the estates surrounding the lake, allied to seasonal occupation of the crannog during the summer and autumn months. Interestingly, the lack of heads indicates that both red and roe deer were being butchered at the site of the kill, with the hindlimbs of the former and the fore- and hindlimbs of the latter being selected and brought back to the crannog.[116] The rest of the carcasses must have been distributed elsewhere, including amongst the hunting party and perhaps the adjacent monastic site that owned the surrounding land. Naomi Sykes has argued that the increasing significance of deer hunting also found amongst the elite in late Anglo-Saxon England demonstrates a growing emphasis on high-status display associated with the rise of thegns and their establishment of more restricted control over the land and its wild resources. In this case, although deer carcasses were earlier divided up, they were now being brought back to elite settlements complete, indicating a more exclusive attitude to consumption than is evident on the royal site at Llangorse where acts of gift-giving seem to have remained of more significance.[117]

In the early ninth-century *Historia Brittonum* the mythical and heroic symbolism of wild boar hunting is demonstrated by the inclusion, amongst the 'Wonders of Britain', of a site in Buellt with a footprint made by Arthur's hound in pursuit of the magical *Twrch Trywyth*.[118] Although domestic pig and wild boar are difficult to distinguish archaeologically, elite hunting of such animals is suggested by some of the larger bones at Llangorse. Evidence of a dog resembling a greyhound was also found and, though insufficiently strong for hunting deer or wild boar, such an animal could have been used to chase hare, the bones of which are likewise found at Llangorse. In such a lake environment waterbirds such as ducks, geese, and swans were similarly exploited,[119] and in England it has been shown that from the mid-ninth century onwards wild bird bones are increasingly found on elite sites, indicating their consumption. Some species were trapped in nets or snares, but others were caught by falcons.[120] No osteological evidence has so far been found for such birds of prey on early medieval sites in Wales, and it has been argued that hunting with hawks was introduced from England. However, this is not necessarily the case. Whilst raptors in

---

[116] Mulville et al. 2019, 178–80, 185–6. Mounds of burnt stone with troughs and pits, most likely used for cooking meat, have in Ireland traditionally been associated with early medieval deer hunting. They are, however, characteristically Late Neolithic and Bronze Age in both Britain and Ireland. A very small number have later radiocarbon dates, notably Pentrefelin (Archwilio GAT prn 34096), Llŷn, with three radiocarbon dates statistically focused on AD 620–55 pointing to occasional early medieval use or reuse in some way, though an association with deer hunting may be discounted as later folklore; see Kenney 2012; Kenney et al. 2014, 5, 9; Hawkes 2018, 221–4.

[117] Sykes 2010, 183–8. On the division of deer carcasses after the hunt in Welsh and earlier Irish legal texts, see Kelly 1997, 275.

[118] Morris 1980, 42, 83, ch. 73.   [119] Mulville et al. 2019, 177–9, 182, 186, table 8.1.1.

[120] Sykes 2004, 86–8.

210 LIFE IN EARLY MEDIEVAL WALES

England were already associated with the warrior elite in the earlier part of the period, in Wales it is clear from Llandaf charters dated to the eighth century that hawks were also highly valued, since they appear in sales of land by kings in the south-east: one is worth six cows, another twelve.[121] In addition, one of the hunting scenes on the mid-tenth century cross at Penmon may include a horseman carrying a hawk.[122]

By contrast, fishing, whether freshwater, estuarine, or coastal, was a much lowlier pursuit, but there is evidence to suggest that through ownership of fishing rights the elite, both ecclesiastical and secular, were major beneficiaries. During the Roman period it has been argued that the quantity of fish consumed on rural sites in Britain gradually increased, though it was still a small part of the diet. There are comparatively few fish bone samples from Wales but there is more evidence from south and south-west England. As a result, it may be suggested that salmon and eels were caught in the Severn estuary, one of several important salmon rivers in Wales, whilst the consumption of coastal fish may have included wrasse, bass, bream, and mullet.[123]

Most of our evidence for early medieval fishing is concentrated along the lower stretches of the Severn and its estuary on either side of Offa's Dyke, which reaches the shore at Sedbury Cliffs on the west bank of the river. The archaeological remains consist of often fragmentary wooden fish-traps and wicker baskets which have been preserved in the mud of the intertidal zone and foreshore. These would have been used to catch migrating salmon and eels as well as flatfish and other coastal species. Hazel wattles or hurdles found in a tidal palaeochannel near Redwick on the Caldicot Level, which seem to have been part of a curved fish-trap radiocarbon-dated to cal. AD 420–660, are so far the only indication of fishing in the post-Roman period.[124] Further examples, beginning in the later seventh or eighth century, include V-shaped structures of stakes with associated catch baskets found on the eastern bank of the river on Oldbury Flats, Aust, Gloucestershire (Fig. 6.3), at Beachley on the opposite bank, and upstream at Woolaston.[125] Possibly contemporary V-shaped fish-traps and baskets have also been recorded on the Caldicot Level west of Sudbrook Point near the outflow of the River Troggy, but here the majority are eleventh- to fourteenth-century in date and this is also true elsewhere in the Severn estuary.[126]

The archaeological evidence may be closely compared with that in the written sources. Several Llandaf charters refer to fishing rights and fish weirs, including two dated to the end of the ninth century granted by King Brochfael ap Meurig of Glywysing of estates west of Sudbrook Point.[127] Another earlier charter, apparently regranted by King Hywel ap Rhys of Glywysing in the later ninth century, claims land

---

[121] Jenkins 2000, 259–61; Davies, W. 1978, 52–3; Evans, J. G., and Rhys 1893, nos 201, 203a.

[122] Edwards 2013, no. AN51, 225.   [123] Smith, A. et al. 2018, 111–14; Locker 2007, 153–4.

[124] Allen and Bell 1999, 58–60 (SWAN-241).   [125] Chadwick and Catchpole 2010, 10–17, 20–1, 25.

[126] Godbold and Turner 1994; Brown et al. 2010.

[127] Davies, W. 1978, 36, n. 3, 183, nos 234, 235b; Evans, J. G., and Rhys 1893, 234, 235b.

Fig. 6.3. Later seventh- or eighth-century fish-trap, Oldbury flats (© Gloucestershire County Council).

at Tidenham, Gloucestershire, located between the Wye and the Severn between Beachley and Woolaston.[128] By the mid-tenth century at the latest, however, Tidenham was in English hands and was granted to Bath Abbey in 954. An undated survey of the estate and a lease to Archbishop Stigand of Canterbury 1061–5 give detailed descriptions of the fishing rights along the Wye and Severn, including mention of over a hundred fish-weirs, some with baskets. These documents therefore testify to the rapidly growing importance of commercial fishing, which also included, by the end of the period, enormous numbers of herring caught off the coast that could be preserved by smoking, salting, or drying, thereby indicating the increasing value to landowners of the fish trade.[129]

Taken together, this evidence supports the view that what has been termed the 'fish-event horizon' around the turn of the millennium was also taking place in the south-east borderlands of Wales. Indeed, the fish-bone evidence from across England argues for a rapid expansion in the commercial fishing trade at this time, especially for marine fish—herring and increasingly cod. This is broadly reflected in Ireland, across

---

[128] Ibid., 174b, 229b; Davies, W. 1978, 173, 182, nos 174b, 229b.
[129] Robertson 1956, nos cix, cxvii; Faith 1994; Banham and Faith 2014, 183–8; Davies, W. 1978, 61.

212 LIFE IN EARLY MEDIEVAL WALES

the Channel, and in Central Europe, though marine fish were exploited at an earlier date in Scandinavia, and in the Northern Isles probably as a result of Viking settlement.[130] Since there were no towns in Wales, the more general expansion in fishing evident in the lower reaches of the Wye and Severn, and in the Severn estuary, was probably primarily focused on the needs of a growing urban population in England prior to the Norman Conquest. In this context Harold Godwinson's brief establishment of a foothold at Portskewett close to Sudbrook Point in 1065[131] may also reflect a bid to control lucrative fishing rights on both sides of the Severn estuary. Monasteries, such as Bath Abbey and Llancarfan,[132] likewise needed to secure supplies of fish as no animal flesh was eaten on fast days.

To what extent the evidence in the south-east borderlands is comparable with the rest of Wales is difficult to say since very little is known, though there is nothing to indicate that marine fish were of significance prior to the end of the period. Fisheries are mentioned on the Ely,[133] and those on the east side of the Dee estuary around Chester were undoubtedly important by the time of Domesday, but there are only a couple of rather vague references in Atiscros Hundred to the west.[134] River fishing for salmon and sea trout may have been carried out at night using a net strung between two coracles, as on several Welsh rivers, including the Dee and Wye into the twentieth century, and on the Teifi, Taf, and Tywi to this day.[135] A few salmon or sea-trout bones were identified at Dinas Powys and, if not intrusive, the small number of fish-bones from Llangorse crannog, in addition to salmon or sea trout, suggest some consumption of freshwater fish, principally pike, but also perch, roach, and bream.[136] Likewise, molluscs have only rarely been recorded and only on sites near the coast. For example, early medieval shell middens sampled at Wylfa Newydd, Anglesey, contained large quantities of limpets that may have been used as bait, as well as oysters, whilst cockles and winkles were found at Llanbedrgoch.[137] On earlier sites in the south only small quantities have been identified. Oysters predominated at Longbury Bank, with some cockles, mussels, limpets, and scallops, whilst limpets, oysters, and whelks were identified at Dinas Powys.[138]

There has been comparatively little stable isotope analysis of human bone from early medieval cemeteries in Wales to cast light on the extent to which marine fish were eaten. However, individuals examined from five early medieval cemeteries in the south showed that even coastal communities had not consumed significant quantities

---

[130] Barrett et al. 2004; on Ireland, see O'Sullivan 2001, 179–81, 186–8.

[131] Douglas and Greenaway 1981, *s.a.* 1065.   [132] Wade-Evans 1944, 78–9, ch. 24.

[133] Evans, J. G., and Rhys 1893, 204a; Davies, W. 1979a, 116.

[134] Terrett 1962, 360–2; Williams, A., and Martin 2002, 736–7.

[135] Jenkins 2006, 58–9, 69, 86; BBC Radio 4, *From Our Home Correspondent*, 2 October 2017.

[136] Mulville et al. 2019, 182; Alcock 1963, 39–40.

[137] Ashley Batten (pers. comm., May 2017); Redknap 2000, illus. 116.

[138] Campbell and Lane 1993, 52; Alcock 1963, 39.

of marine fish, though some freshwater fish and molluscs may have been eaten as part of a predominantly terrestrial protein diet. A similar picture emerged in the north at Coed y Meirw, Llangefni, Anglesey.[139] In contrast, the man buried in a Viking furnished grave at Tanlan, near Talacre, Flintshire, had been consuming large amounts of marine protein, suggesting that he was from Scandinavia where fish, such as herring and cod, were already an important part of the diet.[140]

There is also some evidence to suggest the continuing consumption of wild plants, nuts, and fruit. Seaweed, with its high protein and vitamin content, may have been eaten at Brownslade and other coastal sites. Hazelnuts, likewise a good source of protein, are, however, more commonly found in early medieval contexts ranging from Llangorse crannog to Conkland Hill. Sloe stones were also found at the former and blackberry seeds at the latter, indicating the collecting and consumption of wild fruit.[141]

The pursuit of deer and other game in Wales was therefore primarily an elite pastime that appears to have grown in popularity in the latter part of the period, as in Anglo-Saxon England. Equally, though some freshwater and estuarine fish were probably consumed throughout the period, in the south-east at least this resource grew rapidly in significance from around the turn of the millennium, a phenomenon evident across England and further afield. As a result, control of fishing rights became increasingly important because of the expanding fish trade, probably initially to towns in England, that now began to include marine species such as herring. Although also enjoyed by the elite, a range of wild foods probably provided necessary extra sources of nutrition for those at the other end of the social scale.

DIET AND HEALTH

So far, I have analysed a range of evidence to try and reconstruct aspects of landholding and the changing farming economy over time, whilst also determining the extent to which natural resources were exploited for food. This has also indicated social differences, by around the seventh century onwards, between estate owners, whether secular or ecclesiastical, and the tenants who lived on these estates who supplied the owners with agricultural goods in the form of food renders, resulting in the need to produce regular agricultural surpluses. Here I shall examine archaeological, osteological, and other data to cast light on how food was prepared and eaten, as well as aspects of dietary health that might further illuminate social difference and potentially changes over time.

---

[139] Hemer 2011; Hemer et al. 2017; Joyce 2019, 22.

[140] Higham et al. 2007, S5; Christopher Bronk Ramsey, Oxford University Radiocarbon Accelerator Unit (pers. comm.).

[141] Groom et al. 2011, 183; Hart 2014, 48, 5; Caseldine and Griffiths 2019, 170–1.

214 LIFE IN EARLY MEDIEVAL WALES

As already indicated, limited isotope analysis points to a predominantly terrestrial diet. Similarly, Chad 3 and 4 of the Lichfield marginalia, as well as the Llandaf and Llancarfan charters, show that in south Wales at least food render was paid twice a year and was made up of bread, its accompaniment—flesh in the form of animals, such as a sow or a wether, and/or dairy products in summer—and drink, with sometimes honey as well.[142] Cereals, mainly barley and increasingly oats, were the dietary mainstay, but much less wheat was grown and may have been cultivated largely for render. While there must have been regional differences, the emphasis on oats and barley and the ways in which cereals were prepared point to strong similarities with Ireland and much of northern Britain, preferences that to some extent survived into modern times. It is therefore possible to draw on the wealth of evidence in the early medieval Irish written sources alongside the archaeology.

Regina Sexton has demonstrated that in Ireland cereals were mainly consumed as bread, with porridge and gruel forming lesser elements in the diet. Barley was also important for brewing ale, with fermentation used in brewing and baking alike, both usually carried out by women in a domestic context. Barley and oat flours are low in gluten and, even with a leavening agent, produce flat breads of the kind later described by Gerald of Wales. Wheat, which is higher in gluten, produces a lighter loaf made, for example, with buttermilk like soda bread or leavened with yeast.[143] The dough may have been kneaded in a wooden trough or on a flat stone such as that found embedded in clay at Hedd yr Ynys, Llangefni, Anglesey, which also showed signs of blackening, suggesting it had at some point been placed near the hearth for the loaf to rise or been utilized as a bakestone. There is a similar stone from Longbury Bank, whilst other, thinner bakestones, which would have been set in the embers of the hearth, have been identified there and at Dinas Powys.[144] Some breads were covered during baking to aid rising, most likely with an iron cooking pot to make a simple oven. Alternatively, they might be placed in a lidded iron pot and suspended over the fire and, though none has survived, iron griddles would also have been used to cook oatcakes and bannocks.[145] Baking could be carried out on the domestic hearth or in the open air, but baking for larger numbers may have required a bakehouse and it has been suggested that a sunken-floored structure with an oven close to the spring at Llanbedrgoch may have functioned in this way.[146] Large amounts of bread were also consumed on monastic sites and a bakery is specifically mentioned in Lifris's *Life* of St Cadog.[147]

[142] Davies, W. 1982a, 46; Charles-Edwards 2013, 280–2.

[143] Sexton 1998, 76–80; Thorpe 1978, 237.

[144] Sexton 1998, 81–2; Kenney 2018, 39–40, 51, figs 5, 7; Campbell and Lane 1993, 52; Alcock 1963, 168, fig. 36.

[145] Sexton 1998, 81–2; Minwel Tibbott 1982.   [146] Redknap 2001, 144–5, pl. 3.

[147] Wade-Evans 1944, 120–1, ch. 49.

The bread was then accompanied by whatever was available depending on season, status, and dietary preference. *De Raris Fabulis*, a tenth-century monastic text from Wales or Cornwall used for teaching Latin, lists, for example, butter, lard, and dripping, a range of other dairy products including cheese and curds, vegetables such as leeks and cabbage, and meat in the form of sausages and black puddings.[148] Other accompaniments would have included roasted, boiled, or barbecued meats (fresh or salted), poultry, eggs, fruits, nuts, and honey. Suitable accompaniments could also be added to porridge and gruel cooked in an iron pot on the edge of the hearth.[149]

Drinks included milk and whey but also ale that was generally low in alcohol and consumed by everyone. Archaeological evidence for brewing in the form of sprouted barley grains used for making malt has been found associated with corn-dryers, as at Cefn Du, Llanfihangel Ysgeifiog, Anglesey.[150] Bragget was similarly malted but honey was added making it stronger and of higher status, whilst in poetry mead was considered an elite drink associated with feasting and warbands as, for example, in both *Etmyg Dinbych* and an *englyn* in the Cambridge Juvencus (Chapter 1).[151]

Amongst the elite there was also a taste for exotic food and drink, particularly wine. During the Roman period many new foods, including fruits such as figs, vegetables such as leaf beet, and herbs such as dill and coriander, were brought to Britain for the first time. Such imports had most impact in the south and east, and in some instances, for example apples, these were swiftly adapted to native cultivation. Some vineyards were also planted but wine was normally imported, largely from Gaul in amphorae (and later probably in barrels) alongside olive oil and fish sauces.[152] Whilst it is difficult to prove that such imports persisted into the fifth century, wine at least continued because of its role in the Christian liturgy and it may also have been perceived more widely as a sign of lingering Roman identity. What is clear is that during the later fifth and first half of the sixth century wine and possibly other exotic products were reaching a small number of high-status sites in Wales, such as Dinas Powys, in late Roman amphorae (LRA) from the eastern Mediterranean imported via the Atlantic seaways together with red slipware bowls from Turkey (LRC) and North Africa (ARD-D) which, together with the large number of pig bones, are strongly indicative of feasting. Equally, during the sixth century, grey *Dérivées sigillées paléochrétiennes*, Atlantic Group (DSPA) bowls, including *mortaria* that could have been used for preparing fruit and vegetable purées in the Roman manner (though other functions, including dairying, have also been suggested), were being imported from Bordeaux. Later, in the second half of the sixth and seventh centuries, this was replaced by E ware jars and other vessels, most likely imported for their exotic contents, including coriander and dill. Jars with spouts may have been for pouring wine, which may also have been

---

[148] Gwara 2002, 6–7. [149] Sexton 1998, 83–5. [150] Cuttler et al. 2012, 20, 228–9.
[151] Haycock 2000, 6–17; Gruffydd 2005, 96–9, ll. 6, 32.
[152] Van der Veen 2016, 817–23; Cool 2006, 134–6.

imported from south-west France in barrels alongside delicate glass drinking vessels, particularly cone beakers, also found at Dinas Powys and other sites.[153] Hilary Cool has shown that in the late Roman period in Britain glass drinking vessels were primarily used by adult males[154] and it is possible that this was perpetuated on high-status early medieval sites. However, the importation of glass and ceramics from Bordeaux had ceased by around 750 and this means that we do not know to what extent the wine trade continued, though it would certainly have been required for liturgical use.

At the other end of the scale diet could be strictly regulated as part of a Christian and monastic way of life. The sixth-century penitential attributed to Gildas, for example, prescribes fasting and an abstemious but nourishing diet of bread with butter on Sundays, but otherwise dry bread with a little fat, vegetables, eggs, and cheese as well as milk, buttermilk, and whey. However, the ascetic rule incorporated into Rhygyfarch's *Life* of St David appears much harsher, with only one meal a day taken without pleasure—a dinner of bread and herbs with salt and a temperate drink— though the old and sick were treated more leniently.[155]

In contrast, the comparative lack of cemeteries in Wales where human bone has survived currently makes it very difficult to identify characteristic osteological features indicative of differences in health and nutrition that might point to dietary and social difference, and much more research is needed before broader trends are likely to emerge. Nevertheless, the large mixed cemetery at the major ecclesiastical site of Llandough enabled a pioneering study of over 800 individuals, most of whom were buried during the seventh to ninth centuries or later. The mortality curve reflects that of other contemporary sites beyond Wales, as do the heights of men and women, but it was noted that the greater differentiation between the heights of the two might indicate better nutrition amongst the former, though the inclusion of migrants might also have been a factor. Overall nutrition appears to have been relatively good, though there were more signs of stress amongst those in Areas II and III compared with probably earlier burials in Area 1. It was noted that instances of enamel hypoplasia— lines, furrows, and pitting on the teeth indicative of stress, including malnutrition, during the growing years—were not very high, nor were signs of anaemia. Nor were scurvy and rickets identified but, interestingly, indications of gout—a disease associated with obesity, high alcohol intake, and other health problems—were present, notably in a male of 35–45 years, suggesting overindulgence. Taken together, the results support the notion of a relatively high-status, rural population primarily composed of the monastic inhabitants, patrons, estate workers, and their families, though some were not born locally.[156]

---

[153] Campbell 2007a, 14–73, 81, 83–96, 138–9; Duggan 2018, 65–115; Cool 2006, 45–6, 95.

[154] Ibid., 224–6.   [155] Winterbottom 1978, 84–6, 146–7; Sharpe and Davies 2007, 126–7, ch. 20.

[156] Holbrook and Thomas 2005, 45–51; Hemer et al. 2013, 2355–9.

Other samples so far examined are very much smaller and sometimes poorly preserved. These include mixed cemeteries associated with coastal communities at Brownslade, West Angle Bay, and St Patrick's Chapel, Pembrokeshire; Atlantic Trading Estate, Glamorgan; Bardsey Island, Caernarfonshire; and Coed y Meirw, Llangefni, and Tywyn-y-Capel, Anglesey.[157] These have revealed comparatively little about nutrition, but some cases of anaemia and enamel hyperplasia, together with one instance of rickets as well as other signs of childhood disease and poor diet, are apparent. One burial, however, stands out. A male in his fifties from Brownslade showed signs of DISH (diffuse idiopathic skeletal hyperostosis), which has been linked to a rich diet and obesity. It is therefore notable that his was the only burial with a stone grave-marker indicative of status, and isotope analysis indicated that he had not been born locally but possibly originated from Iberia or the Mediterranean.[158]

Therefore, although it is possible to reconstruct what people ate and to a certain extent how food was prepared and to begin to tease out evidence for social distinctions, the importation of exotic food and drink, and dietary stipulations based on religion, it currently remains much more difficult to use the limited osteological evidence to act as a comparative indicator to illuminate dietary health. In the future increased data of this kind may enable better quantitative analysis illuminating differences and changes over time.

CONCLUSION

Although it currently remains very difficult to recover a detailed picture of the agricultural economy of early medieval Wales and to determine the probably complex reasons underpinning change, the limited increase in archaeological evidence over the last twenty years can be used alongside a better understanding of the environmental record, including pollen analysis and wider climate change, together with the written sources, to indicate certain trends. This enables some broader comparison with the development of agricultural economies elsewhere in Britain and Ireland.

Pollen samples, though mainly from the uplands, indicate an overall contraction in the agricultural economy in Wales during the fifth and sixth centuries. Regional differences are not yet apparent but would certainly have existed, as they did in England. However, varying increases in woodland pollen are evident across both England and Wales.[159] Several factors underlie this. On the one hand, the demise of the Roman administration in Wales and the consequent fragmentation of authority and the

[157] Groom et al. 2011, 146–55; Murphy et al. 2016; Arnold 1998, 111–21; Faillace and Madgwick, in Joyce 2019; Davidson 2009b, 210–19.

[158] Groom et al. 2011, 152–5; Hemer et al. 2013, 2356; Hemer and Verlinden 2020.

[159] Rippon et al. 2015, 309–15.

collapse of the market economy that went with it would have resulted in a major contraction in the need to produce agricultural surpluses, whether in the form of tax or for exchange and trade. On the other hand, it is now thought that a widespread deterioration in the climate took place across Europe during this period, exacerbated by the effects of the 'Late Antique Little Ice Age' that began in 536 and may have persisted until the 660s. Although the climate of Britain is temperate and the direct effects of this are not clearly detectable in Wales, there are indications in the tree-ring data from Ireland (see Chapter 2). A cooler and wetter climate would have increased the chance of crop failure and impacted on yields, particularly in more marginal areas limited by altitude, aspect, geology, and soils, and is likely to have been more serious in eastern inland areas of Wales, where the growing season was already shorter. Climate, and its impact on availability of pasture and winter fodder, would also have affected livestock, making them more dependent upon barley and oats and prone to disease. A contraction in the availability of food would similarly have weakened the human population and this would have allowed epidemics, such as the Justinian bubonic plague of the 540s, to take hold, leading to substantial population decline.

Nevertheless, at this time we can also see changes in the farming economy in Wales designed to mitigate risk. Firstly, from towards the end of the Roman period onwards we see major changes in the types of grain that were grown. Though the cultivation of barley for both human and animal consumption continued, spelt declined sharply, whilst oats expanded until it became the most important crop. Barley and oats, which were both well suited to the prevailing conditions, might also have been grown together to give a greater chance of success. Although free-threshing wheat, which provided a lighter loaf, replaced spelt, the evidence suggests that it was only grown in small amounts and the bristle variety may have been favoured in some regions as it was better adapted to poorer soils. At the same time corn-dryers point to the need to dry partially processed grain prior to storage, to prevent spoiling, though they were also used for malting barley to make ale. Secondly, there are indications that a concentration on cattle rearing for beef gave way to an emphasis on dairying, thereby providing a more reliable form of protein, especially in the summer months. These trends are also apparent in early medieval Ireland, but in southern and eastern England spelt was largely replaced by free-threshing bread wheat and, though cattle were a significant part of the livestock economy, dairying does not appear to have been so important.[160] Nonetheless, the presence of a considerable quantity of pig bones at Dinas Powys and imported amphorae and glass beakers there and at a handful of other sites in Wales points to elite feasting on pork and perhaps exotic foods alongside the drinking of wine and mead.

[160] O'Connor 2011, 367, 370.

During the fifth and sixth centuries, what evidence there is suggests the continuation of earlier settlement forms and field systems, but during the seventh and eighth it is possible to detect some significant changes in the organization of the farmed landscape in Wales. Firstly, whilst some earlier field systems continued in use, there are signs of the advent of new settlements with associated rectangular fields, as at Rhuddgaer on Anglesey. This coincides with the emergence, evident in the Lichfield and Llandaf charters, of smaller landed estates termed *uillae* (and *trefi* in Welsh) in the south that were increasingly being granted by laymen to the Church. At the same time the pollen record across Wales shows a reversal of the decline in pastoral and arable indicators, signalling some expansion in the farming economy. The emergence of ecclesiastical, as well as secular, estates in the documentary record signals the obligation on the part of tenants to produce agricultural surpluses to pay food render to their owners on a regular basis. Nonetheless, it has been demonstrated that in both Ireland and England there was a much greater expansion in the agricultural economy at this time, largely associated with substantial secular and monastic estates, but also, in the latter, driven by the emergence of craft and trading settlements (wics) with semi-urban populations not primarily engaged in agricultural production. In both improvements in agricultural technology, particularly the use of watermills—but also in Kent at Lyminge by the introduction from the Continent of a heavy swivel plough—both around the turn of the seventh century, clearly show this, and such innovations were significant factors that facilitated economic expansion and the accrual of wealth amongst both secular and ecclesiastical elites. This contrasts sharply with the situation in Wales, where so far very little evidence of technical innovation has been identified, though the existence of at least some watermills at estate centres, such as Llanbedrgoch on Anglesey, does imply larger surpluses. It is, however, more difficult to determine why the agricultural expansion in Wales during the seventh and eighth centuries appears so much weaker. The limitations of much of the terrain beyond the coastal lowlands and the likely continuing wetness of the climate were surely significant factors, and to some extent these would have impacted on the amounts of surplus that it was possible to produce. Other factors would have included conflict, leading to the destruction of standing crops and livestock raids, but the comparative weakness of secular rulers and continuing political fragmentation almost certainly played a part (Chapter 12). Elsewhere the Church has been increasingly regarded as at the forefront of technological change, and though the impact of ecclesiastical estates in Wales on the agricultural landscape is clear, lack of excavation means that any evidence remains to be found. Whilst the ascetic rigour of some foundations, notably St Davids, could have been an adverse contributory factor in the pre-Viking period, its subsequent recovery from repeated raids suggests that by then it was a relatively wealthy institution that drew on the resources of extensive estates.[161]

---

[161] See Davies, W., and Flechner 2017 for wider discussion of the economic role of the early medieval Church in Wales and Ireland.

From around the ninth century onwards the pollen evidence from Wales currently fails to show any clear pattern, though there are some indications of an increase in pastoral farming, particularly in the uplands of the north-west. This broadly coincides with a warming climate that may have encouraged increased exploitation of the uplands for summer pasture and an expansion in dairying. However, wider growth in the agricultural economy is not generally evident. Tudur Davies has argued that this reflects an intensification in armed conflict including both Anglo-Saxon and Viking incursions (evident in the Welsh chronicles and other written sources at this time), together with increasing demands for tribute.[162] Food security could also be a problem, as indicated by an outbreak of cattle disease in 987 followed in 989 by famine causing great loss of life, and famine struck again in Gwynedd in 994.[163] Such food shortages would have particularly impacted on the young and the old and would certainly have led to loss of agricultural labour. During the same period, however, we can also begin to see mechanisms of estate organization more clearly and a tightening grip on resources by kings and monastic corporations, such as fisheries along the Severn estuary. Elite display is now increasingly seen in terms of hunting and feasting on venison in addition to pork, as well as consuming food render, as at the royal crannog of Llangorse. This rise in hunting as a pastime is very clearly evident in England, and it is possible that Welsh rulers who submitted to Anglo-Saxon kings took part in the chase on visits to the English court.

[162] Davies, T. L. 2019, 189–93.

[163] Jones, T. 1952, 10. See also a mention of animal mortality in Britain in 810, Harleian Chronicle (B text), Morris 1980, 47, 88.

SEVEN

Craft, Display, and Trade

The study of artefacts in its widest sense—how they were made and used, and the parts they played in social interactions—provides a potentially powerful tool in the reconstruction of how people lived in early medieval Wales. Such studies can also shed light on their role in the wider economy, aiding recognition of change, as well as the nature and significance of a range of contacts with other parts of Britain, Ireland, Europe, and occasionally further afield. Nevertheless, though the evidence is gradually increasing, early medieval artefacts remain comparatively rare discoveries in Wales other than on a handful of high-status sites. Ironworking is, however, an exception, since it leaves features and residues easily recognizable in archaeological investigations that can also be radiocarbon-dated. The rise in finds as a result of the Portable Antiquities Scheme is also notable, but the lack of an archaeological context for most makes understanding their significance more difficult.

In this chapter I shall first examine evidence for craftworking in early medieval Wales, including the exploitation of materials, technology, specialization, and the different locational and social contexts in which this took place. Secondly, the symbolism and influence of objects can be clearly demonstrated through their roles in forms of display, the projection of identities, and as a means of social interaction and belonging. Material evidence, including artefactual assemblages from high-status sites, as well as the written sources, can have a significant role to play in illuminating not only how power and wealth were displayed in early medieval Wales but also the impact of gift-giving and other largesse as a means of social interaction helping to redistribute goods and bind society together. We can also suggest how some artefacts, notably penannular brooches, might have been used to project group identities and a sense of belonging. Discussion will mainly focus on secular contexts and on aspects of dress and personal adornment, weapons, and martial display, as well as the significance of feasting, hospitality, and other pastimes. Lastly, I shall consider the changing pattern of evidence for trade and exchange over the course of the early Middle Ages, particularly long-distance contacts, alongside the increasing use of silver bullion, and less clearly coin, as currency and the places where such interactions took place. The overall aim is to discern the evolution of production and underlying reasons for change over the course of the early Middle Ages, thereby enabling some comparison beyond

Life in Early Medieval Wales. Nancy Edwards, Oxford University Press. © Nancy Edwards 2023.
DOI: 10.1093/oso/9780198733218.003.0007

222 LIFE IN EARLY MEDIEVAL WALES

Wales, as well as its place in a wider economy based on land ownership, farming, and the creation of agricultural surpluses.

MATERIALS, CRAFTWORKING, AND TECHNOLOGY
Organic Materials and Artefacts

Woodworking was a craft of great significance in early medieval Wales, practised in every community for day-to-day needs, though there is also evidence for specialization. Timber in the form of posts and planks, as well as stakes for wattled walling, was the most common identifiable building material. A wide variety of everyday artefacts, including lathe-turned bowls and stave-built barrels and tubs made by skilled craft-workers, would also have been essential, since the only pottery was imported. Even so, our knowledge of woodworking is severely restricted since waterlogged sites are confined to the latter part of the period. Indeed, Llangorse crannog, built in the 890s (Chapter 5), and the early to mid-eleventh century trackway at Llangynfelyn (Fig. 2.4) are the only significant discoveries. In addition, identification of species from charcoal and pollen can likewise be illuminating, and tools or metal fittings can sometimes tell us about wooden artefacts that have been lost.

The management of wood as a resource would have been important to every community. This included a range of timber from mature woodland, such as oak, used in construction, the regular harvesting of coppiced hazel rods for wattles, and the cutting of alder and willow that favoured damper environments to make lathe-turned bowls and baskets. Charcoal produced from substantial amounts of timber was also required for metalworking. The collection of fuel, including gorse which when ignited burns fiercely, was similarly important since it was needed for warmth, cooking, and the drying of grain.

Enormous amounts of timber were used to build Llangorse crannog. Tall oaks 0.8–1.2 metres in diameter, demonstrating the existence of dense, long-lived woodland, were favoured for beams and planks, and smaller trunks for larger piles, whilst other piles and posts were of ash. Wattles were mainly of coppiced hazel, with some ash and willow, and their sizes suggest regular harvesting every four to five or every eight to nine years. Tool-marks indicate that axes and wedges were used for felling and the radial splitting of large trunks into beams and planks. Otherwise preparation was minimal, though some timbers had been trimmed to a point with an axe, including palisade planks driven into the lakebed. Wood was used unseasoned and carpentry techniques were simple, widespread, and long-lived, though construction on this scale would undoubtedly have required considerable planning, knowledge of the available resources, and expertise in how to use them as well as labour. Some planks later reused in the palisade had paired notches, enabling them to be slotted together, perhaps originally as parts of fences or buildings. Other planks and beams had quadrangular holes near one end, enabling them to be anchored with wooden pegs, whilst other planks and posts had smaller holes suitable for treenails.[1] There was a similar pointed oak plank with a quadrangular hole on the Llangynfelyn trackway, whilst a charred hazel example from a smithing site at Abernant, Kemys Inferior, Monmouthshire, was radiocarbon-dated to cal. AD 690–990.[2]

The only major wooden object associated with Llangorse is a well-preserved logboat found in 1925 close to the northern shore, which has been radiocarbon-dated to cal. AD 720–1020 and may therefore be contemporary with the crannog. Made of a substantial, hollowed-out oak trunk, tool-marks suggest that it was fashioned by axe and adze. It is 4.65 metres long, with a maximum width of 0.63 metres, with a curved, upward-pointing, beaked prow that may have been used for mooring and a rounded stern with a seat. It was probably paddled rather than poled like a punt and it has been estimated that it could have carried four people or a substantial load.[3]

Otherwise, apart from two fragments of the shrine of Gwenfrewi made from oak planks originally decorated with metal sheets attached with copper-alloy binding strips and rivets (Fig. 11.2), wooden artefacts have not survived. Nevertheless, iron tools and metal fittings from the fifth-to-seventh-century hillfort at Dinas Powys hint at wooden artefacts that must once have existed and the range of carpentry skills used to make them. In addition to a small file and two probable drill bits, iron nails were found, most likely used in construction, whilst an iron handle, staples, and suspension loops demonstrate the presence of stave-built vessels on the site.[4] Copper-alloy rim fittings found in pre-Viking levels at Llanbedrgoch also indicate wooden vessels, and a fragmentary saw-blade, hammer-head, and socketed-and-tanged chisels from the Viking Age levels also point to woodworking of some sophistication.[5]

In the same way tools can provide significant clues to the ubiquitous tasks associated with domestic textile production necessary for clothing and other household needs, such as blankets, sacks, and ropes. Cloth may also have been manufactured on a grander scale, notably by the end of the period, for the sails of ships of Viking type.[6] As we have seen (Chapter 6), wool and to a lesser extent linen were the main materials, though, as in Roman Britain, goat hair and hemp may have continued in use, and luxury silk was imported ultimately from Byzantium and further east. Because of the need for waterlogged conditions to survive, the only extant textile fragments are again from Llangorse crannog, principally a spectacular but incomplete charred linen

---

[1] Lane and Redknap 2019, 111–48, 274–5.
[2] Page et al. 2012, 302; Tuck 2001.   [3] Lane and Redknap 2019, 340–55.
[4] Alcock 1963, 113, 116, no. 12, 117–18, nos 15–19, 27–8, 31–2.
[5] Redknap 2000, 83, fig. 126; Mark Redknap (pers. comm.).
[6] Wincott Heckett 2010, 558–9; Gruffudd ap Llywelyn's fleet was destroyed at Rhuddlan in 1063; see Douglas and Greenaway 1981.

224 LIFE IN EARLY MEDIEVAL WALES

garment decorated with silk and linen embroidery (see Fig. 7.4, below), though the ornament suggests that it was made in Anglo-Saxon England rather than in Wales.[7] In addition, textile impressions sometimes survive on ironwork as, for example, on the iron bands of a girdle from a fifth- or sixth-century male grave at Llandough. These were of a coarse tabby weave, but whether they belonged to the girdle, clothing, or a shroud is no longer clear (see Chapter 11).[8]

Textile production in the early Middle Ages is very largely associated with women, and the time-consuming domestic tasks of preparing the wool or flax, spinning, weaving, dyeing, finishing, and sewing[9] would likely have been taught to girls from an early age, thereby passing down the generations. Indeed, it has been estimated that a woman may have spent at least 800 hours a year making cloth, and even a simple female dress could have used around 2.5 kilograms of wool.[10] At Dinas Powys finds of spinning and weaving equipment were 'clean' crafts associated with Building IB (Fig. 5.11) and, as elsewhere in early medieval Britain and Ireland, spindle whorls were the most common finds. Those from Dinas Powys were mainly disc-shaped and recycled from Romano-British pottery, with a Samian example probably made on the site. Others were simply fashioned from the head of an ox femur, more elegantly shaped of lathe-turned antler, or cast from lead.[11] The different materials, weights, and shapes, as well as the diameter of the hole for the wooden spindle, may reflect the spinning of different types of yarn. Spindle whorls made from recycled Roman pottery, including Samian, become more common in the late fourth century, particularly on farms in south-west Britain, and this type persisted in both early medieval Wales and in Anglo-Saxon contexts,[12] suggesting some continuity in domestic modes of production. Indeed, examples recycled from Roman pottery were still in use on Llangorse crannog at the turn of the tenth century, suggesting surprisingly little technological change. At Llanbedrgoch, however, lead is the most common type.[13]

Weaving was carried out on a vertical warp-weighted loom indicated by discoveries of fragmentary clay loom weights. During the Roman period warp-weighted looms were largely replaced by more sophisticated two-beam looms, but in less Romanized regions occasional finds of clay loom weights on rural sites, especially in Cornwall, indicate their continued use.[14] This is also probable in Wales, as loom weights have

---

[7] Allen et al. 2017, 225; Edwards 1990, 81; Lane and Redknap 2019, 170, 276–316.

[8] Holbrook and Thomas 2005, 56–7, 62–4.

[9] For discussion of these, see Walton Rogers 2007, 9–41.

[10] Lee 2015, 293–4. These estimates are for Viking societies but probably applied more widely to early medieval northern Europe.

[11] Alcock 1963, 121–2, no. 3, 148–9, 153–4, nos 13–14; Campbell 1991, 431–2.

[12] Cool 2000, 53; Allen et al. 2017, 227–8; Walton Rogers 2007, 25.

[13] Lane and Redknap 2019, 336–8; Redknap 2000, 84, fig. 128. See also a tantalizing reference to a lost limestone disc-shaped spindle whorl from Caergwrle, Flintshire, carved with an imitation of an Athelstan penny; Andrew 1923–4.

[14] Walton Rogers 2007, 28–9; Allen et al. 2017, 229.

been found on Roman-period farmsteads at Biglis, Glamorgan, and near Castell Henllys, Pembrokeshire. This may also signal continuing use of vertical warp-weighted looms into the post-Roman period, since there are fragmentary annular clay loom weights from Longbury Bank and Dinas Powys, both fifth- to seventh-century sites.[15] In Wales, however, they have yet to be found in the large numbers characteristic of Early and Middle Saxon rural settlements where they are often found in sunken-floored buildings which may have been weaving sheds. They die out in urban contexts, such as York, during the Viking period,[16] but a later bun-shaped fragment has been noted in a building at Rhuddlan and, unusually, several, including one complete example of intermediate type, from an undated context at Bryn Llithrig, Flintshire.[17] A glass smoother used for finishing linen and other fine cloth from Rhuddlan has also been dated to the tenth century, and an iron sewing needle was identified at Llanbedrgoch.[18]

In addition to wool a range of other animal products were regularly exploited, including bone, antler, and horn, together with leather, skins, and furs, but comparatively little evidence has survived. Leather would have been an important commodity needed for items such as straps and horse harness, which can be inferred from the associated metal fittings, as well as shoes and bags. The discovery of tools such as iron awls, as, for example, at Dinas Powys, and socketed pronged tools at Llanbedrgoch suggests that leatherworking was being practised, but objects have not survived. However, two waterlogged scraps, one a possible offcut, also point to on-site leather-working at Llangorse crannog, where fragments were also reported in the mid-nineteenth century.[19]

We know rather more about bone- and antler-working, whilst an ornamental copper-alloy drinking-horn terminal from Llangorse demonstrates the use of horn, a material that has not survived (see below). Antler offcuts indicative of on-site working have been found at Dinas Powys, Llanbedrgoch, and Rhuddlan. Here they were associated with the infill of a sunken-floored building (Fig. 5.10, a), suggesting that this may have been a workshop, and the discovery of a bone motif piece with animal ornament of probable tenth-century date indicates bone-working nearby.[20] The assemblage of bone and antler objects from Dinas Powys ranges from the utilitarian, such as the ox femur-head spindle whorl, requiring little expertise to make, to polished bone pins, one with a carved animal head, and composite bone combs held together

---

[15] Robinson 1988, 63; Mytum and Webster 2001, 91; Campbell and Lane 1993, 49–51; Alcock 1963, 149, no. 3.

[16] Walton Rogers 2007, 30–2, including discussion of the typology; 1997, 1752–3.

[17] Quinnell and Blockley 1994, 168–9; Davies, E. 1949, 106–7; Edwards and Lane 1988, 30.

[18] Quinnell and Blockley 1994, 168; Redknap 2000, 84, fig. 128.

[19] Alcock 1963, 113, 118–19; Redknap 2000, fig. 127; Lane and Redknap 2019, 271–2.

[20] Alcock 1963, 150; Redknap 2000, fig. 125; Redknap 2004a, 158; Quinnell and Blockley 1994, 169–72.

with iron rivets, some with ring-and-dot ornament,[21] that were undoubtedly the products of a skilled artisan. The forms of these double-sided combs (Fig. 7.1, top row), some of which have distinctive curved ends, thicker teeth on one side than the other, and drilled holes for suspension from a belt, are clearly derived from a late Roman type, suggesting continuity in craftworking skills.[22] This is supported by the investigation of a probable late Roman workshop in Minchin Hole cave on Gower, where a similar comb was found alongside other bone artefacts, including spoons.[23] Bone and antler combs broadly comparable with those at Dinas Powys and mostly datable to between the fifth and ninth centuries are also found in south-west England[24] as well as in western and northern Scotland and across Ireland, pointing to Irish Sea contacts and the role of peripatetic craftworkers in their spread.[25]

In contrast, incomplete, composite antler combs with iron rivets from seventh- and eighth-century contexts at Llanbedrgoch are single-sided, with the plain tooth plates, one of which is drilled for suspension, forming a crest (Fig. 7.1, bottom left). The connecting plates are incised with lozenges, zigzags or criss-cross designs. Apart from a parallel from the hillfort at Degannwy, suggesting a possible regional type, there are no close comparisons, but high-backed composite combs are occasionally found in both Ireland, for example Lagore crannog, and Atlantic Scotland.[26] By the early tenth century at Llangorse crannog we see a different form of single-sided composite bone comb held together with bone pegs (Fig. 7.1, bottom right). This is much longer, with a slightly curved back and connecting plates either plain or incised with lozenges and ring-and-dot ornament. This form is found widely in Britain, Ireland, and the Scandinavian world from the eighth to mid-tenth centuries, reflecting the wider economic contacts of the Viking Age.[27]

Ironworking and Other Metals

Smithing is usually regarded as a male pursuit[28] and every community needed a wide range of iron artefacts including knives, agricultural implements, and craftworking tools to carry out everyday tasks. Other, more specialized artefacts would have been elite items: for example, an enamel decorated bridle mount from Llanbedrgoch and a

---

[21] Alcock 1963, 150–9; Campbell 1991, 421–2, 439–41.

[22] Allason-Jones 2010, 79–80. On typology see MacGregor 1985, 88–95; Ashby 2009, Type 10 (Roman and post-Roman), Type 11 (early medieval); Dunlevy 1988, Class B (early medieval).

[23] Branigan et al. 1993, 55–61, 67–71, fig. 5 (6.2). See also two combs from Lydney, Glos., Wheeler and Wheeler 1932, pl. 32.

[24] Bantham, Devon; see Fox, A. 1955, 59–61.   [25] Ashby 2009; Dunlevy 1988, 353–6, fig. 3.

[26] E.g. Amgueddfa Cymru–National Museum Wales acc. nos 98.51H [1787, 1925]; Lane and Redknap 2019, 270; Dunlevy 1988, Class C2, 357–8, fig. 4.2; Ashby 2009, Type 1c.

[27] Lane and Redknap 2019, 263–71; Ashby 2009, Type 5; Dunlevy 1988, class F1, 362–4.

[28] For discussion in the context of Anglo-Saxon society, see Hadley 2012, 117–22.

Fig. 7.1. Bone and antler combs from Dinas Powys (top left and right), Llanbedrgoch (bottom left), and Llangorse crannog (bottom right) (© Amgueddfa Cymru–National Museum Wales; photograph: Robin Maggs).

sword from Builth Wells, Radnorshire, which, because of their ornament, are unlikely to have been locally made.[29] Nevertheless, acidic soils mean that iron artefacts seldom survive, making the assemblages where they do, notably Dinas Powys and Llanbedrgoch, all the more important.[30]

Wales and the borders are rich in iron. The Forest of Dean continued to be heavily exploited in the later Roman period, with renewed extraction during the late eighth or ninth century indicated by the iron-smelting complex at Clearwell Quarry, St Briavels, Gloucestershire,[31] though whether the blooms were traded westwards is unknown. In Wales itself there are significant iron deposits in the Vale of Glamorgan, Gower, and south Pembrokeshire, though bog iron is more widely found, especially in the uplands, and is the main source available in the north. The latter is usually high

---

[29] Redknap 2000, 66, fig. 90; 1991, 28.
[30] Alcock 1963, 113–20; Redknap 2000, 80, figs 118, 126–7; 2004a, 161.
[31] Allen et al. 2017, 182–3; Pine et al. 2009.

228   LIFE IN EARLY MEDIEVAL WALES

in phosphorus, making it good for producing the cutting edges of knives and other blades. There is, however, very little evidence for iron-smelting across Britain in the fifth and sixth centuries. As a result it has been argued that, with the collapse of the Roman market economy and declining technology, recycled iron became a major source despite its poor quality.[32] However, some iron production persisted in both England[33] and Wales at this time, at least on high-status sites, probably using techniques available since the Iron Age. At Dinas Powys and Longbury Bank slag and hearth bottoms clearly indicate smithing, with hammer-scale also at the latter, but the presence of lumps of iron ore suggests smelting as well.[34]

The scale of iron production increased in both England and Ireland during the seventh to ninth centuries.[35] In Wales there is also a small but growing number of ironworking sites, but the scale of production appears more limited. Further research is needed, but evidence points, as in England,[36] to the reintroduction of more efficient furnaces indicated by the presence of tapped slag enabling increased production, though when and where from remain unclear. At Borras Quarry, Flintshire, pits with ironworking debris indicated smelting in non-tapping furnaces, demonstrating the persistence of technology available since the Iron Age. Nevertheless, at Cefn Graeanog, Caernarfonshire, whilst the majority of smelting slags, some of which may be associated with furnaces, do not show any signs of tapping, some do, suggesting technological change.[37] The evidence for tapped slag furnaces at South Hook, Pembrokeshire, is, however, unequivocal and demonstrates smelting on a significant scale, pointing to craft specialists amongst this farming community. A subrectangular, slightly sunken building was identified as an iron-smelting workshop (Fig. 7.2) providing shelter, the interior gloom aiding recognition of the changing flame colour in the furnace, essential to the success of the smelting process. At the northern end were two parallel furnaces, one of which was radiocarbon-dated to cal. AD 760–1000. Each consisted of a gully with a D-shaped pit at one end, with debris from their last firing made up of tapped slags and material from the collapsed furnace shafts. The best parallel is provided by one of the furnaces at Ramsbury, Wiltshire. Evidence for fuel included young oak and hazel charcoal with gorse, broom, and bracken probably used for kindling. Two sources of iron were identified but only one had been smelted on site. Since the other is only present in smithing hearth cakes, it indicates the likely importation of

---

[32] Fleming 2021, 122–33.   [33] Ibid., 125; Hinton 2011a, 425.

[34] Alcock 1963, 44–7; Campbell and Lane 1993, 52; Tim Young (pers. comm.). The iron ore at Dinas Powys is from nearby Wenvoe.

[35] Hinton 2011a, 426; O'Sullivan et al. 2014, 222–7.

[36] At Lyminge, Kent, tapped slag from shaft furnaces is present as early as the sixth century and may indicate contacts with Merovingian France; Thomas 2016, 365.

[37] Grant 2012, 9–10; 2014, section 2.10; McNicol 2016; Young 2015a, 3–5; see also Glanfred, Cardiganshire, Jones. I. et al. 2018, 228–9, 233–8.

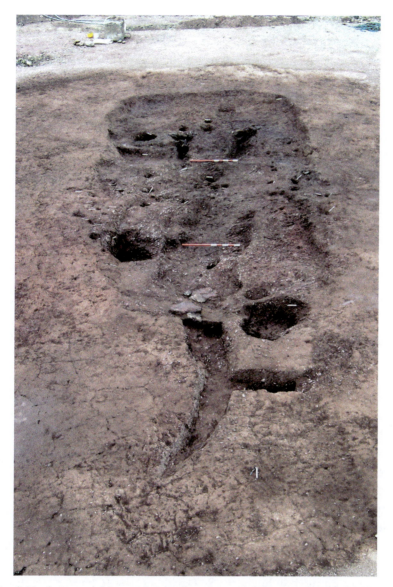

Fig. 7.2. South Hook, iron-smelting workshop, from the south (Photograph: Dyfed Archaeological Trust).

some blooms from elsewhere.[38] Equally, a fine example of a smithing hearth radiocarbon-dated to cal. AD 610–70 was excavated just outside the Roman fort at Gelligaer, Glamorgan. It was figure-of-eight-shaped, one 'bowl' forming the slag-filled hearth, whilst the other was filled with large stones, with hammer-scale showing

---

[38] Crane and Murphy 2010b, 123–8, 145, 158–63, 172–3, 185–90.

the original location of the anvil.[39] Though as yet unrecognized on other Roman sites in Wales, it is possible that this denotes the continuing early medieval scavenging of iron and its reworking, a process increasingly identified on such sites in England.[40]

The contexts for early medieval ironworking are often unclear. At Dinas Powys and Longbury Bank the evidence points to elite patronage of probably itinerant smiths who may also have been engaged in ornamental metalworking. As estate centres developed, the situation may have changed, with more sustained employment of smiths whose skills were also essential in equipping war bands. Nevertheless, the elite context for ironworking at Llangorse crannog[41] appears little different to that at Dinas Powys and Longbury Bank. In contrast, during the ninth and tenth centuries at Llanbedrgoch ironworking is part of a different package of metalworking, craft, and commercial activities signalling a Hiberno-Scandinavian presence on the site (Chapter 5).[42] Whilst South Hook was an agricultural and ironworking community, smelting may also have been practised away from settlements where ore and fuel were close at hand. Smithing evidence sometimes appears isolated from settlements and, in the case of Pentre Farm, Pontarddulais, Glamorgan, the hearth with a fifth-to-seventh-century radiocarbon date was cut into the edge of a Bronze Age burial cairn,[43] a ritual location that might support the concept of the 'otherness' of smiths which has been argued for in some other early medieval societies.[44] In truth, considerably more evidence is needed—it may simply be that, at least on free-draining soils with a long history of exploitation, we are failing to find the settlements associated with them.

The evidence for fine metalworking—the working of copper alloys, silver, and gold to make objects of personal adornment such as pins and penannular brooches, as well as other ornaments associated with horse harness, weapons, and elite display—is almost entirely concentrated on a few high-status sites: Dinas Powys and Longbury Bank at the beginning of the early Middle Ages and Llangorse crannog and Llanbedrgoch towards the end. The only other sites are Pant on the Llŷn peninsula, about which little is known, where sixth- or seventh-century copper-working residues were found, including a crucible fragment,[45] and St Patrick's Chapel. Here fine metal-working likely sprang up in the eighth century because of the traffic of pilgrims but might also be more directly linked to St Davids nearby (Chapter 10). Elsewhere in Britain and Ireland fine metalworking is frequently associated with monastic workshops producing a range of ecclesiastical equipment, but lack of excavation means that there are no such indications from Wales.

---

[39] Young 2015b. For further examples of radiocarbon-dated smithing hearths, see for Abernant, Kemys Inferior, Monmouthshire, Tuck 2001; for Parc Bryn Cegin, Llandygái, Caernarfonshire, Kenney 2008, 106–8.

[40] Fleming 2021, 117–19.   [41] Lane and Redknap 2019, 318–36.   [42] Redknap 2006, 29.

[43] Ward 1978, 56–8, 63; Tim Young (pers. comm.).

[44] Hinton 2011b, 199–200; Wright 2019.   [45] Ward and Smith 2001, 60–4, 66–7, 70.

Evidence for early medieval extraction remains negligible. Even though major deposits of copper in Wales, such as at Parys Mountain, Anglesey, were exploited during both the Bronze Age and the Roman period, there are no signs of early medieval activity—indeed, later mining may well have destroyed the evidence. However, some copper extraction is certainly evident in Ireland and in Wales there was clearly interest in its mineral wealth. The *Historia Brittonum* refers to Lough Leane, Co. Kerry, where the remains of later seventh- or eighth-century copper smelting close to Bronze Age workings on Ross Island point to early medieval extraction.[46] Generally speaking, Roman exploitation of lead deposits available as *galena* in Wales and the Marches was only renewed in the later Middle Ages, but there are hints of small-scale, early medieval smelting at Banc Tynddol, Cwmystwyth, Cardiganshire.[47] Tin may have been imported from Cornwall.[48]

In some instances where metallurgical analysis of copper-alloy droplets, as at Longbury Bank, or artefacts has taken place, as, for example, at Llangorse crannog, it has been shown that bronze containing very little lead was favoured. This would have given a better finish and might also indicate exploitation and smelting of fresh supplies of metal on some elite sites, and this is consistent with other early medieval sites in western Britain and Ireland.[49] It is not, however, universal. A small tinned penannular brooch from Anglesey, a likely local type, contained zinc and a large amount of lead in addition to copper and tin, giving it values closer to those in early Anglo-Saxon England, where recycling of earlier material was significant.[50] In some elite contexts, the importance of recycling is very clear. At Dinas Powys (Fig. 7.3) fragmentary copper-alloy artefacts were found, many of them Anglo-Saxon, as well as part of an ingot and small pieces of sheet metal, one ready-folded for melting in a crucible. A similar array of scrap is evident at Longbury Bank, indicating the availability of different sources of metal.[51] We can also see some of the equipment used. The large number of vitrified clay fragments from Dinas Powys are mainly from small subtriangular crucibles with knobbed lids, similarly found at Longbury Bank. Their residues indicate the melting of gold, silver, and mixed copper-alloys containing tin, zinc, and lead, consistent with reusing scrap. On both sites there were also fragments of heating trays, possibly for enamel- and glass-working, as well as clippings and droplets of molten metal. At Dinas Powys a couple of fragments of what are presumed to be bivalve clay moulds for casting artefacts were identified, together with part of a lead

[46] Comber 2004, 13, 86; Morris 1980, ch. 75; O'Brien 2004, 405–24.
[47] Arnold and Davies 2000, 100–3; Anguilano et al. 2010.   [48] Turner 2006, 74–5.
[49] Campbell and Lane 1993, 30–2, 35; Lane and Redknap 2019, 231.
[50] Edwards 2008, 153–4. Examples have been found at Ty'n y Coed and Pant-y-Saer.
[51] Alcock 1963, 104–12, 120–2; Graham-Campbell 1991, 220–3, pls 1–3; Campbell 1991, 415–19; Campbell and Lane 1993, 30–5.

Fig. 7.3. Dinas Powys, fine-metalworking evidence. Left to right, top row: crucible; bivalve mould fragment; lead die terminal for a Type F penannular brooch. Bottom row: fused glass; millefiori glass rod; scrap metal: Anglo-Saxon, chip-carved, gilded disc; rectangular plaque (© Amgueddfa Cymru–National Museum Wales; photograph: Robin Maggs).

die for making zoomorphic penannular brooches, later cut up as scrap.[52] Overall these assemblages demonstrate the craft of highly skilled metalworkers in the patronage of elites. The notion that they were itinerant and semi-independent is strengthened by the mixture of scrap used: at Dinas Powys this included late Roman silver as well as Anglo-Saxon pieces, and the form of the brooch die is Irish. There could also have been a market in scrap for recycling and, particularly in the case of gold and silver, patrons may have amassed wealth in the form of metals that could then be reworked. This is indicated by the highly fragmented, fifth-century hacksilver hoard from Wem, Shropshire, which included a Type F penannular brooch that had probably secured a bag in which it had been placed.[53]

---

[52] Alcock 1963, 140–7; Campbell 1991, 425–7, 431–2, figs 109–111; Bayley n.d.; Campbell and Lane 1993, 34, 51; Graham-Campbell 1991, 223–5.
[53] White 2020.

CRAFT, DISPLAY, AND TRADE **233**

In Wales during the fifth to seventh centuries the artefacts that have survived, such as penannular brooches, are small and made of copper alloy, occasionally tinned or silvered, or in one case decorated with red enamel showing Irish influence.[54] Gold filigree and glass insets on brooches in the eighth century[55] indicate changing fashions, but in many cases outdated examples were probably simply melted down. The choice of copper alloy with only sparing use of precious metals is very different from much of Anglo-Saxon England at this time. Indeed, the fine-metalworking assemblages from Dinas Powys and Longbury Bank, though on a lesser scale, are closely comparable with those from broadly contemporary high-status sites in Ireland, for example Garranes and Garryduff, Co. Cork, and also with hillforts in western Scotland, such as the Mote of Mark and Dunadd,[56] demonstrating a similar command of labour and resources.

Comparatively little evidence of fine metalworking was recovered from Llangorse crannog, probably because of the short period of occupation and the circumstances of deposition. Only one crucible fragment was identified, but a variety of copper-alloy and lead scrap as well as unfinished artefacts that may have been discarded argue for metalworking on the site. In addition, there is possible evidence of brazing—applying a copper-alloy coating to another metal.[57] Taken together, this demonstrates the continuing significance of elite patronage of fine-metalworkers, as also seen on Irish royal sites such as Lagore crannog and Knowth, Co. Meath.[58] They may have continued to be itinerant, but it is also possible that by this time they had become more permanent fixtures in royal retinues, travelling with them from place to place.

Silver was reaching the Irish Sea region and northern England in increasing quantities from the mid-ninth century onwards as a result of Viking incursions. The fine-metalworking activity at Llanbedrgoch is directly linked to these and is therefore different to that at Llangorse crannog. It includes a range of hacksilver together with copper-alloy waste and silver and copper-alloy droplets, demonstrating that casting was taking place. A fragment of a stamped lead trial-piece resembling part of a broadband arm-ring die might indicate the manufacture of these characteristically Hiberno-Scandinavian ornaments on site, but it might simply be scrap.[59] Though the quantities are smaller, the assemblage may be closely compared with metalworking and associated commercial activities found on the sites of Viking winter camps in England

---

[54] E.g. the brooches from Ty'n-y-Coed, Anglesey (tinned), Edwards 2008; Longbury Bank (silvered), Campbell and Lane 1993, 32–4, and Goodwick, Pembrokeshire (red enamel), Campbell 2013.

[55] E.g. the silver brooch from Newton Moor, Vale of Glamorgan, Redknap 1992, and a fragment from Llanarmon yn Iâl, Denbighshire, PAS no. NMGW-3E31B4.

[56] Ó Ríordáin 1942; O'Brien and Hogan. 2021, 306–8; O'Kelly 1962; Laing and Longley 2006, 25–74; Lane and Campbell 2000, 106–54, 238–9. Garranes and Dunadd are both royal sites.

[57] Lane and Redknap 2019, 318–36.

[58] Hencken 1950, 86, 170–3, 234–41; Comber 2004, 65–91; Eogan 2012, 526–44.

[59] Redknap 2000, 84, fig. 129; 2004a, 156–8.

234 LIFE IN EARLY MEDIEVAL WALES

during the 870s, such as Torksey, Lincolnshire, and in Ireland with a more permanent settlement at Woodstown, Co. Waterford.[60]

Other Inorganic Materials

The working of enamel and glass is closely aligned with ornamental metalworking since these materials were used in decoration. Much of the equipment, such as hearths, crucibles, and heating trays, is also the same, and the same artisans were probably involved. No evidence of early enamel-working has been identified in Wales, though a few artefacts decorated with red and yellow enamel have been found, notably the eighth-century carrying hinge of a house-shaped shrine from Llangorse crannog which is also ornamented with a blue glass stud and blue and white millefiori. This has close stylistic parallels with similar shrines in Ireland, but to what extent similar artefacts were also being made in Wales remains unknown.[61]

In Roman Britain making glass from its raw ingredients was confined to a few towns and military sites, such as Bulmore, outside Caerleon. In the countryside, however, there is some evidence of bead-making from recycled Roman glass, as at Cefn Cwmwd, Anglesey, and it may be suggested that a tradition of bead-making continued into the early Middle Ages that may have been maintained and aided the development of other techniques of ornamental glass-working.[62] Dinas Powys is key to understanding both the sources of glass and the processes being used in the sixth and seventh centuries. A few sherds of Roman glass from the site indicate one likely source for recycling. Nevertheless, the main source was imported: pale yellow, light green, and brown glass vessels, particularly cone beakers, probably made in Bordeaux, with some dark-blue squat jars that may have been made in Kent.[63] Although Leslie Alcock argued that such glass was brought to Dinas Powys as scrap for recycling, Ewan Campbell demonstrated that these delicate drinking vessels arrived whole but were easily broken, and the cullet could then be melted down for reuse.[64] Indeed, there are several fragments of burnt and fused glass vessels at Dinas Powys, demonstrating that glass-working was taking place, probably in the north-western part of the site, with the deeper colours preferred for recycling. In addition, two fragmentary rods of blue glass and a blackish purple and opaque white millefiori rod were found in the metalworking area in the south-eastern corner of the site, where they were probably being used to make insets. Like one of the glass beads, these may have originated in the eastern Mediterranean, though some millefiori rods may also have been made in western

[60] Hadley and Richards 2015, 26–9, 36–43, 51–4; Russell and Hurley 2014, 111–222.
[61] Lane and Redknap 2019, 209–18; for further enamelled objects, see Redknap 2007a 36–7, 72, nos 14–15.
[62] Allen et al. 2017, 199–200; Cuttler et al. 2012, 152; Cool 2000, 49–50.
[63] Alcock 1963, 178–88; Campbell 2007a, 54–73, Groups B–D; 1989b; Stephens 2011, 289.
[64] Alcock 1963, 52–3; Campbell 2000, 37–8.

CRAFT, DISPLAY, AND TRADE   **235**

Britain and Ireland. Other beads from Dinas Powys could have been made on-site since the yellow, brown, and blue examples might all be derived from the remains of the imported glass vessels which probably originated from Bordeaux and Kent.[65]

Although a small number of glass beads are found on a variety of Welsh sites throughout the period, they have been little studied, making it difficult to determine their chronology, to what extent they were locally made, and how they were worn. On the whole they are of one colour but similar to examples from Ireland and Anglo-Saxon England, though few have trails or other ornament.[66] The context of small blue glass beads from graves in cemeteries in the south-west—St Patrick's Chapel, for example[67]—points to contacts with Ireland and may also be compared with the use of blue glass settings in eighth- or early ninth-century penannular brooches, such as that from Newton Moor (Fig. 7.6, bottom left).[68] Plain yellow and plain green beads are also occasionally found.[69] Some more elaborate examples from eastern parts of Wales come from England or the Continent, including a fragmentary cylindrical brick-red bead with yellow and white trails, probably an heirloom, from Llangorse crannog.[70] The impact of Hiberno-Scandinavian settlement is also evident in the range of beads from Llanbedrgoch.[71]

Amber, as an import from the Baltic, similarly signals Viking activity, as indicated by discoveries of beads at Hen Gastell (Briton Ferry), where a polychrome glass 'string bead' was also found, Gateholm Island, and Bacon Hole Cave on Gower.[72] Evidence of amber working at St Patrick's Chapel is, however, of particular significance because of the discovery of pieces of raw amber, amber chips, and part of an amber bead, associated with mid-eighth-century craftworking and other activity, and a later grave.[73] As copper-alloy working was being carried out on-site, amber may also have been used to ornament the objects made. The discovery of amber-working argues for both the long-distance trade of amber from the Baltic prior to the Viking incursions and the presence of artisans in south-west Wales who had acquired the skills to work it. A combination of amber and blue glass insets is found on the Llys Awel

---

[65] Alcock 1963, 185–7; Campbell 1991, 68–9, 433; 2007a, 80–2; Lane and Campbell 2000, 173–4; O'Sullivan et al. 2014, 231. On Roman and later imported gold-in-glass beads similar to that from Dinas Powys, see Guido 1999, 78–80. Vessel recycling was also going on at Hen Gastell (Briton Ferry), with two fragments of fused glass (Wilkinson 1995, 20), and probably at New Pieces with one (Campbell n.d.).

[66] In Britain research has focused on Iron Age, Roman, and early Anglo-Saxon forms; see Guido 1978; 1999; Brugmann 2004. For Ireland see Mannion 2015.

[67] Murphy et al., 2014, 17; 2016, 46–7; 2019, 3, 12; Redknap in Murphy and Hemer 2022, 220–4.

[68] Redknap 1995a, 60–2.

[69] E.g. from north-east Anglesey: Carrog, Smith, G. H. 2014, 61; Wylfa Newydd cemetery, Ashley Batton (pers. comm.).

[70] Lane and Redknap 2019, 259, 262.

[71] Redknap 2000, 81, fig. 119.   [72] Wilkinson 1995, 22–4; Anon. 2012, 15, fig.

[73] Murphy et al. 2016, 16, 47; 2019, 18, 30, 32, context 160 and burial 29; Redknap and Lazzari in Murphy and Hemer 2022, 219–2, 243–7.

236 LIFE IN EARLY MEDIEVAL WALES

pseudo-penannular brooch (Fig. 7.6, bottom right), Denbighshire,[74] and the use of amber in this way may be compared with penannular brooches in Ireland, where it became a characteristic ornament on ninth-century metalwork.[75]

Shale and similar materials were used to make bracelets, finger rings, and beads that were polished with beeswax to give them an attractive, shiny black or dark-grey sheen. Sourcing the materials scientifically can be difficult, making it hard to determine to what extent they were made in early medieval Wales and whether they were items of trade. During the Roman period the Kimmeridge shale industry in Dorset was of particular significance and objects of personal adornment, notably lathe-turned brace-lets, were fashionable up to around the mid-fourth century, as, for example, at the fort in Caernarfon.[76] During the early Middle Ages the only evidence for manufacture in Wales is from Dinas Powys, where there was waste from making a lathe-turned brace-let as well as other objects. The presence of waste argues against the items being scav-enged from a Roman site. Instead, it may demonstrate an element of continuity in production skills passed down through three or four generations.[77] At Llangorse cran-nog four finger rings were found, three definitely turned on a lathe, demonstrating a similar focus on elite sites, though by this period their presence may signal Anglo-Scandinavian or Hiberno-Scandinavian trade contacts. The discovery of part of a nar-row finger ring at Gateholm and a fragmentary bracelet from Llanbedrgoch similarly points to their association with Viking activity. Bracelet fragments have also been found at Borras Quarry and St Patrick's Chapel which may indicate distribution to a broader range of sites.[78] Indeed, shale bracelet production was part of a wider fashion evident also in early medieval Scotland and Ireland, though in the latter, where manu-facture reached its height in the ninth and tenth centuries, they seem to have been made by hand rather than on a lathe. From the tenth century onwards, the manufac-ture of artefacts in Viking Dublin, some from Whitby jet, shows, as with amber, not only wider trade of the finished products but also the raw materials.[79]

Everyday artefacts, such as whetstones and rubbing stones, are widely found on early medieval sites, even where other materials have been lost, but in the absence of additional evidence the longevity of simple forms often makes them very difficult to date. Whetstones were essential for sharpening the blades of knives, weapons, and agricultural and other tools and are sometimes associated with metalworking. Rubbing stones, identifiable by their smooth, polished surfaces, were used in a variety of tasks

---

[74] Redknap 1991, 40.

[75] Youngs 1989, 208; e.g. the Roscrea, Killamery, and Ardagh brooches (Cone 1977, nos 46, 47, 49), and the Derrynaflan Chalice (Ryan 1997, 1003, 1011).

[76] Allen et al. 2017, 198; Cool 2000, 49; Casey and Davies 1993, 206.

[77] Alcock 1963, 22–5, 176–7.

[78] Lane and Redknap 2019, 245–7; Redknap 2008, 105; Murphy et al. 2016, 47, no. 430; Redknap in Murphy and Hemer 2022, 226–7.

[79] Stevens 2017; Wallace 2016, 297–8.

CRAFT, DISPLAY, AND TRADE **237**

such as leather and textile production. Small worked flints are also quite common and, though often regarded as prehistoric, they are most likely early medieval, functioning, for example, as strike-a-lights. The large assemblage of stone from Dinas Powys includes sandstone whetstones, both shaped rectangular examples and long rounded pebbles left in their natural state, their worn surfaces and grooves for sharpening points demonstrating patterns of use.[80] Sandstone was also the preferred material for whetstones at Llangorse crannog and South Hook, with smaller examples probably for personal use. Small rectangular whetstones perforated for suspension from a belt, such as that from Gateholm, are characteristic of Viking sites and became objects of trade from as far away as Norway.[81]

Larger artefacts, such as quernstones, must have been quarried and then transported to local settlements and, where geological identifications have taken place, local sandstones were favoured throughout the period. For example, a large number of quernstones made from a carboniferous sandstone known as Anglesey grit have been found at both Coed-y-Meirw, Llangefni, where it has been suggested that some may be unfinished pointing to their manufacture close by, and later at Llanbedrgoch.[82] From around the beginning of the tenth century, we can see the more systematic quarrying of suitable outcrops of Anglesey grit in the distribution of stone sculpture, which, though clustered in the south and east of the island, was also transported by sea as far afield as Bardsey Island and Dyserth, signalling elite patronage and control of some quarries, notably Penmon. A similar pattern in the exploitation of stone suitable for large crosses with complex carving is indicated in other parts of Wales at this time. However, in Tegeingl there is some evidence for quarried stone crossing the Dee in both directions, probably reflecting the fluid border location rather than it being a traded commodity.[83]

Therefore, although the evidence for materials, craftworking, and technology is constrained by survival and largely confined to a handful of high-status secular settlements with very few artefacts or associated manufacturing debris from other sites, some points may be highlighted. Firstly, many crafts, such as woodworking and textile production, were primarily practised at a domestic level in response to the day-to-day needs of farming communities. However, there were also artisans responsible for more specialized craftworking, for example the making of bone combs in contrast to ox-femur spindle whorls that were simply cut and perforated. The production of iron and the making of iron artefacts were both highly skilled and essential to daily activities across early medieval society, including the elite. Smiths may therefore have been

[80] Alcock 1963, 159–66.

[81] Lane and Redknap 2019, 250–8; Crane and Murphy 2010b, 157–8; Redknap 2008, 105.

[82] Parry and Parry 2016, 7; Joyce 2019, 26; Redknap 2000, 79, fig. 115. See also quernstones from Llangorse crannog and South Hook; Lane and Redknap 2019, 248; Crane and Murphy 2010b, 152.

[83] Edwards 2013, 110–13; 2007a, 29; Redknap and Lewis 2007, 52–3.

either farmers as well or peripatetic and are likely to have operated in line with their skills at different levels in communities, on estates, or subject to the patronage of elites. Fine metalworking with its associated ornamentation and production of other luxury items was not, however, essential, making elite patronage all the more important.

How craftworkers were organized is very difficult to determine. Although the Roman market economy had collapsed, including the technology of mass production, everyday domestic craft skills remained essential, being passed down within families and farming communities. It has been suggested that more specialized crafts, such as bone-comb-making, the working of shale, and the manufacture of glass beads from recycled materials, also persisted and evolved in a similar way, very likely through generations of the same family who may also have fostered apprentices. The role of women as craftworkers remains virtually invisible except in textile production not only in a domestic setting within farming communities but also on high-status sites. Peripatetic specialist craftworkers could have travelled considerable distances, particularly those brought together by elite patronage, presenting important opportunities to develop skills and exchange ideas. At Dinas Powys, for example, the fine-metalworking evidence in the form of materials, including Anglo-Saxon copper-alloy scrap and a fragmentary lead die for a penannular brooch of Irish type, indicates widespread contacts, including travelling artisans.[84] This is equally true at Llangorse crannog two or three centuries later and large ecclesiastical foundations may have acted in a similar way. However, despite the lack of towns in early medieval Wales that would have attracted a range of craftworkers, thereby increasing production for an expanding market, there are some indications of change, pointing to the wider economic horizons of the Viking Age. The smiths at South Hook were involved in iron-smelting on a considerable scale, indicating a market for their blooms, whilst at Llanbedrgoch there was a group of Hiberno-Scandinavian craftworkers and traders engaged in a range of commercial activity. At Rhuddlan textile working and other crafts associated with tenth-century structures also suggest economic activity within the *burh* founded by Edward the Elder, later a Welsh royal *llys*.

Who controlled raw materials remains another very difficult question. Farming communities managed woodland and drew upon the wider environment for their everyday needs alongside the by-products of crops and animal husbandry. The rise of secular and ecclesiastical estates implies some control of the resources on them, such as stone outcrops and iron deposits, as well as by-products from the collection of food render. At Llangorse the amount of mature timber required to build the crannog denotes royal or ecclesiastical control of the resource. Recycling, particularly of metals but also other materials, such as the Roman potsherds made into spindle whorls, remained important throughout the period and ranged from domestic scavenging of

---

[84] Graham-Campbell 1991, 221–5; see also discussion of the fine-metalworking debris from Dunadd, Lane and Campbell 2000, 243–7.

CRAFT, DISPLAY, AND TRADE **239**

useful items to more systematic melting down of metals and the trade in scrap, as well as elite acquisition of luxury goods such as glass vessels that were then recycled in their own right.

DISPLAY, IDENTITY, SOCIAL INTERACTION, AND BELONGING

As the inscription indicates, the man portrayed below the cross on the later tenth-century pillar at Llandyfaelog Fach, Breconshire, is Briamail Flou, the patron who had it set up (Fig. 7.4). An imposing figure with a long narrow beard and knee-length tunic, he engages directly with his audience, holding a possible staff of office and a long knife, thereby demonstrating his authority and martial identity.[85] Similarly, on the late ninth- or early tenth-century cross at Llan-gan, Glamorgan, there is a bearded figure clasping what is probably a sword, and a drinking horn as a symbol of hospitality. Equally, the base of a contemporary cross from Margam set up by Conbelin for the soul of Ric... shows two horsemen, presumably those named in the inscription, hunting a stag with hounds, a popular aristocratic pursuit.[86] Together these depict important aspects of a male elite lifestyle at this time. Women are not, however, represented on carved monuments in this way, making the nature and extent of their participation more difficult to perceive.

Although Briamail Flou is clad in a simple knee-length tunic, it is clear from the Llandaf charters that in the mid-eighth century at least clothing could command considerable economic value as a commodity used in the purchase of land. In one charter, clothes for one man are worth fourteen cows, whilst in a second red linen was included as an item of payment, and in a third a cloak worth six ounces, probably of silver, was given to King Ithel of Glywysing's queen.[87] Nevertheless, the discovery of the Llangorse textile (Fig. 7.5) making up parts of an elaborate belted tunic has been instrumental in transforming our understanding of the resources lavished on royal clothing and the impact such a garment must have had when worn. The cloth itself was simple tabby-woven linen with eyelets for fastening and the seams carefully strengthened with stitching or braided bindings. What stands out, however, is the decoration. Much of the surface was covered with panels of stem-stitched embroidery, the stylized motifs composed of coloured silk threads with the background threads of linen. Borders were made up of paired lions or acanthus leaves, with vine-scroll panels inhabited by a variety of birds and animals. It was suggested that discrepancies in the repetitive motifs indicated several different hands in the work. The combination of

[85] Redknap and Lewis 2007, no. B16; Edwards 2015, 13–14. The incomplete object in his right hand has been reconstructed as a club or mace.

[86] Redknap and Lewis 2007, nos G43, G79; Edwards 2015, 5, 14.

[87] Evans, J. G., and Rhys 1893, 203a, 203b, 204b; Davies, W. 1978, 53–4.

FIG. 7.4. Portrait of an armed man on the cross-slab at Llandyfaelog Fach. The inscription below names him as Briamail Flou, the patron (Crown copyright: Royal Commission on the Ancient and Historical Monuments of Wales).

inhabited vine-scroll and lions emulating Byzantine silks might symbolize Christian kingship and, since that of acanthus and inhabited vine-scroll recalls broadly contemporary manuscript illumination associated with the court of Wessex, it may be argued that the garment was a product of the same cultural environment as the early tenth-century Cuthbert embroideries made for Queen Ælfflæd (d.916), the second wife of Edward the Elder. Moreover, according to Asser, King Elise ap Tewder of Brycheiniog

Fig. 7.5. Parts of the fragmentary Llangorse embroidered garment, showing a seam, the weave, and stem-stitch ornament (© Amgueddfa Cymru–National Museum Wales).

had submitted to King Alfred, making it conceivable that the tunic was a diplomatic gift acknowledging a relationship of this kind.[88]

As items of display, dress accessories are important in seeking to understand identities and social belonging as well as the potential significance of the gift-giving economy and developments in trade and exchange. Penannular brooches, worn by both men and women at the shoulder or centrally on the breast,[89] originated during the Roman period. From around the end of the fourth century new forms, Type F with zoomorphic terminals (Fig. 3.5), and later Type G1 (Fig. 7.6, top left) with faceted terminals, emerge in the lower Severn region as part of a revitalization of native art

---

[88] Lane and Redknap 2019, 276–316; Keynes and Lapidge 1983, 96, ch. 80. The frontispiece to Bede's *Lives of St Cuthbert* presented to the saint's shrine by King Athelstan in 934 has hybrid inhabited vine-scroll/acanthus borders (Cambridge, Corpus Christi College 183, fo. 1v); Backhouse et al. 1984, 26–7. The only known use of vine-scroll and acanthus in Wales is on the crosses at Penally, Pembrokeshire; Edwards 2007a, 81, nos P82–3.

[89] Youngs 1989, 72–89.

Fig. 7.6. Penannular brooches from Longbury Bank (top left), Pant-y-Saer (top right), Newton Moor (bottom left), and Llys Awel (bottom right) (© Amgueddfa Cymru–National Museum Wales; photograph: Robin Maggs).

styles also seen on other ornamental metalwork, notably pins. The fashion for penannular brooches quickly spread to Ireland, where Type F brooches became typical, their terminals often decorated with red enamel and later millefiori glass, whereas Type G1, also found in some later fifth- and sixth-century Anglo-Saxon graves, evolved in western and northern Britain together with the development of some other regional forms.[90] During the eighth century penannular brooches were becoming larger and increasingly ornate, marking them out as symbols of elite identity across Celtic-speaking Britain and Ireland, and subsequently they remained items of prestige with new forms emerging in response to the evolution of a hybrid native and Scandinavian ornamental taste.[91]

In recent years the number of penannular brooches known from Wales and the borders has increased significantly, though many are incomplete. Some have come to light on excavations but many more are chance finds, including metal-detector discoveries, lacking any archaeological context. Only a handful of Type F brooches are

---

[90] On typology, see Fowler 1963; Dickinson 1982. See also Ó Floinn 2001, 2–7; Youngs 2007, 80–5, 90–1, 96–7.

[91] Youngs 1989, 72–116.

known, with rather more Type G1, but during the later sixth and seventh centuries another form develops in this region characterized by spatulate terminals, sometimes decorated with stamped ornament such as ring-and-dot. Two almost plain, tinned copper-alloy brooches are known from from Ty'n y Coed and Pant-y-Saer on Anglesey (Fig. 7.6, top right), whilst stamped examples include those from Shavington cum Gresty, Cheshire, Much Dewchurch, Herefordshire, and Kenfig, Glamorgan. All these early brooches are small with modest ornament: the tinning on the Anglesey brooches may have been intended to emulate silver, and the use of red enamel is rare, pointing to only limited available resources.[92] Type G1 brooches have, for example, been found at Longbury Bank and Hen Gastell (Briton Ferry), both high-status sites, suggesting they were worn by the inhabitants, and it has been argued that ornamental metalworking, including brooch manufacture, would have been concentrated on sites of this kind. Nevertheless, their discovery on farming settlements, notably Pant-y-Saer, and in graves, such as Coed-y-Meirw, Llangefni, Anglesey, demonstrates that they were also reaching the wider population, though the underlying mechanisms remain unclear. Are we seeing widespread elite gift-giving creating ways to bind society together or perhaps more widespread manufacture by peripatetic smiths offering increased opportunities for emulation and the expression of cultural identity? It may also be argued that some brooches or their makers were travelling considerable distances, notably a bird-headed, annular brooch from Llanbedrgoch that reached Anglesey, possibly as a result of contacts with Northumbria in the earlier seventh century.[93]

Although the probably eighth-century penannular brooch from Newton Moor, Glamorgan, is similar in form to earlier Type G1 examples and is therefore of native manufacture, it is on an altogether different scale. Not only is it larger, offering greater scope for ornament—it is also cast from silver and the terminals are decorated with gold foils and twisted filigree wires with central blue glass settings.[94] This brooch is not, however, unique, as indicated by the discovery of a gold foil from the terminal of a brooch from Llanarmon-yn-Iâl, Denbighshire, also decorated with twisted filigree— this time in spirals—and a setting of blue glass, and an incomplete silver brooch with punched ornament and the remains of gilding on the lozenge-shaped terminal from Penllyn, Glamorgan.[95] Other less showy copper-alloy penannular brooches derived from Type G1 are known from Llanmadog, Gower, and south-west Wales, and there are also more idiosyncratic examples suggesting less skilled experimentation with materials, forms, and styles. These include an incomplete silver brooch with gilding, and gold filigree on the terminal, from Weston Rhyn, Shropshire, a second find from

[92] Redknap 2007a, 71, nos 9–11, pl. IV; Youngs 2007, 91–5, figs 4.6–4.11; Edwards 2008; 2017b, 68, figs 2–3. For the Shavington cum Gresty brooch, see PAS no. LVPL2035. There is a fragmentary zoomorphic penannular brooch with missing enamel from Longley Farm, Stowe Green, east of the Wye, Redknap 2007a, 71–2, pl. V.

[93] Ibid., 56–7, 74, no. 24, but see also discussion of seventh-century bird-headed penannulars from Ireland and Scotland, e.g. Dunadd, Lane and Campbell 2000, 114–18.

[94] Redknap 1995a, 60–2.   [95] PAS no. NMGW-3E31B4; Edwards 2017b, 68, fig. 4.

244 LIFE IN EARLY MEDIEVAL WALES

Newton Moor with a stamped hoop and small rectangular terminals decorated with blue glass and possibly red enamel, and one discovered near Tenby, Pembrokeshire, with greatly expanded terminals ornamented with interlace panels.[96] Nonetheless, there is nothing on the scale of some penannular brooches found in Ireland and Scotland at this time.[97] During the course of the ninth century, however, similar forms of penannular brooch become evident on both sides of the Irish Sea, making products native to Wales more difficult to identify. The pseudo-penannular gilded copper-alloy brooch from Llys Awel, Denbighshire, with its expanded terminals decorated with chip-carved interlace and amber and blue glass settings has already been mentioned, but there are also fragmentary penannular brooches with lobed terminals, including another from Llys Awel and one from Trearddur Bay, Anglesey, both of which are gilded, as well as a terminal with a central setting from Llangorse crannog.[98]

The size and complexity of some of these brooches, together with the use of precious metals and different coloured insets, as well as a range of other ornament, demonstrate their role as objects of prestige and display, indicating that, from the eighth century onwards, elites had increasing wealth derived from land, food renders, and other resources to dispose of in this way. The small number of discoveries of such ornate brooches may reflect an increasingly hierarchical society but equally patterns of survival. To what extent they were also part of a system of gift-giving and rewards cementing fidelity and aiding societal cohesion is likewise difficult to determine, as, from the ninth century onwards, is the role of trade and other contacts in promoting the same forms on both sides of the Irish Sea.

Other items of personal adornment included glass beads, shale rings and bracelets, and other copper-alloy ornamental dress fastenings, such as pins and strap-ends, some of which were objects of trade or other mechanisms of exchange (see below). Ornate composite bone and antler combs from high-status sites, such as Dinas Powys, Llanbedrgoch, and Llangorse crannog, were also objects of display, with some having perforations allowing suspension from the waist so they could be seen. That they were regarded in this way signals the significance of hair and how it was cared for in projecting social standing as well as other aspects of identity:[99] priests, for example, were marked out by their tonsures, which initially in Britain and Ireland meant shaving the front of the head rather than the top.[100] In Wales, for sons at least, the first cutting of hair, normally by the father or occasionally a foster father, to acknowledge kinship, and later of the beard at puberty were important rites of passage inherited from the Roman

---

[96] Redknap 1995a, 61–4; PAS nos NMGW-DA579E, NMGW-193AB5; WREX-D5FC73.

[97] See, for example, Youngs 1989, 72–116.

[98] Lewis 1982; Redknap 1995a, 63–5; Lane and Redknap 2019, 218–21. See also examples from Bodfari, Denbighshire, and Llandow, Glamorgan, PAS nos WREX-C2544A, PUBLIC-E95DF8.

[99] Ashby 2014, 153–5.

[100] See Bede, *Historia Ecclesiastica*, v.21, Colgrave and Mynors 1969, 546–53. Also the name *Mailisi* ('the bald/tonsured one of Jesus') on Llanfaelog 2, an early to mid-sixth-century inscribed stone; Edwards 2013, no. AN13, 165.

CRAFT, DISPLAY, AND TRADE **245**

world. Combs (as well as shears and razors) were employed in such ceremonies, explaining the continuation of late Roman forms, and as such it may be argued that they had an important ritual, even a magical, function, making them potentially significant objects in a gift-giving economy.[101] The importance of hair removal is also indicated by the discovery of copper-alloy tweezers at Llangorse crannog.[102] The male figure on the cross at Llan-gan appears to have short hair and that on Llandyfaelog has no signs of hair at all. However, they both have prominent beards, the latter long and thin suggesting careful styling, perhaps plaiting as indicated in Ireland on secular elite figures on the early tenth-century Cross of Scriptures at Clonmacnoise, Co. Offaly.[103] Women certainly had long hair: a decorative braid is shown in the female representation on a whetstone from near Llandudno Junction, and at Tywyn-y-Capel, Anglesey, the woman in grave 214 dated *c.*650–800 still had a thick plait resting on her right shoulder.[104]

In a society where power rested in large part on military prowess[105] and the ability of warlords and rulers to lead and reward their men, weapons and related accoutrements may be regarded as key items of masculine display. However, prior to the ninth century discoveries are rare. In all likelihood this is because of poor survival, especially if sword hilts, for example, were of horn rather than decorated with ornamental metalwork. This contrasts sharply with the situation in early Anglo-Saxon England, where weapons were frequently deposited in adult male graves and swords were an important symbol of masculinity, their ornate fittings, as in the Staffordshire hoard, underlining the importance of military display.[106] Nevertheless, weapons are also rare in Ireland prior to the ninth century. Here it has been argued that initially forms of Roman sword were influential and the discovery of swords at the royal crannog at Lagore, Co. Meath, indicates their elite associations.[107] Apart from a sword worth twelve cows mentioned in one of the Llandaf charters,[108] the only earlier evidence in Wales is also from a high-status site, Llanbedrgoch, where a silver hilt-guard and a small silver pyramidal mount probably once attached to a scabbard have been found.[109]

Spears were, however, used more widely in warfare (as well as in hunting), with spearheads and ferrules identified on several high-status sites in western Britain and Ireland, including Lagore and Dunadd.[110] The discovery of three iron ferrules at Dinas Powys and possible post-Roman examples from the promontory fort at Coygan Camp, Carmarthenshire, is therefore surely significant.[111] Also of interest is a spearhead and javelin, the latter derived from a Roman *pilum*, probably ritually deposited in

[101] Charles-Edwards 2013, 300–3; Ashby 2014, 155–9.   [102] Lane and Redknap 2019, 223.
[103] Harbison 1992, ii, fig. 132, second panel shaft.
[104] Kendrick 1941, pl. 17; Davidson 2009b, 185–90, 198–9.   [105] Davies, W. 1990, 17–18.
[106] Hadley 2012; Fern et al. 2019, and for an Anglo-Saxon horn hilt, see figs 2.26–2.27.
[107] Edwards 1990, 89–90.   [108] Evans, J. G., and Rhys 1893, 202; Davies, W. 1978, 53–4.
[109] Both were found in 2012; Mark Redknap (pers. comm.). For recent discussion of Anglo-Saxon examples of the latter, see Procter 2014.
[110] Edwards 1990, 89; Lane and Campbell 2000, 160–2.
[111] Alcock 1963, 120, no. 47; Wainwright 1967, 97–100; Campbell 1991, 113, 438–9.

246 LIFE IN EARLY MEDIEVAL WALES

a Bronze Age ring ditch with post-Roman inhumations at Four Crosses, Llandysilio, Montgomeryshire.[112] The extent to which the Old Welsh elegiac verses commemorating the fallen brought together in *Y Gododdin* now reflect warfare in northern Britain in the sixth and seventh centuries is highly problematic.[113] Here, however, it is relevant to mention that the main weapons indicated are thrusting spears and javelins thrown from horseback, and it has been argued that this tactic was also used by light cavalry in Roman Britain and earlier, indicating a degree of continuity that persisted in northern and western Britain throughout the early medieval period.[114]

From the ninth century onwards major changes are evident, with Welsh rulers exercising power over greater territorial ranges, the advent of Viking incursions, the greater threat of English expansion westwards, and an increasingly complex web of alliances and factions, including the use of mercenaries (Chapter 12).[115] The importance of martial display as we have seen during this period is reflected in the portrayal of figures with weapons on sculpture. This is seen more widely on Viking Age sculpture in northern England, and there is also a scene with heroic Scandinavian origins on the cross at Whitford, Flintshire, showing a warrior armed with battleaxe, sword, and spear.[116] Equally, the discovery of a spearhead and axe in Caerwent probably indicates a Viking grave.[117] From this time also, though still small, the number of sword fittings found in Wales increases and suggests the adoption of Anglo-Scandinavian types, though the blades, sometimes skilfully pattern-welded to create a decorative effect, only very rarely survive.[118] To date distribution is concentrated in the eastern borderlands and the Vale of Glamorgan with only a couple of pommels further west,[119] but this may reflect metal-detecting activity rather than patterns of conflict at the time. A ninth-century sword found near Builth Wells is Anglo-Saxon since it is decorated with Trewiddle-style silver mounts, and a silver-gilt sword fitting of Carolingian type from Hanmer, Flintshire, likely indicates Viking activity, but there are also plainer swords of ninth- to eleventh-century date from Hawarden, Flintshire, and Llanmihangel, Vale of Glamorgan.[120]

Representations of small round shields in the hunting scene on the Margam cross and on a monument from Eglwysilan, Glamorgan,[121] indicate that these too were items of display. This form, often highly decorated, is also praised in Welsh poetry such as *Y Gododdin*, and similar shields are found elsewhere in Britain and Ireland at

---

[112] Barford et al. 1986; Warrilow et al. 1986, 57–62, 85–6; Redknap 1991, 28.

[113] For recent discussion of the textual and chronological problems, see Charles-Edwards 2013, 364–78.

[114] Rowland 1995, 19–29; Day 2015, 137–40, 143–4.

[115] Davies, W. 1990, 41–89.   [116] Edwards 2013, no. F12, 373.

[117] Knight 1996, 56–8; Redknap 2000, fig. 66. See also a spearhead of Viking type from Ty'n Rhosydd, Anglesey; RCAHMW 1937, xc, lxix illus.

[118] Leahy 2003, 123–4; Redknap 2000, 85–7. Peterson Type L is the main form.

[119] Redknap 2000, 50.

[120] Redknap 1991, 28; 2002; 2022, 91–2; PAS nos HESH-26E9D1, CPAT-3952B8, NMGW-E9F623.

[121] Redknap and Lewis 2007, nos G79, fig. G79g, G17.

CRAFT, DISPLAY, AND TRADE **247**

this time.[122] They were made of wood covered in leather with metal bosses and other ornamental fittings. Therefore, it is normally only the metal elements that are likely to survive. However, these are not always easy to identify. For example, it has been argued that segments of boars' tusks found at Dinas Powys could have been used to decorate the rim of a shield, and whilst three fragments of Anglo-Saxon metalwork are more securely identifiable as shield fittings, they may have arrived as scrap.[123] Otherwise, a zoomorphic shield mount has been tentatively identified at Llanbedrgoch together with a fragmentary edge binding from Llangorse.[124]

In a society where martial display was important whetstones used to sharpen weapons would have had their own significant role. Although the vast majority were everyday items, some were clearly objects of status in a similar manner to the whetstone at Sutton Hoo. The terminal of the seventh- or eighth-century basalt fragment found near Llandudno Junction is on a much more modest scale but is similarly carved with a human head. However, a very large and beautifully finished rectangular example of Viking Age date from Llanbedrgoch weighs almost 500 grams and with its silvered bronze suspension ferrule in the form of a helmet the whetstone conveys power as well as military significance.[125]

The importance of horses as high-status possessions of considerable worth has already been discussed (Chapter 6), as has their role in hunting, an elite pastime that may be viewed as an adjunct to warfare since both involved deft horsemanship and the skilled employment of weapons.[126] In a story in the *Life* of St Cadog, King Rhun presents 'a best stallion with all horse accoutrements', as well as a shield, sword, and spear, to the saint.[127] Such pieces of equestrian metalwork could be highly ornamented, thereby enhancing the impact of both horse and rider in displays of wealth and prestige, whilst also making harnesses ideal gifts. However, discoveries in Wales are still comparatively rare, with distribution focused along the south Welsh coast. The earliest examples of equestrian metalwork are late sixth- and seventh-century, for example a modified copper-alloy bridle-mount from Llysworney, Glamorgan, with a blue glass stud and birds' heads suggesting Anglo-Saxon contacts. Other examples of eighth- and ninth-century date, such as two gilded mounts from Sker Point, Glamorgan, decorated with spirals and interlace, have stylistic connections with Ireland, though they may have been more locally made. From the tenth century onwards the range of equine equipment increases under Viking influence, leading to the introduction of stirrups that made horses easier to mount and ride. The pair of stirrup irons from St Mary Hill, Glamorgan, may come from a Viking burial, and a prick-spur and horseshoe from one of the sunken-floored buildings at Rhuddlan

---

[122] Day 2011.   [123] Alcock 1963, 43–4; Graham-Campbell 1991, 222–3.

[124] Mark Redknap (pers. comm.); Lane and Redknap 2019, 223–5, no. 2512.

[125] Bruce-Mitford 1975–83, ii, 310–24; Kendrick 1941; Redknap 2004b, 170–1.

[126] Rowland 1995, 29.   [127] Wade-Evans 1944, 78–9, ch. 24.

248 LIFE IN EARLY MEDIEVAL WALES

could signal an Anglo-Saxon introduction. Although it has been argued that from the eleventh century onwards in England the increasing amount of equine equipment indicates the use of horses across a wider social spectrum, the small number of finds does not seem to support a similar expansion in Wales.[128]

Feasting was also an important focus of elite largesse to reward retinues and war bands, increasing loyalty and enhancing group identities. As already indicated (Chapter 6), in the earlier part of the period feasting included the display of luxury tableware from the eastern Mediterranean and glass drinking vessels probably from Kent and Bordeaux used for imported wine and other alcoholic drinks. Later, in *Etmyg Dinbych* ('The Praise of Tenby'), the poet eulogizes his dead patron, recalling the throng of men at lavish New Year's Eve feasts.[129] In such a context decorated drinking horns that could be passed from hand to hand were considered important symbols of generosity. It is, however, unclear whether the horns mentioned in two mid-eighth century land sales in the Llandaf charters were for drinking or hunting.[130] Drinking horns with highly ornamented metal fittings are found in high-status Anglo-Saxon graves of the late sixth and early seventh century, including Prittlewell and Sutton Hoo.[131] It has been argued that less elaborately decorated drinking horns with bird-headed terminals, the earliest Irish examples of which are eighth century, may have been inspired by Anglo-Saxon diplomatic gifts, with animal-headed terminals evolving simultaneously.[132] Although there is only one such drinking-horn terminal in Wales from Llangorse, a failed casting of a toothed beast's head,[133] it provides a valuable later glimpse of a shared experience of elite hospitality otherwise only visible in the poetry in a highly idealized form. As *Etmyg Dinbych* indicates, the poet was an important figure at such gatherings, implying his performance and the likely role of songs and music as part of the entertainment. In an additional stanza attached to the poem there is mention of 'wailing on strings' (*och ar dant*) after defeat in battle that may refer to a harp or lyre, but no archaeological evidence for musical instruments in early medieval Wales has been found.[134] However, in an eighth-century Llandaf charter there is an intriguing reference to a *tuba*, perhaps a war trumpet, worth twenty-four cows—a very large sum.[135]

Board games were another leisure pursuit. They were probably initially introduced into Britain and Ireland during the early Roman period and then adapted to more local conditions.[136] Versions continued to be played amongst the early medieval elite

[128] Redknap 2013; 2000, 54, fig. 68. [129] Gruffydd 2005.

[130] Evans, J. G., and Rhys 1893, 202, 203b; Davies, W. 1978, 52–3.

[131] Blackmore et al. 2019, 194–201; Bruce-Mitford 1975–83, iii(i), 324–47, 374–9.

[132] Neuman de Vegvar 2017, 179; e.g. Lismore, Co. Waterford, Moynagh Lough crannog, Co. Meath, Youngs 1989, 62, nos 53–4.

[133] Lane and Redknap 2019, 225–9. [134] Williams, I. 1980, 157, 166, l. 64.

[135] Evans, J. G., and Rhys 1893, 204b; Davies, W. 1978, 54; 1979a, 116–17.

[136] Hall and Forsyth 2011; Blackmore et al. 2019, 252–3.

and must also have been played more widely, including on monastic sites.[137] In Wales *tawlbwrdd*, which has Roman origins and pits a king and his war band against a larger force in the manner of Scandinavian *hnefatafl*, was one board game, but it is probable that there were others with similar antecedents as well.[138] A small number of likely gaming pieces have been found in a secular elite context at Dinas Powys, including shale and bone examples with metal pegs for use on a wooden board with holes and part of a Roman glass counter.[139] Later there is also a recycled Roman glass counter from Llangorse.[140] In an ecclesiastical context a possible siltstone gaming piece has been identified from the cemetery at Llandough.[141] Gaming boards have proved more elusive, but possible fragmentary examples incised on mudstone have recently been found at St Patrick's Chapel and are comparable with gaming boards from a monastic context at Inchmarnock in Scotland.[142] The only other likely example is a poorly recorded fragment for use with pegs found at Caerwent. Unusually, it is made from whalebone, suggesting a Scandinavian origin, and may originally have been associated with a probable group of Viking furnished burials found in the town (Chapter 12).[143]

This discussion has demonstrated that it is possible to identify a range of artefacts and other evidence that used together help us to reconstruct the significance of display as part of an elite lifestyle in early medieval Wales. The emphasis is on projecting masculine identities through clothes, objects of personal adornment, grooming, and the power associated with martial display through a combination of possessions, including weapons, horses, and their accoutrements. Also of significance as a mode of display is the role of feasting and related activities, such as song, storytelling, and poetic recital, not only as a way of rewarding retinues but also as a method of strengthening loyalties and helping to create group identities. In contrast, the position of women in the performance of elite display remains very difficult to discern, though their role in the making of luxury textiles is apparent and penannular brooches were worn by women as well as men.[144]

Personal appearance, and the garments and items of adornment, such as penannular brooches, that were part of it, were likewise instrumental in fashioning identities. We have already explored the complexity of continuing Roman and native British identities

[137] For discussion of evidence for board games in Scotland, Anglo-Saxon England, and the Viking world, see Youngs 1983; Hall 2018; Blackmore et al. 2019, 247–53.

[138] *Tawlbwrdd* and *gwyddbwyllt* (now chess) are first mentioned in the thirteenth century; *Geiriadur Prifysgol Cymru*. Linguistically *gwyddbwyllt* has much earlier origins; see Hall and Forsyth 2011, 1331–3.

[139] Alcock 1963, 151–4, nos 6, 8, 16, 176–7, no. 4, 186, no. 9. On the identification of pegged gaming pieces, see Hall 2017, 13–15.

[140] Lane and Redknap 2019, 205–6.   [141] Holbrook and Thomas 2005, 72, no. 3, fig. 37.

[142] Murphy and Hemer 2022, 200–1, nos 933, 951–2; Lowe 2008, 116–28.

[143] Mark A. Hall and Stephen Greep (pers. comms).

[144] The brooch from the cemetery at Coed y Meirw, Llangefni, was found in a female grave; Edwards forthcoming. See also the woman on horseback who may be wearing a penannular brooch as a symbol of her authority on the Hilton of Cadboll Pictish cross-slab; Nieke 1993, 129; James et al. 2008, 184, illus. 2.1.

as well as aspects of an Irish identity evident in parts of Wales in the fifth and sixth centuries (Chapter 4). The revitalization of native ornamental metalwork also speaks to the display of British identities that evolve into wider Celtic-speaking identities and modes of adornment and personal display that persisted into the Viking Age.

The role of gift-giving and reciprocity in early medieval Welsh society—what has been termed an 'economy of regard'[145]—as a way of transferring wealth and resources and establishing social relationships is more difficult to identify from the artefacts alone. Nevertheless, the written sources, notably the Llandaf charters, can give some insight into their values in specific transactions, demonstrating the importance of donations of land to the Church. Rulers ruled as a result of their military prowess and would have rewarded their followers accordingly, with feasts, equipment, and booty reinforcing loyalty and belonging. Feasts were likely also held as a response to the collection of food renders on estates. Diplomatic gifts between rulers would have served not only as a projection of power, wealth, and generosity but also as tokens sealing relationships. Emulation in terms of personal appearance and generosity was probably also important but remains very difficult to perceive in the archaeological record.

It is possible to see some changes in wealth and display over time. Displays of wealth in Wales in the fifth to seventh centuries are modest, as they were in Scotland and Ireland, but contrast sharply with the wealth exhibited in Anglo-Saxon graves, especially those of the elite in the late sixth and early seventh centuries, though the range of artefacts more widely suggests that in life similar modes of display were important at this time. The available evidence in the form of imported pottery and glass also highlights the role of feasting in elite display. By the eighth century increasing wealth for a few is suggested by the continuing patronage of fine-metalworkers now producing larger and more ornate penannular brooches, as was also happening in Ireland and Scotland, but again the evidence in Wales is much more restricted, suggesting limited resources. From the ninth century onwards, however, there are some indications that the acquisition and projection of wealth were driven by a wider and more complex set of mechanisms, including exchange and trade at a number of different levels, but continued on a modest scale.

TRADE AND EXCHANGE

The discovery of exotic artefacts makes patterns of long-distance trade and exchange much easier to identify than regional or local ones, though these must surely have existed in a variety of different contexts alongside gift-giving, payments of food render, and the exaction of tribute. During the fifth to seventh centuries the importation of

---

[145] Offer 1997, 450–7.

pottery, glass vessels, and occasionally other items signals the persistence or renewal of long-distance trade routes through the Mediterranean and along the Atlantic seaways to western Britain and Ireland. Although the various types of imported pottery and glass vessels are now well studied, as is their British and Irish distribution, there remain significant questions concerning the wider patterns of trade and exchange and the role of sites in Wales within these networks.

The Mediterranean-imported ceramics are dominated by late Roman amphorae traded for their contents—principally wine, but also olive oil and possibly other food-stuffs. The types reaching Britain and Ireland came from southern Turkey, Rhodes, and Cyprus (LRA1); Chios, Cnidos, and the Argolid in Greece (LRA2); western Asia Minor (LRA3); and the Gaza region (LRA4). It is also thought that North African amphorae from the Carthage area arrived, and other unidentified fabrics found in Britain and Ireland may include Iberian examples as well. It is generally argued that alongside the amphorae small amounts of tableware in the form of red-slip bowls and dishes, some decorated with rouletting on the rims and internal basal stamps, also reached Britain and Ireland as a subsidiary cargo. Late Roman C (LRC), sometimes termed Phocaean red slipware (PRSW), from north-western Turkey was the more common Insular import, but later African red slipware (ARS-D), originating from the Carthage region, has also been identified.[146] The small number of other items from the eastern Mediterranean include Menas pilgrim flasks and glass beads from Alexandria, a few Byzantine coins, and a Byzantine intaglio from Cefn Cwmwd, Anglesey.[147] Dating of the red slipware has established that goods found in British and Irish contexts span the period $c.475$–550, with those from the eastern Mediterranean in the later fifth and early sixth century, and those from North Africa during the first half of in the sixth. It has also been plausibly argued that the demise of this trade was hastened by the spread of the Justinian plague.[148] It was originally thought that ships were sailing directly from Byzantium and Carthage to Britain and Ireland,[149] but recent research on ceramic assemblages on the Continent indicates that this is unlikely to have been the case. Instead, distributions of late Roman amphorae and red slipware along the coast of western Iberia, and particularly from Vigo in Galicia, strongly suggest that this was an important intermediary trading place where Mediterranean goods changed hands before their journey northwards, skirting the Bay of Biscay, with Bordeaux in south-west France also emerging as a major entrepôt.[150] Although we do not know who the traders were,[151] their main destination was south-west Britain, particularly the promontory fort at Tintagel on the north Cornish coast and

---

[146] Duggan 2018, 29–52, 193–7.   [147] Campbell 2007a, 74–8.
[148] Ibid., 25–6, 138–9.   [149] Fulford 1989.   [150] Duggan 2018, 91–100, 116–56.
[151] Possible immigrants, both men and women, from Iberia and the Mediterranean have been tentatively identified following oxygen and strontium isotope analysis of burials at Llandough, Glam., and Brownslade and Porthclew, Pembs., but the results may be related to early diet rather than origin; Hemer et al. 2013, 2356–8.

252 LIFE IN EARLY MEDIEVAL WALES

the beach market at Bantham in south Devon. Cornish tin was probably the major export, perhaps alongside other metals and raw materials as well as slaves.[152]

The distribution of late Roman amphorae and red slipware in Wales and the borders is limited almost entirely to high-status hillforts and related sites concentrated along the south coast, with clusters associated with Longbury Bank and particularly Dinas Powys, which also has the greatest range of material (Fig. 7.7, a). This points to elite control and the likely significance beyond the Roman period of trade and other exchange mechanisms operating across the Bristol Channel as well as the role of Tintagel as a nexus in this distribution network. The slipware at New Pieces also suggests that the Severn was a key route north, whilst the amphorae from Dinas Emrys and Degannwy either indicate a coastal route from the south or, perhaps more likely, contacts across the Irish Sea, where Dalkey Island functioned as a gateway for exotic goods.[153] A route along the north Welsh coast may also be suggested, and the discovery of a cluster of sixth-century Byzantine copper coins and two Menas flasks around the Mersey estuary (Fig. 7.7, b) points to some activity at Meols, a coastal trading place with Iron Age and Roman origins. Although some doubt has been cast on whether Byzantine coins in particular are ancient losses, their clustering here and discoveries in south Wales, notably the two gold *solidi* of Justinian (527–65) and Tiberius III (698–705) minted in Constantinople from sand dunes at Tenby, as well as in south-west England may also be indicative of trade.[154]

Continental imports into Britain and Ireland consist of two types of pottery. Firstly, there are small amounts of a grey tableware, occasionally stamped and decorated with grey-black slip, that include *mortaria* for food preparation, known as *Dérivées sigillées paléochrétiennes* Atlantic Group (DSPA), though related types may also be represented. Secondly, there are rather larger amounts of a hard, white, gritty coarseware known as E ware comprising a range of jars used as storage vessels, including for madder and exotic foods, as well as bowls and pitchers.[155] In addition, there are drinking vessels of thin, pale-yellow and yellowish-green glass, principally cone beakers but also bowls, many of which are decorated with opaque white glass trails (Groups C and D).[156] It has been shown that both these and DSPA originate from Bordeaux or its environs and this is now highly likely for E ware as well; all three were probably shipped north as adjuncts to the wine trade.[157] The importation of DSPA into Britain and Ireland is focused on the sixth century and it has been demonstrated that glass vessel production in

[152] Duggan 2018, 65–77, 154–5, 204; Campbell 2007a, 129–30.   [153] Doyle 2009, 28–9.

[154] Griffiths et al. 2007, 58–61, 304, 431–3; James 2016b, 485; Redknap 2019, 343–9, 352, 360–1; Philpott 2020. For a more measured view on authenticity, in opposition to Boon's 1991 highly sceptical approach, see Moorhead 2009, who also lists a copper *follis* of Heraclius, minted in Carthage (611–12), found at Cosmeston, 269, no. 11. On Byzantine coins from Caerwent, see Chapter 4. Eight late sixth- and earlier seventh-century copper *folles* and half *folles* have also been found at the royal centre at Rendlesham, Suffolk, where it has been suggested that they reflect mercantile activity; Scull et al. 2016, 1603–4.

[155] Campbell 2007a, 27–52; Duggan 2018, 52–62.

[156] Campbell 2007a, 64–9, Groups C and D; Duggan 2018, 63–4.   [157] Ibid., 53, 64, 114.

CRAFT, DISPLAY, AND TRADE 253

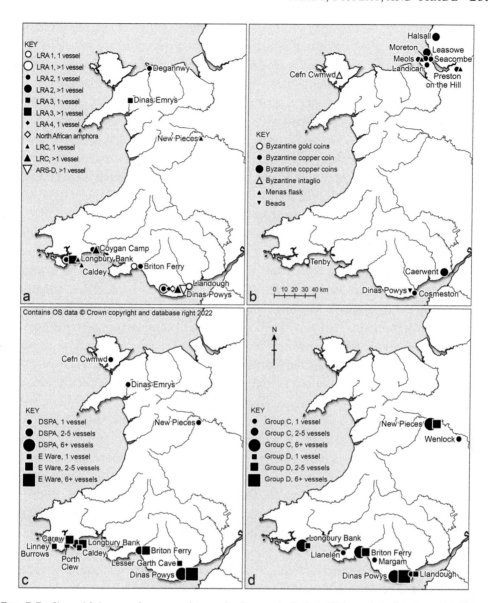

Fig. 7.7. Sites with imported pottery, glass, and other exotic finds in Wales and the borders, mid-fifth to early eighth centuries: a. late Roman amphorae (LRA), Late Roman C and African red slipware (ARS-D); b. Byzantine coins land other finds; c. *Dérivées sigillées paléochrétiennes* Atlantic Group (DSPA) and E ware pottery; d. imported glass.

Bordeaux was largely during the same period, though this also extended well into the seventh century, with undecorated examples more common towards the end of the sequence. E ware importation appears to begin in the later sixth century, reaching a peak in the earlier seventh, before ceasing around the end of the century.[158] In Wales

[158] Campbell 2007a, 46, 139; Duggan 2018, 64.

the distribution of this pottery and glass largely mirrors that of the Mediterranean ceramics (Fig. 7.7, c, d), indicating similar patterns of acquisition. Nonetheless, Dinas Powys has the largest assemblage of DSPA from any site in Britain and Ireland,[159] and in Wales E ware is so far confined to the south coast, with the cluster of glass at New Pieces reflecting the Severn route. The small overall distribution of DSPA, also found at Tintagel, is largely from the west coast of Britain. In contrast, that of E ware, which seemingly begins importation after the abandonment of Tintagel, is more focused on Ireland and the west coast of Scotland. That of the glass vessels is somewhere in between. This realignment points to the reduction of Cornish tin as a major export and the growth of new trade and exchange networks that excluded much of Wales.

As we have seen (Chapter 4), the distribution of ogham and some other inscribed stones points to post-Roman Irish settlement in Dyfed, Gwynedd, and Brycheiniog, leading to strong and continuing links with Ireland as part of a wider cultural zone around and across the Irish Sea. True, artefactual evidence for trade and exchange within this zone remains very difficult to identify, but this is because fine metalwork decorated in the Insular style, the most important extant signifier, is also characteristic across this wider region. However, from the mid-sixth century onwards it is possible to recognize Anglo-Saxon glass vessels and ornamental metalwork, often on the same elite sites where Mediterranean and Continental imports are found. Glass from Dinas Powys includes a sherd from a brown claw beaker, probably made in East Anglia, and another from an early seventh-century, deep blue squat jar, probably from Kent, with a similar sherd from Hen Gastell (Briton Ferry).[160] In addition, some Anglo-Saxon ornamental metalwork found at Dinas Powys, including a Kentish strap-end, may well have arrived as complete artefacts rather than as scrap, and this is also possible in the case of a strap-end and fragment of belt fitting from Longbury Bank, but these are less distinctively Anglo-Saxon in origin.[161] The presence of such glass vessels and dress accessories on high-status sites along the south Wales coast may indicate trade westwards along the Thames or more direct contacts with Anglo-Saxon elites providing opportunities for gift-giving and exchange. Overall, the distribution of these, together with Mediterranean and Continental imports, points to elite control not only of the mechanisms of luxury trade but also of the goods, perhaps including raw materials such as wool, as well as slaves, horses, and cattle probably exchanged in return. Evidence for the wider dissemination of imported goods is also very limited, suggesting that such wealth and the mechanisms of display that went with it were concentrated amongst a comparatively small number of rulers, including the 'tyrants' of Gildas.[162]

By the dawn of the eighth century the cessation of trade in exotic pottery and glass vessels along the Atlantic seaways to western Britain and Ireland means that if, for

[159] Ibid., 55–6.   [160] Ibid., 60; Wilkinson 1995, 20, 22 no. 23.
[161] Graham-Campbell 1991, 221–2; Campbell and Lane 1993, 34.
[162] Winterbottom 1978, chs 28–36.

example, wine continued to be imported in casks, this has left no trace in the archaeological record, even though there is increasing evidence of more general trading activity along the west coast of France, including in the Loire, Charente, and Garonne estuaries.[163] Irish Sea trade, which must have continued, also remains very difficult to identify because of the continuation of a shared cultural identity evident in the production of ornamental metalwork. What is clear is that western Britain and Ireland lay well outside the zone of the burgeoning developments in North Sea and cross-Channel trade networks made possible by the emergence of what have been termed *emporia*, exemplified on the Continent by Quentovic and Dorestad, and in southern and eastern England by *Hamwic* (Southampton), *Lundenwic* (London), and *Gippeswic* (Ipswich) as well as other lesser sites such as Wareham in Dorset.[164] Trade was facilitated by the use of early silver pennies (*sceattas*)[165] minted in both England and on the Continent between the late seventh and mid-eighth centuries, with many imports into England from Frisia. Much greater numbers of early silver pennies are being reported in England as a result of the Portable Antiquities Scheme. Nevertheless, discoveries remain comparatively few in both the west Midlands and the south-west and are mainly earlier in the series, suggesting a connection with the salt trade at Droitwich, with finds around the Severn estuary indicative of riverine networks as well. Significantly, however, there are only four currently known from Wales, all from the borders (Fig. 7.8).[166] Finds of Anglo-Saxon pennies and Northumbrian *stycas* from the second half of the eighth and first half of the ninth centuries in Wales are also very rare, apart from a small number at Llanbedrgoch, suggesting trade along the north Wales coast, but these may well be connected with the Hiberno-Scandinavian activity on the site.[167] Likewise, there is comparatively little clearly identifiable Anglo-Saxon fine metalwork found in Wales between the late seventh and mid-ninth centuries.[168] Nor has any pottery been found, though much of west and south-west England were also aceramic at this time.[169] The lack of coin use should not be seen as a barrier to trade, but overall the dearth of evidence for economic engagement with Anglo-Saxon England at this time is best explained by tensions as a result of the expanding power of Mercia resulting in resistance to changes in cultural identity that trade might have brought. These reached a high-point under Offa (757–96) and Coenwulf

---

[163] Loveluck 2013, 179, 194, 202–4.

[164] Hodges 1982, 50–86; Wickham 2005, 682–5, 687–9; Pestell 2011; Costen and Costen 2016.

[165] On the terminology, see Naismith 2017, 67–8.

[166] Naylor 2011; 2015, 291. The PAS finds from Wales are: Caerwent, Mons., NMGW-9A4808; Churchstoke, Monts., HESH-33C368; Holt, LVPL-20C747, and Bronington, WREX-9F2C2D, Flints.

[167] Besly 2006, 716, nos 1–4. Coins from Llanbedrgoch include a penny (*c.*784–93) of Queen Cynethryth. wife of Offa of Mercia, and two *stycas*. There is also a penny of Coenwulf from Rossett, Flints., PAS no. CPAT-4AAF81. One *styca* was found at *Segontium*, and five in a redeposited context in Llangollen (Lodwick and Besly 2013, 178), as well as four(?) from Meols (Griffiths et al. 2007, 343).

[168] Redknap 2009c, 297–9. [169] Blinkhorn 2013, 159.

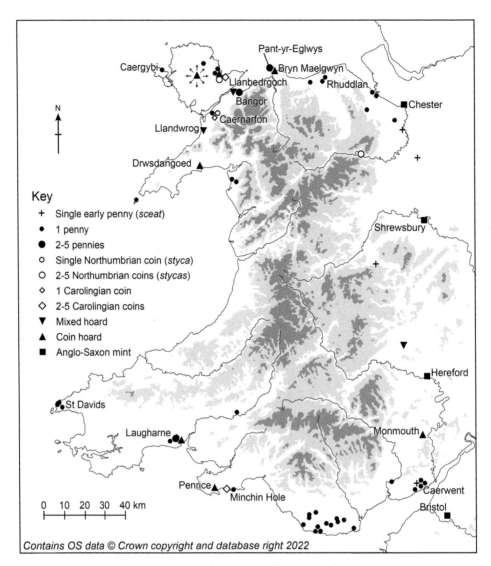

Fig. 7.8. Discoveries of coins and silver/coin hoards in Wales dating from the late seventh to mid-eleventh centuries.

(796–821), leading to the construction of Offa's and subsequently Wat's Dykes acting as both physical and psychological barriers to communication and trade (Chapter 12).

From around the mid-ninth century archaeological evidence for long-distance trade in Wales increases, if only to a limited degree. This should be viewed within the wider context of expanding international trade networks brought about by Viking settlement in Britain and Ireland and the West Saxon reconquest of the Danelaw together resulting in the growth of towns, economic acceleration, and increasing wealth. From the end of the eighth century Viking raids in the Irish Sea were part of a wider spectrum of activity, including the capture and trafficking of slaves, that also embraced opportunities for the trade of exotic goods,[170] though the presence of Baltic amber at St Patrick's Chapel may indicate that trade with Scandinavia had already commenced at an earlier date (see above). The foundation of the *longphort* at Dublin in 841 led, from around the late ninth century onwards, to rapid urban development, with trade contacts stretching from Scandinavia to the Caspian and Mediterranean, as well as to the North Atlantic. Anglesey and the north Wales coast were drawn into the orbit of Hiberno-Scandinavian settlement and other activity associated with the important trade route between Dublin and Chester.[171] At the same time the rise of Wessex and the reconquest of the Danelaw led to the refortification of Chester as a *burh* in 907 by Æthelflæd of Mercia, and in 921 the foundation of the *burh* at *Cledemutha* (Rhuddlan) by Edward the Elder, with the result that Tegeingl, situated between the Clwyd and the Dee, developed as a border region with a mixed Welsh, English, and Scandinavian identity. Equally, the south Wales littoral and Severn estuary were drawn into Anglo-Saxon and Viking activity along the Bristol Channel, with important trade routes developing between Dublin, Waterford, and the emergent town of Bristol in the eleventh century.[172]

We can demonstrate to some extent the impact of these trading networks in Wales by examining evidence for Late Saxon pottery, Hiberno-Scandinavian ringed pins, and silver, but these must act as proxies for a range of other goods that have not survived. The production of Stafford-type ware, consisting mainly of wheel-turned jars and bowls, spans the tenth and first half of the eleventh centuries. Its distribution is centred on the *burh* at Stafford where kilns have been excavated, but it was traded to other parts of west Mercia, including Hereford and Shrewsbury. It is also found in some quantity at Chester, with a few sherds from Rhuddlan and Llanbedrgoch, as well as Dublin, indicating trade along the north Wales coast and across the Irish Sea. St Neots-type ware, widely found in East Anglia and the Midlands, has also been identified in Rhuddlan, underlining its commercial contacts with England.[173] Otherwise evidence for the trade of Late Saxon pottery into Wales remains negligible, with only a few sherds of Cotswolds-type ware from Monmouth, and a sherd similar to examples from Gloucestershire at Portskewett close to the Severn estuary.[174]

David Griffiths has tentatively identified a Hiberno-Scandinavian style of personal adornment centred on Dublin that spreads across the Irish Sea region as a result of trade and other activity.[175] In particular, clay moulds and the large numbers of copper-

---

[170] On the relationship between raids and commercial activity, including selling captives as slaves, see Wormald 1982, 131–4.

[171] Wallace 2016, 9, 352–79.   [172] Griffiths 2010, 130–9; 2006, 153–8; Wallace 2016, 372–4.

[173] Blinkhorn 2013, 162–5; Carver 2010, 76–93; Quinnell and Blockley 1994, 191–2; Redknap 2000, 78, fig. 113; Wallace 2016, 366. Stafford-type ware was formerly called Chester ware. I am grateful to Julie Edwards for discussing this and the Rhuddlan pottery with me.

[174] Blinkhorn 2013, 167; Courtney 1994, 111; Crawford 2011; Brett et al. 2015, 19.

[175] Griffiths 2010, 150–3.

258 LIFE IN EARLY MEDIEVAL WALES

alloy ringed pins from tenth- and eleventh-century levels in Dublin demonstrate their manufacture in the town. These cloak fasteners are also widely distributed across Ireland, Britain, Scandinavia, and the North Atlantic.[176] Though comparatively rare in Wales, their distribution also highlights the northern and southern coastal routes, as they have not been found elsewhere. On Anglesey eleven are known from Llanbedrgoch as well as an isolated example from Llanfairpwll, with further clusters at Meols and in Chester.[177] In the south, there are four from Pembrokeshire, including a fine early to mid-eleventh century decorated pin from St Patrick's Chapel, examples from Port Eynon on Gower and Portskewett that may be regional variants, and several from Caerwent.[178]

The distribution of silver bullion and coins, however, provides the most convincing evidence that, from the mid-ninth century onwards, the north and south coasts of Wales became part of a wider Irish Sea zone of Hiberno-Scandinavian trading and other activity, with signs of wider-flung contacts as well. The assemblage of coins, hacksilver, and lead weights from Llanbedrgoch is particularly significant and, together with other discoveries in the north-west, indicates south-east Anglesey as a key point on the route to Chester, but also the possible significance of the Conwy estuary. Coins from Llanbedrgoch include a small hoard of Carolingian deniers of Louis the Pious (*c*.822–40), Charles the Bald (*c*.848–77), and Pepin II of Aquitaine (839–52), all suggesting Viking contact with western France, as well as the Northumbrian *stycas* and a penny of Archbishop Wulfred of Canterbury (*c*.805–32). In addition to an ingot and ingot fragments, the hacksilver comprises at least two offcuts from Hiberno-Scandinavian broad-band arm-rings signalling trade links with Ireland, part of a Scandinavian oval brooch, as well as part of a 'Permian' arm-ring and two fragmentary Kufic dirhams also demonstrating connections with the Baltic and ultimately further east through the river systems of Russia and beyond. The significance of a bullion economy is also demonstrated by a variety of lead and other metal weights (Fig. 7.9), including two with reused ornamental insets of Insular metalwork that were used with a pair of scales to weigh silver.[179] Together these point to commercial activity during the second half of the ninth and first half of the tenth centuries. A mixed hoard of coins and bullion dated to *c*.925 from the environs of the ecclesiastical site at Bangor shows many of the same links since it includes fragments of a Hiberno-Scandinavian broad-band arm-ring and an ingot together with Kufic coins and Anglo-Saxon pennies of Edward the Elder, but it also contains pennies from Anglo-Scandinavian York, reflecting the significance of economic links between the Irish Sea zone, especially Dublin, and the northern Danelaw at this time. Broadly contemporary mixed hoards of this kind are also found elsewhere in western Britain and Ireland, notably the two

[176] Fanning 1994.

[177] Redknap 2000, fig. 124; 2007b, 70; Fox 1940b; Griffiths et al. 2007, 67–9, pl. V.

[178] St Patrick's Chapel, Murphy et al. 2016, 46, fig. 15; Pen Arthur Farm, St Davids, Redknap 2007c; Gateholm, Redknap 2008, 105; Radford Pill, Carew, PAS no. NMGW-43C072; Porth Eynon, PAS no. NMGW-E8FA8; Portskewett, Redknap 2000, fig. 122; Caerwent, Knight 1996, 56, fig. 7.

[179] Redknap 2009b; 2000, 82, fig. 121; 2016, 163–4; Hårdh 2007.

FIG. 7.9. Balance weights from Llanbedrgoch, two decorated with fragmentary Insular metalwork insets (© Amgueddfa Cymru–National Museum Wales; photograph: Robin Maggs).

enormous hoards from Cuerdale and Silverdale, Lancashire, and Dysart 4, Co. Westmeath.[180]

Hoards from Llandwrog, Drwsdangoed (now lost),[181] and Bryn Maelgwyn, as well as a small group of coins from Pant-yr-Eglwys, all contain pennies of Cnut (1016–35), giving some insight into the continuing economic importance of the Dublin–Chester trade route but also the likely significance of economic contacts with the Isle of Man during the first half of the eleventh century. The first (Fig. 7.10) is an unusually late mixed hoard made up of four ingots, one incomplete, and pennies, some fragmentary, fourteen of Sihtric Anlafsson ('Silkenbeard'), king of Dublin (d.1042), the designs of which are heavily influenced by those of contemporary English pennies, but also three or four of Cnut probably minted in Chester.[182] Almost all of the over 200 coins found at Bryn Maelgwyn were of Cnut and were predominantly minted in Chester, but there are also two Hiberno-Scandinavian pennies from Dublin, a Cnut imitation and

---

[180] Boon 1986b, 92–7. Another hoard from Anglesey, now lost, dates to c.915; Blackburn 2007, 130–1; PAS no. LANCUM-65C1B4.

[181] Nr Chwilog, Anon. 1850, 334; Dolley 1958–9, 257, n. 1.   [182] PAS no. NMGW-038729.

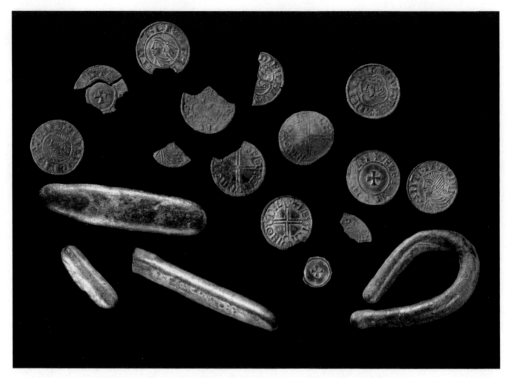

Fig. 7.10. The Llandwrog Hoard (© Amgueddfa Cymru–National Museum Wales).

one of Sihtric Anlafsson. Amongst the Cnut coins found at Pant-yr-Eglwys is another rare imitation modelled on the Chester mint but thought to have been one of a series of imitations of English pennies produced on the Isle of Man where, similarly to Llandwrog, mixed coin and bullion hoards continued well into the eleventh century.[183]

Otherwise, discoveries of single Anglo-Saxon pennies from the north are few and mainly from the north-east, though, interestingly, only two are known from Rhuddlan, and this is also true of finds along the south coast, the majority of which date from the later tenth century onwards.[184] Although there are two deniers of Charles the Bald (c.848–77) and Lothair I (840–55) found with a penny of Ecgberht of Wessex (809–39) at Minchin Hole, Gower, the pattern of hoarding is different from the north since there are no mixed hoards and only three coin hoards, all of Anglo-Saxon pennies dominated by mints in Wessex and the south-west with only a few from elsewhere, reflecting trade in the Severn estuary and further east rather than across the Irish Sea, and they are all later tenth- or early eleventh-century in date. In addition to a hoard (c.975) of Eadgar from Laugharne churchyard, there are two of Æthelræd II (987–1016) from Penrice, Gower, and Monmouth. The former includes coins from

---

[183] Boon 1986b, 1–28; Blackburn 1996; Naismith 2017, 317–22, 329–32.
[184] Besly 2006. Numbers have increased significantly since; see PAS.

CRAFT, DISPLAY, AND TRADE   **261**

Winchester, London, Exeter, Barnstaple, and Bath; the latter from London, Hereford, Gloucester, and Ilchester.[185]

Using the Llandaf charters, Wendy Davies has observed that during the eighth century land was being bought with payments that included cows, horses, dogs, hawks, clothing, and other items. Most values were, however, calculated in numbers of cows, indicating that these were the main unit of value, though ounces of silver were also sometimes used, thereby demonstrating the existence of a dual economy.[186] Cows were likewise the unit of value in a charter that has been dated to the seventh century included in the *Life* of St Cadog, and in the ninth-century Lichfield marginalia payments were made both in livestock and by weight, presumably in silver.[187] Although the concept of cattle as a unit of value likely had its origins in prehistory, the emphasis here on cows reflects the post-Roman rise in dairying (Chapter 6) and is directly comparable with the broadly contemporary system recorded in Irish legal texts where cows are the main unit of value, but which also allows for some payments in silver.[188] Such a system is also supported by the accrual of wealth in the form of penannular brooches and other items of precious metal seen to some degree in Wales, but to a far greater extent in Ireland and Scotland at this time.

The limited influx of precious metals into Wales as a result of Scandinavian settlements in Britain and Ireland that opened up new long-distance trade routes, signalled by the appearance of Kufic dirhams and other bullion, is matched in the written sources by the increasing use of payments in silver and gold but occasionally coins. The last were probably also seen largely in terms of weight, but in certain instances specific sums are recorded, indicating increasing familiarity with a monetary economy by the end of the period.[189] For example, in 989 Maredudd ab Owain of Gwynedd is reported to have paid a penny per head in tribute to the 'Black Host'—the Hiberno-Scandinavians of Dublin—whilst the Old English *Ordinance concerning the Dunsæte* records values of compensation for livestock and slaves in pounds, shillings, and pence, signalling an expectation that the Welsh of Archenfield (Ergyng) would use coin in formal dealings with the English on the other side of the Wye.[190]

As already indicated, silver hoards and other finds in the north point to the importance of a bullion economy well into the eleventh century, whilst in the south the emphasis on coin hoards demonstrating economic contacts with Wessex and the south-west suggests more engagement with the use of money. More generally, the small number of finds, particularly of single pennies, and their limited geographical distribution point to the continuing significance of payments made in livestock and

[185] Dolley 1958–9; 1959; Besly 1993.   [186] Davies, W. 1978, 51–4, 59–61.
[187] Wade-Evans 1944, 132–5, ch. 65; Charles-Edwards 2013, 272–3, 286–8; Evans, J. G., and Rhys 1893, Chad 1, 2, 5, xliii–xlvi; Jenkins and Owen 1983, 50–2, 54.
[188] Kelly 1997, 57–8.   [189] Davies, W. 1978, 59–61.
[190] Jones, T. 1952, 10; Noble 1983, 109; Molyneaux 2011, 256–7.

Fig. 7.11. The Hywel Dda penny (© The Trustees of the British Museum).

other goods, and cows were still appearing as units of value up to the twelfth century.[191] In addition, internal strife and attacks from outside, as well as the large payments of tribute demanded of the Welsh by both English and Hiberno-Scandinavian kings, would inevitably have resulted in depletion of surpluses, creating barriers to economic development.

Nevertheless, the intriguing survival of a single penny (Fig. 7.11) attributed to Hywel Dda ('the Good', d.950), who, towards the end of his life, reigned over Gwynedd as well as Dyfed, signals a brief but very limited experiment with the production of coin. Inscribed +HOþÆL REX, it is entirely of Anglo-Saxon design and was minted by the Chester moneyer Gillys, active in the reign of Eadred (946–55), and was probably found with two pennies of Edmund (939–46). The fact it is unique means that its political and economic significance have been debated. It has been interpreted as an honorific presentation since Hywel is recorded in attendance with other rulers on both Æthelstan (921–39) and Eadred. Most recently, however, his role as the most important of these rulers has been emphasized, and the coin has been seen as English recognition of his position following Hywel's acquisition of Gwynedd in 942. Nevertheless, it almost certainly also had an economic purpose and may thus have been intended to facilitate trade in the Irish Sea zone emanating from Chester and along the north Wales coast.[192] The coin might therefore have been an act of emulation made with English consent, demonstrating both Hywel's considerable authority as ruler of much of Wales and an understanding of the potential of monetary imitation as a means of fostering trade, particularly with England. Indeed, half a century later we see the successful imitation of the coinage of Æthelræd II and Cnut in Hiberno-Scandinavian Dublin during the reign of Sihtric Anlafsson (989–1036), another powerful ruler.[193] Although David Griffiths has made the interesting suggestion that the imitation Cnut penny found at Pant-yr-Eglwys and deposited after c.1023 could have been minted in Rhuddlan, then under the control of the ambitious Llywelyn ap Seisyll (d.1023), no examples have been found there, and in the light of

[191] Charles-Edwards 2013, 287; Naismith 2017, 312–13.
[192] Blunt 1982; Naismith 2017, 311–12; Thomas 2022b.
[193] Naismith 2017, 328–32.

CRAFT, DISPLAY, AND TRADE 263

discoveries in the Isle of Man that origin now appears the most likely.[194] Therefore, apart from the brief experiment with minting coin towards the end of the reign of Hywel Dda, who had exceptional standing amongst Welsh rulers and is later accredited with originating the Welsh law codes, subsequent political instability and the lack of economic infrastructure in the form of towns may have meant that it was not repeated.

Where did trade and exchange take place? As we have seen, during the fifth to seventh centuries the production of high-status artefacts and acquisition of imports were focused on a small number of identifiable hillforts and related sites, pointing to elite control over trade and exchange. These were characteristically located on the coast or close to it. The exceptional concentrations of imported pottery at the promontory fort of Tintagel on the north Cornish coast and the settlement at Bantham near the mouth of the Avon in south Devon are examples of what have been termed 'gateway communities' providing foci for seasonal long-distance trade and exchange.[195] Degannwy, for example, at the mouth of the Conwy, and Coygan Camp near Laugharne on the Taf estuary both have sheltered moorings nearby that may have provided similar opportunities, but on a much smaller scale. Equally, the concentration of imports at Longbury Bank, Caldey Island, and Tenby would suggest a landing place on one of the sandy beaches in the vicinity.

The cessation of imported pottery and glass traded along the Atlantic seaways broadly coincides with the demise of elite hillfort occupation, leaving Llanbedrgoch as the only currently identifiable high-status settlement that may have spanned the seventh to mid-tenth centuries. Whatever the precise interpretation of the Hiberno-Scandinavian presence, Mark Redknap's contention, that from the mid-ninth century onwards it was transformed from a high-status local estate centre into a regional one with more inhabitants, a range of craftworking, and wide-ranging connections remains valid.[196] As such it may have functioned in a similar way to mid-Saxon 'productive' sites where concentrations of coins, metalwork, and other crafts are also present.[197] Although the extent of its role as part of a long-distance trading network remains somewhat opaque, its location near Traeth Coch where boats could be landed is surely relevant, as this might have functioned as a seasonal beach market. Equally, the discovery of fragments of an arm-ring and ingot at Llan-faes near the shores of the Menai Strait, a significant centre of trade during the later twelfth and thirteenth centuries, is thought to be close to *Maes Osfeilion*, the unlocated Hiberno-Scandinavian settlement associated with Ingimund in the early tenth century.[198]

---

[194] Griffiths 2010, 109; Davies, M. 2002, 208; Bornholdt Collins et al. 2014, 494–8; Naismith 2017, 321–2.
[195] Hodges 1982, 23–5; Thomas 1993, 85–8; Reed et al. 2011, 127–31.
[196] Redknap 2004a, 164–9.   [197] Pestell 2011, 562–6.
[198] Redknap 2009b, 34–5; Besly 1995; Jones, T. 1952, 6, 139.

264 LIFE IN EARLY MEDIEVAL WALES

In both instances the impetus behind these economic developments appears to have been Hiberno-Scandinavian activity. The foundation of the *burh* at Rhuddlan was, however, an English endeavour. Its siting at the furthest tidal and lowest fording points on the Clwyd offered important commercial opportunities, but although craftworking and pottery imports indicate some economic development, the very small number of coins[199] signals that this was not sustained. Along the south coast, sandy beaches and sites on river estuaries were likewise places of intermittent and seasonal trade and exchange over a long period of time. Examples include Laugharne, with a cluster of Anglo-Saxon pennies,[200] and Traeth Mawr, probably an important landing place in the Roman period, where craftworking and exotic finds as well as coins from St Patrick's Chapel hint at trading activity.[201] The latter, where pilgrims landed on the way to St Davids, indicates that major churches also had opportunities to promote and control trade and markets, probably timed to coincide with holy days when large crowds were present. However, with the exception of Bangor, located on the Menai Strait, where a silver hoard and other pennies have been found,[202] the lack of excavation at important church sites means that we know almost nothing about their role in this sphere. The locations of secular assembly sites may also have encouraged seasonal markets and local fairs to spring up, as has been suggested at a crossroads at Bayvil not far from the important ancestral site of Crugiau Cemais and the church of St Brynach at Nevern.[203]

Interrogation of the evidence for long-distance trade and exchange reveals that it was focused on sites along the north and south Welsh coasts throughout the early Middle Ages with very little evidence from elsewhere. During the fifth to seventh centuries the continuing significance of the Atlantic seaways is evident in the maintenance or renewal of a long-distance trade network with the Continent and the Mediterranean, though imports found in Wales were probably mediated via south-west Britain, as tin was the major export. By the eighth century, however, the cessation of imported pottery and glass appears to cause a hiatus, though it is possible that goods such as wine, which are invisible in the archaeological record, were still being traded. It is only from the mid-ninth century onwards that we can trace a major realignment in long-distance trade networks brought about by Viking settlements and urban expansion in Ireland and England. Nevertheless, the overall impression is that Wales remained on the fringes of these trade and exchange networks throughout the period.

---

[199] One penny of Æthelræd II and one of Edward the Confessor; Blackburn 2007, 132; Besly 2006, 717, no. 25.

[200] One of Athelstan, Dykes 1976, 28, no. 3; and two cut halfpennies of Æthelræd II, PAS nos PUBLIC-F416D3, PUBLIC-8CC232; Naylor 2012, 304.

[201] One of Eadgar (Besly 2006, 716, no. 13), and one of Edmund (Murphy et al. 2019, 4, 8, 18).

[202] Boon 1986b, 92–7; Edwards 2013, 249.   [203] Comeau 2014.

CRAFT, DISPLAY, AND TRADE   **265**

More generally, the continuing shared cultural identity of western and northern Britain and Ireland, most clearly detectable archaeologically in the stylistic affinities of fine metalwork, points to long-term contacts that would have facilitated trade and exchange around and across the Irish Sea, but these have proved very difficult to identify archaeologically prior to the tenth century. Although finds of metalwork and glass on elite sites such as Dinas Powys signal contacts with Anglo-Saxon kingdoms during the sixth and seventh centuries, the nature of these is less clear. The later limited artefactual evidence fails to support an expansion of trade as a result of English economic and urban development beginning in the long eighth century. This suggests that the rise of Mercia cutting off the Severn as a major riverine route into Wales and the increasing threat of English expansion westwards put up barriers to trade that were exacerbated by the construction of Offa's and Wat's Dykes. Although the Hiberno-Scandinavian phase at Llanbedrgoch and the foundation at *Cledemutha* (Rhuddlan) by Edward the Elder in 921 were defended settlements with craftworking and trading activity, they failed to develop urban characteristics. Indeed, towns were a Norman introduction, and there is little to suggest their development in the parts of Wales that remained under native rule, as in the case of Llan-faes, before the later twelfth century.[204] During the tenth and early eleventh centuries there are signs of acceleration in trade and exchange, with increasing use of silver bullion and to a lesser extent coin for some transactions. Nevertheless, the failed experiment with a native coinage under Hywel Dda in the late 940s, as far as we know unrepeated by subsequent Welsh rulers apart from likely much later imitations minted at Rhuddlan around the turn of the thirteenth century,[205] and the overwhelming continuation of a barter economy based on both cows and silver as units of value, likewise point to comparatively limited economic growth.

CONCLUSION

Although the economy of Wales followed the same very broad trajectories as elsewhere in Britain and Ireland over the course of the early Middle Ages, it remained largely undeveloped despite mineral wealth and agricultural surpluses successfully exploited by the Romans. The closest comparisons are with parts of Scotland and western Ireland, where the physical environment and often poor soils presented many of the same problems and challenges evident in Wales, where the central mountainous massif results in the fragmentation of more fertile lowlands, mostly located close to the sea. Nevertheless, environmental causes, such as geography, and climate deterioration at the beginning of the period, making agricultural surpluses smaller and less

[204] Soulsby 1983, 16–19.   [205] Besly 1995, 53–5.

predictable in all likelihood contributing to major population decline, are only one factor, and human agency must also have played a significant role.

The collapse of the Roman economy included a sharp decline in the exploitation of raw materials, including minerals, and a significant loss of technology leading to recycling and small-scale, local production. At the same time there was a breakdown in the commercial infrastructure associated with markets and trade networks as well as the loss of coins as currency. What replaced it in western Britain, including Wales, was a small-scale economy based on much more limited exploitation of raw materials and production of agricultural surpluses, with the emphasis on domestic crafts practised within farming communities augmented by essential skilled artisans, notably blacksmiths who may have been peripatetic, that was to continue throughout the period. Elites emerged, focused on a comparatively small number of hillforts and related sites, who had sufficient power and command of resources to become the patrons of professional craftspeople producing items for display. These included ornamental metalwork and bone and antler combs, modest articles of personal adornment revealing both an evolution of Roman period forms and a revival in long-standing native stylistic taste. The same elites controlled the import of luxuries, such as glass drinking vessels, acquired via long-distance trade and exchange networks, probably trading cattle, horses, slaves, and raw materials in return. Such luxuries provided the adjuncts to display associated with feasting and the gift-giving economy demanding loyalty and creating group identities.

During the seventh and eighth centuries we begin to see the consolidation of landed estates, new forms of farming settlement associated with *trefi*, the decline of hillforts, and the growing authority of the Church leading to donations of land. The collection of food renders from such estates, if surpluses were sufficient, would have allowed secular and potentially ecclesiastical elites to accumulate wealth and potentially facilitated opportunities for trade and exchange. Such developments would have facilitated increased patronage of skilled craftspeople producing ornate items such as penannular brooches made of precious metals and ecclesiastical equipment. However, personal and military display, together with donations of land and other gifts, as well as acts of almsgiving, could also have significantly depleted increasing but limited surpluses, making the development of other trade and exchange networks more difficult to sustain. There is a hiatus in the evidence for trade along the Atlantic seaways to the Continent in this period, suggesting that, even if some links were maintained, they were at a reduced level, which may also have lessened the incentive for an increase in the exploitation of raw materials and production of goods for trade in return. Furthermore, it has proved very difficult to identify evidence of long-distance trade and sites where such exchange took place. Accumulation of wealth in the form of agricultural surpluses that could be transformed into fine metalwork and other luxury items is much more apparent in southern and eastern Ireland and parts of Scotland than it is in Wales, though the evidence is concentrated in more fertile regions. In contrast, southern and eastern England lay much closer to burgeoning cross-Channel trade networks, facilitating the expansion of coastal craft and trading settlements (*wics*), a hierarchy of 'productive sites', and the minting of coins, none of which are apparent in either western and northern Britain or Ireland before the tenth century. In the case of Wales, the small size of kingdoms and the loss of territory and resources to Mercia, with the consequent impacts on the accumulation of wealth and opportunities for trade and exchange, were further factors curtailing economic growth.

From the ninth century onwards, although there are some definite signs of economic development facilitated by the location of Wales within Irish Sea trade networks, particularly, from the tenth century, between Dublin and Chester, overall expansion appears limited and did not result in either the growth of towns or more than a brief experiment with coinage. Indeed, the increasing significance of Dublin and to a lesser extent Chester with their mixed Scandinavian and native populations as places of burgeoning international trade during the tenth century, and later Bristol, may have made the development of further towns along the north and south Wales coasts more difficult. Despite an improving climate, indications of increased agricultural growth remain comparatively limited, though some expansion in the exploitation of raw materials is suggested by, for example, the reintroduction of the shaft furnace, as at South Hook, which would have increased iron production, presenting opportunities for increased trade and the establishment of settlements with professional artisans to meet a growing market. While it is true that the Hiberno-Scandinavian phase of settlement at Llanbedrgoch demonstrates an upsurge in craft and commercial activity linked to a much wider network stretching across the Irish Sea as well as further afield, this is so far unique, and the economic development of the English *burh* at Rhuddlan was not sustained. The small number of bullion and coin hoards indicates increased accumulations of wealth. Nevertheless, the wealth apparent at Llangorse crannog suggests that much was still concentrated in royal hands or in control of the Church. The rising power of England and the Viking threat, as well as a continuing undercurrent of internecine violence and the instability of many Welsh rulers, including their need to make large payments of tribute and ransoms,[206] would have depleted resources with potentially wide-ranging effects on economic growth and its wider infrastructure. This contrasts sharply with the situation in England, where from the later tenth century onwards, despite the depletion of reserves caused of huge payments of Danegeld, there was a well-organized currency facilitating trade and other transactions in coin, and wealth was increasingly in the hands of urban populations and traders rather than being simply an asset for those with power.[207]

[206] Davies, W. 1990, 57, 75–6.   [207] Sawyer 2013, 100–10.

In Ireland the economic impact of Dublin and other Hiberno-Scandinavian towns with their populations of artisans and merchants is also evident. The comparative lack of economic development in early medieval Wales at this time is, however, more comparable with Scotland, with its often challenging geography, political fragmentation, and likely low population density, but there the Scandinavian impact in the north and west was undoubtedly greater. Towns, some on sites with earlier signs of urbanization, only come to prominence during the reign of David I (1124–53), when coins were also minted for the first time. Prior to this bullion transactions persisted, although there is some evidence to suggest the use of Anglo-Saxon and Scandinavian coins.[208]

[208] Astill 2008, 44–5; Naismith 2017, 312–14.

EIGHT

Christianity: Identifying the Evidence

Christianity was a leading force in the transformation of Europe during the early Middle Ages. For Wales the origins of this transformation lay in the later Roman period, and its development was continuous from then onwards. However, for most of the population conversion probably came during the fifth and sixth centuries as a thread of continuity in the aftermath of the collapse of the Roman economy and during the process of kingdom formation. It is during this period also that we see the origins of monasticism and, by the seventh century, the increasing authority of the Church. With this came the patronage of both rulers and others and, as the period proceeds, the charter evidence, especially for the south-east, indicates the importance of land grants made to ecclesiastical foundations which increased their economic wealth and security, thereby providing a possible impetus for agrarian change. Nonetheless, such grants also served in some measure to protect the property of those who made them, since patronage was a means of control. Indeed, by the end of the period there were important regional family churches later known as *clasau*, and by this time also large numbers of smaller sites serving local communities, though many of these probably had their origins much earlier. The latter were frequently focused on cemeteries and did not necessarily have church buildings at all. It is also possible to trace the wider Christianization of the landscape, for example through the erection of stone crosses, the marking of routeways and landing places, and the appropriation of older ritual sites, such as holy wells, for Christian use. By the end of the period this is also seen in the writing of hagiography, which likewise sought to bind episodes in the lives of the saints to specific places, thereby recording and creating sacred landscapes which would continue to be revered.

The following chapters will consider the development of the early medieval Church in Wales and the impact which Christianity, and all that went with it, had on people and their lives, as well as how they were remembered in death. This chapter will demonstrate the importance of a multidisciplinary approach by focusing on an analysis of the different types of evidence that we can use to identify early medieval ecclesiastical foundations and other sites, such as cemeteries. This will form a critical introduction to the following chapters. Focusing on the archaeology, I will then examine the process of conversion (Chapter 9), before considering evidence for the development

Life in Early Medieval Wales. Nancy Edwards, Oxford University Press. © Nancy Edwards 2023.
DOI: 10.1093/oso/9780198733218.003.0008

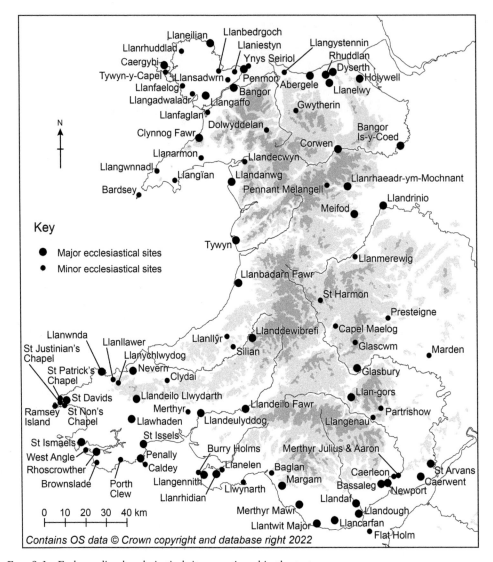

Fig. 8.1. Early medieval ecclesiastical sites mentioned in the text.

of monastic foundations as well as regional churches and *clasau*, together with hermitages and smaller Christian sites and cemeteries as part of a wider Christian landscape (Chapter 10). Lastly, I will discuss the archaeology of belief, focusing on saints' cults, relics, and pilgrimage as well as exploring aspects of burial practice, superstition, and magic (Chapter 11).

There has been much greater success in identifying early medieval church and burial sites in Wales and the borders than with recognizing settlements (Fig. 8.1). Although comparatively few are mentioned in the early medieval written sources, many more can be identified because they underlie existing church sites and were identified, for example, as a result of sculptural and other evidence discovered during

CHRISTIANITY: IDENTIFYING THE EVIDENCE 271

church restoration or other works. Nevertheless, with the exception of Pennant Melangell, Montgomeryshire, this has not led to any major excavations on existing church sites as in England at Monkwearmouth and Jarrow, for example, as well as Winchester and Deerhurst, or in Scotland at sites such as Whithorn and Portmahomack. There have also been several important excavations in Ireland, as at Nendrum, where buildings are no longer in use.[1] In Wales, there has been much more emphasis on the investigation of early medieval cemeteries, some on the sites of former chapels which are now largely unencumbered by standing church buildings, but occasionally in the vicinity of more important ecclesiastical foundations, such as Llandough, Glamorgan.[2] These have left behind archaeological evidence susceptible to discovery, initially through agricultural disturbance but now sometimes detectable from the air, or as a result of housing and other developments, as at Capel Maelog, Radnorshire, or coastal erosion, as at St Patrick's Chapel, Traeth Mawr, Pembrokeshire, or Capel St Ffraid (Tywyn-y-Capel), Trearddur Bay, Anglesey.[3]

The comparative lack of excavation apart from cemeteries means that a multidisciplinary approach remains essential to identify the evidence for both early medieval ecclesiastical foundations and other Christian sites. The critical use of early medieval written sources alongside later medieval documents and antiquarian references, together with place names and dedications, may be combined with a range of archaeological evidence to try and reconstruct the origins and development of the early medieval church in Wales, its impact on the landscape, and the lives of those who lived in it.

CHURCH BUILDINGS

In England and Ireland (and occasionally Scotland) early medieval church fabric and sometimes whole stone buildings have survived, but there is no such evidence from Wales, making early medieval sites more difficult to identify. The only church with possibly early medieval fabric still standing is Presteigne, Radnorshire, where parts of the north wall have tentatively been identified as pre-Norman. However, this is located in a border area east of Offa's Dyke and should therefore be seen as part of a small group of late Anglo-Saxon churches in Herefordshire and south Shropshire and not something we should expect to see more widely to the west.[4] That stone churches existed on some of the more important sites in Wales by the end of the period is,

---

[1] Britnell 1994; Cramp 2005–6; Biddle 2018; Rahtz and Watts 1997; Hill 1997; Carver et al. 2016; McErlean and Crothers 2007.

[2] Holbrook and Thomas 2005.

[3] Britnell 1990; Murphy et al. 2014; 2015; 2016; 2019; Murphy and Hemer 2022; Davidson 2009b.

[4] Taylor and Taylor 1965, ii, 497–9.

nevertheless, likely. The earliest written account is of the cathedral at Llandaf which Bishop Urban replaced in 1120. He describes a small church 28 feet long, 15 feet wide, and 20 feet high, with side-aisles and a *porticus* 12 feet long (most likely a chancel) with a possible apse.[5] Some sculpture fragments identified as architectural from Bangor Cathedral are probably pre-Romanesque and, from the tenth century onwards, there is consistent evidence for the more systematic quarrying of suitable building material, making the construction of stone churches on major sites more likely. Examples include Anglesey grit, used at Bangor, Caerbwdy sandstone found at St Davids, and Sutton stone from the coast of west Glamorgan.[6] However, it is not until the twelfth century, when we see the wider proliferation of Romanesque stone churches, that these are evident on more minor sites. Although wooden churches, either of timber or wattle and possibly turf, were probably relatively common, excavations have produced very little evidence, with only a very small number of possible examples, notably Burry Holms and Llanelen, both on Gower.[7]

Even if evidence for early medieval church buildings is rare, the presence of Romanesque fabric can be indicative of an earlier foundation when used alongside other data, such as the Viking Age stone sculpture at Penmon, Anglesey, which includes a font.[8] Later written accounts indicating the presence of more than one church on a site, as at Meifod, Montgomeryshire, which also has a cross-slab,[9] can likewise be informative since this is also characteristic of major early medieval and some more minor sites across England, such as Jarrow and Heysham, as well as in Scotland at Iona, and in Ireland, for example, at Armagh and Clonmacnoise.[10] Of particular interest, however, are later buildings known in Wales as *capeli-y-bedd* ('grave chapels'), some of which still stand in churchyards, usually south of the main church, as at Caergybi (Holyhead), Anglesey, but are occasionally now part of it, as at Partrishow, Breconshire, where it is at the western end. In other cases, such as Gwytherin, Denbighshire, and Clydai, Pembrokeshire, the former existence of a *capel-y-bedd* is known from antiquarian sources. It has been shown that these were either thought to cover the grave of the founding saint or to house their relics—indeed the *capel-y-bedd* at Clynnog Fawr, Caernarfonshire, contained the shrine of St Beuno until its destruction *c*.1790. Here early twentieth-century excavation in the interior of the early sixteenth-century chapel, which is to the south-west but on a different alignment from the main church, revealed the incomplete drystone foundations of a

[5] Evans, J. G., and Rhys 1893, 86.

[6] Edwards 2013, 73–4, 111–13, nos CN6–CN9; 2007a, 29, 86; Redknap and Lewis 2007, 51, 58.

[7] On Burry Holms, see Hague 1974, 29–32; RCAHMW 1976b, 14–15; for a critique of Hague's interpretation, see Pritchard 2009, 249–51; on Llanelen, see Schlesinger and Walls 1996, 110–12.

[8] Gem 2009; Edwards 2013, nos. AN51–5.   [9] Ibid., no. MT6.

[10] Blair 2005, 199–202, 216; Campbell and Maldonado 2020, 55, figs 2, 12; Ó Carragáin 2010a, 215–21.

smaller, earlier, but undated building measuring around 5.5 × 3 metres internally, and burials, two of which were in long cists.[11]

INSCRIBED STONES AND STONE SCULPTURE

The almost total lack of evidence for church buildings means that the presence of early medieval stone sculpture is the most reliable means of identifying early medieval Christian sites. What survives, however, is only likely to be the tip of the iceberg and we should also assume that woodcarving, though less permanent, was common. Of the approximately 150 fifth- to seventh-century inscribed memorial stones, in addition to those found in cemeteries, as many as 70 per cent may be associated with later church sites in the south-west, though significantly fewer elsewhere, with almost 40 per cent in the north and 36 per cent in the south-east, in each case suggesting that these sites are early foundations. For example, the inscribed stone at Merthyr, Carmarthenshire, was discovered during grave-digging, while at Llandanwg, Merioneth, one stone was preserved in the church fabric, a second was first noted in the church, and a third recently came to light in the churchyard.[12]

With later stone sculpture, the association with church sites becomes more pronounced. More than 420 cross-carved stones and pieces of more ambitious sculpture, such as crosses and cross-slabs, are now known from Wales, and the vast majority of these are associated with Christian sites of some kind (Fig. 8.2). Cross-carved stones, most of which would have functioned as grave-markers or as foci within a cemetery, are frequently very simple monuments and therefore difficult to date other than through typology, sometimes aided by ornament capable of art-historical comparison or the palaeographic and linguistic analysis of infrequent inscriptions. Nevertheless, it has been argued that the production of cross-carved stones commenced round about 600 but came into its own during the seventh century as inscribed stones gave way to largely anonymous grave-markers, a fashion probably introduced into Ireland and western Britain along the Atlantic seaways from Merovingian France. On analogy with the development of more ambitious sculpture and analysis of the inscriptions, monuments with outline crosses, sometimes carved in relief, are more likely to date from around the ninth century onwards, while in most cases those with incised linear crosses seem more likely to be earlier, with some overlap between.[13] Some limited corroboration is also now available from scientific dating. St Ismaels 4, Great Castle Head, Pembrokeshire, a stone with an incised linear cross, was found as a lintel over a grave adjacent to another radiocarbon-dated to cal. AD 660–880, whilst a grave

---

[11] Edwards 2002, 234–5; Petts and Turner 2009; Stallybrass 1914.
[12] Edwards 2007a, 33, no. CM35; 2013, 45, nos MR10–12.   [13] Edwards 2007a, 114–17.

274 LIFE IN EARLY MEDIEVAL WALES

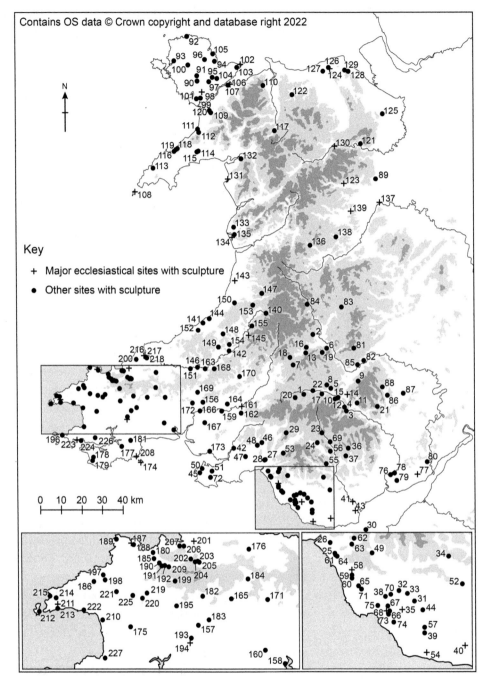

FIG. 8.2. The distribution of early medieval cross-carved stones and stone sculpture.

CHRISTIANITY: IDENTIFYING THE EVIDENCE 275

1 Defynnog
2 Llanafan Fawr
3 Llanddeti
4 Llanddeti (Tal-y-bont)
5 Llan-ddew
6 Llanddewi'r Cwm
7 Llanddulas
8 Llandyfaelog Fach
9 Llaneleu
10 Llanfeugan
11 Llanfihangel Cwm Du
12 Llanfrynach
13 Llangamarch
14 Llan-gors
15 Llanhamlach
16 Llanlleonfel
17 Llanspyddid
18 Llanwrtyd
19 Maesmynys
10 Llywel
21 Partrishow
22 Trallwng
23 Vaynor
24 Ystradfellte
25 Aberafan
26 Baglan
27 Cadocton-juxta-Neath (Court Herbert)
28 Cadoxton-juxta-Neath (Neath Abbey)
29 Cadoxton-juxta-Neath (Coelbren)
39 Flatholm
31 Coety (Tŷ Newydd)
32 Coety (Pen-yr-Allt)
33 Coychurch
34 Eglwysilan
35 Ewenni
36 Gelli-Gaer (Capel Brithdir)
37 Gelli-Gaer (Capel Gwladys)
38 Laleston
39 Llanblethian
40 Llancarfan
41 Llandaf
42 Llandeilo Tal-y-Bont
43 Llandough
44 Llan-gan
45 Llangennith
46 Llangiwg
47 Llangyfelach (Church)
48 Llangyfelach (Mynydd Gellionen)
49 Llangynwyd
50 Llanmadog

51 Llanrhidian
52 Llantrisant
53 Lantwit-juxta-Neath
54 Llantwit Major
55 Llanwonno (Church)
56 Llanwonno (Mynydd Merthyr)
57 Llyswyrny
58 Margam (Abbey)
59 Margam (Cwrt-y-Defaid)
60 Margam (Eglwys Nynnid)
61 Margam (Lower Court Farm)
62 Margam (Penrhydd-fawr)
63 Margam (Penrhydd-waelod)
64 Margam (Port Talbot)
65 Margam (Upper Court Farm)
66 Merthyr Mawr
67 Merthyr Mawr
68 Merthyr Mawr (Church)
69 Merthyr Tydfil
70 Newcastle
71 Pyle and Kenfig
72 Reynoldstown
73 St Brides Major and Wick (Ogmore Castle)
74 St Brides Major and Wick
75 Tythegston
76 Caerleon
77 Caerwent
78 Christchurch
79 Llan-wern
80 St Arvans
81 Bryngwyn
82 Clyro
83 Llanddewi Ystradenni
84 Llansanffraid Cwmteuddwr
85 Llowes
86 Clodock
87 Kenderchurch
88 Llanveynoe
89 Oswestry
90 Cerrig Ceinwen
91 Heneglwys
92 Llanbadrig
93 Llanfachraith
94 Llanfair-Mathafarn-Eithaf
95 Llanffinan
96 Llanfihangel Tre'r Beirdd
97 Llanfihangel Ysgeifiog
98 Llangaffo
99 Llangeinwen
100 Llechgynfarwy

101 Newborough
102 Penmon
103 Penmon
104 Penmynydd
105 Penrhosllugwy
106 Bangor (Cathedral)
107 Bangor (Ffriddoedd)
108 Bardsey Island
109 Bontnewydd
110 Caerhun
111 Clynnog (Church)
112 Clynnog (Capel Uchaf)
113 Llangwnnadl
114 Llangybi (Church)
115 Llangybi (Cefn-coch)
116 Nefyn
117 Penmachno
118 Pistyll (Church)
119 Pistyll (Tŷ Mawr Farm)
120 Waunfawr
121 Llandysilio yn Iâl (Pillar of Eliseg)
122 Llangernyw
123 Llanrhaeadr-ym-Mochnant
124 Dyserth
125 Hope
126 Meliden
127 Rhuddlan
128 Whitford (Church)
129 Whitford (*Maen Achwyfan*)
130 Corwen
131 Llandanwg
132 Llandecwyn
133 Llanegryn
134 Tywyn (Church)
135 Tywyn
136 Carno
137 Llandrinio
138 Llanwyddelan
139 Meifod
140 Caron-uwch-Clawdd
141 Henfynyw
142 Lampeter
143 Llanbadarn Fawr
144 Llanddewi Aber-arth
145 Llanddewibrefi
146 Llandysul
147 Llanfihangel-y-Creuddyn
148 Llanfihangel Ystrad (Llanllŷr)
149 Llanfihangel Ystrad (Maes Mynach)
150 Llangwyryfon

Fig. 8.2. Continued

151	Llanllwchaearn	177	Carew	203	Nevern (Pen Parke)
152	Llannarth	178	Castlemartin (Church)	204	Neven (Tre-bwlch)
153	Llanwnnws	179	Castlemartin (Brownslade)	205	Nevern (Tre-haidd)
154	Silian	180	Fishguard South	206	Newport (Church)
155	Tregaron	181	Jeffreyston	207	Newport (Cnwc-y-Crogwydd)
156	Abergwili	182	Llandeilo Llwydarth	208	Penally
157	Egremont	183	Llandysilio	209	Pontfaen
158	Laugharne	184	Llanfrynach	210	Roch
159	Llanarthne	185	Llanllawer	211	St Davids (Cathedral)
160	Llanddowror	186	Llanrhian	212	St Davids (Ramsey Island)
161	Llandeilo Fawr (Church)	187	Llanwnda (Church)	213	St Davids (St Non's)
162	Llandeilo Fawr (Cefn Cethin Farm)	188	Llanwnda	214	St Davids (Pen-Arthur)
163	Llanfihangel-ar-arth	189	Llanwnda (Llanwnnwr Farm)	215	St Davids (St Patrick's)
164	Llanfynydd	190	Llanychaer (Cilrhedyn Isaf Farm)	216	St Dogmaels (Abbey)
165	Llanglydwen	191	Llanychaer (Clyn Farm)	217	St Dogmaels (Bryngwyn Farm)
166	Llangunnor	192	Llanychlwydog	218	St Dogmaels
167	Llangyndeyrn	193	Llawhaden (Church)	219	St Dogwells (Church)
168	Llanllwni	194	Llawhaden (St Kennox Farm)	220	St Dogwells (Wolf's Castle)
169	Llanpumsaint	195	Llys-y-Frân	221	St Edrins
170	Llansawel	196	Marloes	222	St Elvis
171	Llanwinio	197	Mathry (Rhoslanog Farm)	223	St Ismaels (Church)
172	Newchurch	198	Mathry (Tregidreg Farm)	224	St Ismaels (Great Castle Head0
173	Pembrey	199	Morvil	225	St Lawrence
174	Caldey	200	Moylegrove	226	Steynton
175	Camrose	201	Nevern (Church)	227	Walton West
176	Capel Colman	202	Nevern (Cilgwyn)		

FIG. 8.2. Continued

marked by an *in situ* cross-shaped slab with an incomplete linear cross from St Patrick's Chapel probably dates to the ninth century.[14]

The distribution of cross-carved stones is informative since it demonstrates the continuing importance of Christian contacts around and across the Irish Sea to the end of the early Middle Ages since they are also characteristic of Ireland, the Isle of Man, and Scotland, especially in the west. The majority are found in south-west Wales, with a particular concentration in the northern half of Pembrokeshire, in the same area as where many of the ogham inscriptions are found. In the north-west there is a second and later concentration of grave-slabs with outline crosses on Anglesey, an area with both earlier Irish and later Hiberno-Scandinavian settlement, with a few probably earlier examples on the Llŷn peninsula as well. Other cross-carved stones are scattered more thinly across Cardiganshire, Carmarthenshire, Glamorgan, and Breconshire, including the upper Usk valley where one might expect continuing Irish contacts, but there are very few in Merioneth, the north-east, or the borderlands in the upper reaches of the Severn and further south. Though some are clustered on important foundations, such as St Davids and its environs and at Llanddewibrefi,

[14] Ibid., no. P131 (Wk-14018); Murphy et al. 2016, 11, 45, grave 26, fig. 14 (403); 2019, 31, B18.

Cardiganshire, many more are found in ones and twos on otherwise unknown sites which are now parish churches, such as Llaneleu, Breconshire, and Llangernyw, Denbighshire.[15] However, others, such as that from St Kennox Farm, Llawhaden, Pembrokeshire, and Pembrey, Carmarthenshire, would seem to be associated with the sites of cemeteries or chapels that later failed to reach parish church status. It is therefore clear that these and other cross-carved stones, for example in the vicinity of Nevern, Pembrokeshire, also indicate the Christianization of the wider landscape.[16]

Crosses, cross-slabs, and other sculpture carved in relief with interlace, frets, and sometimes other ornament, but only rarely Christian figural iconography, emerge during the eighth century, and a handful of inscriptions provides the skeleton of a chronological framework. Inscriptions also indicate the importance of patronage by both ecclesiastics and secular rulers, such as Abbot Samson and the kings of Glywysing at Llantwit Major.[17] Such sculpture required considerable resources as well as skill to produce, and the stone was sometimes transported considerable distances. For example, the stone for the cross at Llanbadarn Fawr, Cardiganshire, which outcrops on the slopes of Cadair Idris close to the Mawddach estuary, would have been carried around 40 kilometres south by sea.[18] It is therefore not surprising that such monuments are often concentrated on sites of known significance which are also noted in the written sources, as with Caldey Island and Penally, Pembrokeshire, Llantwit Major and Merthyr Mawr, Glamorgan, Penmon, Anglesey, and Dyserth, Flintshire.[19] This suggests that in some other instances, such as Margam, Glamorgan, which later became a Cistercian house, the presence of such sculpture is also indicative of its former importance even though there is no mention in the documentary record.[20] On sites such as these there is some evidence to suggest that monuments originally stood as foci within the cemetery, as with the cross at Nevern, Pembrokeshire, which still stands to the south of the church.[21] This is underlined by the fact that many of the inscriptions request prayers for the souls of their patrons, though it is unknown whether any marked graves. In some other cases, however, crosses were set up on the boundary of an ecclesiastical site, as at Penmon, with the object of providing symbolic protection, or in the wider landscape where they may have served a variety of other functions, such as marking ecclesiastical land, as at Merthyr Mawr. Towards the end

---

[15] Edwards 2007a, 49, 116–17, nos P93–6, P98, P100–6, CD10–13; Redknap and Lewis 2007, B18–19; Edwards 2013, D3–4.

[16] Edwards 2007a, 56–60, 62, nos CM39, P56. See also Comeau 2016, 217–18.

[17] Edwards 2013, 126–7. Monuments datable by inscriptions naming figures identifiable in the written sources are Llantwit Major 3, mid-eighth century; Llandysilio yn Iâl 1 (Pillar of Eliseg), c.808–54/5; Llantwit Major 1, later ninth century before 886; Llandaf 4, c.1022–45; St Davids 8, post 1078, late eleventh or early twelfth century; Redknap and Lewis 2007, nos G30, G63, G65; Edwards 2013, no. D3; 2007a, no. P97.

[18] Edwards 2013, no. CD4.

[19] Edwards 2007a, nos P6, P82–4; Redknap and Lewis 2007, 575, 577–9; Edwards 2013, nos AN51–4, F2–3.

[20] Redknap and Lewis 2007, 577.   [21] Edwards 2007a, 60–1, no. P73.

278 LIFE IN EARLY MEDIEVAL WALES

of the period there is also a small number of carved stone fonts, for example at Penmon, which undoubtedly stood within church buildings of some kind.[22] The distribution of more ambitious sculpture reflects not only wealth and the skills of those who carved them but also the availability of suitable stone. For example, the concentration of monuments associated with major sites on free-draining soils in the Vale of Glamorgan is matched by the availability of a range of carboniferous sandstones suitable for carving.[23]

BURIALS AND CEMETERIES

More than 130 inhumation cemeteries thought to be of early medieval date have now been recorded in Wales (Fig. 8.3) and since the 1970s there have been almost thirty major excavations as well as several other significant exploratory ones. The cemeteries may be divided into two principal groups: those now associated with parish churches or former chapels of ease, thereby enabling their identification as early medieval foundations, and those, sometimes termed kin or community cemeteries, which do not appear to have had any ecclesiastical connections. The number of radiocarbon dates from cemeteries in Wales is still comparatively small but, on analogy with better dated sequences from Ireland and Scotland, it may be argued that in Wales these cemeteries begin in the later Roman period and increase in numbers during the centuries of conversion, with some of those that did not go on to become ecclesiastical sites continuing in use for some time after this.[24] Moreover, a significant proportion of these sites, some 20 per cent overall, but rising to 36 per cent in the north, are associated with prehistoric ritual and other monuments, particularly Early Bronze Age cairns and barrows, which remained significant nodes in the landscape linked with a mythical ancestral past.[25] Such cemeteries are found across Britain and Ireland in this period, and indeed further afield, but there are important differences between the richly furnished burials characteristic of most parts of southern and eastern Anglo-Saxon England[26] and those elsewhere, where graves are largely findless and otherwise share many other features. As Charles Thomas long ago established, in northern and western Britain as well as Ireland a proportion of these, which he termed 'undeveloped' cemeteries, were abandoned, whilst others, which he termed 'developed cemeteries', evolved into church and chapel sites.[27]

[22] Edwards 2013, nos AN51, AN54; Redknap and Lewis 2007, 578, no. G99.

[23] Ibid., 56–8; Soilscapes.

[24] For the latest published list of radiocarbon dates from Wales, see Longley 2009, 109–10. On Ireland, see O'Sullivan et al. 2014, 283–312; O'Brien 2020; on Scotland, Maldonado 2013.

[25] Longley 2009, 120.

[26] Lucy 2000, fig. 1.1. For the association between Anglo-Saxon cemeteries and prehistoric monuments, see Semple 2013, 13–62.

[27] Thomas 1971, 50–68.

CHRISTIANITY: IDENTIFYING THE EVIDENCE 279

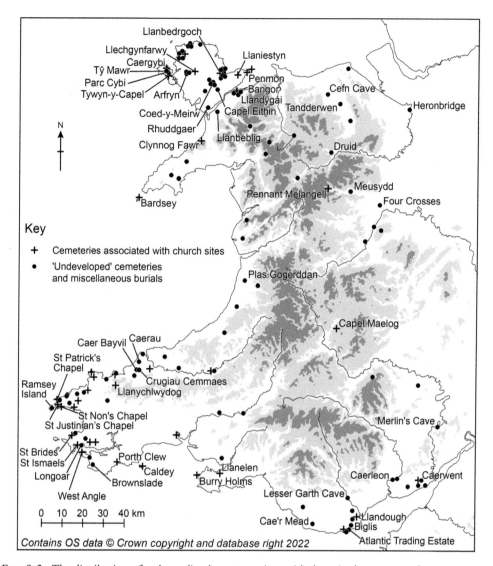

Fig. 8.3. The distribution of early medieval cemetery sites, with those in the text named.

In western and northern Britain and Ireland, early medieval burials are overwhelmingly inhumations. There are no clearly identifiable post-Roman cremations in Wales,[28] though other native practices did continue to some extent (Chapter 9). Inhumations, which have their origins as a later Roman burial rite, are characteristically extended and oriented broadly west–east, with the head at the western end, but frequently with some variation towards south-west/north-east and occasionally north–south burials

---

[28] Pollock 2006, 73, identified a possible post-Roman pyre site adjoining a Bronze Age burial monument at Pentre Farm, Pontarddulais, Glamorgan, radiocarbon-dated to 1500±70BP, cal. AD 400–660 (Har-959); Ward 1978, 56–8. However, a metalworking site seems more likely if the small amount of cremated bone is residual. For discussion of early medieval cremation burials in Ireland and Scotland, see Gleeson and McLaughlin 2020.

280 LIFE IN EARLY MEDIEVAL WALES

as well, as at Arfryn and Capel Eithin, Anglesey, and Llandough.[29] The form of the grave shows considerable variation, often on the same site, and is partially dictated by available materials as well as social status and belief together with the preferences of those conducting the burial. Firstly, there are stone-lined graves, often known as long cists. These may be lined with vertical slabs and sometimes also have paved floors and may be covered by lintels as, for example, at Arfryn. Secondly, a variety of wooden grave linings, lids, and bases are now being recognized. For example, at Tŷ Mawr, Anglesey, small stones lining the grave are thought to have supported wooden boards, while at Capel Maelog one grave contained traces of the upper and lower planks of a coffin, and staining was also thought to represent coffins at Llandough. Thirdly, dug graves are common and occasionally the hunched posture of the skeleton suggests that it was wrapped in a shroud, as at Llandough.[30] In other cases the dead were buried clothed, as indicated by a woman at Coed y Meirw, Llangefni, Anglesey, who had a small Type G1 penannular brooch beneath her right shoulder, presumably fastening her dress, and in another grave there was a probable purse fitting near the hip which would have hung from a belt at the waist.[31] There is seldom clear evidence for changes in grave form over time because of insufficient and imprecise radiocarbon dates, but this does occur at Tywyn-y-Capel, where there were long cists with lintels in the first phase c.650–800, but the second, spanning approximately the eighth to twelfth centuries, was characterized by dug graves, some with signs of shrouds.[32]

There is also evidence that some graves were elaborated in different ways above ground, in some cases indicating family groups as well as custom and status. For example, burials in the first phase at Tywyn-y-Capel were marked above ground by a low mound surrounded by stones. Although so far unique, this practice may have been common elsewhere in the north-west since the inscription on the stone at Penmachno, Caernarfonshire, which was found with two graves, reads 'Carausius lies here in this heap of stones', which probably refers to a cairn.[33] Square-ditched mortuary enclosures containing one and sometimes two or three graves are, however, being increasingly recognized, especially in the north, though they are also occasionally found in south-west England. It is generally thought that the earth removed from the ditches would have been piled over the grave to form a mound or barrow, as at Tandderwen, Denbighshire (Fig. 9.4), though in a few instances it has been argued that there was some kind of wooden superstructure, as for example, at Llandygái,

[29] Hedges 2016, 153–5; White and Smith 1999, 142, fig. 40; Holbrook and Thomas 2005, 38–9, fig. 6.
[30] Longley 2009, 106–12; Hedges 2016, 147–52; Cuttler et al. 2012, 113–21, fig. 10.5; Britnell 1990, 36; Holbrook and Thomas 2005, 27.
[31] Edwards forthcoming; Iwan Parry, Brython Archaeology (pers. comm.).
[32] Davidson 2009b.
[33] Ibid., 175; Edwards 2013, no. CN38: *Caravsivs hic iacit in hoc congeries lapidvm.*

Caernarfonshire.[34] At Druid, Corwen, Merioneth (Fig. 9.4), for example, there is a small cemetery with six square-ditched enclosures, each with a single grave, though a small number of other graves set between them were not marked in this way. It is therefore generally argued that such enclosures were a sign of status and, where there is more than one burial, these are likely to indicate close family links.[35] However, at sites such as Meusydd, Llanrhaeadr-ym-Mochant, Denbighshire, and Atlantic Trading Estate, Glamorgan, there are no such enclosures, but the comparatively neat clusters and rows of graves, together with the lack of intercutting, suggest that they were marked in some way, perhaps by a low mound of earth left over from the grave fill. Nevertheless, in a few instances, as at Arfryn, post-holes indicate wooden markers, and at St Patrick's Chapel a cross-incised cruciform slab had been set up at the western end of a woman's grave.[36]

A glance at the distribution reveals significant differences in the numbers of cemeteries which have been located in different parts of Wales. Although there are concentrations on both Anglesey and in coastal areas of Pembrokeshire, with a couple of clusters in the south-east, very few are known in other eastern regions, a situation commensurate with adjoining parts of England.[37] The two principal reasons that lie behind this are linked. Firstly, skeletal material is seldom well preserved because acidic soils are so common, and this has led to problems of grave recognition. Secondly, the concentrations reflect the common use of long cists, since these are more archaeologically visible than dug graves or those with wooden coffins, especially where no bodily remains have survived and there are no other features aiding recognition, notably the presence of square-ditched mortuary enclosures and the reuse of prehistoric sites, as at Tandderwen, Denbighshire.[38] It is therefore likely that in these areas dug graves, with or without coffins or other wooden linings, were the norm.

The frequent lack of skeletal preservation has further implications since this can result in an absence of suitable samples for radiocarbon dating, making the building and comparison of cemetery chronologies much more difficult.[39] There has also been a tendency to assume that long-cist burials are always of early medieval date and that their discovery in churchyards or under church floors may therefore be taken as reliable evidence of an early medieval foundation. However, this is not in fact the case. Long-cist graves had a very long period of currency, with their origins in the later Roman period, as suggested by the small cemetery at Parc Cybi, Anglesey.[40] That

[34] Longley 2009, 113–15; Webster and Brunning 2004; Brassil et al. 1991, 64; Edwards 1991, fig. 110; Lynch and Musson 2001, 109.

[35] Jones, N. W. et al. 2013b, 78–83.

[36] Ibid., 73–9; James, H. 1992, 96–8; Hedges 2016, 155–6; Murphy et al. 2016, 11, grave 26, fig. 14 (403).

[37] See Lucy 2000, fig. 1.1. For Herefordshire, see Ray 2015, 202–4.

[38] Longley 2009, fig. 6.1; Brassil et al. 1991.

[39] For the most recent list of radiocarbon dates, see Longley 2009, 109–10.

[40] Kenney et al. 2020, i, 198–207.

282 LIFE IN EARLY MEDIEVAL WALES

many from later church and chapel sites are early medieval is indicated by radiocarbon dates and other evidence as, for example, at Llanychlwydog and Porth Clew, Pembrokeshire.[41] Nevertheless, excavations beneath the churchyard boundary at Eglwyswrw, north Pembrokeshire, revealed both dug graves and long cists with lintels, two of which had residual Dyfed gravel-tempered pottery in their fills indicating a post-late-twelfth-century date, though this does not in itself preclude an earlier foundation for the site. Equally, recent excavations underneath the church at Nefyn, Caernarfonshire, uncovered a cist-and-lintel grave radiocarbon-dated to between the late twelfth and mid-thirteenth centuries AD.[42]

ENCLOSURES

Curvilinear churchyard boundaries, sometimes with outer enclosures, have frequently been used to identify early medieval foundations, most convincingly in Ireland but also in other parts of western and northern Britain.[43] In Wales, the recognition of such boundaries can certainly be significant when used alongside other evidence, but it must be acknowledged that remains are often fragmentary and their interpretation is not always as straightforward as might first appear. Such enclosures, usually most clearly visible on aerial photographs, may be retained as the line or the arc of a modern churchyard perimeter. Alternatively, they may still be detectable as relict landscape features, such as field boundaries, and it is also possible to identify examples, now destroyed or only partially extant, with the aid of earlier maps.[44] The first difficulty, however, arises in establishing the original date of their construction since little excavation has taken place. For example, at Llangïan, Caernarfonshire, a site with an early inscribed stone, repairs to the curvilinear churchyard wall indicated stratified deposits radiocarbon-dated to cal. AD 430–670, but this did not date the enclosure itself.[45] It is also becoming clear that some enclosures and the sites associated with them have complex histories. At Porth Clew exploratory excavations revealed that the twelfth-century or later chapel was located within a sequence of earlier enclosures. It overlay a square inner enclosure, a deposit in the ditch of which was radiocarbon-dated to

---

[41] Murphy 1987; Schlee 2009a; 2009b; James 2016b, 443–4.

[42] Ludlow 2000, where comparisons beyond Wales are also discussed; C R Archaeology 2015. For an exceptional and more elaborate example of a late tenth- or earlier eleventh-century stone-lined grave (4231) with stone lintels (and one timber), see the phase 1 cemetery at Haughmond Abbey, Shropshire; West and Palmer 2014, 121–37, 337, 342–5, figs 5.23, 5.27–8.

[43] The evidence for Ireland is summarized in O'Sullivan et al. 2014, 145–8; for Cornwall, see Preston-Jones 1992; for a more general discussion of the western British evidence and possible dating, see Petts 2002. In England minster enclosures likely existed but have proved much harder to find; see Blair 2005, 196–8.

[44] For the use of these methods in Wales, see James, T. A. 1992; Brook 1992; Silvester and Evans 2009, 27–31; Ludlow 2009, 71–6.

[45] Ward, M. 1994; Edwards 2013, no. CN25.

between the mid-sixth and mid-seventh century AD, and this was enclosed within a later, larger, curvilinear enclosure with two ditches dated to cal. AD 660–810 and cal. AD 810–1010 respectively. However, the early medieval burials were located to the south beyond these enclosures with only a couple between the inner and outer curvilinear ditches.[46] In some other instances the sites of later prehistoric settlement enclosures were reused, as at Llanmerewig, Montgomeryshire, where the church of St Llwchaiarn is still surrounded by an impressive curvilinear embankment (Fig. 8.4). Excavations outside this indicated that the earliest phase was in fact a Late Iron Age or early Roman hilltop enclosure with three ditches and a roundhouse. Something similar is also likely at Llanfaglan, Caernarfonshire, where a complex of undated enclosures was recorded from the air.[47] Moreover, while it is clear that many 'undeveloped' cemeteries were never enclosed, there are likely exceptions, notably Caer, Bayvil, Pembrokeshire, where an Iron Age hilltop settlement enclosure was reused for early medieval burial. At Capel Maelog, however, the curvilinear cemetery enclosure is tenth-century or later.[48]

FIG. 8.4. Llanmerewig Church, with its curvilinear embanked enclosure (Crown copyright: Royal Commission on the Ancient and Historical Monuments of Wales).

[46] Schlee 2009a; 2009b; James 2016b, 443–4.

[47] Blockley 2014; Driver and Davidson 2005. For churchyard enclosures with possible late prehistoric origins in the south-west, see Ludlow 2009, 71–4.

[48] James 1987; Britnell 1990, 84.

284 LIFE IN EARLY MEDIEVAL WALES

It is also evident that the size of the curvilinear enclosure has some bearing since important ecclesiastical foundations known from other evidence may still have unusually large enclosures, as, for example, Meifod with an area of around 2 hectares.[49] In other cases parts of outer enclosures may still survive as hedge-lines and field walls, as at Silian, Cardiganshire, and Llandysilio, Pembrokeshire, both sites with carved stone monuments; and at Capel Colman, Pembrokeshire, a late seventh- or eighth-century cross-carved stone still stands close to the line of a possible outer enclosure.[50] However, curvilinear enclosures were not universal, and at Caergybi the walls of the late Roman, rectilinear, fortlet enclosure were reused.[51]

HOLY WELLS AND TREES

It is also relevant to consider holy wells alongside other evidence indicative of early medieval ecclesiastical foundations, and it is highly likely that the sanctity of at least some of these lay in the pre-Christian past. The well of St Gwenfrewi (Winefride) at Holywell, Flintshire, provides a good example. Although there are no early medieval material remains and the well is first clearly mentioned in 1093 when it was granted to St Werburgh's in Chester, the cult site was probably well established by this time. In the twelfth-century *Lives* of Gwenfrewi, when St Beuno restores the severed head of the saint to her body, a spring gushes forth where her blood had stained the ground. This suggests the former existence of a pre-Christian head cult, a memory of which was later Christianized and there are good parallels for this in Ireland.[52] More often a holy well connected with the founding saint is located on the churchyard boundary, as at Llanllawer, Pembrokeshire, and Llandeilo Fawr, Carmarthenshire, or close to it, as with St Seiriol's well at Penmon.[53] As with Penmon, however, such sites are frequently obscured by much later well-houses and other features, and there has been little archaeological excavation.[54] Nonetheless, an inscribed stone was noted near the well of St Owen at Narberth North, Pembrokeshire, and a cross-carved stone with an incised fish symbol is now built into a well near Llandeilo Llwydarth, Pembrokeshire, and may formerly have marked the site.[55]

[49] Silvester and Evans 2009, 28, fig. 2.2.

[50] Edwards and Vousden 2014; James 1997, 5–7, 21–3; Ludlow 2003, prn 46776; Edwards 2007a, nos CD29–31, P8, P25–8.

[51] RCAHMW 1937, 28–34.

[52] Jones, F. 1954, 49; Thomas 1906–13, ii, 179–80; Wade-Evans 1944, chs 8–14, 290–3; de Smedt et al. 1887, 712–14. For a seventh-century Irish hagiographical story concerning St Patrick's Christianization of a pagan well cult, see Tírechán, Bieler 1979, 152–5, ch. 39. For archaeological evidence of a late prehistoric well cult associated with a skull at Inchagreenogue, Co. Limerick, see Bhreathnach 2014, 136.

[53] Ludlow 2003, prn 46817; Edwards 2007a, 238.

[54] Excavations at St Seiriol's well found nothing of any antiquity; Edwards 1986, 26–7.

[55] Ludlow 2003, prn 46842; Edwards 2007a, nos P23, P69.

References to the survival of pre-Christian tree cults and their subsequent Christianization are less evident in Wales than in Ireland, where there is a rich tradition, or Anglo-Saxon England. Nevertheless, a story in the late twelfth-century *Life* of St Brynach, in which an oak produces miraculous wheaten loaves, could reflect an earlier cult of some kind.[56] It has also been claimed that some very large yew trees in Welsh churchyards, such as that at Llangernyw, Denbighshire, could be as much as fifteen hundred years old, though problems with their dating mean that it is very difficult to determine their age.[57] In Ireland at least yew wood had a sacred as well as a functional value, and it was commonly used for making early medieval crozier staffs and reliquaries. However, the surviving fragments of a shrine, probably of eighth- or ninth-century date, known as *Arch Gwenfrewi*, from Gwytherin, Denbighshire, are in fact made of oak.[58]

RELICS, RELIQUARIES, AND OTHER CHRISTIAN METALWORK

Relics and reliquaries can on occasion provide further evidence aiding the identification of early medieval ecclesiastical foundations, but as elsewhere in Britain very few have survived the vicissitudes of the Reformation and its aftermath as well as the Civil War. What is extant indicates the existence in Wales of small house-shaped shrines of Late Antique form but decorated with Insular ornamental metalwork, notably the surviving hinge of likely eighth-century date for a carrying strap attached to such a shrine from Llangorse crannog, and larger triangular shrines, such as *Arch Gwenfrewi* (Fig. 11.2).[59] As Gerald of Wales famously commented, the Welsh, like the Scots and the Irish, revered secondary relics, particularly portable bells and croziers encased in gold, silver, or bronze which were regarded as the possessions of the saints.[60] Indeed, there are clear parallels between the few quadrangular bells still extant in Wales and Herefordshire, such as that from Llangystennin, Caernarfonshire, and those in Ireland, where considerably more have survived, together with examples in Scotland and Brittany.[61] Other, less reliable, references to early medieval relics which have not survived are noted in saints' *Lives*, for example Lifris's *Life* of St Cadog, which records stories associated with a 'mottled bell' at Llancarfan, Glamorgan, or in antiquarian sources, such as St Baglan's crozier from Baglan, Glamorgan, reported to Edward

---

[56] On Ireland, see Lucas 1963, esp. 27–42; on England, Blair 2005, 226, 380–2, 476–7, 481–2; on Wales, Comeau 2016, 220; Wade-Evans 1944, 12–15, ch. 14.

[57] Bevan-Jones 2002, 28–30, 49.

[58] Lucas 1963, 18, 22, 29, 31–2; Murray 2014, 124; 2017, 167; Edwards and Gray Hulse 1992, 95; 1997.

[59] Lane and Redknap 2019, 209–18.   [60] Thorpe 1978, 87.

[61] Bourke 2020, 381–3, 422–6, 504–9, is a catalogue of those from Wales and Herefordshire, including earlier references to possible examples no longer extant.

286 LIFE IN EARLY MEDIEVAL WALES

Lhuyd at the end of the seventeenth century.[62] Other early medieval metalwork decorated with Christian symbols or iconography has also occasionally come to light, mainly as a result of metal-detecting. Finds include a cruciform mount and a fragmentary pendant cross from St Arvans, Monmouthshire, though these were not found on the site of the church itself.[63] In fact early medieval artefacts from church sites are extremely rare other than those from major excavations at Llandough and St Patrick's Chapel.[64]

WRITTEN SOURCES

In contrast to the wide-ranging archaeological evidence which now allows us to identify a considerable number of ecclesiastical foundations (together with cemeteries and other sites), the early medieval written sources note remarkably few outside the southeast, especially when these are compared with the numerous sites mentioned in contemporary sources in both Ireland and England.[65] Firstly, a small number focusing on the most important sites are noted in the Welsh chronicles, with a few of these also mentioned in similar sources beyond Wales. As we have seen (Chapter 1), chronicles were compiled contemporaneously at St Davids from the late eighth century indicating its significance as an intellectual centre by that time. They occasionally record the deaths of prominent churchmen, such as Jonathan *princeps* ('abbot') of Abergele in 856 (= 858) or Asser bishop of St Davids in 908 (= 909). Viking and other raids are also noted in the later chronicle, *Brut y Tywysogion*, for example on Penmon in 971 and Clynnog in 978, which are the earliest mentions of these foundations.[66] Secondly, hagiography can provide important clues to sites associated with a particular saint. The only surviving early *Life* of a Welsh saint, Samson of Dol, probably written in the late seventh century, recounts his training at the monastery of Llantwit Major before his move to the island retreat of Caldey (Ynys Bŷr) in Dyfed. Later, the *Life* of St Cadog by Lifris (d.1104) refers to burial rights at Llancarfan and includes an appendix listing properties then held by various members of the community of canons.[67] Thirdly, the Llandaf charters enable identification of over seventy ecclesiastical sites, monasteries, a few also with bishops, as well as churches, mainly in Gwent and Ergyng. The distribution indicates regional differences—for example, there are fewer but more important sites in Glamorgan, and the cult of St Teilo was originally centred further

---

[62] Wade-Evans 1944, *Vita Sancti Cadoci*, 84–7, ch. 27; Morris 1909–11, iii, 27.

[63] Redknap 2009a, 354–6; 2022, 95–7.

[64] Holbrook and Thomas 2005, 32–5, 52–73; Murphy et al. 2016, 46–7, fig. 15; 2019, 17.

[65] Davies, W. 1982a, 141–6, figs 49–50.   [66] Morris 1980, 48–9, 89–90; Jones, T. 1952, 8.

[67] Taylor 1991 and Flobert 1997, chs 7, 21; Wade-Evans 1944, *Vita Sancti Cadoci*, chs 9, 28, 48–52; Charles-Edwards 2013, 600–1, 604–7.

west on Llandeilo Fawr. The approximate dating framework alongside other evidence also hints at important changes over time—not least the eclipse of Llandeilo Fawr by the later tenth century and the appropriation of the cult of St Teilo by the new bishopric at Llandaf. Such charters can likewise shed significant light on royal and aristocratic patrons and the working estates they donated to the Church as well as the underlying reasons for such grants.[68]

In addition, a number of later medieval sources, when used judiciously alongside other evidence, can help to identify further ecclesiastical foundations and other religious sites with origins in the early Middle Ages. Hagiography, such as the *Lives* of Gwenfrewi (Winefride), has already been mentioned. Some churches, such as Dyserth and Rhuddlan, Flintshire, both of which also have early medieval sculpture and other relevant evidence, are first noted in Domesday Book,[69] and earlier material incorporated into the Welsh laws is also illuminating. For example, Thomas Charles-Edwards has argued that the section in the lawbooks, including in the Cyfnerth Redaction, on the seven bishop-houses of Dyfed should probably be dated to the second half of the ninth or early tenth century. These may be identified as St Davids itself, St Ismaels, Llandeilo Llwydarth, which was later replaced by Llawhaden, Rhoscrowther, Llandeulyddog (Carmarthen), possibly St Issells, and an unlocated site known as *Llan Geneu*; the first four all have early medieval carved stone monuments and other supporting evidence. Some had abbots but, apart from the first, their precise status is more contentious and it is possible that all initially supported independent regional bishops who later came under the authority of or were subsumed by St Davids.[70] Finally, church taxations, notably that of Pope Nicholas IV (1291), can provide valuable clues aiding identification of earlier *clas* sites which retained a portionary status, such as Corwen, the mother church of the commote of Edeirnion, as well as the first recorded forms of some place names and church dedications.[71]

PLACE NAMES AND CHURCH DEDICATIONS

Place names and church dedications are potentially significant additional sources that can be used alongside archaeological and other written evidence to identify early medieval ecclesiastical foundations. However, except for the most important sites, these are usually only recorded from the later Middle Ages onwards and both are subject to change over time. *Merthyr* place names, of which there are only around thirty, mainly in south Wales, are of particular interest because they are regarded as

[68] Davies, W. 1978, 121–63; Davies, J. R. 2002, 365–9.
[69] Edwards 2013, nos F2–3, F9–10; Williams, A., and Martin 2002, 736.
[70] Charles-Edwards 1971; Edwards 2007a, 10, nos P90–8, P128–30, P21–2, P55.
[71] Astle et al. 1802, 286; Edwards 2013, 377–8.

288 LIFE IN EARLY MEDIEVAL WALES

early, most likely fifth- to seventh-century, on analogy with related names in southern France, Brittany, west Cornwall, and Ireland, where they are already known in the seventh. The term, derived from the Latin *martyres*, is usually linked with a personal name, and is thought to refer to relics and may therefore indicate the tomb of a saint.[72] For example, *Merthyr Isw* (Partrishow) still has a later *capel-y-bedd* that may have housed the corporeal relics or overlain the grave of St Issui.[73] The most common ecclesiastical place-name element is *llan*, usually followed by a personal name presumed to be that of the founding saint. It has been argued that a *llan* should be 'typically understood as [a] church-complex plus cemetery in which the laity were buried' and such names became common from the seventh century onwards alongside the growth of churchyard burial,[74] sometimes replacing *merthyr*. For example, *Merthyr Caffo*, Anglesey, a name only recorded in the *Life* of St Cybi *c*.1200, is now known as Llangaffo.[75] Other place-name elements include the Latin *basilica*, which is also early and refers to a church with major relics. The only known example in Wales is Bassaleg, Monmouthshire, where there may have been a *capel-y-bedd*. Dyserth, Flintshire, is also interesting since it is derived from the Latin *desertum*, meaning a 'solitary place' and hence a 'hermitage' or 'retreat'. Equivalents of both are also found in Ireland.[76]

Church dedications are characterized by two things. On the one hand, Welsh churches are frequently still dedicated to obscure local saints with Celtic names rather than to universal saints and many of these are unique, notably on Anglesey. While the antiquity of such names is frequently problematic, there is sometimes other evidence to suggest that they could relate to early founders who later acquired the status of saints, as at Llansadwrn, Anglesey, where a sixth-century inscribed stone commemorates *Saturninus*, the diminutive Latin form of the Welsh name *Sadwrn*.[77] On the other hand the distributions of dedications to particular saints, such as Teilo in the Llandaf charters, can sometimes point to spheres of influence and the growth of cults during the early Middle Ages. It is also possible to trace the impact of the cults of Irish saints in the south-west and northern coastal areas of Wales, indicating the continuing importance of contacts with Ireland, including during the Viking period. As might be expected, there is evidence for the cult of St Patrick as, for example, at Llanbadrig in northern Anglesey and at St Patrick's Chapel at Traeth Mawr, the probable landing place for pilgrims travelling to St Davids from Ireland. It may also be suggested that this was where, according to Rhygyfarch's *Life* of St David, St Patrick raised a man from the dead before embarking for Ireland.[78] The church at Dyserth is still dedicated

---

[72] Sharpe 2002, 141–4; Parsons 2013a.   [73] Ibid., 85–7.

[74] Davies, J. R. 2002, 393; see also Padel 2010, 116–19.   [75] Parsons 2013a, 60–1.

[76] On Bassaleg, see Roberts 1992, 41–2; Sharpe 2002, 137–9; Bhreathnach 2014, 159. On Dyserth, see Owen and Gruffydd 2017, 65.

[77] Yates 1973; Edwards 2013, no. AN45.   [78] Ibid., 354; Sharpe and Davies 2007, 110–13, ch. 3.

to St Brigid (Ffraid) and St Cwyfan (Kevin), both important Hiberno-Scandinavian cults.[79]

CONCLUSION

This discussion has emphasized the need for a multidisciplinary approach allowing us to make the best use of a wide range of archaeological evidence alongside the meagre written record and other sources. Such an approach not only enables the identification of different types of site but can also shed significant light on the evolution of a hierarchy of Christian sites and major changes, as well as continuities, over time, aiding recognition of regional differences and wider comparisons. It likewise enables as far as possible the construction of an analytical narrative of the Christianization of the landscape during the later Roman and early medieval periods in Wales.

[79] On Brigid dedications in Wales, see Bowen 1954, 97–8. On Cwyfan and the wider Scandinavian dissemination of Brigid's cult in coastal regions of north-west England and south-west Scotland, see Edmonds 2019, 134–8, 143.

NINE

Conversion, Commemoration, and Burial

Christianity reached Britain during the Roman period, expanding during the fourth century when it became the official religion of the Empire, and it is now generally accepted that it was from these roots that Christianity in western Britain grew, rather than being reintroduced from southern Gaul during the late fifth and sixth centuries (Chapter 1). The link between the continuation of a Roman identity and the adoption of a Christian one has also been discussed (Chapter 4). Although the processes underlying conversion and the pace and spread of Christianity at this time remain difficult to discern in both the archaeological and written record, interrogation of the evidence for Wales does reveal some more general trends. This discussion will begin by considering what we know of pre-Christian religions and the origins of Christianity in this part of later Roman Britain, before examining the process of conversion focusing on commemoration and burial.

PRE-CHRISTIAN RELIGIONS

By the time Gildas was writing in the second quarter of the sixth century, he presents an already well-established British Church that had become wealthy and corrupt, but he also looks back to the past, referring to the mountains, hills, and rivers once revered as divine.[1] The veneration of such natural features, frequently perceived as liminal in the landscape, and the deities associated with them characterizes many religions and should be seen as part of a culturally constructed cosmology incorporating the realm above, the world where people live, and the underworld. Indeed, such a cosmology, with its sacred mountains and rivers, also became an essential tenet of Christianity.[2] In Britain and Ireland the deposition of metalwork and sometimes human remains in watery places from the later Bronze Age onwards suggests gifts to deities associated with them. Around the same time we also see the beginnings of hillfort construction, and many of these are now seen to have had a sacred dimension involving not only

[1] Davies, W. 1982a, 169, 172; Winterbottom 1978, 17, 90, ch. 4.3.
[2] della Dora 2016, 26–71; Lewis-Williams 2008, 31.

Life in Early Medieval Wales. Nancy Edwards, Oxford University Press. © Nancy Edwards 2023.
DOI: 10.1093/oso/9780198733218.003.0009

offerings of metalwork and sometimes the deposition of human remains or more formal burials but also rituals concerned with animals and crops. It is also thought that hillforts became places for large, possibly seasonal, gatherings of people on sites unsuitable for or with little evidence of year-round habitation.[3]

In Wales the sacred connotations of the Severn and the Dee have already been mentioned (Chapter 2), and the importance of later prehistoric ritual deposition in watery places, such as Llyn Fawr, Glamorgan, and into the early Roman period at Llyn Cerrig Bach, Anglesey, is well known. Equally, there are indications that mountains were revered, as suggested by the La Tène enamelled bowl found on the slopes of Snowdon.[4] The evidence likewise argues for a ritual element in the functions of some hillforts, such as Tre'r Ceiri, and it has been argued that there was an upsurge in activity on some of these sites in the later Roman period that in some cases persisted into the post-Roman centuries, as at Dinorben and Dinas Emrys (Chapters 3 and 5). Wider numinous landscapes remain difficult to perceive, but we can detect a thriving fourth-century cult focused on a healing spring at Llys Awel below the hillfort of

FIG. 9.1. Votive offerings from Llys Awel, near Pen-y-Corddyn Mawr hillfort (© Amgueddfa Cymru–National Museum Wales).

---

[3] Bradley 2007, 200–2, 214–16, 248–51.   [4] Lynch et al. 2000, 179–80, 191; Macdonald 2007, 161–2.

292 LIFE IN EARLY MEDIEVAL WALES

Pen-y-Corddyn Mawr, Denbighshire (Fig. 9.1). Finds include three votive dog figurines and a statuette of the god Mercury, the Roman deity most frequently transported into a native context, together with over 200 Valentinianic (364–78) and fifteen Theodosian (378–402) coins.[5] Other large fourth-century coin hoards have been recovered from both the hillfort and its vicinity.[6] The most interesting discovery is, however, a late Roman belt buckle and plate from above the spring near the hillfort entrance. It is decorated with Christian iconography—two fish and two peacocks facing a tree of life, thereby symbolizing water, earth, and air, as well as eternal life.[7] The significance of such a find in this location is more difficult to unravel. It might indicate syncretic beliefs, a Christian offering for healing, or the deposition of a powerful Christian symbol directed at converting the sacred landscape. As such it is comparable with a votive copper-alloy fragment with Old and New Testament iconography found in the ruins of the modified temple on the hilltop at Uley, Somerset.[8]

In the more Romanized south-east, the discovery of coins spanning the mid-third to late fourth centuries on Portskewett Hill overlooking the Severn estuary suggests it may have been the site of a temple.[9] If so, it might have been a counterpart to the thriving temple and baths complex at Lydney across the Severn, which was also active at this time. The latter, a healing shrine dedicated to the native water god Nodens, who was twinned with Mars, is actually situated within a hillfort, and huge numbers of votives, including dog figurines and other offerings of items of personal adornment, such as bracelets as well as coins, have been found. However, the extent to which religious activity continued beyond the Valentinianic period is unclear, though a later fifth- or sixth-century Type G1 penannular brooch was also found on the site.[10] Indeed, a case can be made for the persistence of this and a number of other hilltop shrines in south-west England, some associated with hillforts, into the post-Roman period, suggesting the continuing strength of Romanized native beliefs in this region. And at Uley, as already mentioned, there are indications of conversion, including the erection of a small stone building thought to be a church which succeeded the ruinous temple of Mercury in the late sixth or early seventh century.[11]

By the early ninth century, however, when the *Historia Brittonum* was written, hillforts had become part of a mythical, pre-Christian past. This is illustrated by an episode in the *Life* of St Germanus recounting how the saint was denied entry to the hillfort of Moel Fenlli, Denbighshire, and its subsequent destruction by heavenly fire alongside the eponymous pagan tyrant Benlli and his followers. Archaeological

[5] Arnold and Davies 2000, 130–1; Henig 1984, 57.

[6] Guest and Wells 2007, 305–7, nos. 938–40, 943.

[7] Burnham 1993, 271, fig. 4; Mawer 1995, 61–2. On ritual deposition of Christian objects elsewhere in late Roman Britain, see Petts 2003, 124–32.

[8] Woodward and Leach 1993, 65, 107–10.   [9] Arnold and Davies 2000, 130.

[10] Wheeler and Wheeler 1932, 89, 100–29; Casey and Hoffmann 1999; Dickinson 1982, 62, no. 20.

[11] Woodward and Leach 1993, 303–35.

evidence from the site includes Roman pottery and other artefacts, and two Constantinian coin hoards suggest that it too was a place of ritual deposition in the late Roman period. The Tale of Emrys, associated with the hillfort of Dinas Emrys, has similar connotations with allusions to wizards, a lake, and human sacrifice.[12] Finds of post-Roman imported pottery from the site include a sherd of DSPA pottery from a vessel stamped with a Christian chi-rho monogram with a sun and moon, alpha and omega, which had been reworked into a roundel, but the lack of an understandable context makes its significance unclear.[13]

Taken together, late Roman forts and towns in Wales and the borders demonstrate a range of evidence for temples, shrines, and cults as well as the continuation of native beliefs and ritual activities. The significance of the Romano-Celtic temple in Caerwent, constructed as late as *c*.330 and that flourished to the end of the century, has already been mentioned, and there was probably a second outside the east gate adjacent to the early medieval extramural cemetery (Chapters 3 and 4). At the other end of the scale in Insula XI, a small domestic shrine of similar date consisted of a stone head set on a platform with a large boulder for offerings. Human remains and votive offerings were also being deposited in pits and wells within the town. Such evidence indicates the continuation of unofficial native rituals and beliefs, probably throughout the Roman period.[14] Equally, in Wroxeter a shrine associated with a votive healing eye cult was excavated in the ruins of the basilica, and a scatter of human skull fragments were later redeposited nearby.[15]

Forts and their associated civilian settlements would undoubtedly have brought together people from a wide range of backgrounds with different beliefs and from different parts of the Empire. This is reflected, for example, in the inscriptions on Roman altars and tombstones from the legionary fortresses at Chester and Caerleon naming people adhering to a variety of gods, official—notably Jupiter and the *genius* of the legion concerned—and otherwise.[16] However, from the second century onwards in such contexts we can also detect evidence for several cults that had been introduced into Roman Britain from the East and that appealed to those seeking a heightened, more personal, religious experience and commitment. The best known in Britain is Mithraism, associated with a god of light, and the Mithraeum outside the auxiliary fort at Caernarfon has already been noted (Chapter 3).[17] From Caernarfon also is a remarkable gold plaque. It was found outside the fort (Fig. 4.1) and is most likely from a burial. Inscribed in Greek, it was owned by a man named Alphianos and

---

[12] Morris 1980, chs 32–5, 40–2.   [13] Campbell 2007a, 27, fig. 19 D1.

[14] Brewer 2006, 22–3, 44–6; Boon 1976; Pollock 2006, 63–8.   [15] Barker et al. 1997, 212–17.

[16] Collingwood and Wright 1995, nos 17–85 and 445–574; Tomlin et al. 2009, nos 3149–51; Henig 1984, 88–94; Haynes 2016, 453–5.

[17] Henig 1984, 97–109; Boon 1960.

functioned as a talisman. The inscription invokes a great variety of gods for protection but also has various mysterious symbols indicative of magic and superstitious belief.[18]

Therefore, even though our knowledge and understanding of native religion and beliefs in the later Roman period in Wales are severely limited, what evidence there is indicates the continuing significance of natural places such as mountains, hills, and springs. Similarly, an upsurge in deposition, principally of later third- and fourth-century coin hoards, as well as other activity on some hillforts, suggests a sacred dimension and the vitality of associated beliefs, some of which show Roman influences, at this time. However, unlike south-west England, there are as yet no identifiable examples of Romano-Celtic temples within hillforts, as at Lydney across the Severn. As might be expected, evidence for Roman polytheistic religion and other cults was concentrated in forts and towns, and at Caerwent the continuing vigour of these as well as an undercurrent of native beliefs and practices are clear.

THE ORIGINS OF CHRISTIANITY

Christianity, a monotheistic religion, was similarly introduced from the East via soldiers and traders into this cosmopolitan, Romanized environment. In *De Excidio* Gildas refers to the martyrdoms of Julius and Aaron at Caerleon, alongside that of Alban at *Verulamium*, which was clearly better known to him. He conjectures that these had occurred during the persecution of Diocletian, which lasted from 303 to 306 in the West, though it is generally argued that they actually took place earlier, during the third century. Julius and Aaron, the second a rare Old Testament name which may have been adopted after baptism, are described by Gildas as *legionum urbis cives* ('citizens of the city of the legions') and were therefore most likely soldiers.[19] As already indicated (Chapter 4), the link with Caerleon is made explicit in a mid-ninth-century Llandaf charter recording the donation of an estate with the *merthyr* of Julius and Aaron. Its bounds and other later evidence point to a location east of the fort on a hill on the far side of the Usk (Fig. 4.2), where possible early medieval cist graves were found in 1785, but recent exploratory excavations remain inconclusive.[20]

The turning point, however, came in 313 with Constantine's and Licinius's Edict of Milan restoring religious toleration and giving imperial favour to Christianity. The Council of Arles, held the following year, was attended by three British bishops from London, York, and probably Lincoln, as well as a priest and deacon who may have

---

[18] Peers and Hemp 1919; Collingwood and Wright 1995, no. 436; Henig 1984, 187; Pollock 2006, 174, C1.3.

[19] Winterbottom 1978, ch. 10. On Gildas and martyrdoms, see Thomas 1981, 42–50; Stephens 1985; Boon 1992, 11–15; Sharpe 2002, 105–30; see also Livingstone 2014, on persecution.

[20] Evans, J. G., and Rhys 1893, 225–6, 377; Davies, W. 1978, 181, no. 225. For detailed discussion, see Seaman 2015; 2018. On the *merthyr* name, see Parsons 2013a, 52–3, 87–8.

represented the province of *Britannia Prima*.[21] It is therefore not surprising that archaeological evidence for Christianity in Roman Britain is very largely datable to the fourth century, testifying to its expansion at this time. However, in contrast to most other regions, evidence for Christianity in Wales and the borders is sparse and has generally been viewed as an extension of that further east, particularly within the ambit of Cirencester.[22] In addition to the martyrs at Caerleon, George Boon identified a group of vessels found in House IX.7N in Caerwent as a possible, later fourth-century, Christian *agape* set used for religious meals after celebration of the Eucharist. The pottery, probably originally wrapped in a woollen cloth, consisted of two sooted jars and three bowls, as well as a fragmentary pewter plate and flanged bowl with a knife and double swivel-hook. These had been placed in a larger pot set into the floor and then sealed with an inverted *mortarium* which had been cemented into place. Identification of an *agape* set rests on the presence of a chi-R graffito on the base of the pewter bowl, but it has also been suggested that the swivel-hook might be for the suspension of a lamp lit at the beginning of the meal.[23] The combination of objects, their careful deposition, and the chi-R graffito makes Boon's identification an attractive one, pointing to a Christian congregation in the fourth-century town. Such a community would have needed a place to worship, but in Britain late Roman church buildings have proved notoriously difficult to identify with any certainty.[24] Both Boon's suggestion of a house church in House V.12N where the objects were found[25] and Nash-Williams's tentative identification of a small apsidal church north of the baths[26] lack any clear supporting evidence. Following geophysics, a basilica-plan church has also been mooted in Wroxeter but no excavation has taken place, so it is impossible to say.[27]

Christian artefacts have generally been easier to identify than buildings. Late Roman vessels, plate, and other items such as spoons, which were often deposited in hoards, as well as objects of personal adornment such as rings and belt fittings, were sometimes decorated with Christian symbols and iconography. Such hoards and other finds are known across much of Britain south of the Forth and Clyde, the most significant being the spectacular hoard of altar plate and votive plaques from Water Newton (*Durobrivae*), Cambridgeshire, but they are almost unheard of in Wales.[28] Indeed, the

---

[21] Sharpe 2002, 77; Petts 2003, 36–7.

[22] For full discussion of the range of archaeological evidence, see Thomas 1981, also figs 15–16; Mawer 1995, also fig. 1; Petts 2003.

[23] Boon 1962; 1992, 17–18; Ashby 1907, 459–60; Knight 1984a, 357, n. 3; for a more cautious interpretation, see Mawer 1995, 19.

[24] For discussion of the problems, supporting evidence, and those identified, see Petts 2003, 56–86.

[25] Boon 1992, 18–19. On the discovery of a decorated lead coffin lid nearby, see Pollock 2006, 57–61.

[26] Nash-Williams 1930, 235–6.

[27] White and Barker 1998, 107–8, pl. 14. On villas and possible Christian continuity in south-east Wales, see Chapter 4.

[28] Mawer 1995, fig. 1; Painter 1977.

296 LIFE IN EARLY MEDIEVAL WALES

Caerwent pewter bowl and Pen-y-Corddyn Mawr buckle and plate are the only items with Christian symbols and iconography from known contexts. The only other is an antiquarian find, thought to have come from Monmouthshire, of a silver spoon with a Constantinian chi-rho, alpha, and omega, alongside the fragmentary name of the Christian owner.[29] Two further objects from the borders are, however, also of significance here. Firstly, a lead salt-pan from Shavington, Cheshire, with an incomplete inscription reading VIVENTI [S]COPI has been interpreted as *Viventi Episcopi*, most likely meaning 'of Viventius the bishop'. The name likewise has Christian connotations, and it has been argued that his diocese may have been centred on the late Roman fortress at Chester and, if so, this has important implications for the strength of late Roman Christianity in this area. The second is a strap-end ornamented with a peacock, a tree of life, and a possible solar roundel, which may indicate syncretic beliefs, from the Roman town of Kenchester (*Magnis*) in Herefordshire.[30]

Thus, while we might expect Christianity in Wales to be growing in strength amongst communities in Romanized environments, including forts and towns, by the later fourth century, the scarcity of the data currently does little to support this view. Moreover, with one possible exception, namely the Rhuddgaer lead coffin discussed below, it is confined to areas within easy reach of more Romanized parts of Britain centred on Chester and Cirencester to the east. Archaeological invisibility of Christian communities could be a factor, possibly in the face of the continuing vibrancy of polytheistic and native beliefs and contemporary economic collapse, but arguing from such negative evidence is problematic. Instead, we need to look for the expansion of Christianity in Wales in the post-Roman period.

COMMEMORATION

It is the fifth- to mid-seventh-century inscribed memorial stones that provide the clearest evidence of conversion since many of them undoubtedly marked the graves of the Christian dead. Nevertheless, probably the earliest Christian commemorative inscription is on an incomplete lead coffin from Rhuddgaer, Anglesey (Fig. 9.2). This was found in 1878, probably within a larger Roman period cemetery, close to the mouth of the Braint, a name in all likelihood derived from the goddess Brigantia, pointing to a sacred river with long-standing religious connotations. The coffin is thought to have contained a plaster burial providing maximum protection for the body, and this Roman rite, usually regarded as fourth-century, is also seen as Christian in some contexts, but not all. The two long sides originally had identical reverse inscriptions reading *Camvloris hoi* ('Camuloris here'). *Hoi* is thought to derive from

---

[29] Mawer 1995, 48.   [30] Penney and Shotter 1996; Mawer 1995, 63.

CONVERSION, COMMEMORATION, AND BURIAL 297

FIG. 9.2. The Rhuddgaer lead coffin (Crown copyright: Royal Commission on the Ancient and Historical Monuments of Wales).

Primitive Old Irish *xoi*, the equivalent of the vulgar Latin, Christian *hic iacit* formula, though *xoi* is not known in Ireland until the fifth century. Therefore, the combination of the inscriptions and the burial rite suggests that Camuloris was a Christian. These practices, and the beliefs which went with them, probably emanated from the fort at Caernarfon across the Menai Strait around the end of the fourth century, though the closeness of the Braint suggests that older beliefs continued to pervade the landscape in which the site lay.[31]

It has been proposed that a handful of fourth-century inscribed memorials associated with Roman forts and towns in northern Roman Britain might be Christian,[32]

---

[31] Edwards 2016b, 183–5; Sims-Williams 2003, 27.   [32] Handley 2001, 183–4; Petts 2003, 150–5.

and this is certainly possible. However, the Christian formulae, notably *hic iacit* ('here lies') and more complex variations of this, on inscribed stones in post-Roman western Britain are first found in Rome in the fourth century. These would have reached Britain, probably in the earlier fifth century, perhaps from Trier in north-east Gaul, or along the Atlantic seaways from the Rhône valley in the south, or from Bordeaux or the Loire on the western seaboard. Their introduction should be seen as part of a wider spectrum of continuing Christian contacts between Britain and Gaul during the fifth century, notably Constantius's account of Germanus of Auxerre's visit to Britain in 429 to combat the Pelagian heresy and probably again somewhat later, in his early *Life* of the saint.[33]

As already indicated (Chapter 4), inscribed stones with the *hic iacit* formula and variations of it are most commonly found in north-west Wales and it may be argued that in this region the projection of a continuing or assumed Roman identity amongst members of the elite and their families went hand in hand with the adoption of a Christian one. Indeed, if conversion was seen as part of their elite status, this is likely to have had a trickle-down effect, persuading others to follow suit. Trawsfynydd 2, Merioneth, originally located beside a Roman road where it was visible to passers-by, is a particularly interesting example of a fifth-century monument projecting a Christian identity. The horizontal inscription, which has a more elaborate version of the *hic iacit* formula, may be reconstructed to read *Porivs hic in tvmvlo iacit homo [x]p(ist)ianvs fvit* ('Porius, here in the tomb he lies, he was a Christian man'), thereby drawing attention to his baptized status. *Xpistianvs* incorporates a Greek chi and rho as the first two letters, and the lack of patronym may emphasize the significance of a heavenly father rather than an earthly one.[34] Similarly, an incomplete inscription on a sixth-century monument from Llansadwrn, Anglesey, commemorating a Christian couple reads *Hic beatvs...Satvrninvs se[pvltvs] iacit · et sva sa[ncta] conivx · pa...* ('Here lies buried blessed...Saturninus. And his saintly wife...'). Again we see elaboration of the *hic iacit* formula and, as on the Continent, attention is drawn to their pious characters by the addition of suitable adjectives. It is also possible that the inscription ended with the blessing *pa(x vobiscum sit)* ('peace be with you both'), demonstrating a further link.[35] Other Christian formulae are also occasionally found. In the south-west the horizontal Latin inscription on the bilingual stone from Castell Dwyran, Carmarthenshire, which has been dated to the late fifth or earlier sixth century, reads *Memoria Voteporigis protictoris* ('The memorial/tomb of Voteporix the Protector').

---

[33] Edwards 2013, 122–3. Christian contacts between fifth-century Britain and Gaul are discussed by Chadwick 1959, 200–32, and summarized in Sharpe 2002, 79–81, 98–9. On Germanus, see Thompson 1984; Higham 2014. The historicity of the link, also made on the Pillar of Eliseg (Edwards 2013, no. D3), with the origins of the kingdom of Powys, is suspect since it is the product of hagiography incorporated into the early ninth-century *Historia Brittonum*; Morris 1980, chs 32–5, 39, 47–9; see also Edwards 2016a, 93–4.

[34] Matt. 23:9; Edwards 2013, no. MR23.   [35] Ibid., no. AN45.

Memoria is primarily found in Italy and North Africa but also occasionally in Gaul and Spain. Above the inscription is an early example of a simple ring cross, a feature also found on the Continent, mainly in the sixth century.[36] Near St Davids a stone of similar date has *nomena* following the name of the man commemorated. This is literally the plural of 'name', but here it means the 'remains' or 'relics' of the deceased and is likewise found on the Continent and in North Africa. Comparisons have also been drawn with later ogham-inscribed stones in Ireland, with Old Irish *anm* meaning 'name', indicating the importance of Christian contacts not only via the Atlantic seaways but also across the Irish Sea.[37] A small number of other monuments also have a Christian symbol, usually, as on the Continent, above the inscription. These include the only examples of a chi-rho monogram cross on Penmachno 4 and at Treflys, Caernarfonshire, and the crosses on the monuments from Margam Mountain, Glamorgan (Fig. 4.5), and Llangadwaladr, Anglesey, which commemorates King Catamanus of Gwynedd who died *c.*625 (Fig. 1.1).[38]

In *De Excidio*, Gildas indicates three principal orders of clergy: bishops (*episcopi*), priests (*presbyterii*), and deacons (*diacones*). He also uses the term *sacerdos* to refer to the priestly office and its sacramental functions rather than a specific rank. A century earlier St Patrick tells us that his father was a deacon and his grandfather a priest, pointing to the existence of clerical families in the early British Church. As with St Patrick, such men would have been an essential part of the conversion process in their roles as missionaries, in some instances at least aided by the patronage of the secular elite. Gildas also makes it clear that clergy were included in the entourages of his tyrants. Moreover, as adherents grew, the need for consolidation would have necessitated the expansion of pastoral care, especially the provision of baptism, though Gildas criticizes clergy for their pastoral neglect. He also mentions both monks and monasticism.[39] From around the later fifth century onwards the Latin-inscribed stones similarly provide important evidence for churchmen and church organization, with four examples from north-west Wales. Both Aberdaron 1 and 2 (Fig. 4.4, d), Caernarfonshire, commemorate priests using the abbreviations PBR and PRSB for *presbyter*, and *sacerdos* is found on a monument from Llandudno commemorating Sanctinus, a suitable name for a man of his vocation, as well as on Llantrisant 1, Anglesey. Although there is no reference to bishops or deacons on the Welsh stones, examples are known elsewhere: an *episcopus* is commemorated at Cardinham, Cornwall, and a 'subdeacon' was reported on a lost stone from Lower Curgie, Galloway, with

---

[36] Edwards 2007a, no. CM3. For an example of *memoria* in Cornwall, see Lewannick 1; Macalister 1945, no. 466.

[37] *Rinaci nomena*, Edwards 2007a, no. P107. See also *Eqvestri nomine* ('of Equester by name') on Llandanwg 2, Merioneth; Edwards 2013, no. MR11.

[38] Ibid., 66–7, nos CN38, CN41, AN26; 2007a, 47–8; Redknap and Lewis 2007, no. G77.

[39] Hood 1978, *Confessio*, ch. 1; Winterbottom 1978, chs 28, 32, 34–5, 66–7, 109–10; Thomas 2010, 70.

300 LIFE IN EARLY MEDIEVAL WALES

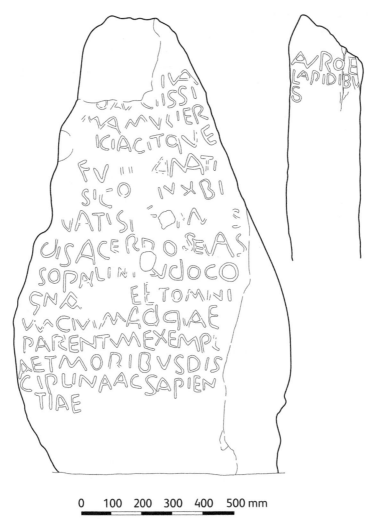

FIG. 9.3. The Llantrisant inscribed stone commemorating the wife of a priest, possibly a bishop (Crown copyright: Royal Commission on the Ancient and Historical Monuments of Wales).

two further examples of *sacerdos* from Kirkmadrine.[40] Similarly, the deceased on the bilingual inscription Llanfaelog 2, Anglesey, is named Mailisus, which Patrick Sims-Williams has identified as the early Irish name *Máel Ísu*, 'the bald one of Jesus', referring to his clerical tonsure.[41]

The inscription on the stone from Llantrisant (Fig. 9.3), dating to around the second half of the sixth century, is particularly illuminating because of its unusual length. It commemorates the 'most loving wife' of Bivatisus but is almost entirely

---

[40] Edwards 2013, 55, nos CN2–3, CN21, AN46; Macalister 1945, no. 459; Craig 1997, 619.
[41] Edwards 2013, no. AN13.

about her husband.[42] It begins by setting out his clerical status and background, though frustratingly we cannot identify his origin. He was not only a *sacerdos* but also a *famulus dei* ('servant of God') and *vasso Paulini* ('disciple of Paulinus'), though we do not know who this was. Though unique in Britain, these epithets are comparable with examples on inscriptions in Iberia and Gaul, again highlighting the significance of contacts via the Atlantic seaways. Both might indicate that he had taken monastic vows, and this is not necessarily at odds with his marital status, since in fifth-century Gaul such couples might live as brother and sister rather than as husband and wife. The final part consists of a succession of phrases praising his character and ending with an allusion to Old Testament passages extolling wisdom above silver and gold and precious stones. Such phrases may have been derived from a collection of exemplars, but the form of the inscription also indicates at least passing knowledge of a tradition of Latin Christian panegyric poetry found in Gaul, though it is possible this had also persisted in Britain amongst an educated clerical elite typified by Gildas himself.[43] There is a further possible reference to monasticism on Aberdaron 2—Senacus the priest is buried *cvm mvltitvdinem fratrvm* ('with the multitude of the brethren').[44]

Almost 70 per cent of the inscribed stones in north Wales are explicitly Christian, but this contrasts with only a third in the south-east and a fifth in the south-west. This reflects the more characteristic use of ogham and bilingual inscriptions, particularly in the south-west and Breconshire, and the preference for the religiously neutral *X fili Y* ('of X son of Y') formula and variations of it, emphasizing the ties of family and kin. Other inscriptions simply give the name of the deceased. This means that almost 60 per cent of the inscribed stones have no religious affiliation and raises the important question as to whether at least some of those commemorated were pagans. There are no definitive answers since the Church only began to exert more control over burial from the seventh century onwards, but that some were pagan, seems inherently likely, especially amongst the earlier monuments with oghams. In Ireland a significant proportion of these were probably pagan, as indicated by contemporary burial customs, some of which also have parallels in Wales. Bridell, Pembrokeshire, for example, uses a formula commonly found in Ireland and reads *Nettasagri maqi mucoi Briaci* ('of Nettasagri son of the kindred of Briaci'), thereby linking the man commemorated with the mythical ancestor of an Irish *túath*, perhaps a deity as well as a protective patron (Fig. 4.4, b). A small number of inscribed stones in south-west Wales, including

---

[42] *...iva* (or *...ina*) / *sanctissi/ma mvlier* / *[h]ic iacit qve* / *fvit amati/[s?]si(ma) co[n]ivx Bi/vatisi f[a]mv[lv]s* / *d(e)i sacerdos et vas/so Pavlini Avdo* (or *Ando*) *cog/na[tion]e et omni/vm civivm adqvae* / *parentvm exempl/a et moribvs dis/ciplina ac sapien/tiae* // *avro e[t]* / *lapidibv/s* ('*...iva* (or *...ina*), a most holy woman lies here, who was the most loving wife of Bivatisus, servant of God, priest and disciple of Paulinus, from Avdus (*or* Andus) by kindred, and of all citizens and kinsfolk an example and in (his) character of(?) discipline and of wisdom as gold in stones' *or* '(better than) gold and precious stones'); Edwards 2013, no. AN46.

[43] Job 28:12–19; Proverbs 8:10–11; Wisdom 7:7–9; Tedeschi 2005, 179; Sims-Williams 1984, 170–1.

[44] Edwards 2013, no. CN3.

Bridell, also had crosses subsequently added to them, perhaps by descendants later seeking to provide their ancestors with a retrospective or overt Christian identity, or at the instigation of the Church.[45] It is also interesting that during the sixth century we see the *hic iacit* formula being used in conjunction with the *X fili Y* one, thereby Christianizing it, as, for example, on Capel Brithdir, Gelli-gaer, Glamorgan, which reads *Tegernacus filius Marti hic iacit* ('Tegernacus son of Martius lies here').[46]

Therefore, although the inscribed stones in the north-west clearly demonstrate the conversion of a significant number of the elite and provide evidence by the sixth century of ordained clergy and possibly monasticism, the picture across the rest of Wales is less clear. In the north-east there are few inscribed stones, though the fifth-century inscription from Llanerfyl, Montgomeryshire, is certainly Christian. However, the comparative lack of overtly Christian inscribed stones amongst the elite in the south-west could suggest that conversion was initiated later or was more drawn out. This is also true of monuments in Breconshire and Glamorgan, where the combination of the *hic iacit* formula with *X fili Y* is characteristic, suggesting that overtly Christian commemoration was only adopted from the sixth century onwards amongst some of the elite.

BURIAL

By its nature, burial evidence that is broadly contemporary with the inscribed memorial stones is more representative of the population as a whole. Therefore, an examination of archaeological context as well as changes in burial practices over time can provide a wider understanding not only of conversion to Christianity but also of the continuation of other customs and beliefs. Two broad traditions, native and Roman, are evident for the disposal of the dead in later Roman Britain and in some contexts these became intertwined. Firstly, in the countryside in particular, we can detect the continuation of a range of burial practices and other customs with their origins in the Iron Age, demonstrating the persistence of native beliefs. In Wales at this time less separation is evident between the living and the dead, with burials sometimes located within or more often on the edges of settlements or close to boundary ditches. There is also some evidence for continuing burial associated with hillforts, such as Coygan Camp, Carmarthenshire, which also has early medieval activity, together with occasional barrow burial and continuing skeletal fragmentation.[47] Secondly, from the second century onwards, as elsewhere in the Empire, we see in Roman Britain the gradual abandonment of cremation and the introduction of inhumation burial, particularly in association with Romanized sites such as forts and towns. This cannot, however,

[45] Edwards 2007a, 47–8, no. P5. [46] Redknap and Lewis 2007, no. G28.
[47] Weekes 2016, 434, 440; Pollock 2006, 73–101, 179–80.

be linked to changes in religious belief and reasons need to be sought in differing societal attitudes to death and commemoration as well as status and display. By the end of the fourth century two patterns of inhumation are apparent which are either completely separated or in different parts of the same cemetery. The first is characterized by north–south orientation of the graves, various modes of burial including crouched and prone, objects of personal adornment, and grave goods such as coins and hobnail footwear to facilitate the journey to the next world. The second, which occasionally succeeds the first, is typified by west–east orientation of graves set in carefully ordered rows, sometimes with enclosures or mausolea. Burials are extended and supine with protection for the body evident in the use of plaster coverings, wood or lead coffins, and stone grave linings; there are few if any grave goods. It has been proposed that the latter, exemplified by Poundbury, Dorset, and the second phase of Butt Road, Colchester, are Christian, thereby indicating a growing number of adherents by the end of the Roman period. It has also been argued that this type continues into the post-Roman period in south-west Britain, exemplified by Cannington, Somerset. The excavators were, however, rightly more cautious about identifying Christian belief from the burial evidence in this case since they also found a possible Romano-Celtic shrine. Nevertheless, their interpretation does suggest that conversion was taking place during the lifetime of the cemetery which persisted into the seventh century and possibly beyond.[48]

In Wales, our understanding of later Roman inhumation cemeteries associated with forts and towns, notably Caerleon and Caerwent, is severely limited since there has been little modern excavation, though in the case of the latter the early medieval use of the extramural east gate cemetery may reflect continuity of a community with earlier Christian associations. At Carmarthen it has also been suggested that possibly Roman lead coffins unearthed in the grounds of the later medieval Augustinian priory might be Christian, likewise suggesting an element of continuity, and the proximity of the parish church and Roman cemetery at Caernarfon has already been noted (Fig. 4.1).[49] There is, however, no clear evidence of Christian burial before the Rhuddgaer lead coffin around the turn of the fifth century. What we can discern is the spread of extended inhumation cemeteries beyond the environs of Roman sites, such as Abernant, near Bulmore, outside Caerleon, into more rural settings, and this trend is clearest in the more Romanized south-east.[50] For example, radiocarbon dates suggest that a small, probably family, cemetery at Atlantic Trading Estate, Vale of Glamorgan, commenced in the late Roman period and continued for at least a couple of centuries. Over forty broadly west–east, findless inhumations were excavated, some

---

[48] Watts 1991, 36–89; Woodward 1993; Quensel-von Kalben 1999, 90–4; Petts 2003, 138–49; 2004; Rahtz et al. 2000, 397–420.

[49] Pollock 2006, 31–3, 67–9.　　[50] Ibid., 74; Tuck 2003; 2006.

304 LIFE IN EARLY MEDIEVAL WALES

in cists, others with wooden coffins; some skeletons were also hunched, suggesting shrouds, a trait that has been linked more specifically with Christian belief.[51]

In other, less Romanized regions of Wales, we can also trace the spread of similar extended inhumation cemeteries into the countryside, but to what extent this had, as at Parc Cybi, near Holyhead,[52] already commenced during the later Roman period, as in Scotland,[53] rather than subsequently remains more difficult to determine because of our current limited understanding of their chronology. What we are seeing, however, is the adaptation of a later Roman burial rite, with many of the traits potentially identifiable as Christian, to the concerns of a rural population during a period of rapid change in power structures and the economy as well as in religious belief. Two aspects are of interest here: firstly, the landscape context of a proportion of these cemeteries is highly significant since they are sited with reference to a range of prehistoric monuments, and secondly, only some cemeteries go on to become the sites of later chapels or churches.

The importance of memory and its role in relation to the reinvention of prehistoric sites through their reuse for post-Roman burial should be understood as a reflection of people's perceptions of and broader ties to the inhabited landscape, including the continuing significance of ritual foci, stretching back into the deep past (Chapter 2). At Plas Gogerddan, Cardiganshire, for example, the cemetery seems to have been focused on one of two Late Neolithic or Early Bronze Age standing stones (Fig. 9.4, d). There were also three later Bronze or Iron Age burial monuments with ring ditches as well as three crouched inhumations, one of which, dating to the first century BC or AD, had been inserted into one of the ring ditches. In the final phase there were over twenty broadly west–east, extended inhumations, some with coffin stains, one of which was radiocarbon-dated to cal. AD 340–610. There were also the remains of three square-ditched mortuary enclosures; the best preserved was interpreted as having plank walling set into the base of the ditch, with two posts marking the eastern entrance. A stone-lined pit was sited between the grave and the entrance and it was suggested that this had held a wooden box, the significance of which is unknown, though such a feature would not normally be regarded as Christian.[54]

Capel Eithin, Anglesey, is equally complex (Fig. 9.4, a). Neolithic activity was succeeded by Early Bronze Age cremation burials in urns and later by others associated with charcoal-filled pits and a cairn. During the late first and early second century AD a small square stone structure, interpreted as a likely Romano-Celtic shrine, was built within a circular enclosure in the south-west corner of the site, and there was also evidence of bronze-working. The early medieval cemetery consisted of over a hundred graves—adults, juveniles, and infants. Both dug graves and wholly or partially encisted burials were represented with a range of alignments and in various groupings indicative

[51] Price 1987; James, H. 1992, 96–8, 103. On shrouds and Christianity, see O'Brien 2017, 272.
[52] Kenney et al. 2020, i, 198–207.   [53] Maldonado 2013.   [54] Murphy 1992.

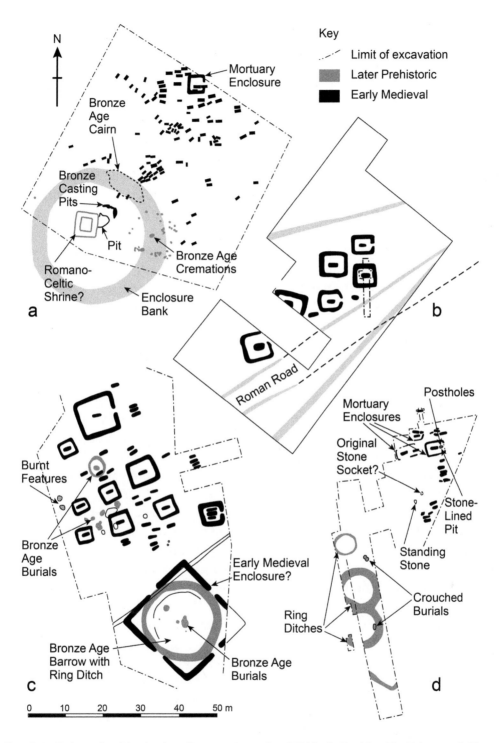

Fig. 9.4. Early medieval 'undeveloped' cemeteries: a. Capel Eithin; b. Druid; c. Tan Dderwen; d. Plas Gogerddan (after Longley 2009, fig. 6.5; Jones, N. W. et al. 2013b, fig. 4; Brassil et al. 1991, fig. 2; Murphy 1992, illus. 3).

306 LIFE IN EARLY MEDIEVAL WALES

of families, some of which were focused on the cairn. A square-ditched mortuary enclosure, which was likewise interpreted as having a timber superstructure, housed three graves, one of which had been set into the eastern entrance. However, the only indication of date is a likely sixth-century inscribed stone, now lost, commemorating a man by the name of Devorix, meaning 'divine king', but this cannot necessarily be taken to signal any particular religious affiliation.[55]

Other significant examples of the reuse of prehistoric monuments for early medieval burial include Arfryn, Anglesey, which also has an inscribed stone commemorating Ercagnus, a man with an Irish name but no Christian affiliation. The cemetery was on the site of a curvilinear Middle Bronze Age hilltop enclosure which was probably subsequently mistaken for a burial monument, and this site has been compared with the contemporary reuse of prehistoric burial monuments known as *ferta* in Ireland.[56] Groups of likely early medieval inhumations on Anglesey have also been found associated with barrows and in some cases the barrow itself was reused for later burial.[57] In another case, the cemetery at Trefollwyn was located close to the find-spot of a large phallic pillar decorated with La Tène ornament, suggesting some sort of later Iron Age sacred site; a lost inscribed stone with a *hic iacit* formula was also recorded nearby.[58]

On the mainland at Llandygái, Caernarfonshire, the cemetery overlay a Neolithic cursus, part of a much wider ritual landscape. The cemetery at Tan Dderwen, Denbighshire, contained several square-ditched mortuary enclosures, and it was proposed that a large Bronze Age barrow with a ring ditch had later been incorporated into it by the construction of a square-ditched enclosure around it (Fig. 9.4, c).[59] However, for others the maintenance of a tradition of Roman roadside burial appears to have been more important, as at Druid, Corwen, Merioneth (Fig. 9.4, b), which is located beside a Roman road. In other instances Roman and native customs were brought together. For example, two inscribed stones, both Christian, one commemorating Cantiorix, 'a citizen of Gwynedd' (Fig. 4.4, a), come from a moorland site known as Beddau Gwŷr Ardudwy ('The Graves of the Men of Ardudwy'), Merioneth. The place name refers to the former existence of prehistoric burial mounds located near the Iron Age and Roman hillfort of Bryn-y-Castell, which was in turn beside the Roman road running north from the fort at Tomen-y-Mur.[60]

Recent extensive excavations at Wylfa Newydd, Anglesey, have investigated three cemeteries, each comprising a mixture of long cists and dug graves with occasional signs of wooden coffins. Together they demonstrate the complexity of some burial landscapes and suggest that different populations were being buried in different

[55] White and Smith 1999; Longley 2009, 120, fig. 6.5; Edwards 2013, no. AN20.
[56] Hedges 2016; Edwards 2013, no. AN1. On reuse of *ferta* in Ireland, see O'Brien and Bhreathnach 2011.
[57] Edwards 1986, 31–3; Cuttler et al. 2012, 104–21.
[58] Edwards 1997c; 2013, no. AN40; Davidson et al. 2002, 46–8, 73–7.
[59] Lynch and Musson 2001, 106–15; Brassil et al. 1991, 86–7.
[60] Jones, N. W. et al. 2013b, 78–83; Longley 1996; Edwards 2013, nos MR8–9.

locations, perhaps reflecting different beliefs and practices, though poor bone survival has made radiocarbon dating difficult. The first, located on a hilltop, which focused on the site of a small, later prehistoric, enclosed farmstead, included four square-ditched mortuary enclosures but altogether there were over forty burials, mostly of infants and children.[61] The second was located on lower ground overlooked by the first and again there was some evidence of prehistoric activity. The cemetery consisted of more than twenty graves aligned west–east that probably represented an extended family group.[62] By contrast, the third cemetery was much larger, with over 300 graves aligned broadly west–east but with comparatively few infants. Located 1.4 kilometres to the north-east on a slight rise, it was sited with reference to a settlement of Late Iron Age and Roman date, and the graves were initially focused on a small enclosure indicated by a circle of wooden posts, possibly indicating a ritual function. Initial radiocarbon dates suggest this cemetery may have been in use over a comparatively long period between the fifth and eighth centuries AD.[63]

In the south-west continuing use or reuse of Iron Age enclosures for early medieval cemeteries is also apparent, as at Caer, Bayvil, Pembrokeshire, and at Caerau, Moylgrove, where long-cist burials, some with quartz pebbles, were located between the ramparts of a trivallate enclosure. Two fifth- or earlier sixth-century inscribed stones, one with oghams, the other bilingual, were also found outside a similar multivallate enclosure at Caswilia, Brawdy, and a square-ditched enclosure has been recorded near the hillfort at Castell Perthi-mawr, Cardiganshire.[64]

Indeed, as already demonstrated, a significant number of early inscribed stones, both those with Christian formulae and those without, are associated with these 'undeveloped' cemeteries, but it is rare that they are found *in situ* and where this does occur, they appear to be in a secondary context. For example, at Llannor, Caernarfonshire, two inscribed stones were reused to form the sides of a later long-cist grave, part of a cemetery associated with a Late Neolithic or Early Bronze Age standing stone. One inscription is certainly Christian since it combines the *hic iacit* and *X fili Y* formulae; the other simply gives the name of the deceased, Vendesetl, meaning 'white' or 'holy life', which likewise suggests a Christian affiliation.[65] That at least some of those buried in these cemeteries were Christian is therefore not in doubt, but it would be rash to think that this was necessarily the norm. It seems more sensible to view these as family, kin, and community cemeteries, where both Christian and non-Christian might be buried, and these were perceived as inserted into lived landscapes with a deep past. Ancient burial mounds and other prehistoric monuments were

---

[61] Area 7, Nelson-Viljoen et al. 2021a.   [62] Hotspot 11–13, Nelson-Viljoen et al. 2021b.

[63] Wylfa Head, Nelson-Viljoen et al. 2021–2.

[64] James 1987; Vincent 1864, 302–4; Coflein NPRN 304072, 305306, 405314; Edwards 2007a, nos P2–3; Driver 2006, 145.

[65] Edwards 2013, nos CN30–31; CN 32 is probably from the same site.

308 LIFE IN EARLY MEDIEVAL WALES

associated with mythic and heroic protectors that might therefore be reinvented to support contemporary concerns such as rights to the land, whether long-held or only recently acquired, and this is certainly comparable with the reuse of *ferta* in Ireland.[66]

Customs concerning burial of the dead are frequently highly conservative and it is only from around the seventh century onwards that the Church seems to have had sufficient authority to influence these more deeply. Even so, some of these 'undeveloped' cemeteries may have continued in use for some time. To what extent if any the presence of the graves of the Christian dead were seen as converting the landscape and retrospectively others who had lived and died within it is now difficult to say. However, in the continuing use and reuse of these sacred sites we may be witnessing both their adoption and their transformation, thereby facilitating both conversion and the accommodation of older customs and beliefs.

Nevertheless, it is also possible to catch a glimpse of the continuation of burial rites that are certainly not Christian. At Biglis, a Roman farmstead in the Vale of Glamorgan, an early fourth-century corn-dryer set into the south-eastern boundary of the settlement had been reused for the burial of an elderly woman with a bangle on each wrist, who lay in a north–south, slab-lined grave radiocarbon-dated to cal. AD 400–650, a practice also found in Ireland.[67] This suggests a link with fertility and the harvest, and it is worth noting that sometimes other burials are found near corn-dryers, as at Buttington Cross, Montgomeryshire, a trait also sometimes noted during the Roman period.[68] The deposition of quernstones may also be significant. At Coed-y-Meirw, Llangefni, Anglesey, these were reused in the sides and as lintels of fifth- to seventh-century long cists in one part of the cemetery.[69]

There are likewise indications that burials associated with hillforts and sometimes earlier settlements persisted for some time. A shallow east–west, rock-cut grave containing the remains of a child about 5 years old with early medieval crucible fragments in the fill was located between two hearths in the south-east quadrant of the hillfort at Dinas Powys, and it is possible that the association with metalworking was deliberate. Burials, sometimes isolated, are also sometimes found associated with earlier Roman period sites, as at Sudbrook Road, Portskewett, where a north-west–south-east, crouched burial of a juvenile, possibly with a brooch, had been interred in colluvium overlying an earlier rubble bank associated with late Roman pottery and coins; the burial was radiocarbon-dated to cal. AD 660–780.[70]

[66] On kin and community cemeteries in Ireland and reuse of *ferta* to lay claim to the land, see O'Brien 2017, 263–4.

[67] Robinson 1988, 16, feature 387. For Irish parallels, see O'Brien 2020, 152–3, including Raystown, Co. Meath, where a male buried in a disused corn-dryer was dated to cal. AD 410–570; Seaver 2006, 78–80; 2016, 20–1, 80 (B2398; Wk-16819).

[68] Mann and Hurst 2014, 138; the grave was set into a Bronze Age ring ditch; Pollock 2006, 73.

[69] Parry and Parry 2016, 7–9.

[70] Alcock 1963, 30; Pollock 2006, 83; Brett et al. 2015, 11, 24–5.

CONVERSION, COMMEMORATION, AND BURIAL 309

Burial in caves is apparent at various times in Wales and more widely, but the evidence is often poorly dated and therefore poorly understood. A handful of such burial sites are known from the Roman period, all of which have inhumations, with one exception in small groups,[71] but identifiable early medieval examples are rare. Of particular interest is Merlin's Cave, Herefordshire, sited in an inaccessible location above the Wye gorge. Earlier, mainly antiquarian, excavations within the cave revealed large quantities of human and other bones and artefacts, including a Constantinian coin, suggesting periodic activity from the Neolithic to the later Roman period. Recent limited excavations on the steep slope outside the cave entrance revealed two prone burials of elderly men, one aligned south–north, the other east–west. A cattle knuckle and rib fragments radiocarbon-dated to the Late Bronze Age had deliberately been deposited in the first grave, whilst the second included a human jawbone and part of a used quernstone. An adjacent pit contained a further piece of worn quernstone and animal bones together with the fragmented, reinterred remains of three adults, two females and a male, and one infant. The skull of the male had been burnt and there were possible signs of handling the bones. Radiocarbon dates demonstrated that those in both the graves and the pit dated to between the mid-fifth and mid-sixth century AD.[72] What is the significance of this intriguing site? Caves are often thought to represent entrances into the underworld and in this case the inaccessible location overlooking the Wye is indicative of a sacred and ritual significance enhanced over millennia of use and reuse. The fragmentation of the bodies in the pit signals the persistence of Iron Age modes of treating the dead, and the inclusion of the quernstone fragments and animal bones suggests the concerns of an agricultural community with fertility and ties to the land. However, the particular significance of the curated cattle bones in grave 1, most likely relocated from the cave, remains more difficult to divine, though it is possible that they held some particular symbolic resonance or were simply food for the journey to the next world. Also of relevance here is the dating of the burials to a period when the authority of the Church was beginning to increase, since their interment is the last known activity on the site.

Lesser Garth Cave, Glamorgan, provides an instructive comparison, as it is similarly sited overlooking the Taff gorge. Artefacts recovered from the cave indicate activity in the Neolithic, Early Bronze Age, and later Roman periods when metalworking was taking place. There were also a small number of badly disturbed burials in the first chamber, indicating episodic use beginning in the post-Roman period. Of those that were radiocarbon-dated, two, probably laid on the cave floor, particularly concern us here. One was a young male, the second a young female. Isotope analysis indicated that both had probably been brought up comparatively locally, and copper staining showed that the woman may have been wearing bracelets. The first was dated to cal.

[71] Pollock 2006, 87–9, fig. 6.4.   [72] Hoverd 2015. The place name was coined in the 1920s.

AD 425–545, the second to cal. AD 570–655. However, a later fragmentary burial dated to cal. AD 880–1000 demonstrates further reuse of this liminal location and artefacts included a slotted-pointed craft tool and a later eighth- or early ninth-century brooch pin.[73] The only other identifiable example is from Cefn Cave, Denbighshire, above the Elwy, where a femur was radiocarbon-dated to cal. AD 430–675. This suggests that early medieval cave burial may have been more widespread, particularly in areas of limestone geology.[74] Nevertheless, the very limited evidence to date suggests a concentration during the conversion period and the continuation of older beliefs. This is comparable with Ireland, where there is growing evidence that burial and votive use of caves persisted into the early Middle Ages. Similarly, in eastern Scotland a small number of seaward-looking caves were used for episodic burial, including in the Roman Iron Age, but were also adorned with Pictish symbols and other graffiti accentuating their ritual significance in a time of religious change. By contrast, in Anglo-Saxon England caves and rock fissures were considered places of danger, and early medieval burials associated with them are virtually non-existent.[75]

It may therefore be argued that in Wales the origins of broadly west–east inhumations, often protected by stone cists or wooden coffins, lay in the later Roman period beginning in Romanized environments and gradually spreading into the countryside, though the continuation of earlier native practices is also evident. Indeed, some burials, sometimes on the margins, suggest a persistence of some pagan beliefs and superstitions, including links with fertility, for some time. Although there are some issues with dating, these inhumation cemeteries, some of which are associated with inscribed stones, some with Christian formulae, often demonstrate in their locations a clear link with the prehistoric past, though in some cases the continuation of Roman roadside burial also remained important. It may be suggested that such cemeteries, many of which never acquired churches or chapels, were primarily kin and community burial places which spanned the post-Roman centuries, and that it is only once the Church had more control over burial that the process of conversion was complete.

CONCLUSION

Overall, the evidence suggests that the origins of Christianity in Wales clearly lie in the later Roman period focusing on forts and towns with diverse populations open to a range of external influences. However, in a society where indigenous farming communities remained strong, it may also be argued that, in the countryside especially, a range of native and Romanized native beliefs and their associated practices continued to be important, as at Pen-y-Corddyn Mawr and Llys Awel, and may have persisted

---

[73] Madgwick et al. 2016.   [74] Ibid., 220 (OxA-6234); Archwilio CPAT prn 19306.
[75] Dowd 2015, 199–207; Büster and Armit 2018; Semple 2013, 71–2.

well into the post-Roman period. This, combined with the lack of archaeological evidence for Roman Christianity in Wales beyond the south-east and the environs of Chester, suggests that its growth amongst rural communities may have been comparatively slow. Nonetheless, the Rhuddgaer lead coffin and inscribed stones in the north indicate the presence of a Christian elite during the fifth century, with increasing evidence for an organized Church in the course of the sixth. In other regions the adoption of Christianity could have been slower but also becomes increasingly visible on inscriptions during the sixth century, though the lack of inscribed stones in the more Romanized south-east makes the spread of Christianity in this area from likely nuclei in Caerleon and Caerwent more difficult to document. Nevertheless, the inscriptions, particularly in the north-west, demonstrate the significance of external contacts—most likely via the Atlantic seaways—with the Church and Christian communities in Gaul and probably Iberia, and possibly in the Mediterranean as well. The Christian elite would thus have perceived themselves as part of a wider Christian world which increasingly also spanned the Irish Sea to include Christian communities beyond the former Roman Empire. Significant comparisons may also be drawn with the south-west, particularly Cornwall. Here, although archaeological evidence for Christianity in the Roman period is entirely lacking, military activity may have resulted in pockets of Christian believers. Subsequently, inscribed memorial stones indicate the spread of Christianity amongst the elite and a similar range of Christian contacts beginning in the fifth century and increasing during the sixth, though as in south Wales, the religiously neutral *X fili Y* formula is more common, which may indicate a similar trajectory.[76]

A second major theme is accommodation. Native burial customs and beliefs were deeply embedded in the ties between farming communities and the landscapes in which they lived. Although rural communities came to adopt the later Roman burial rite of increasingly findless inhumation, often in long cists or wooden coffins and usually oriented broadly west–east, the locations of these burials and cemeteries clearly demonstrate wider links with the lived landscape as well as with landholding, community, and kin. The significance of the association between cemeteries and prehistoric monuments and landscapes, part of a much wider phenomenon seen across Britain and Ireland at this time, is most apparent in the less Romanized parts of Wales. It seems appropriate to link it to the dynamics of a period of rapid change when it was important for societies to accommodate and reinvent their pasts as part of a process of adaptation, one strand of which was conversion to Christianity. The presence of grave monuments with Christian formulae in some of these cemeteries indicates this process in action. How long conversion took to penetrate such rural communities more widely and its impact on belief are more difficult to determine, however, and it is likely

---

[76] Herring et al. 2011, 269; Tedeschi 2005, 225–85.

that older practices survived on the margins for some time. The reasons underpinning conversion to Christianity are therefore inevitably very difficult to perceive in terms of the archaeological record alone. For some at all levels of society it must have been a process of transformation that gave hope and meaning to their lives in a period of rapid change and uncertainty, as well as the prospect of life after death. For others, it was a process of adhesion arising from a number of factors, cultural and economic as well as social and political.[77] Nonetheless, a key to understanding the development of a deeper integration between the Church and the wider population is the foundation of church sites, including monasteries, from around the late fifth century onwards. The spread of these is visible across the landscape but should also be viewed in terms of their impact on communities which led to patronage, the acquisition of land and resources, and the provision of pastoral care.

[77] Edwards and Ní Mhaonaigh 2017, 2–3.

TEN

Christian Sites and Christian Landscapes

If the process of conversion was sustained by a hierarchy of bishops, priests, and deacons, and the Christian communities they served, it was consolidated by the establishment of a wide range of Christian sites. As these developed and multiplied they would have had an increasing impact on people's lives at every level. The aim here is to analyse the archaeological and other evidence for a hierarchy of Christian sites, beginning with major monastic foundations that later evolved into regional mother churches, often termed *clasau*. Island sites and hermitages will then be addressed, touching on the scanty evidence for female religious establishments, before discussion of the complex evolving pattern of lesser churches, chapels, and cemeteries. The relationship between major foundations and other Christian sites will be considered in conjunction with aspects of the wider impact of Christianity on the landscape indicated by the donation of land to the Church and the growing authority of St Davids in particular, before comparing the evidence from Wales with that of other parts of Britain and Ireland.

MAJOR MONASTERIES, MOTHER CHURCHES, AND *CLASAU*

There has been extensive discussion of the evolving organization of the early medieval Church in Wales based on the written sources and to what extent it is comparable with that in Ireland and Anglo-Saxon England, about which more is known.[1] From the sixth century onwards the best-evidenced religious foundations in Wales were those with a monastic nomenclature. This is demonstrated by the use of terms such as *podum* and later *monasterium*, as well as *princeps* and later *abbas*, meaning abbot, found in the Llandaf charters and other sources. It has, however, proved far more difficult to determine how these were organized and operated, since there are likely to have been considerable variations in practice from place to place as well as over time.[2]

---

[1] See Lloyd 1939, 202–19; Davies, W. 1978, 121–34; 1982a, 141–68; Pryce 1992, 48–61; Charles-Edwards 2013, 583–624.

[2] Davies, W. 1978, 121–6; 1982a, 149–50; Pryce 1992, 49–51.

Life in Early Medieval Wales. Nancy Edwards, Oxford University Press. © Nancy Edwards 2023.
DOI: 10.1093/oso/9780198733218.003.0010

314 LIFE IN EARLY MEDIEVAL WALES

A small number of these major foundations were clearly also the seats of bishops—Bangor and St Davids, Llandeilo Fawr and later Llandaf—though there were almost certainly others at one time or another. These may have included Glasbury in the south-east, for which a list of bishops has survived, Llanbadarn Fawr in Ceredigion, and Llanelwy (St Asaph) in the north-east, which only emerges as a see in 1141, and the situation prior to this is unclear. Dioceses may initially have been associated with the spheres of influence of particular saints and their foundations or with small kingdoms but gradually came to be broadly equated with major ones. There are also hints of an episcopal hierarchy: Elfoddw is termed *archiepiscopus Guenedotau regione* ('archbishop of the kingdom of Gwynedd') in the Harleian Chronicle (*s.a.*, 809), and later that century Archbishop Nobis of St Davids is noted by his kinsman Asser. There are also other signs, including a passage in the lawbooks, which probably originates in the later ninth or early tenth century, relating to the seven bishop-houses of Dyfed. This suggests that the regional foundations named may once have had bishops of their own.[3]

In the earlier part of the period there are indications of the attraction and promotion of an ascetic lifestyle, at least in some institutions, but also of others that were more liberal, and in the mid-sixth century Gildas was critical of those that were too extreme.[4] Strict monastic practices are clearly attested both in the later seventh-century *Life* of St Samson of Dol and, at the end of the eleventh century, in Rhygyfarch's *Life* of St David. The former portrays aspects of religious, including ascetic, practice and monastic education at Llantwit Major and on Caldey around a century and a half earlier, and the brothers are also shown labouring in the fields and growing herbs.[5] The latter incorporates material thought to derive from an earlier rule emphasizing a communal life and the role of manual labour in providing day-to-day needs, together with the importance of poverty, reading, writing, prayer, and attention to the liturgical round.[6] At some institutions, including St Davids, a strict monastic, even ascetic, life of this kind seems to have been maintained through the establishment of an island or other hermitage as an offshoot of the main foundation. In this the Irish ascetic monastic movement known as the *Céli Dé* ('Clients of God'), which emerged in the later eighth century with a major centre at Tallaght, appears to have been influential, since some 400 years later Gerald of Wales mentions adherents on Bardsey Island (Ynys Enlli) and at Beddgelert, as well as hermits on Ynys Seiriol (Priestholm) off Penmon.[7]

[3] Davies, W. 1982a, 158–60; Davies, J. R. 2007b; Keynes and Lapidge 1983, 94–6; Morris 1980, 47, 88; Charles-Edwards 1971; 2013, 583–98.

[4] Sharpe 1984, 196–8; Winterbottom 1978, 80–2, 143–5.

[5] Taylor 1991 and Flobert 1997, i, chs 9–21, 36.   [6] Sharpe and Davies 2007, chs 21–32.

[7] Follett 2006, 1–8, 212–15; Thorpe 1978, 183–4, 190, where Ynys Seiriol is called Ynys Lannog; Davidson 2009a, 50–1. Today in English it is often known as Puffin Island.

Ties of family and kin, as well as patronage, are central to our understanding of church foundations at all levels, though most of the evidence we have is from the latter half of the period and the larger foundations. Charters added to the Lichfield Gospels while they were at Llandeilo Fawr in the ninth century, those incorporating earlier material in the early twelfth-century Book of Llandaf, and those appended to Lifris's *Life* of St Cadog of Llancarfan all testify to the importance of donating landed estates to churches. In return, in addition to the accrual of spiritual benefits, alliances were formed providing donors with an element of continuing control. Moreover, since ruling families were prominent patrons, they might also place their kin as heads of these institutions as, for example, Idwal, the son of Gruffudd ap Cynan of Gwynedd (d.1137), who became abbot of Penmon. Clergy of all kinds might be married, and distinguished clerical families include that of Sulien of Llanbadarn Fawr, who was bishop of St Davids twice, in the 1070s and 1080s.[8]

The mid-tenth century reform imposing the Benedictine Rule on religious houses, mainly important minsters in Wessex, did not take place in Wales. However, this was by no means universal in England and many, including in the West Midlands, evolved into mother churches run by clergy rather than monks who were rooted in the life of local communities, a situation widely comparable with that in Ireland, Scotland, Brittany, and some other parts of France.[9] In Wales, from around the tenth century onwards, it is also possible to detect the emergence of mother churches such as Llanbadarn Fawr, which are sometimes termed *clasau* in modern scholarship.[10] By the end of the early Middle Ages, if not before, these seem in many instances to be linked with territories coterminous with major secular administrative areas known as *cantrefi* or smaller ones known as commotes, particularly in the north and south-west.[11] Essentially, these foundations, commonly associated with a local saint, were made up of a community of clerics and their families who were ruled by an abbot. However, the list of prebends of Llancarfan attached to Lifris's later eleventh-century *Life* of St Cadog describes each cleric and some other members of the community as holding a portion of agricultural land with its associated settlements, a pattern attested more widely in some later sources, as for example at Llanrhaeadr-ym-Mochnant, Denbighshire.[12] It has also been suggested that lay appropriation and hereditary transmission of landed property may have accelerated after 1100.[13]

Archaeologically, our understanding of the origins and growth of monasticism in Wales is very limited. Nevertheless, the Christian links with Gaul, probably Iberia, and possibly the Mediterranean indicated in the formulae of the inscribed stones, together

---

[8] Bartrum 1966, 99; Edwards 2011, 81.   [9] Blair 2005, 341–67.

[10] On the term *clas*, see Lloyd 1939, 205.

[11] Evans, J. R. 1992; Davidson 2009a, 48–9, fig. 3.2; Silvester and Evans 2009, 31–6; Edwards 2007a, 10.

[12] Wade-Evans 1944, 118–23, chs 48–50; Charles-Edwards 2013, 602–8; Silvester and Evans 2009, 22–4, 28–9, 36; Astle, Ayscough, and Cayley 1802, 286.

[13] Pryce 1992, 53.

316 LIFE IN EARLY MEDIEVAL WALES

with evidence of trade demonstrated by Mediterranean and Gaulish pottery and glass, especially during the later fifth and sixth centuries, testify to the significance of ongoing external contacts with western Britain and Ireland via the Atlantic seaways. Weight is added to these if the fragmentary written record of contacts with Gaul is also brought into play, and in this context the career of Faustus of Riez is of particular note. Born in Britain, he became abbot of the monastery of Lérins off Marseilles *c.*433 and later bishop of Riez and is known to have sent theological works back to Britain in the late 470s via Riochatus, another British monk–bishop. Nearly 400 years later a confused memory is still evident in the *Historia Brittonum* which makes a link between Faustus and St Germanus.[14] The significance of continuing Christian contacts with Brittany is also highlighted by the *Life* of the sixth-century bishop St Samson of Dol, who spent his early life in Wales, initially at the monastery of Llantwit Major before retiring to the island of Caldey and subsequently to a cave near the Severn.[15]

There are only two major ecclesiastical sites in Wales with long if patchy archaeological sequences complemented to some degree by other forms of evidence: Bangor and Llandough. The latter is located beside a stream on a low ridge overlooking the Ely estuary indicating the importance of contacts with the outside world (Fig. 10.1). It was also very close to a Roman villa located on the opposite side of the stream, where further early medieval burials have been found. It is likely that a monastery was established on the villa estate during the later fifth or earlier sixth century, possibly by Dochdwy, to whom the modern church is dedicated. Sherds of late Roman amphorae (LRA) of this date from the north-east Mediterranean and two fragments of sixth- or seventh-century glass from western Gaul were found in residual contexts within graves to the north of the church. These indicate not only the kind of outside contacts that may have fostered the establishment of monasticism but also the elite status of the occupants. They are likewise comparable with imports from the nearby hillfort of Dinas Powys, pointing to a significant link between the two.[16] The archaeological evidence is focused on the cemetery immediately north of the parish church, probably the original ecclesiastical focus of the site. Excavation recovered over 800 broadly west–east inhumations and many other disturbed burials, revealing a mixed population that suggests interment of a lay community, though there were more male burials in the earliest phase. It is also notable that most had been adequately nourished and overall had a higher life expectancy than normal, which also signals a high-status population. One area (iii) was very tightly packed with many intercutting graves, implying concentration on a sacred focus of some kind. The small number of radiocarbon dates from this cemetery suggests that burial spanned the early Middle Ages, but most are

---

[14] Stancliffe 2004; Chadwick 1959, 224–5; Morris 1980, 31, 74, ch. 47.

[15] Taylor 1991 and Flobert 1997, i, chs 9–41.

[16] Holbrook and Thomas 2005, 20–2, 66–7, 80–1; Campbell 2007a, LR1, Groups C and D glass, 19, 64–9; Knight 2005, 100, 104.

CHRISTIAN SITES AND CHRISTIAN LANDSCAPES 317

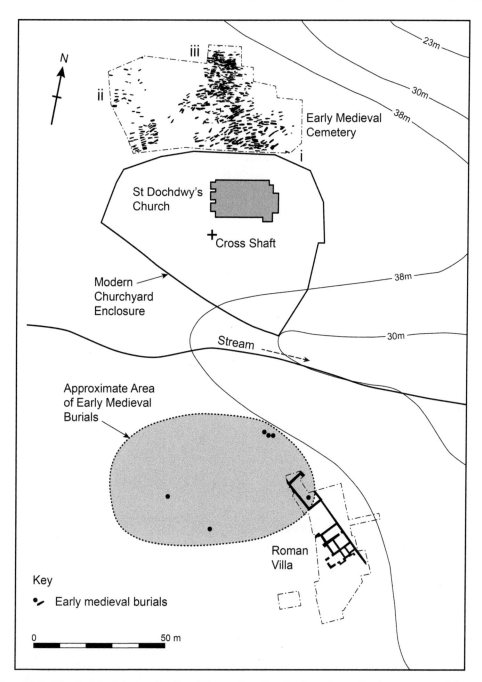

FIG. 10.1. Llandough, showing the site of the modern church, the early medieval cemetery, and the Roman villa, with other burials nearby (after Holbrook and Thomas 2005, fig. 2).

seventh-century or later.[17] This would support the view of the increasing power of the Church over burial from this time, with members of the elite and their families attracted to the site by its perceived sanctity and the prospect of prayers for their souls, a pattern also seen in Gaul and Iberia as well as Ireland.[18] From around this time also the names of abbots of Llandough appear in the witness lists of the Llandaf and Llancarfan charters, but it seems that by the eleventh century the foundation had lost much of its status and the terminology used is indicative of a community of clergy in the manner of a mother church. Nevertheless, a now incomplete cross of late tenth- or early eleventh-century date still stands in the churchyard inscribed with the name Irbic, perhaps a member of the community or a secular patron. The iconography on the base includes a horseman, who may be the donor, and a group of clerics holding processional crosses who may represent the ecclesiastical community.[19]

The evidence from Bangor, the most important foundation in Gwynedd, is in many ways complementary (Fig. 10.2). The site is located in the narrow valley of the Afon Adda close to the Menai Strait and, as in the case of St Davids, it now forms the focus of the cathedral city. Indeed, it is likely that the present High Street follows the original line of the monastic enclosure on its southern side. The one-time existence of

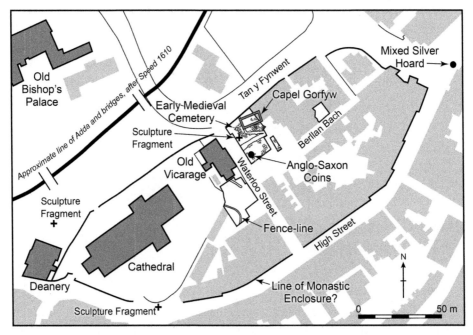

FIG. 10.2. Bangor, showing the cathedral and associated buildings, the probable line of the monastic enclosure, and other early medieval remains (after David Longley, in Edwards 2006, fig. 1).

---

[17] Holbrook and Thomas 2005.   [18] Edwards 2007a, 114–15; Effros 2002, 169–208.
[19] Redknap and Lewis 2007, no. G42. Lettering on the opposite face is now illegible.

an enclosure is also preserved in the place name, which refers to a woven wattle fence.[20] The earliest documentary reference in the Harleian Chronicle gives the death of the founding saint Bishop Deiniol as 584, and though retrospective, probably reflects its sixth-century origins. Thereafter the foundation swiftly grew in significance, as indicated by an entry recording a fire in the Chronicle of Ireland in 632.[21] There have been several excavations north-east of the cathedral and the earliest identifiable feature was a curvilinear fence-line radiocarbon-dated to cal. AD 540–780. However, as at Llandough, the most significant archaeological discovery was part of the cemetery comprising over seventy graves, probably of pre-tenth-century date.[22] If Elfoddw, 'archbishop of the kingdom of Gwynedd' (d.809), who introduced the Roman method of calculating Easter into Wales, was based in Bangor with his pupil Nennius, credited as the author of the *Historia Brittonum*, this also indicates the significance of Bangor as a seat of learning by that time. The foundation retained a reputation in Ireland, too, as the feast day of St Deiniol is included in the Martyrology of Tallaght *c*.830.[23] Later the significance of Hiberno-Scandinavian contacts is also evident. A hoard of coins and hacksilver dated to *c*.925 was deposited just beyond the probable enclosure and at least two Anglo-Saxon pennies of Edgar have also been found, suggesting the possibility of commercial activities in the vicinity. The foundation was also the victim of a Hiberno-Scandinavian raid in 1073.[24] The patronage of the rulers of Gwynedd was probably important from an early date but only becomes evident with the burial of Gruffudd ap Cynan in the new Romanesque cathedral in 1137. A few carved stone fragments from what may have been an earlier stone church have survived, as well as parts of broadly contemporary tenth- or eleventh-century crosses that may originally have stood in the cemetery and possibly outside the enclosure.[25] Although we know nothing further concerning the early medieval layout of the site, there are indications of multiple churches, since the later medieval foundations of Capel Gorfyw were discovered in the cemetery and a further chapel with associated burials was investigated north of the Adda.[26]

In other instances, however, the overall development of such major foundations is less clear. The parish church of Llantwit Major (Llanilltud Fawr), for example, is similarly located in a fertile river valley close to the coast. The later seventh-century *Life* of St Samson depicting monastic life in the time of St Illtud over a century before has already been mentioned. However, the only material evidence is the impressive collection of stone sculpture found either in the churchyard or during church restoration. The inscriptions demonstrate the continuing intellectual significance of the foundation

[20] Speed 1610; Geiriadur Prifysgol Cymru, *bangor*.
[21] Morris 1980, 45, 86; Charles-Edwards, T. M. 2006, i, 138.   [22] Longley 1995.
[23] Morris 1980, 1–2, 47, 88; Best and Lawlor 1931, 71.
[24] Boon 1986b, 92–7; Besly 2006, 717, H4; Jones, T. 1952, 16.   [25] Edwards 2013, nos CN4–9.
[26] RCAHMW 1960, 1–4, 10–11; Longley 1995, 56–61, 66–8.

320 LIFE IN EARLY MEDIEVAL WALES

and the strong ties between it and the rulers of Glywysing, which are also reflected in witness lists in the Llancarfan and Llandaf charters. That on a probably late eighth-century cross-shaft asks for prayers for the souls of Abbot Samson, King *Iuthalel*, *Artmal* his son, and *Tecan*, whilst a cross set up by King *Houelt* (Hywel, d.886) was for the soul of his father *Res* (Rhys), suggesting that members of the royal house were also buried in the cemetery. A later grooved cylindrical pillar could be architectural or part of some other fixture within the church.[27]

The origins of some other major sites can be traced back to the fifth or sixth centuries because they are associated with inscribed stones. Their presence seems to be characteristic of later mother churches in Merioneth, such as Tywyn and Llandanwg, but is also found in the south-west, for example at Nevern, and at Merthyr Mawr in the south-east.[28] Frequently, however, their origins and early histories are obscure and they only emerge towards the end of the early Middle Ages as mother churches. For example, by this time on Anglesey there were four mother churches: Caergybi (Holyhead) in the *cantref* of Aberffraw, Llaneilian in Cemais, and Penmon and Llangaffo at opposite ends of Rhosyr. Caergybi and Penmon overlook the sea, with the other two a little further inland. By the time the *Life* of St Cybi was written *c.*1200, it was thought that the earlier sixth-century king Maelgwn of Gwynedd had gifted the Roman fort to the saint for his foundation. However, the earliest reference to it is as the victim of a Hiberno-Scandinavian raid in 961, indicating that it was well established by this time. Penmon is first noted for the same reason a decade later.[29] Llangaffo only appears for the first time in the *Life* of St Cybi, but the then place name, *Merthyr Caffo*, suggests an early site. The earliest reference to the *abadaeth* ('abbot's land') at Llaneilian is even later.[30] Penmon has an important collection of stone sculpture, which formerly included three crosses, one with clear Hiberno-Scandinavian influences, whilst Llangaffo has both fragmentary crosses and late grave-markers.[31] By contrast, neither Caergybi nor Llaneilian have any known sculpture but both have later *capeli-y-bedd* that once housed the relics of their respective saints.[32] At the former the early medieval bell and crozier of St Cybi may also have survived beyond the Reformation, and an Anglo-Saxon penny of Edward the Martyr (975–8) was found in the churchyard now bounded by the walls of the small, late Roman fort.[33] Penmon has in Welsh terms an unusually large Romanesque church, probably built under the patronage of Gruffudd ap Cynan, and Romanesque fabric is also

[27] Redknap and Lewis 2007, nos G63, G65, G67, see also G66; Sims-Williams 2002, 277–80.

[28] Pryce 2001b, 266–7; Edwards 2013, 47, nos MR 10–12, MR24; 2007a, 33, nos CM18, P70–1; Redknap and Lewis 2007, no. G100.

[29] Wade-Evans 1944, 248–9, ch. 19; Jones, T. 1952, 8.

[30] Wade-Evans 1944, 246–7, ch. 17; Carr 2011, 217–18; Phillipps 1863; Longley 2005, 11–13, 16.

[31] Edwards 2013, nos AN27–38, AN51–5.

[32] RCAHMW 1937, 31–2, 60–1; Gruffydd 1992a, 8–13; 1992b; Longley 2005, 48–54.

[33] Edwards 2002, 254, n. 12; Dolley and Knight 1970, 80–1.

CHRISTIAN SITES AND CHRISTIAN LANDSCAPES 321

evident at both Llaneilian and Caergybi. Possible early medieval cist-graves have also been recorded beyond their present churchyards both there and at Penmon. Finally, all four sites had nearby holy wells, but only those at Penmon and Llaneilian are still extant.[34]

It is also possible to trace the rise of some major foundations and the eclipse of others. By the end of the early Middle Ages St Davids, known in Welsh as *Mynyw* (Latin: *Menevia*), meaning a 'thicket',[35] was the most important church in Wales. As such its impact in the written record is greater than any other ecclesiastical site, ranging from Latin chronicles and hagiography to vernacular poetry. Although the death of David is retrospectively noted as 601 in the Harleian Chronicle, the foundation only emerges from obscurity in the late eighth century and by this time annals were being compiled contemporaneously on the site, demonstrating its significance as an intellectual centre.[36] From the ninth century onwards the names and obits of several bishops are recorded, including Morgeneu in 999 and Abraham in 1080, both victims of Viking raids.[37] The foundation was, however, also subject to native attacks, indicating both its wealth and, more importantly, its role in the politics of power both in Wales and beyond.[38] The cult of St David had reached both Ireland and Brittany by the ninth century and later spread to Wessex under the influence of Asser, whose scholarly reputation had resulted in his invitation to Alfred's court.[39] In contrast, by the second quarter of the tenth century, the poem *Armes Prydein Vawr* ('The Great Prophecy of Britain'), possibly written at St Davids, presents anti-English feeling as well as demonstrating the author's ambitions for the cult. David is depicted as the leading British saint, and it is prophesied that the Welsh and their allies will overcome the English with the power of his prayers, and his holy banner (*lluman glan Dewi*) will lead them into battle.[40] At the end of the period Rhygyfarch's *Life*, written in the early 1090s to promote the cult in the face of the Norman threat, emphasizes the continuing importance of contacts with Ireland as well as giving us a valuable picture of the contemporary Christian landscape of St Davids and its environs linked to episodes in the life of the saint (see below).[41]

The early medieval site, in the narrow, steep-sided valley of the Alun, was focused on the later medieval cathedral, the building of which almost certainly destroyed earlier archaeological levels. Although fragments of stone sculpture that together span the ninth to late eleventh or early twelfth century have been found reused as masonry, either in the cathedral or in the walls of the close, there is no earlier evidence. Monumental sculpture includes part of a cross carved from dolerite that had been

[34] Gem 2009; Llwyd 1833, 101; Jones, H. L. 1847; Jones, F. 1954, 141–3; RCAHMW 1937, 123; Edwards 1986, 26–7.

[35] Charles 1992, 283–4.

[36] Morris 1980, 46, 86, but 589 is given for David's death in some Irish sources; see Dumville 2001, 3.

[37] Guy 2015, 22–3; Davies, J. R. 2007b, 298–300, 303–4; Jones, T. 1952, 10, 17.

[38] See Asser's comments on King Hyfaidd of Dyfed in this regard; Keynes and Lapidge 1983, chs 79–80.

[39] Ibid., chs 77–9; Edwards 2007a, 427.   [40] Isaac 2007, 164–8.   [41] Sharpe and Davies 2007.

transported by sea from the Preseli Hills, probably on the orders of the patron, though the fragmentary inscription is now illegible. There are also several grave-markers, including three local water-worn boulders dated to the ninth century incised with crosses, two of which also have elegant Greek-letter inscriptions with an alpha and omega and the abbreviated sacred monogram IHC XPC ('Jesus Christ'). The combination of cross and inscriptions draws attention not only to Christ's triumph over death but also to the passage in Revelation 21:6 relating to eternal life, as well as demonstrating the scholastic outlook of the St Davids community. A later large upright tombstone with a double cross on one face is surmounted by a crosslet with similar inscriptions that recall these earlier monuments; however, the main inscription commemorates Hed and Isaac, the sons of Bishop Abraham, who died in 1080. The use of three Old Testament names, probably adopted upon ordination, is also noteworthy as a long-standing trait amongst ecclesiastics in early medieval Wales and Cornwall that makes a direct link with both the biblical past and the origins of Christianity in Roman Wales.[42]

In contrast, the earliest evidence for Llandeilo Fawr, the most important foundation dedicated to St Teilo, is an early inscribed stone.[43] The parish church now stands within a large raised curvilinear enclosure (1.2 hectares) above the River Tywi, with both a Roman fort and Dinefwr Castle located nearby. It is possible that the latter was originally an important early medieval secular site and, if so, it suggests significant links between the two; it later emerges as the principal royal stronghold in the kingdom of Deheubarth.[44] The surviving evidence indicates that Llandeilo Fawr reached its zenith in the ninth century. At that time the Lichfield Gospels were displayed on the altar of St Teilo, and the marginalia added to it include charters recording the donation of estates to the foundation and witnesses include Nobis, *epicopus teiliav* ('bishop of Teilo'). An unusual cross-head and a decorated cross-slab are also from this period.[45] Nevertheless, by around a century later its fortunes had declined to such an extent that it had lost possession of its gospel-book. Moreover, by the early twelfth century the Book of Llandaf indicates that the church of Llandaf in the south-east had subsumed the cult of Teilo and claimed Nobis as an earlier bishop as well as ownership of former estates in Dyfed associated with the saint. It is also noteworthy that Joseph, who became Teilo's bishop in 1023, seems to have transferred to Llandaf, where his likely memorial stone, now lost, was recorded by Edward Lhuyd. The rise of Llandaf around this time is also signalled by other stone sculpture, including the upper part of a cross similar to that at Llandough.[46]

[42] Edwards 2007a, nos P90–8; Davies, J. R. 2012. Other Old Testament names include the martyr Aaron at Caerleon, David (Welsh: Dewi), and Daniel (Welsh: Deiniol) at Bangor.

[43] Edwards 2007a, no. CM18.

[44] Burnham and Davies 2010, 251–3; Edwards and Lane 1988, 62–3.

[45] Jenkins and Owen 1983, 48–55; Edwards 2007a, nos CM19–20.

[46] Davies, J. R. 2003, 11–13, 17, 71–2; Redknap and Lewis 2007, nos G36–40.

These examples demonstrate the importance of location to the success of such major ecclesiastical foundations. They are situated in or on the lower slopes of river valleys, frequently close to estuaries, as at Bangor and Llandough, though sometimes, as at Penmon and Caergybi, which has an excellent harbour, on the coast itself. Inland river-valley locations remain important, as at Llandeilo Fawr, and this is also true of major sites further east, such as the mother churches at Llanrhaeadr-ym-Mochnant, which overlooks the Rhaeadr, and Llandrinio, east of Offa's Dyke, which is located close to a possible crossing point over the Severn.[47] Riverine locations above the floodplain or coastal situations were likewise those favoured for Anglo-Saxon minsters, and in Ireland similar places were chosen, though here the relationship of major monasteries to inland routes has also been noted.[48] Little has been done to investigate this in Wales, but Llandeilo Fawr, for example, lay close to more than one Roman road as well as the River Tywi. The Welsh sites are likewise located on free-draining soils, sometimes, as with Llantwit Major and Llandough in the Vale of Glamorgan, of the highest quality. What this reveals is that major foundations of this kind were not cut off from the world but were close to other settlements, thereby facilitating the development of networks of patronage and pastoral care as well as agricultural wealth. As already indicated, the coastal locations of many also offered opportunities for long-distance religious, intellectual, and economic contacts with both the Continent and around and across the Irish Sea, though from the ninth century onwards this also made them vulnerable to Viking attacks.

Though dating remains problematic, the vestiges of large curvilinear enclosures still sometimes survive, as in the street layout at Bangor, or in the plan of the modern churchyard, as at Meifod or Llandeilo Fawr. Curvilinearity was not, however, essential, as indicated by Caergybi where the walls of the rectilinear fortlet provided an impressive boundary adapted to a different purpose whilst retaining a link with the Roman past. In this instance the enclosure was important from the outset and the Bangor place name, also found at an early date at Bangor-is-y-Coed, Flintshire, and Bangor, Co. Down, underlines this. Such enclosures not only provided a measure of physical security but were also symbolically important as places of sanctuary, and crosses located on such boundaries signalled protection. At Penmon, for example, a tenth-century cross originally stood above the site which has a scene more common in Ireland, showing St Anthony tempted by beast-headed demons—a suitable choice that would have emphasized both its monastic status and the apotropaic power of the cross.[49] The symbolism of boundary crosses is, however, clearer in Ireland, and a diagram showing concentric circles with crosses in the eighth-century Book of Mulling may represent an idealized monastic plan. There is also much more archaeological evidence for curvilinear enclosures surviving in Ireland than in Wales, where it has

---

[47] Silvester and Evans 2009, 28–9.   [48] Blair 2005, 193; Hughes and Hamlin 1977, 22–8.
[49] Edwards 2013, no. AN51.

324 LIFE IN EARLY MEDIEVAL WALES

been argued that these were mainly constructed between the sixth and eighth centuries and some had more than one enclosure.[50]

In Wales, as in Ireland, the enclosure of a major church came to have a legal significance that could also extend to any outer enclosures and ecclesiastical land. This is made plain in references to *noddfa* and *refugium* (meaning 'sanctuary') in the thirteenth-century Welsh lawbooks which incorporate earlier material originating in the Old Testament model of *civitates refugii* ('cities of refuge'), also found in the eighth-century Irish ecclesiastical law text *Collectio Canonum Hibernensis*. This indicates that probably from around the same period in Wales there was a similar conception of sanctuary, which provided legal protection for certain people seeking refuge from their enemies, with the prospect of compensation if ecclesiastical sanctuary was violated.[51] There is also other evidence to support this. The now fragmentary inscription of ninth-century date from the important early foundation of Llanddewibrefi, Cardiganshire, reads *Hic iacet Idnert filivs Iacobi qvi occisvs fvit propter predam sancti David* ('Here lies Idnert son of Iacobus who was slain on account of the plundering of St David'). This implies that he was killed in an act of violation of the sanctuary of St David, the saint to whom the site was dedicated.[52] Some Llandaf charters from the eighth century onwards are more explicit: one of 955 refers to the revenge killing of Eli the deacon, who had murdered a peasant and then sought refuge in the church of St Arvans, Monmouthshire.[53]

On major sites the interior of the main enclosure encapsulated the sacred core of the foundation and contained at least one church, which must normally have been constructed of wood, with multiple churches probably fulfilling different functions. It also included the cemetery and in some instances the grave identified as that of the founding saint, which, as at Clynnog and Llaneilian, was later enclosed within or translated into a *capel-y-bedd*, though in the twelfth-century *Life* of St Brynach of Nevern his grave is noted as lying under the east wall of the church. The *Life* of St Cadog makes it clear that the cemetery at Llancarfan was reserved for the elite, including kings and other leading men and their families, and this is also suggested by the osteological evidence at Llandough.[54] Carved stone crosses likewise stood in the cemetery, though it is unclear whether any marked graves. Nevertheless, the inscriptions, as at Llantwit Major, underline the significance of alliances made between ecclesiastical communities and their patrons, in this instance the kings of Glywysing. In contrast, simple, anonymous, cross-carved grave-markers are surprisingly rare on

[50] O'Sullivan et al. 2014, 145–8; Harney 2020, 17–46.

[51] Pryce 1993, 163–74. There is much less evidence for legally defined protective zones associated with minsters in England before the tenth century; see Blair 2005, 221–5.

[52] Edwards 2007a, no. CD9.

[53] Pryce 1993, 170–3; Evans, J. G., and Rhys 1893, 218–19; Davies, W. 1979a, 120; Redknap and Lewis 2007, 581–2.

[54] Wade-Evans 1944, 14–15, ch. 16, 90–1, ch. 28; Charles-Edwards 2013, 600–1.

these sites, and the examples noted at St Davids, which may have marked the graves of the ecclesiastical community, are much more sophisticated than is the norm.

In Ireland archaeological evidence suggests that for the larger sites domestic and other buildings associated with craft and agricultural activities lay in outer enclosures, as at Nendrum, Co. Down, and Clonfad, Co. Westmeath, but at Portmahomack in northern Pictland, whilst there is a broadly similar layout, no inner enclosure line was detected.[55] In Wales archaeological remains for domestic buildings and associated activities are lacking, though the early tenth-century mixed silver hoard from Bangor, which might be associated with a market, was indeed found just beyond the line of the enclosure. Corn-dryers have also been excavated beyond the churchyard at Llanwnda, Pembrokeshire, and may point to the significance of agricultural production in its environs.[56]

These foundations therefore had varied histories and fulfilled a range of functions that developed and changed over time. Some, such as Llandough and Bangor, were founded in the late fifth and sixth centuries, bringing monasticism to Wales as part of a Christian toolkit that was essential to the consolidation of conversion. It is also possible that a monastic lifestyle was attractive in a period of rapid change and uncertainty. Equally, the establishment of a clerical hierarchy, including bishops, based in these foundations was central to the development of pastoral care that would have reached out to communities on monastic estates and in the surrounding countryside. At the same time these sites were themselves foci of pastoral care, and from around the seventh century onwards increasing provisions were being made for the burial of the elite and their families who sought prayers for their souls. In return, they donated land which, with the renders of those who lived on it, led to increasing wealth as well as the growing significance of alliances, both of which resulted in exposure to manipulation and attacks by native rulers and Vikings alike. By the end of the period, it is clear that many of these major sites, frequently now termed mother churches or *clasau*, had essentially become hereditary family corporations, but this does not necessarily mean that pastoral and other religious duties were set aside. Furthermore, the significance of major sites as places of education, scholarship, and learning is evident throughout the period and, in the later eleventh century, may be exemplified by the family of Sulien at Llanbadarn Fawr. His son Rhygyfarch's *Life* of St David also demonstrates the development of such sites and their surrounding landscapes as places of pilgrimage,[57] and sources as late as Gerald of Wales indicate that some continued to maintain a strict monastic lifestyle on islands and in other places set apart from the world into the later Middle Ages.

[55] McErlean and Crothers 2007, 324–96; Stevens 2014, 260–5; Carver et al. 2016, 178–93, fig. 5.1.1.
[56] Crane 2006.
[57] Lapidge 1973–4; 1986; Edwards 1995; Sharpe and Davies 2007; James 1993.

326 LIFE IN EARLY MEDIEVAL WALES

Overall, the picture presented argues for similarities, both in organization and layout, with major churches in Ireland, though the archaeological evidence suggests that sites in Wales were generally on a smaller scale. There appear to be fewer parallels with major churches in Anglo-Saxon England. Though minsters fulfilled many of the same functions as major churches in Wales and Ireland, monasticism arrived in southern and eastern England a century or more later, and in material terms the impact of Rome and monasteries in Gaul on layout and ecclesiastical stone architecture is much greater. Whilst many of these minsters evolved into communities of clerics rather than monks, clear differences—architectural, material, and organizational—are also apparent in the later tenth century as the impact of the Benedictine monastic reform centred on Wessex took hold.

ISLAND MONASTERIES, HERMITAGES, AND FEMALE RELIGIOUS SITES

According to the *Life* of St Samson, the saint left the monastery at Llantwit Major for one founded by Piro, identified as Caldey Island (Ynys Bŷr), where he is said to have lived as a hermit rather than as a member of the monastic community; he later occupied caves overlooking the Severn and in Cornwall. St Dubricius is also said to have retired to Caldey for Lent, reflecting Christ's sojourn in the wilderness and suggesting periods of withdrawal rather than long-term seclusion.[58] The island is depicted as removed from the world, with some monks living communally whilst others pursued a stricter eremitic life. The only other hagiographical representation is in the *Life* of Elgar the Hermit, who lived on Bardsey (Ynys Enlli) in the late eleventh century and whose teeth were translated to Llandaf in 1120. This tale, influenced by the lives of the early desert fathers, similarly portrays a liminal existence on an island sanctified by the presence of the 20,000 saints buried there, thus promoting it as a place of pilgrimage.[59] The earliest reference to Bardsey is in 1012 in *Brut y Tywysogion*, noting the death of a monk, indicating the presence of a religious community on the island.[60]

It is relatively easy to reach Caldey, which lies off the Pembrokeshire coast near Tenby, but the passage to Bardsey, off the end of the Llŷn peninsula, is much harder in adverse conditions because of the strong currents. The early medieval nucleus of both foundations is indicated by the siting of later medieval monastic remains. In the case of Caldey early origins are suggested by a fifth-century ogham stone discovered in the priory ruins. Single sherds of later fifth- or earlier sixth-century Phocaean red slipware and later sixth- or earlier seventh-century Gaulish E ware have also been

---

[58] Taylor 1991 and Flobert 1997, i, chs 20, 33, 36, 41, 50.
[59] The *Life* is in the Book of Llandaf; see Jankulak and Wooding 2010.
[60] Jones, T. 1952, 11; 1955, 19.

found to the north-west in the vicinity of St David's Church, which may indicate a second area of activity closer to the earlier shoreline. This suggests the possibility of direct Mediterranean and Continental contacts, though such pottery was also identified at Longbury Bank on the mainland, pointing to local elite patronage as well. Long-cist graves have been found at both the priory and St David's Church. In the eighth or early ninth century the ogham stone was reworked as a cross-carved monument, with an elegantly executed inscription requesting a prayer for the soul of Catuoconus, which may have stood in the main cemetery.[61] There are also coastal caves on the island and the adjacent islet of St Margaret's where hermits could have lived, but, though activity of various dates has been recorded, no early medieval evidence has been found.[62]

On Bardsey the origins of the early medieval foundation are, however, less clear. A small number of early medieval graves indicating a mixed cemetery, including one with a coin (959–75) of Eadgar, were excavated south of the abbey ruins which nestle in the lea of Mynydd Enlli, but whether they were island residents or had been brought over for burial is currently unknown and further undated human remains have also been exposed periodically nearby.[63] The earliest evidence is a seventh- to ninth-century cross-carved stone which probably functioned as a grave-marker, but there is also a tenth- or eleventh-century cross-shaft. Both were found near the abbey. The latter is carved from Anglesey grit that had been transported around 80 kilometres by sea, which also suggests the increasing importance of the site as a place of pilgrimage and burial by this time since only powerful patrons, perhaps those named in the inscription, would have had access to both quarries and a suitable boat.[64] As at Caldey there are also several coastal caves, as well as hut sites which could have accommodated hermits, but these have yet to be archaeologically explored.

These two examples suggest that from the beginnings of monasticism in Wales some sought the spiritual life of a community more removed from the world, and the sanctity of these sites meant that they became a focus of patronage, burial, and ultimately pilgrimage. Others chose to live as hermits removed from the main community, probably in isolated huts or caves. Such practices emanated ultimately from the stories of the desert fathers but are also evident in Gaul, notably on the island of Lérins.[65] Island sites, some very remote, are also a characteristic feature of western Ireland, for example High Island, Skellig Michael, and Inishmurray, and of Scotland, as at Inchmarnock and the Isle of May, and excavations on these sites have given a much better impression of their functions and monastic island life.[66] In Northumbria

[61] Campbell 1989a, 59–63; Edwards 2007a, no. P6.
[62] Leach 1916; 1917; Walker 2016, 19, 21–3; Darvill and Wainwright 2016, 95–6, 122–3; Murphy 2016, 275.
[63] Arnold 1998; Kenney and Hopewell 2015, 19–21.   [64] Edwards 2013, nos CN11–12.
[65] Leyser 1984, 7–15; Klingshirn 1994, 23–4, 26–31.
[66] For Ireland, see Scully 2014, Horn et al. 1990, O'Sullivan and Ó Carragáin 2008; for Scotland, Lowe 2008, James and Yeoman 2008.

328 LIFE IN EARLY MEDIEVAL WALES

at Lindisfarne, itself a tidal island, the islet of St Cuthbert's was a Lenten retreat, whilst the saint sought seclusion as a hermit on the Inner Farne.[67] In Wales the nature of the geography meant that island monasteries were set apart from the world but not really remote. To what extent caves—by their very nature liminal spaces that might be perceived as entrances to other worlds—were utilized by hermits is more a matter for debate. Current evidence suggests that post-Roman use persisted on the margins in Wales for burials which certainly lay outside the norm (Chapter 9). In south-west Scotland Christian use is clearly indicated by the presence of carved crosses, as at St Molaise's cave on Holy Island off Arran and the coastal cave associated with St Ninian near Whithorn, both of which became places of pilgrimage. Otherwise, while it remains likely that caves were used more widely in Britain and Ireland for eremitic seclusion, other than hagiography and place names associated with particular saints there is virtually no archaeological evidence to corroborate this and more investigation is needed.[68]

Elsewhere in Wales we can see the twinning of a major ecclesiastical foundation with an island hermitage where members of the community might retire, supplied to some degree by the resources of the mainland site, as, for example, Ramsey Island (Ynys Dewi), which, though close to St Davids, is separated by a treacherous sound. There are two later medieval chapels noted on the island. The first, dedicated to St David, has been equated with a site close to the landing place facing the mainland. A likely stone sundial signalling a strict monastic ordering of time was found on the site, probably associated with an early medieval cemetery. It has an unusual inscription in Insular geometric capitals giving the name *Saturnbiu*. This might refer to *Saturnbiu Hail* ('Saturnbiu the Generous'), a bishop of St Davids who died in 831. The possible site of the chapel of St Defynnog has also been identified to the north and there are several coastal caves, including Ogof Mynachdy ('The Cave of the Monastery'), though the name has been thought an antiquarian confection.[69]

In other cases, though the presence of an early medieval eremitic foundation seems likely, it is impossible to prove due to the lack of dating evidence. Burry Holms, a tidal islet off the tip of Gower, was probably a hermitage associated with Llangennith, an early medieval foundation re-established in the early twelfth century as a Benedictine house.[70] Unpublished excavations during the 1960s uncovered a twelfth-century stone church within an oval enclosure with domestic buildings nearby. There were, however, at least two earlier, undated phases. Post-holes beneath the church were

[67] Blair 2005, 217; Colgrave and Mynors 1969, iv.25–9.

[68] Fisher 2001, 62–3; St Ninian's cave: Canmore ID 63133; Ahronson and Charles-Edwards 2010, 455–9; Dowd 2018.

[69] James 1993, 107; Ludlow 2003, prn 2712; Edwards 2007a, no. P99; Driver 2007, 84–6; Coflein NPRN 404188; Archwilio DAT prn 10100.

[70] RCAHMW 1976b, 14–16; Redknap and Lewis 2007, 572–3, nos G47a and b.

interpreted as a small wooden oratory on a slightly different alignment, with an earlier grave beneath. A small wooden roundhouse and a larger subsquare building were also excavated at different levels beneath the later dwellings. While early medieval occupation seems likely, the chronological sequence is unclear. Only Roman and later medieval artefacts were identified, and the former may relate to the promontory fort nearby.[71] The closest parallels for Burry Holms remain better-dated sequences at Church Island, Co. Kerry, and Ardwall Isle, Dumfries and Galloway. However, these iconic sites, usually seen as eremitic monasteries, may have skewed details of earlier interpretations of the evidence at Bury Holms.[72]

Similarly, the offshore island of Ynys Seiriol (Priestholm), associated with Penmon, and Flat Holm in the Bristol Channel, which has been linked with Llancarfan, lack any convincing early medieval evidence, though both were later owned by Augustinian houses, a pattern repeated elsewhere that may have continued or re-established eremitic activity on an already sanctified site. In 1191 Gerald of Wales noted hermits on Ynys Seiriol, and the remains of the church and nearby buildings on the island are twelfth-century or later.[73] Flat Holm is generally identified as *Echni*, where St Cadog is said to have sometimes resided during Lent, and though a chapel dedicated to the saint is known on the island by the mid-twelfth century, excavations have yet to reveal any datable earlier remains.[74]

Therefore, hagiography enables us to establish the existence of more ascetic, early medieval monastic communities and hermits on offshore islands. With Caldey, Bardsey, and Ramsey Island, this is also supported by the archaeological evidence, and in each case they continued to be regarded as places of sanctity in the later Middle Ages. These and some others, including Burry Holms, Ynys Seiriol, and Flat Holm where evidence for early medieval archaeological occupation is less certain, would therefore fit into a wider pattern of eremitic island sites comparable with those in Ireland and Scotland which have been more fully investigated.

Similar sites must also have existed on the mainland, but have proved very difficult to identify, though a proportion of the smaller ecclesiastical foundations in all likelihood originated as places of monastic seclusion. For example, Dyserth, meaning a 'solitary place', is sited close to an impressive waterfall, but, by the time of Domesday Book, it had evolved into an important local church under Hiberno-Scandinavian patronage.[75] Equally, a later eighth- or earlier ninth-century inscription on a cross-carved stone from the site of the later Cistercian nunnery at Llanllŷr, Cardiganshire, records a donation of land to the Church. It reads *Tesquitus Ditoc Madomnuaco Aon filius Asa*

---

[71] Hague 1974, 29–33; RCAHMW 1976b, 14–15; Coflein NPRN 301302.

[72] O'Kelly 1958; Thomas 1967; Pritchard 2009, 249–51.

[73] Thorpe 1978, 190 where it is termed Ynys Lannog; RCAHMW 1937, 141–4; Gem 2009, 303–4, 308–9.

[74] Wade-Evans 1944, 62–3, ch. 18; see also 90–3, 96–7, chs 29, 34; Redknap and Lewis 2007, 565, no. G11.

[75] Edwards 2013, nos F2–3.

Itgen dedit ('The *tesquitus* of Ditoc (which) Aon son of Asa Itgen gave to Madomnuac').
Tesquitus may simply indicate 'a small waste plot', but if a 'small deserted place' is
intended, the site may also have originated as a hermitage.[76]

We know remarkably little about early medieval female monasticism in Wales, presumably because it was less prestigious and therefore courted less patronage. This is
suggested by an early tenth-century Llandaf charter recording a dispute between
Bishop Cyfeiliog and Brochfael ap Meurig, who had given land to his daughter, a holy
virgin. At her death he tried unsuccessfully to reclaim the church and its estate, which
might indicate that female establishments were often short-lived because of the lack
of women's rights to inherit.[77] There are no traces of monastic foundations overseen
by abbesses of the kind recorded in seventh-century Northumbria at Hartlepool and
Whitby or at Kildare in Ireland.[78] What little evidence there is might, however, suggest that some sites associated with Celtic female saints had a link with pre-Christian
cult sites. Pennant Melangell is one example that might have originated as a hermitage.
It is located in a remote valley near the falls of the Nant Gwyn (meaning the 'White'
or 'Holy' Brook) but also close to the spectacular waterfall at Blaen-y-Cwm. It is possible
that both here and at Dyserth, which has a later dedication to Brigid, the proximity of
the waterfalls relates to an earlier sacred landscape.[79] Brigid may have originated as a
pre-Christian deity in Ireland, and this is also likely with Gwenfrewi at Holywell,
where the site of a gushing spring with a pre-Christian severed head cult may have
been reinvented in a Christian guise.[80] In the case of Pennant Melangell, the church
overlay Bronze Age mortuary activity, and it has also been argued that the hare with
which St Melangell is associated in late medieval hagiography was a sacred animal of
pre-Christian significance.[81]

LESSER CHURCHES, CHAPELS, AND CEMETERIES

Lesser churches are rarely noted in the written sources before the thirteenth century,
by which time the parish system had fully evolved; minor sites may be mentioned even
later, if at all. Equally, there has only been occasional archaeological investigation of
parish church sites, and instead the emphasis has been on those of ruinous later medieval chapels with early medieval cemeteries which never achieved parish church status.
Several questions arise. What are the origins of these lesser churches and other sites,
and to what extent is it possible to identify their early medieval status and trace their
development over time? Is the sometimes relatively dense distribution of such sites an
early medieval phenomenon and, if so, when in the period did this take place? Did

[76] Edwards 2007a, no. CD20.   [77] Davies, W. 1979a, 122–3, no. 231.
[78] Blair 2005, 212–13, 255; Ó Carragáin 2010a, 33–4, fig. 175.   [79] Bradley 2000, 26.
[80] Edwards 2017a, 390–1.   [81] Britnell 1994, 90–1; Pryce 1994, 37, 39; Ross 1967, 435–6.

they have church buildings or were at least some of these simply cemeteries where churches and chapels were only constructed during the later Middle Ages?

The origins of lesser churches and chapels are undoubtedly complex, and the shortage of major excavations makes the more detailed development of individual sites often very difficult to discern. This also has an impact upon our ability to identify regional and chronological differences and the reasons that may lie behind them, especially as there has been more archaeological investigation in the west, whilst the foundations mentioned in the Llandaf charters are concentrated in Gwent and Ergyng, where very little excavation has taken place.

In the west the sites of some later parish churches clearly had their origins during the fifth and sixth centuries as kin and community cemeteries or other places of burial, indicated by the discovery of graves radiocarbon-dated to this period or inscribed stones. On Anglesey, for example, the recent exposure of a large, long-cist cemetery outside the churchyard at Llanbedrgoch provided an opportunity for one burial to be sampled giving a radiocarbon date of cal. AD 430–600, but how long this cemetery remained in use and whether there was ever any early medieval church are unknown. The elevated promontory location is unusual for a parish church but is comparable with contemporary 'undeveloped' cemeteries with inscribed stones at Arfryn and Capel Eithin.[82] Inscribed stones associated with parish churches on the island include one from Llangefni discovered beneath the foundations of the later medieval church. The inscription, with its Christian *hic iacit* formula, has been dated to the fifth century and commemorates Culidor and his wife Orvvite. The incomplete sixth-century inscription commemorating 'blessed...Saturninus...and his saintly wife' unearthed in the graveyard of Llansadwrn Church is also of interest since the dedication gives a Welsh form of his name, indicating that he was later regarded not only as the founder but also as a local saint. Similarly, the Irish name Mailisus ('the bald one of Jesus') on the bilingual monument from Llanfaelog survives in its Welsh form as the dedication of the parish church. In the *Life* of St Cybi *c*.1200 Maelog is depicted as his disciple, which may signal an earlier, possibly monastic, foundation later eclipsed or subsumed by the major church at Caergybi.[83] The earlier seventh-century cross-inscribed stone commemorating King Cadfan of Gwynedd at Llangadwaladr (Fig. 1.1) likewise provides a *terminus ante quem* for the establishment of a place of royal burial. The dedication is usually equated with his grandson, Cadwaladr, and by this time we could be dealing with a monastic establishment founded and patronized by the ruling family but which later fell out of favour, perhaps as Bangor or one of the major foundations on Anglesey grew in significance.[84]

[82] Evans, R., and Jones 2019, 137–40, 146.
[83] Edwards 2013, nos AN39, AN45, AN13; Wade-Evans 1944, 236–7, ch. 5.
[84] Edwards 2013, no. AN26.

332 LIFE IN EARLY MEDIEVAL WALES

However, the sites of some other churches and chapels on Anglesey most likely originated somewhat later. At Llechgynfarwy, for example, a cross-carved stone, which has been dated between the seventh and ninth century, was found outside the churchyard close to a group of long-cist graves.[85] Recent excavations in a similar location at Llaniestyn also revealed a mixed cemetery of nearly fifty stone-lined and dug graves, two of which were set within a mortuary enclosure, with a later burial inserted into the northern side of the ditch (Fig. 11.1a). Radiocarbon dates from a grave within the mortuary enclosure spanned the late seventh to late ninth centuries.[86] At Tywyn-y-Capel (Capel St Ffraid), which never achieved parish status, it has proved possible to recover a more complex sequence. Limited excavations because of destruction by the sea uncovered two phases. The first consisted of a small number of burials, both men and women, in cist-and-lintel graves marked by mounds ringed with boulders. These were dated to c.650–800 and, after a short episode of sand inundation, the second phase of more than 100 dug graves probably continued into the twelfth century. The mixed burials in both phases indicate the presence of a local community, but the relationship between the two phases is difficult to establish. The dates of both phases and the use of shrouds, suggested by the positions of some skeletons during the second phase, are indicative of a Christian population, and the skeletal evidence hints that the later population was less healthy and of lower status than its predecessors. The dedication to St Ffraid (Brigid) also suggests Hiberno-Scandinavian contacts in the later phase, but whether there was ever an early medieval church building is unclear; the remains of the later stone chapel on top of the mound were washed away by the sea in 1868.[87]

Towards the end of the period there is an upsurge in stone sculpture fashioned from Anglesey grit. Monuments include small crosses, cross-carved grave-markers (probably those of local elites), and fonts ornamented with frets and interlace that would have stood within church buildings. These are all associated with later parish churches, some with Celtic dedications, such as Cerrig Ceinwen and Llangeinwen (a female saint), that may signal the redevelopment of older sites. Others have universal dedications, such as Llanfair-Mathafarn-Eithaf to the Virgin Mary and Llanfihangel Ysgeifiog to St Michael, which, if the original dedications survive, suggest a further phase of new foundations, perhaps on secular estates, in the eastern and southern half of the island. However, the comparative lack of stone sculpture in the north and west makes similar sites much more difficult to detect. Indeed, it is only in the twelfth and early thirteenth centuries with the erection of Romanesque and later stone churches on the island, as well as the production of Romanesque fonts, that the dense pattern of small

[85] Ibid., no. AN48.

[86] Evans, R. et al. 2015; 2016; Evans, R., and Jones 2019, 140–6, Grave 19: SUERC 71027, cal. AD 680–880, SUERC 71028, cal. AD 680–890.

[87] Davidson 2009b, 167–81, 205–11, 219.

parishes (approximately one church to every 10 square kilometres) becomes clear, though many of these sites were probably in existence long before.[88]

Two of the trends apparent on Anglesey are more clearly visible in the south-west. Here as many as 70 per cent of the fifth- to early seventh-century inscribed stones are associated with the sites of later parish churches and chapels of ease, indicating the early origins of these sites compared with less than 40 per-cent in the north and only 36 per cent in the south-east.[89] For example, at Eglwys Gymyn, Carmarthenshire, possible Bronze Age cremation urns were recorded together with a bilingual inscribed stone (Fig. 4.4), suggesting reuse of a prehistoric site, while at Llanwinio, which has a similar monument later upended and carved with a cross, it has been proposed that the hilltop church is situated within an earlier hillfort enclosure. The combination of a Latin-inscribed stone and the place name at Merthyr similarly indicates the early origins of the site.[90]

The large number of cross-carved stones in the south-west, 40 per cent of which are associated with lesser churches and chapels, indicates a second phase in the inception of these sites during the seventh to ninth centuries, since comparatively few are found in conjunction with inscribed stones. Others found on farms, such as St Kennox, Llawhaden, point to further unidentified sites.[91] The most significant site is St Patrick's Chapel overlooking Porth Mawr, near St Davids, where the western part was fully excavated, indicating various stages in its development (Figs 10.3 and 10.4). The earliest phase, dating to the eighth century, consisted of a small oval enclosure made of stone, with the western entrance facing the sea. Within this was a low rectangular structure, similar to those known as *leachta* in Ireland,[92] constructed of slabs located over a shallow pit. One slab was a probably reused cross-carved stone, whilst others had graffiti, including two inscriptions, a boat, and a plaitwork ring cross. The enclosure had a quartz floor, and quartz pebbles had been placed on top of the structure. It may therefore have functioned as a place of prayer for those who had landed or who were setting out to sea. In the same phase there were also areas of fine metal and amber-working, suggesting craft and trading activities near the shore. The burial of infants commenced as soon as sand began to accumulate within the enclosure and on top of the altar, the location of which continued to be marked by a slab, thereby demonstrating its ongoing significance in the development of the site. Sand built up between several layers of burials, the earliest associated with a rectilinear stone-walled enclosure. Radiocarbon dates indicate a comparatively short lifespan during the eighth to tenth centuries for this phase of the cemetery. Several cross-carved slabs had been incorporated into cist graves

---

[88] Edwards 2011; 2013, nos AN2–4, AN14–15, AN21–4, AN41–4; 2016b, 200.

[89] Edwards 2013, 45.

[90] Edwards 2007a, 33, nos CM7, CM34–5; James, T. A. 1992, 69–70; Parsons 2013a, 55–6.

[91] Edwards 2007a, 56–7, no. P56.

[92] See, for example, the excavation of Trahanareear, Inishmurray, Co. Sligo; O'Sullivan, J., and Ó Carragáin 2008, 216–39, 323. For wider discussion, see O'Sullivan, A. et al. 2014, 161–4.

Fig. 10.3. St Patrick's Chapel, showing the eleventh- or twelfth-century building, with the rectangular burial enclosure beneath, during excavation in 2016 (photograph: Stephen Rees, by permission of Dyfed Archaeological Trust).

Fig. 10.4. St Patrick's Chapel, showing the eighth-century *leacht* during excavation in 2021 (by permission of Dyfed Archaeological Trust).

as lintels or side-stones—there is nothing to suggest that they had been reused. A small free-standing cross marked the head of a woman's grave, another was found on the beach. Later the cemetery was partially sealed by rubble dated by an early eleventh-century Hiberno-Scandinavian ringed pin, and it was only at this point that a stone chapel was constructed; subsequently the cemetery was only used for the burial of children.[93] These excavations demonstrate the potential complexity of individual site histories, but on others with cross-carved stones only exploratory excavation has been possible. For example, at Longoar Bay, another chapel site, only a handful of graves were revealed, one of which had a lintel with a linear cross. An adjacent grave was radiocarbon-dated to cal. AD 660–880.[94] A rare excavation on a parish church site at Llanychlwydog in the Gwaun valley, where four cross-carved stones had been found in the nineteenth century, revealed long-cist graves in the churchyard, one of which was radiocarbon-dated to cal. AD 740–1070.[95]

In the borderlands of the south-east there has been little archaeological investigation of the sites of parish churches or chapels of ease, and inscribed and cross-carved stones as well as early medieval cemeteries are rare. However, the Llandaf charters indicate that in Ergyng there were already a considerable number of churches and monasteries during the seventh and eighth centuries, with a similar distribution evident in Gwent during the ninth to eleventh.[96] In West Glamorgan seventh- to ninth-century and later sculpture points to a similar density in the vicinity of major sites at Merthyr Mawr and Margam (Fig. 8.2). However, in the eastern Vale sculpture is only found on a few major sites, such as Llantwit Major, though the significance of this in terms of the origins and development of more minor sites is less clear.[97] In western Herefordshire, formerly Ergyng, a further wave of foundations is suggested during the mid-eleventh century. Bishop Herewald of Llandaf consecrated several new churches, some with dedications to universal saints, probably on secular estates with tenants, and he also ordained priests to serve them, a situation directly comparable with many parts of England.[98]

Our current understanding of the origins and development of lesser churches and chapels elsewhere in the eastern half of Wales is very limited indeed, though taken together the comparatively high incidence of parishes with *llan* names, Celtic dedications, and curvilinear churchyards is indicative of early medieval sites.[99] Capel Maelog is also of seminal importance as the site was totally excavated, allowing us to understand its development more clearly (Fig. 10.5). In this case it originated as a late

[93] Murphy et al. 2014; 2015; 2016; 2019; Murphy and Hemer 2022. On *leachta*, see Ó Carragáin 2021.

[94] Edwards 2007a, no. P131; Mower 2003.   [95] Murphy 1987; Edwards 2007a, nos P51–4.

[96] Davies, W. 1978, 124.   [97] Redknap and Lewis 2007, 260, fig. 86.

[98] Evans, J. G., and Rhys 1893, 275–80; Herewald is an English name. On Late Saxon estate churches, see Blair 2005, 385–96.

[99] On Breconshire and Radnorshire, see Silvester 1997, 114–17.

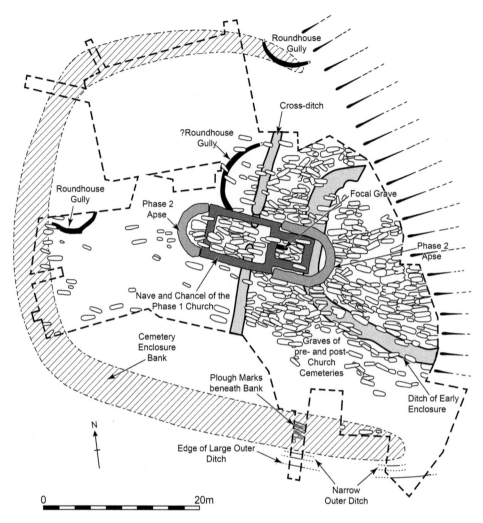

Fig. 10.5. Capel Maelog, showing evidence for the earlier settlement, the cemetery, the enclosure, and the late twelfth- or early thirteenth-century chapel, sited with reference to the focal grave (after Britnell 1990, fig. 3).

Roman and early medieval farming settlement (Chapter 5). Burial commenced sometime after the seventh century and initially a small cemetery was located on either side of a ditch with a causeway over it and a focal grave on the eastern side. The initiation of burial marks a significant change in the function of the site, most likely the establishment of a cemetery associated with a settlement nearby, and it has been proposed that the special grave could be that of the founder, perhaps with the burials of other family members focused on it. The curvilinear cemetery enclosure bank was only constructed in the tenth century or later and the small stone chapel was not built until the late twelfth or early thirteenth. Even so, the significance of the focal grave was maintained by its location on the junction between the nave and chancel. The chapel never became a parish church and was probably abandoned during the sixteenth century.[100]

The complexity of Capel Maelog and St Patrick's Chapel, where stone chapels only appear late in the sequence, demonstrates that establishing the status of these and other lesser early medieval Christian sites is difficult and, in many instances, this will have changed over time. Central to this problem, however, is the extent to which more minor sites had church buildings of any kind. A church with its associated cemetery would surely have been the focal point of a small monastic site, but where the emphasis was on family, kin, or community burial, perhaps with only intermittent pastoral care, this would not necessarily have been the case. *Ecclesia* ('church') and *oraculum* ('oratory'), terms used in the Llandaf charters, imply the existence of church buildings, presumably constructed of timber or wattles and turf, and in the rare instances where a settlement term such as *uilla* or *castellum* is associated with *ecclesia*, this may point to a church serving a secular community. Unusually, the mid-eleventh-century list of probable estate churches in Ergyng consecrated by Herewald specifically mentions a wooden church.[101] Furthermore, although it has been argued that *llan* names become more common from the seventh century onwards because of the growth of churchyard burial,[102] this does not necessarily mean that there was a church building, since the term has connotations associated with the surrounding land as well.[103] *Llan* is often linked with a personal name, but though this later forms the church dedication, this might equally refer to a secular founder (rather than a monastic one), later revered as a saint.

The problem is compounded by the difficulties encountered in identifying sites with wooden churches archaeologically. This is well illustrated by Llanelen on the Gower peninsula, which was probably a chapel belonging to Llanrhidian that went out of use by the fourteenth century. Underlying the later medieval stone church with its small cemetery was an earlier phase which, it was argued, included seven post-holes beneath the platform on which the stone church was built. These were interpreted as an earlier wooden church on analogy with Burry Holms, the only other possible example in Wales; eight graves, some covered with mounds, which had been cut through an occupation layer, were regarded as contemporary with it.[104] However, even if one accepts the existence of a wooden church, the absence of radiocarbon

---

[100] Britnell 1990.   [101] Davies, W. 1978, 121–3; Evans, J. G., and Rhys 1893, 277.
[102] Davies, J. R. 2002, 393.   [103] *Geiriadur Prifysgol Cymru, llan.*
[104] Schlesinger and Walls 1996, 104–14. The suggestion that a large pit at the north-east corner of the presumed phase 1 church was a baptistery seems untenable, since baptisteries, though common on the Continent, are virtually unknown in Britain or Ireland. Here baptism in rivers, springs, or holy wells prevailed until the introduction of fonts within churches; see Blair 2005, 70, 201–2, 459–62; Whitfield 2007; Ó Carragáin 2010a, 197–206.

dates means that a site chronology is very difficult to establish. Dating of the earlier phase hinges on a handful of early medieval high-status artefacts, including a fragment of sixth- or seventh-century imported glass cone beaker found in a later context. Part of an unidentified glass phial and a fragmentary zoomorphic copper-alloy fitting also came from a deposit overlying what was tentatively identified as a founder's grave.[105] If the artefacts are contemporary, this suggests a sixth- or seventh-century church foundation with associated graves that was re-established as a chapel of ease with further burials in the later Middle Ages. In some cases traces of wooden churches could therefore still lie beneath later stone buildings or may have been totally destroyed during their construction. In others, a cross-carved stone or an altar may have provided a suitable focus for worship in the open air.

Therefore, although our understanding of the early medieval origins and development of lesser churches and other more minor sites is steadily increasing, it is limited by the patchy and restrictive nature of the archaeological and written evidence and continuing difficulties with chronological precision. In the west some fifth- and sixth-century family, kin, and community cemeteries and other places of burial with inscribed stones, some of which were also associated with prehistoric monuments, clearly developed into the sites of parish churches and chapels of ease, thereby emphasizing the culmination of their Christian transformation. However, a significant number of others simply went out of use. Equally, some secular settlements and some earlier enclosures acquired a burial function before developing into parish churches and chapels of ease. A second phase is likewise detectable during the seventh to ninth centuries with the establishment of new Christian sites in the west and some other parts of Wales as well. These are indicated by cemeteries and cross-carved stones which, it may be argued, signal both the expansion of monasticism and the establishment of a wider pattern of family and community cemeteries, only some of which had churches, and this process is likely also reflected by the spread of *llan* names around this time. This would have underpinned the consolidation of Christian belief alongside the increasing authority of the Church, since churches and cemeteries would have formed the focus of pastoral care for the wider population, including the rites of baptism and burial, thereby helping to bind local communities together. To what extent there may have been a third phase of church foundation, suggested on Anglesey by the presence of sculpture spanning the tenth to early twelfth centuries, is more difficult to establish. Such evidence may indicate the founding of further family and estate churches, but it might also indicate earlier sites that are becoming archaeologically visible for the first time. Indeed, all too often it is only possible to see the pattern of later medieval parish formation with associated chapels of ease and not the underlying distribution that preceded it.

---

[105] Schlesinger and Walls 1996, 112, 125–9, 136–8; Campbell 2007a, 63.

CHRISTIANITY AND THE WIDER LANDSCAPE

The discussion so far has focused on establishing a hierarchy of Christian sites—major foundations with a monastic nomenclature as well as island monasteries and hermitages, including possible female establishments, and a range of lesser churches and cemeteries. The evidence has also shed light on how these developed and changed over time, reflecting wider religious and societal change. Together the sites in a particular locality constituted an evolving Christian landscape that also incorporated both natural features and earlier sacred sites and monuments. The aim here is to consider key examples of such landscapes and evidence aiding their identification at different spatial levels. I shall first discuss landscapes associated with the environs of major churches, thereby illuminating their relationship with lesser sites and cemeteries and the communities they served. I shall then touch on evidence for ecclesiastical estates, before examining examples of wider spheres of ecclesiastical power and influence.

St Davids and its environs provides an excellent example of the evolution of a Christian micro-landscape, partially encapsulated in Rhygyfarch's late eleventh-century *Life* of the saint, but more extensively revealed in a range of other evidence.[106] As already indicated, St Davids only emerges from obscurity in the late eighth century and the hermitage on Ramsey Island (Ynys Dewi) is first apparent at a similar date. Nonetheless, discoveries east of St Davids suggest that Christianization had begun in the fifth and sixth centuries with kin cemeteries and the erection of inscribed stones. At Carnhedryn, for example, there is a Christian inscribed stone reading *Rinaci nomena* ('The remains (or relics) of Rinacus') as well as crop-marks suggesting it was originally sited within a prehistoric funerary landscape.[107] In the second phase, beginning in the seventh century, we see the foundation of Christian sites with later medieval chapels on the coast. These may originally have been associated with communities who became ecclesiastical tenants, but by the time the *Life* was written, some had an important role to play in the promotion of St David's cult. St Patrick appears in the *Life* of the saint, and the significance of the remains at the chapel dedicated to him has already been discussed. There is also St Non's, dedicated to the mother of the saint and where she reputedly gave birth, a chapel with a large cross-carved stone, likely long-cist graves, and a holy well. However, some other sites suggested by *capel* place names, cross-carved stones, or long cists are not in Rhygyfarch's *Life*.[108] Amongst these a somewhat later burial ground is suggested by four cross-carved stones of ninth- to eleventh-century date from ecclesiastical land on Pen-Arthur Farm.[109]

---

[106] James 1993; Sharpe and Davies 2007.

[107] James 1993, 108–9; Edwards 2007a, no. P107; Ludlow 2003, prn 46860.

[108] Sharpe and Davies 2007, chs 3, 6–7; James 1993, 105–8; Ludlow 2003, prn 46863; Edwards 2007a, no. P100.

[109] Ibid., nos P103–5.

340 LIFE IN EARLY MEDIEVAL WALES

The wider Christianization of the earlier inhabited landscape is also implied in the *Life* by the deaths of the warlord Baia and his wife, stories associated, amongst other sites, with Clegyr Boia, an enclosed rocky hilltop with prehistoric occupation west of St Davids.[110]

The modern parish of St Davids is coterminous with the *cantref* of Pebidiog, and some other major foundations are similarly located within large parishes that may reflect earlier patterns of ecclesiastical landholding. Nevern, the most important church in the *cantref* of Cemais, is a good example. It nestles in the valley of the Afon Nyfer but the parish stretches from the coast right up into the Preseli Hills, and the distribution of seventh- to ninth-century cross-carved stones can be used to reconstruct the wider Christian landscape. In the south-east of the parish these include two at Cilgwyn, one of several chapels of ease which may have early origins, and others are associated with farms on the lower slopes of the Preselis, thereby suggesting a network of chapels and cemeteries serving agricultural communities living on the ecclesiastical estate.[111] Although no sculpture has been found, to the east in the parish of Bayvil later medieval place names indicate the survival of both *clas* lands and an area of sanctuary.[112] By contrast, in the Gwaun valley to the south-west where there is a dense pattern of small parishes, the distribution of cross-carved stones is mostly associated with later churches, suggesting similar origins to sites in the south-east, but their subsequent histories and landownership diverged. In the Gwaun valley an unusual late eighth- or ninth-century pillar carved with a Crucifixion from Cilrhedyn Isaf also hints at the one-time existence of a small monastery eclipsed by the rise of Nevern, but later dedications point to the increasing reach of St Davids.[113]

These two examples enable the identification of major churches in other parts of Wales with dependent chapels and other sites where less evidence has survived. The impressive sculpture from Margam in western Glamorgan, for example, points to a significant foundation, though nothing is known of it until a Cistercian house was established there in 1147. Nevertheless, the distribution of Cistercian granges signals an earlier pattern of landholding associated with Christian foci, some of which are marked by cross-slabs, some with inscriptions, mainly of tenth- or eleventh-century date. One from Eglwys Nynnid tells us that the cross had been made for the soul of Drim..., possibly a patron and donor of the land.[114]

In the north-east, where the comparative lack of sculpture and long-cist graves makes identification of minor sites all the more difficult, later documentation has been

[110] Sharpe and Davies 2007, chs 15–18; Vyner 2001, 78–83; Archwilio, DAT prn 2655.

[111] Edwards 2007a, 61–2, nos P74–9; 2013, no. P140.

[112] Comeau 2016, 212; Charles 1992, i, 139–40.

[113] Edwards 2007a, 61–2, nos P32–5, P49–54, P85–7; Edwards 2013, no. P50; James 2007, 44–5, 55.

[114] Evans, E. M. 2009, 96, fig. 5.4; Redknap and Lewis 2007, nos G78–97. The inscription on no. G87, Margam (Eglwys Nynnid) 2, reads *i(n) nomine dei crucam proparare(t) pro anime Drim...eci*. Much of the coastal landscape has been destroyed by industrialization.

CHRISTIAN SITES AND CHRISTIAN LANDSCAPES 341

used to reconstruct areas of influence associated with major churches and to hint at the dependent chapels linked with them, though dating is problematic. For example, remarkably little is known about Bangor Is-y-Coed, the famous early monastery on the Dee mentioned in Bede's *Historia Ecclesiastica*. By the end of the early Middle Ages, it was probably a mother church that was later sited within a large parish, though it may originally have controlled a greater area on either side of the river. Further up the Dee is Corwen, another mother church with a large parish, the authority of which probably later extended throughout the commote of Edeirnion.[115]

Patterns of ecclesiastical landholding, as well as some information concerning donation, are also evident in the surviving charter material, enabling the locations of estates to be pinpointed and, where boundary clauses survive, these can also be plotted on the ground (Chapter 6). Ninth-century charters added to the Lichfield Gospels while it was at Llandeilo Fawr include two relating to the donation of Trefwyddog to God and St Teilo. This estate was located to the north between the Camddwr stream and the Afon Twrch in the later parish of Llanycrwys, later a grange of Talley Abbey, which had inherited land formerly owned by Llandeilo Fawr. What may have been long-standing boundary markers in the charter included prehistoric monuments, notably the still prominent late Neolithic or early Bronze Age standing stone, *Hirfaen Gwyddog*, which now played significant roles as landmarks in a Christian landscape.[116]

Though more difficult to use, charters in the Book of Llandaf also enable the reconstruction of ecclesiastical estates, and in some cases landholding is further illuminated by the surviving sculpture. For example, a charter, the core of which is datable to *c*.935, records a donation by King Cadwgan of three *modii* of land (about 50 hectares) near Merthyr Mawr, which is located on the Ogmore river in west Glamorgan. The bounds stretched 'by length from Merthyr Glywys as far as the river Ogmore and by width from Tir i Cair as far as the settlement (*uillam*) of Oufreu'.[117] What is particularly interesting here is that two inscribed crosses dated to the eleventh century also appear to record donations of land to Merthyr Mawr, and these were probably originally set up on the land concerned as permanent reminders of this as well as visible Christian symbols in the landscape. The first, which is fragmentary, was found south of the Ogmore reused as masonry. On one face the incomplete inscription reads…*est…quod ded[it] Arthmail agrum d(e)o et Gligius et Nertat et Fili*…('(Be it known) that Arthmail gave (this) field to God and Glywys and Nertat and Fili…'). The second, which originally stood in a field nearly 1.25 kilometres north of Merthyr Mawr, also has two inscriptions: the latter is incomplete but ends with the phrase…· *loco*

[115] Colgrave and Mynors 1969, ii.2; Silvester and Evans 2009, 32–5.

[116] Evans, J. G., and Rhys 1893, xlv (Chad 3 and 4); Jones, G. R. J. 1972, 311–16; Richards 1974, 116–17; Evans, E. M. 2009, 90.

[117] Evans, J. G., and Rhys 1893, 224; Davies, W. 1979a, 121; Coe 2001, 1004; Parsons 2013a, 80, has suggested that Merthyr Glywys was located in the parish of Newton Nottage.

342   LIFE IN EARLY MEDIEVAL WALES

isto · in grefium · in proprium · usque in diem · iudici ('for that place in a legal document, in perpetuity until the Day of Judgement'). Both therefore echo the terminology and phrasing of charters. *S(a)nc(t)i Gliuissi* ('saintly Glywys') is also mentioned on a third cross found close to Merthyr Mawr and it is possible that, as this foundation grew in significance, it subsumed the cult of the saint originally focused on the early site of Merthyr Glywys nearby.[118]

Another earlier eighth-century Llandaf charter recording the redonation of Llandeilo'r-fân, Breconshire, notes a boundary cross which seems to have stood beside a drove road coming off the Epynt, therefore drawing the attention of passers-by.[119] The cross-carved pillar known as *Maen Dewy* ('David's Stone') that still stands near the crest of the hill at Penwaun, Pembrokeshire, probably marked the boundary of the *cantref* of Pebidiog in which St Davids is located.[120] To the west approaches to the church at Llanwnda seem to have been marked by cross-carved stones, one of which is still extant.[121] To the east in the parish of Dinas field names suggest that crosses also once indicated the boundaries of secular agricultural land but, since they no longer survive, when they were originally erected is unclear.[122] Nevertheless, the placing of crosses on boundaries and the marking of Church land drew attention not only to ecclesiastical ownership but also to Christianization of the landscape itself.

From the ninth century onwards St Davids had more than local significance. This is apparent in Asser's reference to the *parochiam Sancti Degui* ('jurisdiction of St David'), meaning its dependent territory,[123] and in this instance sculpture can also help to determine its wider sphere of influence. Details of crosses, cross-slabs, and grave-markers dating to this period from St Davids, their forms, ornament, and inscriptions (as well as sometimes their geology), are comparable with sculpture in both Pebidiog and neighbouring *cantrefi*. This points to the wider religious, cultural, and artistic influence of St Davids and also drew on continuing contacts around and across the Irish Sea. For example, the form of the cross-head on St Davids 1 is the same as that on a cross-carved pillar from Llawhaden. This became a major church in the *cantref* of Daugleddau and was dedicated to St Aidan of Ferns (the Irish saint Máedóc), one of David's disciples in Rhygyfarch's *Life*. It is also one of the seven bishop-houses of Dyfed listed in a law text thought to originate in the later ninth or early tenth century, suggesting that St Davids had by then extended its authority over 30 kilometres to the east. St Ishmael was similarly seen as a disciple of St David, with a major church

[118] Redknap and Lewis 2007, nos G98–9, G117; on *in grefium in proprium* (literally 'in a writing into ownership'), see Davies, W. 1998, 103–5, n. 29.

[119] Evans, J. G., and Rhys 1893, 154; Davies, W. 1979a, 101; Seaman 2019a, 168–9, fig. 9.5.

[120] Edwards 2007a, Fishguard South 1, no. P16.

[121] Anon. 1883, 343. The cross-carved pillar was rediscovered by the author in July 2020.

[122] Comeau 2009, 241; 2016, 217–18. The setting up of crosses in connection with land disputes remained important in later medieval Welsh land law: see Pryce 1993, 220; Roberts 2001, 311–14.

[123] Stevenson 1959, ch. 79, l. 55; Keynes and Lapidge 1983, 262, n. 181.

dedicated to him on the north side of Milford Haven, later identified as a bishop-house in the *cantref* of Rhos. The sculpture here is also comparable. Indeed, one stone probably originates from Caerfai Bay near St Davids and was likely carved there and then transported to St Ismaels by sea. However, no sculpture is known from the other bishop-houses listed—Rhoscrowther and possibly St Issels in the *cantref* of Penfro, *Llandeulyddog* (Carmarthen) in Cantref Gwarthaf, *Llan Teilaw* (Llandeilo Llwydarth), which was replaced by Llawhaden, and the unidentified site of *Llan Geneu*—and it is therefore possible that ties with St Davids were less strong.[124] Further sites in Pebidiog, such as St Edrins and St Lawrence, appear less significant since they are not mentioned in the written sources, but they too have early medieval sculpture comparable with St Davids, including monuments carved from Caerfai sandstone.[125]

The nature of early links between St Davids and Ceredigion is more difficult to unravel. By the time Rhygyfarch was writing, there was an important connection between Llanbadarn Fawr, where he lived, and St Davids, where his father Sulien was twice bishop. Indeed, Llanbadarn Fawr may have been an earlier bishopric, later subsumed within the diocese of St Davids.[126] Rhygyfarch depicts David's father as ruler of Ceredigion, David's education as taking place at *Vetus Rubus* (subsequently identified as Henfynyw on the coast), and in later chapters David's primacy is established when his preaching defeats the Pelagian heresy at a synod in Llanddewibrefi.[127] Such hagiographic ties are necessarily suspect other than as a means of fostering links between Ceredigion and St Davids in the late eleventh century.[128] However, in the case of Llanddewibrefi, an important early monastic foundation located inland on a tributary of the Teifi, a clear link is also suggested by the sculpture.[129] A Latin-inscribed stone indicates that the origins of the site go back to the sixth century, and cross-carved stones, two with inscriptions, show that it flourished during the seventh to ninth. The most important of these, dating to the early ninth century, commemorates Idnert son of Iacobus and records a raid on the site, equating it with an attack on St David himself.[130] Whether the cult began here and later grew at St Davids, a place with much better land and sea access, is pure speculation. It was, however, a significant outlying foundation clearly associated with the saint. Widely distributed foundations and their

[124] Edwards 2007a, 84–7, nos P55, P90, P128–30; Sharpe and Davies 2007, chs 15, 35–7, 42, n. 68; Charles-Edwards 1971, 250–2.

[125] Edwards 2007a, nos P122–6, P132.

[126] In his poem on the Life and Family of Sulien, Rhygyfarch's brother Ieuan refers to Llanbadarn Fawr as the seat of the holy bishop Padarn; see Lapidge 1973–4, 84–5, l. 70. Gerald of Wales also alludes to a tradition that Llanbadarn Fawr was formerly the seat of a bishop; Thorpe 1978, 181.

[127] Sharpe and Davies 2007, chs 2, 7, 49–54. On the identification of Henfynyw, ibid., 117, n. 35. On Henfynyw, see James 2007, 76; Edwards 2007a, no. CD2. Two cross-carved stones, one a water-worn boulder with a cross similar to St Davids 5, no. P94, have recently been found nearby; Robert Gapper (pers. comm.).

[128] Ó Riain 1994, 385–6.   [129] Edwards 2007a, nos CD 8–13.

[130] Ibid., no. CD9. The now fragmentary inscription read: *Hic iacet Idnert filivs Iacobi qvi occisvs fvit propter predam sancti David* ('Here lies Idnert son of Iacobus who was slain on account of the plundering of St David').

344 LIFE IN EARLY MEDIEVAL WALES

changing patronage and fortunes are a feature of the Columban *familia* of monasteries in both Ireland and northern Britain.[131] The early medieval influence of St Davids was on an altogether smaller scale, but it is the only example in Wales where this can be clearly detected archaeologically well outside the area in which the foundation is located, probably reflecting the active patronage of the rulers of Dyfed.[132] Distributions of saints' dedications may also give some indication of the later sphere of influence of a particular foundation or cult. Dedications to St Teilo, for example, may broadly reflect the former sphere of influence of sites dependent on Llandeilo Fawr centred on Ystrad Tywi, though, by the early twelfth century, these were claimed by Llandaf.[133]

The evolution of a Christian landscape therefore coincides with the consolidation of the religion, commencing with the establishment of a range of monastic sites from around the late fifth century onwards as part of a continuing network of Christian and other contacts with Gaul and probably Iberia and the Mediterranean, as well as significant links with Ireland. Some of these, aided by patronage, developed into major foundations that, from around the seventh century onwards, attracted elite burial and began to acquire estates as donations of land. Those with bishops might initially have represented areas of authority commensurate with the patrimony of particular founding saints or small kingdoms. A small number of these expanded their authority at the expense of others, notably St Davids from the ninth century onwards, a tactic similarly actively pursued by Llandaf at the end of the early Middle Ages. The ordination of priests by bishops, the accrual of monastic estates with their resident farming communities, alongside the patronage of the secular elite, likewise the owners of land, provided not only increasing wealth but also expanding opportunities for administering to the lay population in the surrounding area. Some kin and community cemeteries characteristic of the conversion period were eventually abandoned, but in the southwest in particular many others eventually became the sites of later medieval parish churches and chapels of ease. Indeed, in the west more generally and also in parts of the south-east there is now sufficient evidence to indicate a proliferation of lesser sites and cemeteries during the seventh to ninth centuries that became the day-to-day Christian foci of farming communities, and again, a significant number of these developed into later medieval parish churches and chapels. However, there are also indications that some smaller monastic establishments failed to flourish and were later abandoned, or were brought under lay control or the sway of larger foundations. From about the early tenth century onwards we can see the development of mother churches (*clasau*), many of which had probably evolved from earlier monastic foundations, that had regional authority, often commensurate, by around the end of the period, with *cantrefi* or commotes. While elements of monastic terminology survived,

[131] Herbert 1988, 26–97; Charles-Edwards 2000, 282–343.
[132] For further discussion of the geographical expansion of the cult of St David, see James 2007.
[133] Davies, W. 1982a, 162–3.

these were communities of clerics and their families, each probably living on their own portion of land. It is, however, unclear at what point priests started to be resident within their local communities rather than based in larger establishments. Around the end of the period another wave of foundations, most likely secular estate churches, has been hinted at on Anglesey that led to the completion of a network of small parishes across the island. This process is more clearly evident in Ergyng where Bishop Herewald of Llandaf (d.1104) was consecrating what appear to have been new churches, alongside the ordination of their priests. The proliferation of Christian sites providing increasing opportunities for pastoral care, the acquisition of ecclesiastical land, and the development of saints' cults also resulted in the wider Christianization of the landscape, which could be marked with crosses and linked with hagiographical events. Earlier monuments and the stories associated with or reinvented for them were also incorporated alongside the appropriation of natural features such as springs and wells, thereby embracing the pre-Christian past.

CONCLUSION

Even with a multidisciplinary approach, our understanding is constrained by the nature of the evidence and there have been few archaeological excavations outside the west. Nevertheless, the evolution of a landscape of early medieval Christian sites, as outlined above, has much in common with that in Ireland. The early British Church, alongside that in Gaul, was instrumental in the initial stages of the conversion of the Irish.[134] Yet, in contrast to northern Britain, the role of the Irish in Wales, where there were also Irish settlements, is harder to detect. By around 800 in most parts of Ireland it is possible to discern a dense pattern of Christian sites and this is comparable with that in parts of Wales during the seventh to ninth centuries, especially in the south-west. Here the distribution of cross-carved stones, a wider trend found on both sides of the Irish Sea, and a small number of well-dated excavations makes site identification easier. The likely foundation of further churches in south-east Anglesey suggested by the sculpture is related to Hiberno-Scandinavian links with Dublin and its hinterland, including Rathdown, where there is also a proliferation of sculpture over a greater range of sites around this time.[135] Continuing connections with Ireland are also apparent amongst the mother churches (*clasau*) that emerged in Wales from around the tenth century onwards. For example, the community at Caergybi had links with Macop, Co. Meath, whilst Sulien of Llanbadarn Fawr was partly educated in Ireland with resulting influences evident in the works of his sons, including Rhygyfarch's *Life* of St David.[136] Connections between north Wales and the Isle of Man may also be

---

[134] Dumville 1993.   [135] Edwards 2011; Boazman 2019, 53–62.
[136] Wade-Evans 1944, 240–1, ch. 13; Edwards 2013, 159; 1995.

significant. The major monastery at Maughold was active by the seventh century, while the large number of chapel sites with cemeteries known as keeills, often with simple linear cross-carved stones, may likewise indicate the proliferation of Christian sites from around the late sixth or early seventh century onwards.[137]

Links across the Bristol Channel are also to be expected, allowing comparisons with the Christianization of the landscape in south-west Britain, especially Cornwall, in the period prior to the Anglo-Saxon takeover. Here, as in much of Wales, inscribed stones, some also with oghams, indicate both an Irish element in the population and the process of conversion to Christianity that grew from Roman roots. As in Wales also, some inscribed stones are associated with parish churches, suggesting their origins as places of burial in the fifth and sixth centuries. There are likewise unenclosed, undeveloped cemeteries with long-cist graves, especially along the north Cornish coast. Although there are no early cross-carved stones, there are *lann place names, the equivalent of llan in Welsh. Many, such as Lanhydrock, are paired with local saints' names and there are also examples in Devon, Somerset, and even Dorset, which came under the control of Wessex at an earlier date. This has led to the suggestion that the term was in use by the seventh century at the latest, possibly slightly earlier than in Wales or Ireland.[138] There are similarly some indications of important early monastic foundations, notably St Petroc's at Padstow (probably also an early bishopric), and St Kew, associated with Docco, mentioned in the Life of St Samson.[139]

It is, however, much harder to gauge what comparisons may be made with the evolution of the Christian landscape in Anglo-Saxon England, since we know considerably more about the development of churches in the south and east than in the west, parts of which remained in British hands into the seventh century, and it is likely that there were significant regional differences. Similarly, we have consistently less understanding of the development of Christian sites and the archaeological evidence for them in the eastern half of Wales, where we might expect most contact. Although a bishopric has been mooted in late Roman Chester with further possible sees in other Roman towns in the west Midlands, including Wroxeter, evidence remains inconclusive. Nevertheless, the argument for continuity of Christian belief amongst the Britons in this region and their early conversion of the small number of incoming settlers remains compelling, since Anglo-Saxon cemeteries are rare.[140] Bede's reference to the religious community at Bangor Is-y-Coed, now just within the modern border of Wales, also demonstrates that monasticism had taken root before the early seventh

---

[137] Wilson 2018, 23–50, but he is reticent about dating such simple cross-carved stones; see 48–9. Two keeills, Speke and Cronk Keillane, now have burials radiocarbon-dated to the late sixth or early seventh centuries; Andrew Johnson (pers. comm.).

[138] Padel 2010; Herring et al. 2011, 269–76; Preston-Jones and Okasha 2013, 40–4, 46–7, 158–9.

[139] Padel 2010, 121–3; Olson 1989, 14, 66–78, 81–3, 105–7; Taylor 1991 and Flobert 1997, i, ch. 45.

[140] Bassett 1992; Blair 2005, 31.

century.[141] It has been argued that, around the 670s, the Mercian diocese of Lichfield was broken up, leading to the foundation of Worcester in the kingdom of the Hwicce and Hereford in that of the Magonsætan. However, Anglo-Saxon monasteries were being established earlier, notably, in the latter, the double house at Much Wenlock, founded in 654 on land donated by King Merewahl as a daughter house of Iken in East Anglia, which also probably had links with Kent.[142] At Much Wenlock the stone walls and plaster of a possible mid-Saxon church have been found, suggesting that this minster looked very different from its counterparts in Welsh-held lands to the west.[143] However, we know almost nothing archaeologically of others in this border region, most of which were probably built of wood, as sculpture west of the Severn is rare.[144] Nevertheless, imposition of an Anglo-Saxon minster of this kind was part of a wider political, social, and religious change that impacted on the landscape, however superficial earlier Christian penetration may have been. This separation from the west (visible ideologically in the late acceptance of the Roman calculation of Easter), was completed by the construction of Offa's and Wat's Dykes in the late eighth and earlier ninth centuries. Many minsters in this border region probably evolved into mother churches as the Benedictine monastic reform movement had only limited impact, and, as such, those in rural locations may have been little different from their counterparts further west.[145] Churches also changed hands. Llandrinio, for example, the mother church of the commote of Deuddwr, is located east of Offa's Dyke, suggesting that it was formerly under Mercian authority, and Anglo-Saxon influence is also indicated by a fragment of ninth- or early tenth-century sculpture with probable traces of plant ornament.[146] From the tenth century onwards, both English and Hiberno-Scandinavian power and influence emanating from Chester and Wirral were also increasing in Tegeingl and are seen, for example, in the sculpture associated with churches at Rhuddlan and Dyserth.[147]

By contrast, the proliferation of Christian sites in the west, including Wales from the seventh century, is not generally a feature of Anglo-Saxon England, though in some western regions, including parts of Herefordshire and Shropshire, the presence of otherwise undated curvilinear churchyards may signal sites established under the direction of the British Church.[148] Towards the end of the early Middle Ages, however, the rapid increase in proprietary estate churches with cemeteries is most clearly evident in the east of England. Though there are fewer in the west Midlands,

[141] Colgrave and Mynors 1969, ii.2. [142] Sims-Williams 1990a, 4–6, 97–8.

[143] Interpretation of the Anglo-Saxon remains at Much Wenlock has proved controversial: see Taylor and Taylor 1965, i, 453–5; Woods 1987 (who sees them as Roman); repost in Fletcher et al. 1988. Finds include two glass sherds, one Campbell Group B, Germanic tradition, one Group C, imported, sixth- or seventh-century, Atlantic tradition cone beaker; Woods 1987, 64–5, fig. 18(2–3); Campbell 2007b, signalling a high-status site.

[144] Sims-Williams 1990a, 168–74; Bryant 2012, 19–22. [145] Ibid., 17.

[146] Silvester and Evans 2009, 28; Edwards 2013, nos MT2–3. [147] Ibid., 109–10, nos F2–3, F9–10.

[148] Brook 1992; Blair 2005, 27.

as indicated in Domesday Book, the number of such local churches was nonetheless increasing around this time and is also detectable in the survival of late Anglo-Saxon fabric in churches in Herefordshire and south Shropshire, as well as Presteigne in Radnorshire.[149] Bishop Herewald of Llandaf's consecration of churches in Ergyng would fit into a similar scenario, but to what extent this was also happening west of Offa's Dyke is unclear.

[149] Ibid., 368–425; Bryant 2012, 18; Taylor and Taylor 1965, ii, 497–9.

ELEVEN

Ritual and Belief

So far, discussion of the impact of Christianity on early medieval society in Wales has focused on what archaeological and other evidence can tell us about the processes of conversion, integration, and consolidation of the religion, primarily through identification and analysis of a developing hierarchy of sites, ranging from major monastic foundations to cemeteries and holy wells, that together transformed the religious landscape. By contrast, this chapter is concerned with aspects of Christian belief and the rituals associated with them.

At the simplest level, belief was expressed in objects of personal adornment. As early as the later sixth or early seventh century, penannular brooches such as that from Kenfig, Glamorgan, were occasionally decorated with small terminal crosses.[1] Such brooches could have been worn by both ecclesiastics and the laity as visible symbols of Christian belief and identity but may also have been valued for their apotropaic powers. From the seventh century onwards, some objects of Anglo-Saxon type with more overt Christian symbolism suggest a possible market for such items, particularly in the south-east. For example, a piece of horse harness from Llysworney, Vale of Glamorgan, may have been adapted as a pendant cross. The arm of a pendant cross has also been found near St Arvans, Monmouthshire, together with a small cruciform mount with a chi-rho hook and a face mask on each arm suggesting both Christ on the cross and an intention to ward off the evil eye. An eighth- or ninth-century disc-headed pin from St Florence, Pembrokeshire, ornamented with a cross surrounded by triquetra knots symbolizing the Trinity, shows a continuing taste for personal objects of this kind.[2] In the north, however, the only examples of such metalwork are small lead pendant crosses of Hiberno-Scandinavian type from Llanbedrgoch and Abergele, which may be compared with similar finds from Dublin and Meols.[3]

---

[1] Redknap 2007a, 71, no. 10; Edwards 2017b, fig. 3; for an unprovenanced parallel, see Youngs 2007, 93, fig. 4.8b. For Irish parallels, see Youngs 1989, 31–2, no. 16; Kilbride-Jones 1980, nos 110, 121; Hunt Museum 2002, 135.

[2] Redknap 2009a, 352–6.

[3] Ibid., 357–8; PAS no. GAT-6E2F79; Wallace 2016, 243; Griffiths et al. 2007, 157–8, pl. 28.

Life in Early Medieval Wales. Nancy Edwards, Oxford University Press. © Nancy Edwards 2023.
DOI: 10.1093/oso/9780198733218.003.0011

Even so, archaeologists have sometimes been reluctant to engage with both religious beliefs and the ways in which these can give meaning and order to emotions such as hope and anxiety, ecstasy and grief. Nevertheless, this perceived psychological dimension goes hand in hand with the notion of a shared religious experience that helps to control such emotions and contributes to a sense of societal belonging and identity.[4] In the case of early medieval Christianity this was primarily conveyed through the Bible and other religious texts such as penitentials and hagiography, as well as liturgical and other rituals related to the monastic round, the Christian year, and the life cycle. The devotional experience was also sustained and enhanced through performance and the environment in which it took place, encouraging engagement with the senses. At the same time practices would have been more effectively controlled in religious foundations, though in some cases older beliefs may have been Christianized and in others elements of magic may also have persisted. Discussion here will consider both archaeological and written evidence but will centre on aspects of ritual and belief most clearly detectable in the material record: saints' cults, relics, and pilgrimage, together with devotional and other practices associated with death and commemoration.

SAINTS' CULTS, RELICS, AND PILGRIMAGE

The development of saints' cults in Wales should be viewed against the backdrop of their evolution across Western Europe, and in Rome in particular. Here the cults of Christian martyrs that originated during the third century were more systematically promoted during the later fourth, centred on their graves outside the city.[5] In Wales, Julius and Aaron were also martyrs and the growth of their cults, probably focused on a hill outside the legionary fortress at Caerleon, is apparent by the mid-sixth century when Gildas was writing. The reference to the antiquarian discovery of possible early medieval cist-graves on the likely site of the *merthyr* of Julius and Aaron, mentioned in a Llandaf charter, may signal a wish to be buried close to the remains of these early saints (Chapters 4 and 9). However, from around the later sixth century we can begin to trace the evolution of cults based around local saints who were not martyred for their faith, and some of these acquired a wider following. In contrast to Gaul, they were not urban bishops like St Germanus of Auxerre, who visited Britain and whose cult was probably later influential in north-east Wales (Chapter 9), or Samson, whose spiritual life began in the south before his journey to Brittany, where he became bishop of Dol.[6] Rather, they were later perceived as the founders of monasteries and churches. As such they became the spiritual patrons and guardians of these places and

---

[4] Lewis-Williams 2008; Tarlow 2012; Beit-Hallahmi and Argyle 1997, 1–32, 230–55.
[5] Thacker 2002, 2–5. [6] Taylor 1991 and Flobert 1997, i, chs 44, 52, 61.

their communities, functioning as heavenly mediators between them and God.[7] By the end of the early Middle Ages, hagiography and other literature portray male saints as heroic figures who, in the case of David, could lead his followers to victory against the English. More generally, they wielded their authority by cursing and destroying those who failed to obey them, thereby reflecting their protective role in a violent age, whilst also demonstrating miraculous powers of healing and command of the natural world.[8] By contrast, as elsewhere in Western Europe, there were few female saints and no early lives have survived other than the brief appearance of Non, the mother of David, in Rhygyfarch's *Life*, who, very unusually, is portrayed as a victim of rape.[9] By contrast, in the twelfth century Gwenfrewi (Winefride) is depicted as a target of male violence in order to protect her virginity, a common trope, though she was dependent on St Beuno to destroy her aggressor and restore her head to her body.[10]

Although saints acted as mediators between the heavenly and earthly spheres, the growth of their cults was facilitated by the presence of their bodily remains, which offered protection to the foundation where they lay, and these primary relics became foci of prayer and veneration. In Rome, prior to the second half of the eighth century, there was a reluctance to disturb the graves of martyrs, and what evidence there is from Wales suggests a similar unwillingness that resulted in a conservative attitude to primary relics that persisted until the advent of Norman influence, a situation also evidenced in Brittany.[11] This would appear to contrast with that in Merovingian France where, from the later sixth century, there is evidence for the elevation of the bodily remains of saints and their display in free-standing shrines within churches on the sites where they had originally been buried. Elevation also seems more prevalent in Ireland, with notable examples including Cogitosus's late seventh-century reference to the sarcophagi of St Brigid and Abbot Conlaed in the church at Kildare.[12] A century later elaborate translations were also being practised in Anglo-Saxon England, and these were not only performances with emotional force but also went hand in hand with the promotion of the cult, as shown by the accounts relating to St Æthelthryth at Ely and St Cuthbert at Lindisfarne.[13]

In Wales there are no such accounts. Nevertheless, the early significance of holy graves and their associated corporeal relics is suggested by *merthyr* place names,

---

[7] Thacker 2002, 24–34.   [8] Isaac 2007; Davies, W. 1982a, 174–8.

[9] Schulenburg 1998, 404–5; Sharpe and Davies 2007, 112–13, ch. 4; Cartwright 2007, 182–3, 200–6; Charles-Edwards 2013, 622.

[10] Wade-Evans 1944, 292–3, chs 12–14; de Smedt et al. 1887, 712–14.

[11] Thacker 2002, 14–20; Edwards 2002, 236–8; Smith, J. M. H. 1990, 335–7.

[12] Connolly and Picard 1987, 25, ch. 32.1; Edwards 2002, 238–9, 243. In Ireland later archaeological evidence indicates both shrine chapels thought to overlie the graves of saints and outdoor shrines overlying special graves; see Ó Carragáin 2003, 130–40; and for Illaunloughan, Co. Kerry, an excavated example of the latter, see White Marshall and Walsh 2005, 55–66, 166–71.

[13] Colgrave and Mynors 1969, iv.19, 390–7, iv.30, 442–5; Williams, Howard 2007, 110–11; Karkov 2003, 399–401; Thacker 2016.

352 LIFE IN EARLY MEDIEVAL WALES

usually combined with a personal name linked with the founding saint. Equally, we have already seen how early inscribed stones that once marked graves, such as that commemorating Saturninus and his holy wife at Llansadwrn and that naming Mailisus from Llanfaelog, Anglesey, were later associated with churches and the cults of founding saints (Chapter 10). In the *Historia Brittonum*, amongst the 'Wonders of Britain' is the story of the body of a holy man with a miraculous altar brought by ship to Llwynarth on Gower. St Illtud built a church over his grave, indicating that by the early ninth century churches were being constructed around special graves and their associated relics.[14] Indeed, a cross-inscribed stone from Llandecwyn, Merioneth, dated between the ninth and eleventh centuries, could record the consecration of such a church. The graffiti inscriptions in Latin with initial crosses separating the phrases were executed by Heli the deacon and include the name of the saint, Tetquin, who may have been buried on the site, a possible invocation 'to the most glorious Lord', and the first six letters of the alphabet. It has been argued that these may recall a symbolic liturgical act made during church consecration ceremonies where alphabets were written in ashes on the floor of the new church, a practice also possibly referred to in connection with St Patrick in the *Historia Brittonum*.[15]

By the late eleventh and twelfth centuries, the hagiography suggests that the graves of many saints in Wales still remained undisturbed, as in the case of St Brynach, whose body lay buried under the eastern wall of his church at Nevern, whilst that of St Gwynllyw was in the floor of his church at Newport.[16] Some other ecclesiastical communities, however, did not seem to know the precise location of the grave of their founding saint, though the lack of corporeal remains does not appear to have detracted from the development of the cult. For example, St Padarn was thought to have been buried in Brittany and St Deiniol on Bardsey Island.[17] It is also unclear whether the *Archa Sancti David*, stolen *c.*1088 and destroyed for its metal covering, contained any corporeal remains of the saint; Rhygyfarch only states that St David was buried within his own monastery.[18] It is only with the Normans that a change in attitudes becomes apparent. For example, in the absence of the corporeal relics of the patron saint, Bishop Bernard of St Davids had the remains of Caradog the Hermit taken to the cathedral in 1124. This was very likely in response to Bishop Urban of Llandaf, who four years earlier had arranged for the purported relics of St Dyfrig and the teeth of Elgar the Hermit to be translated from Bardsey Island to Llandaf.[19]

---

[14] Morris 1980, 41, 83, ch. 73; Edwards 2002, 236.

[15] Edwards 2013, no. MR15; Morris 1980, 34, 75, ch. 54.

[16] Wade-Evans 1944, 14–15, ch. 16, 180–1, ch. 10.   [17] Ibid., 262–7, chs 23–9; Thorpe 1978, 184.

[18] Ab Ithel 1860, *s.a.* 1088; Jones, T. 1952, *s.a.* 1087 (= 1089); Sharpe and Davies 2007, 150–1, ch. 65; Cowley 2007, 274–5.

[19] Ibid., 275–6; Jankulak and Wooding 2010, 41–2, 47, ch. 11.

It should be said, however, that in the acidic soils so common in Wales the corporeal remains of those later regarded as saints would seldom have survived. Nevertheless, the mere fact of their burial would have provided protection and enhanced the sanctity of the site, thereby attracting further burials even if there were no primary relics. Initially square-ditched and other grave enclosures in 'undeveloped' cemeteries, notably at Llandygái and Capel Eithin which were interpreted as having superstructures, were seen as the specially marked graves of holy men or women that became places of veneration and the foci of other burials. It was argued that these were modelled on *cellae memoriae*, structures erected over the graves of early Christian martyrs in parts of the Late Antique world.[20] Nonetheless, it is now generally accepted that such square-ditched and other grave enclosures are primarily a sign of status rather than belief and that more than one grave within an enclosure or a cluster of surrounding graves may represent a family group. It is, however, potentially important to make a distinction between those enclosures associated with 'undeveloped' cemeteries and examples found on the sites of later parish churches with cults of early medieval founder saints. The early medieval cemetery adjacent to Llaniestyn Church, Anglesey, included a ditched mortuary enclosure that formed the focus for a cluster of other graves (Fig. 11.1, a). The enclosure was oriented approximately east–west, with a causewayed entrance. It contained two graves, one of which was radiocarbon-dated to between the late seventh and late ninth centuries, with some signs of subsequent disturbance, including insertion of a third grave into the northern side of the ditch. What is unusual about the two graves is their monumentality. No bone survived, but after each body had been laid in the grave, probably in a wooden coffin, stones, some with visible tool-marks, were placed around each to form a kerb. It was suggested that these carefully chosen masonry blocks might have been recycled from a Roman site, but whether they remained visible above ground is unclear.[21] Even though we shall never know whether this mortuary enclosure included the grave of the founding saint, or was later perceived to do so, the finely carved effigy of St Iestyn, probably once part of a later fourteenth-century altar tomb, demonstrates the subsequent development of the cult.[22]

It is also clear that early medieval burials beneath later churches influenced their location and spatial design. The special grave already mentioned at Capel Maelog lay undisturbed beneath the chancel arch of the late twelfth- or early thirteenth-century church (Fig. 10.5). No bone survived, but its unusually elaborate form, consisting of a coffin with edging stones above marking the outline of the grave, is similar to those

[20] On Llandygái, see Houlder 1968, 221, reinterpreted in Lynch and Musson 2001, 109, 116; on Capel Eithin, see White and Smith 1999, 133–45, 156. For more general discussion, see Thomas 1971, 137–41; Edwards 2002, 230–2.

[21] Evans, R. et al. 2015, 14–15, 20–1; 2016, 15–21; Evans, R. and Jones 2019, 145–8.

[22] RCAHMW 1937, cxxxiii, 107, pl. 83; Edwards 2002, 235–6.

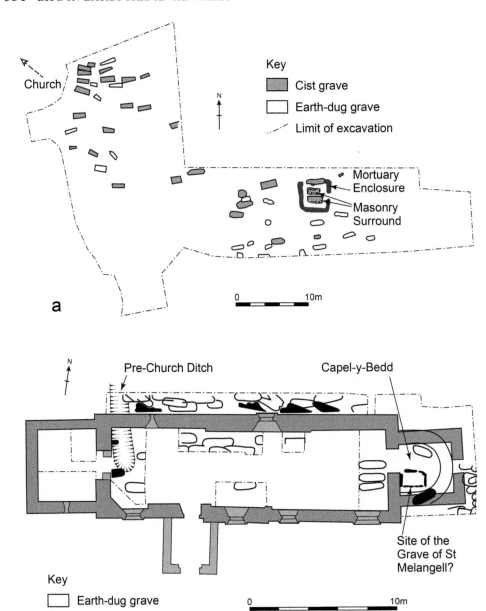

FIG. 11.1. a. Llaniestyn, early medieval cemetery and mortuary enclosure; b. Pennant Melangell Church, with its eastern apse, the grave later associated with St Melangell, and other burials (after Edwards 2002, fig. 6.1).

at Llaniestyn. In this case, however, there were scattered quartz pebbles within the stone setting and the grave may still have been visible when the church was built. The date of the grave is unknown, though the coffin in a nearby grave was radiocarbon-dated to cal. AD 770–1040.[23]

Nevertheless, the most significant evidence is from the church at Pennant Melangell, the site of a possible hermitage associated with the female saint, Melangell, whose elaborate, though incomplete, Romanesque shrine still stands in the church, which also dates back to the twelfth century. Excavations in 1958 and again, during major church renovations, in 1989 allow us to reconstruct an important sequence of events in the development of the site and the cult of its patron saint (Fig. 11.1, b). Middle Bronze Age mortuary evidence was followed by renewed activity in the early Middle Ages, consisting of a ditch and undated graves, some scattered with quartz pebbles, underlying the walls of the church. The only early medieval artefact was a fragmentary sixth- or seventh-century red glass bead of Anglo-Saxon type. The church, possibly preceded by a wooden one set on stone footings, had an eastern apse which was later known as the *cell-y-bedd* ('cell of the grave'). Within this was a stone-edged grave covered by a large slab later perceived as that of the saint. Consequently, it has been plausibly argued that the Romanesque church was built so that the apse, with its offset eastern opening, enclosed the special grave and, at the same time, any bodily remains were translated to the shrine which was probably located in the apse above.[24]

Around the same time *capeli-y-bedd* ('grave chapels') were also being built over the perceived graves of founding saints elsewhere in Wales, either in the form of separate small churches or as part of the main church. In some instances, as at Pennant Melangell, this was also associated with the construction of shrines. Few buildings have survived but these include separate *capeli-y-bedd*, as at Clynnog Fawr, where the shrine of St Beuno lay in a separate chapel south of the main church, and at Caergybi. Both were probably first built in the twelfth century.[25] Separate *capeli-y-bedd* are characteristic of both north and west Wales and are comparable with similar but earlier shrine chapels in Ireland, such as Labbamolaga, Co. Cork, and Clonmacnoise, Co. Offaly, where St Ciarán's shrine later housed the saint's secondary relics. Both were probably constructed between the eighth and tenth centuries.[26] A further parallel of a similar date may be drawn with St Columba's shrine at Iona and there are other likely examples in Cornwall, as at Crantock, as well as in west Normandy and Brittany, again suggesting the significance of ecclesiastical contacts along the western seaways. In eastern Wales and the borders, however, the incorporation of grave chapels at the eastern or western ends of the main church, as at Pennant Melangell and Merthyr

---

[23] Britnell 1990, 36–7, CAR 939.
[24] Radford and Hemp 1959; Britnell 1994; Heaton and Britnell 1994; Britnell and Watson 1994.
[25] Stallybrass 1914; Gruffydd 1992a; 1992b; Edwards 2002, 234–5.
[26] Ó Carragáin 2003, 130–140; 2010a, 66–70.

356 LIFE IN EARLY MEDIEVAL WALES

Issau (Partrishow) respectively, may have more in common with the linear arrangement of churches found in Anglo-Saxon England.[27]

Even if in Wales during the early Middle Ages the graves of the saints remained largely undisturbed, material evidence and hagiography together indicate the significance of more portable secondary relics and their perceived power since they too were imbued with the authority and virtue of the saint. Although few such secondary relics have survived from Wales and the borders, the picture they and the written evidence presents is very similar to that in Ireland, where there are many extant examples of bells and croziers, as well as some books, that were sometimes enshrined and were later regarded as the possessions of the saint. These distinctive relics were similarly revered in Scotland, the Isle of Man, Cornwall, and Brittany, but, as in Wales, comparatively few have come down to us, though some others survived beyond the Reformation and were noted by antiquarians. This indicates similar attitudes to secondary relics across the Celtic-speaking regions of Britain as well as Ireland and Brittany.

Nevertheless, the earliest reliquaries in Britain and Ireland, datable to between the seventh and early ninth centuries, were small house-shaped containers usually made of wood with ornamental metalwork, which—in all but their decoration—are broadly comparable with portable shrines the shape of Late Antique sarcophagi found across early medieval Europe and the eastern Mediterranean. It has been argued that Insular reliquaries of this type are unlikely to have contained fragmented corporeal relics at such an early date but instead pieces of cloth, known as *brandea* or *palliola*, that had touched the graves of Roman martyrs, notably Peter, Paul, Lawrence, and Stephen. In other instances, however, they may have held material linked with local saints, such as holy soil or splinters of wood, and one Anglo-Saxon house-shaped box may originally have contained the consecrated host.[28] Though the majority of these have been preserved in Ireland, with further examples in Scotland, Italy (indicating the significance of contacts with Rome), and Scandinavia (most likely as a result of Viking raids),[29] fragments indicate that they were also in use in Wales. Part of a bronze hinge ornamented with red and yellow enamel, blue and white millefiori, and a blue glass stud was found with a binding strip at the royal crannog at Llangorse. The hinge is similar to Irish examples and was once attached to a house-shaped shrine so it could be carried, in processions for example, on a strap around the neck. The binding strip came from the roof. The reliquary may originally have been housed in the church at Llan-gors on the mainland, where the kings of Brycheiniog were patrons. A gilt bronze

---

[27] RCAHMS 1982, 41–3, 137–8; Petts and Turner 2009.

[28] Edwards 2002, 245–8; Rollason 1989, 26–7. On the Anglo-Saxon container (now at Mortain, Normandy), see Webster and Backhouse 1991, 175–6.

[29] For Insular examples, see Youngs 1989, 134–40.

interlace roundel discovered near Din Lligwy, Anglesey, also probably came from a shrine of this kind.[30]

The reliquary known as *Arch Gwenfrewi* from Gwytherin, Denbighshire, is a different form of box shrine of triangular shape with small feet. A late seventeenth-century drawing in Edward Lhuyd's *Parochialia* shows it still largely complete (Fig. 11.2), but only two fragments of one of the gable ends now survive. The box was made of oak and the drawing shows it still partially covered with metal sheets, riveted binding strips, roundels with cruciform shapes and interlace ornament, and other mounts, as well as a small cross attached to the ridge of the lid. The fact that so little now survives has led to considerable debate about its original size and function, as well as its date, which in the absence of scientific dating cannot be entirely resolved. The decoration may also have been of more than one period. It may have been similar in function to house-shaped shrines but somewhat larger, and the best parallels for the roundels are with eighth- and early ninth-century roundels of Anglo-Saxon type.[31] Alternatively, it has been compared with the early twelfth-century triangular shrine of St Manchán from Lemanaghan, Co. Offaly, which has Hiberno-Scandinavian Urnes-style bosses

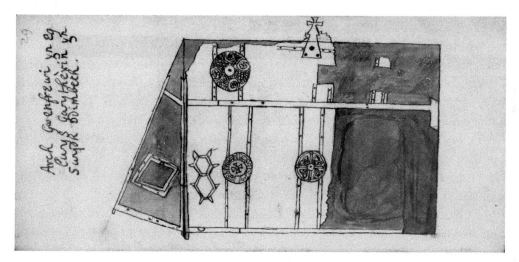

Fig. 11.2. The reliquary known as *Arch Gwenfrewi*, recorded by Edward Lhuyd at Gwytherin (Bodleian Library Oxford, MS Rawl, B 464, fol. 29r).

---

[30] Lane and Redknap 2019, 209–18; Redknap 2009a, 366. On a further possible fragmentary hinge-plate of eleventh-century date with Irish parallels from east of the Wye at the Roman site of Weston under Penyard (*Ariconium*), see La Niece and Stapleton 1993; Redknap 1995a, 70; Murray 2014, 140.
[31] Butler and Graham-Campbell 1990; Edwards and Gray Hulse 1992; 1997.

358 LIFE IN EARLY MEDIEVAL WALES

rather than roundels and is large enough to have carried his disarticulated remains. Robert of Shrewsbury's *Life* of Gwenfrewi (Winefride) gives a first-hand account of how in 1137 her remains at Gwytherin were exhumed and translated to Shrewsbury, and it has been argued that this shrine could have been used for their transportation.[32]

Gerald of Wales famously remarked upon the reverence of both the common people and the clergy in Wales, as well as in Ireland and Scotland, for secondary relics in the form of 'portable bells [and] staffs crooked at the top and encased in gold, silver or bronze'.[33] Such objects originated as ecclesiastical equipment and are first noted in Adomnán's late seventh-century *Life* of Columba,[34] but they were later perceived as secondary relics. Although no enshrined relics of this kind have survived in Wales, six bells are still extant, with a further example from Herefordshire (Fig. 11.3). They were intended to be rung by hand and it has been suggested that the more common form in Ireland and Scotland had Roman antecedents. This was made from an iron sheet folded into a quadrangular shape and then riveted together, with a separate handle and suspension loop for the clapper. Such bells would, however, have had the appearance of bronze since they were then coated with copper alloy. Archaeological evidence of this brazing process has been discovered at the monastic site of Clonfad, Co. Westmeath, indicating their manufacture there sometime in the late eighth or ninth century. It is probable that iron bells were once more common in Wales, but the only extant example of this type is from Llangenau, Breconshire. That from Marden, Herefordshire, is also iron but is made from two sheets riveted together rather than one, suggesting local manufacture.[35] The other five are made from cast copper alloy, and it has been suggested that this type, which is probably derived from iron bells and has a more limited distribution in Ireland and Scotland, was made contemporaneously, but their manufacture began somewhat later. The Welsh examples, which are all from the north-west, demonstrate considerable variety and range widely in size from 100 millimetres in height at Llanrhuddlad to 220 millimetres at Dolwyddelan, and the form of the latter may indicate Irish manufacture. Unusually, the example from Llangwnnadl has animal-headed terminals on the handle, suggesting a ninth-century date, whilst that from Llanarmon may be as late as the twelfth.[36] That such bells were

---

[32] Bourke 2009; for Robert of Shrewsbury's account, see de Smedt et al. 1887, 730. On St Manchán's shrine, see Murray 2014, 230–61.

[33] Thorpe 1978, 87.

[34] Sharpe 1991, ii.14, 164–5, ii.42, 197, iii.13, 215, iii.23, 229. On their monastic and liturgical functions, see Bourke 2020, 154–63.

[35] Bourke 2008; 2020, 26–7, 34–5, 56–64, 381–3 nos 77–8. On Clonfad, see Stevens 2014, 265–8.

[36] Redknap 2009a, 360–2; Bourke 2020, 32–6, 64–71, 80, 422–6, nos 123–7. The fifth bell is from Llangystennin.

Fig. 11.3. An iron bell from Llangenau (left), and a copper-alloy bell from Llangwnnadl (© Amgueddfa Cymru–National Museum Wales).

the valued possessions of early medieval churches in Wales is also shown in the hagiography. For example, Lifris's late eleventh- or early twelfth-century *Life* of St Cadog of Llancarfan describes a 'beautiful mottled bell' reputedly made by Gildas and taken to Rome for the Pope's blessing before being given to St Cadog; the word 'mottled' (*uaria*) could refer to a brazed iron bell.[37]

No other early medieval relics have survived in Wales, but later written sources give us an inkling of what once existed. In both Ireland and Scotland, however, wooden croziers with highly ornamented metal casings are still extant, giving an idea of what has been lost. Their primary function was as staffs of office associated with particular churches and their founding saints, and their origins are early. A late sixth-century crooked wooden staff, the drop of which is incised with a cross, was excavated at Lemanaghan, and a tinned metal drop-plate ornamented with spirals found at Kilpatrick, Co. Westmeath, is around the same date, though the majority of enshrined

---

[37] Wade-Evans 1944, 84–7, ch. 27; Redknap 2009a, 362.

360 LIFE IN EARLY MEDIEVAL WALES

examples are tenth-century or later.[38] References to croziers in Wales include a late eleventh-century Old Welsh *englyn* praising the relic known as *Cyrwen*—St Padarn's *bachal* or staff. This was written by Ieuan of Llanbadarn Fawr in the margin of his illuminated manuscript of St Augustine's *De Trinitate*.[39] Likely examples of early medieval croziers that may have survived the Reformation include the staff of St Curig at St Harmon, Radnorshire, which Gerald of Wales describes as 'completely encased in gold and silver', as well as that from Baglan, Glamorgan, mentioned by Edward Lhuyd at the end of the seventeenth century.[40] From both Ireland and Scotland there is also evidence that manuscripts associated with particular saints were enshrined. An early example of a book shrine found in Lough Kinale, Co. Westmeath, probably dates to the late eighth or early ninth century.[41] It is not known whether the Lichfield Gospels, kept on the altar of St Teilo at Llandeilo Fawr in the early ninth century, were perceived as a relic, though they clearly fulfilled some of the same functions. Gerald of Wales also mentions a gospel-book reputedly copied by David but miraculously completed by an angel that was enshrined in gold and silver. This is likely the same as the 'worm-eaten book covered with silver plate' listed amongst the relics of St David at the Reformation.[42] Other early medieval secondary relics may have included St Cynog's torque, which was also noted by Gerald of Wales, and St Padarn's tuni*c*.[43]

The functions of relics in early medieval Wales seem broadly similar to those in Ireland, where much more is known.[44] By the ninth century in Wales the authority of the saint was being sought in making agreements and taking oaths, as indicated in the story in the *Historia Brittonum* concerning the altar suspended over the grave of the saint at Llwynarth.[45] The ninth-century marginalia added to the Lichfield Gospels demonstrate its role in recording the donation of land and other agreements, a practice also found in other Insular gospel-books such as the Book of Kells. The acquisition of the Gospels by Gelli son of Arthudd from Cyngen son of Gruffudd and its donation to Llandeilo Fawr are finalized with their names, and in the settlement of a land dispute St Teilo heads the list of witnesses, thereby demonstrating his authority from on high.[46] By the end of the early Middle Ages the miraculous powers of relics and their role in healing are also apparent. Rhygyfarch demonstrates St David's command over the elements when he places the point of his staff in the ground and a spring gushes forth. His staff and bell are also famed for their miracles. Lifris's *Life* of St Cadog indicates his bell should be used in oath-taking and claims that it was instrumental

---

[38] On Irish croziers, see Murray 2007; on Scottish ones, Michelli 1986. For the Lemanaghan staff, see O'Carroll 2000; for Kilpatrick, Murray 2017, 173–5.

[39] Russell 2012.   [40] Thorpe 1978, 78–9; Edwards 2002, 254, n. 127.

[41] Ibid., 258–61; Kelly 1993.   [42] Pryce 2018, 24; Williams, Glanmor 1967, 120.

[43] Thorpe 1978, 86; Russell 2012, 10, 14.   [44] Lucas 1986, 13–36.

[45] Morris 1980, 41, 82, ch. 71.

[46] Evans. J. G., and Rhys 1893, xliii; Jenkins and Owen 1983, 50–2, 61–5.

in raising two individuals from the dead. It was also taken into the countryside, its miraculous bridging of a river enabling peace with a neighbouring king.[47]

The surviving evidence for relics also allows us to go some way towards perceiving their impact on those who saw and venerated them.[48] We know almost nothing of early medieval church interiors in Wales but we can suggest a combined sensory effect that would have enhanced the ritual experience of the believer and contrasted greatly with the sights, sounds, and smells of everyday life. Ornamental metalwork on reliquaries and liturgical equipment would have sparkled in the light of candles or oil lamps. Some relics, however, might have been concealed from view, thus increasing emotional tension: an altar associated with St David was, according to Rhygyfarch, hidden under leather coverings.[49] Singing and chanting in Latin punctuated by the ringing of a handbell would have created a sacred soundscape: St Cadog's bell is described as having 'a sweet sound' and was even alleged to have spoken with a human voice.[50] The heady smell of incense and beeswax candles would have added a further sensory dimension.[51] Touch was, however, of the greatest significance since this was how the virtue of the saint was imparted to the believer. Oaths and agreements were concluded in this way and touch was similarly used to convey the power of the saint's relics to prevent those who potentially intended harm. According to Lifris's *Life*, when Danish and English raiders tried to seize St Cadog's shrine, they could not lift it and, when struck, it bellowed, causing an earthquake, and the man who had broken its 'gilded wing' 'melted away'.[52]

As indicated above, saints' cults in Wales have their origins in the sixth century, but these and their associated relics become more visible from the ninth century onwards, with the surge in hagiography around the end of the early Middle Ages indicating the promotion of cults as an adjunct to the increasing popularity of pilgrimage. Initially crowds may have congregated on major sites on saints' feast days and other Christian festivals. The feast days of both St David and St Deiniol are recorded in the early ninth-century Martyrology of Tallaght, indicating the spread of their cults to Ireland.[53] Hiberno-Scandinavian raids, such as those on St Davids in the late tenth and late eleventh centuries, may have targeted such holy days to maximize the capture of slaves.[54] While many pilgrimages must have been to local churches, where such

[47] Wade-Evans 1944, 86–7, 114–17, chs 37, 44.   [48] See, for example, Wells 2018.

[49] Sharpe and Davies 2007, 140–1, ch. 45.

[50] Wade-Evans 1944, 86–7, ch. 27. The latter might indicate a role in prophecy.

[51] Asser, writing *c*.893, mentions King Alfred's earlier gift of 'incense weighing as much as a stout man' before his return home to St Davids; Keynes and Lapridge 1983, ch. 81. See also allusions to incense in the Stowe Missal (*c*.792–803); Hunwicke 2002, 6, 8, 17. The sixth- or seventh-century eastern Mediterranean censer associated with Glastonbury (Webster and Backhouse 1991, 94, no. 68) is of doubtful provenance (Gilchrist and Greene 2015, 416), but Late Saxon censer covers are known, e.g. Pershore, Glos. (Backhouse *et al.* 1984, no. 74).

[52] Wade-Evans 1944, 111–13, ch. 40.   [53] Best and Lawlor 1931, 20, 71.

[54] Jones, T. 1952, *s.a.* 981 (= 982), 998 (= 999), 1078 (= 1080). On such targeting in Ireland, see Smyth 1999, 21.

362 LIFE IN EARLY MEDIEVAL WALES

gatherings would have helped to promote a shared sense of identity, those to more major sites could also involve lengthy journeys. Pilgrims to Rome included the Welsh rulers Cyngen of Powys, who died there in 854, and Hywel Dda in 928.[55] It is also possible that pilgrims reached the eastern Mediterranean. In addition to trade contacts indicated by later fifth- and sixth-century imported pottery and occasional Byzantine coins, the discovery of two flasks for holy oil from the shrine of St Menas near Alexandria—one at Meols, the other at Preston-on-the-Hill near the Mersey estuary (Fig. 7.7, b)—suggests these were brought back by returning pilgrims as souvenirs.[56]

Some early saints, such as Samson of Dol, embarked on a *peregrinatio* or pilgrimage by gradually adopting a more ascetic lifestyle, abandoning first kin, then homeland by setting out on a journey, in this case finally reaching Brittany. Pilgrims embarking on journeys to Christian sites and shrines likewise underwent a phase of separation as they travelled towards their destination with an increasing sense of emotional anticipation of the spiritual and curative benefits they might accrue.[57] One of the objectives of Rhygyfarch's *Life* of St David was to describe the devotional landscape around St Davids associated with the saint and, as we have seen, these sites and others are identifiable on the ground (Chapter 10). *Maen Dewy* ('David's Stone') marks the spot where pilgrims approaching by land along the north coast first looked out over the *cantref* of Pebidiog where St Davids lay. It is incised with a simple ring cross later elaborated with further carving, including a small cross likely added by a passing pilgrim. Equally, those travelling to St Davids along the southern route probably stopped at Llawhaden, dedicated to St Aidan (Máedóc) of Ferns, represented by Rhygyfarch as one of David's most devoted disciples. Here there is a ninth-century cross-carved pillar also with additional graffiti crosses probably incised by pilgrims.[58] Many others would have arrived at St Davids by sea. A cross-carved stone of ninth- or tenth-century date at Martin's Haven may have functioned as a prayer-station for those embarking on the voyage northwards across St Bride's Bay to Porth Clais.[59] Those arriving from Ireland probably headed for Porth Mawr, mentioned by Rhygyfarch as the place where St Patrick brought a man who had been buried close to the beach back to life, before sailing off to evangelize Ireland.[60] This must be a reference to the site of St Patrick's Chapel, the earliest, eighth-century phase of which has an enclosed rectangular stone structure or *leacht* that functioned as a prayer-station, again with graffiti added to some of the slabs (Fig. 10.3). Contemporary evidence of bronze-casting and amber-working hints at workshops that likely sprung up because of opportunities for trade with passing pilgrims. This hypothesis is strengthened by the discovery of bone

---

[55] Morris 1980, 48–9, 89–90.   [56] Griffiths et al. 2007, 58–60.

[57] Turner and Turner 1978, 1–17.

[58] Edwards 2007a, nos P16 (Fishguard South 1), P55; Sharpe and Davies 2007, chs 15, 35–6, 42, n. 68.

[59] Edwards 2007a, no. P59.   [60] Sharpe and Davies 2007, ch. 3.

bead-making waste. It has been suggested that such beads had a devotional function and similar waste is known on Irish ecclesiastical and cemetery sites such as Killeany, Co. Laois.[61]

The ultimate destination was St Davids, the impact of which was heightened because its valley location largely shields it from view, and large stone crosses may have greeted pilgrims when they finally reached the ecclesiastical boundary.[62] Nevertheless, they would also have visited and perhaps taken part in processions to other sites in the immediate vicinity associated with episodes in the life of the saint. These doubtless included St Non's Chapel, which, according to Rhygyfarch, was the site of David's birth, where a rock with the imprints of his mother's hands made during her labour was hidden in the base of the altar. The earliest archaeological evidence from the site with its adjacent holy well is a large cross-carved stone of seventh- or eighth-century date.[63]

The archaeological evidence from the environs of St Davids shows that during the eighth century the construction of a devotional landscape was already underway. By the end of the early Middle Ages there was an ordered pilgrimage landscape with a range of sites that inspired an emotional engagement between the devotee and the saint. It has, however, proved much more difficult to reconstruct such pilgrimage landscapes elsewhere in Wales, especially as there is frequently an accretion of much later folklore and evidence of post-Reformation revival. By the early twelfth century Bardsey Island was already promoted as a pilgrimage destination, 'the Rome of Britain' where 20,000 saints were buried.[64] Equally, some vestiges of an earlier pilgrim landscape may survive at Caergybi. The island on which Caergybi is located is now called Ynys Cybi, demonstrating the impact of the saint on the surrounding landscape. It is ringed with later chapels, including one dedicated to the Irish saint Ffraid (Brigid) with its early medieval cemetery. Nevertheless, it is dominated by Mynydd Cybi (Cybi's Mountain) with its distinctive, white quartz slopes and a later prehistoric hillfort on its summit. Neolithic and Bronze Age ritual and burial monuments on the island also hint at the Christian reinvention of an earlier ritual landscape.[65]

It is therefore possible to trace the origins of and changing attitudes to the commemoration of saints and the growth of the cult of relics back to Continental beginnings, but also to see how these were adapted to more local circumstances. In Wales apparent reluctance to disturb the graves of saints reflects a conservative attitude to corporeal relics which, it has been argued, may stem from a wish to uphold the Roman

---

[61] O'Sullivan et al. 2014, 292. See also Illaunloughan, White Marshall and Walsh 2005, 185–7, Clonfad, Stevens 2014, 268–9, and Raystown, Seaver 2016, 147–8.

[62] Edwards 2007a, no. P91. For discussion of crosses and the devotional landscape of Iona, see Campbell and Maldonado 2020, 55–8.

[63] James 1993; Sharpe and Davies 2007, ch. 6; Edwards 2007a, no. P100.

[64] Jankulak and Wooding 2010, 39, 45, ch. 2.

[65] Stumpe 2014, 31–49; Davidson 2009b; Cuttler et al. 2012, 104–21; Kenney et al. 2020, 315–16, 319–22.

origins of the Church. There is evidence of a similar attitude to such relics in both Cornwall and Brittany.[66] The use of incorporeal relics and reliquaries in the form of house shrines initially conformed to Continental and Mediterranean practices. Nevertheless, ecclesiastical contacts with Ireland were particularly significant in leading to the adoption and veneration of bells, books, and croziers in other Celtic-speaking regions, including Wales, and were sometimes later enshrined. These were regarded as the possessions of saints, imbuing them with their own agency and, when displayed on the altar or taken in ritual procession within or beyond the boundaries of an ecclesiastical foundation, on feast days for example, their emotional impact on believers may have been profound.

Christian pilgrimage too has Mediterranean and Continental origins, but in western Britain and Ireland the concept was initially adopted as part of an ascetic monastic lifestyle, though the subsequent focus on local saints and the promotion of their cults by local and regional churches helped attract wealth and patronage as well as binding communities together. The liminality of the pilgrimage journey leading to the final goal was also enhanced by an unfolding devotional landscape enhancing the spiritual experience. Indeed, the cult of St David was already growing in significance from the eighth century onwards, with an organized pilgrimage landscape evident by the end of the period in both a network of Christian sites and in the hagiography.

DEATH AND COMMEMORATION

From the seventh century we can discern the increasing role of the Church in the way the dead were commemorated. This change also originated on the Continent, and in Merovingian Gaul for example, the funerary liturgy shows a growing concern with the passage of the dead to the afterlife. This goes hand in hand with the development of the concept of purgatory and with it a need for the prayers of the living to liberate the souls of the dead from suffering.[67] The introduction along the western seaways of frequently anonymous cross-carved grave-markers replacing inscribed memorial stones reflects changes in commemoration on the Continent, and those with inscriptions now seek prayers for the souls of those they remember.[68] At the same time, major ecclesiastical sites were becoming places of burial for the Christian elite, including patrons and their families. It is in this context that churchmen had the most direct influence on funerary practices. With smaller sites (unless they were monastic), family and kin would have had a much greater role in the preparation of the body and its interment, and the degree to which the Church was involved depended on the reach and impact of pastoral care.

---

[66] Padel 2010, 115. [67] Paxton 1990, 66–8; Effros 2002, 112–32, 169–204.
[68] Edwards 2007a, 49, 116.

Skeletal material rarely survives in Wales, making the detailed reconstruction of burial practices more difficult. This discussion will therefore focus primarily on church and chapel sites with cemeteries with good skeletal preservation, enabling better analysis of burial practices to cast light on aspects of Christian belief as well as magic. The increasing impact of the Church on attitudes to death that is evident on the carved stone monuments, some with inscriptions and related iconography, will also be considered.

As already argued, the practice of inhumation burial, with the graves usually orientated broadly west–east, has its origins in the later Roman period in Britain, and in Wales this custom spread from Roman sites into rural areas (Chapters 8 and 9). The use of stone-lined cists and wooden coffins demonstrates the importance of protecting the corpse, a concept central to Christian belief since it was expected that the dead would rise and their bodies would be reunited with their souls on the Day of Judgement.[69] The use of linen shrouds and winding sheets, almost certainly made by women, is more clearly associated with Christianity,[70] though they are more difficult to identify in the archaeological record as the position of the body normally provides the only clue. However, in this regard the inscription on a ninth-century grave-marker from Llanlleonfel, Breconshire, is particularly revealing, while also appearing to convey a sense of apocalyptic imminence. It reads, 'Silent in the shroud, Ioruert and Ruallaun in their graves await in peace the dreadful coming of the Judgement'.[71]

At the monastic site of Llandough, for example, over 800 graves were excavated, the majority of which were seventh-century or later (Fig. 10.1). They were often intercut, suggesting the popularity of this sacred space. Many were cut through the natural limestone bedrock, which in itself gave protection to the body, and a few had large boulders placed round the body or had head-support stones. There is also evidence of wooden coffins in the form of staining and in one grave seven probable coffin nails were found, while numerous other burials were hunched, suggesting the former presence of shrouds.[72]

Cemeteries associated with chapel sites show considerable variation, indicating regional and community preferences. At Tywyn-y-Capel (Capel St Ffraid) on Anglesey graves were rarely intercut. The earliest, radiocarbon-dated to c.650–800, were interred in cist-and-lintel graves marked by mounds, whilst in the second phase there were around a hundred dug graves, some with bodily positions, for example wrists

---

[69] Revelation 20–1. On Continental attitudes to the protection of the body, see Effros 2002, 62–75, 133–4.

[70] Luke 23:53. See the late eighth- or early ninth-century representations of shrouded bodies in the Last Judgement scene on an Anglo-Saxon ivory (Beckwith 1972, 118–9, fig. 1), and Christ in the tomb wrapped in a winding sheet on later ninth- and early tenth-century crosses in Ireland (O'Brien 2009, 146; Harbison 1992, iii, fig. 909).

[71] Redknap and Lewis 2007, no. B34: *[In s]indone muti Ioruert Ruallaunq(ue) sepulc(h)ris + Iudicii adventum specta(n)t i(n) pace trem(en)dum.*

[72] Holbrook and Thomas 2005, 25–31.

crossed at the pelvis and crossed ankles, indicative of shrouds.[73] In contrast, at St Patrick's Chapel, within the ambit of St Davids, radiocarbon dating has shown that in the period 3 cemetery spanning the late eighth, ninth, and tenth centuries, there were initially dug graves within a rectangular stone-walled enclosure, but in later phases as wind-blown sand accumulated, there were also more protective long cists, some with lintels of local schist or occasionally water-worn beach pebbles. One young woman buried in a cist-and-lintel grave with stone markers at the head and foot also seems to have been laid to rest in a shroud, since a copper-alloy pin was found amongst her hand bones, which lay crossed on her pelvis. The positions of other bodies and a bone pin from another grave indicate that they too were probably buried in shrouds.[74]

Excavated cemeteries with skeletal remains associated with church and chapel sites are all mixed but infants are in most cases under-represented, suggesting that in some instances they were buried elsewhere, and in some cases a continuation of burials in domestic contexts, as at Dinas Powys, may have prevailed for those who were not baptized.[75] At Llandough, for example, a high-status cemetery associated with a monastic site, 30 per cent were male, 25 per cent were female, and 26 per cent were children, but of these only 8.4 per cent were infants, many of whom were buried in one particular area of the cemetery.[76] In contrast, though there are also signs of cemetery organization at St Patrick's Chapel, the excavated western part commenced with infants and children but later contained mainly young women, as well as a considerable number of infants and children who were carefully buried in a similar manner to adults, demonstrating the protective concern of grieving parents and kin. After a break in burial, in the final eleventh- or twelfth-century phase associated with the chapel, this area was again exclusively used for children, probably in the manner characteristic of many Irish cemeteries after other burials had ceased.[77] At Brownslade, Pembrokeshire, where there is also a likely later medieval chapel, the broadly mid-seventh to mid-ninth-century cemetery was clustered round a Bronze Age barrow. Here, however, it was argued that there was some age profiling, with older individuals held in higher esteem. There were both dug graves and cists, but older adults were buried in the best cist-and-lintel graves, whilst cists without lintels were the graves of infants and children.[78]

Although the vast majority of burials are supine and oriented broadly west–east with the head at the western end, there are exceptions which indicate that some individuals were treated differently for reasons of status or belief by those who were interring them. Firstly, a few burials are oriented differently, for example north–south with the head to the north, as with some early Period 3 graves at St Patrick's Chapel. Secondly, on this site also there were a small number of prone burials, one with a

---

[73] Davidson 2009b, 173–208.   [74] Murphy and Hemer 2022, 30–46, 73, 248.

[75] Page 2011, 107; Alcock 1963, 30.   [76] Holbrook and Thomas 2005, 91; Page 2011, 103.

[77] Murphy et al. 2016; 2019; Murphy and Hemer 2022, 51–4.   [78] Groom et al. 2011, 142–5.

stone slab over the base of the skull and another on the body. Prone burials are likewise occasionally found in Christian cemeteries in both Ireland and later Anglo-Saxon England, where it has been argued that they may be a symbol of humility or penitence. However, it was also noted that some individuals had died a violent death and, in the case of St Patrick's Chapel, the slabs on the body may point to concerns about the dead walking.[79]

Though the majority were interred in individual graves, multiple burials are also sometimes found and it has been noted that multiple and consecutive burials within the same grave became more common in Anglo-Saxon England from the seventh century onwards. Both adults, as at St Patrick's Chapel and Llandough, and children, as at St Patrick's Chapel and Tywyn-y-Capel, might be buried in the same grave, probably reflecting family relationships or other close ties.[80] As one might expect, neonates were sometimes buried alongside their mothers who had died in childbirth, as, for example, at West Angle, Pembrokeshire, where there was an adult female with a neonate interred on her left side in a late cist-and-lintel grave from within the probable chapel enclosure. The upper fill contained an unusual amount of plant material, mainly scrub woodland species such as hazel, thorn, and bramble, but also gorse and a small amount of cereals. Their inclusion could be fortuitous, but such a concentration is highly unusual and might have a more symbolic meaning, representing material brought from a domestic context, or even an array of branches with flowers and fruits and other plants strewn on the grave.[81] Hazel may also have been favoured for its regenerative qualities.[82]

The burial at West Angle also contained several small quartz pebbles, a remarkably common ritual practice found not only in Wales but more widely in early medieval and later cemeteries in Ireland, Scotland, the Isle of Man, Cornwall, and occasionally in Anglo-Saxon England.[83] At Llandough, for example, around forty graves containing quartz pebbles were recorded. Most had been thrown into the grave fill, but others had been deliberately deposited, and therefore their inclusion should be considered a significant part of the funeral ritual. A single pebble placed on the chest might be sufficient, or sometimes more on different parts of the body.[84] They might also be laid on top of the grave to form a visible marker, as at Tywyn-y-Capel, where the phase 1 cist-and-lintel grave of a young woman was covered by a slab-edged mound with a

---

[79] Murphy and Hemer 2022, 61, 88; O'Brien 2020, 153–5; Channing 2012, 97; Hadley 2010, 107–8. For wider discussion of such burials in mainland Europe and concerns about 'revenants', see Gilchrist 2022, 134–6.

[80] Holbrook and Thomas 2005, fig. 7 (10/11) (212/206); Davidson 2009b, 195, grave 292; Murphy et al. 2016, 25, 36.

[81] Groom et al. 2011, 171–7, 180 (the grave was radiocarbon-dated, Beta-229575, to cal. AD 890–1045 (93.5 per cent probability).

[82] Gilchrist 2008, 127, 137.

[83] O'Sullivan and Ó Carragáin 2008, 270; Hill 1997, 472–3; Gilchrist 2008, 138–9.

[84] Holbrook and Thomas 2005, 35–7.

368 LIFE IN EARLY MEDIEVAL WALES

row of quartz pebbles on the top.[85] At St Patrick's Chapel, the quartz pebbles found around and on top of the eighth-century prayer-station were probably deposited as part of the devotions of pilgrims and other travellers visiting the site, a practice comparable with the ritual use of quartz pebbles in association with *leachta* in Ireland, as on Inishmurray and Inishark. Deposition of quartz pebbles associated with graves at St Patrick's Chapel appears more common over time, and one late cist-and-lintel infant burial had been covered by a layer of quartz and other pebbles.[86] In a Christian context the inclusion of white quartz pebbles within the grave probably reflects the reference to a 'white stone' as a sign of redemption associated with the judgement of souls and perhaps also as symbolic tokens representing prayers for the dead.[87] However, the ritual use of quartz, which glows faintly when rubbed or struck, has its origins in prehistory, when it was probably associated with water and regeneration, and therefore its perceived magical qualities were inherited by Christianity through linking it with death and resurrection.[88]

Though rare, other items are also occasionally found in graves. Knives, for example at Llandough,[89] suggest that some were laid to rest in their clothes with knives at their belts, but some other artefacts may have been chosen specifically for their talismanic powers. Amber, like quartz, may have been selected not only for its appearance but also for its electrostatic properties. At St Patrick's Chapel amber chips suggest on-site working, but in one instance half an amber bead and another piece of amber may have been intentionally placed beneath the body.[90] Glass beads, some Roman, were found in graves at Llandough and occasionally elsewhere. There is some evidence to indicate that blue beads in particular, sometimes worn by infants as at St Patrick's Chapel, probably functioned as amulets, which possibly took on more specifically Christian connotations as the colour can symbolize the boundary between the human and divine.[91] Roman coins were also found in a few graves at Llandough (Chapter 4) and it has been proposed more generally that apotropaic value may have increased with the age of the object.[92] On Bardsey Island an Anglo-Saxon penny of Eadgar had been placed within the mouth of a mature male, perhaps to facilitate his passage to the next world. The deposition of Roman or Anglo-Saxon coins within graves is not common

---

[85] Davidson 2009b, 185–90, 208–9.

[86] Murphy et al. 2016, 13; Murphy and Hemer 2022; Lash 2018, 90–6; O'Sullivan and Ó Carragáin 2008, pl. 81.

[87] Revelation 2:17; Holbrook and Thomas 2005, 37.   [88] Gilchrist 2008, 138–9, 151.

[89] Holbrook and Thomas 2005, 32.   [90] Gilchrist 2008, 139; Murphy et al. 2016, 16.

[91] Holbrook and Thomas 2005, 32–3, 35, 65–6; Murphy et al. 2016, 36 (infant burial 289), 47; 2019, 12, 18; Gilchrist 2008, 148–9; Gannon 2017, 67–8; Mannion 2017, 149, 153–7. Blue glass beads associated with infant burials are also found in Ireland, e.g. Raystown, Co. Meath; Seaver 2016, 50, 136.

[92] Gilchrist 2008, 141.

but has also been noted in later Anglo-Saxon and post-Conquest burials, with occasional examples in the mouth.[93]

A particularly interesting object was found in a fifth- or sixth-century grave at Llandough which contained a young adult male. He was wearing a girdle made of two iron bands hooked together at the back with traces of a textile which may have covered them. This is most likely a hernia truss, and the deceased may have travelled to Llandough seeking healing, or it might even have been retained on the body to encourage healing after death. Hernia trusses have also been identified in broadly contemporary graves on the Continent, including in France and Spain. Nevertheless, the monastic context reminds us that a penitential purpose is also possible, thereby reflecting an ascetic lifestyle also indicated by an early eighth-century reference in a letter of Boniface claiming that a visionary at the monastery of Much Wenlock 'wore a girdle round his loins for the love of God'.[94]

Burial markers and other stone sculpture can also be informative about attitudes to death and commemoration. Unusually, at St Patrick's Chapel several cross-carved stones were found *in situ*. An upright cruciform slab incised with a cross marked the head of the grave of a young woman, with a further stone at her feet. Such markers would have helped to ensure that the grave remained undisturbed by later burials, as well as indicating her status. However, four other cross-carved stones were not grave-markers but instead formed the lintels or side-stones of infant long-cist graves; three of the crosses faced inwards, emphasizing their protective function. All are of local mudstone roughly scratched with a knife. This indicates that they were not made by a professional mason but probably by a grieving family member. Placing the cross-carved slab in or over the grave would have been part of the funeral ceremony, with the cross likely symbolizing both a prayer for the soul and that the infant had been baptized. This practice may be a regional one, as a similar cross-carved stone scratched with a knife is known from Brownslade.[95]

From the late eighth century onwards some cross-carved stones as well as more ambitious crosses and cross-slabs have dedicatory and commemorative inscriptions in Latin, demonstrating a significant change in Christian attitudes to death and the after-life. These monuments are mostly associated with major church sites in the south, and the formulae used indicate an increasing ecclesiastical role in the commemoration of the dead. This is linked with the need to pray for the salvation of souls, thereby demonstrating developing ideas about purgatory. The late eighth- or early ninth-century cross-carved stone from Caldey asks '...all walking there that they pray for the soul of

---

[93] Arnold 1998, 106; Hadley 2009, 477–80; Gilchrist and Sloane 2005, 79, 100–2.

[94] Holbrook and Thomas 2005, 53–64; Gilchrist and Sloane 2005, 104–5; Gilchrist 2008, 149–50; Sims-Williams 1990a, 246.

[95] Murphy et al. 2016, 11, 20, 27, 66; 2019, 10–11, 28; Edwards in Murphy and Hemer 2022, 182–8; Edwards 2007a, nos P11, P101.

370 LIFE IN EARLY MEDIEVAL WALES

Catuoconus'. Blessings are also requested, either from those reading the inscription, as on a ninth-century cross-carved stone from Llanwnnws, or from God, as on a contemporary monument from Llanddewibrefi. The inscription on the later ninth-century cross at Llantwit Major actually begins with a benedictory invocation—'In the name of God the Father and of the Holy Spirit...'—which is followed by the name of the patron, Hywel, the ruler of Glywysing, who had commissioned the monument for the soul of his father, Rhys.[96]

In contrast, the only known inscriptions in Old Welsh are incised on a ninth-century cross-carved grave-marker at Tywyn in the north-west (Fig. 11.4). These are exceptional, not only because the language used is different, suggesting a different mindset, but also because there is no indication of the redemption of souls or the liturgical role of the Church. Instead, the inscriptions refer to the mortal remains of four, probably related, individuals including, very unusually, two women—Tengr(um)ui, wife of Addian, and Cun, wife of Celyn—which is possibly why Welsh rather than Latin was chosen. The latter is followed by the phrase *tricet nitanam* ('a mortal wound remains'), a unique and emotive expression of grief.[97]

In Carolingian Europe it is possible to detect an increasing theological interest in meditation on Christ's death, with the consequent production of devotional images of the Crucifixion. Contacts between the Continent and Ireland from the ninth century and with southern England somewhat later also led to the introduction of iconographical models for the depiction of the Crucifixion which were adapted to local concerns, and this is also evident on stone sculpture in Wales. For example, the figure of Christ crucified between the spear and sponge bearers on the late ninth- or early tenth-century cross at Llan-gan has been influenced by sculptural representations in Ireland. Such scenes are, however, remarkably rare, as is biblical iconography more generally, perhaps reflecting a more conservative attitude to depicting images of the divine in line with the injunction against them in the Second Commandment. This reluctance to show Christ crucified is clearly demonstrated by the cross at Margam (Fig. 11.5), which has also been dated to the late ninth or early tenth century. Here there is no figure of Christ but simply a cross ornamented with interlace, suggesting that it functioned as a symbol, not of his death, but of his victorious resurrection. Nevertheless, St John the Evangelist and the Virgin Mary stand on either side of the cross, suggesting the influence of Anglo-Saxon crucifixion images, and the presence of the Virgin also indicates the increasing significance of her cult. Monuments such as these were commissioned not simply as acts of piety to benefit the souls of those named and commemorated in their inscriptions. They would also have functioned as foci for prayer and contemplation, and the occasional depiction of angels, as on the cross-slab at St Arvans, points to their role as intercessors between heaven and earth.

[96] Ibid., 92–6, nos P6, CD13, CD27; Redknap and Lewis 2007, no. G63; Nash-Williams 1950, 40–1.
[97] Edwards 2013, 103, no. MR25.

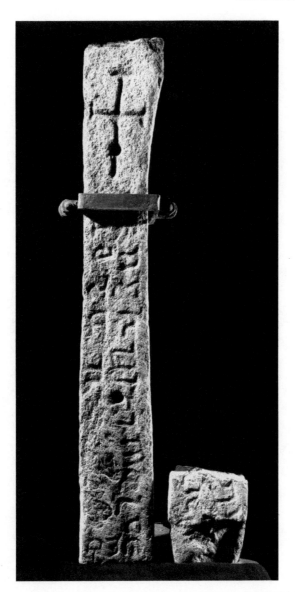

Fig. 11.4. Tywyn cross-carved stone with commemorative inscriptions in Old Welsh (Crown copyright: Royal Commission on the Ancient and Historical Monuments of Wales).

Some would also have had a more public function as stations for liturgical processions, during Holy Week for example.[98]

Therefore, for Christians the prospect of resurrection at the Last Judgement and the hope of everlasting life became important tenets of belief fostered and increasingly controlled by the Church through the encouragement of prayers for the souls of the

---

[98] Edwards 2015; Redknap and Lewis 2007, nos G43, G79, MN1.

FIG. 11.5. Disc-headed cross, Margam, with the figures of St John the Evangelist and the Virgin Mary. Inscriptions on the cross-head identify the patron as Conbelin, who set it up for the soul of Ric... (© Amgueddfa Cymru–National Museum Wales).

dead. From the later eighth century onwards such attitudes were clearly articulated in ecclesiastical circles and amongst the Welsh elite through the patronage of ambitious stone sculpture, with Latin inscriptions requesting prayers and blessings, and were also sought by those who were buried on major ecclesiastical sites. The rite of west–east inhumation burial was inherited from a later Roman past. The use of long cists and coffins and the introduction of shrouds, often regarded as specifically Christian, all facilitated the protection of the body, enabling it to be reunited with the soul on Judgement Day. Individual graves might also be marked with crosses, providing protection whilst also signalling status and Christian identity. The roughly incised crosses on cist slabs at St Patrick's Chapel also show a special concern by the grieving family for the well-being of infants in the afterlife. Other practices, notably the deposition of quartz pebbles, were inherited from a prehistoric past but were given Christian meaning that enhanced what were seen as their magical properties and apotropaic value. The occasional burial of other items, such as blue glass beads or a coin in the mouth, might be interpreted in the same way, reflecting an undercurrent of belief in the efficacy of charms as well as prayers for the dead. Above all the Tywyn inscription in Old Welsh articulates the raw emotion of continuing grief in very different terms from the measured requests in Latin for prayers for the dead.

CONCLUSION

This discussion has focused on two aspects of ritual and belief in early medieval Wales, where archaeological evidence from the seventh century onwards can be used alongside the written sources to illuminate the increasing influence of the Church on all levels of society. These go some way to helping us perceive the emotional and sensory impact of Christianity in the form of the Latin liturgy and its associated accoutrements on those who performed and witnessed it. The cult of relics, pilgrimage, and later the concepts of purgatory and prayers for the soul were initiated in the Late Antique world of Rome and the Mediterranean. Their acceptance in Wales therefore demonstrates the continuation of wider Christian contacts as well as the influence of Christian practices in Ireland, notably in the adoption of bells, books, and croziers as the relics of local saints. Nevertheless, the roots of Christianity in Wales had Roman foundations, and it has been shown that some aspects of ritual and belief, including the very late adoption in 768 of the 'Roman' calculation of when Easter should be celebrated, continuing use of archaic liturgy and the Old Latin Bible (*Vetus Latina*) in the ninth century, and a reticence concerning the representation of Christ, were highly conservative.[99] In burial practices, whilst we can also see the material impact of new ideas about the afterlife—in the use of white quartz pebbles, for example—there are also clear indications of an undercurrent of older beliefs and the Christianization of earlier practices.

[99] Davies, W. 1992, 17–18, 21; Lapidge 1986, 92–3, 102; Edwards 2015, 17–19.

TWELVE

Power and Authority

In earlier chapters I considered evidence for the fragmentation of power that took place as a result of the demise of Roman control and the likely resurgence of native authority and identity alongside the impact of Irish settlers in some parts of Wales, particularly the south-west (Chapters 3 and 4). The spheres of authority that evolved may initially have been very small and may have coalesced on lands around the power bases, typically hillforts such as Dinas Powys, of the leaders who emerged. By the mid-sixth century, however, as Gildas makes clear, there were also larger regional kingdoms, such as Dyfed, and by implication Gwynedd (first mentioned on the inscribed stone from Beddau Gwŷr Ardudwy), ruled by 'tyrants' who exercised power over others through violence and coercion.[1] These larger entities, notably Gwent, the name of which is derived from *Venta Silurum* (Caerwent) (Chapter 4), seem to have their origins in the Roman *civitates* and areas administered by the military, pointing to some continuity in regional identities that have their roots in the tribal organization of later prehistory. Equally, authority over the rulers of smaller territories amongst others was sustained by the formation of patron–client relationships maintained through a system of gift-giving and reciprocity. At the same time, as Christianity gained in strength, the Church sought to provide checks and balances by promoting the ideals of Old Testament kingship, as the early seventh-century inscription commemorating Cadfan of Gwynedd implies (Fig. 1.1).[2] Major ecclesiastical sites were often located close to hillforts and other secular power bases, as in the case of Llandough and Dinas Powys,[3] and more generally the evidence indicates that from the seventh century onwards the patronage of secular rulers and their families is increasingly apparent, including the donation of land to the Church, demonstrating the importance of the symbiotic relationship between the two.

During the eighth and ninth centuries the written sources frequently refer to kings (*reges*) of named regions and in some instances there are indications of lesser kingdoms as well. In contrast, between the mid-tenth and early eleventh centuries this term virtually ceases and instead rulers across Wales are simply identified by their

---

[1] Winterbottom 1978, chs 28–36, 29–36, 99–104; Edwards 2013, Ffestiniog 1, no. MR5, 288.
[2] Ibid., no. AN 26, 182. [3] Seaman and Sucharyna Thomas 2020, 556–7.

Life in Early Medieval Wales. Nancy Edwards, Oxford University Press. © Nancy Edwards 2023.
DOI: 10.1093/oso/9780198733218.003.0012

names and patronyms, suggesting that perceptions of power and authority were adapting as circumstances changed. Although the identities of particular regions persisted, from the tenth century onwards rulers were increasingly mobile and the most powerful exercised authority more widely, a situation comparable with Ireland and, to a lesser extent, England as well.[4] For example, Hywel Dda (d.950) initially ruled Dyfed, but towards the end of his reign his authority had extended to most of Wales apart from the south-east, a position gained through a mixture of violence and negotiation.[5] Conflict between the various competing branches of ruling families was also common.[6]

From the mid-seventh century onwards, the expansion of Mercia westwards led to the increasing loss of British territory, creating a frontier zone defined in the late eighth and early ninth centuries by Offa's and Wat's Dykes. Even so, parts of Wales, especially the north-east and south-east, remained an object of English territorial ambitions, leading to conflict ranging from raids to the construction of the *burh* of *Cledemutha* at Rhuddlan by Edward the Elder in 921. Equally, Welsh rulers entered into client relationships with their English counterparts, perhaps with Mercian kings as early as the mid-seventh century, but, as Asser indicates, certainly during the reigns of Alfred and his successors.[7] By the mid-ninth century and subsequently Wales was also the object of Viking raids and other aggression, leading to limited settlement, particularly in the north-west, which may have become an object of Scandinavian political ambitions. Nevertheless, some Welsh rulers also sought alliances and, by the mid-eleventh century, the complexity of these is demonstrated by Gruffudd ap Llywelyn of Gwynedd, who made use of bands of Hiberno-Scandinavian mercenaries and their fleets under the command of his ally, Ælfgar, the exiled son of the Earl of Mercia, against the forces of Edward the Confessor.[8]

In addition to English and Viking depredations, events recorded in the written sources and other evidence point to endemic violence and coercion in Welsh society. For example, a late sixth- or early seventh-century inscribed stone from Llanboidy, Carmarthenshire, records the killing of Mavohenus son of Lunaris.[9] The chronicles list many raids and battles, and note the mutilation and violent deaths of rulers and their rivals, and the holding of others for ransom. The impacts on farming communities of the laying waste of territories that included slave-taking, destruction of crops, and driving away livestock seriously affected food security.[10] Nevertheless, the role of the Church in encouraging rulers and others to settle disputes and atone for violent

---

[4] Davies, W. 1990, 9–18, 41.   [5] Thornton 2004a.   [6] Davies, W. 1990, 44–6.

[7] Charles-Edwards 2013, 387–96, 412–13, 424–8, 497–519; Keynes and Lapidge 1983, 96, ch. 80.

[8] Davies, M. 2002, 208–9, 223–9.

[9] Edwards 2007a, no. CM13, *Mavoheni fili Lvnari hic occisus*. See also, Llanddewibrefi 2, no. CD9 (Chapter 10).

[10] Dumville 2002; Jones, T. 1952.

376 LIFE IN EARLY MEDIEVAL WALES

acts is also apparent in charters and other documents. The *surexit* memorandum, written mainly in Welsh and added to the Lichfield gospels in the early ninth century, records the resolution of a land dispute and payments made in compensation to the loser.[11] Similarly, several Llandaf charters have additional explanatory narrations: in one *c*.900, March ap Peibio returned an estate near Bishton in Gwent, following his pardon for the killing of his cousin, whilst two mid-eleventh-century charters record restoration and donation of estates to Llandaf after the seizure of Seisyll's wife and the wounding of one of Bishop Joseph's men by King Meurig ap Tewdrig of Morgannwg and his associate.[12]

David Wyatt has demonstrated a strong connection in the patriarchal societies of early medieval Britain and Ireland between elites and their war bands, masculinity, violence, and the taking of slaves.[13] For Wales, as most of the evidence is late, it is difficult to assess change over time, though what there is suggests the likely impact, as in Ireland, of Scandinavian incursions on modes of behaviour. Gruffudd ap Cynan, for example, made use of Hiberno-Scandinavian forces, and there is a reference in his mid-twelfth-century Latin *Life* to the taking of captives who may have been sold into slavery by these mercenaries. In 1081, after his victory at Mynydd Carn against Trahaearn ap Caradog of Gwynedd, he devastated his opponent's home territory of Arwystli, 'where raging with slaughter and fire, he dragged their wives and daughters off into captivity'.[14] Though propaganda, such actions indicate what was considered acceptable, and violence against women was commonplace in a patriarchal society of this kind. That royal women were vulnerable is indicated by the capture of the wife of the ruler of Brycheiniog in a Mercian raid on Llangorse crannog in 916,[15] while, following his defeat of Hywel ab Edwin at Pencadair in 1041, Gruffudd ap Llywelyn 'seized his wife and made her his own'.[16] For the vast majority paying ransoms would not have been possible and those retained as slaves by their captors became a marketable commodity. It is notable that the slave market in Hiberno-Scandinavian Dublin, where a possible pair of manacles has been found, reached its zenith in the late tenth and eleventh centuries, overlapping with the rise of Bristol as a slave market during the eleventh century.[17]

So far it has not proved possible to locate any early medieval battle sites on the ground,[18] but we can occasionally detect the impact of violence in the osteological

[11] Jenkins and Owen 1983, 51, 56; 1984.

[12] Davies, W. 1979a, nos 235a, 259, 261. For other examples of violent acts noted in the Llandaf charters, see Davies, W. 1978, 112, 116.

[13] Wyatt 2009, 61–171.   [14] Russell 2005, 70–1, ch. 18.   [15] Whitelock 1979, *s.a.* 914.

[16] Jones, T. 1952, 13.

[17] Holm 1986, 331–45. A possible slave collar from Dublin is now regarded as a horse hobble; Wallace 2016, 325–6.

[18] None is listed in the RCAHMW, *Inventory of Historic Battlefields in Wales*. The site, marked by a plaque, of St Germanus of Auxerre's hagiographic mid-fifth-century 'Hallelluya victory' over the Saxons at Maes Garmon, near Gwernaffield, Flintshire, is eighteenth-century myth-making; Edwards 2016a, 93–4.

record. The most dramatic evidence comes from Heronbridge near Chester on the west bank of the Dee. Here, within an earthwork enclosure, a mass grave was found cut through Roman buildings between Watling Street and the river. The individuals had died from head wounds and recent examination of a man in his forties and another in his early twenties revealed the extent of their injuries. Both skeletons were radiocarbon-dated to the sixth or early seventh century, and isotope analysis indicated that they may have come from north-east England or south-east Scotland. As a result, it has been suggested that they could have been buried, perhaps where they died, in the aftermath of Æthelfrith of Bernicia's victory against the Britons in the Battle of Chester, fought in 616. According to Bede, the victors suffered heavy losses and many from the monastery of Bangor-on-Dee were also slaughtered.[19] In contrast, in the church cemetery at Llandough, where over 800 burials were excavated, only three, all adult males, show clear signs of violence in the form of injuries to the head. In each case, however, the wounds have signs of healing, demonstrating that they were not the immediate cause of death. One had probably been made with a blade, the other two were the result of blunt force trauma.[20]

Six mid- to late tenth-century burials, including one woman and two adolescents, were found in shallow graves in the upper levels of the enclosure ditch at Llanbedrgoch (Fig. 5.5). These are significant because of their unconventional disposal as well as unmistakable signs of violence. One adult male was in a crouched position, his hands tied behind his back, and had suffered a post-mortem blade cut to the back of the head. A second, probably also with his hands tied, had taken a blow to his left eye, and then been thrown into the grave on top of an adolescent, whilst another was buried slightly twisted with his head face down. Isotope analysis indicated that none was locally born, and in three cases they might have come from Scandinavia or Scotland. We cannot tell why they died in this way, though they could have been slaves, hostages, or the victims of summary or judicial execution who could not be disposed of more publicly.[21] The lack of parallels elsewhere in Wales is problematic, but their unceremonious end makes them in some ways comparable with groups of late Anglo-Saxon execution burials, though these are not associated with settlements but are found in public locations on administrative boundaries, beside routeways, and outside towns.[22]

In recent years there has been an upsurge of interest in using a multidisciplinary approach, including archaeology, to cast a different light on our understanding of aspects of early medieval power and authority such as conflict, justice, and punishment. This also allows us to identify material evidence for administrative practice and so to begin to analyse the significance of associated sites and monuments, such as places of

[19] Mason, D. J. P. 2007, 43–56, pls 3–19; Colgrave and Mynors 1969, ii.2, 140–3.
[20] Loe 2003, 327–30; Holbrook and Thomas 2005, 50, 52.   [21] Redknap 2004a, 154–5; 2016, 161–3.
[22] Reynolds 2009, 240–7.

378 LIFE IN EARLY MEDIEVAL WALES

assembly, in their wider landscape settings.[23] Another aspect receiving renewed attention is the reordering of landscapes in the early Middle Ages through the establishment of boundaries and frontiers involving the construction of linear earthworks, routeways, and other infrastructure, and the nature of change over time.[24] Therefore this discussion will focus on aspects of early medieval power and authority where the archaeological record has a clear role to play. Firstly, to what extent is it now possible to identify evidence for assembly sites and other meeting places in early medieval Wales? How did these develop and change over time, and how far does this reflect patterns of increasing administrative complexity that were beginning to emerge from around the ninth century onwards? Secondly, I shall discuss some features of the changing relationship between Wales and England, principally the role and significance of Offa's and Wat's Dykes as part of an evolving frontier landscape. Finally, I shall consider the wider Scandinavian impact in different regions of Wales. A significant aspect of both is the extent to which the changing nature of cultural identities brought about by these interactions is visible in the archaeological record.

ASSEMBLY SITES AND OTHER MEETING PLACES

We can now identify several different types of early medieval meeting place. Firstly, there were power bases, the homes of rulers and their families where retinues, clients, war bands, and other guests gathered, where food render was collected, feasting took place, luxury goods were received and commissioned, and gifts exchanged. In the fifth to seventh centuries such bases were characterized by hillforts and related sites, and this is part of a wider phenomenon found across western and northern Britain and in some other parts of Europe at this time. Dinas Powys, for example, was one of a network of elite sites strategically located to facilitate control of their wider hinterlands—perhaps small kingdoms—in the fertile coastal lowlands between the Taff and the Thaw.[25] From the eighth century onwards, however, whilst some hillfort locations, such as Degannwy, remained strategic nodes in the landscape, there is a major shift away from hillforts as elite places of residence, and the power bases that replaced them become much more difficult to identify. The continuation of enclosed sites on fertile lowlands that functioned as estate centres, as indicated by Llanbedrgoch, seems likely, but the lack of parallels is problematic. As rulers attempted to spread their authority more widely, the picture also changes, with the need for a greater range of meeting places. In the late ninth and early tenth centuries Llangorse crannog—with its calculated reference to and reinvention of ancestral links with Ireland—was a

---

[23] Smith, K. P., and Reynolds 2013, 687–92; Carroll et al. 2019a; Reynolds 2019.

[24] For reference to the range of recent research, see Williams, Howard, and Delaney 2019, 1–12.

[25] Seaman and Sucharyna Thomas 2020.

seasonal residence of the rulers of Brycheiniog but was also located very near the monastery at Llan-gors, suggesting that the provision of hospitality was expected and demonstrating the close cooperation between secular and ecclesiastical power. Nor can it be coincidental that by the mid-eleventh century Rhuddlan, formerly the site of the English *burh* of *Cledemutha*, had become a major residence of Gruffudd ap Llywelyn of Gwynedd (Chapter 5).

The written sources also point to the sites of major churches as important meeting places. The presence of literate clergy to make records and relics on which oaths might be sworn facilitated dispute resolution and the donation of land to the Church, the resources of which would have fed attendees. The phraseology of charters and other documents also reflects the biblical learning of the clerics who composed them, and the witness lists note the men assembled to make the agreement. For example, the *surexit* memorandum in the Lichfield gospels records a dispute settlement made by a group of 'good men' and the witness list includes both the ecclesiastical household of Llandeilo Fawr and four laymen.[26] Similarly, a Llandaf charter dated to *c.*925 appears to show the settlement of a 'great dispute' between Bishop Libiau and King Tewdwr ab Elise of Brycheiniog that took place at Llan-gors monastery. The king had stolen the bishop's food rent but could not pay the agreed compensation, so, upon the intervention of the bishop of St Davids, he donated land instead. The witness list is headed by clerics, beginning with the two bishops, followed by laymen led by the king.[27]

Other communal sites of meeting and assembly in early medieval Wales were in the open air and, as a result, have proved more difficult to locate. There have, however, been major breakthroughs in identifying such sites, not only in Anglo-Saxon England but also in Scotland and Ireland, as well as in Scandinavia and Iceland, and these offer valuable comparative evidence potentially aiding recognition.[28] Place names and historical references, including antiquarian sources, have been used alongside topographical and archaeological research to pinpoint sites within their wider landscape contexts and to analyse spatial relationships and chronological change. In Wales, however, adopting these methods still presents a considerable challenge because of the limited written record and the comparative lack of detailed place-name research.

It is now thought that in later prehistory hillforts functioned as seasonal meeting places associated with food storage, as well as ritual activities indicated by shrines and depositional offerings. Thus they also had a ceremonial role, and this may have been combined with decision-making.[29] We have already seen that in Wales there is evidence

---

[26] Jenkins and Owen 1984. [27] Evans, J. G., and Rhys 1893, 237b; Davies, W. 1979a, 124.

[28] E.g. Pantos and Semple 2004; Semple 2013, 63–107, 193–223; Semple and Sanmark 2013; Baker and Brookes 2015; O'Grady 2014; FitzPatrick 2004; Gleeson 2018.

[29] Bradley 2007, 247–52, 256.

380 LIFE IN EARLY MEDIEVAL WALES

for continuing or renewed activities associated with some hillforts in the later Roman period, particularly in the north. Examples include Dinorben and Pen-y-Corddyn Mawr, demonstrated by finds of coins, pottery, and other artefacts, with some indications of ritual activity and continuing use into the post-Roman period. There are hints also, as at Dinas Emrys, that not all hillforts with evidence of early medieval occupation were simply the homes and power bases of the ruling elite. Instead, it may be suggested that some hillforts remained important markers in the landscape and symbols of enduring regional and communal identities.

In addition, however, we are now beginning to identify other places of open-air communal meeting and assembly that, from around the ninth century onwards, may have functioned at regional and local levels in connection with the settlement of disputes, military musters, royal inaugurations, and legislation. It should, however, be noted that the often-cited reference to an assembly convened by Hywel Dda at Whitland in Dyfed to reform the laws of Wales appears to be a later medieval construct.[30]

To date the most convincing example of an assembly and perhaps a royal inauguration site to have been identified in Wales is marked by the Pillar of Eliseg, which was once a cross (Fig. 12.1). The monument is sited strategically in the narrow valley of the Nant Eglwyseg on an important land route linking the east–west corridor of the Dee with the Vale of Clwyd and the coastal plain to the north.[31] Excavation has demonstrated that it stands on top of an impressive, multiphase, Early Bronze Age burial cairn, thereby dominating the valley, but also making a symbolic connection with a broader mythical and heroic past indicated, for example, in the verses of *Englynion y Beddau* ('Stanzas of the Graves') (Chapter 2).[32] The incomplete Latin inscription once visible on the shaft informs us that the cross was set up at the instigation of Concenn (Cyngen, d.854), the last early medieval ruler of Powys and the great-grandson of Eliseg. It was intended to be read out loud and incorporates legal terminology, as well as phraseology showing a strong link between secular and ecclesiastical authority. However, it is also a piece of royal propaganda conveying a series of messages about Concenn, his family, and, by implication, their right to rule at a time when Powys was under increasing external threat. Beginning with a genealogy establishing the link between Concenn and his great-grandfather, the inscription then tells us that the cross was erected to commemorate Eliseg and extols his military success against the English. Next it appears to trace the purported origins of the kingdom back to the Roman past—perhaps in an attempt to accrue imperial prestige in a manner comparable

---

[30] Pryce 1986.

[31] For analysis of its location and landscape context, see Murrieta-Flores and Williams 2017.

[32] Edwards et al. 2015; Jones, T. 1967.

Fig. 12.1. The Pillar of Eliseg (photograph: the author).

with Carolingian rulers and Offa—before proclaiming God's blessing on Concenn, his household, and the kingdom of Powys in perpetuity.[33]

Comparison with assembly sites elsewhere is instructive. As a matter of convenience, most, including those associated with hundreds and wapentakes in late Saxon England, were located close to routeways. A key feature of some was the reuse of prehistoric monuments, such as cairns and barrows, or their incorporation into wider landscapes of early medieval power, demonstrating their reinvention to serve new ends. In other instances natural or purpose-built mounds were also used.[34] In the case of the Pillar of Eliseg, the Early Bronze Age cairn may have functioned as a performative focus, and the glacial spur on which it stands is part of a natural amphitheatre, making the location suitable for ceremonies and gatherings. Crosses in England and carved stones in Scotland likewise marked places of assembly and judicial activity.[35] On the Pillar of Eliseg the royal genealogy—and indeed the whole inscription—could

---

[33] Edwards 2009c; 2013, Llandysilio yn Iâl 1, no. D3; Jones, O. W. 2009.

[34] Baker and Brookes 2015, 13–15; Skinner and Semple 2016. On Scotland, see O'Grady 2014.

[35] Semple 2013, 214, 218–19; Baker and Brookes 2015, 15; see also, for Cleulow cross, Wincle, Cheshire, Kirton 2015. For Scotland, e.g. Mortlach, Banffshire, O'Grady 2014, 120; for Monreith cross, Wigton, Allen and Anderson 1903, iii, 482, 485–6.

382 LIFE IN EARLY MEDIEVAL WALES

have been recited as part of a royal inauguration ceremony, as in the case of Alexander III of Scotland when he was proclaimed king at Scone in 1249.[36] The valley of the Nant Eglwyseg is large enough for temporary camps and associated activities, such as feasting and fairs, but their ephemeral nature would not necessarily have left any trace in the archaeological record.[37] The locality would have provided plentiful resources—fertile lowland, woodland, and upland pasture suitable for hunting, and the river for fish.[38] The wider landscape is also significant. The nearby Cistercian abbey of Valle Crucis may be on the site of an earlier church foundation implied by the name Llanegwestl. This would have provided a Christian focus and from here the dramatic hillfort of Dinas Brân is visible towering over the Dee, its prominence indicative of a continuing symbolic role as a marker of wider territorial identity.[39]

The locations of other crosses may provide important clues in identifying further sites. In the border territory of Tegeingl, Domesday Book records Atiscros as the name of an English hundred. In the sixteenth century the cross, which marked the hundred meeting place, still stood not far from the west bank of the Dee estuary.[40] Also in Tegeingl is the tenth-century cross known as *Maen Achwyfan* ('Cwyfan's Stone'),[41] which stands in a field near a crossroads with several prehistoric barrows nearby. Geophysics has shown that it may be in the centre of a curvilinear enclosure approached by a double-ditched trackway. Tegeingl was an area of Viking settlement and it is therefore intriguing that the cross (Fig. 12.2) is carved with heroic iconography derived from Norse mythology, including an armed warrior, scenes that would have been well suited to a secular assembly location.[42] The later tenth- or early eleventh-century cross at Carew, Pembrokeshire, is also a good candidate. This imposing monument (now in the grounds of the castle), was originally sited with reference to the earlier promontory fort, thereby making a symbolic link with the past as well as providing a large gathering space.[43]

Other potential assembly sites and meeting places marked by prehistoric cairns and barrows, or natural or artificial mounds, doubtless existed but are currently almost impossible to identify. For example, the term *gorsedd*, sometimes found in place names, refers to a 'mound', 'barrow', 'court' or 'over-seat'. The story *Pwyll Pendefig Dyfed* in the Mabinogi includes a mythical tale of place relating to *Gorsedd Arberth*. From there Pwyll first sees his future wife, Rhiannon, riding by on a magical horse. Her name is derived from Rigantona, meaning a great or divine queen, identifiable as a Celtic

---

[36] Edwards 2009c, 168–9. On Scone, see also O'Grady 2018, 139–43.

[37] For sites in England with artefacts and other evidence, see Baker and Brookes 2015, 9.

[38] Murietta-Flores and Williams 2017, 93. On the connection between Irish assembly sites and deer hunting, see FitzPatrick 2012, 116–17.

[39] Edwards et al. 2015, 52; Murrieta-Flores and Williams 2017, 21–2; Semple 2013, 204.

[40] Edwards 2013, Flint 1, no. F4, 470; Owen and Gruffydd 2017, 57.

[41] This refers to the Hiberno-Scandinavian saint to whom the church at Dyserth is dedicated.

[42] Edwards 2013, Whitford 2, no, F12; Griffiths 2006.   [43] Edwards 2007a, no. P9.

Fig. 12.2. *Maen Achwyfan*, with the figure of an armed warrior on the cross-shaft (Crown copyright: Royal Commission on the Ancient and Historical Monuments of Wales.

goddess. It is therefore possible that *Gorsedd Arberth* was perceived as a place of royal inauguration in the manner of Tara in Ireland but, assuming it existed, it has proved another matter to locate it on the ground.[44] It is also possible that in the earlier part of the period Bronze Age cairns and barrows associated with later 'undeveloped'

---

[44] Charles-Edwards 2004, 96–8; Davies, S. 2007, 8–11, 230.

384 LIFE IN EARLY MEDIEVAL WALES

cemeteries could have acted as foci for community meeting places, as suggested in Anglo-Saxon England.[45] Tan Dderwen, Denbighshire, is a good candidate (Fig. 9.4). Here the site of a Bronze Age ring ditch was the later focus of an early medieval cemetery, with many of the graves set in small square-ditched enclosures. What is unusual, however, is that the ring ditch was also enclosed within a larger rectilinear ditched enclosure, with causeways giving access to the monument, and, though there is no dating evidence, it has been plausibly interpreted as a place of assembly.[46] The transformation of an assembly mound into a Christian context is also evident in a miracle in Rhygyfarch's *Life* of St David: the saint addresses a synod at Llanddewibrefi from a hill that rises up out of the ground, reflecting the natural topography of the site.[47]

Other place names may also provide a clue: for example, the earliest Welsh name for the Great Orme is *Cyngreawdr Fynydd* ('Hill of the Assembly'). This dramatic promontory has a rich archaeological landscape including Bronze Age copper mines and Pen-Dinas hillfort, but there is also a small church dedicated to St Tudno close to where early eleventh-century coins were found.[48] *Dadl* is another relevant place-name element, meaning a 'case' or 'dispute', and by analogy an 'assembly site'. There is, for instance, tantalizing evidence associated with the site of *Croes y Ddadl* on Kenfig burrows, in the Vale of Glamorgan. This is first mentioned in 1397, but the base of the cross survived well into the twentieth century, standing very close to a large, oval, bivallate enclosure of unknown date.[49]

In some other instances it may be possible to trace polyfocal landscapes of meeting and assembly that evolved over time. For example, multidisciplinary analysis of the medieval and earlier landscape of Bayvil in the *cantref* of Cemais in north Pembrokeshire revealed Crugiau Cemais as an early focus (Fig. 12.3).[50] The site originated as a group of Early Bronze Age barrows clustered on two prominent hillocks with extensive views over the surrounding countryside. This became the focus of a likely hillfort and an Iron Age enclosed settlement, within which is a square-ditched burial enclosure, signalling reuse in the post-Roman period.[51] However, it has been suggested that the increasing power of the Church meant that Crugiau Cemais was gradually eclipsed as a place of assembly and burial and these moved elsewhere. Two ogham- and Latin-inscribed stones from the major church at Nevern (Nanhyfer), dedicated to St Brynach, also point to the origins of that site as a place of fifth- or sixth-century burial.[52] Another was Caer Bayvil, similarly a reused earlier enclosure known as Caereglismore ('Fort of the Great Church')—referring to Nevern—and the place name, Llwyn Dyn Waeth

---

[45] Williams, Howard 2004; Semple 2013, 89–94.   [46] Brassil et al. 1991, 50–62, 86–7.

[47] Sharpe and Davies 2007, ch. 52.

[48] Richards 1975, 59; Williams, R. A., and Le Carlier de Veslud 2019; Archwilio, GAT prn 637, 6961; Boon, 1986b, 11–12, 27.

[49] Charles-Edwards 2004, 101–4; Coflein NPRN 307293, 405397; see also Edwards and Lane 1988, 85.

[50] Comeau 2014.   [51] Murphy and Murphy 2015.   [52] Edwards 2007a, nos P70–1.

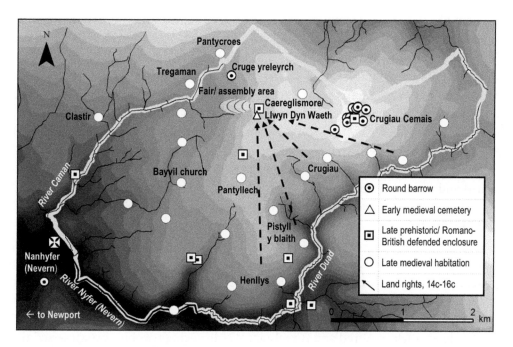

Fig. 12.3. The polyfocal landscape of Bayvil in the *cantref* of Cemais (© Rhiannon Comeau).

('Grove of Acclamation'), is indicative of an assembly place nearby. Standing stones marking a crossroads on a 'sarn' (track) connecting Nevern with Caer Bayvil suggest a further focus, since this was the site of a midsummer fair first noted in 1348 but likely earlier associated with the feast of the translation of St Brynach. The ogham inscriptions identify the locality as an area of post-Roman Irish settlement and it is therefore significant that similar evolving polyfocal landscapes of assembly and meeting are far more clearly evidenced in Ireland as at Teltown, Co. Meath.[53]

More research to identify assembly sites and other meeting places is clearly needed. However, the limited evidence to date points to increasing administrative complexity over time. Whilst some hillforts and related sites emerged as the post-Roman power bases of the rulers of small territories, others may have endured or been reinvented as places of regional communal identity. In time the increasing authority of the Church created a further institution of power aligned with rulers and their kin. As some kingdoms expanded, enveloping smaller entities, and rulers ranged more widely, there was a need to create systems of administration that facilitated the maintenance of power and the more systematic gathering of food render and other resources, and, from around the ninth century onwards, sites such as the Pillar of Eliseg signal a move towards such increasing complexity.

[53] Comeau 2014; Gleeson 2017; 2018.

386 LIFE IN EARLY MEDIEVAL WALES

There has been considerable debate about the origins of the administrative system of *cantrefi*, and their probably subsequent division into commotes. Both terms are first seen in twelfth-century sources,[54] but some of their boundaries may be older since they reflect the natural topography, often following river courses.[55] Locations where *cantrefi* boundaries met also acted as assembly places. For example, Garn Turne is a rocky summit with a Neolithic chambered tomb at the point where Cemais, Pebidiog (Dewisland), and Daugleddau met, and, although it is only first mentioned in 1326, it could be considerably older.[56] Should we see *cantrefi* as emerging from the ninth century onwards alongside assembly sites as some smaller kingdoms were subsumed and rulers became more mobile?[57] Or was the system one of imposition by a powerful ruler as a further step on the road to statehood, possibly during the reign of Gruffudd ap Llywelyn of Gwynedd who, by the 1050s, exercised authority throughout Wales?[58] Or were *cantrefi* only beginning to emerge in the late eleventh century, perhaps as a response to Norman invasion? Comparisons with the system of late Saxon hundreds with their meeting places may be instructive here, since influence is evident in the frontier territory of Tegeingl and assembly mounds were also a feature of Hiberno-Scandinavian communities east of the Dee.[59] As *subreguli* who submitted to English kings such as Alfred and Æthelstan, Welsh rulers probably also witnessed the late Saxon administrative system, with its network of assembly sites and meeting places, at first hand. Therefore, *cantrefi* were almost certainly established before the Norman invasion. Although they are mentioned for the first time in twelfth-century sources, which could point to the intervention of Gruffudd ap Llywelyn, this may only have been the final step in the piecemeal evolution of an administrative system with origins in the tenth century or even earlier.

Some wider comparisons can also be made with England, where Andrew Reynolds has drawn attention to the changing spatial configuration of power and increasing social complexity over the course of the early Middle Ages, likewise suggesting three main phases of development. In the sixth century power was centred on small-scale polities and localities such as the royal vills of Yeavering or Rendlesham. However, from the seventh century onwards, alongside kingdom expansion, the evidence suggests the development of dispersed administrative frameworks that also embraced minsters, a growing economy, and grand infrastructure projects, such as the construction of Offa's and Wat's Dykes defining the Mercian frontier. Finally, from the tenth century onwards, though they were built on earlier foundations,

---

[54] *Cantref* literally means a unit of 'a hundred townships'; *Geiriadur Prifysgol Cymru*. For discussion of these terms in the sources, see Stokes 2004, 83–94.

[55] Seaman 2019b, 329–31.

[56] SM 9793 2725; Charles 1992, ii, 396; Comeau 2020, 118–21, 123. The site is still marked on the road by a modern boundary stone.

[57] Jones, R. 1998.   [58] Charles-Edwards 2013, 568–9.

[59] On the place name Thingwall, see Harding et al. 2015, 6, 44, 56.

POWER AND AUTHORITY 387

we can see both large-scale political formations and increasing territorial and administrative complexity.[60]

BUILDING BORDERS AND FRONTIERS: CHANGING RELATIONS WITH ANGLO-SAXON ENGLAND

The construction of Offa's and Wat's Dykes marked a watershed in the changing relationship between first Mercia, then England, and the kingdoms of Wales. Before their construction Wales was part of a greater Britain, the memory of which, in the early ninth-century *Historia Brittonum*, was still clear. Indeed, the idea of the Welsh as Britons and of their being the rightful heirs of the Britons continued long after this.[61] Nevertheless, by the end of the ninth century when Asser was writing, the reality had changed. The dykes had sliced through the landscape from north to south, helping to define a wider frontier region between England and Wales. Offa's Dyke is the largest earthwork in Britain, with some very impressive surviving stretches (Fig. 12.4), and parts of Wat's Dyke are also well preserved. There nevertheless remain significant unresolved questions relating to their dating, extent, and purpose, as well as regarding their longer-term impact in terms of cross-border interactions and the emerging cultural identity of the Welsh Marches.

Asser's *Life of King Alfred*, written in 893, states that Offa 'ordered a great dyke to be built between Wales and Mercia from sea to sea' (*vallum magnum inter Britanniam atque Merciam de mari usque ad mare fieri imperavit*).[62] This is not only the earliest mention of the dyke but also the earliest reference to *Britannia* in the narrower sense of Wales.[63] There seems little reason to question Asser's attribution to Offa, king of Mercia (757–96), since he was writing only around a century later. It is also supported to some extent by place names, though the earliest known record, *Offedich*, near Womaston, Radnorshire, is only in 1184.[64] As yet clear scientific dating is lacking. What archaeological evidence there is does, however, point to a post-Roman date.[65]

---

[60] Reynolds 2019, 452–4.   [61] Williams, Glanmor 1979, 73.

[62] Stevenson 1959, 12, ch. 14. The southern section of the dyke across the Beachley peninsula is mentioned in an Anglo-Saxon charter of 956, but not specifically linked with Offa; Sawyer 1968, no. S 1555. For discussion of Offa's Dyke in later sources, see Williams, A. 2009, 32–6.

[63] Pryce 2001a, 777.   [64] Noble 1983, 40.

[65] The only radiocarbon dates are from a salvage excavation near Chirk. These (cal. AD 880–1020 (SUERC-51224); cal. AD 540–660 (SUERC-51225); cal. AD 470–660 (SUERC-51225); cal. AD 430–650 (SUERC-51230)) were from redeposited material at the base of the bank and only provide a date after which it was constructed. As three dates are consistent, the first may be aberrant; Grant and Jones 2014. Optically stimulated luminescence (OSL) and radiocarbon dates are forthcoming from an excavation at Chirk Castle; Belford 2019, 86–90. Roman ceramics etc. were found in the dyke bank at Ffrith, Flintshire, but as there is a Roman settlement beneath, they are residual, as Fox, C. 1955, 40–4, originally argued, supporting a post-Roman date. See also Hill and Worthington 2003, 83–5; Ray and Bapty 2016, 19.

388   LIFE IN EARLY MEDIEVAL WALES

Fig. 12.4. Offa's Dyke from the air between Rhosllanerchrugog and Coedpoeth near Wrexham (Crown copyright: Royal Commission on the Ancient and Historical Monuments of Wales).

Nor does this preclude the possibility that some sections of the dyke could have a more complex construction history, but this can only be investigated by a systematic programme of scientific dating on different parts of the monument.[66]

---

[66] For how scientific dating has impacted on unravelling the construction history of the Danevirke, north Germany, see Dobat 2008.

The problems associated with establishing a more complete understanding of the dating are compounded by continuing debate about the extent of the dyke (Fig. 12.5). During the 1920s and 1930s Cyril Fox surveyed the line of surviving earthworks from near Treuddyn in the north to Sedbury cliffs, which overlook the Severn estuary, in the south, though he also noted significant gaps where no archaeological remains were visible. More specifically, he was persuaded that the lengthy gap north of Treuddyn was partially filled by a smaller earthwork, the Whitford Dyke, separating the hinterland west of the Dee from the Vale of Clwyd, and the line of this indicated that Offa's Dyke had originally ended at the coast in the vicinity of Prestatyn. Hence, in line with Asser, he argued that it stretched from sea to sea.[67] From the 1970s onwards aerial photography and work by David Hill and Margaret Worthington, including further survey and a large number of sections across the dyke, filled in some of the smaller gaps and confirmed a more-or-less unbroken line between north of Treuddyn and Rushock Hill over 100 kilometres to the south in Herefordshire, apart from an 8-kilometre stretch along the Severn between Trederwen and Buttington, an important fording point on the river. The major gap south of Rushock Hill and along the Wye past Hereford led them to argue that the southern part running high above the east bank from Redbrook, Gloucestershire, down to the Sedbury cliffs was not associated with Offa's Dyke.[68] However, more recent research by Keith Ray and Ian Bapty has rehabilitated Fox's original view that the southern part is of a similar build to those in the central and northern sections. Whilst the major gap along the Wye remains a real one, likely stretches have been located between Rushock Hill and the river.[69] In the north, however, there are still no confirmed stretches beyond Treuddyn,[70] and further survey and excavation work on the Whitford Dyke, which remains undated, has revealed that, although it is probably a coherent earthwork, it appears much slighter with a shallow ditch on either side.[71] Therefore it is not part of Offa's Dyke.

In order to consider the functions of the dyke and set it in a wider historical context, it is necessary to understand its construction and relationship to the topography. Survey and excavation have demonstrated a number of distinctive features, but there is likewise quite a lot of variation to suit local topographical conditions. The overall similarities between different parts of the dyke, which is characterized by a substantial bank with a western ditch, demonstrate a great deal of planning and an understanding of how to use the often challenging upland terrain to the best advantage, pointing to an overseer with considerable engineering skill. It is very carefully placed in the landscape to allow surveillance from it but also to inhibit movement eastwards. Moreover, it is highly visible from the west and, though some stretches are more

[67] Fox. C. 1955.   [68] Hill 2000; Hill and Worthington 2003, 47–87.

[69] Ray and Bapty 2016, 10–92, discuss the line of the dyke and critique earlier research.

[70] On recent fieldwork examining a possible line reaching the coast west of Gronant, see Ray et al. 2021, 61–77.

[71] Jones, N. W. et al. 2013a; Jones, N. W. 2015.

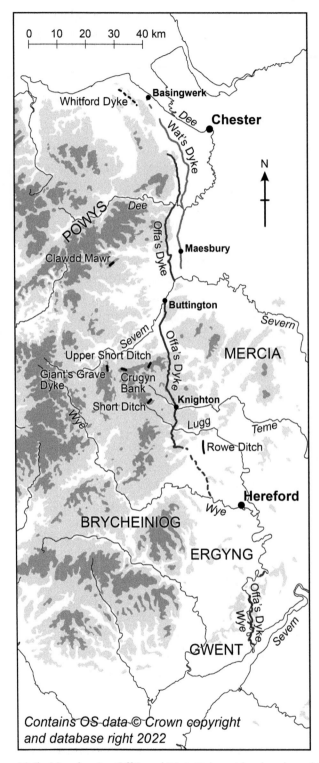

Fig. 12.5. Map showing Offa's and Wat's Dykes with other short dykes.

dramatic than others, it can present a formidable barrier. For most of its length the dyke hugs the high ground, running along the crest or below it along the western slopes. But it also descends often steep gradients to traverse river valleys, creating barriers to movement along them as, for example, the stretch from Llanfair Hill southwards to cross the Teme at Knighton. Here and at Dudston, Chirbury, it is possible to detect short sections on slightly different alignments, suggesting the complex adjustments required to achieve the overall result. Nevertheless, it has proved exceptionally difficult to distinguish any original gateways, with the possible exception of that at Bwlch, Discoed, west of Presteigne.[72]

Short sections and variations in construction also indicate that the dyke was built by different gangs of workers. The bank, though frequently denuded, can still be more than 3.5 metres tall, and the impression of height is sometimes increased by scarping the slope on the crest of which the bank is located. It is made up of the material dug from the ditch, though quarry scoops have also occasionally been found. The base was sometimes marked out by a row or layer of boulders or turves, and the façades might be strengthened with turves or drystone walling, but there are no traces of any superstructure along the top of the bank. The adjacent western ditch, where excavated, is often around 5 metres wide and at least 2 metres deep, usually with a V- or U-shaped profile. In one case an 'ankle-breaker' slot was found in the bottom to make crossing more difficult, and sometimes there is a counterscarp bank beyond.[73]

To date, however, it has proved impossible to identify any associated structures, though temporary camps must have existed, and the possible reuse of some hillforts has been mooted. There has also been speculation about the use of lookout posts and beacons as part of a process of surveillance. This lack of infrastructure contrasts sharply with Hadrian's Wall and the Antonine Wall, with which Offa's Dyke has sometimes been compared, raising questions about the extent to which it was manned, though Mercian patrols on horseback, perhaps organized by a reeve, would have been an appropriate solution to the distances involved and the often rugged terrain.[74]

Before discussing some of the wider issues concerning Offa's Dyke, Wat's Dyke also requires consideration, since the two need to be examined together. Unlike the former, Wat's Dyke is not named after any known historic figure and is only first mentioned by name in the fifteenth century. Place names also indicate that it has often been confused with Offa's Dyke.[75] This is not surprising, as much of the line of the dyke runs parallel but some kilometres to the east of Offa's Dyke along the western edge of the lowlands. However, it then continues northwards, reaching the sea at Basingwerk on the Dee estuary, thereby appearing to conform to Asser's statement.

---

[72] Ray and Bapty 2016, 122–63, 192–208, 228–34.   [73] Ibid., 164–222; Belford 2019, 88.

[74] Ray and Bapty 2016, 225–7, 244–50; Williams, A. 2009, 47–9; Hill and Worthington 2003, 99, 121, 127; Noble 1983, 47.

[75] Fox, C. 1955, 225–7; Owen and Gruffydd 2017, 50.

Fox, with further work, including many small excavations by Hill and Worthington, traced much of the line southwards as far as the Morda Brook at Maesbury, Shropshire, a distance of 61 kilometres, though in built-up areas little now survives.[76] There are also indications that the dyke was sited with reference to strategic points, including Old Oswestry hillfort. Maesbury was a significant place in Mercian history since here Oswald of Northumbria had been killed by Penda of Mercia in the Battle of *Maserfelth* in 642, suggesting that its location was close to a contested border.[77] Secondly, excavation of a 40-metre stretch of the dyke at Gobowen has gone a considerable way to clarify the dating of the dyke. At this point, which is fairly typical, it consisted of part of a marking-out bank that preceded the construction of a V-profile western ditch up to 8 metres wide and 2.7 metres deep with an 'ankle-breaker' slot in the bottom and a turf-covered gravel bank over 5 metres wide that rested on a cobble foundation. There were no signs of later refurbishment. Optically stimulated luminescence (OSL) dates from the base of the ditch point to construction of the dyke at the end of the eighth century or during the first half of the ninth. It seems therefore to have been built very soon after Offa's Dyke and it has been argued that this is most likely to have taken place during the reign of Coenwulf of Mercia (*c*.798–821),[78] whose death at Basingwerk—probably a fortification marking the end of the dyke—is noted in a twelfth-century source.[79]

The construction of both dykes would have been an enormous undertaking, with each requiring a very large workforce, as well as the means to organize it. During the reigns of Æthelbald and Offa military and other obligations, including fortress building, become evident, signalling an increase in royal power and the administrative control necessary for undertaking enterprises of this kind.[80] We can also learn something of Offa's military ambitions against the Britons. The Harleian Chronicle records a battle at Hereford in 760 and raids in 778 and 784, whilst the inscription on the Pillar of Eliseg implies the recovery of land from the English by force.[81] Pressure continued under Coenwulf, including attacks penetrating far into north Wales, on Snowdonia and Rhufoniog in 816, and the destruction of Degannwy in 822 with Powys being brought under English control.[82] It is against this background that the functions of the dykes need to be viewed, and the likely terminal of Offa's Dyke near Treuddyn may have been initially to facilitate movement west and the annexation of territory along the north Wales coast, a strategy subsequently modified by the construction of Wat's Dyke, which allowed Mercian domination of the west bank of the

[76] Fox, C. 1955, 227–53; Worthington Hill 2019, 58–69.   [77] Stancliffe 1995.

[78] Hayes and Malim 2008. A mid-Saxon loom weight was also found in the base of the ditch at Mynydd Isa, Flintshire.

[79] Lawson 2004. The Welsh form of Basingwerk is Dinas Basing 'Fortification of Basa', an Old English personal name; Owen and Gruffydd 2017, 61.

[80] Williams, Gareth 2005.   [81] Morris 1980, 47, 88; Edwards 2013, 326, 329–30.

[82] Morris 1980, 48, 89.

Dee, protecting the lowlands of Cheshire to the east and strengthening control of the land between the dykes further south. The western ditch, positioning, scale, and visibility of Offa's Dyke make it plain that Fox's view of an agreed boundary cannot be sustained.[83] Instead, the construction of both dykes was intended as one of a range of actions aimed at expanding a Mercian hegemony. Their visual effect combined with surveillance doubtless had a psychological as well as a physical impact, breaking apart communities that created a lasting memory of losing a sense of place as well as emphasizing Mercian authority. The barriers formed not only deterred Welsh raiding and other aggression but also other means of social and economic interaction with communities to the east. However, the problems with identifying gateways make it more difficult to assess mechanisms, such as tolls, that may have existed to regulate crossings and the movement of goods.[84]

David Hill argued that the line of Offa's Dyke from near Treuddyn to Rushock Hill was marking a frontier between Mercia and Powys, though it would also have included the region to the south between the Severn and Wye.[85] The border between the former territories of the *Wreocensætan* and the *Magonsætan*, which had been absorbed into Mercia, appears to have run east along the Severn where Offa's Dyke reaches the river at Trederwen, and the gap as far as Buttington may also indicate a significant boundary with land further west. Equally, the southern section seems to mark the frontier between Gwent and the southern part of the territory of the *Magonsætan* or the lands of the *Hwicce*, including much of Gloucestershire, which Offa had brought under Mercian control.[86] The gap in the dyke along the Wye with Hereford on its eastern bank corresponds with the region of Ergyng (Archenfield) to the west, which had originally been on both sides of the river, suggesting that this part of the frontier had a different status, a position still evident later in the period. The origins of Hereford are not well understood, but the earliest phase of activity, sealed by a substantial gravel bank which is the earliest phase of the late Saxon defences, dates to between the mid-eighth and mid-ninth centuries, broadly coinciding with the construction of the dykes.[87]

The significance of what are termed the 'short dykes' also needs consideration before examining the longer-term impact of Offa's and Wat's Dykes on the evolution of frontier communities. More than thirty have been identified, mainly west of Offa's Dyke in Montgomeryshire and Radnorshire, but there is also the Rowe Ditch to the

---

[83] Fox, C. 1955, 279–81. [84] Ray and Bapty 2016, 298–364. [85] Hill 2000, 203.

[86] Sims-Williams 1990a, xiv, 16–53. It has also been argued that Wansdyke, a comparable but undated linear earthwork, might mark a broadly contemporary frontier between Wessex and the expanding territory of Mercia; see Reynolds and Langlands 2006.

[87] According to Gerald of Wales and later tradition, Offa also had an estate at Sutton, where in 794 King Æthelbert of East Anglia was murdered and his head thrown into the Lugg, but no archaeological evidence has been found. Æthelbert was regarded as a saint and Hereford Cathedral is dedicated to him; Ray 2015, 212–15, 219–31; Whitelock 1979, [*s.a.*] 794; Brewer 1863, 420.

east in Herefordshire and a group on the fringes of the Glamorgan uplands, with one or two elsewhere.[88] These dykes, which often but not always consist of a bank and ditch, were characteristically constructed either across upland ridges or valley floors. Cyril Fox argued that those west and east of Offa's Dyke were slightly earlier than it and were part of more localized efforts to defend Mercian communities from Welsh raiding when the frontier was in flux.[89] The Glamorgan dykes which traverse ridgeway routes, thereby deterring or controlling access from the north, were similarly regarded as early medieval, since cross-carved stones and other sculpture were located nearby.[90] More recent work, including radiocarbon dates from underneath the banks of five dykes west of Offa's Dyke providing a *terminus post quem* after which each was built, has also tended to support an early medieval horizon for their construction.[91] The same applies to the very limited dating evidence from the Glamorgan dykes.[92] However, their wider context and roles remain enigmatic and continue to spark debate, with both defensive and boundary functions suggested,[93] or, indeed, a combination of the two. The Rowe ditch, for example, which runs for 3 kilometres blocking the Arrowe valley west of Leominster, is first mentioned in a charter in 958. It consists of a substantial bank and west-facing ditch that cut across the earlier prehistoric and Roman landscape. As a result it is seen as a significant but short-lived division in the frontier zone as English control moved westwards.[94]

What was the longer-term impact of Offa's and Wat's Dykes on the evolution of the frontier landscape? To what extent did the lines of the dykes become fossilized into boundaries and how far is it possible to identify changing cultural identities as a result? More work is needed, but if we begin to compare material and other evidence from different parts of the wider frontier zone west and east of Offa's and Wat's Dykes, some interesting points emerge. In the north, the foundation of the *burh* of *Cledemutha* at Rhuddlan by Edward the Elder in 921 (Chapter 5) may now be viewed as a more permanent step in the movement of English control westwards along the coast. This should be seen in the context of both earlier Mercian attacks and the re-establishment of English authority in Chester and on Wirral, areas of significant Hiberno-Scandinavian settlement. This move was not, however, permanent, indicating the inherent insecurity of this frontier zone. Rhuddlan was back in Welsh hands for much of the first half of

---

[88] Hankinson and Caseldine 2006, illus. 1. [89] Fox, C. 1955, 164–8.

[90] RCAHMW 1976b, 2–11.

[91] The dated dykes are Giant's Grave: cal. AD 340–530 (Beta 186676); Short Ditch: cal. AD 400–540 (Beta 290094)—under bank, cal. AD 430–620 (Beta 290093)—edge of bank, cal. AD 410–590 (Beta 223798); Clawdd Mawr: cal. AD 420–610 (Beta 290092), cal. AD 630–710 (Beta 211075); Upper Short Ditch: cal. AD 540–660 (Beta 212488), cal. AD 660–780 (Beta 290095); Crugyn Bank: cal. AD 610–90 (Beta 290091), cal. AD 650–780 (Beta 212487); Hankinson and Caseldine 2006, 260; Caseldine 2011, 136.

[92] Lewis 2006.

[93] For a defensive function against raids, see Grigg 2018, 120–5. On boundaries, see Hankinson and Caseldine 2006, 268–9.

[94] White 2003, 43–7; Ray 2015, 209–10.

the eleventh century, becoming the principal seat of Gruffudd ap Llywelyn, who also held lands east of the Dee in Exestan hundred. In 1063 Harold Godwinson attacked Rhuddlan, forcing Gruffudd to flee. His subsequent murder by a rival meant that, on the eve of the Norman Conquest, Tegeingl was again under English control.[95] The creation of the hundred of Atiscros west of the Dee with its own meeting place signals the intention of exercising English law and authority, but it was not divided into hides in the English manner. Indeed, English place names in the wider area of Tegeingl—Englefield in English—between the Dee and the Clwyd are confined to the west bank of the former, the coastal strip, and the adjacent hill slopes.[96] Nonetheless, the range of tenth- and eleventh-century artefacts from this area suggests a mixed cultural identity, and the slightly larger number of single coins indicates increased economic exchange (Fig. 7.8). A notable stray find from further west is the Trewhiddle-style gold ring found on Llysfaen Common between the Conwy and the Clwyd. Inscribed with the name Alhstan, possibly the bishop of Sherbourne (824–67), it might reflect the custom of ring-giving by the powerful to their clients.[97]

To the south the east–west corridor of the Dee into the Vale of Llangollen remained an important access point westwards from the Cheshire plain protected by both Offa's and Wat's Dykes, from which much of the landscape of this part of the frontier zone could be surveyed.[98] The inscription on the earlier ninth-century Pillar of Eliseg, which is broadly contemporary with Wat's Dyke, refers to military success against the English in the time of Offa. English cultural influence in this frontier zone west of the dykes is harder to detect, but the round cross-shaft is of Anglo-Saxon type. Later, a tenth- or eleventh-century cross-shaft further west at Corwen shows similar influence but also has an otherwise unparalleled runic inscription, a personal name, that may be either English or Scandinavian.[99]

South of the Dee, Wat's Dyke appears to take on the role of a more permanent administrative boundary. Domesday Book entries for Shropshire indicate that land east of Wat's Dyke was divided into hides, and it is surely no coincidence that the hundred of the *Mersete* at Maesbury near its terminus refers to 'the people on the boundary'. Nevertheless, identities east of the dyke were clearly mixed. Details in the entries for this hundred show that *Walenses* ('Welshmen') were a majority of the free population, but the administrative superstructure was English, with English villeins confined to five manors, three of which were mixed.[100] Therefore, *Mersete* hundred was still substantially Welsh-speaking, and more generally the survival of

[95] Williams, A., and Martin 2002, 717; Davies, M. 2002, 229–36, 239–40.

[96] Williams, A., and Martin 2002, 737; Lewis 2007, 137; Owen 1994, xxxii.

[97] V&A, no. 627–1871.

[98] Murrieta-Flores and Williams 2017. Vantage points offering surveillance from the Welsh side are also suggested.

[99] Edwards 2013, nos D3, MR7.   [100] Lewis 2007, 134–6.

pre-English river names across Shropshire also suggests this was so amongst the farming population more widely, with English settlement names in *tún* representing the speech of Mercian, or later English, administrators.[101] At the same time finds of early medieval metalwork recorded by the Portable Antiquities Scheme in Shropshire, such as strap-ends and harness fittings of late Saxon type, are becoming more common, particularly in the east of the county, but are only occasionally found west of Wat's Dyke, suggesting that it remained not just an administrative boundary but also a barrier to trade and other transactions, though the extent of the movement of stock and other raw materials remains impossible to gauge.

In this area ecclesiastical sites with stone sculpture are also rare on both sides of the dykes, suggesting limited patronage and resources. To the west, the ninth- or early tenth-century cross-slab at Llanrhaeadr-ym-Mochnant in the Tanat valley shows no sign of Anglo-Saxon influence, but subsequently an inscription was incised across the centre of the cross-head, perhaps obliterating an earlier one. It reads + *Cocom filiu Edestan*, '(The cross of) Cocom son of Edestan'. Cocom seems to be a Welsh name, but Edestan is the Old English Æthelstan, indicative of a mixed identity which may imply Anglo-Saxon penetration into this part of Powys and intermarriage amongst frontier communities. Further south again, close to where Offa's Dyke reaches the Severn, is Llandrinio. This mother church is clearly in a border location *west* of the Severn but *east* of Offa's Dyke. The *llan* name and dedication to St Trinio show links further west, but the ninth- or early tenth-century sculpture fragments demonstrate more mixed affinities. One has fret and interlace ornament but the other has a curlicue characteristic of Anglo-Saxon plant-scroll comparable with a Mercian cross-shaft at Wroxeter.[102]

South of the crossing point at Buttington, Offa's Dyke re-emerges to the east of the Severn, and together the dyke and river form a narrow frontier corridor with the ford of Rhydwhyman, a long-term strategic marker in the landscape, also providing access westwards. The dyke then heads south-east across the lowlands of the Vale of Montgomery, and here its fossilization as a boundary might be indicated as, unusually, the modern Welsh border still follows this line. South again, the dyke climbs into the uplands, which must always have presented a physical barrier, making east–west communication difficult except in valley crossings such as Knighton.[103]

Although no evidence of Offa's Dyke has been found along the course of the Wye, by the end of the eighth century the river formed a significant boundary. The existence of the British kingdom of Ergyng, which had originally spanned both sides of the river, is indicated by early kings named in Llandaf charters relating to churches on the southern side between the Wye and the Monnow. However, after the mid-ninth century there are no longer charters from the northern half of this area, suggesting

[101] Parsons 2013b, 120–1.   [102] Edwards 2013, nos D7, MT2–3.   [103] Ray and Bapty 2016, 39–47.

that subsequently it was no longer under Welsh control.[104] Indeed, tensions were inherent in this frontier zone, as the late Saxon fortifications at Hereford imply.[105] Asser tells us that during the 880s King Elise ap Tewdwr of Brycheiniog had submitted to King Alfred to escape Mercian tyranny. Æthelflæd of Mercia's attack in June 916 on *Brecenanmere*, the crannog at Llangorse, capturing the king of Brycheiniog's wife and over thirty others, had probably been sparked by the murder of Abbot Egbert three days earlier.[106] On the other hand, in 914 Edward the Elder paid forty pounds to ransom Bishop Cyfeiliog of Archenfield (Ergyng), a man with a Welsh name, who had been captured by Vikings.[107] Stock raiding was a further problem but, as the *Ordinance concerning the Dunsæte* makes clear, there were also agreed mechanisms for conflict resolution and compensation between English and Welsh on either side of the river.[108] Later in Domesday Book Archenfield, which had been laid waste by Gruffudd ap Llywelyn of Gwynedd when he sacked Hereford in 1055, was neither a hundred nor hidated, with Welshmen still following their own customs including continuing to make payments in food renders such as honey.[109] Archaeologically, however, there is little evidence of cultural identity. Finds of late Saxon metalwork recorded by the Portable Antiquities Scheme in Herefordshire are less frequent south and west of the Wye, but an ecclesiastical bell of Celtic type is known from Marden.[110] Nevertheless, in contrast to Anglo-Saxon sculpture in the north and east of the county, notably the cross-shaft at Acton Beauchamp, monuments south of the Wye are more similar to those further west, and inscriptions at Clodock and Llanveynoe have Welsh personal names.[111]

The Wye, still navigable north of Hereford in the early Middle Ages, flows south into Gwent, where Offa's Dyke recommences on the eastern side, overlooking it from the ridge above, before descending and crossing the Beachley peninsula to reach the mouth of the Severn.[112] As we have already seen, the economic development of the fishing industry on the lower reaches of the Wye and Severn and along the Severn estuary towards the end of the period was probably a response to the needs of ecclesiastical centres and a growing urban population in England. At the same time late Saxon coins and coin hoards indicate an expansion in trade along the south Wales littoral (Chapters 6 and 7). The growing power of Wessex and attempts to control both trade and economic development were therefore important factors in this

---

[104] Copplestone-Crow 2009, 12–15; Davies, W. 1978, 76, 88, 90–1, 93; Charles-Edwards 2013, 251.

[105] Ray 2015, 224–6.   [106] Lane and Redknap 2019, 412–14.   [107] Whitelock 1979, [*s.a.*] 914.

[108] Noble 1983, 106–9; Molyneaux 2011.

[109] Douglas and Greenaway 1981 *s.a.* 1055; Jones, T. 1952, 14; Davies, M. 2002, 221–9, for the wider context; Williams, A., and Martin 2002, 493–4, 499; Lewis 2007, 132–3.

[110] Bourke 2020, 382–3, no. 78. On Marden and its possible association with King Offa, see Ray 2015, 219–21.

[111] Bryant 2012, 276–99, pls 496–501; Redknap and Lewis 2007, 529–35, nos H1, H4.

[112] Ray and Bapty 2016, 50–4.

frontier zone. The rulers of Gwent and Glywysing had submitted to King Alfred in the 880s and the payment of tribute by the people of Gwent to the West Saxons, who also took hostages, is noted in the *Ordinance concerning the Dunsæte*.[113] During the first half of the eleventh century border raiding seems to have been endemic and on the eve of the Norman Conquest Harold Godwinson attempted to establish a foothold for hunting at Portskewett on the eastern edge of the Gwent Levels. It was, however, destroyed before it was finished by Caradog ap Gruffudd, king of south Wales, whose family had close ties to the area.[114]

Therefore, though the 'short dykes' may mark earlier local and short-lived attempts to defend and define border landscapes, the construction of Offa's and Wat's Dykes was a decisive step in the creation of a frontier separating the kingdoms of Wales from first Mercia, then England. This zone, marked geographically by stretches of upland and natural river boundaries which might also act as conduits—the Dee, the Severn, and the Wye—was brought into much sharper focus by the disruptive presence and visibility of the dykes. Together these formed both physical and psychological barriers, demonstrating the extent and ambition of Mercian power. With the exception of English expansion west of the Dee in the north-east, this frontier zone remained largely unchanged until the end of the period, later contributing to the creation of the Welsh March. It was clearly a zone of conflict and contention, and we can now begin to see how this played out regionally. However, the continuing scarcity of the archaeological evidence means that cultural distinctions in different parts of the frontier to the west and east of the dykes can only be perceived to a limited degree. Nevertheless, Domesday Book indicates that in Shropshire at least, though separated from similar communities further west, Welsh speakers continued to be a significant element of the farming population, with an elite Anglo-Saxon administrative overlay. However, apart from the north and south coasts, finds of late Saxon metalwork and coins seem remarkably rare, suggesting that, although livestock and raw materials such as salt may have been traded, there is otherwise little evidence of either economic or cultural exchange.

THE VIKING IMPACT

From the ninth century onwards the Viking impact on different parts of Wales was an important extension of the continuing cultural and other contacts around and across the Irish Sea. It also reflects the shifts of power and economic expansion that resulted from the establishment of settlements, particularly Dublin, within a wider maritime zone that, originating in Scandinavia, stretched from Atlantic Scotland southwards

---

[113] Keynes and Lapidge 1983, 96, ch. 80; Noble 1983, 109.
[114] Douglas and Greenaway 1981 *s.a.* 1065; Walker 2006.

through the Irish Sea to Brittany and beyond. Raids and other violence were undoubtedly destructive, but changing alliances between native and incomer and the development of hybrid identities were no less significant. These are clearly demonstrated in the life of Gruffudd ap Cynan, who was born in Dublin *c*.1055 and brought up in Swords nearby. After a long struggle for power, he went on to rule Gwynedd until his death in 1137. Gruffudd's father was Cynan, the son of Iago, a ruler of Gwynedd, but his mother, Raghnell, was Hiberno-Scandinavian. She was the daughter of Olaf, the son of Sihtric Anlafsson ('Silkenbeard'), king of Dublin, and was related via her mother to various Irish ruling families as well.[115]

The nature and extent of the Viking impact on Wales remain a matter of debate. Henry Loyn used the written sources to establish a chronological framework for Viking raids and other activity in Wales and set it within a wider context. He proposed two principal phases—*c*.800–950 and *c*.950 to the late eleventh century. This was linked with the evidence of Scandinavian place names focused on navigation points, islands, and likely trading settlements along the north and south Welsh coasts. He also recognized the significance of the then very limited archaeological evidence in the form of coins, silver hoards, and sculpture. Together these allowed him to construct a model for Viking activity in Wales, which he regarded as peripheral to events elsewhere. He not only recognized the impact of Viking raiding and other acts of violence and coercion but also emphasized the important role of the Vikings in establishing the trade routes linking Dublin with Chester and later Ireland with the Severn estuary, making the existence and identification of associated settlements more likely.[116] Building on this, more nuanced interpretations of the written sources and a growing body of archaeological evidence, including the settlement at Llanbedrgoch, have led to the view that there were more sustained attempts at bringing parts of north Wales, particularly Anglesey, under Scandinavian control.[117]

My aim here is to assess the Viking impact regionally, beginning with the northwest, but first some explanation of Scandinavian place names is required. On the border these may be noted in Domesday Book, but otherwise they only appear in the written sources from the thirteenth century onwards, so when they were first used is less clear and some may date from the twelfth century rather than earlier. It is also sometimes difficult to distinguish between Old English and Old Norse names. Nevertheless, a significant group of Old Norse names has been identified as earlier on the grounds that the Welsh and Scandinavian forms of the names are completely different, suggesting that the latter were coined independently of the former at a time before any integration had taken place. However, it should also be noted that some,

---

[115] Russell 2005, chs 1–6; Etchingham 2001, 157–61; 2007, 150–1; Edwards 2013, 11. Cynan ap Iago has been plausibly identified as instrumental in the killing of Gruffudd ap Llywelyn; Hudson 1990, 340–8; Davies, M. 2002, 230–6.

[116] Loyn 1976.   [117] Davies, W. 1990, 48–60; Etchingham 2001; 2007.

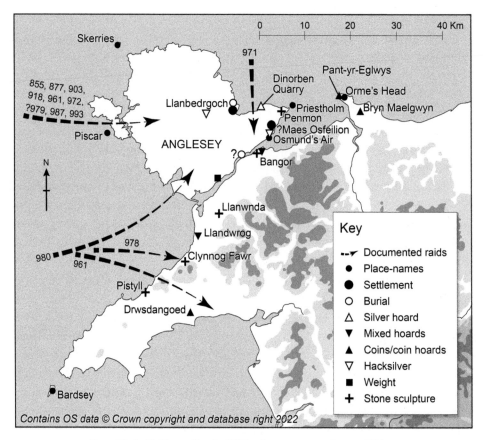

Fig. 12.6. Evidence for the Viking impact on north-west Wales.

such as Orme's Head, from *ǫrmr*, a serpent, which has no Welsh equivalent, may indicate coastal navigation points rather than landing sites and therefore need not have necessitated interaction between Scandinavian and Welsh speakers. The wider influence of Old Norse words on the Welsh language is remarkably slight.[118]

The impact of the Vikings on north-west Wales (Fig. 12.6) was concentrated on Anglesey but is also reflected in evidence of coastal activity as far west as Bardsey Island, the Old Norse name for Ynys Enlli, and eastwards to Orme's Head. Overall there are few place names, but Anglesey itself is Scandinavian, derived from *Ǫngull* + *ey*, meaning 'Ongull's Island', but this was used alongside the earlier Môn, which is first recorded in its Latin form, *Mona*, during the Roman period.[119] Not only was Anglesey a target because of its pivotal location on Irish Sea routes, principally that from Dublin to Chester and Wirral; also attractive was its relative wealth, including fertile soils suitable for grain found mainly in the southern half of the island.

[118] Charles 1992, xxxv–xxxviii; Richards 1975, 55, 58–9.
[119] Jones, G. T., and Roberts 1996, 89–90.

Interrogation of entries in the Harleian Chronicle, *Brut y Tywysogion*, and the Irish annals indicates that Anglesey and the mainland coast were the object of first Hiberno-Scandinavian and later Gaelic-Scandinavian attentions also linked to events and political struggles in Gwynedd and elsewhere in the Irish Sea region.

The first phase is focused on the second half of the ninth and early tenth centuries. From the 820s onwards Viking raids on Ireland intensified and became increasingly widespread, eventually leading to the first permanent settlements, notably the *longphort* at Dublin in 841. This was a likely trigger for the first recorded attack on Anglesey in 855 followed by the killing of Orm, 'chief of the Dark Foreigners', by Rhodri Mawr, king of Gwynedd, but in 877 the tables were turned and he was forced to flee to Ireland.[120] Later, in 902, events in Dublin that led to the expulsion of Ingimund and his followers were instrumental in their seizure of *Maes Osfeilion*, probably located near Llan-faes. Whether this was more than a temporary foothold is unknown, but Ingimund was driven out by Rhodri's son Cadell and the following year is credited with founding settlements on Wirral. A further raid on Anglesey launched from Dublin is noted in 918.[121]

During the second phase spanning the latter half of the tenth and eleventh centuries renewed pressure on Anglesey and coastal Gwynedd should be seen as part of wider claims over Ireland, the Isle of Man, and western Scotland. Recorded raids begin again in the 960s,[122] but during the 970s and 980s attacks were led by Godfrith and Maccus Haraldsson, brothers based in the Isles who also had interests in Limerick and were taking advantage of alliances with different hostile factions amongst the ruling family of Gwynedd.[123] These commenced in 971 with Maccus raiding Penmon. The following year Godfrith laid waste and subdued the whole island and in 980 joined forces with Custennin ap Iago, whose father had been exiled from Gwynedd and seized by Vikings, to attack Llŷn and Anglesey. He ravaged the island once more in 987 and is reported to have captured 2,000 men, who were only freed two years later after ransom payments of a penny a head.[124] In the earlier eleventh century Gruffudd ap Cynan's maternal grandfather, Olaf Sihtricsson, is credited with building a stronghold in Gwynedd known as Bon y Dom.[125] In the latter part of the century Gruffudd ap Cynan maintained his links with Dublin but failed to dislodge the

---

[120] Dumville 2002, 12–13, *s.a.* 853; Jones, T. 1952, *s.a.* 853 (= 855); CELT, Annals of Ulster, U856.6, U877.3.

[121] Etchingham 2001, 163–4; CELT, Annals of Ulster, U902.2; Morris 1980, 49, 90, [*s.a.*] 902; Jones, T. 1952, *s.a.* 900 (= 903), 918; Wainwright 1948. This last account (in the Fragmentary Annals of Ireland) of Ingimund's settlement on Wirral is problematic, as it survives only in a mid-seventeenth-century copy (Radner 1978, vii), but is supported by the 902 entry in the Harleian Chronicle (*s.a.* 900 (= 903) in *Brut y Tywysogion*) mentioning Ingimund's capture of *Maes Osfeilion*. On its location, see Charles-Edwards 2013, 328, n. 95.

[122] Jones, T. 1952, *s.a.* 959 (= 961), 961 (= 963).

[123] Etchingham 2001, 171–81; Charles-Edwards 2013, 146–7.

[124] Jones, T. 1952, *s.a.* 970 (= 972), 978 (= 979), 979 (= 980), 986 (= 987), 988 (= 989).

[125] Russell 2005, 54–5, ch. 4.

402 LIFE IN EARLY MEDIEVAL WALES

Normans, who had won a foothold in south-east Anglesey. It was Magnus Barelegs of Norway who defeated them, paving the way for Gruffudd's return from Ireland.[126]

Archaeological evidence is also concentrated in the south-east of the island. During the first phase this points to the establishment of settlements associated in part with controlling the seaways, including the eastern approach to the Menai Strait and the Dublin–Chester route. It may be argued that the final phase settlement at Llanbedrgoch (Chapter 5), with its imposing defensive enclosure, rectangular buildings, and typically Viking metalwork assemblage, which includes hacksilver, is an important example of the takeover of an elite estate and the resources and renders that went with it. Violence and exaction of tribute may have resulted in wider control. Radiocarbon and artefactual dating indicate that the settlement was occupied in the later ninth and tenth centuries, and fragments of characteristically Hiberno-Scandinavian silver broad-band arm-rings and a lead trial piece signal contacts with Ireland (Chapter 7). These may have been made in Dublin and date to the later ninth and earlier tenth century and are also found in several mixed silver hoards, notably Cuerdale, Lancashire, associated with the expulsion from Dublin in 902. There are other finds close to Llanbedrgoch, notably a hoard of similar but complete broad-band arm-rings from Dinorben quarry below Din Sylwy hillfort, an important coastal vantage point. Whilst fragmented arm-rings could be used in commercial transactions and payments of tribute, the complete ornaments had a social function as markers of status and may therefore have been used as gifts to seal alliances as well.[127] There is also an isolated silver drachm of the Sassanian king Chosroes II (591–628) from Llanddyfnan. It was found rolled up in the manner of hacksilver and, though early, its association with Viking activity is strengthened by the discovery of a second but later example of a drachm in the Herefordshire silver hoard dating to c.979.[128] Also close by was a grave of furnished Viking type, suggesting the burial of someone who was yet to be more fully integrated into a Christian society. The body had been placed in a wooden coffin accompanied by a comb. The grave was located on a low sandy cliff overlooking the landing place at Traeth Coch and this is typical of many other later ninth- and early tenth-century Insular Scandinavian furnished graves in Ireland, Atlantic Scotland, and the Isle of Man. Such burials are clearly linked with settlement and would seem to symbolize both land ownership and authority.[129] Further south, the discovery of two pieces of hacksilver near Llan-faes hints that the settlement of *Maes Osfeilion* may have been nearby. Also in the vicinity is the Scandinavian place name Osmund's Air,

---

[126] Jones 1952, *s.a.* 1096 (= 1098); Russell 2005, 82–5, chs 28–9; Power 1986.

[127] Boon 1986b, 99–102; Sheehan 2009, 58–61; 2004, 183–4.

[128] PAS no. LVPL2174; Jane Kershaw (pers. comm.); Abdy and Williams 2006, 57, no. 253; Hoverd et al. 2020, 48.

[129] Edwards 1985; Harrison 2008, 174–6, 179. A ringed pin, used to fasten a cloak or shroud, found in the parish church cemetery at Llanfairpwll overlooking the Menai Strait, may indicate a second Insular Scandinavian furnished grave on Anglesey; see Fox 1940b.

referring to a gravel bank where boats might beach.[130] The early tenth-century mixed silver hoard from Bangor also points to an extension of Hiberno-Scandinavian activity or influence on the opposite side of the Menai Strait.[131]

Evidence broadly relating to the second phase is distributed more widely from the Conwy estuary to the Llŷn peninsula, but to what extent this indicates any further settlement as part of a more sustained attempt at subjection by Hiberno- and Gaelic-Scandinavian leaders remains more open to question. What is clear is a greater degree of acculturation evident in the stone sculpture. The concentration in south-east Anglesey shows increased investment in sculpture over a greater range of Christian sites, pointing to the longer-term consolidation, integration, and mixing of identities apparent in other areas of Viking settlement including south of Dublin, the Isle of Man, and parts of south-west Scotland. Most monuments are simple cross-carved stones, the grave-markers of landholding families (Chapter 10). However, at Penmon, the most important church in the area, there are two circle-head crosses, a form found mainly in Hiberno-Scandinavian areas of settlement in north-west England, including Chester and Wirral. One is decorated with a distinctive Viking Borre-style ring chain also found on Manx cross-slabs, whilst the figural scenes have more in common with crosses in Ireland. These and others are carved from the local Anglesey grit and examples are also found on the mainland, notably an eleventh- or early twelfth-century font at Pistyll decorated with a later form of Borre ring chain, indicating a wider sphere of continuing Hiberno-Scandinavian cultural influence.[132]

Interestingly, the silver hoards are all from the mainland, one mixed from Llandwrog and three with coins from Drwsdangoed (now lost), Bryn Maelgwyn, and Pant-yr-Eglwys. The latter all contain pennies of Cnut, which date them to the 1020s, but coins from Hiberno-Scandinavian Dublin and probably the Isle of Man are also represented, indicating the economic importance of the Dublin–Chester route (Chapter 7). Equally, the larger hoards may signify wealth derived from plunder or tribute, but who buried them it is no longer possible to say. Nevertheless, they date to around the same time as Gruffudd ap Cynan's Hiberno-Scandinavian grandfather, Olaf Sihtricsson, who is said to have built Bon y Dom, which was probably located somewhere on the Gwynedd mainland.[133]

In contrast, the Viking impact on the frontier zone of Tegeingl is closely linked but peripheral to Scandinavian settlements east of the Dee and around the Mersey estuary, including those of Ingimund and his followers on Wirral (Fig. 12.7). Viking interest in Chester is first noted in 893 when a Danish army captured the 'deserted city' but left the following year to raid Wales. Later Ingimund and his allies are reported to have received land from Æthelflæd of Mercia, but subsequently a combined force

[130] Redknap 2009b, 34–5; Jones, B. L., and Roberts 1980.   [131] Boon 1986b, 92–7.
[132] Edwards 2011; 2013, 109–14, nos AN51–2 (see also the lost cross-shaft, no. AN53), CN39.
[133] RCAHMW 1937, cxlvi.

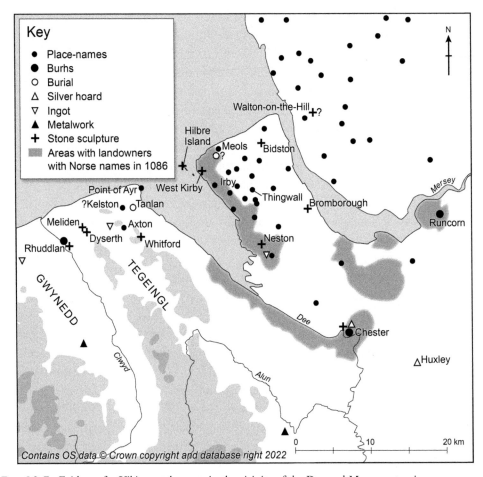

Fig. 12.7. Evidence for Viking settlements in the vicinity of the Dee and Mersey estuaries.

besieged Chester, which was fortified as a *burh* in 907.[134] It developed into a thriving late Saxon trading town with an identifiable Scandinavian element amongst the population, probably concentrated south of the Roman fortress. This is indicated by two probably eleventh-century church foundations dedicated to St Olaf of Norway and St Brigid of Kildare, saints popular amongst Hiberno-Scandinavian communities, as well as that dedicated to St John, which has a sizable collection of Viking Age sculpture.[135] Artefacts from Chester include decorated metalwork such as Hiberno-Scandinavian ringed pins, ingot moulds, and silver, including a mixed hoard from the town and the Huxley hoard of flattened Hiberno-Scandinavian broad-band arm-rings and ingots that was found some way to the south-east.[136]

---

[134] Whitelock 1979, *s.a.* 894–5 (= 893–4) 907; Wainwright 1948, 167–9; Radner 1978, 168–73.
[135] Thacker 1987, 257–8; Mason, D. J. P. 2007, 89–123; Bailey 2010, 62–9.
[136] Thacker 1987, 258; Mason, D. J. P. 2007, 114–17, pls 30, 40; Graham-Campbell and Philpott 2009, 45–69.

POWER AND AUTHORITY 405

Turning to Wirral, Bromborough is the most likely location of the Battle of Brunanburh in 937. This was Æthelstan's decisive victory against a combined force of Scots, British from Strathclyde, and Hiberno-Scandinavians from Dublin—in the lead-up to which *Armes Prydein Vawr* had probably been written, urging the Welsh to join them (Chapter 1).[137] The strength of Hiberno-Scandinavian settlement on Wirral and north of the Mersey is indicated by a considerable number of place names. These include Irby, from *Íri-býr* ('the farmstead of the Irishman'), where evidence for a Viking Age settlement has been found, but also the trading site of Meols, from *melr*, a 'sandbank', and Thingwall, from *þing-vǫllr*, meaning 'the field where the assembly meets'. In Domesday Book land on both banks of the Dee and around Chester was still owned by men with Norse names,[138] and taken together the evidence points to an identifiable landowning population of Hiberno-Scandinavian descent.

Between the Dee and the Clwyd there is a small but significant cluster of evidence indicating a Hiberno-Scandinavian presence radiating in an arc south of Point of Ayr. This was an important landmark at the western tip of the Dee estuary and settlement here would have helped secure access to both Wirral and Chester. Point of Ayr is a Scandinavian place name incorporating *eyrr*, meaning a 'gravel sandbank', but there is only one definite settlement name, Axton, with Old Norse *askr* (referring to an ash tree) plus Old English *tūn*.[139] The only archaeological evidence likely to be associated with settlement during the second half of the ninth or earlier tenth centuries is a furnished grave at Tanlan, near Talacre. Here, on a sandy slope, a stone cist was found containing the skeleton of a young man with a spearhead and knife. A radiocarbon date of cal. AD 660–880 from the skeleton might seem rather early, but this has been caused by the marine reservoir effect resulting from a substantial marine component in his diet, which also suggests that he was not brought up locally since a terrestrial diet was the norm.[140] However, discoveries of silver are surprisingly rare—the only example is an ingot from Trelawnydd.[141]

We can surmise a continuing Hiberno-Scandinavian sphere of influence in the area from the distribution of tenth- and eleventh-century stone sculpture. There are characteristic Viking Age circle-head crosses at Whitford (known as *Maen Achwyfan*) and Dyserth, as well as fragments from Meliden and Rhuddlan, and these are comparable with others from West Kirby and Bromborough on Wirral, as well as monuments at St John's Chester. As we have seen, *Maen Achwyfan* may mark a place of assembly and is carved with heroic scenes from Norse mythology, suggesting the patrons were of Scandinavian descent. Such iconography is otherwise unknown in Wales but is more

[137] Whitelock 1979, *s.a.* 939; Foot 2009, 169–79; Cavill 2015.
[138] Philpott 2015, 110–13; Jesch 2000, 3–4; Cavill 2000, 138, 142; Griffiths 2006, 156.
[139] Owen and Gruffydd 2017, 8, 138, see also Kelston, a possible settlement name, 103.
[140] Smith, F. G. 1931–3; Higham et al. 2007, S5, OxA-12899.
[141] PAS no. NMGW-799430.

406 LIFE IN EARLY MEDIEVAL WALES

common on sculpture in areas of Scandinavian settlement in northern England and the Isle of Man.[142] Cwyfan is the Irish saint Cóimgen (Kevin) of Glendalough, and the church at Dyserth is dedicated jointly to him and St Brigid (Welsh: Ffraid). Both were popular in Dublin and its hinterland, with dedications also to the latter in West Kirby and Chester.[143] Like the circle-head crosses at Penmon, the later cross and cross-base at Dyserth are carved from Anglesey grit, pointing to the patronage of rulers of Gwynedd at a time when Tegeingl was back under Welsh control. In contrast, the sandstone used for the earlier Meliden fragment is probably from the Cheshire basin, signalling the significance of contacts with Hiberno-Scandinavian communities east of the Dee during the tenth century when this region was under English authority.[144]

In south Wales the nature of the Viking impact appears somewhat different (Fig. 12.8). Though raiding is well documented and coastal place names comparatively common, there are fewer signs of permanent settlement since archaeological evidence is rare. The virtual absence of large silver hoards is likewise noteworthy. During the later ninth and early tenth century recorded Scandinavian attacks were

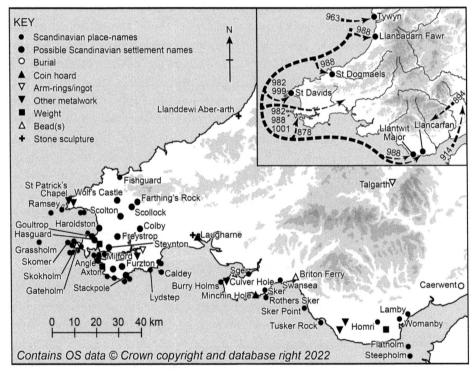

FIG. 12.8. Evidence for the Viking impact on south Wales.

---

[142] Meliden probably had similar scenes, now lost; Edwards 2013, nos F2, F8, F9, F12; Bailey 2010, 53–4, 62–71, 134–5, illus. 34–8, 75–114, 349–54.
[143] Edmonds 2019, 132–8, 143.   [144] Edwards 2013, 351–2, 355, 360.

POWER AND AUTHORITY 407

initially part of campaigns in south-west England against Alfred and Edward the Elder. Asser notes that in 878 a Viking fleet of twenty-three ships, most likely from Ireland, led by the brother of Hálfdan and Ívarr the Boneless, had overwintered in Dyfed before their defeat in Devon. Though no camp has been found, Milford Haven—a place name combining Old Norse *fjǫrðr* ('fjord') preceded by *melr*, a 'sandbank', recalling the sandy shores of the inlet—remains a plausible location.[145] Further attacks were focused on the south-east. The concealment of the large Herefordshire mixed silver hoard near Leominster *c.*879 strongly suggests a Viking intrusion, and in 894 a Danish army plundered Brycheiniog, Gwent, and Glywysing. More is, however, known about the campaign of 914, when Vikings from Brittany penetrated the Severn estuary and captured Cyfeiliog, the bishop of Archenfield (Ergyng), compelling Edward the Elder to pay the ransom for his release. The force was eventually subdued and the remnants became trapped on the island of Steepholm before escaping, via Dyfed, to Ireland.[146]

From the 960s onwards the south-west was the focus of attention, and to some extent events here are connected with those in the north-west. Indeed, in 982 Godfrith Haraldsson's men plundered Dyfed and raided St Davids, which then became a prime target. The attack in 999 was severe enough to result in the murder of Bishop Morgenau and nearly a century later, in 1080, Bishop Abraham was killed, forcing the previous incumbent, Sulien of Llanbadarn Fawr, to return to his post. Such raids were part of a wider pattern of attacks on churches, such as St Dogmaels and Llancarfan in 988.[147] However, there is also evidence during the eleventh century that, as in north Wales, the rulers of Deheubarth were hiring Hiberno-Scandinavian fleets and mercenaries in order to defend their kingdom. In 1044 Hywel ab Edwin gathered a fleet from Ireland but it was defeated at the mouth of the Tywi by Gruffudd ap Llywelyn and Hywel was killed.[148]

In the south-west there are far more Scandinavian place names than in the north, but to what extent these are early medieval is very difficult to establish. B. G. Charles plausibly argued that most were coined during the eleventh century and are largely linked with trading and other mercantile activity at a time when alliances with Hiberno-Scandinavians would also have fostered integration.[149] The majority are coastal and concentrated in western Pembrokeshire, especially in the south around Milford Haven: for example, the offshore islands of Skomer (from *skalm* + *ey*, meaning 'cleft island') and Skokholm, referring to the sound between them, as well as Goultrop which combines *gǫltr*, 'boar', with *hop* meaning 'bay'. In the north, the important

---

[145] Keynes and Lapidge 1983, 83–4, ch. 54; Charles 1992, xxxv–xxxvi, 23.

[146] Hoverd et al. 2020; Whitelock 1979, *s.a.* 915–17 (= 914); Morris 1980, *s.a.* 895, 913; Jones, T. 1952, *s.a.* 894 (= 896).

[147] Ibid., *s.a.* 981 (= 982), 987 (= 988), 998 (= 999), 1078 (= 1080); 1955, *s.a.* 980 (= 982), 988, 999, 1080.

[148] Jones, T. 1952, *s.a.* 1042 (= 1044).   [149] Charles 1992, xxxvii–xxxviii.

408 LIFE IN EARLY MEDIEVAL WALES

harbour at Fishguard (Welsh: Abergwaun) similarly has an Old Norse name derived from *fiskigarðr*, referring to a fish-trap. However, there are also a small number of likely inland settlements including Colby, which combines the personal name *Koli* with *by*, a 'farm'.[150]

Nonetheless, the relatively large number of place names remains at odds with the paucity of archaeological evidence, at present confined to a few stray artefacts from the vicinity of Milford Haven and St Davids, which both have other evidence of Scandinavian activity. Finds from around Milford Haven, including two capped lead weights and a fragment of Hiberno-Scandinavian broad-band arm-ring, suggest, as with Llanbedrgoch, activity in the later ninth and earlier tenth centuries emanating from Ireland.[151] Later tenth- and eleventh-century ringed pins found near St Davids were almost certainly made in Dublin.[152] The amber bead from Gateholm suggests it was a stopping-off point for ships sailing up the Bristol Channel and might also have acted as a temporary refuge. Tenth- and eleventh-century stone sculpture with overt Viking affinities is also rare. However, two grave-slabs from St Davids, including that commemorating the sons of Bishop Abraham, have Irish parallels. The other is probably of more than one phase with the addition of poorly executed plaitwork reminiscent of motif pieces in Hiberno-Scandinavian Dublin. Also significant is the mid- to late tenth-century hogback grave-cover at Llanddewi Aber-arth Church, which, unusually for Wales, is sited on high ground overlooking the shore. This continues the tradition of earlier furnished Viking graves, such as Benllech and Tanllan, and might therefore indicate Hiberno-Scandinavian patronage associated with a coastal place of trade. Similarly, the small circle-head cross at Laugharne points to mercantile communities that included wealthy individuals of Scandinavian descent.[153]

Further east again, the Scandinavian place names mostly relate to offshore islands and other landmarks along the coast that probably arose from increasing mercantile activity in the eleventh century associated with expanding trade between Ireland and the developing town of Bristol. The origins of both Swansea and Cardiff may also date to this period. Swansea (Welsh: Abertawe) comprises the Old Norse personal name *Sveinn*, probably with *ey* denoting 'Swein's Island', though exactly where this was in the Tawe estuary is unclear. Womanby Street in Cardiff is derived from Old Norse **hundamaðr*, referring to a 'hound keeper' + *by*, which, together with the probable Old Norse names of Homri and Lamby nearby, indicates a small cluster of likely Scandinavian settlements in the area, though their date remains problematic.[154]

---

[150] Ibid., 50, 456, 587–8, 616, 660.
[151] Redknap 2000, pl. 81; PAS no. NMGW-22CFAA.
[152] Redknap 2007c; Murphy et al. 2016, fig. 15; Fanning 1994, 54–6, 84, fig. 54, 94–106.
[153] Edwards 2007a, nos P97–8, CD7, CM10.
[154] Pierce 2002, 99–100, 181–4.

Some of the place names may, however, be earlier, and archaeological evidence dating to the first phase may indicate the activities of Viking war bands who sought temporary hideaways along the coast. Finds from two caves on Gower point to their use in this way. Three coins from Minchin Hole—two mid-ninth-century Carolingian deniers and a penny of Ecgbert of Wessex (809–39)—may be compared with Carolingian deniers at Llanbedrgoch and are also found in silver hoards in Ireland at this time. Though usually made of silver, the copper-alloy penannular brooch with ball terminals from Culver Hole is also a characteristic Viking type.[155] The contemporary use of caves as hideaways is paralleled in Ireland, exemplified by arm-rings discovered in Alice and Gwendoline Cave, Co. Clare, and pieces of dismantled ecclesiastical loot found in caves at Kilgreany and Park North, Co. Waterford. Such lairs are also known in Scandinavia and Iceland.[156] Equally, the amber and string beads found at Hen Gastell (Briton Ferry) might indicate that this strategic hillfort overlooking the mouth of the Neath was temporarily in Viking hands (Chapter 5).

Though caves in Ireland were also occasionally used for Viking burials,[157] there is no sign of this in Wales. Nor have burials in similar locations to those at Tanlan and Traeth Coch been found in the south. However, in Caerwent, the poorly recorded discovery of human remains with part of an axe, a tenth-century spearhead, an arrowhead, sheers, and what might have been lead weights suggests a small group of Viking furnished burials.[158] The artefacts came to light in the ruins of a Roman temple on the northern edge of the cemetery associated with the church of St Tatheus (Fig. 4.2). Similar graves in or close to places of Christian burial are also known more widely— for example, at Kilmainham and other sites in Dublin, as well as cemeteries in the Isle of Man and northern England, such as Kildale, Yorkshire. Their location signals not only settlement but also the dual processes of conversion and integration into a Christian society.[159] Although it has been claimed that a pair of stirrups from St Mary Hill, Glamorgan, also came from a Viking grave, nothing is known of their context. Therefore they should be regarded as stray finds in a similar way to the lead weight with an Insular metalwork inset from Wenvoe in the Vale of Glamorgan.[160] Later finds are very rare and the lack of tenth- and eleventh-century stone sculpture with characteristically Viking Age features is also noteworthy. This suggests that there were few settlements east of the Tywi, and those of Scandinavian descent were swiftly integrated into their local communities.

Therefore, the Viking impact on Wales is clearly related to the wider Scandinavian impact on the Atlantic seaways and the Irish Sea region as well as attacks on England

---

[155] Dykes 1976, 27; Branigan et al. 1993, 44; Redknap 2000, pl. 123.
[156] Dowd 2015, 190–4; Madgwick et al. 2016, 222.   [157] Dowd 2015, 201–7.
[158] Hudd 1911, 438–9, figs 2(2), 4(1), pl. LX; Knight 1996, 56–8.
[159] Harrison and Ó Floinn 2014, 294–6, ill. 140; Wilson 2008, 46–52; Richards 2000, 149–51.
[160] Redknap 2013, 193–5; 2022, 93–4; PAS no. NMGW-07268F.

and settlement of the Danelaw. In that sense, as Loyn argued, it is peripheral to events elsewhere, but this is also to underplay the effects on people's lives. So, what was the Scandinavian impact on Wales? Firstly, whilst the destruction caused by Viking raiding needs to be understood within the broader context of the inherent violence of the time, the terminology used in the sources marks these out as different. In 853, when Anglesey was laid waste, the Harleian Chronicle refers to the 'Black Gentiles', thereby underlining their non-Christian, outsider status.[161] Indeed, the derogatory term 'Gentiles' was still used for Hiberno-Scandinavians two hundred years later, by which time they had been Christian for over a century.[162] What stands out is that, whether pagan or Christian, as outsiders they would not have been subject to the checks and balances that helped to regulate native Welsh society. The emphasis on raiding ecclesiastical foundations, particularly noted during the second half of the tenth century, may have been because the chronicles were written by churchmen. Nevertheless, such sites were also largely undefended, and killing leading clerics, as at St Davids, would have had a major impact. Raids may well have taken place on feast days, when crowds gathered and relics were displayed, offering maximum opportunities for slave-taking and seizing other booty. Equally, the economic and psychological impacts of ravaging the countryside, living off the land, and hostage-taking for ransom should not be underestimated.

Secondly, the combination of archaeological and other evidence demonstrates that during the second half of the ninth and early tenth centuries some Hiberno-Scandinavian land-taking and settlement did take place in south-east Anglesey, related to wider bids to control the Irish seaways and establish the lucrative Dublin–Chester trade route. However, the lack of settlement place names suggests numbers were low, and incomers were therefore swiftly linguistically integrated with the local population, who likely lived on lands they had seized. The evidence similarly points to limited Hiberno-Scandinavian settlement west of the Dee, mainly near Point of Ayr, but this appears peripheral to the main concentrations on Wirral and around Chester and was also subject to the uncertainties created by vacillating native and Anglo-Saxon control in this frontier zone. The degree of settlement in the south remains difficult to determine, though here Loyn's model suggesting the initial establishment of temporary or more permanent staging posts on islands and other places along the coast, eventually leading to the opening up of trade routes between Ireland along the Severn Sea to Bristol, remains attractive.[163] There are pointers to later ninth- or earlier tenth-century activity around Milford Haven, but that around St Davids, including possible farming settlements in the wider hinterland, may be considerably later. Other coastal communities may also have included merchants and traders of Scandinavian descent.

---

[161] Morris 1980, 48, 89, *s.a.* 853. On the related term 'Dark Foreigners', who arrived in Ireland in the mid-ninth century, see Downham 2007, 12–15.

[162] Jones, T. 1952, *s.a.* 1040 (= 1042).   [163] Loyn 1976, 17.

During the course of the tenth century, in the north signs of Scandinavian cultural influence—notably in the sculpture—seem to have gone hand in hand with the integration of settled landholding communities, which would also have fostered the growth of trade. This is seen in south-east Anglesey, raising questions about the nature of continuing Scandinavian ambitions to control the whole island and perhaps parts of the adjacent mainland as well. At the same time, there were also alliances between native rulers and their rivals with Hiberno- and Gaelic-Scandinavian leaders, who would doubtless have expected payments in land, silver, and other goods, as well as making elite marriages, in return. Indeed, the *Life* of Gruffudd ap Cynan emphasizes his mixed Welsh and Hiberno-Scandinavian identity, which may also have been a feature of some landholding elites, notably on Anglesey. However, there is little other evidence for the persistence of this amongst the rest of society in the material culture. This contrasts with the emergence of an Anglo-Scandinavian identity in much of the Danelaw, where Scandinavian cultural influence, as well as language and place names, were much more pervasive.[164] It is, however, in some ways similar to Ireland beyond Hiberno-Scandinavian Dublin and other trading centres where archaeological evidence, place names, and the impact on the language are more limited.[165]

[164] Kershaw and Røyrvik 2016, 1675–7; Hadley and Richards 2021, 117–40, 178–99.
[165] Bradley, John 1988.

THIRTEEN

Conclusion

This study set out to explore how people lived in Wales over the period *c.* AD 300–1050, how their lives changed, and why, placing this where possible within a wider comparative context focusing on other parts of Britain and Ireland. Although centring on the early Middle Ages, this slightly longer timespan allows consideration of the later Roman period and the changes that came about with the end of Roman rule, which is essential to understanding what came afterwards and the nature of the changes that took place. This chapter brings together some of the key themes examined earlier to enable a broader chronological discussion of the major changes and underlying continuities that helped to shape people's lives *c.* AD 300–1050 and indicates some areas for future research.

With excavation and other research, the archaeological resource for early medieval Wales has grown steadily over the past half-century (Chapter 1) and this will continue. Increasingly sophisticated methods of scientific dating, particularly radiocarbon dating, have been instrumental in the identification of sites with few or no diagnostic early medieval artefacts. This is now enabling the refinement of site chronologies, thereby aiding our understanding of wider changes and the underlying reasons for them and helping to facilitate comparison both within and beyond Wales. Equally, the rapid developments in other scientific techniques, notably the study of pollen and plant remains, animal bones, and human osteology, have opened new avenues for archaeological research. These are now helping us to reconstruct past landscapes and recognize climatic and environmental change. We can also detect trends in the evolution of farming economies and exploitation of the natural world that will lead to a better understanding of the diet and health of past populations. Even so, there are still very significant gaps in the archaeological evidence, especially in relation to the recognition of early medieval settlements. Regionally, the distribution of evidence more generally is often concentrated in the coastal lowlands, particularly in north-west and south-west Wales, rather than in the east where the difficulties in locating farming settlements, for example, are also reflected on the English side of Offa's and Wat's Dykes (Chapter 5).

The multidisciplinary approach adopted here has allowed the expanding archaeological resource to be analysed where possible in conjunction with the often

Life in Early Medieval Wales. Nancy Edwards, Oxford University Press. © Nancy Edwards 2023.
DOI: 10.1093/oso/9780198733218.003.0013

challenging written sources. These are primarily in Latin but also occasionally in Welsh, with fifth- and sixth-century inscriptions indicating that Irish was being spoken in some parts of Wales, as well as British and some Latin, at this time (Chapter 4). Most surviving written sources are, however, ninth-century or later, with an upsurge in the late eleventh and twelfth centuries probably reflecting the impact of Norman incursions and settlement in some parts of Wales from the 1070s onwards (Chapter 1). These written sources have in turn received increased scholarly attention over the past half-century with the result that we now have a more critical and nuanced understanding of their date, content, purpose, and the context in which the works were produced and how they have come down to us. Though usually first noted in the later Middle Ages, place names have also been discussed where appropriate. This approach has combined to give both a wider and a more detailed picture of how people lived in early medieval Wales as well as how they thought. It can also illuminate changes in identity, power, and authority, together with how Christianity came to have an increasing impact on people's lives. Nevertheless, as we might expect, the emphasis is still very largely on the secular and ecclesiastical elite in a society dominated by men (Chapter 7), and this is underlined by the nature of the written sources. The relative material poverty of farming communities has meant that their ways of living are only now becoming a little clearer through excavation and the analysis of a range of environmental evidence. Equally, the lives of women (other than their association with specific domestic tasks and crafts) and children remain more difficult to perceive except through interrogation of burials and the osteological record (Chapter 11). We can only glimpse the existence of slaves when they are occasionally mentioned in the written sources (Chapters 6 and 12).

Wales is shaped by its Irish Sea location that, in the early Middle Ages, allowed communication with other parts of western and northern Britain, Ireland, and the Isle of Man, leading in many ways to the evolution of a shared cultural identity as well as giving access to the wider Atlantic seaways facilitating contact with western France, Iberia, and ultimately the Mediterranean, as well as Scandinavia to the north (Chapter 2). Whilst the landscape could be altered over time by human endeavour, the land itself with its central mountainous core helped to fragment the more fertile coastal lowlands facing the Irish Sea and Bristol Channel, as well as breaking up the borderlands to the east. Here the Severn, Wye, and Dee were initially important conduits, but, with the construction of Offa's and Wat's Dykes in the later eighth and early ninth centuries and the continuing threat of English expansion, access eastwards became more difficult. It is therefore no coincidence that the *Historia Brittonum* (829/30), which sought to construct a history of the Britons from their origins to the end of the seventh century before the rise of Mercia, was written at this time; this combined a strong sense of British identity with an emerging awareness of Welsh national consciousness (Chapter 1). The geographical fragmentation of Wales also led to strong regional identities, evident from late prehistory onwards, that are likewise

414 LIFE IN EARLY MEDIEVAL WALES

seen in the archaeological evidence throughout the period under discussion. They are similarly reflected in the evolving pattern of early medieval kingdom formation that made it difficult to bring Wales together as a political entity in more than a very fleeting way at the end of Hywel Dda's reign in the mid-tenth century, and again during that of Gruffudd ap Llywelyn in the mid-eleventh.

Chris Wickham has suggested that Wales might be comparable with other early medieval European 'mountain societies', ranging from Italy at the heart of the Western Roman Empire to Scotland on the changing northern boundary and Norway well outside. In all, fragmentation of the more fertile coastal lowlands is a characteristic, though both Scotland and Norway achieved limited royal hegemony by around the end of the early Middle Ages.[1] Ireland, which remained outside the Roman Empire, also provides a useful comparison. Though geographically very different, with its central bogs and peripheral uplands, this too is a fragmented landscape with both larger areas and smaller pockets of fertile lowland. This was surely influential in the evolution, by the sixth century, of a complex pattern of small kingdoms (*túatha*) and the rise of provincial overkings leading, in the early eleventh century, to the ascendancy of the Dál Cais in Munster and King Brian Boru's ultimately failed attempt to gain control of the whole island.[2] Like Ireland also, the climate of Wales is temperate, though wet and windy, but in Wales the growing season is noticeably shorter in the east (Chapter 2).

In Wales the apparent focus of early medieval settlement on free-draining soils in the more fertile coastal lowlands and river valleys was part of a long continuum stretching back into prehistory (Chapters 3 and 5). This sense of place in a lived landscape with its fields, a range of pastures that might include water meadows, saltmarshes, heaths, woodlands, and uplands, as well as wild places, also provided day-to-day resources and an underlying continuum in people's lives. This was linked not only to seasonal time that marked the cyclical events of the farming year but also to earlier monuments—prehistoric barrows, cairns, standing stones, hillforts, and Roman remains—that continued to have a resonance in the landscape, inviting links with an often mythical ancestral past and opportunities for their reinvention to serve the needs of the present (Chapter 2). This has been recognized as a widespread phenomenon in Britain and Ireland in the early Middle Ages as well as further afield, for example in Scandinavia. However, it would be a mistake to see these landscapes as static: settlements were rebuilt, abandoned, or moved, and new ones might spring up. Farming methods also changed in response to environmental factors, dietary preference, the demands of the elite, obligations to produce a surplus to pay food renders, or openings for exchange and trade. The physical environment, particularly in more marginal terrains, as well as the changing climate also created constraints on agricultural

[1] Wickham 2010, 204–8.
[2] Edwards 1990, 6–8; Downham 2018, 11, 81–3, maps 2–3.

production. However, the mineral wealth of Wales—iron, copper, lead, silver, and gold—was also a valuable resource, providing potential opportunities for exploitation ranging from the piecemeal to an industrial-scale (Chapters 3, 6, and 7).

By the beginning of the fourth century Wales had been under Roman control for more than two centuries, with the consequent long-term impacts of continuing military occupation on indigenous ways of living (Chapter 3). Regional differences are important, including, in the south, the introduction of urban settlements at Caerwent (*Venta Silurum*) and Carmarthen (*Moridunum*), the *civitas* capitals respectively of the Silures and probably the Demetae. In the south-east there is also plenty of evidence for villa estates, reflecting proximity to the Cotswolds further east, though other more modest villas are also known in other parts of Wales. Above all, we see the impact of the Roman stimulus to and overarching control of the economy through requisition and taxation, exploitation of mineral resources, a ramping up of agrarian production to supply the army and other non-producers, the introduction of a market economy based on industrial production of goods such as pottery, use of currency alongside barter, and both regional and long-range trade networks that potentially reached across the empire. We can also see the impact of Rome and the culture that went with this on the use of written and spoken Latin, on the calculation of time (Chapter 2), and on the built environment, as well as on religious practice, with, from the fourth century onwards, Christianity beginning to gain a foothold (Chapter 9).

At the same time, the archaeological evidence allows us to see the continuation of indigenous ways of living (Chapter 3). Though there is some variation from region to region, farming communities continued to live in roundhouses in a variety of enclosed and unenclosed settlements, albeit sometimes influenced by Roman forms. Hillforts also continued as important markers in the landscape. Though some of these were now functioning as farms, others seem to have retained a significance as places of assembly and locales with sacred connotations, suggesting the continuation or reinvigoration of some long-standing societal structures (Chapters 5, 9, and 12). Across a range of sites, we can also detect contacts with the Roman market economy, mainly in the form of varying amounts of pottery and sometimes coins, as well as in the crops grown, with an emphasis on spelt and barley (Chapter 6).

Wales provides a good case study for our understanding of crossing the divide between Roman and post-Roman Britain (Chapter 3), as well as of what happened subsequently. Over the course of the fourth century the archaeological evidence demonstrates a continuing Roman military presence focused on the north and south coasts, with the primary aim of countering Irish raiders and keeping the seaways open. However, the increasing stresses inherent in holding the wider empire together in the face of barbarian and other threats were also taking their toll. Indeed, in Wales the more limited, urban market economy in the south-west was already faltering in the earlier fourth century. It is unknown how long mineral extraction under military auspices prevailed or to what extent its cessation contributed, from the mid-fourth

416 LIFE IN EARLY MEDIEVAL WALES

century onwards, to a much wider and accelerating economic decline. This is evident in the contraction of market networks and the availability of goods, such as pottery, leading, increasingly, to a culture of recycling and make do and mend. Some specialist artisans, such as blacksmiths and comb-makers, continued, and their skills were passed down the generations, but the emphasis now turned to crafts such as woodworking and textile production based in the home (Chapter 7). As indicated in Caerwent, with falling living standards and a declining population urban structures, including tax collection, were also breaking down. Nevertheless, there are some signs of occupation into the fifth century and beyond, as well as a sense of continuity as *Venta Silurum*, the *civitas* capital of the Silures, was preserved in the name of the kingdom of Gwent and later became the site of a monastery (Chapters 3 and 4). Equally, with the withdrawal of troops to other parts of Britain and the empire, continued military defence increasingly depended on those left behind who may have morphed into local militias or war bands led by their former military commanders, a pattern also suggested on Britain's northern frontier.[3]

In the countryside, a lavish villa lifestyle could no longer be maintained but, even with the collapse of the market economy, the rural population would have continued to farm in order to sustain their households, though the need or incentive to produce a surplus to feed the military, urban populations, and other non-producers would have substantially declined. The demise of pottery and coins, often only found in small quantities, combined with the small numbers of radiocarbon dates, as well as the radiocarbon plateau *c.* AD 425–550, means that it is often thought that settlements were abandoned when Roman artefacts ceased. However, this need not have been the case. As I have argued (Chapters 3 and 5), the pattern of dispersed enclosed farmsteads first seen in Wales in late prehistory and also evident throughout the Roman period almost certainly continued, though in declining numbers, well into the early Middle Ages. To what extent the loss of markets and a slump in the agrarian economy from around the mid-fourth century led to significantly reduced standards of living amongst farming communities is more difficult to discern. Climate deterioration was another significant factor, now clearly indicated in the pollen record in the post-Roman centuries, leading to less land, especially in more marginal areas, under the plough. It would certainly have reduced yields, with the consequent effects on food security and nutrition (Chapter 6, and see below). It is noticeable that the change from spelt and barley to barley and oats, both better suited to the climate, with smaller quantities of free-threshing wheat requiring less effort to process than spelt, began in the late Roman period but accelerated thereafter. Corn-dryers were also used more widely in the post-Roman centuries. Equally, there is an important move from

[3] Collins 2012, 156–67.

raising cattle for meat to dairying, thereby providing a more sustainable source of protein as well as an important measure of wealth (Chapters 6 and 7).

At first the loosening and, ultimately, the loss of Roman control led to the fragmentation of authority, with all the consequent uncertainty and tensions, as the old order faded and new patterns of power were established. Leaders—the 'tyrants' of Gildas—and their war bands may ultimately have emerged from both the Roman military and Romanized civic dignitaries. That there were Latin speakers amongst the post-Roman elite is implied by the continuation of Latin as a spoken language for some and Latin-inscribed memorial stones, some of which commemorate men and women with Roman names, suggesting the persistence of a Roman identity (Chapters 3 and 4). At the same time, the survival or re-emergence of indigenous structures of power seems to have gone hand in hand with a resurgence of a British cultural identity, evident, for example, in elite occupation of hillforts (Chapter 5).

Irish immigration was a further significant factor in the mix, taking advantage of both the comparative material wealth of the former province of *Britannia Prima* as well as the breakdown of Roman control. Irish raids had long been a problem, but settlement may also have been facilitated by the presence of Irish recruits in the Roman army (Chapters 3 and 4). Numbers may have been small, as spoken Irish and the use of ogham had ceased by around 600. The distribution of ogham-inscribed stones and others with Irish names points to the main concentration in the far south-west, which may have resulted in men of Irish descent emerging as rulers of the kingdom of Dyfed, with further settlers mainly in north-west Anglesey and Brycheiniog (Chapter 4). Irish immigrants also served to strengthen cultural and other contacts across the Irish Sea, seen, for example, in similar fashions of personal adornment (Chapter 7).

As elsewhere in western and northern Britain, by the later fifth century elites and possibly some more prosperous farming communities were living in hillforts and related sites, reflecting status and the need for defence as well as a continuation or reinvention of earlier settlement forms (Chapter 5). In Wales much of what we know about elite lifestyle is still typified by the artefactual assemblage from Dinas Powys, the home of a local leader and his household, who could command the surrounding countryside—perhaps a very small kingdom—with access to a range of produce and other raw materials (Chapter 12). In a society where gift-giving helped maintain loyalty and bind communities together, such resources and, very likely, the proceeds of coercion and conflict also provided the means allowing patronage of highly skilled craftworkers, feasting, and the acquisition of luxury goods, such as wine, from southwest France, western Iberia, and the Mediterranean (Chapter 7). Therefore wealth and power were concentrated in the hands of small elites and their retinues, and the lives of the rest of the population remain very difficult to discern.

What little evidence there is suggests that the earliest Christians in Roman Wales were living in forts and towns alongside adherents to a range of other deities and cults.

In the countryside indigenous beliefs, sometimes Romanized, continued to focus on natural places, such as springs, whilst some hillforts also persisted as sacred nodes and gathering places (Chapter 9). The subsequent course of Christian conversion amongst the elite is clearly visible in the epitaphs on the inscribed stones which also demonstrate continuing contacts with Gaul, probably Iberia, and the Mediterranean indicating that believers in Wales were part of a wider Christian community. In the north-west, from around the turn of the sixth century, there is increasing evidence of Christian commemoration and an organized clergy as well as signs of monasticism, but in some other regions, notably the south-west, conversion may have been slower and more drawn out. Most epitaphs, whether overtly Christian or not, also continue to emphasize the significance of kinship in binding society together (Chapters 4 and 9).

The cemetery evidence, which is often difficult to date with any precision, remains less easy to interpret, but I have argued for a process of accommodation (Chapter 9). Although farming communities gradually adopted the later Roman burial rite of inhumation, it would be wrong to associate this with conversion and there are also indications of the persistence of some older customs and beliefs. The locations of cemeteries, which are often associated with prehistoric monuments, indicate deep ties to what were perceived as ancestral landscapes that underscored rights to the land as well as the strength of kin and community, whether long-standing or reinvented, in a period of rapid change. The discovery of Christian inscribed stones in such locations signals that conversion was taking place, whilst also referencing the past.

What was the impact of the 'Late Antique Little Ice Age' that commenced with a volcanic eruption causing a dust veil in 536, with further episodes in 539/40 and probably 547, as well as the Justinian bubonic plague that followed it, in all likelihood arriving via the Atlantic seaways in the later 540s with further outbreaks in the later seventh century? Though climate deterioration in Wales is made clear in the pollen record during the post-Roman centuries, pollen sequences only show broad trends, not specific episodes, and this problem is exacerbated by the radiocarbon plateau *c.* AD 425–550. Apart from the tree-ring evidence in Ireland, this leaves us with a few terse and retrospective references in the written record (Chapters 2 and 6). Nevertheless, the rapidly accumulating scientific evidence for the wider impact of climatic forcing leading to significantly lower temperatures in the northern hemisphere in the years following 536 cannot be ignored, with likely longer-term effects lasting into the mid-seventh century. Indeed, it has recently been argued that in Scandinavia the volcanic eruptions had a devastating effect, leading to settlement abandonment and a serious drop in the population.[4] Whilst the temperate climate of Wales would have brought some amelioration, the impact, particularly in more marginal areas and parts of the east with a shorter growing season, is likely to have been harsh, with failed harvests

---

[4] Price 2020, 74–7, 524–5.

and potential loss of livestock bringing hunger and disease, especially to those living on or at little above the level of subsistence. Whether the Justinian plague can also be directly linked to these climatic events is less clear, though its impact on an already weakened population may have been severe as well as severing the trade route that brought luxury goods from the eastern Mediterranean (Chapter 7). Both sudden climatic cooling and plague point to substantial loss of human life, still evident more generally in estimates of population levels in the time of Domesday half a millennium later (Chapter 5).

Gildas was probably writing *De Excidio Britanniae* c.530 × 545 (Chapter 1), and though it has been suggested that he may allude to the volcanic dust veil of 536–7, and that this may have precipitated him into writing, this is certainly not conclusive.[5] Nevertheless, David Dumville has drawn attention to the long hiatus between Gildas, with his Roman rhetorical education, and the early ninth-century *Historia Brittonum*, by which time sources for the fifth century were few and far between. He attributes this to both the impact of plague and Anglo-Saxon expansion,[6] though it may now be argued that wider societal disruption caused by climate forcing was also a significant factor. In Gildas's day some larger kingdoms in Wales, such as Dyfed and Gwynedd, were already expanding, but, in the course of the seventh century, we also see the steady Anglo-Saxon erosion of a greater Britain of which Wales was a part (Chapter 12).

The role of the 'Late Antique Little Ice Age' and its aftermath in providing a context for or accelerating longer-term developments in Welsh society is more difficult to determine. Nevertheless, by the later seventh century major changes in settlement forms were already in motion that may in part be linked to land reorganization following earlier abandonment and a decline in population (Chapter 5). By this time also, pollen cores point to a reversal of the decrease in arable and pastural indicators seen in the post-Roman period alongside a gradual increase in the exploitation of landed estates and their resources to produce the surpluses necessary for payment of food renders (Chapter 6). From the eighth century onwards, there are likewise indications in the written sources that may signal the development of a more complex society that included rulers of kingdoms and subkingdoms, the landed aristocracy, hereditary tenants, and slaves, whilst also accommodating the increasing power of the Church.

Although some remained significant places in the landscape, it appears that most hillforts and related sites had ceased as elite settlements by the later seventh century, if not before. What replaced them is still far from clear, though the location of Llanbedrgoch on fertile lowland and its developing role as an estate centre give some indications of the nature of this important change. At the same time, whilst some earlier farmsteads were rebuilt or reoccupied, new open settlements with subrectangular

---

[5] Woods 2010.   [6] Dumville 1986, 9–11.

buildings are also apparent, as at Rhuddgaer, with its associated field system, and South Hook. It may be argued that these were part of an evolving dispersed settlement pattern and were the *trefi* of the written record. This term is also found in some other parts of western Britain, notably Cornwall, where similar changes in settlement forms were also taking place (Chapter 5).

Whilst there are signs of modest growth in agrarian production and in ironworking during the seventh and eighth centuries, the economy essentially remained small-scale, with none of the signs of rapid expansion witnessed in southern and eastern England facilitated by the upsurge in cross-Channel and North Sea trade (Chapter 7). Cows were the main unit of value, though references to payments probably in silver bullion suggest the existence of a dual economy. Farming surpluses may have increased, but wealth accrued from the land and its resources remained in the hands of a comparatively small elite and, increasingly, the Church. Their patronage of fine-metalworkers continued, producing objects for display such as ornate penannular brooches and reliquaries, but the scale of production appears significantly less when compared with Ireland and parts of Scotland at this time. Opportunities for long-distance trade may also have been curtailed. Beyond the seventh century, there is no evidence of luxury products arriving from south-west France, probably with raw materials and slaves traded in return. However, continuing links around and across the Irish Sea and Bristol Channel, and with parts of Anglo-Saxon England, make small-scale trade connections likely, though archaeologically these can be hard to trace.

Christianity in Wales grew from Roman roots, with inscribed stones pointing to its subsequent spread amongst the elite. Its consolidation is evident from the seventh century onwards in the transformation of the landscape made possible by the proliferation of Christian sites, a pattern also evident in Ireland and Cornwall (Chapter 10). To what extent this acceleration was brought about by the vicissitudes of the 'Late Antique Little Ice Age' and the impact of plague and their aftermath must remain a matter of speculation, though for some Christian belief in a loving God and the prospect of life after death may have given hope in difficult times (Chapter 9). Nonetheless, it was the establishment of monastic foundations from the late fifth century onwards that provided the impetus for consolidation and the means for the provision of pastoral care (Chapter 10). This was driven by foundations, such as Llandough, that were not shut away from the world, though others in remote places and on islands, such as Caldey, were probably more ascetic in their outlook. At the former, from the seventh century onwards, we can begin to trace the promotion of local saints' cults, the concept of monastic enclosures as places of sanctuary, and their cemeteries as the burial places of lay patrons and their families who were seeking prayers for their souls, indicated, by the late eighth century, in inscriptions on stone sculpture (Chapter 11). In return, patrons donated landed estates, with their scattered farmsteads and hereditary tenants, to these foundations, thereby increasing their wealth. This exchange was instrumental in bringing the secular elite and monastic communities together.

Whether, in the wake of the crises of the mid-sixth century, monasteries might have been the beneficiaries of land that could not be adequately exploited by the secular elite, whilst their donation also maintained some control through kinship ties, is very difficult to say because of lack of evidence. Nevertheless, we should also ask to what extent these foundations, as seems likely in Ireland and England, were catalysts for wider agrarian development and technological innovation (Chapter 6). The advent of charter writing, for example, also points to the role of churchmen in the development of both ecclesiastical and secular administration (Chapter 12). Equally, their intellectual engagement with biblical learning and computistics was instrumental in the implementation of Christian time, which integrated the seasons and the agricultural year with a new pattern of festivals and commemoration in people's lives (Chapter 2).

From the seventh century onwards, we also see the increasing impact of Christianity on the wider population, though the archaeological evidence is mainly from western parts of Wales. Many cemeteries, some associated with prehistoric monuments, were abandoned. Some, however, ultimately became the sites of later medieval parish churches, and new cemeteries were also established, but neither necessarily had church buildings until a later stage. Some new sites may have been founded as small monasteries. Others were the burial places of farming communities that lived close by (Chapter 10). Christian belief was no longer expressed through inscribed memorial stones. Instead, reflecting contacts with Ireland and ultimately the Continent, we see the advent of mostly anonymous cross-carved stones, some of which were the foci of these cemeteries, though the majority marked the graves of the Christian dead (Chapter 11). It has also been argued that the proliferation of *llan* place names for church sites in Wales may be linked to this expansion, though these are also found in south-west England, possibly slightly earlier (Chapter 10). At the same time the wider Christianization of the landscape was also underway. Springs and wells became places of baptism. Cross-carved stones were set up on routeways and at landing places, as, in the eighth century, at St Patrick's Chapel, which may herald the initiation of a pilgrimage landscape associated with St Davids that only becomes visible in the hagiography at the end of the early Middle Ages (Chapters 1, 2, 8, and 11).

The construction of Offa's and Wat's Dykes in the late eighth and early ninth centuries marks a watershed in the evolution of Wales as an entity (Chapter 12). Their initial impact as physical and psychological barriers that broke up landscapes and communities was a realization of the power and ambition of an expanding Mercian hegemony. In effect, this finally brought to an end the prospect of a greater Britain, though a *hiraeth* or 'longing' for it remained for some considerable time. In the longer term we also see the evolution of a frontier zone with its inherent tensions that might easily lead to conflict, with an inevitable impact on people's lives. The evidence as it stands similarly suggests comparatively few opportunities for cross-border trade and exchange but, if the focus was on livestock with raw materials such as salt in return, these are difficult to trace in the archaeology (Chapter 12).

By the mid-ninth century Wales was also being drawn into the Viking world as part of the wider Scandinavian impact on the Atlantic seaways, Ireland, and the Danelaw (Chapter 12). Attacks and some settlement in south-east Anglesey, most clearly evidenced at Llanbedrgoch, as well as west of the Dee should be seen in the context of early tenth-century settlements on Wirral and around the Mersey estuary. These were integral in the development of the Dublin–Chester trade-route and the quest for wider control of the Irish Sea region that in the longer term brought integration and acculturation as well as renewed conflict and the exaction of ransoms and tribute. At the same time, we see attempts at bringing the north-east coastal lowlands of Wales under English control that reached a high point in 921 with the establishment of a *burh* at Rhuddlan (*Cledemutha*) by Edward the Elder, though by around a century later these inroads had been lost (Chapter 5). The Scandinavian impact on the south is less clear and, though some earlier raiding and other activity that may have included settlement are evident, this seems largely related to the opening-up of trade routes between Ireland and Bristol in the course of the eleventh century (Chapter 12).

The relative increase in documentation from the ninth century onwards, including the Harleian Chronicle and later *Brut y Tywysogion*, together with entries in the Irish annals and the Anglo-Saxon Chronicles, provides a chronological framework unavailable earlier (Chapter 1). These shed valuable light upon kingdoms and their rulers, including the expansion of Gwynedd that began in 825 when Merfyn Frych, who probably came from the Isle of Man, came to power. He succeeded in establishing a new dynasty and his descendants subsequently ruled much of Wales.[7] We also gain some understanding of the nature and limitations of their power and authority, and the inherent rivalries and political complexity of the times. Military success remained all-important, but we can similarly see an intricate set of changing alliances that included Welsh rulers submitting to English kings, including both Alfred and Æthelstan. Alliances are also evident with Hiberno-Scandinavian groups which, by the end of the early Middle Ages, may be seen in Welsh rulers' use of mercenaries and their fleets, indicating a wider and more complex theatre of armed conflict, and in the Cambro-Hiberno-Scandinavian identity of Gruffudd ap Cynan of Gwynedd (Chapter 12).

Archaeological evidence for the lives of these rulers, their families, and retinues is only occasionally revealed, making the discoveries at Llangorse crannog all the more significant. Built in the early 890s, it was a summer residence of Elise ap Tewdwr, ruler of Brycheiniog, and was abandoned in 916 following a Mercian attack (Chapter 5). Here we catch glimpses of a lavish lifestyle, the consumption of wheaten bread and pork, probably brought as food render, and venison hunted in the surrounding countryside. Feasting and the sharing of drink are likewise suggested, the festivities accompanied by songs and poetry, perhaps including the Llywarch cycle which is

---

[7] Thornton 2004b; Charles-Edwards 2013, 467–79.

associated with the adjacent landscape. Patronage of craftworkers is also evident, as are the trappings of power in the fragmentary embroidered garment with its Anglo-Saxon style ornament indicating a possible diplomatic gift (Chapters 1, 6, and 7). We similarly see links with the church of Llan-gors, on whose estate the crannog was built, demonstrating their close alliance. The construction of the crannog indicates not only command of labour and resources but also reinvention of an identity rooted in the memory of Irish settlement in Brycheiniog in the fifth and sixth centuries (Chapter 4).

The wider performance of power and increased administrative complexity are seen, from the ninth century onwards, in places of open-air regional and local assembly that may also have been used for royal inauguration, though to date very few have been identified archaeologically (Chapter 12). Some were marked by crosses—for example, the Pillar of Eliseg, set up by Concenn (Cyngen), the last early medieval ruler of Powys, on top of an Early Bronze Age cairn. As elsewhere in Britain, Ireland, and Scandinavia, such places may have reinvented or augmented older landscape foci, including prehistoric burial mounds and hillforts, imbued with the mystique of heroic tales and mythical histories. Equally, they were likely influenced by contact with the late Saxon administrative system of hundreds and their meeting places, and, by the end of the early Middle Ages, the Welsh regional *cantrefi* were also in place, with a secondary division into commotes first visible in the twelfth century (Chapter 12).

From the ninth century onwards, it is also clear that the authority of some ecclesiastical foundations was being extended over larger areas, incorporating and sometimes eclipsing other churches, some of which had bishops, and their saints' cults (Chapter 10). The most significant of these was St Davids, which grew to be the most important church in Wales, and the names of several bishops are known, as is its reputation as a centre of learning. From the eleventh century we are also aware of the rise of Llandaf, later made plain in the ambitions of Urban, its first Norman bishop. Across Wales we can also detect a pattern of smaller but still significant regional foundations that came to be known as mother churches, many of which, such as Llantwit Major, had much earlier monastic roots, while others, particularly in the north, only become evident from the tenth century onwards. Smaller churches may also have been established on secular estates at this time. We should understand that, in a society where patronage and kinship were key, the fortunes of the larger foundations are likely to have been increasingly intertwined with those of ruling families and other members of the landed elite, though this also made them vulnerable to native as well as Viking attacks. The importance of patronage is visible archaeologically in the increasing monumentality of stone sculpture, as at Llantwit Major, the probable burial place of the kings of Glywysing, and stone churches may also have been built on the most important sites, such as Bangor and Llandaf (Chapter 8). At St Davids we also see the active promotion of a wider pilgrimage landscape (Chapter 11). Whilst some indications of monastic practices continued, sometimes on islands more removed from the world, many mother churches had, by the end of the period, evolved into hereditary, landed, family corporations, as at Llanbadarn Fawr, that continued as foci of both pastoral care and learning, but that may also reflect aspects of secular, landed society at this time.

Evidence for secular, as opposed to ecclesiastical, landed estate centres remains sparse. The only extensively excavated example, Llanbedrgoch, seems unlikely to be typical because of the Hiberno-Scandinavian intrusion resulting in a wider range of craftworking and external contacts pointing to mercantile activity (Chapters 5 and 7). Its rebuilt enclosure was clearly impressive, and occupation of a small number of later enclosed sites in the north-west similarly indicates a wider need for defence, as well as a demonstration of status. The lives of less wealthy farming communities also remain very difficult to reconstruct. However, the continuation of a dispersed pattern of open settlements with subrectangular buildings, such as South Hook and Conkland Hill, is suggested. A proportion of these evolved into the dispersed farmsteads of the later Middle Ages with chapels of ease or small parish churches nearby (Chapters 5 and 10). As the climate improved, there were also more opportunities to exploit marginal land that may reflect a rising population as well as improvements in crop and animal husbandry. For example, the presence of bristle oats, found in association with stinking chamomile, on sites in the south-west suggests utilization of more poorly drained soils, possibly aided by improved plough technology. Pollen diagrams, particularly in the north-west, signal increased upland exploitation to provide pasture for dairy herds in the summer months. Farming communities consistently made use of a range of seasonal pastures, but increasing transhumance, by the end of the period, may already have been leading to more permanent upland settlements (Chapters 5 and 6).

Although, from the ninth century onwards, there are increasing signs in Wales of developments in the economy, these were not on the same scale as those in Ireland with the foundation of Dublin and other Hiberno-Scandinavian coastal trading towns, and England with its accelerating urban growth towards the end of the early Middle Ages. The situation is, however, more comparable with Scotland, which continued to lack towns and did not mint coins at this time (Chapter 7). Rhuddlan (*Cledemutha*) was a comparatively small, fortified, English *burh*, planted at the highest fording point across the Clwyd, and though there are some indications of craftworking and trade, these appear modest in scale. The most compelling evidence for craft and more far-flung trading connections comes from Llanbedrgoch, though by the end of the period there are also hints of small coastal trading places, such as Laugharne (Chapters 5 and 7). Churches, such as Bangor, may also have encouraged markets to develop (Chapter 10). Nevertheless, there are few signs of independent craftworking communities, and the emphasis on secular or ecclesiastical patronage appears to be sustained. Overall, the evidence is focused along the north and south coasts with very little from the interior, and the impression given is that Wales was always on the margins of developing trade between Ireland and England (Chapters 7 and 12). Nevertheless, increased coastal and riverine fishing, mainly around the Severn estuary, suggests that Welsh landowners were now benefiting from exploitation of this valuable resource which could also be traded eastwards to supply markets in England (Chapter 6). However, in Wales we are still dealing with a predominantly barter economy at this time. Nonetheless, from the tenth century onwards silver hoards indicate that the use of bullion was increasing, thereby signalling some engagement with the wider Viking Age economy. Transactions in Anglo-Saxon and occasionally other coins still appear rare, though a few coin hoards in the south point to expanding trade with south-west England. Whilst the Hywel Dda penny, minted by a Chester moneyer in the late 940s, is a recognition of the ruler's power and ambition, economically the experiment was clearly short-lived (Chapter 7).

Although there are some signs of an upturn in agricultural production, there is little evidence of increased mineral extraction at this time, apart from iron, the processing of which was facilitated by improving technology, as at South Hook. Overall, the impression given is that the economy in Wales was still comparatively weak (Chapter 7). The underlying reasons are likely to have been complex. The very few settlements with artefact concentrations suggest that wealth and resources were still concentrated in the hands of rulers and a comparatively small landholding elite. Though more land was being brought into production, yields would have been limited by soil fertility, weather, and the control of pests. Once food renders were exacted, surpluses may still have been insufficient to allow the widespread development of more independent trade networks and insufficient agricultural labour may also have been a restraint. Raiding and other forms of conflict brought slave-taking, livestock stealing, and the destruction of crops, leading to increased instability and the loss of livelihoods. Anglo-Saxon kings and Viking leaders as well as native rulers were also demanding payments of tribute and ransom. Such a combination of environmental constraint, economic instability, violence, and extortion could have a devastating impact on the poor, the wealthy, and the Church alike (Chapter 12).

The sack of Rhuddlan by Harold Godwinson in 1063 brought Tegeingl back into English hands and, with his brother Tostig, he went on to campaign in Wales more widely. This ultimately led to the murder of Gruffudd ap Llywelyn of Gwynedd, whose head and ship's figurehead were brought to Harold as trophies. In 1065 he attempted to gain a foothold in Gwent.[8] The Norman invasion of England in 1066 was followed by a rapid advance, leading to the establishment of strongholds under Norman earls in Hereford, Chester, and Shrewsbury in 1067–71, opening the way for inroads into Wales. This was made easier by Gruffudd ap Llywelyn's death, which resulted in a political vacuum and internecine strife. Hiberno-Scandinavian raids were a continuing problem in the west. By the 1090s, however, the Normans had made

[8] Douglas and Greenaway 1981, *s.a.* 1063, 1065.

426 LIFE IN EARLY MEDIEVAL WALES

considerable advances into the south-east, the central borderlands, and the north-east, and even into Gwynedd, Ceredigion, and Dyfed, but ultimately the scale was too ambitious and the geography proved too challenging.[9] Indeed, it was not until 1282 that Wales in its entirety finally succumbed to Edward I.

Nevertheless, from the 1060s onwards the landscape and built environment of Wales were rapidly changing and, as a result, the archaeological evidence becomes much easier to identify. This is seen most clearly in areas that came under sustained Norman control but is also visible in those that remained or came back into Welsh hands and signals widespread societal change and a more rapidly expanding economy. Motte-and-bailey castles, such as Hen Domen, marked the lines of the Norman advance, and the impressive Romanesque stone keep built at Chepstow signified William the Conqueror's power and intention.[10] Some had associated boroughs, for example the motte-and-bailey castle at Rhuddlan, where there was also a mint.[11] In Norman-occupied areas Continental religious orders were introduced and older foundations were brought under those in England, such as St Peter's, Gloucester, or Normandy. Romanesque stone churches, such as Llandaf Cathedral, also sprang up, not only in Norman held areas but also more widely across Wales, aided by the patronage of Welsh princes. This is seen in Gwynedd in the construction of a Romanesque cathedral in Bangor, the churches at Penmon and Tywyn, and a string of smaller churches across Anglesey that were eventually incorporated into the parish system.[12] The princes of Gwynedd also established an administrative system focused on *llysoedd* ('courts'), such as Rhosyr, which may also have spread more widely.[13] Trading settlements also begin to develop, as at Llan-faes (Chapter 7). Whilst the dispersed pattern of farming settlements remained in many parts of Wales, in Norman-occupied areas of the south we also see the plantation of nucleated villages with open-field systems, as at Cosmeston in the Vale of Glamorgan. Continuing climatic improvement also facilitated increasing upland settlement.[14]

In this discussion, I have suggested that, although underlying continuities are also evident, there were four periods that brought more rapid change to people's lives: firstly, the collapse of the market economy and end of Roman rule focused on the second half of the fourth and first half of the fifth centuries; secondly, the century following the onset of the 'Late Antique Little Ice Age' in 536 that may have precipitated steeper population decline, contributing to settlement change and landscape reorganization and leading in the longer term to modest agricultural expansion as well as the consolidation of Christianity; thirdly, the late eighth and first half of the ninth century marked by the construction of Offa's and Wat's Dykes that began to

---

[9] Davies, R. R. 1987, 27–34.   [10] Higham and Barker 2000; Bates 2006, 21–2.
[11] Quinnell and Blockley 1994, 214–16.
[12] Davies, R. R. 1987, 39–40; Edwards 1996, 59–61; 2013, 421–2; Gem 2009.   [13] Johnstone 1997.
[14] Edwards 1997a, 5–8.

define the frontier of Wales and the advent of Viking incursions, but also wider signs of an expanding economy; and lastly, the Norman conquests and settlement. In the future, increased and more accurate radiocarbon dating and Bayesian analysis gained from well-stratified early medieval sites and deposits will enable a more nuanced understanding, allowing us to build on this chronological framework, but only if we can recognize them in the first place. Priority should therefore be given to the identification and excavation of settlements with good environmental preservation, not only those of the elite but also those of farming communities, in order to understand more clearly the longer-term evolution of settlements within a wider landscape, the exploitation of resources, and the changing economy. Equally, there have still been remarkably few excavations on larger ecclesiastical sites and more research should be directed to identifying places of assembly. We also need more lowland pollen samples to understand long-term environmental change and the analysis of cemetery populations to gain insights into health, kin, diet, migration, and belief.[15] At the same time new theoretical interpretations of the data and other interdisciplinary and multidisciplinary studies will provide new insights, and we should consider not simply the changing dynamics of elite male society in early medieval Wales but also the changing lives of others, including women and children, more fully. Ultimately, however, it is only with more data, particularly from a range of excavations, that we will be able to test and refine current interpretations and formulate new and more sophisticated questions in the future.

---

[15] See Edwards et al. 2016 for further discussion of a research framework for the archaeology of early medieval Wales.

REFERENCES

Abdy, R. (2006), 'After Patching: imported and recycled coinage in fifth- and sixth-century Britain', in Cook and Williams (eds) (2006), 75–98.

Abdy, R., and Williams, G. (2006), 'A catalogue of hoards and single finds from the British Isles, *c.* AD 410–675', in Cook and Williams (eds) (2006), 11–73.

Ab Ithel, J. Williams (ed.) (1860), *Annales Cambriae* (London: Longman, Green, Longman, and Roberts).

Adlam, R., and Wysocki, M. (2009), 'Appendix I: the human skeletal remains', in A. Davidson (2009b), 210–19.

Ahronson, K., and Charles-Edwards, T. M. (2010), '*Prehistoric Annals* and early medieval monasticism: Daniel Wilson, James Young Simpson and their cave sites', *Antiquaries Journal*, 90, 455–66.

Alcock, L. (1958), 'Post-Roman sherds from "Longbury Bank" Cave, Penally (Pemb.)', *Bulletin of the Board of Celtic Studies*, 18(1), 77–8.

Alcock, L. (1963), *Dinas Powys: An Iron Age, Dark Age and Early Medieval Settlement in Glamorgan* (Cardiff: University of Wales Press).

Alcock, L. (1967), 'Excavations at Degannwy Castle, Caernarvonshire, 1961–6', *Archaeological Journal*, 124, 190–201.

Alcock, L. (1971), *Arthur's Britain: History and Archaeology AD 367–634* (London: Allen Lane).

Alcock, L. (1972), '*By South Cadbury, is that Camelot...': The Excavation of Cadbury Castle 1966–1970* (London: Thames & Hudson).

Alcock, L. (1975–6), 'A multi-disciplinary chronology for Alt Clut, Castle Rock, Dumbarton', *Proceedings of the Society of Antiquaries of Scotland*, 107, 103–13.

Alcock, L. (1987), *Economy, Society and Warfare among the Britons and Saxons* (Cardiff: University of Wales Press).

Alcock, L. (1995), *Cadbury Castle, Somerset: The Early Medieval Archaeology* (Cardiff: University of Wales Press).

Alcock, L., and Alcock, E. A. (1987), 'Reconnaissance excavations on early historic fortifications and other royal sites in Scotland 1974–84: 2, Excavations at Dunollie Castle, Oban, Argyll, 1978', *Proceedings of the Society of Antiquaries of Scotland*, 117, 119–47.

Alcock, L., Alcock, E. A., and Driscoll, S. T. (1989), 'Reconnaissance excavations on early historic fortifications and other royal sites in Scotland: 3, Excavations at Dundurn', *Proceedings of the Society of Antiquaries of Scotland*, 119, 189–226.

Allason-Jones, L. (2010), 'Personal appearance', in R. Collins and L. Allason-Jones (eds) (2010), 78–85.

Allen, J. R. (1899), 'Early Christian art in Wales', *Archaeologia Cambrensis*, ser. 5, 16, 1–69.

Allen, J. R., and Anderson, J. (1903), *The Early Christian Monuments of Scotland*, 3 pts (repr. 1993 with an introduction by I. Henderson) (Balgavies: Pinkfoot Press).

430 REFERENCES

Allen, J. R. L., and Bell, M. G. (1999), 'A Late Holocene tidal palaeochannel, Redwick, Gwent: late Roman activity and a possible early medieval fish trap', *Archaeology in the Severn Estuary*, 10, 53–64.

Allen, M., Lodwick, L., Brindle, T., Fulford, M., and Smith, A. (2017), *New Visions of the Countryside of Roman Britain, Vol. 2: The Roman Economy of Britain* (London: Society for the Promotion of Roman Studies, Britannia monograph 30).

Andrew, W. J. (1923–4), 'A spindle-whorl carved in imitation of a penny of Athelstan A.D. 925–941', *British Numismatic Journal*, 17, 305–6.

Andrews, M. (1989), *The Search for the Picturesque* (Aldershot: Scolar Press).

Anguilano, L., Timberlake, S., and Rehren, T. (2010), 'An early medieval lead-smelting bole from Banc Tynddol, Cwmystwyth, Ceredigion', *Historical Metallurgy*, 44, 85–103.

Anon. (1850), 'Fourth annual meeting, Dolgellau', *Archaeologia Cambrensis*, ser. 2, 1, 315–34.

Anon. (1883), 'Fishguard meeting report', *Archaeologia Cambrensis*, ser. 4, 14, 333–48.

Anon. (2012), *Watery Bay and Gateholm Island, Pembrokeshire, Wales: Archaeological Evaluation and Assessment of Results* (Wessex Archaeology, report 77508.1).

Anon. (2021), 'Roman villa revealed near Wrexham', *Current Archaeology*, 371, 10.

Archif Melville Richards, http://www.e-gymraeg.co.uk/enwaulleoedd/amr/cronfa_en.aspx [accessed 11 December 2020].

Archwilio: The Historic Environment Records of Wales, https://www.archwilio.org.uk/arch/ [accessed 15 October 2021].

Arnold, C. J. (1998), 'Excavation of "Ty Newydd", Ynys Enlli (Bardsey Island), Gwynedd', *Archaeologia Cambrensis*, 147, 96–132.

Arnold, C. J., and Davies, J. L. (2000), *Roman and Early Medieval Wales* (Stroud: Sutton).

Arnold, C. J., and Huggett, J. W. (1997), *New Pieces, Criggion, Powys: Interim Report on the Archaeological Investigations 1997* (Glasgow University, unpublished report).

Arnold, C. J., and Huggett, J. W. (2000), *New Pieces, Criggion, Powys. Interim Report on the Archaeological Investigations 2000* (Glasgow University, unpublished report).

Ashby, S. P. (2009), 'Combs, contact and chronology: reconsidering the combs in early-historic and Viking-Age Atlantic Scotland', *Medieval Archaeology*, 53, 1–33.

Ashby, S. P. (2014), 'Technologies of appearance: hair behaviour in early medieval Europe', *Archaeological Journal*, 171(1), 151–84.

Ashby, T. (1907), 'Excavations at Caerwent, Monmouthshire, on the site of the city of Venta Silurum, in the year 1906', *Archaeologia*, 60, 451–64.

Ashby, T., Hudd, A. E., and King, F. (1911), 'Excavations at Caerwent, Monmouthshire, on the site of the Romano-British city of Venta Silurum, in the years 1909 and 1910', *Archaeologia*, 62, 405–48.

Astill, G. (2008), 'General survey 600–1300', in D. P. Palliser (ed.), *The Cambridge Urban History of Britain, Vol. 1: 600–1540* (Cambridge: Cambridge University Press), 51–78.

Astle, T., Ayscough, S., and Cayley, J. (eds) (1802), *Taxatio ecclesiastica Angliae et Walliae auctoritate P. Nicholai IV. circa A.D. 1291* (London: Record Commission).

Atkin, C. W. (1954), 'Herefordshire', in H. C. Darby and I. B. Terrett (eds), *The Domesday Geography of Midland England*, 1st ed. (Cambridge: Cambridge University Press), 57–112.

Austin, D. (ed.) (1995), *Carew Castle Archaeological Project 1994 Season Interim Report* (Dept of Archaeology, University of Wales, Lampeter).

REFERENCES 431

Backhouse, J., Turner, D. H., and Webster, L. (1984), *The Golden Age of Anglo-Saxon Art* (London: British Museum).

Bailey, R. N. (2010), *Corpus of Anglo-Saxon Stone Sculpture Vol. IX, Lancashire and Cheshire* (Oxford: Oxford University Press).

Baillie, M. (1995), *A Slice through Time: Dendrochronology and Precision Dating* (London: B. T. Batsford).

Baker, J., and Brookes, S. (2015), 'Identifying outdoor assembly sites in early medieval England', *Journal of Field Archaeology*, 40(1), 3–21.

Banham, D., and Faith, R. (2014), *Anglo-Saxon Farms and Farming* (Oxford: Oxford University Press).

Barber, A. (2008), *Land at Cwrt Llechrhyd, Llanelwedd, Powys, Archaeological Evaluation* (Cotswold Archaeological Trust, report 08220).

Barber, A., Leonard, C., and Hart, J. (2014), *South Wales Gas Pipeline Project: Site 512, Land North of Steynton, Milford Haven, Pembrokeshire* (Cotswold Archaeology, report 13255).

Barber, J. W., and Crone, B. A. (1993), 'Crannogs; a diminishing resource? A survey of the crannogs of southwest Scotland and excavations at Buiston crannog', *Antiquity*, 67, 520–33.

Barford, P. M., Owen, W. G., and Britnell, W. J. (1986), 'Iron spearhead and javelin from Four Crosses, Llandysilio, Powys', *Medieval Archaeology*, 30, 103–6.

Baring-Gould, S., and Burnard, R. (1904), 'An exploration of some cytiau in Tre'r Ceiri', *Archaeologia Cambrensis*, 6th ser., 4, 1–16.

Baring-Gould, S., and Fisher, J. (1907–13), *The Lives of the British Saints*, 4 vols (London: Hon. Soc. Cymmrodorion).

Barkan, L. (1999), *Unearthing the Past: Archaeology and Aesthetics in the Making of Renaissance Culture* (New Haven, London: Yale University Press).

Barker, P., and Higham, R. (1982), *Hen Domen Montgomery: A Timber Castle on the English-Welsh Border, Vol. I* (London: Royal Archaeological Institute).

Barker, P., and Lawson, J. (1971), 'A pre-Norman field-system at Hen Domen, Montgomery', *Medieval Archaeology*, 5, 58–72.

Barker, P., White, R., Pretty, K., Bird, H., and Corbishley, M. (1997), *The Baths Basilica at Wroxeter* (London: English Heritage).

Barker, S., Coombe, P., and Perna, S. (2018), 'Re-use of Roman stone in London city walls', in C. Coquelet, G. Creemers, R. Dreesen, and E. Goemaere (eds), *Roman Ornamental Stones in North-Western Europe* (Namur: Études et Documents Archéologie 38), 327–48.

Barrett, J. C., Freeman, P. W. M., and Woodward, A. (2000), *Cadbury Castle Somerset: The Later Prehistoric and Early Historic Archaeology* (London: English Heritage).

Barrett, J. H., Locker, A. M., and Roberts, C. M. (2004), ' "Dark Age Economics" revisited: the English fish bone evidence AD 600–1600', *Antiquity*, 78, 618–36.

Barrowman, R. C., Batey, C. E., and Morris, C. D. (2007), *Excavations at Tintagel Castle, Cornwall, 1990–1999* (London: Society of Antiquaries of London).

Bartrum, P. C. (ed.) (1966), *Early Welsh Genealogical Tracts* (Cardiff: University of Wales Press).

Bassett, S. (1992), 'Church and diocese in the West Midlands: the transition from British to Anglo-Saxon control', in J. Blair and R. Sharpe (eds), *Pastoral Care Before the Parish* (Leicester, London, and New York: Leicester University Press), 13–40.

432 REFERENCES

Bates, D. (2006), 'William the Conqueror, William fitz Osbern and Chepstow Castle', in R. Turner and A. Johnson (eds), *Chepstow Castle: Its History and Buildings* (Logaston: Logaston Press), 15–22.

Bateson, J. D. (1973), 'Roman material from Ireland: a re-consideration', *Proceedings of the Royal Irish Academy*, 73C, 21–97.

Bateson, J. D. (1976), 'Further finds of Roman material in Ireland', *Proceedings of the Royal Irish Academy*, 76C, 171–80.

Bayley, J. (n.d.), *Crucibles and Related Finds from Dinas Powys* (English Heritage: Ancient Monuments Laboratory, unpublished report).

Bayliss, A., Bronk Ramsey, C., van der Plicht, J., and Whittle, A. (2007), 'Bradshaw and Bayes: towards a timetable for the Neolithic', *Cambridge Archaeological Journal*, 17(S1, Feb.), 1–28.

Bayliss, A., Hines, J., Høilund Nielsen, K., McCormac, G., and Scull, C. (2013), *Anglo-Saxon Graves and the Grave Goods of the 6th and 7th Centuries AD: A Chronological Framework* (London: Society for Medieval Archaeology).

Baynes, E. N. (1908), 'The excavations at Din Lligwy', *Archaeologia Cambrensis*, 6th ser., 8, 183–210.

Baynes, E. N. (1930), 'Further excavations at Din Lligwy', *Archaeologia Cambrensis*, 85, 375–93.

Beckwith, J. (1972), *Ivory Carvings in Early Medieval England* (London: Harvey Miller).

Beit-Hallahmi, B., and Argyle, M. (1997), *The Psychology of Religious Behaviour: Belief and Experience* (London and New York: Routledge).

Belford, P. (2019), 'Hidden earthworks: excavation and protection of Offa's and Wat's Dykes', *Offa's Dyke Journal*, 1, 80–95.

Berks, T., Davidson, A., Kenney, J., Roberts, J. A., and Smith, G. (2007), 'A497 improvement: prehistoric sites in the vicinity of Abererch and Chwilog', *Archaeology in Wales*, 47, 3–17.

Besly, E. (1993), 'Recent coin hoards from Wales', *British Numismatic Journal*, 63, 84–90.

Besly, E. (1995), 'Short cross and other medieval coins from Llanfaes, Anglesey', *British Numismatic Journal*, 65, 46–82.

Besly, E., (2006), 'Few and far between: mints and coins in Wales to the middle of the thirteenth century', in Cook and Williams (eds) (2006), 701–19.

Best, R. I., and Lawlor, H. J. (eds.) (1931), *The Martyrology of Tallaght* (London: Henry Bradshaw Society 68).

Bevan-Jones, R. (2002), *The Ancient Yew* (Macclesfield: Windgather).

Bhreathnach, E. (2014), *Ireland and the Medieval World AD 400–1000: Landscape, Kingship and Religion* (Dublin: Four Courts).

Bick, D. (2004), 'Holloways in the Welsh border', *Archaeology in Wales*, 44, 100–4.

Biddle, M. (2018), *The Search for Winchester's Anglo-Saxon Minsters* (Oxford: Archaeopress).

Bieler, L. (ed. and trans.) (1979), *The Patrician Texts in the Book of Armagh* (Dublin: Dublin Institute of Advanced Studies).

Birth, K. K. (2014), 'The Vindolanda timepiece: time and calendar-reckoning in Roman Britain', *Oxford Journal of Archaeology*, 33(4), 395–411.

Blackburn, M. (1996), 'Hiberno-Norse and Irish Sea imitations of Cnut's *quatrefoil* type', *British Numismatic Journal*, 66, 1–20.

Blackburn, M. (2007), 'Currency under the Vikings, Part 3: Ireland, Wales, Isle of Man and Scotland in the ninth and tenth centuries', *British Numismatic Journal*, 77, 119–49.

Blackmore, L., Blair, I., Hirst, S., and Scull, C. (2019), *The Prittlewell Princely Burial: Excavations at Priory Crescent, Southend-on-Sea, Essex, 2003* (London: MOLA monograph 73).

Blair, J. (2005), *The Church in Anglo-Saxon Society* (Oxford: Oxford University Press).

Blair, J. (2013), *The British Culture of Anglo-Saxon Settlement* (University of Cambridge, Department of Anglo-Saxon, Norse and Celtic, H. M. Chadwick Memorial Lectures 24).

Blair, J. (2018), *Building Anglo-Saxon England* (Princeton and Oxford: Princeton University Press).

Bland, R., and Loriot, X. (2010), *Roman and Early Byzantine Gold Coins found in Britain and Ireland* (London: Royal Numismatic Society).

Blinkhorn, P. (2013), 'No pots please, we're Vikings: pottery in the southern Danelaw, 850–1000', in L. ten Harkel and D. M. Hadley (eds), *Everyday Life in Viking Age Towns* (Oxford: Oxbow), 157–71.

Blockley, K. (1990), 'Excavations in the vicinity of Forden Gaer Roman fort, Powys 1987', *Montgomeryshire Collections*, 78, 17–46.

Blockley, K. (2014), 'Archaeological excavations adjacent to St Llwchaiarn's churchyard, Llanmerewig', *Montgomeryshire Collections*, 102, 53–70.

Blockley, K., and Taverner, N. (2002), 'Excavations at Sarn-y-bryn-caled, Welshpool, Powys in 1998–9', *Montgomeryshire Collections*, 90, 41–68.

Blunt, C. E. (1982), 'The cabinet of the Marquess of Ailesbury and the penny of Hywel Dda', *British Numismatic Journal*, 52, 117–22.

Boazman, G. (2019), 'Medieval culture and identity in the southern hinterland of Hiberno-Scandinavian Dublin', in S. Duffy (ed.), *Medieval Dublin XVII* (Dublin: Four Courts), 15–62.

Bollard, J. K. (2009), 'Landscapes of the Mabinogi', *Landscapes*, 2, 37–60.

Bollard, J. K. (ed. and trans.), and Griffiths, A. (2015), *Englynion y Beddau: Stanzas of the Graves* (Llanrwst: Gwasg Carreg Gwalch).

Boon, G. C. (1958), 'A note on the Byzantine Æ coins said to have been found at Caerwent', *Bulletin of the Board of Celtic Studies*, 17(4), 316–19.

Boon, G. C. (1960), 'A temple of Mithras at Caernarvon–Segontium', *Archaeologia Cambrensis*, 119, 136–72.

Boon, G. C. (1962), 'A Christian monogram at Caerwent', *Bulletin of the Board of Celtic Studies*, 19(4), 338–44.

Boon, G. C. (1976), 'The shrine of the head, Caerwent', in G. C. Boon and J. M. Lewis (eds), *Welsh Antiquity* (Cardiff: National Museum Wales), 163–75.

Boon, G. C. (1977), 'A Greco-Roman anchor-stock from north Wales', *Antiquaries Journal*, 57, 10–30.

Boon, G. C. (1981–2), 'Three bones of St Tatheus: or, Duw yn anghyfiawn ni rann', *Monmouthshire Antiquary*, 3–4, 1–5.

Boon, G. C. (1986a), 'Theodosian coins from north and south Wales', *Bulletin of the Board of Celtic Studies*, 33, 429–35.

Boon, G. C. (1986b), *Welsh Hoards, 1979–81* (Cardiff: National Museum of Wales).

Boon, G. C. (1991), 'Byzantine and other exotic ancient bronze coins from Exeter', in N. Holbrook and P. T. Bidwell (eds), *Roman Finds from Exeter* (Exeter: Exeter City Council and University of Edinburgh), 38–45.

Boon, G. C. (1992), 'The early Christian church in Gwent, I: the Romano-British church', *Monmouthshire Antiquary*, 8, 11–24.

Bornholdt Collins, K., Fox, A., and Graham-Campbell, J. (2014), 'The 2003 Glenfaba hoard (*c*.1030), Isle of Man', in R. Naismith, M. Allen, and E. Screen (eds), *Early Medieval Monetary History: Studies in Memory of Mark Blackburn* (Farnham: Ashgate), 471–514.

Borst, A. (1993), *The Ordering of Time: From the Ancient Computus to the Modern Computer* (Cambridge: Polity Press).

Bourke, C. (2007), 'The monastery of Saint Mo-Choi of Nendrum: the early medieval finds', in McErlean and Crothers (2007), 406–21.

Bourke, C. (2008), 'Early ecclesiastical hand-bells in Ireland and Britain', *Journal of the Antique Metalware Society*, 16 (June), 22–8.

Bourke, C. (2009), 'The shrine of St Gwenfrewi from Gwytherin, Denbighshire: an alternative interpretation', in Edwards (ed.) (2009b), 375–88.

Bourke, C. (2020), *The Early Medieval Hand-Bells of Ireland and Britain* (Sandyford: National Museum of Ireland).

Bowen, E. G. (1954), *The Settlements of the Celtic Saints in Wales* (Cardiff: University of Wales Press).

Bowen, E. G. (1969), *Saints, Seaways and Settlements in the Celtic Lands*, 2nd ed. (Cardiff: University of Wales Press).

Boyle, S. D. (1991), 'Excavations at Hen Waliau, Caernarfon, 1952–1985', *Bulletin of the Board of Celtic Studies*, 38, 191–212.

Bradley, Jeremy (2013), *Land off Penrhos Road, Bangor, Gwynedd* (Oxford Archaeology North report 2013–14/1386).

Bradley, John (1988), 'The interpretation of Scandinavian settlement in Ireland', in J. Bradley (ed.), *Settlement and Society in Early Medieval Ireland* (Kilkenny: Boethius Press), 49–78.

Bradley, R. (1987), 'Time regained: the creation of continuity', *Journal of the British Archaeological Association*, 140, 1–17.

Bradley, R. (2000), *An Archaeology of Natural Places* (Abingdon: Routledge).

Bradley, R. (2007), *The Prehistory of Britain and Ireland* (Cambridge: Cambridge University Press).

Brady, N. (2016), 'What the plough can reveal about the role of agrarian technology in the changing nature of early medieval Ireland' in J. Klápště (ed.), *Agrarian Technology in the Medieval Landscape* (Turnhout: Brepols, Ruralia 10), 143–55.

Branigan, K., Dearne, M. J., and Rutter, R. G. (1993), 'Romano-British occupation of Minchin Hole Cave, Gower', *Archaeologia Cambrensis*, 142, 40–73.

Brannlund, L. (2013), *South Wales Gas Pipeline Project, Site 25.08, Land South of Brynwgan, Manorbier and Salem, Carmarthenshire, Archaeological Excavation* (Cotswold Archaeology report 13276).

Brassil, K. S., Owen, W. G., and Britnell, W. J. (1991), 'Prehistoric and early medieval cemeteries at Tandderwen, near Denbigh, Clwyd', *Archaeological Journal*, 149, 46–97.

Breen, T. C. (1988), 'Excavation of a roadway at Bloomhill Bog, County Offaly', *Proceedings of the Royal Irish Academy*, 88C, 321–39.

Breese, C. E. (1930), 'The fort at Dinas Emrys', *Archaeologia Cambrensis*, 85, 342–54.

Brereton, J. M. (1990), *The Brecon Beacons National Park* (Newton Abbot and London: David & Charles).

REFERENCES   435

Brett, M., Holbrook, N., and McSloy, E. R. (2015), 'Romano-British and medieval occupation at Sudbrook Road, Portskewett, Monmouthshire: excavations in 2009', *Monmouthshire Antiquary*, 31, 3–43.

Brewer, J. S. (ed.) (1863), *Geraldi Cambrensis Opera*, Vol. 3 (London: Longman, Roberts and Green).

Brewer, R. (1993), 'Venta Silurum: a civitas capital', in S. J. Greep (ed.), *Roman Towns: The Wheeler Inheritance, A Review of 50 Years' Research* (York: Council for British Archaeology), 56–65.

Brewer, R. (2004), 'The Romans in Gwent', in M. Aldhouse-Green and R. Howell (eds), *Gwent County History, Volume 1: Gwent in Prehistory and Early History* (Cardiff: University of Wales Press), 205–43.

Brewer, R. (2006), *Caerwent Roman Town*, 3rd ed. (Cardiff: Cadw).

Britnell, W. J. (1989), 'The Collfryn hillslope enclosure, Llansantffraid Deuddwr, Powys: excavations 1980–1982', *Proceedings of the Prehistoric Society*, 55, 89–134.

Britnell, W. J. (1990), 'Capel Maelog, Llandrindod Wells, Powys: excavations 1984–87', *Medieval Archaeology*, 34, 27–96.

Britnell, W. J. (1994), 'Excavation and recording at Pennant Melangell Church', *Montgomeryshire Collections*, 82, 41–102.

Britnell, W. J., and Silvester, R. J. (eds), (2012), *Reflections on the Past: Essays in honour of Frances Lynch* (Welshpool: Cambrian Archaeological Association).

Britnell, W. J., and Silvester, R. J. (2018), 'Hillforts and defended enclosures in the Welsh borderland', *Internet Archaeology*, 48.

Britnell, W. J., and Watson, K. (1994), 'Saint Melangell's shrine, Pennant Melangell', *Montgomeryshire Collections*, 82, 147–66.

Bromwich, R., and Evans, D. S. (eds) (1992), *Glossary to Culhwch ac Olwen* (Lewiston and Lampeter: Edward Mellon).

Brook, D. (1992), 'The early church east and west of Offa's Dyke', in Edwards and Lane (eds) (1992), 77–89.

Brooks, N. (2010), 'Why is *The Anglo-Saxon Chronicle* about kings?', *Anglo-Saxon England*, 39, 43–70.

Brown, A., Turner, R., and Pearson, C. (2010), 'Medieval fishing structures and baskets at Sudbrook Point, Severn Estuary, Wales', *Medieval Archaeology*, 54, 346–61.

Brown, I. (2004), *Discovering a Welsh Landscape: Archaeology in the Clwydian Range* (Macclesfield: Windgather).

Brown, P. (2013), *Through the Eye of a Needle: Wealth, the Fall of Rome, and the Making of Christianity in the West, 350–550 AD* (Princeton: Princeton University Press).

Browne, D. (2007), 'From antiquarianism to archaeology: the genesis and achievement of the Royal Commission's Anglesey volume', *Archaeologia Cambrensis*, 156, 33–49.

Browne, D., and Griffiths, R. A. (2008), 'One hundred years of investigation', in P. Wakelin and R. A. Griffiths (eds), *Hidden Histories: Discovering the Heritage of Wales* (Aberystwyth: RCAHMW), 19–29.

Browne, D., and Hughes, S. (eds) (2003), *Archaeology of the Welsh Uplands* (Aberystwyth: RCAHMW).

Bruce-Mitford, R. L. S. (1975–83), *The Sutton Hoo Ship-Burial*, 3 vols (Cambridge: British Museum Press).

436 REFERENCES

Brugmann, B. (2004), *Glass Beads in Early Anglo-Saxon England* (Oxford: Oxbow).

Brunning, R. (2010), 'Taming the floodplain: river canalisation and causeway formation in the Middle Anglo-Saxon period at Glastonbury, Somerset', *Medieval Archaeology*, 54, 319–29.

Bryant, R. (2012), *Corpus of Anglo-Saxon Stone Sculpture, Vol. X, The Western Midlands* (Oxford: Oxford University Press).

Bully, S., and Picard, J.-M. (2017), '*Mensa in deserto*: reconciling Jonas's *Life of St Columbanus* with recent archaeological discoveries at Annegray and Luxeuil', in Edwards et al. (eds) (2017), 119–43.

Büntgen, U., Myglan, V. S., Ljungvist, F. C., McCormick, M., Di Cosmo, N., et al. (2016), 'Cooling and societal change during the Late Antique Little Ice Age from 536 to around 660 CE', *Nature Geoscience*, 9 (March), 231–6.

Burgess, R. (2012), 'The Gallic Chronicle of 452: a new critical edition with a brief introduction', in R. W. Mathisen and D. Shanzer (eds), *Society and Culture in Late Antique Gaul* (Aldershot: Ashgate), 52–84.

Burnham, B. C. (1993), 'Sites explored: Wales', in B. C. Burnham, L. J. F. Keppie, A. S. Esmond Cleary, M. W. C. Hassall, and R. S. O. Tomlin, 'Roman Britain in 1992', *Britannia*, 24, 269–76.

Burnham, B. C., and Davies, J. L. (eds) (2010), *Roman Frontiers in Wales and the Marches* (Aberystwyth: RCAHMW).

Burnham, B. C., and Wacher, J. (1990), *The 'Small Towns' of Roman Britain* (London: B. T. Batsford).

Büster, L., and Armit, I. (2018), 'Signs from the Pictish underground: early medieval cave ritual at Sculptor's Cave, north-east Scotland', in K. Andreas Bergsvik and M. Dowd (eds), *Caves and Ritual in Medieval Europe, AD 500–1500* (Oxford and Philadelphia: Oxbow), 85–96.

Butler, L., and Graham-Campbell, J. (1990), 'A lost reliquary casket from Gwytherin, north Wales', *Antiquaries Journal*, 70, 40–8.

Cahill Wilson, J. (2014), 'Romans and Roman material in Ireland: a wider perspective', in *Late Iron Age and 'Roman' Ireland*, Discovery Programme Reports 8 (Dublin: Wordwell), 11–58.

Cahill Wilson, J., Standish, C., and O'Brien, E. (2014), 'Investigating mobility and migration in the later Irish Iron Age', in *Late Iron Age and 'Roman' Ireland*, Discovery Programme Reports 8 (Dublin: Wordwell), 127–49.

Camden, W. (1594), *Britannia siue Florentissimorum regnorum, Angliae, Scotiae, Hiberniae, et insularum adiacentium ex intima antiquitate chorographica descriptio* (London: George Bishop).

Camden, W. (1695), *Camden's Britannia newly translated into English with large additions and improvements* (Oxford: Edmund Gibson).

Campbell, E. (1989a), 'New finds of post-Roman imported pottery and glass from south Wales', *Archaeologia Cambrensis*, 138, 59–66.

Campbell, E. (1989b), 'A blue glass squat jar from Dinas Powys, south Wales', *Bulletin of the Board of Celtic Studies*, 36, 239–45.

Campbell, E. (1991), *Imported Goods in the Early Medieval Celtic West: with special reference to Dinas Powys* (unpublished PhD thesis, University College of Wales Cardiff).

REFERENCES **437**

Campbell, E. (2000), 'A review of glass vessels in western Britain and Ireland AD 400–800', in J. Price (ed.), *Glass in Britain and Ireland AD 350–1100*, Occasional Paper 127 (London: British Museum), 33–46.

Campbell, E. (2007a), *Continental and Mediterranean Imports to Atlantic Britain and Ireland, AD 400–800* (York: Council for British Archaeology).

Campbell, E. (2007b), *Imported Material in Atlantic Britain and Ireland, AD 400–800* [data set] (York: Archaeology Data Service), https://doi.org/10.5284/1000293.

Campbell, E. (2013), 'Hybridity and identity in early medieval Wales: an enamelled Class G brooch from Goodwick, Pembrokeshire', in A. Reynolds and L. Webster (eds), *Early Medieval Art and Archaeology in the Northern World* (Leiden and Boston: Brill), 163–75.

Campbell, E. (n.d.), *Early Medieval Imported Pottery and Glass from New Pieces* (unpublished report).

Campbell, E., and Lane, A. (1989), 'Llangorse: a 10th-century royal crannog in Wales', *Antiquity*, 63, 675–81.

Campbell, E., and Lane, A. (1993), 'Excavations at Longbury Bank, Dyfed, an early medieval settlement in south Wales', *Medieval Archaeology*, 37, 15–77.

Campbell, E., and Macdonald, P. (1993), 'Excavations at Caerwent Vicarage Orchard Garden 1973: an extra-mural post-Roman cemetery', *Archaeology Cambrensis*, 142, 74–98.

Campbell, E., and Maldonado, A. (2020), 'A New Jerusalem "at the ends of the earth": interpreting Charles Thomas's excavations at Iona Abbey 1956–63', *Antiquaries Journal*, 100, 33–85.

Canmore: National Record of the Historic Environment, Historic Scotland, https://canmore. org.uk/ [accessed 25 October 2021].

Cantrill, T. C. (1910), 'Hut-circles on Gateholm, Pembrokeshire', *Archaeologia Cambrensis*, 6th ser., 10, 271–82.

Carr, A. D. (2011), *Medieval Anglesey*, 2nd ed. (Llangefni: Anglesey Antiquarian Society).

Carr, L. C. (2012), *Tessa Verney Wheeler: Women and Archaeology before World War Two* (Oxford: Oxford University Press).

Carroll, J., Reynolds, A., and Yorke, B. (2019a), 'Introduction', in Carroll et al. (2019b), 1–33.

Carroll, J., Reynolds, A., and Yorke, B. (eds) (2019b), *Power and Place in Europe in the Early Middle Ages* (Oxford: Oxford University Press).

Carruthers, W. (2010), 'Charred plant remains, in Crane and Murphy (2010b), 163–81.

Cartwright, J. (2007), 'The cult of St Non: rape, sanctity and motherhood in Welsh and Breton hagiography', in Evans and Wooding (eds) (2007), 182–206.

Carver, M. (2010), *The Birth of a Borough: An Archaeological Study of Anglo-Saxon Stafford* (Woodbridge: Boydell).

Carver, M. (2019), *Formative Britain: An Archaeology of Britain, Fifth to Eleventh Century AD* (Abingdon and New York: Routledge).

Carver, M., Garner-Lahire, J., and Spall, C. (2016), *Portmahomack on Tarbat Ness: Changing Ideologies in North-East Scotland, Sixth to Sixteenth Century AD* (Edinburgh: Society of Antiquaries of Scotland).

Caseldine, A. E. (1990), *Environmental Archaeology in Wales* (Lampeter: Saint David's University College).

Caseldine, A. E. (2011), 'Environmental archaeology', *Archaeology in Wales*, 50, 135–6.

Caseldine, A. E. (2015), 'Environmental change and archaeology – a retrospective view', *Archaeology in Wales*, 54, 3–14.

Caseldine, A. E., and Griffiths, C. J. (2019), 'The plant remains', in Lane and Redknap (2019), 158–73.

Casey, P. J. (1974a), 'Excavations outside the north-east gate of Segontium, 1971', *Archaeologia Cambrensis*, 123, 54–77.

Casey, P. J. (1974b), 'A coin of Valentinian III from Wroxeter', *Britannia*, 5, 383–6.

Casey, P. J. (1983), 'Caerwent (*Venta Silurum*): the excavation of the north-west corner tower and an analysis of the structural sequence of the defences', *Archaeologia Cambrensis*, 132, 49–77.

Casey, P. J. (1989), 'Coin evidence and the end of Roman Wales', *Archaeological Journal*, 146, 320–9.

Casey, P. J., and Davies, J. L. (1993), *Excavations at Segontium (Caernarfon) Roman Fort, 1975–1979* (London: Council for British Archaeology).

Casey, P. J., and Hoffmann, B. (1999), 'Excavations at the Roman temple in Lydney Park, Gloucestershire in 1980 and 1981', *Antiquaries Journal*, 79, 81–143.

Cavill, P. (2000), 'Place-names of the Wirral: a gazetteer', in P. Cavill, S. E. Harding, and J. Jesch (eds), *Wirral and its Viking Heritage* (Nottingham: English Place-Name Society), 125–47.

Cavill, P. (2015), 'The Battle of Brunanburgh in 937 – battlefield dispatches', in Harding et al. (eds) (2015), 95–108.

CELT: *Corpus of Electronic Texts* (*Documents of Ireland*, University College Cork), https://celt.ucc.ie/ [accessed 4 November 2020].

Chadwick, A. M., and Catchpole, T. (2010), 'Casting the net wide: mapping and dating fish traps through the Severn Estuary Rapid Coastal Zone Assessment Survey', *Archaeology in the Severn Estuary*, 21, 47–80.

Chadwick, N. K. (1958a), 'Early culture and learning in north Wales', in N. K. Chadwick, K. Hughes, C. Brooke, and K. Jackson (eds), *Studies in the Early British Church* (Cambridge: Cambridge University Press), 29–120.

Chadwick, N. K. (1958b), 'Intellectual life in west Wales in the last days of the Celtic Church', in N. K. Chadwick, K. Hughes, C. Brooke, and K. Jackson (eds), *Studies in the Early British Church* (Cambridge: Cambridge University Press), 121–82.

Chadwick, N. K. (1959), 'Intellectual contacts between Britain and Gaul in the fifth century', in H. M. Chadwick, N. K. Chadwick, K. Jackson, R. Bromwich, P. Hunter Blair, and O. Chadwick, *Studies in the Early British Church* (Cambridge: Cambridge University Press), 189–263.

Channing, J. (2012), 'Ballykilmore – living with the dead, the development and continuity of an early medieval graveyard', in P. Stevens and J. Channing, *Settlement and Community in the Fir Tulach Kingdom: Archaeological Excavation on the M6 & N52 Road Schemes* (Dublin: National Roads Authority and Westmeath County Council).

Charles, B. G. (1948), 'The second book of George Owen's *Description of Penbrokeshire*', *National Library of Wales Journal*, 5(4), 265–85.

Charles, B. G. (1992), *The Place-names of Pembrokeshire*, 2 vols (Aberystwyth: National Library of Wales).

Charles-Edwards, G. (2002), 'The Springmount bog tablets: their implications for Insular epigraphy and palaeography', *Studia Celtica*, 36, 27–45.

REFERENCES **439**

Charles-Edwards, G. (2006), *The Origins and Development of Insular Geometric Letters* (unpublished PhD thesis, University of Wales, Bangor).

Charles-Edwards, G., and McKee, H. (2008), 'Lost voices from Anglo-Saxon Lichfield', *Anglo-Saxon England*, 37, 79–89.

Charles-Edwards, T. M. (1971), 'The seven bishop-houses of Dyfed', *Bulletin of the Board Celtic Studies*, 24(2), 247–62.

Charles-Edwards, T. M. (1976), 'Boundaries in Irish law', in P. H. Sawyer (ed.), *Medieval Settlement* (London: Arnold) 83–7.

Charles-Edwards, T. M. (1993), *Early Irish and Welsh Kinship* (Oxford: Clarendon Press).

Charles-Edwards, T. M. (2000), *Early Christian Ireland* (Cambridge: Cambridge University Press).

Charles-Edwards, T. M. (2004), 'Cadwallon (Cædwalla) *ap* Cadfan (*d.* 634)', *Oxford Dictionary of National Biography*, https://doi-org.ezproxy.bangor.ac.uk/10.1093/ref:odnb/4322 [accessed 14 November 2017].

Charles-Edwards, T. M. (trans.) (2006), *The Chronicle of Ireland*, 2 vols (Liverpool: Liverpool University Press).

Charles-Edwards, T. M. (2012), 'The use of the book in Wales, *c.* 400–1100', in R. Gameson (ed.) (2012), 389–405.

Charles-Edwards, T. M. (2013), *Wales and the Britons 350–1064* (Oxford: Oxford University Press).

Christie, N., and Herold, H. (eds) (2016), *Fortified Settlements in Early Medieval Europe: Defended Communities 8th–10th Centuries* (Oxford and Philadelphia: Oxbow).

Ciarialdi, M. (2012), 'Charred plant remains', in Cuttler, R., Davidson, A., and Hughes, G., *A Corridor through Time: The Archaeology of the A55 Anglesey Road Scheme* (Oxford: Oxbow), 222–42.

Clarke, S. (2008), *Down the Dig, Monmouth—An Adventure in Archaeology* (Monmouth: Monmouth Archaeology Society).

Clay, C. (2004), 'Iconoclasm in Roman Chester: the significance of the mutilated tombstones from the north wall', *Journal of the British Archaeological Association*, 157(1), 1–16.

Clwyd-Powys Archaeological Trust, *Historic Landscapes: The Vale of Clwyd*, http://www.cpat.org.uk/projects/longer/histland/clwyd/clnatura.htm [accessed 12 October 2021].

Coe, J. B. (2001), *The Place-Names of the Book of Llandaf* (unpublished PhD thesis, University of Wales Aberystwyth).

Coflein: National Monuments Record of Wales, https://coflein.gov.uk/ [accessed 15 October 2021].

Colgrave, B., and Mynors, R. A. B. (eds and trans.) (1969), *Bede's Ecclesiastical History of the English People* (Oxford: Clarendon Press).

Collingwood, R. G., and Wright, R. P. (1995), *The Roman Inscriptions of Britain, I: Inscriptions on Stone*, 2nd ed. (Oxford: Oxford University Press).

Collins, R. (2010), 'Brooch use in the 4th- to 5th-century frontier', in R. Collins and L. Allason-Jones (eds) (2010), 64–77.

Collins, R. (2012), *Hadrian's Wall and the End of Empire: The Roman Frontier in the 4th and 5th Centuries* (London: Routledge).

Collins, R., and Allason-Jones, L. (eds) (2010), *Finds from the Frontier: Material Culture in the 4th–5th Centuries* (York: Council for British Archaeology).

Collis, J. (2003), *The Celts: Origins, Myths and Inventions* (Stroud: Tempus).

Comber, M. (2004), *Native Evidence of Non-ferrous Metalworking in Early Historic Ireland* (Oxford: British Archaeological Reports, Int. ser. 1296).

Comeau, R. (2009), 'Cytir and crosses: the archaeological landscape of the parish of Dinas', *Archaeologia Cambrensis*, 158, 225–53.

Comeau, R. (2014), 'Bayvil in Cemaes: an early medieval assembly site in south-west Wales?', *Medieval Archaeology*, 58, 270–84.

Comeau, R. (2016), 'Feeding the body and claiming spirit(s): early Christian landscapes in west Wales', in T. Ó Carragáin and S. Turner (eds), *Making a Christian Landscape in Atlantic Europe* (Cork: Cork University Press), 205–24.

Comeau, R. (2019), 'The practice of "in rodwallis": medieval Welsh agriculture in north Pembrokeshire', in Comeau and Seaman (eds) (2019), 130–52.

Comeau, R. (2020), *Land, People and Power in Early Medieval Wales: The Cantref of Cemais in Comparative Perspective* (Oxford: British Archaeological Reports, Brit. ser. 659).

Comeau, R. (2021), 'Crop processing and early medieval settlement: the evidence for Bayvil, Pembrokeshire', *Medieval Settlement Research*, 36, 61–7.

Comeau, R., and Burrow, S. (2021a), 'Corn-drying kilns in Wales: a review of the evidence', *Archaeologia Cambrensis*, 170, 111–49.

Comeau, R., and Burrow, S. (2021b), 'Corn-drying kilns in Wales: a gazetteer', https://doi.org/10.5284/1085018.

Comeau, R., and Seaman, A. (eds) (2019), *Living off the Land* (Oxford: Windgather).

Cone, P. (ed.) (1977), *Treasures of Irish Art 1500 B.C. to 1500 A.D.* (New York: Metropolitan Museum of Art).

Connolly, S., and Picard, J.-M. (trans.) (1987), 'Cogitosus: *Life of St Brigit*', *Journal of the Royal Society of Antiquaries of Ireland*, 117, 11–27.

Cook, B., and Williams, G. (eds) (2006), *Coinage and History in the North Sea World c. 500–1250: Essays in honour of Marion Archibald* (Leiden: Brill).

Cool, H. E. M. (2000), 'The parts left over: material culture into the fifth century', in T. Wilmott and P. Wilson (eds), *The Late Roman Transition in the North* (Oxford: British Archaeological Reports, Brit. ser. 299), 47–65.

Cool, H. E. M. (2006), *Eating and Drinking in Roman Britain* (Cambridge: Cambridge University Press).

Copplestone-Crow, B. (2009), *Herefordshire Place-Names*, 2nd ed. (Little Logaston: Logaston Press).

Costen, M. D., and Costen, N. P. (2016), 'Trade and exchange in Anglo-Saxon Wessex, c AD 600–780', *Medieval Archaeology*, 60(1), 1–26.

Courtney, P. (1994), *Medieval and Later Usk* (Cardiff: University of Wales Press).

Cowley, F. G. (2007), 'The relics of St David: the historical evidence', in Evans, J. W., and Wooding (eds) (2007), 274–81.

Coyle McClung, L., and Plunkett, G. (2020), 'Cultural change in the climate record in final prehistoric and early medieval Ireland', *Proceedings of the Royal Irish Academy*, 120C, 1–30.

Craig, D. (1997), 'The provenance of the early Christian inscriptions of Galloway', in P. Hill, *Whithorn and St Ninian: The Excavation of a Monastic Town 1984–91* (Stroud: Whithorn Trust and Sutton), 614–23.

Cramp, R. (2005–6), *Wearmouth and Jarrow Monastic Sites*, 2 vols (Swindon: English Heritage).

Cramp, R. (2009), 'Milestones in early medieval archaeology', in Gilchrist and Reynolds (eds) (2009), 47–63.

Crane, P. (2004), 'Excavations at Newton, Llanstadwell, Pembrokeshire', *Archaeology in Wales*, 44, 3–32.

Crane, P. (2006), *Ty Isaf, Llanwnda, Goodwick, Pembrokeshire* (Cambria Archaeology, report 2006/70).

Crane, P. (2008a), 'Felindre Varchog A487', *Archaeology in Wales*, 48, 138.

Crane, P. (2008b), *A487 Castell Cadw, Felindre Farchog, Pembrokeshire Road Improvements: Archaeological Watching Brief* (Dyfed Archaeological Trust, report 2008/32).

Crane, P., and Murphy, K. (2010a), 'The excavation of a coastal promontoty fort at Porth y Rhaw, Solva, Pembrokeshire 1995–98', *Archaeologia Cambrensis*, 159, 53–98.

Crane, P., and Murphy, K. (2010b), 'Early medieval settlement, iron smelting and crop processing at South Hook, Herbranston, Pembrokeshire, 2004–05', *Archaeologia Cambrensis*, 159, 117–95.

C R Archaeology (2015), 'St Mary's Church, Nefyn, Lleyn Peninsular [*sic*]', *Archaeology in Wales*, 54, 203–5.

Craw, J. H. (1929–30), 'Excavations at Dunadd and other sites on the Poltalloch estates', *Proceedings of the Society of Antiquaries of Scotland*, 64, 111–46.

Crawford, J. (2011), 'MONMOUTH, William Jones Almshouses', *Archaeology in Wales*, 50, 107.

Crew, P. (1980), 'Holyhead Mountain', *Archaeology in Wales*, 20, 42–4.

Crone, A. (1993), 'Crannogs and chronologies', *Proceedings of the Society of Antiquaries of Scotland*, 123, 245–54.

Crone, A. (2000), *The History of a Scottish Lowland Crannog: Excavations at Buiston, Ayrshire 1989–90* (Edinburgh: Scottish Trust for Archaeological Research).

Crone, A., and Campbell, E. (2005), *A Crannog of the 1st Millennium AD: Excavations by Jack Scott at Loch Glashan, Argyll, 1960* (Edinburgh: Society of Antiquaries of Scotland).

Cunliffe, B. (2001), *Facing the Ocean: The Atlantic and its Peoples* (Oxford: Oxford University Press).

Curle, A. O. (1913–14), 'Report on the excavation, in September 1913, of a vitrified fort at Rockcliffe, Dalbeattie, known as the Mote of Mark', *Proceedings of the Society of Antiquaries of Scotland*, 48, 125–68.

Cuttler, R., Davidson, A., and Hughes, G. (2012), *A Corridor through Time: The Archaeology of the A55 Road Scheme* (Oxford: Oxbow).

Darby, H. C. (1954), 'Gloucestershire', in H. C. Darby and I. B. Terrett (eds), *The Domesday Geography of Midland England*, 1st ed. (Cambridge: Cambridge University Press), 1–56.

Darby, H. C. (1977), *Domesday England* (Cambridge: Cambridge University Press).

Darby, H. C. (1987), 'Domesday: 1086 – 1836 – 1986', *National Library of Wales Journal*, 25(1), 1–17.

Dark, K. R. (1990), *Interim Report on the Excavation at Brawdy Hill-Fort, Dyfed, Wales* (unpublished report).

Dark, K. R. (1994a), *From Civitas to Kingdom* (Leicester: Leicester University Press).

Dark, K. R. (1994b), *Discovery by Design: The Identification of Secular Élite Settlements in Western Britain A.D. 400–700* (Oxford: British Archaeological Reports, Brit. ser. 237).

442 REFERENCES

Dark, K. R. (2000), *Britain and the End of the Roman Empire* (Stroud: Tempus).

Dark, P. (2000), *The Environment of Britain in the First Millennium* A.D. (London: Duckworth).

Darvill, T., David, A., Griffiths, S., Hart, J., James, H., Murphy, K., and Rackham, J. (2020), *Timeline: The Archaeology of the South Wales Gas Pipeline* (Cirencester: Cotswold Archaeology Monograph 13).

Darvill, T., and Wainwright, G. (2016), 'Neolithic and Bronze Age Pembrokeshire', in H. James et al. (eds) (2016), 55–222.

Davidson, A. (2009a), 'The early medieval church in north-west Wales', in Edwards (ed.) (2009b), 41–60.

Davidson, A. (2009b), 'Excavations at Tywyn y Capel, Trearddur Bay, Anglesey, 1997 and 2002–3', *Archaeologia Cambrensis*, 158, 167–223.

Davidson, A., Hopewell, D., Kenney, J., and Longley, D. (2002), *Early Medieval Burial and Ecclesiastical Sites 2001–2002* (Gwynedd Archaeological Trust, report 451).

Davies, E. (1929), *The Prehistoric and Roman Remains of Denbighshire* (Cardiff: William Lewis).

Davies, E. (1949), *The Prehistoric and Roman Remains of Flintshire* (Cardiff: William Lewis).

Davies, J. L. (1967), 'Excavations at Caer Dynnaf, Llanblethian, Glam. 1965–1967', *Morgannwg*, 11, 77–8.

Davies, J. L. (2002), 'Land use and military supply in the Highland Zone of Roman Britain', in M. Aldhouse-Green and P. Webster (eds), *Artefacts and Archaeology: Aspects of the Celtic and Roman World* (Cardiff: University of Wales Press), 44–61.

Davies, J. L. (2012a), 'Roman Anglesey: a survey and recent research', in Britnell and Silvester (eds) (2012), 369–89.

Davies, J. L. (2012b), 'The Romans in mid Wales: Montgomeryshire', *Montgomeryshire Collections*, 100, 45–66.

Davies, J. L., and Driver, T. (2018), 'The Romano-British villa at Abermagwr, Ceredigion: excavations 2010–15', *Archaeologia Cambrensis*, 167, 143–209.

Davies, J. L., Hague, D. B., and Hogg, A. H. A. (1971), 'The hut-settlement on Gateholm, Pembrokeshire', *Archaeologia Cambrensis*, 120, 102–10.

Davies, J. R. (2002), 'The saints of south Wales and the Welsh church', in Thacker and Sharpe (eds) (2002), 361–95.

Davies, J. R. (2003), *The Book of Llandaf and the Norman Church in Wales* (Woodbridge: Boydell).

Davies, J. R. (2007a), 'Some observations on the "Nero", "Digby", and "Vespasian" recensions of *Vita S. David*', in J. W. Evans and Wooding (eds) (2007), 156–60.

Davies, J. R. (2007b), 'The archbishopric of St Davids and the bishops of *Clas Cynidr*', in J. W. Evans and Wooding (eds) (2007), 296–304.

Davies, J. R. (2012), 'Old Testament personal names among the Britons: their occurrence and significance', *Viator*, 43(1), 175–92.

Davies, M. (2002), 'Gruffudd ap Llywelyn, king of Wales', *Welsh History Review*, 21(2), 207–48.

Davies, R. R. (1987), *Conquest, Coexistence, and Change: Wales 1063–1415* (Oxford: Clarendon Press; Cardiff: University of Wales Press).

Davies, S. (trans.) (2007), *The Mabinogion* (Oxford: Oxford University Press).

Davies, T. L. (2015), *Early Medieval Llyn Tegid: An Environmental Landscape Study* (unpublished PhD thesis, University of Sheffield).

Davies, T. L. (2019), 'Culture, climate, coulter and conflict: pollen studies from early medieval Wales', in Comeau and Seaman (eds) (2019), 174–98.

Davies, W. (1974–5), 'The Celtic Church', *Journal of Religious History*, 8, 406–11.

Davies, W. (1978), *An Early Welsh Microcosm: Studies in the Llandaff Charters* (London: Royal Historical Society).

Davies, W. (1979a), *The Llandaff Charters* (Aberystwyth: National Library of Wales).

Davies, W. (1979b), 'Roman settlements and post-Roman estates in south-east Wales', in P. J. Casey (ed.), *The End of Roman Britain* (Oxford: British Archaeological Reports, Brit. ser. 71, 153–73.

Davies, W. (1981), 'Property rights and property claims in Welsh "Vitae" of the eleventh century', in E. Patlagean and P. Riché (eds), *Hagiographie, Cultures et Sociétés IVe–XIIe Siècles* (Paris: Études Augustiniennes), 515–33.

Davies, W. (1982a), *Wales in the Early Middle Ages* (Leicester: Leicester University Press).

Davies, W. (1982b), 'The Latin charter-tradition in western Britain, Brittany and Ireland in the early medieval period', in D. Whitelock, R. McKitterick, and D. N. Dumville (eds), *Ireland in Early Medieval Europe* (Cambridge: Cambridge University Press), 258–80.

Davies, W. (1983), 'A historian's view of Celtic archaeology', in D. A. Hinton (ed.), *25 Years of Medieval Archaeology* (Sheffield: University of Sheffield and Society for Medieval Archaeology), 67–73.

Davies, W. (1990), *Patterns of Power in Early Wales* (Oxford: Clarendon Press).

Davies, W. (1992), 'The myth of the Celtic Church', in Edwards and Lane (eds) (1992), 12–21.

Davies, W. (1998), 'Charter-writing and its uses in early medieval Celtic societies', in H. Pryce (ed.), *Literacy in Medieval Celtic Societies* (Cambridge: Cambridge University Press), 99–112.

Davies, W. (2001), 'Thinking about the Welsh environment a thousand years ago', in G. H. Jenkins (ed.), *Wales and the Welsh 2000* (Aberystwyth: Centre for Advanced Welsh and Celtic Studies), 1–18.

Davies, W. (2004), 'Looking backwards to the early medieval past: Wales and England, a contrast in approaches', *Welsh History Review*, 22(2), 197–221.

Davies, W., and Flechner, R. (2017), 'Conversion to Christianity and economic change: consequence or coincidence?', in Edwards et al. (eds) (2017), 377–96.

Davies, W., Graham-Campbell, J., Handley, M., Kershaw, P., Koch, J. T., Le Duc, G., and Lockyer, K. (2000), *The Inscriptions of Early Medieval Brittany* (Oakville, CT, and Aberystwyth: Celtic Studies Publications).

Davis, O. (2011), 'A LiDAR survey of Skokholm Island, Gateholm islet and Marloes peninsular [*sic*], Pembrokeshire', *Archaeologia Cambrensis*, 160, 115–32.

Davis, O., and Sharples, N. (2014), *Excavations at Caerau Hillfort, Cardiff, South Wales, 2013: Interim Report* (Cardiff Studies in Archaeology, report 34).

Davis, O., and Sharples, N. (2015), *Excavations at Caerau Hillfort, Cardiff, South Wales, 2014: Interim Report* (Cardiff Studies in Archaeology, report 35).

Davis, O., Sharples, N., and Wyatt, D. (2014), 'The Caer Heritage Project: fieldwork at Caerau', *Archaeology in Wales*, 54, 35–42.

Davis, O., Sharples, N., Wyatt, D., Brook, D., and Young, T. (2015), 'The Caer Heritage Project: a preliminary note on recent research and community engagement at Caerau hillfort, Cardiff', *Archaeology in Wales*, 55, 13–19.

Day, J. (2011), 'Shields in Welsh poetry up to *c.* 1300: decoration, shape and significance', *Studia Celtica*, 45, 27–52.

Day, J. (2015), 'Weapons and fighting in *Y Gododdin*', *Studia Celtica*, 49, 121–47.

Deliyannis, D. M. (2001), 'Year-dates in the early Middle Ages', in C. Humphrey and W. M. Ormrod (eds), *Time in the Early Medieval World* (Woodbridge: York Medieval Press and Boydell), 5–22.

della Dora, V. (2016), *Mountain, Nature and Culture* (London: Reaktion).

de Smedt, C., van Hoofe, G., and de Backer, J. (eds) (1887), *Acta Sanctorum quotquot Toto Orbe coluntur vel a Catholicis Scriptoribus celebrantur...*, Nov. vol. 1 (Paris: Victorem Palmé), 691–759.

Díaz-Andreu, M. (2007), *A World History of Nineteenth-Century Archaeology: Nationalism, Colonialism and the Past* (Oxford: Oxford University Press).

Dickinson, T. M. (1982), 'Fowler's Type G penannular brooches reconsidered', *Medieval Archaeology*, 26, 41–68.

Dobat, S. (2008), 'Danevirke revisited: an investigation into military and socio-political organization in south Scandinavia (*c.* AD 700–1100)', *Medieval Archaeology*, 52, 27–67.

Dolley, R. H. M. (1958–9), 'A hoard of pennies of Eadgar from Laugharne churchyard in south Wales', *British Numismatic Journal*, 29, 255–8.

Dolley, R. H. M. (1959), 'Two unpublished finds of English eleventh-century pence', *Numismatic Chronicle*, 19, 187–92.

Dolley, R. H. M., and Knight, J. K. (1970), 'Some single finds of tenth- and eleventh-century English coins from Wales', *Archaeologia Cambrensis*, 119, 75–82.

Donovan, E. (1805), *Descriptive Excursions through South Wales and Monmouthshire in the year 1804 and the Four Preceding Summers*, 2 vols (London: author).

Dooley, A. (2007), 'The plague and its consequences in Ireland', in Little (ed.) (2007a), 215–28.

Douglas, D. C., and Greenaway, G. W. (eds) (1981), English Historical Documents Online 1042–1189, *The Anglo-Saxon Chronicle (1042–1155)* (London: Routledge), http://www.englishhistoricaldocuments.com/document/view.html?id=268 [accessed 20 October 2020].

Dowd, M. (2015), *The Archaeology of Caves in Ireland* (Oxford and Philadelphia: Oxbow).

Dowd, M. (2018), 'Saintly associations with caves in Ireland from the early medieval period (AD 400–1169) through to recent times', in K. N. Bergsvik and M. Dowd (eds), *Caves and Ritual in Medieval Europe, AD 500–1400* (Oxford and Philadelphia: Oxbow), 116–30.

Downham, C. (2007), *Viking Kings of Britain and Ireland* (Edinburgh: Dunedin Academic Press).

Downham, C. (2018), *Medieval Ireland* (Cambridge: Cambridge University Press).

Doyle, I. W. (2009), 'Mediterranean and Frankish imports from early medieval Ireland', *Journal of Irish Archaeology*, 18, 17–62.

Driscoll, S. T. (2011), 'Pictish archaeology: persistent problems and structural solutions', in Driscoll et al. (eds) (2011), 245–79.

Driscoll, S. T., Geddes, J., and Hall, M. A. (eds) (2011), *Pictish Progress: New Studies on Northern Britain in the Early Middle Ages* (Leiden and Boston: Brill).

Driver, T. B. (2006), 'RCAHMW aerial reconnaissance 2006', *Archaeology in Wales*, 46, 143–52.

Driver, T. B. (2007), *Pembrokeshire: Historic Landscapes from the Air* (Aberystwyth: RCAHMW).

Driver, T. B. (2016), *The Hillforts of Cardigan Bay* (Little Logaston: Logaston Press).

REFERENCES **445**

Driver, T. B., and Davidson, A. (2005), 'New discoveries at St. Baglan's Church, Llanfaglan (Bontnewydd), Gwynedd', *Archaeology in Wales*, 45, 104–5.

Duckworth, C. N., and Wilson, A. (eds) (2020), *Recycling and Reuse in the Roman Economy* (Oxford: Oxford University Press).

Duggan, M. (2018), *Links to Late Antiquity: Ceramic Exchange and Contacts on the Atlantic Seaboard in the 5th to 7th Centuries AD* (Oxford, British Archaeological Reports, Brit. ser. 639).

Dull, R. A., Southon, J. R., Kutterolf, S., et al. (2019), 'Radiocarbon and geologic evidence reveal Ilopango volcano as source of the colossal "mystery" eruption of 539/40 CE', *Quaternary Science Reviews*, 222, 105855.

Dumbleton, E. N. (1870), 'On a crannoge, or stockaded island, in Llangorse Lake, near Brecon', *Archaeologia Cambrensis*, ser. 4, 1, 192–8.

Dumville, D. N. (1977), 'Sub-Roman Britain: history and legend', *History*, 62, 173–92.

Dumville, D. N. (1986), 'The historical value of the *Historia Brittonum*', *Arthurian Literature*, 6, 1–26.

Dumville, D. N. (1993), 'British missionary activity in Ireland', in D. N. Dumville (ed.), *St Patrick A.D. 493–1993* (Woodbridge: Boydell), 133–45.

Dumville, D. N. (2001), *Saint David of Wales*, Kathleen Hughes Memorial Lecture 1 (Cambridge: University of Cambridge).

Dumville, D. N. (2002), *Annales Cambriae, A.D. 682–954: Texts A–C in Parallel* (Cambridge: University of Cambridge).

Dunlevy, M. (1988), 'A classification of early Irish combs', *Proceedings of the Royal Irish Academy*, 88C, 341–422.

Dykes, D. W. (1976), *The Anglo-Saxon Coins in the National Museum of Wales* (Cardiff: National Museum of Wales).

Eckhardt, H., and Williams, Howard (2003), 'Objects without a past? The use of objects in early Anglo-Saxon graves', in Howard Williams (ed.), *Archaeologies of Remembrance? Death and Memory in Past Societies* (New York, Boston, Dordrecht, London, and Moscow: Kluwer Publications and Plenum Publishers), 141–70.

Edmonds, F. (2019), *Gaelic Influence on the Northumbrian Kingdom: The Golden Age and the Viking Age* (Woodbridge: Boydell).

Edwards, N. (1985), 'A possible Viking grave from Benllech, Anglesey', *Transactions of the Anglesey Antiquarian Society*, 19–24.

Edwards, N. (1986), 'Anglesey in the early Middle Ages: the archaeological evidence', *Transactions of the Anglesey Antiquarian Society*, 19–42.

Edwards, N. (1990), *The Archaeology of Early Medieval Ireland* (London: B. T. Batsford).

Edwards, N. (1991), 'The Dark Ages', in J. Manley, S. Grenter, and F. Gale (eds), *The Archaeology of Clwyd* (Mold: Clwyd County Council), 129–41.

Edwards, N. (1995), '11th-century Welsh illuminated manuscripts: the nature of the Irish connection', in C. Bourke (ed.), *From the Isles of the North: Early Medieval Art in Britain and Ireland* (Belfast: HMSO), 147–55.

Edwards, N. (1996), 'Identifying the archaeology of the early church in Wales and Cornwall', in J. Blair and C. Pyrah (eds), *Church Archaeology: Research Directions for the Future* (York: Council for British Archaeology), 49–62.

Edwards, N. (1997a), Landscape and settlement in medieval Wales: an introduction', in Edwards (ed.) (1997b), 1–11.

Edwards, N. (ed.) (1997b), *Landscape and Settlement in Medieval Wales* (Oxford: Oxbow).

Edwards, N. (1997c), 'Two carved stone pillars from Trefollwyn, Anglesey', *Archaeological Journal*, 154, 108–17.

Edwards, N. (2001), 'Early medieval inscribed stones and stone sculpture in Wales: context and function', *Medieval Archaeology*, 45, 15–39.

Edwards, N. (2002), 'Celtic saints and early medieval archaeology', in Thacker and Sharpe (eds) (2002), 225–65.

Edwards, N. (2007a), *A Corpus of Early Medieval Inscribed Stones and Stone Sculpture in Wales, Vol. II: South-West Wales* (Cardiff: University of Wales Press).

Edwards, N. (2007b), 'Edward Lhuyd and the origins of early medieval Celtic archaeology', *Antiquaries Journal*, 87, 165–96.

Edwards, N. (2008), 'An early medieval penannular brooch from Ty'n y Coed, Pentraeth, Anglesey', *Archaeologia Cambrensis*, 157, 153–6.

Edwards, N. (2009a), 'The archaeology of the early medieval Celtic churches: an introduction', in Edwards (ed.) (2009b), 1–18.

Edwards, N. (ed.) (2009b), *The Archaeology of the Early Medieval Celtic Churches* (Leeds: Maney).

Edwards, N. (2009c), 'Rethinking the Pillar of Eliseg', *Antiquaries Journal*, 89, 143–77.

Edwards, N. (2010), 'Edward Lhuyd: an archaeologist's view', *Welsh History Review*, 25(1), 20–50.

Edwards, N. (2011), 'Viking-age sculpture in north-west Wales: wealth, power, patronage and the Christian landscape', in F. Edmonds and P. Russell (eds), *Tome: Studies in Medieval Celtic History and Law in honour of Thomas Charles-Edwards* (Woodbridge: Boydell), 73–87.

Edwards, N. (2012), 'Roman continuity and reinvention: the early medieval inscribed stones of north Wales', in Britnell and Silvester (eds) (2012), 390–405.

Edwards, N. (2013), *A Corpus of Early Medieval Inscribed Stones and Stone Sculpture in Wales, Vol. III: North Wales* (Cardiff: University of Wales Press).

Edwards, N. (2015), *The Early Medieval Sculpture of Wales: Text, Pattern and Image*, Kathleen Hughes Memorial Lectures 13 (Cambridge: Hughes Hall and Department of Anglo-Saxon, Norse and Celtic, University of Cambridge).

Edwards, N. (2016a), 'Perspectives on conversion in Wales', in Flechner and Ní Mhaonaigh (eds) (2016), 93–107.

Edwards, N. (2016b), 'Christianising the landscape in early medieval Wales: the island of Anglesey', in T. Ó Carragáin and S. Turner (eds), *Making Christian Landscapes—Conversion and Consolidation in Early Medieval Europe* (Cork: Cork University Press), 177–203, 482–8.

Edwards, N. (2016c), 'New discoveries of early medieval carved stones in Wales', *Archaeologia Cambrensis*, 165, 187–99.

Edwards, N. (2017a), 'Chi-rhos, crosses and Pictish symbols: inscribed stones and stone sculpture in early medieval Wales and Scotland', in Edwards et al. (eds) (2017), 381–407.

Edwards, N. (2017b), 'The archaeology of early medieval Wales: a matter of identity', *Studia Celtica*, 51, 65–87.

Edwards, N. (forthcoming), 'The penannular brooch', in *Llangefni Linkroad Early Medieval Cemetery* (Brython Archaeology, report).

Edwards, N., Davies, T., and Hemer, K. A. (2016), 'Research framework for the archaeology of early medieval Wales *c.* AD 400–1070', http://www.archaeoleg.org.uk/pdf/refresh2016/earlymedrefresh2016.pdf [accessed 8 January 2021].

Edwards, N., and Gould, J. (2013), 'From antiquarians to archaeologists in nineteenth-century Wales: the question of prehistory', in N. Evans and H. Pryce (eds), *Writing a Small Nation's Past: Wales in Comparative Perspective, 1850–1950* (Farnham: Ashgate), 143–63.

Edwards, N., and Gray Hulse, T. (1992), 'A fragment of a reliquary casket from Gwytherin, Denbighshire', *Antiquaries Journal*, 72, 91–101.

Edwards, N., and Gray Hulse, T. (1997), 'Gwytherin (Denbs.): a second fragment of *Arch Gwenfrewi*', *Archaeology in Wales*, 37, 87–8.

Edwards, N., and Lane, A. (eds) (1988), *Early Medieval Settlements in Wales AD 400–1100* (Bangor and Cardiff: University College of North Wales and University College Cardiff).

Edwards, N., and Lane, A. (eds) (1992), *The Early Church in Wales and the West* (Oxford: Oxbow).

Edwards, N., Lane, A., Bapty, I., and Redknap, M. (2005), 'Early medieval Wales: a framework for archaeological research', http://www.archaeoleg.org.uk/pdf/earlymed/VERSION%2001%20EARLY%20MEDIEVAL.pdf [accessed 8 January 2021].

Edwards, N., Lane, A., and Redknap, M. (2010), 'Early medieval Wales: an updated framework for archaeological research', http://www.archaeoleg.org.uk/pdf/reviewdocs/earlymedreview.pdf [accessed 8 January 2021].

Edwards, N., and Ní Mhaonaigh, M. (2017), 'Transforming landscapes of belief in the early medieval Insular world and beyond: an introduction', in Edwards et al. (eds) (2017), 1–17.

Edwards, N., Ní Mhaonaigh, M., and Flechner, R. (eds) (2017), *Transforming Landscapes of Belief in the Early Medieval Insular World and Beyond: Converting the Isles II* (Turnhout: Brepols).

Edwards, N., Robinson, G., and Williams, H. (2015), *Excavations at the Pillar of Eliseg, Llangollen, 2010–2012* (Bangor University, University of Chester, unpublished report).

Edwards, N., and Vousden, N. (2014), 'A rediscovered piece of early medieval sculpture from Silian, Ceredigion', *Archaeology in Wales*, 53, 125–30.

Effros, B. (2002), *Caring for Body and Soul: Burial and the Afterlife in the Merovingian World* (Pennsylvania: Pennsylvania State University Press).

Eogan, G. (2012), *Excavations at Knowth 5: The Archaeology of Knowth in the First and Second Millennia AD* (Dublin: Royal Irish Academy).

Esmonde Cleary, A. S. (1989), *The Ending of Roman Britain* (London: B. T. Batsford).

Esmonde Cleary, A. S. (2013), *The Roman West, AD 200–500* (Cambridge: Cambridge University Press).

Etchingham, C. (2001), 'North Wales, Ireland and the Isles: the Insular Viking zone', *Peritia*, 15, 145–87.

Etchingham, C. (2007), 'Viking-age Gwynedd and Ireland: political relations', in Jankulak and Wooding (eds) (2007), 149–67.

Evans, D. R., and Metcalf, V. M. (1992), *Roman Gates: Caerleon* (Oxford: Oxbow).

Evans, E. M. (2000), *The Caerleon Canabae: Excavations in the Civil Settlement 1984–90* (London: Society for the Promotion of Roman Studies, Britannia Monograph 16).

Evans, E. M. (2001), *Romano British South East Wales Settlement Survey: Final Report* (Glamorgan Gwent Archaeological Trust, report 2001/23).

Evans, E. M. (2009), 'Continuity and renewal of monastic landholding in Wales before and after the Anglo-Norman conquest', in Edwards (ed.) (2009b), 85–103.

Evans, E. M. (2018), 'Romano-British settlements in south-east Wales', *Internet Archaeology*, 48.

Evans, E. M., Dowdell, G., and Thomas, H. J. (1985), 'A third-century maritime establishment at Cold Knap, Barry, South Glamorgan', *Britannia*, 16, 57–125.

Evans, J. G., and Rhys, J. (eds.) (1893), *The Book of Llan Dâv* (Oxford, facsimile ed.; Aberystwyth: National Library of Wales, 1979).

Evans, J. W. (1992), 'The survival of the *clas* as an institution in medieval Wales: some observations on Llanbadarn Fawr', in Edwards and Lane (eds) (1992), 33–40.

Evans, J. W., and Wooding, J. M. (eds) (2007), *St David of Wales: Cult, Church and Nation* (Woodbridge: Boydell).

Evans, P. (2004), 'Excavations at Cardiff Castle 2003', *Archaeology in Wales*, 44, 43–60.

Evans, R., Davidson, J., Kennaway, K., and Jones, B. M. (2016), *St. Iestyn, Llanddona, Anglesey, Proposed Churchyard Extension, Archaeological Excavation: Interim Report* (Gwynedd Archaeological Trust, report 1308).

Evans, R., and Jones, B. (2019), 'Early medieval cemeteries at Llanbedrgoch and Llaniestyn, Anglesey', *Archaeologia Cambrensis*, 168, 137–51.

Evans, R., Oates, A.-M., McNicol, D., Lynes, M., and Smith, S. G. (2015), *St. Iestyn, Llanddona, Anglesey, Proposed Churchyard Extension: Archaeological Watching Brief* (Gwynedd Archaeological Trust, report 1277).

Evans, R. P. (1991), 'Thomas Pennant (1726–1798) "The father of Cambrian tourists"', in Pennant, T., *A Tour of Wales*, 2 vols (Wrexham: Bridge Books, facsimile ed.), i, no pagination.

Everson, P. (1991), 'Offa's Dyke at Dudston in Chirbury, Shropshire. A pre-Offan field system?', *Landscape History*, 13, 53–65.

Faith, R. (1994), 'Tidenham, Gloucestershire, and the history of the manor in England', *Landscape History*, 16, 39–51.

Fanning, T. (1994), *Viking Age Ringed Pins from Dublin* (Dublin: Royal Irish Academy).

Farley, M. (1984), 'A six hundred metre long section through Caerwent', *Bulletin of the Board of Celtic Studies*, 31, 209–49.

Farrell, R. (1991), 'The Crannóg Archaeology Project (CAP): Archaeological field research in the lakes of the West Midlands of Ireland', in C. Kharkov and R. Farrell (eds), *Studies in Insular Art and Archaeology* (Oxford, OH: American Early Medieval Studies 1), 99–105.

Fasham, P. J., Kelly, R. S., Mason, M. A., and White, R. B. (1998), *The Graeanog Ridge: The Evolution of a Farming Landscape and Settlements in North-West Wales* (Aberystwyth: Cambrian Archaeological Monograph 6).

Faulkner, N. (2000), *The Decline and Fall of Roman Britain* (Stroud: Tempus).

Fear, A. T. (trans.) (2010), *Orosius: Seven Books against Pagans* (Liverpool: Liverpool University Press).

Fenton, R. (1903), *A Historical Tour through Pembrokeshire* (Brecknock: Davies and Co., new ed.).

Fern, C., Dickinson, T., and Webster, L. (eds) (2019), *The Staffordshire Hoard: An Anglo-Saxon Treasure* (London: Society of Antiquaries of London).

Fisher, I. (2001), *Early Medieval Sculpture in the West Highlands and Islands* (Edinburgh: RCAHMS and the Society of Antiquaries of Scotland).

FitzPatrick, E. (2004), *Royal Inauguration in Gaelic Ireland c.1100–1500* (Woodbridge: Boydell).

FitzPatrick, E. (2012), '*Formaoil na Fiann*: hunting preserves and assembly places in Gaelic Ireland', *Proceedings of the Harvard Celtic Colloquium*, 32, 95–118.

Fitzpatrick-Matthews, K. J., and Fleming, R. (2016), 'The perils of periodization: Roman ceramics in Britain after 400 CE', *Fragments*, 5, 1–33.

Flechner, R. (2013), 'The Chronicle of Ireland: then and now', *Early Medieval Europe*, 21(4), 422–54.

Flechner, R., and Ní Mhaonaigh, M. (eds) (2016), *The Introduction of Christianity into the Early Medieval Insular World: Converting the Isles I* (Turnhout: Brepols).

Fleming, A. (2010), 'Horses, elites…and long-distance roads', *Landscapes*, 11(2), 1–20.

Fleming, R. (2010), *Britain After Rome* (London: Allen Lane).

Fleming, R. (2012), 'Recycling in Britain after the fall of Rome's metal economy', *Past & Present*, 217 (Nov.), 3–45.

Fleming, R. (2021), *The Material Fall of Roman Britain 300–525 CE* (Philadelphia: University of Pennsylvania Press).

Fletcher, E., Biddle, M., and Kjølbye-Biddle, B. (1988), 'The churches of Much Wenlock', *Journal of the British Archaeological Association*, 141, 178–83.

Flobert, P. (ed. and trans.) (1997), *La Vie Ancienne de Saint Samson de Dol* (Paris: Centre National de la Recherche Scientifique Éditions).

Follett, W. (2006), *Céli Dé in Ireland: Monastic Writing and Identity in the Early Middle Ages* (Woodbridge: Boydell).

Foot, S. (2009), *Æthelstan: The first King of England* (Newhaven and London: Yale University Press).

Ford, P. K. (trans.) (1977), *The Mabinogi and other Welsh Medieval Tales* (Berkeley, Los Angeles, and London: University of California Press).

Forsyth, K. (2005), '*Hic memoria perpetua*: the early inscribed stones of southern Scotland in context', in S. M. Foster and M. Cross (eds), *Able Minds and Practised Hands: Scotland's Early Medieval Sculpture in the 21ˢᵗ Century* (Leeds: Maney), 113–34.

Foster, S. M. (2004), *Picts, Gaels and Scots*, 2ⁿᵈ ed. (London: B.T. Batsford and Historic Scotland).

Fowler, E. (1963), 'Celtic metalwork of the fifth and sixth centuries A.D.', *Archaeological Journal*, 120, 98–160.

Fowler, P. (2002), *Farming in the First Millennium AD* (Cambridge: Cambridge University Press).

Fowles, J. (ed.), and Legg, R. (1980–2), *Monumenta Britannica by John Aubrey*, 3 vols (Sherborne: Dorset Publishing Co.).

Fox, A. (1939), 'The siting of some inscribed stones of the Dark Ages in Glamorgan and Breconshire', *Archaeologia Cambrensis*, 94, 30–41.

Fox, A. (1946), 'Early Christian Period, i. Settlement sites and other remains', in V. E. Nash-Williams (ed.), *A Hundred Years of Welsh Archaeology* (Gloucester: Cambrian Archaeological Association), 105–22.

Fox, A. (1955), 'Some evidence for a Dark Age trading site at Bantham, near Thurlestone, south Devon', *Antiquaries Journal*, 35, 55–67.

450 REFERENCES

Fox, C. (1940a), 'The re-erection of Maen Madoc, Ystradfellte, Breconshire', *Archaeologia Cambrensis*, 95, 210–16.

Fox, C. (1940b), 'An Irish bronze pin from Anglesey', *Archaeologia Cambrensis*, 95, 248.

Fox, C. (1943), *The Personality of* Britain, 4th ed. 1959 (Cardiff: National Museum of Wales and University of Wales Press).

Fox, C. (1955), *Offa's Dyke: A Field Survey of the Western Frontier-Works of Mercia in the Seventh and Eighth Centuries A.D.* (London: Oxford University Press for the British Academy).

Frere, S. (1987), *Britannia*, 3rd ed. (London and New York: Routledge & Kegan Paul).

Frere, S., Hassall, M. W. C., and Tomlin, R. S. O. (1986), 'Roman Britain in 1985', *Britannia*, 17, 363–454.

Fulford, M. G. (1989), 'Byzantium and Britain: a Mediterranean perspective on post-Roman Mediterranean imports in western Britain and Ireland', *Medieval Archaeology*, 33, 1–6.

Fulford, M. G., Allen, J. R. L., Rippon, S. J., Wild, J. P., Aldhouse-Green, S. H. R., Hamilton-Dyer, S., Keith-Lucas, M., Robinson, M., and Gale, R. (1994), 'The settlement and drainage of the Wentlooge Level, Gwent: excavation and survey at Rumney Great Wharf 1992', *Britannia*, 25, 175–211.

Fulford, M. G., Handley, M., and Clark, A. (2000), 'An early date for ogham: the Silchester ogham stone rehabilitated', *Medieval Archaeology*, 44, 1–24.

Gaffney, V. L., and White, R. H. (2007), 'Wroxeter, the *Cornovii*, and the Urban Process', *Journal of Roman Archaeology*, sup. ser. 68.

Gameson, R. (ed.) (2012), *The Cambridge History of the Book, Vol. I* c. *400–1100* (Cambridge: Cambridge University Press).

Gannon, A. (2017), 'The Ennabeuren reliquary casket: reckoning on redemption', in C. Newman et al. (eds) (2017), 65–74.

Gardner, A. (1999), 'Military identities in late Roman Britain', *Oxford Journal of Archaeology*, 18, 403–18.

Gardner, A. (2007), *An Archaeology of Identity: Soldiers and Society in Late Roman Britain* (Walnut Creek: Left Coast Press).

Gardner, A. (2016), 'Changing materialities', in Millett et al. (eds) (2016), 481–509.

Gardner, A., and Guest, P. (2010), *Caerleon, Excavations in Priory Field and the Southern Canabae, 2010: Interim Report* (Cardiff University and University College London, unpublished report).

Gardner, A., and Guest, P. (2011), *Caerleon Legionary Fortress, Excavations in Priory Field and Golledge's Field, 2007–2010: Assessment Report* (Cardiff University and University College London, unpublished report).

Gardner, W., and Savory, H. N. (1964), *Dinorben: A Hill-fort occupied in Iron Age and Roman Times* (Cardiff: National Museum of Wales).

Geiriadur Prifysgol Cymru [A Dictionary of the Welsh Language], http://www.geiriadur.ac. uk/ [accessed 1 May 2020].

Gelling, P. S., and Stanford, S. C. (1967), 'Dark Age pottery or Iron Age ovens?', *Transactions of the Birmingham Archaeological Society*, 82, 77–91.

Gem, R. (2009), 'Gruffudd ap Cynan and the Romanesque church of Penmon, Anglesey', in Edwards (ed.) (2009b), 301–12.

Gerrard, C. (2003), *Medieval Archaeology, Understanding Traditions and Contemporary Approaches* (London and New York: Routledge).

Gerrard, J. (2013), *The Ruin of Roman Britain* (Cambridge: Cambridge University Press).

Gerrard, S. (1987), 'Carew Castle', *Archaeology in Wales*, 27, 62–4.

Gibson, A. (1995), 'The Carreg Beuno prehistoric landscape, Berriw', *Montgomeryshire Collections*, 83, 41–58.

Gifford, E., and Gifford, J. (1999), 'The art of Anglo-Saxon shipbuilding', in J. Hawkes and S. Mills (eds), *Northumbria's Golden Age* (Stroud: Sutton), 73–86.

Gilchrist, R. (1988), 'A reappraisal of Dinas Powys: local exchange and specialized livestock production in 5th- to 7th-century Wales', *Medieval Archaeology*, 32, 50–62.

Gilchrist, R. (2008), 'Magic for the dead? The archaeology of magic in later medieval burials', *Medieval Archaeology*, 52, 119–59.

Gilchrist, R. (2012), *Medieval Life: Archaeology and the Life Course* (Woodbridge: Boydell).

Gilchrist, R. (2013), 'Courtenay Arthur Ralegh Radford 1900–1998', *Biographical Memoirs of Fellows of the British Academy*, 12, 341–58.

Gilchrist, R. (2022), 'Voices from the cemetery: the social archaeology of late medieval burial', *Medieval Archaeology*, 66(1), 120–50.

Gilchrist, R., and Greene, C. (2015), *Glastonbury Abbey: Archaeological Investigations 1904–1979* (London: Society of Antiquaries of London).

Gilchrist, R., and Reynolds, A. (eds) (2009), *Reflections: 50 Years of Medieval Archaeology 1857–2009* (Leeds: Maney).

Gilchrist, R., and Sloane, B. (2005), *Requiem: The Medieval Monastic Cemetery in Britain* (London: Museum of London Archaeology Service).

Gleeson, P. (2017), 'Converting kingship in early Ireland: redefining practices, ideologies, and identities', in Edwards et al. (eds) (2017), 287–317.

Gleeson, P. (2018), 'Gathering communities: locality, governance and rulership in early medieval Ireland', *World Archaeology*, 50(1), 100–20.

Gleeson, P., and McLaughlin, R. (2020), 'Ways of death: cremation and belief in first-millennium AD Ireland', *Antiquity*, 95, 382–99.

Godbold, S., and Turner, R. C. (1994), 'Medieval fishtraps in the Severn estuary', *Medieval Archaeology*, 38, 19–54.

Gordon-Williams, J. P. (1926), 'Note on a bronze stag from Gateholm and various stray finds from Pembrokeshire', *Archaeologia Cambrensis*, 81, 191–2.

Gosden, C. (1994), *Social Being and Time* (Oxford: Blackwell).

Grace, P. A. (2018), 'From *blefed* to *scamach*: pestilence in early medieval Ireland', *Proceedings of the Royal Irish Academy*, 118C, 67–93.

Graham-Campbell, J. (1991), 'Dinas Powys metalwork and the dating of enamelled zoomorphic penannular brooches', *Bulletin of the Board of Celtic Studies*, 38, 220–32.

Graham-Campbell, J., and Philpott, R. (eds) (2009), *The Huxley Viking Hoard: Scandinavian Settlements in the North West* (Liverpool: National Museums).

Grant, F. (2008), 'Human impact and landscape change at Moel Llys y Coed in the Clwydian Hills, north Wales: the Mesolithic – present day', *Archaeology in Wales*, 48, 3–15.

Grant, I. (2004), 'The excavation of a double-ditched enclosure at Arddleen, Powys, 2002–03', *Montgomeryshire Collections*, 92, 1–31.

452 REFERENCES

Grant, I. (2007), 'Excavations in Betws yn Rhos, Conwy, 2004 and 2007', *Archaeology in Wales*, 47, 18–26.

Grant, I. (2012), *Borras Quarry, Wrexham: Archaeological Watching Brief 2012* (Clwyd-Powys Archaeological Trust, report 1161).

Grant, I. (2014), *Borras Quarry, Wrexham: Archaeological Watching Brief and Excavation 2014* (Clwyd-Powys Archaeological Trust, report 1295).

Grant, I., and Jones, N. (2014), 'Chirk, Offa's Dyke', *Archaeology in Wales*, 53, 213–14.

Gregson, N. (1985), 'The multiple estate model: some critical questions', *Journal of Historical Geography*, 11(4), 339–51.

Griffiths, D. (2006), 'Maen Achwyfan and the context of Viking settlement in north-east Wales', *Archaeology Cambrensis*, 155, 143–62.

Griffiths, D. (2010), *Vikings of the Irish Sea* (Stroud: History Press).

Griffiths, D., Philpott, R. A., and Egan, G. (2007), *Meols: The Archaeology of the North Wirral Coast* (Oxford: Oxford University School of Archaeology).

Griffiths, W. E. (1954), 'Excavations at Caer Gybi, Holyhead, 1952', *Archaeologia Cambrensis*, 103, 113–16.

Grigg, E. (2013), '"Mole rain" and other natural phenomena in the Welsh annals: can *mirabilia* unravel the textual history of *Annales Cambriae*?', *Welsh History Review*, 24(4), 1–40.

Grigg, E. (2018), *Warfare, Raiding and Defence in Early Medieval Britain* (Ramsbury: Robert Hale).

Grimes, W. F. (1931), 'Romano-British pottery from Crockysdam Camp, Warren, Pemb.', *Bulletin of the Board of Celtic Studies*, 5(4), 394–5.

Grinsell, L. V. (1981), 'The later history of Tŷ Illtud', *Archaeologia Cambrensis*, 130, 131–9.

Groom, P., Schlee, D., Hughes, G., Crane, P., Ludlow, N., and Murphy, K. (2011), 'Two early medieval cemeteries in Pembrokeshire: Brownslade Barrow and West Angle Bay', *Archaeologia Cambrensis*, 160, 133–203.

Gruffydd, A. (1992a), *Investigations at Caer Gybi: Holyhead Environmental Improvement Scheme—Phase 2* (Gwynedd Archaeological Trust, report 041a).

Gruffydd, A. (1992b), 'St Cybi environmental improvement scheme, Caer Gybi', *Archaeology in Wales*, 32, 76–7.

Gruffydd, R. G. (1978), 'Canu Cadwallon ap Cadfan', in R. Bromwich and R. B. Jones (eds), *Astudiaethau ar yr Hengerdd* (Cardiff: University of Wales Press), 25–43.

Gruffydd, R. G. (1989–90), 'From Gododdin to Gwynedd: reflections on the story of Cunedda', *Studia Celtica*, 24–5, 1–14.

Gruffydd, R. G. (2005), '"The Praise of Tenby": a late-ninth-century Welsh court poem', in J. F. Nagy and L. E. Jones (eds), *Heroic Poets and Poetic Heroes in Celtic Tradition: A Festschrift for Patrick K. Ford* (Dublin: Four Courts, CSANA Yearbook 3–4), 91–102.

Guest, P. (2022), 'The Forum-Basilica at Caerwent (Venta Silurum): a history of the Roman Silures', *Britannia*, 53, 227–67.

Guest, P., and Wells, N. (2007), *Iron Age and Roman Coins from Wales* (Wetteren: Moneta).

Guido, M. (1978), *The Glass Beads of the Prehistoric and Roman Periods in Britain and Ireland* (London: Society of Antiquaries of London).

Guido, M. (1999), *The Glass Beads of Anglo-Saxon England c.AD 400–700*, ed. M. Welch (Woodbridge: Boydell).

Guilbert, G. (1979a), 'Dinorben 1977–8', *Current Archaeology*, 65, 182–8.

Guilbert, G. (1979b), 'Dinorben', *Archaeology in Wales*, 19, 14.

Guilbert, G. (1980), 'Dinorben C14 dates', *Current Archaeology*, 70, 336–8.

Guilbert, G. (2018), 'Historical excavation and survey of hillforts in Wales: some critical issues', *Internet Archaeology*, 48.

Guy, B. (2015), 'The origins of the compilation of Welsh historical texts in Harley 3859', *Studia Celtica*, 49, 21–56.

Guy, B. (2020), *Medieval Welsh Genealogy* (Woodbridge: Boydell).

Gwara, S. (ed. and trans.) (2002), *De Raris Fabulis, 'On Uncommon Tales': A glossed Latin Colloquy-Text from a tenth century Cornish Manuscript* (Cambridge: University of Cambridge, Department of Anglo-Saxon, Norse, and Celtic).

Hadley, D. M. (2009), 'Burial, belief and identity in later Anglo-Saxon England', in Gilchrist and Reynolds (eds) (2009), 465–88.

Hadley, D. M. (2010), 'Burying the socially and physically distinctive in later Anglo-Saxon England', in J. Buckberry and A. Cherryson (eds), *Burial in Later Anglo-Saxon England c. 650–1100 AD* (Oxford and Oakville: Oxbow), 103–15.

Hadley, D. M. (2012), 'Masculinity', in J. Stodnick and R. R. Trilling (eds), *A Handbook of Anglo-Saxon Studies* (Oxford: Blackwell), 115–32.

Hadley, D. M., and Richards, J. D. (2015), 'The winter camp of the Viking Great Army, AD 872–3, Torksey, Lincolnshire', *Antiquaries Journal*, 96, 23–67.

Hadley, D. M., and Richards, J. D. (2021), *The Viking Great Army and the Making of England* (London and New York: Thames & Hudson).

Hague, D. B. (1974), 'Some Welsh evidence', *Scottish Archaeological Forum*, 5 (1973), 17–35.

Hall, M. A. (2017), *Playtime in Pictland: The Material Culture of Gaming in Early Medieval Scotland* (Rosemarkie: Groam House Lecture).

Hall, M. A. (2018), 'Matters of life and death: aspects of board games and their interaction with Picts, Anglo-Saxons and Vikings', in *Il Gioco nella Società e nella Cultura dell'alto medievo* (Spoleto: Fondazione Centro Italiano di Studi Sull'Alto Medievo), 196–218.

Hall, M. A., and Forsyth, K. (2011), 'Roman rules? The introduction of board games to Britain and Ireland', *Antiquity*, 85, 1325–38.

Hamerow, H. (2012), *Rural Settlements and Society in Anglo-Saxon England* (Oxford: Oxford University Press).

Hamerow, H., Bogaard, A., Charles, M., Forster, E., et al. (2020), 'An integrated biological approach to the medieval "Agricultural Revolution": a case-study from Stafford, England, c. AD 800–1200', *European Journal of Archaeology*, 23(4), 585–609.

Hamerow, H., Hinton, D. A., and Crawford, S. (eds) (2011), *The Oxford Handbook of Anglo-Saxon Archaeology* (Oxford: Oxford University Press).

Handley, M. A. (2001), 'The origins of Christian commemoration in Late Antique Britain', *Early Medieval Europe*, 10(2), 177–99.

Handley, M. A. (2003), *Death, Society and Culture: Inscriptions and Epitaphs in Gaul and Spain, AD 300–750* (Oxford: British Archaeological Reports, Int. ser. 1135).

Hankinson, R., and Caseldine, A. (2006), 'Short dykes in Powys and their origins', *Archaeological Journal*, 163, 264–9.

Hannah, R. (2005), *Greek and Roman Calendars: Constructions of Time in the Classical World* (London: Duckworth).

Hanning, R. W. (1966), *The Vision of History in Early Britain: From Gildas to Geoffrey of Monmouth* (New York and London: Columbia University Press).

Harbison, P. (1992), *The High Crosses of Ireland*, 3 vols (Bonn: Dr Rudolf Habelt GMBH).

Hårdh, B. (2007), 'Oriental-Scandinavian contacts on the Volga, as manifested by silver rings and weight systems', in J. Graham-Campbell and G. Williams (eds), *Silver Economy in the Viking Age* (Walnut Creek: Left Coast Press), 135–47.

Harding, S. E., Griffiths, D., and Royles, E. (eds) (2015), *In Search of Vikings: Interdisciplinary Approaches to the Scandinavian Heritage of North-West England* (Boca Raton, London, and New York: CRC Press).

Harney, L. (2020), 'The early medieval ecclesiastical enclosures of Dublin: exploring their character, chronology and evolving function in light of excavations across Ireland', in S. Duffy (ed.), *Medieval Dublin XVIII* (Dublin: Four Courts), 17–127.

Harper, K. (2017), *The Fate of Rome: Climate, Disease and the End of an Empire* (Princeton and Oxford: Princeton University Press).

Harrison, S. H. (2008), 'Separated from the foaming maelstrom: landscapes of Insular "Viking" burial', *Anglo-Saxon Studies in Archaeology and History*, 14, 173–82.

Harrison, S. H., and Ó Floinn, R. (2014), *Viking Graves and Grave-Goods in Ireland* (Dublin: National Museum of Ireland).

Hart, J. (2014), *South Wales Gas Pipeline Project, Site 508, Land at Conkland Hill, Wiston, Pembrokeshire: Archaeological Excavation* (Cotswold Archaeology, report 13251).

Harvey, A. (2017), 'Languages and literacy in mid-first-millennium Ireland', in Edwards et al. (eds) (2017), 47–63.

Hawkes, A. (2018), *The Archaeology of Prehistoric Burnt Mounds in Ireland* (Oxford: Archaeopress).

Hawkes, J. (1982), *Mortimer Wheeler: Adventurer in Archaeology* (London: Weidenfeld & Nicolson).

Haycock, M. (2000), *'Where cider ends, there ale begins to reign': Drink in Medieval Welsh Poetry* (Cambridge: Department of Anglo-Saxon, Norse, and Celtic, H. M. Chadwick Memorial Lectures 10).

Hayes, L., and Malim, T. (2008), 'The date and nature of Wat's Dyke: a reassessment in the light of recent investigation at Gobowen, Shropshire', *Anglo-Saxon Studies in Archaeology and History*, 15, 147–79.

Haynes, I. (2016), 'Identity and the military community in Roman Britain', in Millett et al. (eds) (2016), 448–63.

Heaton, R. B., and Britnell, W. J. (1994), 'A structural history of Pennant Melangell', *Montgomeryshire Collections*, 82, 103–25.

Hedges, J. D. (2016), 'Bronze Age settlement and early medieval cemetery at Arfryn, Bodedern, Anglesey', *Archaeologia Cambrensis*, 165, 113–85.

Hemer, K. A. (2011), 'Stable isotope analysis of human remains: Brownslade and West Angle Bay', in Groom et al. (2011), 182–7.

Hemer, K. A., Evans, J. A., Chenery, C. A., and Lamb, A. L. (2013), 'Evidence of early medieval trade and migration between Wales and the Mediterranean Sea region', *Journal of Archaeological Science*, 40, 2352–9.

Hemer, K. A., Evans, J. A., Chenery, C. A., and Lamb, A. L. (2014), 'No man is an island: evidence of pre-Viking Age migration to the Isle of Man', *Journal of Archaeological Science*, 52, 242–9.

Hemer, K. A., Lamb, A. L., Chenery, C. A., and Evans, J. A. (2017), 'A multi-isotope investigation of diet and subsistence amongst island and mainland populations from early medieval western Britain', *American Journal of Physical Anthropology*, 162, 423–40.

Hemer, K. A., and Verlinden, P. (2020), 'Vitamin D deficiency rickets in early medieval Wales: a multi-methodological case-study', *Childhood in the Past*, 13(1), 20–37.

Hemp, W. (1918), 'A Roman gold brooch from Caernarvon', *Proceedings of the Society of Antiquaries of London*, 30, 184–7.

Hencken, H. (1950), 'Lagore crannog: an Irish royal residence of the 7th to 10th centuries A.D.', *Proceedings of the Royal Irish Academy*, 53C, 1–247.

Henderson, I. (2004), 'Allen, John Romilly (1847–1907)', *Oxford Dictionary of National Biography*, https://doi-org.ezproxy.bangor.ac.uk/10.1093/ref:odnb/30388 [accessed 5 January 2021].

Henig, M. (1984), *Religion in Roman Britain* (London: B. T. Batsford).

Herbert, M. (1988), *Iona, Kells and Derry: The History and Hagiography of the Monastic Familia of Columba* (Oxford: Clarendon Press).

Herendeen, W. H. (2007), *William Camden, A Life in Context* (Woodbridge: Boydell).

Herring, P. (2012), 'Shadows of ghosts: early medieval transhumance in Cornwall', in S. Turner and R. J. Silvester (eds), *Life in Medieval Landscapes: People and Places in the Middle Ages* (Oxford: Windgather), 89–105.

Herring, P., Preston-Jones, A., Thorpe, C., and Wood, I. (2011), 'Early medieval Cornwall', *Cornish Archaeology*, 50, 263–86.

Higham, N. J. (2014), 'Constantius, Germanus and fifth-century Britain', *Early Medieval Europe*, 22(2), 113–37.

Higham, R., and Barker, P. (2000), *Hen Domen Montgomery, A Timber Castle on the English-Welsh Border: A Final Report* (Exeter: Exeter University Press).

Higham, T. F. G., Bronk Ramsey, C., Brock, F., and Baker, D. (2007), 'Radiocarbon dates from Oxford AMS system: Archaeometry datelist 32', *Archaeometry*, 49(1), S1–60.

Hill, D. (2000), 'Offa's Dyke: pattern and purpose', *Antiquaries Journal*, 80, 195–206.

Hill, D., and Worthington, M. (2003), *Offa's Dyke: History and Guide* (Stroud: Tempus).

Hill, P. (1997), *Whithorn and St Ninian: The Excavation of a Monastic Town 1984–91* (Stroud: Sutton).

Hills, C. (2011), 'Overview: Anglo-Saxon identity', in Hamerow et al. (eds) (2011), 3–12.

Hingley, R. (2008), *The Recovery of Roman Britain 1586–1906: A Colony so Fertile* (Oxford: Oxford University Press).

Hinton, D. A. (2011a), 'Raw materials: sources and demand', in Hamerow et al. (eds) (2011), 423–39.

Hinton, D. A. (2011b), 'Weland's work: metals and metalsmiths', in M. Clegg Hyer and G. Owen-Crocker (eds), *The Material Culture of Daily Living in the Anglo-Saxon World* (Exeter: University of Exeter Press), 185–200.

Hodges, R. (1982), *Dark Age Economics: The Origins of Towns and Trade A.D. 600–1000* (London: Duckworth).

Hogg, A. H. A. (1974), 'The Llantwit Major villa: a reconsideration of the evidence', *Britannia*, 5, 225–50.

Holbrook, N., and Thomas, A. (2005), 'An early-medieval monastic cemetery at Llandough, Glamorgan: excavations in 1994', *Medieval Archaeology*, 49, 1–92.

Holm, P. (1986), 'The slave trade of Dublin, ninth to twelfth centuries', *Peritia*, 5, 317–45.

456 REFERENCES

Hood, A. B. E. (ed. and trans.) (1978), *St Patrick: His Writings and Muirchu's Life* (London and Chichester: Phillimore).

Hooke, D. (2019), 'Resource management of seasonal pasture: some English/Welsh comparisons', in Comeau and Seaman (eds) (2019), 37–56.

Hope, V. (2016), 'Inscriptions and identity', in Millett et al. (eds) (2016), 285–302.

Hopewell, D. (2013), 'Carmel Head', *Archaeology in Wales*, 52, 224–6.

Hopewell, D. (2016), 'A Roman settlement at Tai Cochion, Llanidan, on Anglesey', *Archaeologia Cambrensis*, 165, 21–112.

Hopewell, D. (2018), 'Roman Anglesey: recent discoveries', *Britannia*, 49, 313–22.

Hopewell, D., and Edwards, N. (2017), 'Early medieval settlement and field systems at Rhuddgaer, Anglesey', *Archaeologia Cambrensis*, 166, 213–42.

Horn, W., Marshall, J. W., and Rourke, G. R. (1990), *The Forgotten Hermitage of Skellig Michael* (Berkeley: University of California Press).

Houlder, C. H. (1968), 'The henge monuments at Llandegai', *Antiquity*, 42(2), 216–21.

Hourihan, S., Long, P., and Simpson, H. (2015), *Archaeological Report for Ysgol Bro Dinefwr, Love Lodge Farm, Ffairfach, Carmarthenshire*, 2 vols (AB Heritage and Rubicon Heritage Services).

Hoverd, T. (2015), *A Report on the Post-Roman Cemetery at Merlin's Cave, Symond's Yat West, Herefordshire* (Hereford Archaeological Report 351).

Hoverd, T., Reavill, P., Stevenson, J., and Williams, G. (2020), 'The Herefordshire Viking hoard', *Current Archaeology*, 361 (April), 46–51.

Howell, R. (2012), 'Roman past and medieval present: Caerleon as a focus for continuity and conflict in the Middle Ages', *Studia Celtica*, 46, 11–21.

Hudd, A. E. (1911), 'Excavations at Caerwent, Monmouthshire, on the site of the Romano-British city of Venta Silurum, 1909 and 1910', *Archaeologia*, 67, 405–47.

Hudd, A. E. (1913), 'Excavations at Caerwent, Monmouthshire in 1911 and 1913', *Archaeologia*, 64, 437–52.

Hudson, B. T. (1990), 'The destruction of Gruffudd ap Llywelyn', *Welsh History Review*, 15(1), 331–50.

Hudson, R. (1970–8), 'Roman coins from the Severn estuary at Portskewett', *Monmouthshire Antiquary*, 3, 179–85.

Hughes, G. (1996), *The Excavation of a Late Prehistoric and Romano-British Settlement at Thornwell Farm, Chepstow, Gwent, 1992* (Oxford: British Archaeological Reports, Brit. ser. 244).

Hughes, H. H. (1907), 'Report on the excavation carried out at Tre'r Ceiri in 1906', *Archaeologia Cambrensis*, 6th ser., 7, 38–62.

Hughes, K. (1973), 'The Welsh Latin chronicles: *Annales Cambriae* and related texts', *Proceedings of the British Academy*, 59, 233–58.

Hughes, K., and Hamlin, A. (1977), *The Modern Traveller to the Early Irish Church* (London: SPCK).

Hunt, R. W. (ed.) (1961), *Saint Dunstan's Classbook from Glastonbury, Umbrae Codicum Occidentalium* IV (Amsterdam: North Holland Pub. Co.).

Hunt Museum (2002), *Essential Guide* (London: Scala and the Hunt Museum).

Hunwicke, J. W. (2002), 'Kerry and Stowe revisited', *Proceedings of the Royal Irish Academy*, 102C, 1–19.

Hutchinson, G. (1984), 'A plank fragment from a boat find from the River Usk at Newport', *International Journal of Nautical Archaeology and Underwater Exploration*, 13, 27–32.

Isaac, G. R. (2007), '*Armes Prydain Fawr* and St David', in Evans, J. W. and Wooding (eds) (2007), 161–8.

James, H. (1987), 'Excavations at Caer, Bayvil, 1979', *Archaeologia Cambrensis*, 136, 51–76.

James, H. (1992), 'Early medieval cemeteries in Wales', in Edwards and Lane (eds) (1992), 90–103.

James, H. (1993), 'The cult of St. David in the Middle Ages', in M. Carver (ed.), *In Search of Cult: Archaeological Investigations in honour of Philip Rahtz* (Woodbridge: Boydell), 105–12.

James, H. (1997), 'Llandysilio Church and parish 500–1543 AD: from heartland to border-land', *Carmarthenshire Antiquary*, 33, 5–26.

James, H. (1998), 'Gwaen Henllan: the oldest recorded meadow in Wales?', in S. Taylor (ed.), *The Uses of Place-names* (Edinburgh: Scottish Cultural Press), 169–79.

James, H. (2003), *Roman Carmarthen: Excavations 1978–83* (London: Britannia Monograph 20).

James, H. (2007), 'The geography of the cult of St David: a study of dedication patterns in the medieval diocese', in Evans, J. W., and Wooding (eds) (2007), 41–83.

James, H. (2016a), 'Roman Pembrokeshire AD 75–410', in James et al. (eds) (2016), 293–339.

James, H. (2016b), 'Early medieval Pembrokeshire AD 400–1100', in James et al. (eds) (2016), 340–532.

James, H., John, M., Murphy, K., and Wainwright, G. (eds) (2016), *Pembrokeshire County History Vol. 1* (Haverfordwest: Pembrokeshire County History Trust).

James, H., and Thorne, D. (2020), ' "Mensura Med Diminih": boundary place-names of a ninth century estate at Llandybïe, Carmarthenshire', *Carmarthenshire Antiquary*, 56, 13–34.

James, H. F., Henderson, I., Foster, S. M., and Jones, S. (2008), *A Fragmented Masterpiece: Recovering the Biography of the Hilton of Cadboll Pictish Cross-slab* (Edinburgh: Society of Antiquaries of Scotland).

James, H. F., and Yeoman, P. (2008), *Excavations at St Ethernan's Monastery, Isle of May, Fife* (Perth: Tayside and Fife Archaeological Committee).

James, T. A. (1992), 'Air photography of ecclesiastical sites in south Wales', in Edwards and Lane (eds) (1992), 62–76.

Jankulak, K., and Wooding, J. M. (eds) (2007), *Ireland and Wales in the Middle Ages* (Dublin: Four Courts).

Jankulak, K., and Wooding, J. M. (2010), 'The Life of St Elgar of Ynys Enlli', in J. M. Wooding (ed.), *Solitaries, Pastors and 20,000 Saints: Studies in the Religious History of Bardsey Island (Ynys Enlli), Trivium*, 39, 15–47.

Jarrett, M. G. (1962), 'Excavations at Llys Brychan, Llangadog, 1961', *Carmarthenshire Antiquary*, 4, 2–8.

Jarrett, M. G., and Mann, J. C. (1968), 'The tribes of Wales', *Welsh History Review*, 4(2), 161–74.

Jarrett, M. G., and Wrathmell, S. (1981), *Whitton: An Iron Age and Roman Farmstead in South Glamorgan* (Cardiff: University of Wales Press).

Jenkins, D. (ed. and trans.) (1986), *The Law of Hywel Dda* (Llandysul: Gomer).

Jenkins, D. (2000), 'Hawk and hound: hunting in the Laws of Court', in T. M. Charles-Edwards, M. R. Owen, and P. Russell (eds), *The Welsh King and his Court* (Cardiff: University of Wales Press), 255–80.

458 REFERENCES

Jenkins, D., and Owen, M. E. (1983), 'The Welsh marginalia in the Lichfield Gospels: part I', *Cambridge Medieval Celtic Studies*, 5 (Summer), 37–66.

Jenkins, D., and Owen, M. E. (1984), 'The Welsh marginalia in the Lichfield Gospels: part II', *Cambridge Medieval Celtic Studies*, 7 (Summer), 91–120.

Jenkins, J. G. (2006), *The Coracle* (Llanrwst: Gwasg Carreg Gwalch).

Jesch, J. (2000), 'Scandinavian Wirral', in P. Cavill, S. E. Harding, and J. Jesch (eds), *Wirral and its Viking Heritage* (Nottingham: English Place-Name Society), 1–10.

Johnston, E. (2013), *Literacy and Identity in Early Medieval Ireland* (Woodbridge: Boydell).

Johnston, E. (2017), 'Literacy and conversion on Ireland's Roman frontier: from emulation to assimilation?', in Edwards et al. (eds) (2017), 23–46.

Johnstone, N. (1997), 'An investigation of the royal courts of thirteenth-century Gwynedd', in Edwards (ed.) (1997b), 55–69.

Jones, B. L., and Roberts, T. (1980), 'Osmund's Air: a Scandinavian place-name in Anglesey', *Bulletin of the Board of Celtic Studies*, 28(4), 602–3.

Jones, F. (1954), *The Holy Wells of Wales* (Cardiff: University of Wales Press).

Jones, G. R. J. (1961), 'The tribal system in Wales: a reassessment in the light of settlement studies', *Welsh History Review*, 1(2), 111–32.

Jones, G. R. J. (1972), 'Post-Roman Wales', in H. P. R. Finberg (ed.), *The Agrarian History of England and Wales, Vol. I(ii), A.D. 43–1042* (Cambridge: Cambridge University Press), 281–382.

Jones, G. R. J. (1985), 'Multiple estates perceived', *Journal of Historical Geography*, 11(4), 352–63.

Jones, G. T., and Roberts, T. (1996), *The Place-Names of Anglesey* (Bangor: Isle of Anglesey Council and University of Wales Bangor, Research Centre Wales).

Jones, H. L. (1847), 'Communications received', *Archaeologia Cambrensis*, 2, 180–1.

Jones, I. (2013), 'Ulster's early medieval houses', *Medieval Archaeology*, 57, 212–22.

Jones, I., Williams, D., and Williams, S. (2018), 'Early medieval enclosure at Glanfred, near Llandre, Ceredigion', *Archaeologia Cambrensis*, 167, 221–43.

Jones, N. W. (2011), 'Roman-British settlement at Plas Coch, Wrexham: excavations 1994–96', *Archaeologia Cambrensis*, 160, 51–113.

Jones, N. W. (2015), 'Pentre-Ffyddion, Whitford Dyke', *Archaeology in Wales*, 54, 201–2.

Jones, N. W. (2020), 'Roman settlement and industry along the Dee estuary: recent discoveries at Pentre Ffrwrndan, Flintshire', *Archaeologia Cambrensis*, 169, 127–63.

Jones, N. W., Grant, I., and Hankinson, R. (2013a), *The Whitford Dyke, Flintshire: Excavation and Survey 2012* (Clwyd-Powys Archaeological Trust, report 1182).

Jones, N. W., Hankinson, R., and Grant, I. (2013b), 'The excavation and survey of two early medieval cemeteries in north-east Wales', *Archaeology in Wales*, 52, 75–93.

Jones, O. W. (2009), '*Hereditas Pouoisi*: the Pillar of Eliseg and the history of early Powys', *Welsh History Review*, 24(4), 41–80.

Jones, O. W., and Pryce, H. (2019), 'Historical writing in medieval Wales', in J. Jahner, E. Steiner, and E. M. Tyler (eds), *Medieval Historical Writing: Britain and Ireland, 500–1500* (Cambridge: Cambridge University Press), 208–24.

Jones, R. (1998), 'The formation of the *cantref* and the commote in medieval Gwynedd', *Studia Celtica*, 32, 169–77.

Jones, T. (1936), 'Y tri bed yng Nghefn Celfi', *Bulletin of the Board of Celtic Studies*, 8(3), 239–42.

Jones, T. (ed. and trans.) (1952), *Brut y Tywysogyon or The Chronicle of the Princes: Peniarth MS. 20 Version* (Cardiff: University of Wales Press).

Jones, T. (ed. and trans.) (1955), *Brut y Tywysogyon or The Chronicle of the Princes: Red Book of Hergest Version* (Cardiff: University of Wales Press).

Jones, T. (1967), 'The Black Book of Carmarthen "Stanzas of the Graves"', *Proceedings of the British Academy*, 53, 97–107.

Jones, T. (ed. and trans.) (1971), *Brenhinedd y Saesson or The Kings of the Saxons* (Cardiff: University of Wales Press).

Joyce, R. (2019), *Llandrillo Campus Extension Llangefni (Anglesey)* (Archaeology Wales, report 1806).

Karkov, C. E. (2003), 'The body of St Æthelthryth: desire, conversion and reform in Anglo-Saxon England', in M. Carver (ed.), *The Cross Goes North* (York: York Medieval Press), 397–411.

Keller, M., Spyrou, M. A., Scheib, C. L., et al. (2019), 'Ancient *Yersina pestis* genomes from across Western Europe reveal diversification during the First Pandemic (541–750)', *Proceedings of the National Academy of Sciences*, 116:25, 12363–72.

Kelly, E. P. (1993), 'The Lough Kinale book-shrine', in R. M. Spearman and J. Higgitt (eds), *The Age of Migrating Ideas: Early Medieval Art in Northern Britain and Ireland* (Stroud: National Museums of Scotland and Alan Sutton), 168–74.

Kelly, F. (1997), *Early Irish Farming* (Dublin: Dublin Institute of Advanced Studies).

Kelly, R. (1982), 'The excavation of a medieval farmstead at Cefn Graeanog, Clynnog, Gwynedd', *Bulletin of the Board of Celtic Studies*, 29(4), 859–908.

Kendrick, T. D. (1941), 'Portion of a basalt hone from north Wales', *Antiquaries Journal*, 21(1), 73.

Kendrick, T. D., and Hawkes, C. F. C. (1932), *Archaeology in England and Wales 1914–1931* (London: Methuen).

Kenney, J. (2001), *Cefn Graianog Quarry Extension: Archaeological Watching Brief* (Gwynedd Archaeological Trust, report 424).

Kenney, J. (2008), 'Recent excavations at Parc Bryn Cegin, Llandygai, near Bangor, north Wales', *Archaeologia Cambrensis*, 157, 9–142.

Kenney, J. (2012), 'Burnt mounds in north-west Wales: are these ubiquitous monuments really so dull?', in Britnell and Silvester (eds) (2012), 254–79.

Kenney, J. (2014), 'Survey and excavation at Hen Gastell, Llanwnda, Gwynedd', *Archaeology in Wales*, 53, 113–18.

Kenney, J. (2015), *Medieval Field Systems in North-West Wales Scheduling Enhancement 2014–2015, Part 1: Report and Gazetteer* (Gwynedd Archaeological Trust, report 1236).

Kenney, J. (2016), *Evaluation of Scheduling Proposals, Hen Gastell, Llanwnda: Excavation Report* (Gwynedd Archaeological Trust, report 1306).

Kenney, J. (2018), 'Excavations at Hedd yr Ynys, Lôn Fron, Llangefni', *Transactions of the Anglesey Antiquarian Society*, 30–57.

Kenney, J., Bale, R., Grant, F., Hamilton, D., McKinley, J. I., Nayling, N., and Rackham, J. (2014), 'Archaeological work along a gas pipeline replacement route from Pwllheli to Blaenau Ffestiniog', *Archaeology in Wales*, 53, 3–26.

Kenney, J., and Hopewell, D. (2015), *Ynys Enlli Survey and Evaluation 2014–15* (Gwynedd Archaeological Trust, report 1232).

Kenney, J., and Longley, D. (2012), 'Tŷ Mawr, Holyhead, Neolithic activity, ring ditch and early medieval cemetery', in Cuttler et al. (2012), 104–21.

Kenney, J., McGuinness, N., Cooke, R., Rees, C., and Davidson, A. (2020), *Parc Cybi: Final Report on Excavations*, 3 vols (Gwynedd Archaeological Trust, report 1512).

Kenney, J., and McNicol, D. (2017), 'A small medieval settlement at Dolbenmaen, Gwynedd, with hints of a preceding early medieval settlement', *Archaeology in Wales*, 56, 51–62.

Kenney, J., and Parry, L. (2012), 'Excavations at Ysgol yr Hendre, Llanbeblig, Caernarfon: a possible construction camp for *Segontium* fort and early medieval cemetery', *Archaeologia Cambrensis*, 161, 249–84.

Kershaw, J. (2013), *Viking Identities: Scandinavian Jewellery in England* (Oxford: Oxford University Press).

Kershaw, J., and Røyrvik, E. C. (2016), 'The "People of the British Isles" project and Viking settlement in England', *Antiquity*, 90, 1670–80.

Keynes, S., and Lapidge, M. (trans.) (1983), *Alfred the Great: Asser's Life of King Alfred and Other Contemporary Sources* (Harmondsworth: Penguin).

Kilbride-Jones, H. (1980), *Zoomorphic Penannular Brooches* (London: Society of Antiquaries of London).

Kingsley, S. (2009), 'Great voyages, great ocean-going ships?', in M. Mundell Mango (ed.), *Byzantine Trade, 4ᵗʰ–12ᵗʰ Centuries* (Farnham: Ashgate), 323–6.

Kirton, J. (2015), 'Locating the Cleulow Cross: materiality, place and landscape', in H. Williams, J. Kirton, and M. Gondek (eds), *Early Medieval Stone Monuments: Materiality, Biography, Landscape* (Woodbridge: Boydell), 35–61.

Kirton, J., and Young, G. (2017), 'Excavations at Bamburgh: new revelations in light of recent investigations at the core of the castle complex', *Archaeological Journal*, 174(1), 146–210.

Klingshirn, W. E. (1994), *Caesarius of Arles: The Making of a Christian Community in Late Antique Gaul* (Cambridge: Cambridge University Press).

Knight, J. K. (1970–1), 'St Tatheus of Caerwent: an analysis of the Vespasian Life', *Monmouthshire Antiquary*, 3(1), 29–36.

Knight, J. K. (1984), 'Glamorgan, A.D. 400–1100: archaeology and history', in Savory (ed.) (1984), 315–64.

Knight, J. K. (1996), 'Late Roman and post-Roman Caerwent: some evidence from metalwork', *Archaeologia Cambrensis*, 145, 34–66.

Knight, J. K. (2005), 'From villa to monastery, Llandough in context', *Medieval Archaeology*, 49, 93–108.

Koch, J. (ed.) (2006), *Celtic Culture: A Historical Encyclopedia*, 5 vols (Santa Barbara, Denver, and Oxford: ABC Clio).

Laing, L. (1985), 'The Romanization of Ireland in the fifth century', *Peritia*, 4, 261–78.

Laing, L., and Longley, D. (2006), *The Mote of Mark: A Dark Age Hillfort in South-West Scotland* (Oxford: Oxbow).

Lambert, T., and Leggett, S. (2022), 'Food and power in early medieval England: Rethinking *feorm*', *Anglo-Saxon England*, https://doi.org/10.1017/S0263675122000084.

Lane, A. (2014), 'Wroxeter and the end of Roman Britain', *Antiquity*, 88, 501–15.

REFERENCES   461

Lane, A., and Campbell, E. (2000), *Dunadd: An Early Dalriadic Capital* (Oxford: Oxbow).

Lane, A., and Redknap, M. (2019), *Llangorse Crannog: The Excavation of a Royal Site in the Early Medieval Kingdom of Brycheiniog* (Oxford: Oxbow).

La Niece, S., and Stapleton, C. (1993), 'Niello and enamel on Irish metalwork', *Antiquaries Journal*, 73, 148–51.

Lapidge, M. (1973–4), 'The Welsh-Latin poetry of Sulien's family', *Studia Celtica*, 8–9, 68–106.

Lapidge, M. (1984), 'Gildas's education and the Latin culture of sub-Roman Britain', in Lapidge and Dumville (eds) (1984), 27–50.

Lapidge, M. (1986), 'Latin learning in Dark Age Wales: some prolegomena', in D. E. Evans, J. G. Griffith, and E. M. Jope (eds), *Proceedings of the Seventh International Congress of Celtic Studies, Oxford, 1983* (Oxford: Cranham Press), 91–107.

Lapidge, M., and Dumville, D. N. (eds) (1984), *Gildas: New Approaches* (Woodbridge: Boydell).

Lash, R. (2018), 'Pebbles and *peregrinatio*: the taskscape of devotion on Inishark Island, Ireland', *Medieval Archaeology*, 62(1), 83–104.

Lawlor, H. C. (ed.) (1914), *The Psalter and Martyrology of Ricemarch*, 2 vols (London: Henry Bradshaw Society, 47).

Lawlor, H. C. (1925), *The Monastery of St Mochaoi at Nendrum* (Belfast: Belfast Natural History and Philosophical Society).

Laws, E. (1895), 'Discovery of the tombstone of Vortipore, prince of Demetia', *Archaeologia Cambrensis*, ser. 5, 12, 303–7.

Lawson, M. K. (2004), 'Cenwulf', *Oxford Dictionary of National Biography*, https://doi-org.ezproxy.bangor.ac.uk/10.1093/ref:odnb/37273 [accessed 10 November 2021].

Leach, A. L. (1916), 'Nanna's Cave, Isle of Caldey', *Archaeologia Cambrensis*, 6th ser., 16, 155–80.

Leach, A. L. (1917), 'Supplementary notes on Nanna's Cave, Isle of Caldey', *Archaeologia Cambrensis*, ser. 6, 17, 71–7.

Leahy, K. (2003), *Anglo-Saxon Crafts* (Stroud: Tempus).

Lee, C. (2015), 'Costume and contact: evidence for Scandinavian women in the Irish Sea region', in H. B. Clarke and R. Johnson (eds), *The Vikings in Ireland and Beyond: Before and After the Battle of Clontarf* (Dublin: Four Courts), 284–96.

Leech, P., and Evans, C. (2001), *Fosse Lane, Shepton Mallet, 1990: Excavation of a Romano-British Roadside Settlement in Somerset* (London: Society for the Promotion of Roman Studies, Britannia Monograph 18).

Leighton, D. (2012), *The Western Brecon Beacons: The Archaeology of Mynydd Du and Fforest Fawr*, 2nd ed. (Aberystwyth: RCAHMW).

Leonard, C. (2013), *South Wales Gas Pipeline Project, Site 293, Land South-West of Felindre Mawr, Swansea* (Cotswold Archaeology, report 9150).

LeQuesne, C. (1999), *Excavations at Chester: The Roman and Later Defences, Part 1* (Chester: Chester City Council Cultural Services).

Lethbridge, T. C., and David, H. E. (1930), 'Excavation of a house-site on Gateholm, Pembrokeshire', *Archaeologia Cambrensis*, 85, 366–74.

Lewis, B. (2016), 'The saints in narratives of conversion from Brittonic-speaking regions', in Flechner and Ní Mhaonaigh (eds) (2016), 431–56.

Lewis, C. P. (1996), 'Gruffudd ap Cynan and the Normans', in K. L. Maund (ed.), *Gruffudd ap Cynan: A Collaborative Biography* (Woodbridge: Boydell), 61–77.

Lewis, C. P. (2007), 'Welsh territories and Welsh identities in late Anglo-Saxon England', in N. J. Higham (ed.), *Britons in Anglo-Saxon England* (Woodbridge: Boydell) 130–43.

Lewis, J. (2015), 'Metal detector finds', in R. Hankinson, J. Lewis, E. Chapman, H. Toller, P. Webster, W. Owen, and R. J. Silvester, 'Recent work in the environs of Brecon Gaer Roman fort', *Archaeologia Cambrensis*, 164, 106–18.

Lewis, J. M. (1982), 'Recent finds of penannular brooches in Wales', *Medieval Archaeology*, 25, 151–4.

Lewis, R. (2006), *Cross-ridge Dykes of Southeast Wales* (Glamorgan-Gwent Archaeological Trust, report 2006/103).

Lewis-Williams, J. D. (2008), 'Religion and archaeology: an analytical materialist account', in K. Hays-Gilpin and D. Whitley (eds), *Belief in the Past: Theoretical Approaches to the Archaeology of Religion* (Walnut Creek: Left Coast Press), 23–42.

Leyser, H. (1984), *Hermits and the New Monasticism* (London: Macmillan).

Lieberman, M. (2008), *The March in Wales 1067–1300: A Borderland of Early Medieval Britain* (Cardiff: University of Wales Press).

Lindsay, W. M. (1912), *Early Welsh Script* (Oxford: James Parker).

Little, L. K. (ed.) (2007a), *Plague and the End of Antiquity: The Pandemic of 541–750* (Cambridge: Cambridge University Press).

Little, L. K. (2007b), 'Life and after-life of the first plague pandemic', in Little (ed.) (2007a), 3–32.

Livingstone, E. A. (ed.) (2014), *The Concise Oxford Dictionary of the Christian Church*, 3rd (online) ed. (Oxford: Oxford University Press).

Lloyd, J. E. (1911), *A History of Wales from the Earliest Times to the Edwardian Conquest*, 2 vols, 1st ed. (London: Longmans).

Lloyd, J. E. (ed.) (1935–9), *A History of Carmarthenshire*, 2 vols (Cardiff: London Carmarthenshire Society).

Lloyd, J. E. (1939), *A History of Wales from the Earliest Times to the Edwardian Conquest*, 2 vols, 3rd ed. (London: Longmans, Green).

Lloyd, J. E. (1941), 'Bishop Sulien and his family', *National Library of Wales Journal*, 2(1), 1–6.

Llwyd, A. (1833), *A History of the Island of Mona* (Ruthin: R. Jones; repr. Llansadwrn: Magma, 2007).

Locker, A. (2007), '*In piscibus diversis*: the bone evidence for fish consumption in Roman Britain', *Britannia*, 38, 141–80.

Lockyer, K. (2012), 'Dating coins, dating with coins', *Oxford Journal of Archaeology*, 31(2), 191–211.

Lodwick, M. (2009), 'Metal detecting and archaeology in Wales', in S. Thomas and P. G. Stone (eds), *Metal Detecting and Archaeology* (Woodbridge: Boydell), 107–18.

Lodwick, M., and Besly, E. (2013), 'Portable antiquities', *Archaeology in Wales*, 52, 175–83.

Loe, L. K. (2003), *Health and Socio-Economic Status in Early Medieval Wales: An Analysis of Health Indicators and their Socio-Economic Implications in an Early Medieval Skeletal Population in the Cemetery Site at Llandough, Glamorgan* (unpublished PhD thesis, University of Bristol).

Loe, L. K., and Robson-Brown, K. (2005), 'Summary report on the human skeletons', in Holbrook and Thomas (2005), 42–52.

Longley, D. (1991), 'The excavation of Castell, Porth Trefadog, a coastal promontory fort in north Wales', *Medieval Archaeology*, 35, 64–85.

Longley, D. (1995), 'Excavations at Bangor, Gwynedd 1981–1989', *Archaeologia Cambrensis*, 114, 52–70.

Longley, D. (1996), 'Archaeological survey and excavation near Ffestiniog and Gellilydan', *Journal of the Merioneth History and Record Society*, 12(3), 211–20.

Longley, D. (1997), 'The royal courts of the Welsh princes of Gwynedd AD 400–1283', in Edwards (ed.) (1997b), 41–54.

Longley, D. (2005), *St Eilian's Church Llaneilian* (Gwynedd Archaeological Trust, report 559).

Longley, D. (2006), 'Deserted rural settlements in north-west Wales', in K. Roberts (ed.) (2006a), 61–82.

Longley, D. (2009), 'Early medieval burial in Wales', in Edwards (ed.) (2009b), 105–32.

Longley, D., Johnstone, N., and Evans, J. (1998), 'Excavation at two farms of the Romano-British period at Bryn Eryr and Bush Farm, Gwynedd', *Britannia*, 29, 185–246.

Longley, D., and Laing, L. (1997), 'Bryn Euryn hillfort', *Archaeology in Wales*, 37, 88–91.

Loveluck, C. (2013), *Northwest Europe in the Early Middle Ages, c. AD 600–1150: A Comparative Archaeology* (Cambridge: Cambridge University Press).

Lowe, C. (2008), *Inchmarnock: An Early Historic Island Monastery and its Archaeological Landscape* (Edinburgh: Society of Antiquaries of Scotland).

Loyn, H. (1976), *The Vikings in Wales* (London: Viking Society for Northern Research).

Lucas, A. T. (1963), 'The sacred trees of Ireland', *Transactions of the Cork Historical and Archaeological Society*, 68, 16–54.

Lucas, A. T. (1986), 'The social role of relics', *Journal of the Royal Society of Antiquaries of Ireland*, 116, 5–37.

Lucy, S. (2000), *The Anglo-Saxon Way of Death* (Stroud: Sutton).

Ludlow, N. (2000), 'St Cristiolus' churchyard, Eglwyswrw, Pembrokeshire: a post-Conquest cist cemetery', *Archaeologia Cambrensis*, 149, 20–48.

Ludlow, N. (2003), *Cadw: Welsh Historic Monuments, Early Medieval Ecclesiastical Sites Project. Stage 2: Assessment and Fieldwork Pembrokeshire, part 2a: Gazetteer of Sites* (Cambria Archaeology, report 2003/39).

Ludlow, N. (2009), 'Identifying early medieval ecclesiastical sites in south-west Wales', in Edwards (ed.) (2009b), 61–84.

Lynch, F. (1991), *Prehistoric Anglesey*, 2nd ed. (Llangefni: Anglesey Antiquarian Society).

Lynch, F., Aldhouse-Green, S., and Davies, J. L. (2000), *Prehistoric Wales* (Stroud: Sutton).

Lynch, F., and Musson, C. (2001), 'A prehistoric and early medieval complex at Llandegai, near Bangor, north Wales', *Archaeologia Cambrensis*, 150, 17–142.

Lynn, C. J., and McDowell, J. A. (2011), *Deer Park Farms: The Excavation of a Raised Rath in the Glenarm Valley, Co. Antrim* (Belfast: Stationery Office, Northern Ireland Environment Agency).

Macalister, R. A. S. (1945), *Corpus Inscriptionum Insularum Celticarum*, Vol. I (Dublin: Stationery Office; repr. 1996, Dublin: Four Courts, with preface by D. McManus).

MacCarthaigh, C. (2008), 'Irish skin boats, introduction', in C. MacCarthaigh (ed.), *Traditional Boats of Ireland* (Cork: Collins Press), 419–27.

McClatchie, M. (2014), 'The plant remains from early medieval Ireland', in F. McCormick, T. R. Kerr, M. McClatchie, and A. O'Sullivan, *The Archaeology of Livestock and Cereal*

Production in Early Medieval Ireland, AD 400–1100 (Oxford, British Archaeological Reports, Int. ser. 2647), 39–60.

McClatchie, M., McCormick, F., Kerr, T. R., and O'Sullivan, A. (2019), 'Changing perspectives on early medieval farming in Ireland', in Comeau and Seaman (eds) (2019), 57–77.

McCormick, F., and Murray, E. (2007), *Excavations at Knowth Vol. 3: Knowth and the Zooarchaeology of Early Christian Ireland* (Dublin: Royal Irish Academy).

McCormick, M., Dutton, P. E., and Majewski, P. A. (2007), 'Volcanoes and climate forcing in Carolingian Europe, A.D. 750–950', *Speculum*, 82, 865–95.

Macdonald, P. (2001), 'Langstone', *Archaeology in Wales*, 41, 138–9.

Macdonald, P. (2007), *Llyn Cerrig Bach: A Study of the Copper Alloy Artefacts from the Insular La Tène Assemblage* (Cardiff: University of Wales Press).

McErlean, T., and Crothers, N. (2007), *Harnessing the Tides: The Early Medieval Tide Mills at Nendrum Monastery, Strangford Lough* (Belfast: Northern Ireland Archaeological Monographs 7).

McGrail, S. (1998), *Ancient Boats of North-West* Europe, 2nd ed. (London and New York: Longman).

MacGregor, A. (1985), *Bone Antler Ivory and Horn* (London and Sydney: Croom Helm).

McKee, H. (2000), 'Scribes and glosses from Dark Age Wales: the Cambridge Juvencus manuscript', *Cambrian Medieval Celtic Studies*, 39 (Summer), 1–22.

McKee, H. (2012), 'Script in Wales, Scotland and Cornwall', in R. Gameson (ed.) (2012), 167–73.

McKerracher, M. (2018), *Farming Transformed in Anglo-Saxon England: Agriculture in the Long Eighth Century* (Oxford: Windgather).

McManus, D. (1983), 'The chronology of Latin loanwords in early Irish', *Ériu*, 34, 21–71.

McManus, D. (1991), *A Guide to Ogam* (Maynooth: St Patrick's College, Maynooth Monographs 4).

McNicol, D. (2016), *Cefn Graianog Quarry, Gwynedd* (Gwynedd Archaeological Trust, report 1312).

McNicol, D., Kenney, J., and Smith, S. (2017), *Archaeological Excavation in Advance of the Extension of the Dolbenmaen Water Treatment Works and Dolbenmaen to Cwmystradllyn Water Pipeline* (Gwynedd Archaeological Trust, report 1371).

Maddern, C. (2013), *Raising the Dead: Early Medieval Name Stones in Northumbria* (Turnhout: Brepols).

Maddicott, J. R. (1997), 'Plague in seventh-century England', *Past & Present*, 156, 7–54.

Maddicott, J. R. (2000), 'Two frontier states: Northumbria and Wessex, *c.* 650–750', in J. R. Maddicott and D. M. Palliser (eds), *The Medieval State: Essays presented to James Campbell* (London and Rio Grande: Hambledon Press), 25–45.

Madgwick, R., Redknap, M., and Davies, B. (2016), 'Illuminating Lesser Garth Cave, Cardiff: the human remains and post-Roman archaeology in context', *Archaeologia Cambrensis*, 165, 201–29.

Maldonado, A. (2013), 'Burial in early medieval Scotland: new questions', *Medieval Archaeology*, 57, 1–34.

Malim, T., and Hayes, L. (2008), 'The date and nature of Wat's Dyke: a reassessment in the light of recent investigations at Gobowen, Shropshire', *Anglo-Saxon Studies in Archaeology and History*, 15, 147–79.

Maltby, M. (2016), 'The exploitation of animals in Roman Britain', in Millett et al. (eds) (2016), 791–806.

Manley, J. (1987), '*Cledemutha*: a late Saxon burh in north Wales', *Medieval Archaeology*, 31, 13–46.

Manley, J. (1994), 'Excavations at Caergwrle Castle, Clwyd, north Wales: 1988–1990', *Medieval Archaeology*, 38, 83–133.

Manley, J., Otlet, R. L. A., Walker, A. J., and Williams, D. (1985), 'Early medieval radiocarbon dates and plant remains from Rhuddlan, Clwyd', *Archaeologia Cambrensis*, 134, 106–19.

Mann, A., and Hurst, D. (2014), 'Buttington Cross, Powys: a Bronze Age barrow and post-Roman grain processing site', *Archaeology in Wales*, 53, 130–8.

Mann, A., and Vaughan, T. (2008), *Archaeological Evaluation at Bullingham Lane, Bullinghope, Herefordshire* (Historic Environment and Archaeology Service, Worcestershire County Council, report 1632).

Mann, J. C. (1976), 'What was the Notitia Dignitatum for?', in R. Goodburn and P. Bartholomew (eds), *Aspects of the Notitia Dignitatum* (Oxford: British Archaeological Reports, Supp. ser. 15), 1–9.

Manning, W. H. (2003), 'The defences of Caerwent', in P. Wilson (ed.), *The Archaeology of Roman Towns: Studies in honour of John S. Wacher* (Oxford: Oxbow), 168–83.

Mannion, M. (2015), *Glass Beads from Early Medieval Ireland: Classification, Dating, Social Performance* (Oxford: Archaeopress).

Mannion, M. (2017), 'Symbolism, performance, and colour: the use of glass beads in early medieval Ireland', in Newman et al. (eds) (2017), 149–58.

Marshall, P., and Kenney, J. (2008), 'Appendix I: the radiocarbon dates', in J. Kenney, 'Recent excavations at Parc Bryn Cegin, Llandygai, near Bangor, north Wales', *Archaeologia Cambrensis*, 157, 123–32.

Marvell, A. G., and Owen-John, H. S. (1997), *Leucarum: Excavations at the Roman Auxiliary Fort at Loughor, West Glamorgan 1982–84 and 1987–88* (London: Society for the Promotion of Roman Studies, Britannia monograph 12).

Marzinzik, S. (2013), 'The Coleraine treasure from Northern Ireland: a consideration of the fittings', in F. Hunter and K. Painter (eds), *Late Roman Silver: The Traprain Treasure in Context* (Edinburgh: Society of Antiquaries of Scotland), 175–91.

Mason, D. J. P. (1985), *Excavations at Chester, 26–42 Lower Bridge Street 1974–6: The Dark Age and Anglo-Saxon Periods* (Chester: Chester City Council and Grosvenor Museum).

Mason, D. J. P. (2001), *Roman Chester: City of Eagles* (Stroud: Tempus).

Mason, D. J. P. (2007), *Chester AD 400–1066* (Stroud: Tempus).

Mason, R. (2007), 'Representing the nation', in J. Osmond (ed.), *Myths, Memories and Futures: The National Library and the National Museum in the Story of Wales* (Cardiff: Institute of Welsh Affairs), 23–37.

Mattingly, D. (2006), *An Imperial Possession: Britain and the Roman Empire* (London: Penguin).

Mawer, C. F. (1995), *Evidence for Christianity in Roman Britain: The Small-Finds* (Oxford: British Archaeological Reports, Brit. ser. 243).

Meaney, A. (1981), *Anglo-Saxon Amulets and Curing Stones* (Oxford: British Archaeological Reports, Brit. ser. 96).

Meek, J. (2017), 'The newly-identified Roman fort and settlement at Wiston, Pembrokeshire', *Archaeologia Cambrensis*, 166, 175–212.

Meier, M. (2016), 'The "Justinian Plague": the economic consequences of the pandemic in the eastern Empire and its cultural and religious effects', *Early Medieval Europe*, 24(3), 267–92.

Meyer, A. (2019), 'The Vindolanda calendrical clepsydra: time-keeping and healing waters', *Britannia*, 50, 185–202.

Meyer, K. (1900), 'The Expulsion of the Dessi', *Y Cymmrodor*, 14, 101–35.

Michelli, P. E. (1986), 'Four Scottish crosiers and their relation to the Irish tradition', *Proceedings of the Society of Antiquaries of Scotland*, 116, 375–92.

Miller, M. (1975), 'Bede's use of Gildas', *English Historical Review*, 90, 241–61.

Miller, M. (1980), 'Consular years in the *Historia Brittonum*', *Bulletin of the Board of Celtic Studies*, 29(1), 17–34.

Millett, M. (1990), *The Romanization of Britain* (Cambridge: Cambridge University Press).

Millett, M., Revell, L., and Moore, A. (eds) (2016), *The Oxford Handbook of Roman Britain* (Oxford: Oxford University Press).

Millward, R., and Robinson, A. (1978), *The Welsh Borders* (London: Eyre Methuen).

Minwel Tibbott, S. (1982), *Cooking on the Open Hearth* (Cardiff: National Museum of Wales).

Molyneaux, G. (2011), 'The *Ordinance concerning the Dunsæte* and the Anglo-Welsh frontier in the late tenth and eleventh centuries', *Anglo-Saxon England*, 40, 249–72.

Mommsen, T. (ed.) (1892), *Monumenta Germaniae Historica: Chronica Minora, Saec. IV. V. VI. VII.*, Vol. 1 (Berlin: Weidmann).

Monk, M. A., and Kelleher, E. (2005), 'An assessment of the archaeological evidence for Irish corn-drying kilns in the light of results of archaeological experimental archaeobotanical studies', *Journal of Irish Archaeology*, 14, 73–114.

Monk, M. A., and Power, O. (2012), 'More than a grain of truth emerges from a rash of corn-drying kilns?', *Archaeology Ireland*, 26(2), 38–41.

Mook, W. G. (1986), 'Business Meeting: recommendations/resolutions adopted by the twelfth international radiocarbon conference', *Radiocarbon*, 28, 799.

Moore, D. (1998), 'Cambrian meetings 1847–1997: a society's contribution in a changing archaeological scene', *Archaeologia Cambrensis*, 147, 3–55.

Moore, F. (1998), 'Munster ogham stones: siting, context and function', in M. A. Monk and J. Sheehan (eds), *Early Medieval Munster: Archaeology, History and Society* (Cork: Cork University Press), 23–32.

Moorhead, S. (2006), 'Roman Bronze coinage in sub-Roman and early Anglo-Saxon England', in Cook and Williams (eds) (2006), 99–109.

Moorhead, S. (2009), 'Early Byzantine copper coins found in Britain: a review in the light of new finds recorded with the Portable Antiquities Scheme', in O. Tekin (ed.), *Ancient History, Numismatics and Epigraphy in the Mediterranean World: Studies in memory of Clemens E. Bosch and Sabahat Atlan and in honour of Nezahat Baydur* (Istanbul: Ege), 263–74.

Mordechai, L., and Eisenberg, M. (2019), 'Rejecting catastrophe: the case of the Justinian plague', *Past & Present*, 244, 3–50.

Morgan, K. O. (1981), *Rebirth of a Nation: Wales 1880–1980* (Oxford and New York: Oxford University Press; Cardiff: University of Wales Press).

Morgan, O. (1882), 'Ancient Danish vessel discovered at the mouth of the Usk', in O. Morgan, *Goldcliff and the Ancient Roman Inscribed Stone found there in 1878; together with other papers* (Newport: Monmouthshire and Caerleon Antiquarian Association), 23–6.

Morgan, P. (2007), 'The creation of the National Museum and National Library', in J. Osmond (ed.), *Myths, Memories and Futures, the National Library and the National Museum in the Story of Wales* (Cardiff: Institute of Welsh Affairs), 13–22.

Morris, E. (1985), 'Prehistoric salt distributions: two case-studies from western Britain', *Bulletin of the Board of Celtic Studies*, 32, 336–79.

Morris, J. (1973), *The Age of Arthur* (London: Weidenfeld & Nicolson).

Morris, J. (ed. and trans.) (1980), *Nennius: British History and the Welsh Annals* (London and Chichester: Phillimore).

Morris, R. H. (ed.) (1909–11), *Parochialia; being a summary of answers to 'Parochial Queries' issued by Edward Lhwyd*, 3 vols (London: *Archaeologia Cambrensis* supplement).

Morris-Jones, J. (1925), *Sir John Rhys*, British Academy Sir John Rhys memorial lecture (London: Oxford University Press).

Mower, J. (2003), 'Longoar Bay', *Archaeology in Wales*, 43, 142–3.

Mulville, J., Powell, A., and Best, J. (2019), 'The animal bones from Llangorse crannog', in Lane and Redknap (2019), 174–86.

Murphy, F., and Murphy, K. (2015), 'Survey and excavation of multi-period sites at Crugiau Cemmaes, Nevern, Pembrokeshire, 2009–13', *Archaeologia Cambrensis*, 154, 37–56.

Murphy, K. (1987), 'Excavations at Llanychlwydog church, Dyfed', *Archaeologia Cambrensis*, 136, 77–93.

Murphy, K. (1992), 'Plas Gogerddan, Dyfed: a multi-period burial and ritual site', *Archaeological Journal*, 149, 1–38.

Murphy, K. (2016), 'Late Prehistoric Pembrokeshire', in H. James et al, (eds) (2016), 223–92.

Murphy, K., and Hemer, K. A. (2022), *Excavation of an Early Medieval Cemetery at St Patrick's Chapel, St Davids, Pembrokeshire* (Dyfed Archaeological Trust, report 2022–46).

Murphy, K., and Mytum, H. (2011), 'Iron Age enclosed settlements in west Wales', *Proceedings of the Prehistoric Society*, 78, 263–313.

Murphy, K., and Mytum, H. (2013), 'Excavations at Troedyrhiw enclosure Ceredigion 2005', *Archaeology in Wales*, 52, 57–67.

Murphy, K., Page, M., Crane, P., and Wilson, H. (2014), *Excavation at St Patrick's Chapel 2014: Interim Report* (Dyfed Archaeological Trust, report 2014/26).

Murphy, K., Shiner, M., and Wilson, H. (2015), *Excavation at St Patrick's Chapel 2015: Interim Report* (Dyfed Archaeological Trust, report 2015/35).

Murphy, K., Shiner, M., Wilson, H., and Hemer, K. A. (2016), *Excavation at St Patrick's Chapel 2016:, Interim Report* (Dyfed Archaeological Trust, report 2016/59).

Murphy, K., Wilson, H., Comeau, R., and Hemer, K. A. (2019), *Excavation at St Patrick's Chapel 2019: Interim Report* (Dyfed Archaeological Trust, report 2019/51).

Murray, G. (2007), 'Insular-type crosiers: their construction and characteristics', in R. Moss (ed.), *Making and Meaning in Insular Art* (Dublin: Four Courts), 79–94.

Murray, G. (2014), *The Cross of Cong: A Masterpiece of Early Medieval Irish Art* (Sallins: Irish Academic Press with National Museum of Ireland).

Murray, G. (2017), 'Insular crosiers: an independent tradition?', in Newman et al. (eds) (2017), 167–77.

Murray, H. (1983), *Viking and Early Medieval Buildings in Dublin* (Oxford: British Archaeological Reports, Brit. ser. 119).

Murrieta-Flores, P., and Williams, H. (2017), 'Placing the Pillar of Eliseg: movement, visibility and memory in the early medieval landscape', *Medieval Archaeology*, 61(1), 69–104.

Musson, C. R. (1984), 'The Welsh Archaeological Trusts: a ten year perspective', *Archaeology in Wales*, 24, 5–10.

Musson, C. R. (1991), *The Breiddin Hillfort: A Later Prehistoric Settlement in the Welsh Marches* (London: Council for British Archaeology).

Musson, C. R., and Spurgeon, C. J. (1988), 'Cwrt Llechrhyd, Llanelwedd: an unusual moated site in central Powys', *Medieval Archaeology*, 32, 97–109.

Musson, C. R., Taylor, J. A., and Heyworth, A. (1989), 'Peat deposits and a medieval trackway at Llanaber, near Barmouth, Gwynedd', *Archaeology in Wales*, 29, 22–6.

Mytum, H. (2013), *Monumentality in Later Prehistory: Building and Rebuilding Castell Henllys Hillfort* (New York: Springer).

Mytum, H., and Webster, C. (2001), 'Survey and excavation at Henllys Top Field and Cwm Gloyne enclosures', *Studia Celtica*, 35, 89–108.

Naismith, R. (2017), *Medieval European Coinage with a Catalogue of Coins in the Fitzwilliam Museum, Cambridge, Vol. 8: Britain and Ireland c. 400–1066* (Cambridge: Cambridge University Press).

Nash-Williams, V. E. (1923), 'The coins found at Caerwent and Caerleon', *Bulletin of the Board of Celtic Studies*, 2(1), 92–100.

Nash-Williams, V. E. (1930), 'Further excavations at Caerwent, Monmouthshire', *Archaeologia*, 80, 229–88.

Nash-Williams, V. E. (1950), *The Early Christian Monuments of Wales* (Cardiff: University of Wales Press).

Nash-Williams, V. E. (1953), 'The Roman villa at Llantwit Major, Glamorgan', *Archaeologia Cambrensis*, 120(2), 89–163.

Nash-Williams, V. E. (1969), *The Roman Frontier of Wales*, 2nd ed., rev. M. Jarrett (Cardiff: University of Wales Press).

Nayling, N., and McGrail, S. (2004), *Barland's Farm Romano-Celtic Boat* (London: Council for British Archaeology).

Naylor, J. (2011), 'The circulation of sceattas in western England and Wales', in Naylor and Geake (eds) (2011), 296–9.

Naylor, J. (ed.) (2012), 'Portable Antiquities Scheme', *Medieval Archaeology*, 56, 301–21.

Naylor, J. (2015), 'Portable Antiquities Scheme: focus on coinage', *Medieval Archaeology*, 59, 291–6.

Naylor, J., and Geake, H. (eds) (2011), 'Portable Antiquities Scheme', *Medieval Archaeology*, 55, 284–303.

Nelson-Viljoen, C., Macrow, K., and Parry, I. G. (2021a), *Post-excavation Assessment of Potential: Wylfa Area 7* (Brython Archaeology report).

Nelson-Viljoen, C., Macrow, K., and Parry, I. G. (2021b), *Post-excavation Assessment of Potential: Wylfa Newydd Hotspot 11–13* (Brython Archaeology report).

Nelson-Viljoen, C., Macrow, K., and Parry, I. G. (2021-2), *Post-excavation Assessment of Potential: Wylfa Head* (Brython Archaeology report).

Neuman de Vegvar, C. (2017), 'Wayfaring strangers: a case study in island identity in Insular metalwork', in Newman et al. (eds) (2017), 178–88.

Newman, C., Mannion, M., and Gavin, F. (eds) (2017), *Islands in a Global Context: Proceedings of the Seventh International Conference on Insular Art* (Dublin: Four Courts).

Nicolaisen, W. F. H. (1997), 'On Pictish rivers and their confluences', in D. Henry (ed.), *The Worm, The Germ and the Thorn: Pictish and Related Studies presented to Isabel Henderson* (Balgavies: Pinkfoot Press), 113–18.

Nieke, M. (1993), 'Penannular and related brooches: secular ornament or symbol of action?', in R. M. Spearman and J. Higgitt (eds), *The Age of Migrating Ideas: Early Medieval Art in Northern Britain and Ireland* (Stroud: National Museums of Scotland and Alan Sutton), 128–34.

Noble, F. (1983), *Offa's Dyke Reviewed*, ed. M. Gelling (Oxford: British Archaeological Reports, Brit. ser. 114).

Noble, G. (2016), 'Fortified settlement and the emergence of kingdoms in northern Scotland in the first millennium AD', in Christie and Herold (eds) (2016), 26–36.

Noble, G., Gondek, M., Campbell, E., and Cook, M. (2013), 'Between prehistory and history: the archaeological detection of social change amongst the Picts', *Antiquity*, 87, 1136–50.

O'Brien, E. (2009), 'Pagan or Christian? Burial in Ireland during the 5th to 8th centuries AD', in Edwards (ed.) (2009b), 135–54.

O'Brien, E. (2017), 'From burial among the ancestors to burial among the saints: an assessment of some burial rites in Ireland in the fifth to eighth centuries AD', in Edwards et al. (eds) (2017), 259–86.

O'Brien, E. (2020), *Mapping Death: Burial in Late Iron Age and Early Medieval Ireland* (Dublin: Four Courts).

O'Brien, E., and Bhreathnach, E. (2011), 'Irish boundary *ferta*, their physical manifestation and historical context', in F. Edmonds and P. Russell (eds), *Tome: Studies on Medieval Celtic History and Law* (Woodbridge: Boydell), 53–64.

O'Brien, W. (2004), *Ross Island: Mining, Metal and Society in Early Ireland* (Galway: National University of Ireland).

O'Brien, W., and Hogan, N. (2021), *Garranes: An Early Medieval Site in South-West Ireland* (Oxford: Archaeopress).

Ó Carragáin, T. (2003), 'The architectural setting of the cult of relics in early medieval Ireland', *Journal of the Royal Society of Antiquaries of Ireland*, 133, 130–76.

Ó Carragáin, T. (2010a), *Churches in Early Medieval Ireland* (New Haven and London: Yale University Press).

Ó Carragáin, T. (2010b), 'Cemetery settlements and local churches in pre-Viking Ireland in light of comparison with England and Wales', in J. Graham-Campbell and M. Ryan (eds), *Anglo-Saxon/Irish Relations before the Vikings* (Oxford: Oxford University Press), 329–66.

Ó Carragáin, T. (2022), 'Altars, graves and cenotaphs: *leachta* as foci for ritual in early medieval Ireland', in N. NicGhabhann and D. O'Donovan (eds), *Mapping New Territories in Art and Architectural Histories: Essays in honour of Roger Stalley* (Turnhout: Brepols), 129–46.

O'Carroll, E. (2000), 'Ireland's earliest crozier?', *Archaeology Ireland*, 14(2), 24–5.

O'Carroll, E. (2001), *The Archaeology of Lemanaghan—the Story of an Irish Bog* (Bray: Wordwell).

Ó Cathasaigh, T. (1984), 'The Déisi and Dyfed', *Éigse*, 20, 1–33.

O'Connor, T. (2011), 'Animal husbandry', in Hamerow et al. (eds) (2011), 361–76.

Offer, A. (1997), 'Between gift and the market: the economy of regard', *Economic History Review*, 50(3), 450–76.

Ó Floinn, R. (2001), 'Patrons and politics: art, artefact and methodology', in M. Redknap, N. Edwards, S. Youngs, A. Lane, and J. Knight (eds), *Pattern and Purpose in Insular Art* (Oxford: Oxbow), 1–14.

Ogham in 3D, https://ogham.celt.dias.ie/menu.php?lang=en&menuitem=00 [accessed 31 October 2016].

O'Grady, O. J. T. (2014), 'Judicial assembly sites in Scotland: archaeological assembly and place-name evidence of the Scottish court hill', *Medieval Archaeology*, 58, 104–35.

O'Grady, O. J. T. (2018), 'Accumulating kingship: the archaeology of elite assembly in medieval Scotland', *World Archaeology*, 50(1), 137–49.

Okasha, E. (1993), *Corpus of Early Christian Inscribed Stones of South-West Britain* (Leicester: Leicester University Press).

O'Kelly, M. J. (1958), 'Church Island, near Valencia, Co. Kerry', *Proceedings of the Royal Irish Academy*, 59C, 57–136.

O'Kelly, M. J. (1962), 'Two ring-forts at Garryduff, Co. Cork', *Proceedings of the Royal Irish Academy*, 63C, 17–125.

O'Loughlin, T. (1997), 'Living in the ocean', in C. Bourke (ed.), *Studies in the Cult of St Columba* (Dublin: Four Courts), 11–23.

Olson, L. (1989), *Early Monasteries in Cornwall* (Woodbridge: Boydell).

Olson, L. (2017), 'Introduction: "getting somewhere" with the First Life of St Samson of Dol', in L. Olson (ed.), *St Samson of Dol and the Earliest History of Brittany, Cornwall and Wales* (Woodbridge: Boydell), 1–18.

O'Meara, J. J. (trans.) (1982), *Gerald of Wales: The History and Topography of Ireland*, rev. ed. (Harmondsworth: Penguin).

O'Neil, B. H. St J. (1937), 'Excavations at Breiddin Hill camp, Montgomeryshire, 1933–35', *Archaeologia Cambrensis*, 92, 86–128.

Ó Riain, P. (1990), 'The Tallaght Martyrologies, redated', *Cambrian Medieval Celtic Studies*, 20 (Winter), 21–38.

Ó Riain, P. (1994), 'The saints of Cardiganshire', in J. L. Davies and D. P. Kirby (eds), *Cardiganshire County History, Vol. 1: From the Earliest Times to the Coming of the Normans* (Cardiff: University of Wales Press), 378–96.

Ó Ríordáin, S. P. (1942), 'The excavation of a large earthen ring-fort at Garranes, Co. Cork', *Proceedings of the Royal Irish Academy*, 47C, 77–150.

O'Sullivan, A. (1998), *The Archaeology of Lake Settlement in Ireland* (Dublin: Royal Irish Academy).

O'Sullivan, A. (2001), *Foragers, Farmers and Fishers in a Coastal Landscape* (Dublin: Royal Irish Academy).

O'Sullivan, A., McCormick, F., Kerr, T. R., and Harney, L. (2014), *Early Medieval Ireland, AD 400–1100: The Evidence of Archaeological Excavations* (Dublin: Royal Irish Academy).

O'Sullivan, J., and Ó Carragáin, T. (2008), *Inishmurray: Monks and Pilgrims in an Atlantic Landscape* (Cork: Collins Press).

Owen, H. W. (1994), *The Place-Names of East Flintshire* (Cardiff: University of Wales Press).

Owen, H. W., and Gruffydd, G. L. (2017), *The Place-Names of Flintshire* (Cardiff: University of Wales Press).

Owen-John, H. (1988), 'Llandough: the rescue excavation of a multiperiod site near Cardiff, South Glamorgan', in Robinson (ed.) (1988), 123–77.

Padel, O. J. (1985), *Cornish Place-Name Elements* (Nottingham: English Place-Name Society).

Padel, O. J. (2010), 'Christianity in medieval Cornwall: Celtic aspects', in N. Orme (ed.), *The Victoria History of the Counties of England. A History of the County of Cornwall, Vol. 2: Religious History to 1560* (Woodbridge: Boydell), 110–25.

Page, M. R. (2011), '*Ble mae'r babanod?* (Where are the babies?): infant burial in early medieval Wales', in M. Lally and A. Moore (eds), *(Re)Thinking Little Ancestors: New Perspectives on the Archaeology of Infancy and Childhood* (Oxford: British Archaeological Reports, Int. ser. 2271), 100–9.

Page, N., Hughes, G., Jones, R., and Murphy, K. (2012), 'Excavations at Erglodd, Llangynfelyn, Ceredigion: prehistoric/Roman lead smelting site and medieval trackway', *Archaeologia Cambrensis*, 161, 285–356.

Painter, K. S. (1977), *The Water Newton Early Christian Silver* (London: British Museum).

Pantos, A., and Semple, S. (eds) (2004), *Assembly Places and Practices in Medieval Europe* (Dublin: Four Courts).

Parkhouse, J. (1988), 'Excavations at Biglis, South Glamorgan', in Robinson (ed.) (1988), 1–64.

Parkhouse, J., and Evans, E. M. (eds) (1996), *Excavations in Cowbridge, South Glamorgan, 1977–88* (Oxford: British Archaeological Reports, Brit. ser. 245).

Parry, G. (1995), *The Trophies of Time: English Antiquarians of the Seventeenth Century* (Oxford: Oxford University Press).

Parry, I. G., Williams, T., and Hopewell, D. (2012), *Dinas Dinllaen: Preliminary Excavation Report*, appendix in I. Parry, L. Parry, R. Evans, et al., *Afordir Coastal Heritage: Final Report* (Gwynedd Archaeological Trust, project 2072).

Parry, L. W., and Kenney, J. (2013), 'Archaeological discoveries along the Porthmadog bypass', *Archaeology in Wales*, 52, 113–32.

Parry, L. W., and Parry, I. G. (2016), *Early-Medieval Cemetery, Llangefni Link-Road: Interim Field Report* (Brython Archaeology).

Parsons, D. N. (2013a), *Martyrs and Memorials: Merthyr Place-Names and the Church in Early Medieval Wales* (Aberystwyth: University of Wales Centre for Advanced Welsh and Celtic Studies).

Parsons, D. N. (2013b), 'Pre-English river-names and British survival in Shropshire', *Nomina*, 36, 107–22.

PAS = Portable Antiquities Scheme, https://finds.org.uk/ [accessed 7 October 2021].

Paterson, C., Parsons, A. J., Newman, R. M., Johnson, N., and Davis, C. H. (2014), *Shadows in the Sand: Excavation of A Viking-Age Cemetery at Cumwhitton, Cumbria* (Lancaster: Oxford Archaeology North).

Paxton, F. S. (1990), *Christianizing Death: The Creation of Ritual Process in Early Medieval Europe* (Ithaca and London: Cornell University Press).

Pearson, A. (2002), *The Roman Shore Forts* (Stroud: Tempus).

472 REFERENCES

Peers, C. R., and Hemp, W. P. (1919), 'Thursday, 27th February 1919 [Inscribed gold sheet from *Segontium*]', *Proceedings of the Society of Antiquaries of London*, ser. 2, 31, 127–31.

Pennant, T. (1778–83), *A Tour in Wales*, 2 vols (Wrexham: Bridge Books, facsimile ed. 1991).

Penney, S., and Shotter, D. C. A. (1996), 'An inscribed Roman salt-pan from Shavington, Cheshire', *Britannia*, 27, 360–4.

Penniman, T. K. (1936), 'Twlc Point shell-heap, Broughton Bay, Llangennith, Gower', *Bulletin of the Board of Celtic Studies*, 8(3), 275–6.

Pestell, T. (2011), 'Markets, *emporia, wics*, and "productive" sites: pre-Viking trade centres in Anglo-Saxon England', in Hamerow et al. (2011), 556–79.

Petts, D. (2002), 'Cemeteries and boundaries in western Britain', in S. Lucy and A. Reynolds (eds), *Burial in Early Medieval England and Wales* (London: Maney), 24–46.

Petts, D. (2003), *Christianity in Roman Britain* (Stroud: Tempus).

Petts, D. (2004), 'Burial in western Britain AD 400–800: Late Antique or early medieval?', in R. Collins and J. Gerrard (eds), *Debating Late Antiquity AD 300–700* (Oxford: British Archaeological Reports, Brit. ser. 365), 77–87.

Petts, D. (2007), '*De Situ Brecheniauc* and *Englynion y Beddau*: writing about burial in early medieval Wales', *Anglo-Saxon Studies in Archaeology and History*, 14, 165–72.

Petts, D. (2009), *The Early Medieval Church in Wales* (Stroud: History Press).

Petts, D., and Turner, S. (2009), 'Early medieval church groups in Wales and western England', in Edwards (ed.) (2009b), 281–99.

Phillipps, D. T. (1863), 'Charta Sti. Eliani, in Anglesey', *Cambrian Journal*, 4, 319–23.

Phillips, C. W. (1934), 'The excavation of a hut group at Pant-y-Saer in the parish of Llanfair-Mathafarn-Eithaf, Anglesey', *Archaeologia Cambrensis*, 89, 1–36.

Phillips, C. W. (1987), *My Life in Archaeology* (Gloucester: Sutton).

Philpott, R. A. (1991), *Burial Practices in Roman Britain: A Survey of Grave Treatment and Furnishing, A.D. 43–410* (Oxford: British Archaeological Reports, Brit. ser. 219).

Philpott, R. A. (2015), 'Viking Age rural settlement in lowland north-west England: identifying the invisible?' in Harding et al. (2015), 109–25.

Philpott, R. A. (2020), 'Early Byzantine copper coins from north-west England: new finds from Wirral, Cheshire and west Lancashire', *Journal of the Chester Archaeological Society*, 90, 51–70.

Pierce, G. O. (1968), *The Place-Names of Dinas Powys Hundred* (Cardiff: University of Wales Press).

Pierce, G. O. (2002), *Place-Names in Glamorgan* (Whitchurch: Merton Priory Press).

Pine, J., Allen, J. R. L., and Chalinor, D. (2009), 'Saxon iron smelting at Clearwell Quarry, St. Briavels, Lydney, Gloucestershire,' *Archaeology in the Severn Estuary*, 20, 9–40.

Platnauer, M. (trans.) (1922), *Claudian*, 2 vols (Cambridge, MA: Harvard University Press; London: Heinemann).

Pohl, W. (2014), 'Romannes: a multiple identity and its changes', *Early Medieval Europe*, 22(4), 406–18.

Pohl, W. (2018), 'Introduction: early medieval Romanness – a multiple identity', in W. Pohl, C. Gantner, C. Griffoni, and M. Pollheimer-Mohaupt (eds), *Transformations of Romanness: Early Medieval Regions and Identities* (Berlin and Boston: de Gruyter), 3–39.

Pollard, J., Howell, R., Chadwick, A., and Leaver, A. (2006), *Lodge Hill Camp, Caerleon and the Hillforts of Gwent* (Oxford: British Archaeological Reports, Brit. Ser. 407).

Pollock, K. J. (2006), *The Evolution and Role of Burial Practice in Roman Wales* (Oxford: British Archaeological Reports, Brit. ser. 426).

Power, R. (1986), 'Magnus Barelegs' expeditions to the west', *Scottish Historical Review*, 65(2), 107–32.

Preston-Jones, A. (1992), 'Decoding Cornish churchyards', in Edwards and Lane (eds) (1992), 105–24.

Preston-Jones, A., and Okasha, E. (2013), *Early Cornish Sculpture*, Corpus of Anglo-Saxon Stone Sculpture, Vol. 11 (Oxford: Oxford University Press).

Preston-Jones, A., and Rose, P. (1986), 'Medieval Cornwall', *Cornish Archaeology*, 25, 135–85.

Price, C. (1987), 'Atlantic Trading Estate, Barry', *Archaeology in Wales*, 27, 60–1.

Price, N. (2020), *The Children of Ash and Elm: A History of the Vikings* (UK: Allen Lane).

Pritchard, A. (2009), 'The origins of ecclesiastical stone architecture in Wales', in Edwards (ed.) (2009b), 245–64.

Procter, L. (2014), 'Two early Anglo-Saxon silver pyramidal mounts from NE England', *Medieval Archaeology*, 58, 352–3.

Pryce, H. (1986), 'The Prologues of the Welsh Lawbooks', *Bulletin of the Board of Celtic Studies*, 33, 151–87.

Pryce, H. (1992), 'Pastoral care in early medieval Wales', in J. Blair and R. Sharpe (eds), *Pastoral Care before the Parish* (Leicester: Leicester University Press), 41–62.

Pryce, H. (1993), *Native Law and the Church in Medieval Wales* (Oxford: Clarendon Press).

Pryce, H. (1994), 'A new edition of the *Historia Divae Monacellae*', *Montgomeryshire Collections*, 82, 23–40.

Pryce, H. (2001a), 'British or Welsh? National identity in twelfth-century Wales', *English Historical Review*, 116, 775–801.

Pryce, H. (2001b), 'The medieval church', in J. B. Smith and L. B. Smith (eds), *History of Merioneth, Vol. 2: The Middle Ages* (Cardiff: University of Wales Press), 254–96.

Pryce, H. (2011), *J. E. Lloyd and the Creation of Welsh History: Renewing a Nation's Past* (Cardiff: University of Wales Press).

Pryce, H. (2018), 'Gerald of Wales and the Welsh past', in G. Henley and A. J. McMullen (eds), *Gerald of Wales: New Perspectives on a Medieval Writer and Critic* (Cardiff: University of Wales Press), 19–45.

Pryce, H. (2020), 'Chronicling and its contexts in medieval Wales', in B. Guy, G. Henley, O. W. Jones, and R. Thomas (eds), *The Chronicles of Medieval Wales and the March* (Turnhout: Brepols), 1–32.

Pryce, H. (2022), *Writing Welsh History: From the Early Middle Ages to the Twenty-First Century* (Oxford: Oxford University Press).

Quensel-von Kalben, L. (1999), 'The British Church and the emergence of Anglo-Saxon kingdoms', *Anglo-Saxon Studies in Archaeology and History*, 10, 89–97.

Quinnell, H. (2004), *Trethurgy* (Cornwall: Cornwall County Council).

Quinnell, H., and Blockley, M. R. (1994), *Excavations at Rhuddlan, Clwyd 1969–73, Mesolithic to Medieval* (York: Council for British Archaeology).

Rackham, J. (2013), 'The palaeoenvironmental evidence', in J. Hart, *South Wales Gas Pipeline Project Site 25.07, Land South-West of Brynwgan, Manordeilo and Salem, Carmarthenshire: Archaeological Excavation* (Cotswold Archaeology, report 13310), 12–28.

474 REFERENCES

Radford, C. A. R. (1935), 'Tintagel: the castle and Celtic monastery', *Antiquaries Journal*, 15, 401–19.

Radford, C. A. R. (1937), 'The early mediæval period', in RCAHMW, *Anglesey* (London: HMSO), xci–ciii.

Radford, C. A. R. (1956), 'Imported pottery found at Tintagel, Cornwall', in D. B. Harden (ed.), *Dark Age Britain: Studies presented to E. T. Leeds* (London: Methuen), 59–70.

Radford, C. A. R., and Hemp, W. J. (1959), 'Pennant Melangell: the church and shrine', *Archaeologia Cambrensis*, 108, 81–113.

Radner, J. N. (ed.) (1978), *Fragmentary Annals of Ireland* (Dublin: Dublin Institute of Advanced Studies).

Rahtz, P. (ed.) (1974), *Rescue Archaeology* (Harmondsworth: Penguin).

Rahtz, P., Hirst, S., and Wright, S. M. (2000), *Cannington Cemetery* (London: Society for the Promotion of Roman Studies, Britannia monograph 17).

Rahtz, P., and Watts, L. (1997), *St Mary's Church, Deerhurst, Gloucestershire: Fieldwork, Excavations and Structural Analysis, 1971–1984* (Woodbridge: Boydell).

Rahtz, P., Woodward, A., Burrow, I., Everton, A., Watts, L., Leach, P., Hirst, S., Fowler, P., and Gardner, K. (1992), *Cadbury Congresbury 1968–73: A Late/Post-Roman Hilltop Settlement in Somerset* (Oxford: British Archaeological Reports, Brit. ser. 223).

Rance, P. (2001), 'Attacotti, Déisi and Magnus Maximus: the case for Irish federates in late Roman Britain', *Britannia*, 32, 243–70.

Randall, H. J. (1956), 'V. E. Nash-Williams 1897–1955', *Archaeologia Cambrensis*, 105, 150–1.

Ray, K. (2015), *The Archaeology of Herefordshire: An Exploration* (Woonton Almeley: Logaston Press).

Ray, K., Bailey, R., Copeland, T., Davies, T., Delaney, L., Finch, D., Heaton, N., Hoyle, J., and Maddison, S. (2021), 'Offa's Dyke: a continuing journey of discovery', *Offa's Dyke Journal*, 3, 33–81.

Ray, K., and Bapty, I. (2016), *Offa's Dyke: Landscape and Hegemony in Eighth-Century Britain* (Oxford: Oxbow).

RCAHMS (1982), *Argyll: An Inventory of Monuments, Vol. 4, Iona* (Edinburgh: HMSO).

RCAHMW (1911), *An Inventory of the Ancient Monuments in Wales and Monmouthshire, I County of Montgomery* (London: HMSO).

RCAHMW (1912), *An Inventory of the Ancient Monuments in Wales and Monmouthshire, II County of Flint* (London: HMSO).

RCAHMW (1913), *An Inventory of the Ancient Monuments in Wales and Monmouthshire, III County of Radnor* (London: HMSO).

RCAHMW (1914), *An Inventory of the Ancient Monuments in Wales and Monmouthshire, IV County of Denbigh* (London: HMSO).

RCAHMW (1917), *An Inventory of the Ancient Monuments in Wales and Monmouthshire, V County of Carmarthenshire* (London: HMSO).

RCAHMW (1921), *An Inventory of the Ancient Monuments in Wales and Monmouthshire, VI County of Merioneth* (London: HMSO).

RCAHMW (1925), *An Inventory of the Ancient Monuments in Wales and Monmouthshire, VII County of Pembroke* (London: HMSO).

RCAHMW (1937), *An Inventory of the Ancient Monuments in Anglesey* (London: HMSO, 3rd ed. 1968).

REFERENCES 475

RCAHMW (1960), *Caernarvonshire, Vol. 2: Central* (London: HMSO).

RCAHMW (1976a), *An Inventory of the Ancient Monuments in Glamorgan, Vol. I(ii): The Iron Age and Roman Occupation* (Cardiff: HMSO).

RCAHMW (1976b), *An Inventory of the Ancient Monuments in Glamorgan, Vol. I(iii): The Early Christian Period* (Cardiff: HMSO).

RCAHMW (1986), *An Inventory of the Ancient Monuments in Brecknock (Brycheiniog): The Prehistoric and Roman Monuments, Part ii: Hill-forts and Roman Remains* (London: HMSO).

RCAHMW, *Inventory of Historic Battlefields in Wales*, https://battlefields.wales/ [accessed 22 February 2023].

Redknap, M. (1991), *Christian Celts* (Cardiff: National Museums of Wales).

Redknap, M. (1992), 'Excavations at Newton Moor, South Glamorgan: an interim statement', *Severn Estuary Levels Research Committee Annual Report 1991*, 23–6.

Redknap, M. (1994), 'Glyn, Llanbedrgoch, Anglesey', *Archaeology in Wales*, 34, 58–60.

Redknap, M. (1995a), 'Insular nonferrous metalwork from Wales of the 8th to 10th centuries', in C. Bourke (ed.), *From the Isles of the North: Early Medieval Art in Britain and Ireland* (Belfast: HMSO), 59–73.

Redknap, M. (1995b), 'Glyn, Llanbedrgoch, Anglesey', *Archaeology in Wales*, 35, 35, 50, 55–6.

Redknap, M. (1996), Glyn, Llanbedrgoch', *Archaeology in Wales*, 36, 59, 72, 81–2.

Redknap, M. (1997), 'Glyn, Llanbedrgoch', *Archaeology in Wales*, 37, 94–6.

Redknap, M. (1999), 'Further work at Glyn, Llanbedrgoch, Anglesey', *Archaeology in Wales*, 39, 56–61.

Redknap, M. (2000), *Vikings in Wales: An Archaeological Quest* (Cardiff: National Museums and Galleries of Wales).

Redknap, M. (2001), 'Glyn, Llanbedrgoch', *Archaeology in Wales*, 41, 120, 133, 144–7.

Redknap, M. (2002), 'Llanmihangel, Pen-y-bryn Farm', *Archaeology in Wales*, 42, 158–9.

Redknap, M. (2004a), 'Viking-age settlement in Wales and the evidence of Llanbedrgoch', in J. Hines, A. Lane and M. Redknap (eds), *Land, Sea and Home* (Leeds: Maney), 139–75.

Redknap, M. (2004b), 'Glyn, Llanbedrgoch', *Archaeology in Wales*, 44, 149, 155–6, 168.

Redknap, M. (2004c), 'Llangors crannog', *Archaeology in Wales*, 44, 177–8.

Redknap, M. (2006), 'Viking-Age settlement in Wales: some recent advances', *Transactions of the Honourable Society of Cymmrodorion*, new ser. 12, 5–35.

Redknap, M. (2007a), 'Crossing boundaries – stylistic diversity and external contacts in early medieval Wales and the March: reflections on metalwork and sculpture', *Cambrian Medieval Celtic Studies* (*Proceedings of the 12th International Congress on Celtic Studies, 2003*), 53–4, 23–86.

Redknap, M. (2007b), 'Llanbedrgoch: an early medieval settlement and its significance', *Transactions of the Anglesey Antiquarian Society*, 53–72.

Redknap, M. (2007c), 'St Davids and a new link with the Hiberno-Norse world', in J. W. Evans and Wooding (eds) (2007), 84–9.

Redknap, M. (2008), 'An early medieval settlement: Gateholm Island', in P. Wakelin and R. A. Griffiths (eds), *Hidden Histories: Discovering the Heritage of Wales* (Aberystwyth: RCAHMW), 104–5.

Redknap, M. (2009a), 'Early medieval metalwork and Christianity: a Welsh perspective', in Edwards (ed.) (2009b), 351–73.

Redknap, M. (2009b), 'Silver and commerce in Viking-Age north Wales', in Graham-Campbell and Philpott (eds) (2009), 29–41.

Redknap, M. (2009c), 'Glitter in the dragon's lair: Irish and Anglo-Saxon metalwork from pre-Viking Wales, *c*.400–850', in J. Graham-Campbell and M. Ryan (eds), *Anglo-Saxon/Irish Relations before the Vikings* (Oxford: Oxford University Press), 281–309.

Redknap, M. (2013), 'Ring rattle on swift steeds: equestrian equipment from early medieval Wales', in A. Reynolds and L. Webster (eds), *Early Medieval Art and Archaeology of the Northern World: Studies in honour of James Graham-Campbell* (Leiden and Boston: Brill), 177–210.

Redknap, M. (2016), 'Defining identities in Viking Age north Wales: new data from Llanbedrgoch', in V. E. Turner, O. A. Owen, and D. J. Waugh (eds), *Shetland in the Viking World: Papers from the Seventeenth Viking Congress* (Lerwick: Shetland Heritage), 159–66.

Redknap, M. (2019), 'Unveiling Byzantium in Wales', in S. Tougher (ed.), *The Emperor in the Byzantine World* (London and New York: Routledge), 341–71.

Redknap, M. (2022), 'Early medieval metalwork from south-east Wales: patterns and potential', *Archaeologia Cambrensis*, 171, 73–114.

Redknap, M., and Lane, A. (1994), 'The early medieval crannog at Llangorse, Powys: an interim statement on the 1989–1993 seasons', *International Journal of Nautical Archaeology*, 23(3), 189–205.

Redknap, M., and Lane, A. (1999), 'The archaeological importance of Llangorse Lake: an environmental perspective', *Aquatic Conservation: Marine and Freshwater Ecosystems*, 9, 377–90.

Redknap, M., and Lewis, J. M. (2007), *A Corpus of Early Medieval Inscribed Stones and Stone Sculpture in Wales, Vol. I: Breconshire, Glamorgan, Monmouthshire, Radnorshire, and geographically contiguous areas of Herefordshire and Shropshire* (Cardiff: University of Wales Press).

Redknap, M., Rees, S., and Aberg, A. (eds) (2019), *Wales and the Sea: 10,000 Years of Maritime History* (Aberystwyth and Tal-y-Bont: RCAHMW and Y Lolfa).

Reed, S., Bidwell, P., and Allan, J. (2011), 'Excavations at Bantham, south Devon, and post-Roman trade in south-west England', *Medieval Archaeology*, 55, 82–138.

Rees, S. E. (1979), *Agricultural Implements in Prehistoric and Roman Britain*, 2 vols (Oxford: British Archaeological Reports, Brit. ser. 69).

Revell, L. (2016), *Ways of being Roman: Discourses of Identity in the Roman West* (Oxford: Oxbow).

Reynolds, A. (2009), *Anglo-Saxon Deviant Burial Customs* (Oxford: Oxford University Press).

Reynolds, A. (2019), 'Spatial configurations of power in Anglo-Saxon England: sidelights on the relationships between boroughs, royal vills and hundreds', in J. Carroll et al. (eds) (2019b), 436–55.

Reynolds, A., and Langlands, A. (2006), 'Social identities on the macro-scale: a maximum view of Wansdyke', in W. Davies, G. Halsall, and A. Reynolds (eds), *People and Space in the Early Middle Ages 300–1300* (Turnhout: Brepols), 13–44.

Reynolds, A., and Langlands, A. (2011), 'Travel *as* communication: a consideration of overland journeys in Anglo-Saxon England', *World Archaeology*, 43(3), 410–27.

Rhys, J. (1895), 'Notes on the inscriptions on the tombstone of Voteporis, prince of Demetia', *Archaeologia Cambrensis*, ser. 5, 307–13.

Richards, J. D. (2000), *Viking Age England*, 2ⁿᵈ ed. (Stroud: Tempus).

Richards, M. (1960), 'The Irish settlements in south-west Wales', *Journal of the Royal Society of Antiquaries of Ireland*, 90, 133–62.

Richards, M. (1962), 'Welsh *meid(i)r, moydir*, Irish *bothár* "lane, road"', *Lochlann*, 2, 129–34.

Richards, M. (1974), 'The Carmarthenshire possessions of Talyllychau', in T. Barnes and N. Yates (eds), *Carmarthenshire Studies: Essays presented to Major Francis Jones* (Carmarthen: Carmarthenshire County Council), 110–21.

Richards, M. (1975), 'Norse place-names in Wales', in B. Ó Cuiv (ed.), *The Impact of the Scandinavian Invasions on the Celtic-Speaking Peoples* c. *800–1100 A.D.* (Dublin: Institute of Advanced Studies, repr.), 51–60.

Richards, M. P., and Montgomery, J. (2012), 'Isotope analysis and paleopathology: a short review and future developments', in J. E. Buikstra and C. A. Roberts (eds), *The Global History of Paleopathology: Pioneers and Prospects* (Oxford: Oxford University Press), 718–31.

Ridley, R. T. (trans.) (1982), *Zosimus: New History* (Canberra: Australian Association for Byzantine Studies).

Rippon, S. (1996), *The Gwent Levels: The Evolution of a Wetland Landscape* (York: Council for British Archaeology).

Rippon, S. (2008), *Beyond the Medieval Village: The Diversification of Landscape Character in Southern Britain* (Oxford: Oxford University Press).

Rippon, S. (2009), 'Understanding the medieval landscape', in Gilchrist and Reynolds (eds) (2009), 227–54.

Rippon, S. (2018), 'Changing landscapes? Land, people and environment in England, AD 350–600', in P. Diarte-Blasco and N. Christie (eds), *Interpreting Transformations of People and Landscapes in Late Antiquity and the Early Middle Ages: Archaeological Approaches and Issues* (Oxford: Oxbow), ch. 9.

Rippon, S. (2019), 'The fields of Britannia: continuity and change within the early medieval landscape', in Comeau and Seaman (eds) (2019), 15–36.

Rippon, S., Smart, C., and Pears, B. (2015), *The Fields of Britannia* (Oxford: Oxford University Press).

Rivet, A. L. F., and Smith, C. (1979), *The Place-Names of Roman Britain* (London: B. T. Batsford).

Roberts, B. F. (1991), '*Culhwch ac Olwen*, the Triads, saints' lives', in R. Bromwich, A. O. H. Jarman, and B. F. Roberts (eds), *The Arthur of the Welsh* (Cardiff: University of Wales Press), 73–95.

Roberts, B. F. (2022), *Edward Lhwyd* c.*1660–1709: Naturalist, Antiquary, Philologist* (Cardiff: University of Wales Press).

Roberts, B. K., and Barnwell, P. S. (eds) (2011a), *Britons, Saxons and Scandinavians: The Historical Geography of Glanville R. J. Jones* (Turnhout: Brepols).

Roberts, B. K. with Barnwell, P. S. (2011b), 'The multiple estate of Glanville Jones: epitome, critique and context', in Roberts and Barnwell (eds) (2011a), 25–128.

Roberts, J. G., and Peterson, R. (1989), 'Crannog sites in Wales and the Marches', *Archaeology in Wales*, 29, 40.

Roberts, K. (ed.) (2006a), *Lost Farmsteads: Deserted Rural Settlements in Wales* (York: Council for British Archaeology).

Roberts, K. (2006b), 'The deserted rural settlements project: background and methodology', in Roberts (ed.) (2006a), 1–9.

Roberts, R. (1999), 'Gwent Levels wetland reserve', *Archaeology in Wales*, 39, 105–6.

Roberts, S. E. (2001), 'Legal practice in fifteenth-century Brycheiniog', *Studia Celtica*, 35, 307–23.

Roberts, T. (1992), 'Welsh ecclesiastical place-names and archaeology', in Edwards and Lane (eds) (1992), 41–4.

Robertson, A. J. (ed. and trans.) (1956), *Anglo-Saxon Charters* (Cambridge: Cambridge University Press).

Robertson, A. S., Hobbs, R., and Buttrey, V. T. (2000), *An Inventory of Romano-British Coin Hoards* (London: Royal Numismatic Society).

Robinson, D. M. (ed.) (1988), *Biglis, Caldicot and Llandough: Three Late Iron Age and Romano-British Sites in South-East Wales, Excavations 1977–79* (Oxford: British Archaeological Reports, Brit. ser. 188).

Rolfe, J. C. (trans.) (1950), *Ammianus Marcellinus*, 3 vols, 2nd ed. (Cambridge, MA: Harvard University Press; London: Heinemann).

Rollason, D. (1989), *Saints and Relics in Anglo-Saxon England* (Oxford: Basil Blackwell).

Ross, A. (1967), *Pagan Celtic Britain* (London: Routledge & Kegan Paul).

Rowland, J. (1990), *Early Welsh Saga Poetry* (Cambridge: Brewer).

Rowland, J. (1995), 'Warfare and horses in the *Gododdin* and the problem of Catraeth', *Cambrian Medieval Celtic Studies*, 30 (Winter), 13–40.

Russell, I., and Hurley, M. F. (2014), *Woodstown: A Viking-Age Settlement in County Wateford* (Dublin: Four Courts).

Russell, P. (ed. and trans.) (2005), *Vita Griffini Filii Conani: The Medieval Latin Life of Gruffudd ap Cynan* (Cardiff: University of Wales Press).

Russell, P. (2012), 'The *englyn* to St Padarn revisited', *Cambrian Medieval Celtic Studies*, 63 (Summer), 1–14.

Ryan, M. (1997), 'The Derrynaflan hoard and early Irish art', *Speculum*, 72, 995–1017.

Rynne, C. (2018), 'Technological change in the agrarian economy of early medieval Ireland: new archaeological evidence for the introduction of the coulter plough', *Proceedings of the Royal Irish Academy*, 118C, 37–66.

St Joseph, J. K. (1980), 'Air reconnaissance: recent results, 49', *Antiquity*, 54, 47–51.

Sallares, R. (2007), 'Ecology, evolution, and epidemiology of plague', in Little (ed.) (2007a), 231–89.

Salway, P. (1981), *Roman Britain* (Oxford: Clarendon Press).

Savory, H. N. (1956), 'Some sub-Romano-British brooches from south Wales', in D. B. Harden (ed.), *Dark Age Britain: Studies presented to E. T. Leeds* (London: Methuen), 40–58.

Savory, H. N. (1960), 'Excavations at Dinas Emrys, Beddgelert (Caern.), 1954–56', *Archaeologia Cambrensis*, 109, 13–77.

Savory, H. N. (1971), *Excavations at Dinorben, 1965–9* (Cardiff: National Museum of Wales).

Savory, H. N. (ed.) (1984), *Glamorgan County History, Vol. 2: Early Glamorgan* (Cardiff: Glamorgan County History Trust).

Sawyer, P. H. (1968), *Anglo-Saxon Charters: An Annotated List and Bibliography* (London: Royal Historical Society); see also *The Electronic Sawyer: Online Catalogue of Anglo-Saxon Charters*, https://esawyer.lib.cam.ac.uk/about/index.html [accessed 30 September 2021].

Sawyer, P. H. (2013), *The Wealth of Anglo-Saxon England* (Oxford: Oxford University Press).

Schlee, D. (2007), 'Maenclochog Castle', *Archaeology in Wales*, 47, 157.

Schlee, D. (2008), *The Maenclochog Community Excavation* (Cambria Archaeology, report 2008/27).

Schlee, D. (2009a). *The Pembrokeshire Cemeteries Project: Excavations at Porthclew Chapel, 2008 interim report* (Dyfed Archaeological Trust, report 2009/17).

Schlee, D. (2009b), 'Porthclew Chapel', *Archaeology in Wales*, 49, 124–5.

Schlesinger, A., and Walls, C. (1996), 'An early church and medieval farmstead site: excavation at Llanelen, Gower', *Archaeological Journal*, 153, 104–47.

Schulenburg, J. T. (1998), *Forgetful of their Sex: Female Sanctity and Society c. 500–1100* (Chicago: University of Chicago Press).

Scott-Fox, C. (2002), *Cyril Fox: Archaeologist Extraordinary* (Oxford: Oxbow).

Scull, C., Minter, F., and Plouviez, J. (2016), 'Social and economic complexity in early medieval England: a central place complex in the East Anglian kingdom at Rendlesham, Suffolk', *Antiquity*, 90, 1594–612.

Scully, G. (2014), *High Island (Ardoileán), Co. Galway: Excavation of an Early Medieval Monastery* (Dublin: Stationery Office).

Scurr, R. (2015), *John Aubrey: My Own Life* (London: Vintage).

Seaman, A. (2010a), *The Roman to Early Medieval Transition in South-East Wales: Settlement, Landscape and Religion* (unpublished PhD thesis, Cardiff University).

Seaman, A. (2010b), 'Towards a predictive model of early medieval settlement location: a case study from the Vale of Glamorgan', *Medieval Settlement Research*, 25, 11–20.

Seaman, A. (2012), 'The multiple estate model reconsidered: power and territory in early medieval Wales', *Welsh History Review*, 26(2), 163–85.

Seaman, A. (2013), 'Dinas Powys in context: settlement and society in post-Roman Wales', *Studia Celtica*, 47, 1–23.

Seaman, A. (2015), 'Julius and Aaron "Martyrs of Caerleon": in search of Wales' first Christians', *Archaeologia Cambrensis*, 164, 201–19.

Seaman, A. (2016), 'Defended settlement in early medieval Wales: problems of presence, absence and interpretation', in Christie and Herold (eds) (2016), 37–51.

Seaman, A. (2017), 'Further research on a predictive model of early medieval settlement location in south Wales: exploring the use of place-names and proxy data', *Medieval Settlement Research*, 32, 27–34.

Seaman, A: (2018), 'The church of Julius, Aaron, and Alban at Caerleon', *Monmouthshire Antiquary*, 34, 17–38.

Seaman, A. (2019a), 'Landscape, settlement and agriculture in early medieval Brycheiniog: the evidence of the Llandaff charters', in Comeau and Seaman (eds) (2019), 153–73.

Seaman, A. (2019b), 'Power, place and territory in early medieval south-east Wales', in J. Carroll et al. (eds) (2019b), 325–45.

Seaman, A. (2019c), 'Llywarch Hen's Dyke: place and narrative in early medieval Wales', *Offa's Dyke Journal*, 1, 96–113.

Seaman, A., and Lane, A. (2019), 'Excavation of the Ty'n-y-Coed earthworks 2011–14: the Dinas Powys "Southern Banks"', *Archaeologia Cambrensis*, 168, 109–35.

Seaman, A., and Sucharyna Thomas, L. (2020), 'Hillforts and power in the British post-Roman west: a GIS analysis of Dinas Powys', *European Journal of Archaeology*, 23(4), 547–66.

480 REFERENCES

Seaver, M. (2006), 'Through the mill: excavation of an early medieval settlement at Raystown, Co. Meath', in J. O'Sullivan and M. Stanley (eds), *Settlement, Industry and Ritual* (Dublin: National Roads Authority), 73–87.

Seaver, M. (2016), *Meitheal: The Archaeology of Lives, Labours and Beliefs at Raystown, Co. Meath* (Dublin: Transport Infrastructure Ireland).

Semple, S. (2013), *Perceptions of the Prehistoric in Anglo-Saxon England: Religion, Ritual, and Rulership in the Landscape* (Oxford: Oxford University Press).

Semple, S., and Sanmark, A. (2013), 'Assembly in North West Europe: collective concerns for early societies?', *European Journal of Archaeology*, 16(3), 518–42.

Severin, T. (1978), *The Brendan Voyage* (London: Hutchinson & Co.).

Sexton, R. (1998), 'Porridges, gruels and breads: the cereal foodstuffs of early medieval Ireland', in M. A. Monk and J. Sheehan (eds), *Early Medieval Munster: Archaeology, History and Society* (Cork: Cork University Press), 76–86.

Sharpe, R. (1984), 'Gildas as a father of the Church', in Lapidge and Dumville (eds) (1984), 193–205.

Sharpe, R. (trans.) (1991), *Adomán of Iona: Life of St Columba* (Harmondsworth: Penguin).

Sharpe, R. (2002), 'Martyrs and local saints in Late Antique Britain', in Thacker and Sharpe (eds) (2002), 75–154.

Sharpe, R., and Davies, J. R. (ed. and trans.) (2007), 'Rhygyfarch's *Life* of St David', in J. W. Evans and Wooding (eds) (2007), 107–55.

Sheehan, J. (2004), 'Social and economic integration in Viking-age Ireland: the evidence of the hoards', in J. Hines, A. Lane, and M. Redknap (eds), *Land, Sea and Home* (Leeds: Maney), 177–88.

Sheehan, J. (2009), 'The Huxley hoard and Hiberno-Scandinavian arm-rings', in Graham-Campbell and Philpott (eds) (2009), 58–69.

Sherratt, A. (1996), 'Why Wessex? The Avon route and river transport in later British prehistory', *Oxford Journal of Archaeology*, 15(2), 211–34.

Shiner, M. (2016), 'Recent archaeological discoveries in Carmarthenshire', *Carmarthenshire Antiquary*, 52, 5–23.

Shiner, M. (2021), 'Burial in early medieval Wales: identifying multifunctional cemeteries', *Oxford Journal of Archaeology*, 40(3), 268–85.

Shoesmith, R. (2008), 'Reports of sectional recorders: archaeology, 2008', *Transactions of the Woolhope Naturalists' Field Club*, 56, 114–31.

Sigl, M., Winstrup, M., McConnell, J. R., et al. (2015), 'Timing and climate forcing of volcanic eruptions for the past 2,500 years', *Nature*, 523, 543–9.

Silvester, R. J. (1992), *Montgomeryshire Historic Settlements Part 1* (Clwyd-Powys Archaeological Trust, report 40).

Silvester, R. J. (1997), 'Historic settlement surveys in Clwyd and Powys', in Edwards (ed.) (1997b), 113–22.

Silvester, R. J. (2006), 'Deserted rural settlements in central and north-east Wales', in Roberts (ed.) (2006a), 13–39.

Silvester, R. J. (2011), 'Recent research on late prehistoric and Romano-British enclosures in Montgomeryshire', *Montgomeryshire Collections*, 99, 1–26.

Silvester, R. J. (2019), 'Medieval field systems in north Wales', in Comeau and Seaman (eds) (2019), 93–111.

Silvester, R. J., and Evans, J. W. (2009), 'Identifying the mother churches of north-east Wales', in Edwards (ed.) (2009b), 21–40.

Silvester, R. J., and Hankinson, R. (2013), *Farms and Farming, Scheduling Enhancement Programme* (Clwyd-Powys Archaeological Trust, report 1199).

Sims-Williams, P. (1984), 'Gildas and vernacular poetry', in Lapidge and Dumville (eds) (1984), 169–92.

Sims-Williams, P. (1990a), *Religion and Literature in Western England 600–850* (Cambridge: Cambridge University Press).

Sims-Williams, P. (1990b), 'Dating the transition to Neo-Brittonic: philology and history', in A. Bammesberger and A. Wollmann (eds), *Britain 400–600: Language and History* (Heidelberg: Carl Winter Universitätsverlag), 217–61.

Sims-Williams, P. (1991), 'The emergence of Old Welsh, Cornish and Breton orthography, 600–800: the evidence of archaic Old Welsh', *Bulletin of the Board of Celtic Studies*, 38, 20–86.

Sims-Williams, P. (1993), 'The provenance of the Llywarch Hen poems: a case for Llan-gors, Brycheiniog', *Cambrian Medieval Celtic Studies*, 26 (Winter), 27–63.

Sims-Williams, P. (1998), 'The uses of writing in early medieval Wales', in H. Pryce (ed.), *Literacy in Medieval Celtic Societies* (Cambridge: Cambridge University Press), 15–38.

Sims-Williams, P. (2001), 'Clas Beuno and the Four Branches of the Mabinogi', in B. Maier and S. Zimmer (eds), *150 Jahre 'Mabinogion'—Deutsch-Walisische Kulturbeziehungen* (Tübingen: Max Niemeyer), 111–30.

Sims-Williams, P. (2002), 'The five languages of Wales in the Pre-Norman inscriptions', *Cambrian Medieval Celtic Studies*, 44 (Winter), 1–36.

Sims-Williams, P. (2003), *The Celtic Inscriptions of Britain: Phonology and Chronology, c. 400–1200* (Oxford and Boston: Philological Society Publication 37).

Sims-Williams, P. (2019a), *The Book of Llandaf as a Historical Source* (Woodbridge: Boydell).

Sims-Williams, P. (2019b), 'John Rhys and the Insular inscriptions', *Cambrian Medieval Celtic Studies*, 77 (Summer), 47–64.

Sims-Williams, P. (2020), 'An alternative to "Celtic from the East" and "Celtic from the West"', *Cambridge Archaeological Journal*, 30(3), 511–29.

Skinner, A. T., and Semple, S. (2016), 'Assembly mounds in the Danelaw: place-name and archaeological evidence in the historic landscape', *Journal of the North Atlantic*, 8, 115–33.

Smith, A., Allen, M., Brindle, T., and Fulford, M. (2016), *New Visions of the Countryside of Roman Britain, Vol. 1: The Rural Settlement of Roman Britain* (London: Society for the Promotion of Roman Studies, Britannia monograph 29).

Smith, A., Allen, M., Brindle, T., Fulford, M., Lodwick, L., and Rohnbogner, A. (2018), *New Visions of the Countryside of Roman Britain, Vol. 3: Life and Death in the Countryside of Roman Britain* (London: Society for the Promotion of Roman Studies, Britannia monograph 31).

Smith, C. (1985), 'Excavation at the Ty Mawr hut-circles, Holyhead, Anglesey Part II', *Archaeologia Cambrensis*, 134, 11–32.

Smith, C. (1987), 'Excavation at the Ty Mawr hut-circles, Holyhead, Anglesey Part IV', *Archaeologia Cambrensis*, 136, 20–38.

Smith, F. G. (1931–3), 'Talacre and the Viking grave', *Proceedings of the Llandudno, Colwyn Bay and District Field Club*, 27, 42–9.

Smith, G. H. (2005), *Prehistoric Defended Enclosures in North-West Wales, 2004–5: West Conwy, Gwynedd (Arfon) and Anglesey* (Gwynedd Archaeological Trust, report 580).

Smith, G. H. (2006), *Prehistoric Defended Enclosures in North-West Wales, 2005–6: Gwynedd, Dwyfor and Meirionydd* (Gwynedd Archaeological Trust, report 634).

Smith, G. H. (2012a), 'Re-assessment of two hillforts in north Wales: Pen-y-Dinas, Llandudno and Caer Seion, Conwy', *Archaeology in Wales*, 51, 63–78.

Smith, G. H. (2012b), 'A medieval defended enclosure at Llanfairpwllgwyngyll', *Transactions of the Anglesey Antiquarian Society*, 21–39.

Smith, G. H. (2013), 'Llanfechell: a prehistoric funerary and ritual landscape in north Anglesey', *Transactions of the Anglesey Antiquarian Society*, 51–88.

Smith, G. H. (2014), 'A Late Bronze Age/Early Iron Age hilltop enclosure with evidence of early and middle Neolithic and early medieval settlement at Carrog, Llanbadrig, Anglesey', *Studia Celtica*, 48, 55–92.

Smith, G. H., Caseldine, A., Hopewell, D., and Macphail, R. (2011), *The North West Wales Early Fields Project* (Gwynedd Archaeological Trust, report 933).

Smith, G. H., and Thompson, D. (2006), 'Results of the project excavations', in Roberts (ed.) (2006a), 113–32.

Smith, J. M. H. (1990), 'Oral and written: saints, miracles and relics in Brittany *c.* 800–1250', *Speculum*, 65(2), 309–43.

Smith, K. P., and Reynolds, A. (2013), 'Introduction: the archaeology of legal culture', *World Archaeology*, 45(5), 687–98.

Smyth, A. P. (1999), 'The effect of Scandinavian raiders on the English and Irish churches: a preliminary reassessment', in B. Smith (ed.), *Britain and Ireland 900–1300: Insular Responses to European Change* (Cambridge: Cambridge University Press), 1–39.

Soilscapes (Cranfield Soil and Agrifood Institute, Cranfield University), http://www.landis. org.uk/soilscapes/ [accessed 17 April 2018].

Soulsby, I. (1983), *The Towns of Medieval Wales* (Chichester: Phillimore).

Southern, P., and Dixon, K. R. (1996), *The Late Roman Army* (London: B. T. Batsford).

Speed, Gary (2014), *Towns in the Dark? Urban Transformations from Late Roman Britain to Anglo-Saxon England* (Oxford: Archaeopress).

Speed, Greg, and Walton Rogers, P. (2004), 'A burial of a Viking woman at Adwick-le-Street, South Yorkshire', *Medieval Archaeology*, 48, 51–90.

Speed, J. (1610), *Caernarvon both Shyre and Shire-Towne with the Ancient Citie Bangor*, National Library of Wales Map 5128, https://www.library.wales/discover/digital-gallery/ maps/county-maps/speeds-county-maps-of-wales/ [accessed 9 July 2018].

Stafford, P. (2008), '"The Annals of Æthelflæd": annals, history and politics in early tenth-century England', in J. Barrow and A. Wareham (eds), *Myth, Rulership, Church and Charters: Essays in honour of Nicholas Brooks* (Aldershot: Ashgate), 101–16.

Stallybrass, B. (1914), 'Recent discoveries at Clynnog Fawr', *Archaeologia Cambrensis*, ser. 6, 14, 271–96.

Stancliffe, C. (1995), 'Where was Oswald killed?', in C. Stancliffe and E. Cambridge (eds), *Oswald: From Northumbrian King to European Saint* (Stamford: P. Watkins), 84–96.

Stancliffe, C. (2004), 'Faustus [Faustus of Riez] (400 × 10–c. 490), bishop of Riez and theologian', *Oxford Dictionary of National Biography*, https://doi-org.ezproxy.bangor.ac. uk/10.1093/ref:odnb/51403 [accessed 17 November 2021].

REFERENCES   483

Stephens, G. R. (1985), 'Caerleon and the martyrdoms of SS. Aaron and Julius', *Bulletin of the Board of Celtic Studies*, 32, 326–35.

Stephens, W. (2011), 'The bright cup: early medieval vessel glass', in M. Clegg Hyer and G. Owen-Crocker (eds), *The Material Culture of Daily Living in the Anglo-Saxon World* (Exeter: University of Exeter Press), 275–92.

Stephenson, D. (2016), *Medieval Powys: Kingdom, Principality and Lordships, 1132–1293* (Woodbridge: Boydell).

Stevens, P. (2014), 'Clonfad, Co. Westmeath: an early Irish production centre', in C. Corlett and M. Potterton (eds), *The Church in Early Medieval Ireland in the Light of Recent Archaeological Excavations* (Dublin: Wordwell), 259–72.

Stevens, P. (2017), 'Early medieval jet-like jewellery in Ireland: production, distribution and consumption', *Medieval Archaeology*, 61(2), 239–75.

Stevenson, W. H. (ed.) (1959), *Asser's Life of King Alfred*, 2nd ed. (Oxford: Clarendon Press).

Stokes, K. L. (2004), *Welsh Kingship, A.D. 383–1063: A Reassessment of Terminology and Political Formation* (unpublished PhD thesis, University of Cambridge).

Stokes, W. (ed.) (1905), *The Martyrology of Oengus the Culdee* (London: Henry Bradshaw Society 29).

Stumpe, L. H. (2014), *To what extent can we reconstruct an Early Medieval Pilgrimage Landscape relating to St Cybi on Ynys Gybi, Ynys Môn?* (unpublished MA dissertation, Bangor University).

Sumner, G. N. (1977), 'Climate and vegetation', in D. Thomas (ed.), *Wales: A New Study* (Newton Abbot and London: David & Charles), 36–69, 320–1.

Sumner, G. N. (1997), 'Wales', in D. Wheeler and J. Mayes (eds), *Regional Climates of the British Isles* (London and New York: Routledge), 131–57.

Survey of English Place-Names, https://epns.nottingham.ac.uk/ [accessed 11 December 2020].

Swift, C. (1997), *Ogham Stones and the Earliest Irish Christians* (Maynooth: St Patrick's College).

Swift, E. (2012), 'The analysis of reused material culture for Late Antique studies', *Late Antique Archaeology*, 9, 91–119.

Swift, E. (2020), 'Reuse of Roman artefacts in Late Antiquity and the early medieval west: a case-study from Britain of bracelets and belt fittings', in Duckworth and Wilson (eds) (2020), 425–46.

Sykes, N. (2004), 'The dynamics of status symbols: wildfowl exploitation in England AD 410–1550', *Archaeological Journal*, 161, 82–105.

Sykes, N. (2010), 'Deer, land, knives and halls: social change in early medieval England', *Antiquaries Journal*, 90, 175–93.

Symonds, L., Price, T. D., Keenleyside, A., and Burton, J. (2014), 'Medieval migrations: isotope analysis of early medieval skeletons on the Isle of Man', *Medieval Archaeology*, 58, 1–20.

Symonds, M. (2015), 'Fourth-century fortlets in Britain: sophisticated systems or desperate measures?', in R. Collins, M. Symonds, and M. Weber (eds), *Roman Military Architecture on the Frontiers: Armies and their Architecture in Late Antiquity* (Oxford: Oxbow), 46–61.

Tarlow, S. (2012), 'The archaeology of emotion and affect', *Annual Review of Anthropology*, 41, 169–85.

Taylor, H. M., and Taylor, J. (1965), *Anglo-Saxon Architecture*, 2 vols (Cambridge: Cambridge University Press).

484 REFERENCES

Taylor, J. (2007), *An Atlas of Roman Rural Settlement in England* (York: Council for British Archaeology).

Taylor, T. (trans.) (1991), *The Life of St Samson of Dol* (Felinfach: Llanerch, repr.).

Tedeschi, C. (2001), 'Some observations on the palaeography of early Christian inscriptions in Britain', in J. Higgitt, K. Forsyth, and D. N. Parsons (eds), *Roman, Runes and Ogham: Medieval Inscriptions in the Insular World and on the Continent* (Donington: Shaun Tyas), 16–25.

Tedeschi, C. (2005), *Congeries Lapidum: Iscrizioni Britanniche dei Secoli V–VII*, 2 vols (Pisa: Scuola Normale Superior di Pisa).

Terrett, I. B. (1962), 'Cheshire', in H. C. Darby and I. S. Maxwell (eds), *The Domesday Geography of Northern England* (Cambridge: Cambridge University Press), 330–91.

Thacker, A. (1987), 'Anglo-Saxon Cheshire', in B. E. Harris (ed.), *Victoria County History: A History of the County of Cheshire, Vol. 2* (Oxford: Oxford University Press), 237–92.

Thacker, A. (2002), '*Loca sanctorum*: the significance of place in the study of the saints', in Thacker and Sharpe (eds) (2002), 1–43.

Thacker, A. (2016), 'Shaping the saint: rewriting tradition in the early *Lives* of St Cuthbert', in Flechner and Ní Mhaonaigh (eds) (2016), 399–429.

Thacker, A., and Sharpe, R. (eds) (2002), *Local Saints and Local Churches in the Early Medieval West* (Oxford: Oxford University Press).

The List of Historic Place Names of Wales (*Rhestr o Enwau Lleoedd Hanesyddol Cymru*), https://historicplacenames.rcahmw.gov.uk/ [accessed 14 July 2022].

Thomas, B. (2010), 'Priests and bishops in Bede's ecclesiology: the use of *sacerdos* in the *Historia Eccleisastica Gentis Anglorum*', *Ecclesiology*, 6, 68–93.

Thomas, B. B. (1978), 'The Cambrians and the nineteenth-century crisis in Welsh studies, 1847–1870', *Archaeologia Cambrensis*, 127, 1–15.

Thomas, C. (1959), 'Imported pottery in Dark-Age western Britain', *Medieval Archaeology*, 3, 89–111.

Thomas, C. (1967), 'The early Christian cemetery and chapel on Ardwall Isle, Kirkcudbright', *Medieval Archaeology*, 11, 127–88.

Thomas, C. (1971), *The Early Christian Archaeology of North Britain* (Oxford: Oxford University Press).

Thomas, C. (1981), *Christianity in Roman Britain to AD 500* (London, B. T. Batsford).

Thomas, C. (1993), *English Heritage Book of Tintagel, Arthur and Archaeology* (London: B. T. Batsford and English Heritage).

Thomas, C. (1994), *And Shall These Mute Stones Speak? Post-Roman Inscriptions in Western Britain* (Cardiff: University of Wales Press).

Thomas, C. (2007), 'Stone: the inscribed slate from the Site C building', in R. C. Barrowman, C. E. Batey, and C. D. Morris (eds) (2007), *Excavations at Tintagel Castle, Cornwall, 1990–1999* (London: Society of Antiquaries of London), 192–200.

Thomas, D. R. (1906–13), *The History of the Diocese of St Asaph*, 3 vols (Oswestry: Caxton Press).

Thomas, G. (2012), 'The prehistory of medieval farms and villages: from Saxons to Scandinavians', in N. Christie and P. Stamper (eds), *Medieval Rural Settlement: Britain and Ireland, AD 800–1600* (Oxford: Windgather), 43–62.

Thomas, G. (2016), 'Downland, marsh, and weald: monastic foundation and rural intensification in Anglo-Saxon Kent', in Flechner and Ní Mhaonaigh (eds) (2016), 349–76.

REFERENCES   485

Thomas, G., McDonnell, G., Merkel, J., and Marshall, P. (2016), 'Technology, ritual and Anglo-Saxon agriculture: the biography of a plough-coulter from Lyminge, Kent', *Antiquity*, 90, 742–58.

Thomas, R. (2022a), *History and Identity in Early Medieval Wales* (Cambridge: D. S. Brewer).

Thomas, R. (2022b), 'The context of the Hywel Dda penny', in M. Allen, R. Naismith, and H. Pagan (eds), *Interpreting Early Medieval Coinage: Studies in Memory of Stewart Lyon* (London: Spink), 87–98.

Thompson, E. A. (1984), *Saint Germanus of Auxerre and the End of Roman Britain* (Woodbridge: Boydell).

Thornton, D. E. (2004a), 'Hywel Dda [Hywel Dda ap Cadell]', *Oxford Dictionary of National Biography*, https://doi-org.ezproxy.bangor.ac.uk/10.1093/ref:odnb/13968 [accessed 7 August 2020].

Thornton, D. E. (2004b), 'Merfyn Frych', *Oxford Dictionary of National Biography*, https://doi-org.ezproxy.bangor.ac.uk/10.1093/ref:odnb/18587 [accessed 30 December 2020].

Thorpe, L. (trans.) (1978), *Gerald of Wales: The Journey through Wales/The Description of Wales* (Harmondsworth: Penguin).

Tipper, J. (2004), *The* Grubenhaus *in Anglo-Saxon England* (Yedingham: Landscape Research Centre).

Tomlin, R. S. O. (2001), 'A Roman will from north Wales', *Archaeologia Cambrensis*, 150, 143–56.

Tomlin, R. S. O., Wright, R. P., and Hassall, M. W. C. (2009), *The Roman Inscriptions of Britain, III Inscriptions on Stone* (Oxford and Oakville: Oxbow).

Toulmin Smith, L. (ed.) (1906), *The Itinerary in Wales of John Leland in or about the Years 1536–1539* (London: G. Bell & Sons).

Turner, S. (2006), *Making a Christian Landscape: The Countryside in Early Medieval Cornwall, Devon and Essex* (Exeter: Exeter University Press).

Turner, V., and Turner, E. L. B. (1978), *Image and Pilgrimage in Christian Culture*, 2nd ed. (New York: Columbia University Press).

Tyers, P. (1996), *Roman Pottery in Britain* (London and New York: Routledge).

V&A, 'Signet ring', http://collections.vam.ac.uk/item/O122079/signet-ring-unknown/ [accessed 28 September 2020].

Vale of Glamorgan Council, 'Archaeological Work on land at Five Mile Lane', https://www.valeofglamorgan.gov.uk/en/living/Roads/Five-Mile-Lane/Archaeological-Work-on-Land-at-Five-Mile-Lane.aspx [accessed 16 August 2022].

Van der Veen, M. (2016), 'Arable farming, horticulture, and food: expansion, innovation, and diversity', in Millett et al. (eds) (2016), 807–33.

Vincent, H. J. (1864), 'Caerau in the parish of St Dogmells', *Archaeologia Cambrensis*, ser. 3, 10, 299–314.

Vyner, B. E. (2001), 'Clegyr Boia: a potential Neolithic enclosure and associated monuments on the St David's peninsula', in T. Darvill and J. Thomas (eds), *Neolithic Enclosures in Atlantic Northwest Europe* (Oxford: Oxbow), 578–90.

Vyner, B. E., and Allen, D. W. H. (1988), 'A Romano-British settlement at Caldicot, Gwent', in Robinson (ed.) (1988), 65–122.

Waddington, K. (2013), *The Settlements of Northwest Wales: From the Late Bronze Age to the Early Medieval Period* (Cardiff: University of Wales Press).

Wade-Evans, A. W. (1906), 'The Brychan documents', *Y Cymmrodor*, 19, 18–50.

Wade-Evans, A. W. (ed. and trans.) (1944), *Vitae Sanctorum Britanniae et Genealogiae* (Cardiff: University of Wales Press).

Wainwright, F. T. (1948), 'Ingimund's invasion', *English Historical Review*, 63, 145–69.

Wainwright, F. T. (1950), '*Cledemutha*', *English Historical Review*, 65, 203–12.

Wainwright, F. T. (ed.) (1955), *The Problem of the Picts* (Edinburgh: Nelson).

Wainwright, G. J. (1967), *Coygan Camp* (Cardiff: Cambrian Archaeological Association).

Walker, D. (2006), 'Caradog ap Gruffudd ap Rhydderch', *Oxford Dictionary of National Biography*, https://doi-org.ezproxy.bangor.ac.uk/10.1093/ref:odnb/48539 [accessed 27 October 2020].

Walker, E. A. (2016), 'The Palaeolithic and Mesolithic hunter-gatherers of Pembrokeshire', in James et al. (eds) (2016), 1–54.

Wallace, P. F. (2016), *Viking Dublin: The Woodquay Excavations* (Sallins: Irish Academic Press).

Wallis, F. (2010), 'Bede and science', in S. DeGregorio (ed.), *The Cambridge Companion to Bede* (Cambridge: Cambridge University Press), 113–26.

Walton, P., and Moorhead, S. (2016), 'Coinage and collapse? The contribution of numismatic data to understanding the end of Roman Britain', *Internet Archaeology*, 45.

Walton Rogers, P. (1997), *Textile Production at 16–22 Coppergate*, The Archaeology of York Vol. 17 (York: Council for British Archaeology).

Walton Rogers, P. (2007), *Cloth and Clothing in Early Anglo-Saxon England AD 450–700* (York: Council for British Archaeology).

Ward, A. H. (1978), 'The excavation of a Bronze Age composite mound on Pentre Farm, Pontardulais, West Glamorgan', *Archaeologia Cambrensis*, 127, 40–74.

Ward, A. H. (1997), 'Transhumance and settlement on the Welsh uplands: a view from the Black Mountain', in Edwards (ed.) (1997b), 97–111.

Ward, J. (1907), 'Roman remains at Cwmbrwyn, Carmarthenshire', *Archaeologia Cambrensis*, ser. 6, 7, 175–212.

Ward, M. (1994), 'Llangian, Llangian Church', *Archaeology in Wales*, 34, 60.

Ward, M., and Smith, G. (2001), 'The Llŷn crop marks project: aerial survey and ground evaluation of Bronze Age, Iron Age and Romano-British settlement and funerary sites in the Llŷn Peninsula of north-west Wales', *Studia Celtica*, 35, 1–87.

Ward, S. W. (1994), *Excavations at Chester, Saxon Occupation within the Fortress: Sites excavated 1971–81* (Chester: Chester City Council).

Ward-Perkins, B. (2005), *The Fall of Rome and the End of Civilization* (Oxford: Oxford University Press).

Warrilow, W., Owen, G., and Britnell, W. J. (1986), 'Eight ring-ditches at Four Crosses, Llandysilio, Powys, 1981–85', *Proceedings of the Prehistoric Society*, 52 (S2), 53–88.

Watts, D. (1991), *Christians and Pagans in Roman Britain* (London amd New York: Routledge).

Watts, J. (2017), 'Watermills and waterwheels', in M. Clegg Hyer and D. Hooke (eds), *Water and the Environment in the Anglo-Saxon World* (Liverpool: Liverpool University Press).

Webley, R. (2014), 'Strap-end mounts', *Medieval Archaeology*, 58, 353–4.

Webster, C. J., and Brunning, R. A. (2004), 'A seventh-century AD cemetery at Stoneage Barton Farm, Bishop's Lydeard, Somerset and square-ditched burials in post-Roman Britain', *Archaeological Journal*, 161, 54–81.

Webster, L., and Backhouse, J. (eds) (1991), *The Making of England: Anglo-Saxon Art and Culture AD 600–900* (London: British Museum).

Webster, P. (1984), 'The Roman period', in Savory (ed.) (1984), 277–314.

Webster, P. (2002), 'The late Roman fort at Cardiff', in M. Aldhouse-Green and P. Webster (eds), *Artefacts and Archaeology: Aspects of the Celtic and Roman World* (Cardiff: University of Wales Press), 62–75.

Webster, P. (2011), 'Roman pottery in the north west', in T. Saunders (ed.), *Roman North West England: Hinterland or 'Indian County'?* (Council for British Archaeology North West, new ser. 2), 58–73.

Weekes, J. (2016), 'Cemeteries and funerary practice', in Millett et al. (eds) (2016), 425–47.

Weigel, B. (2015), *Burbo Bank Extension Offshore Wind Farm, Denbighshire* (Oxford Archaeology North, report 2014–15/1598).

Weiss, R. (1969), *The Renaissance Discovery of Classical Antiquity* (Oxford: Blackwell).

Wells, E. J. (2018), 'Overview: the medieval senses', in C. M. Gerrard and A. Gutiérrez (eds), *The Oxford Handbook of Later Medieval Archaeology* (Oxford: Oxford University Press), 681–96.

Welsh Archaeological Trusts (2016), *Archaeology in Trust: 40 Years of the Welsh Archaeological Trusts* (Llandeilo: Dyfed Archaeological Trust).

West, J. J., and Palmer, N. (2014), *Haughmond Abbey: Excavation of a 12th-century Cloister in its Historical and Landscape Context* (Swindon: English Heritage).

Westwood, J. O. (1846), 'Ogham characters in Glamorganshire', *Archaeologia Cambrensis*, ser. 1, 1, 182–3.

Westwood, J. O. (1876–9), *Lapidarium Walliae: The Early Inscribed and Sculptured Stones of Wales* (Oxford: Oxford University Press).

Wheeler, R. E. M. (1923), *Segontium and the Roman Occupation of Wales*, *Y Cymmrodor*, 33.

Wheeler, R. E. M. (1925), *Prehistoric and Roman Wales* (Oxford: Clarendon Press).

Wheeler, R. E. M. (1926), *The Roman Fort near Brecon*, *Y Cymmrodor*, 37.

Wheeler, R. E. M., and Wheeler, T. (1932), *Report on the Excavation of the Prehistoric, Roman, and Post-Roman Site in Lydney Park, Gloucestershire* (London: Society of Antiquaries of London).

White, P. (2003), *The Arrow Valley, Herefordshire: Archaeology, Landscape Change and Conservation* (Hereford: Herefordshire Archaeology).

White, R. B. (1971–2), 'Excavations at Arfryn, Bodedern, long-cist cemeteries and the origins of Christianity', *Transactions of the Anglesey Antiquarian Society*, 10–45.

White, R. B., and Longley, D. (1995), 'Excavations at Aberffraw', *Transactions of the Anglesey Antiquarian Society*, 13–21.

White, R. H. (1990), 'Scrap or substitute: Roman material in Anglo-Saxon graves', in E. Southworth (ed.), *Anglo-Saxon Cemeteries: A Reappraisal* (Stroud: Alan Sutton), 125–52.

White, R. H. (2007), *Britannia Prima: Britain's Last Roman Province* (Stroud: Tempus).

White, R. H. (2020), 'A 5th-century hacksilver hoard from Wem, Shropshire', *Medieval Archaeology*, 64(2), 365–9.

White, R. H. (in press), 'Shropshire in an age of transition', in *Medieval Art, Architecture, and Archaeology in Shrewsbury and Mid-Shropshire: Papers from a Conference of the British Archaeological Association 2019* (London: Routledge).

488 REFERENCES

White, R. H., and Barker, P. (1998), *Wroxeter: Life and Death of a Roman City* (Stroud: Tempus).

White, S. I., and Smith, G. (1999), 'A funerary and ceremonial centre at Capel Eithin, Gaerwen, Anglesey', *Transactions of the Anglesey Antiquarian Society*, 9–166.

White, T. H. (1958), *The Once and Future King* (London: Collins).

Whitelock, D. (ed. and trans.) (1979), *The Anglo-Saxon Chronicle (60 B.C.–A.D. 1042), Vol. I, c.500–1042* (London: Routledge), http://www.englishhistoricaldocuments.com/document/view.html?id=5 [accessed 15 September 2020].

White Marshall, J., and Walsh, C. (2005), *Illaunloughan Island: An Early Medieval Monastery in County Kerry* (Bray: Wordwell).

Whitfield, N. (2007), 'A suggested function for the holy well?', in A. Minnis and J. Roberts (eds), *Text, Image, Interpretation: Studies in Anglo-Saxon Literature and its Insular Context in honour of Éamonn Ó Carragáin* (Turnhout: Brepols), 495–514.

Wickham, C. (2005), *Framing the Early Middle Ages: Europe and the Mediterranean, 400–800* (Oxford: Oxford University Press).

Wickham, C. (2010), 'Medieval Wales and European history', *Welsh History Review*, 25(2), 201–8.

Wigley, A. (2007), 'Rooted to the spot: the "smaller enclosures" of the later first millennium BC in the central Welsh Marches', in C. Haselgrove and T. Moore (eds), *The Later Iron Age in Britain and Beyond* (Oxford: Oxbow), 173–89.

Wilkinson, P. T. (1995), 'Excavations at Hen Gastell, Briton Ferry, West Glamorgan 1991–92', *Medieval Archaeology*, 39, 1–50.

Williams, A. (2009), 'Offa's Dyke: a monument without history?', in N. Fryde and D. Reitz (eds), *Walls, Ramparts and Lines of Demarcation: Selected Studies from Antiquity to Modern Times* (Münster: LIT Verlag), 31–56.

Williams, A., and Martin, G. H. (eds and trans.) (2002), *Domesday Book* (London: Penguin).

Williams, D., and Marvell, A. G. (1995), 'A470 Cwmbach – Newbridge-on-Wye', *Archaeology in Wales*, 35, 59.

Williams, Gareth (2005), 'Military obligations and Mercian supremacy in the eighth century', in D. Hill and M. Worthington (eds), *Æthelbald and Offa: Two Eighth-Century Kings in Mercia* (Oxford: British Archaeological Reports, Brit. ser. 383), 103–9.

Williams, Gareth (2010), 'Anglo-Saxon gold coinage, Part 1: the transition from Roman to Anglo-Saxon coinage', *British Numismatic Journal*, 80, 51–75.

Williams, George, and Mytum, H. (1998), *Llawhaden, Dyfed: Excavations on a Group of Small Defended Enclosures, 1980–4*, ed. K. Blockley (Oxford: British Archaeological Reports, Brit. ser. 275).

Williams, Glanmor (1967), *Welsh Reformation Essays* (Cardiff: University of Wales Press).

Williams, Glanmor (1979), *Religion, Language and Nationality in Wales* (Cardiff: University of Wales Press).

Williams, Howard (1998), 'Monuments and the past in early Anglo-Saxon England', *World Archaeology*, 30(1), 90–108.

Williams, Howard (2004), 'Assembling the dead', in Pantos and Semple (eds) (2004), 109–34.

Williams, Howard (2006), *Death and Memory in Early Medieval Britain* (Cambridge: Cambridge University Press).

Williams, Howard (2007), 'The emotive force of early medieval mortuary practice', *Archaeological Review from Cambridge*, 22(1), 107–20.

REFERENCES **489**

Williams, Howard, and Delaney, L. (2019), 'The Offa's Dyke Collaboratory and the Offa's Dyke Journal', *Offa's Dyke Journal*, 1, 1–31.

Williams, Hugh (ed.), (1899–1901), *Gildas*, 2 vols. (London: Honourable Society of Cymmrodorion).

Williams, I. (1927), 'The Computus fragment', *Bulletin of the Board of Celtic Studies*, 3(4), 245–72.

Williams, I. (ed.) (1951), *Pedeir Keinc y Mabinogi*, 2nd ed. (Cardiff: University of Wales Press).

Williams, I. (ed.) (1972), *Armes Prydein: The Prophecy of Britain from the Book of Taliesin*, trans. R. Bromwich (Dublin: Dublin Institute of Advanced Studies).

Williams, I. (1980), *The Beginnings of Welsh Poetry*, ed. R. Bromwich (Cardiff: University of Wales Press).

Williams, R. A., and Le Carlier de Veslud, C. (2019), 'Boom and bust in Bronze Age Britain: major copper production from the Great Orme mine and European trade *c*. 1600–1400 BC', *Antiquity*, 93, 1178–96.

Williams, W. W., and Prichard, H. (1866), 'Excavations at Caerleb', *Archaeologia Cambrensis*, ser. 3, 12, 209–14.

Williamson, T. (2013), *Environment, Society and Landscape in Early Medieval England: Time and Topography* (Woodbridge: Boydell).

Wilson, D. M. (2008), *The Vikings in the Isle of Man* (Aarhus: Aarhus University Press).

Wilson, D. M. (2018), *Manx Crosses* (Oxford: Archaeopress and Manx Heritage).

Wincott Heckett, E. (2010), 'Textiles that work for their living: a late eleventh-century cloth from Cork', in J. Sheehan and D. Ó Corráin (eds), *The Viking Age in Ireland and the West* (Dublin: Four Courts), 555–64.

Winterbottom, M. (ed. and trans.) (1978), *Gildas: The Ruin of Britain and other Works* (London and Chichester: Phillimore).

Withers, C. W. J. (2007), 'Pennant, Thomas (1726–1798)', *Oxford Dictionary of National Biography*, https://doi-org.ezproxy.bangor.ac.uk/10.1093/ref:odnb/21860 [accessed 5 January 2021].

Wmffre, I. (2004), *The Place-Names of Cardiganshire*, 3 vols (Oxford: Archaeopress, British Archaeological Reports, Brit. ser. 379).

Wmffre, I. (2007), 'Post-Roman Irish settlement in Wales: new insights from a recent study of Cardiganshire place-names', in Janculak and Wooding (eds) (2007), 46–61.

Wood, I. (1984), 'The end of Roman Britain: Continental evidence and parallels', in Lapidge and Dumville (eds) (1984), 1–25.

Wood, J. G. (1912), *Saint Tathan, the Patron Saint of Caerwent, written on the Occasion of the Translation of his Supposed Remains* (Newport: Mullock & Sons).

Woods, D. (2010), 'Gildas and the mystery cloud of 536–7', *Journal of Theological Studies*, new ser., 61(1), 226–34.

Woods, H. (1987), 'Excavations at Wenlock Priory, 1981–6', *Journal of the British Archaeological Association*, 140, 36–75.

Woodward, A. (1993), 'Discussion', in D. E. Farwell and T. I. Molleson, *Excavations at Poundbury 1966–80, Vol. II: The Cemeteries* (Dorchester: Dorset Natural History and Archaeological Society), 215–49.

Woodward, A., and Leach, P. (1993), *The Uley Shrines* (London: English Heritage and British Museum).

Wormald, P. (1982), 'Viking studies: whence and whither?', in R. T. Farrell (ed.), *The Vikings* (Chichester: Phillimore), 128–53.

Worthington Hill, M. (2019), 'Wat's Dyke: an archaeological and historical enigma', *Offa's Dyke Journal*, 1, 58–79.

Wright, D. H. (2019), 'Crafters of kingship: smiths, elite power, and gender in early medieval Europe', *Medieval Archaeology*, 63(2), 271–97.

Wyatt, D. (2009), *Slaves and Warriors in Early Medieval Britain and Ireland 800–1200* (Leiden: Brill).

Yates, W. N. (1973), 'The distribution and proportion of Celtic and non-Celtic church dedications in Wales', *Journal of the Historical Society of the Church in Wales*, 23, 5–17.

Young, G. (2010), 'A 9th-century industrial area at Bamburgh Castle', *Medieval Archaeology*, 55, 311–17.

Young, T. P. (2010), 'Archaeometallurgical residues', in Crane and Murphy (2010b), 158–63.

Young, T. P. (2015a), *Assessment of Archaeometallurgical Residues from Cefn Graianog G1598 (2014)*, rev. 2015 (GeoArch, report 2015/19), http://www.geoarch.co.uk/reports/2015–19%20Residues%20from%20Cefn%20Graianog%202014%20revised.pdf [accessed 6 March 2020].

Young, T. P. (2015b), *Archaeological Watching Brief: Gelligaer Cemetery Extension (Phase 1), Gelligaer, Caerphilly* (GeoArch, report 2014/22), http://www.geoarch.co.uk/reports/2014–22%20Watching%20Brief%20Gelligaer.pdf [accessed 6 March 2020].

Youngs, S. (1983), 'The gaming-pieces' in R. L. S. Bruce-Mitford, *The Sutton Hoo Ship Burial, Vol. 3(2)* (London: British Museum), 853–74.

Youngs, S. (ed.) (1989), *'The Work of Angels' Masterpieces of Celtic Metalwork, 6th–9th Centuries AD* (London: British Museum).

Youngs, S. (2007), 'Britain, Wales and Ireland: holding things together', in Jankulak and Wooding (eds) (2007), 80–101.

INDEX

For the benefit of digital users, indexed terms that span two pages (e.g., 52–53) may, on occasion, appear on only one of those pages.

Aberdaron, inscribed stones 54–5, 118–20, 299–301
Aberffraw, early medieval settlement 152
Abergavenny, Roman settlement 76–8
Abergele 23–4, 349
Abermagwr, Roman villa 77, 83–4
Abraham, bishop of St Davids 28, 30, 321, 407
administrative complexity 377–9, 385–7, 392–3, 423
Ælfflæd, queen of Wessex 239–41
Ælfgar 375
aerial photography 16–17, 138–9, 282–3, 389
Æthelbald, king of Mercia 392–3
Æthelflæd, 'Lady of the Mercians' 91–2, 137, 157–9, 256–7, 396–7, 403–4
Æthelfrith, king of Bernicia 376–7
Æthelstan, king of England 27–9, 157, 262–3, 386, 422
Æthelthryth, St, of Ely, cult of 351
Afon Wen, hearth 161–3
'Age of the Saints' 12–13
Aidan of Ferns, St (Máedóc) 342–3, 362–3
Alcock, Leslie 13–14
alcoholic drinks 192–5, 214–15, 218, 248, 254–6, 264, 422–3
Alfred, king 43–4, 386, 397–8, 406–7, 422
    see also Asser, Life of King Alfred
Allen, J. Romilly 6–7
almsgiving 183, 266–7
amber 235–6, 243–4, 256–7, 333–5, 362–3, 368–9, 408–9
Ammianus Marcellinus 66–7
amulets 368–9
Aneirin 24–5
Anglesey (Môn), Hiberno-Scandinavian impact on 400–3, 410–11
Anglo-Saxon Chronicles 29, 137, 422
Annales Cambriae, see Harleian Chronicle
Annals of Ulster 28–9, 111
antiquarians 3–7
antler working 175, 225–6, 238

Antonine Wall 391
Arch Gwenfrewi, see Gwenfrewi
Archenfield, see Ergyng
Arddleen, enclosed settlement 94–5, 170
Ardwall Isle, hermitage 328–9
Arfryn, cemetery 14–15, 115–16, 279–81, 306, 331
    see also Bodedern inscribed stone
arm-rings 258–9, 263–4
    Hiberno-Scandinavian broad-band 154, 233–4, 402–4, 408
Armes Prydein Vawr ('The Great Prophecy of Britain') 27–8, 321, 405
ascetic lifestyle 314, 326, 362–4, 369, 420–1
Ashby, Thomas 10
assembly sites 150–1, 263–4, 377–87, 415, 423, 426–7
Asser of St Davids 43–4, 110, 286–7, 314, 321
    Life of King Alfred 3–4, 29, 157, 239–41, 342, 375, 387–9, 391–2, 396–7, 406–7
Atcham, 'great hall complex' 174
Atiscros hundred (Englefield) 212, 382, 394–5
Atlantic seaways 35–7, 120, 215–16, 254–6, 263–4, 266–7, 273–6, 297–301, 310–11, 315–16, 355–6, 364, 398–9, 409–10, 413–14, 418–19
Atlantic Trading Estate, cemetery 217, 280–1, 303–4
Aubrey, John 3–4

Bacon Hole, cave 235–6
Baglan, crozier 285–6, 359–60
bakestones 214
Balline, Roman silver hoard 98–9
Ballinrees, Roman silver hoard 98–9
Banc Tynddol, Cwmystwyth 231
Bangor, major ecclesiastical site and bishopric 271–2, 314, 318–19, 323–5, 331, 423–6
    silver hoard 258–9, 263–4, 325, 402–3

492 INDEX

Bangor-is-y-Coed, monastery 323–4, 340–1, 346–7, 376–7
Bantham, Devon 251–2, 263
baptism 58–60
'Barbarian Conspiracy' 97–8
Bardsey Island (Ynys Enlli) 5–6, 314, 326–7, 329, 352, 363, 400–1
  cemetery 217
  sculpture 237
Barland's Farm, 'Romano-Celtic' boat 37
barter economy 265, 424–5
Basingwerk 391–2
Bassaleg, ecclesiastical site 287–8
Bath Abbey 210–12
Bayvil, corn-dryer 196, 198–200
  market 263–4
  polyfocal landscape of assembly 384–5
beads, early medieval 368–9, 409
  amber 148, 408
  bone 362–3
  glass 78, 94–6, 165, 234–6, 238, 244–5, 355, 371–3
    imported 251–2
  Roman 113, 234–5
  shale 236
Beddau Gwŷr Ardudwy ('Graves of the Men of Ardudwy'), see Ffestiniog inscribed stone
Beddgelert 314
Bede
  De Temporum Ratione 57–8
  Historia Ecclesiastica 29, 38, 55–6, 346–7, 376–7
bees 189
  honey 214–15, 396–7
  wax 361
beliefs, pre-Christian 75, 284, 290–4, 301–3, 308–11, 330, 350, 363, 367–8, 373, 418
  see also Christianity
bells 58
  see also relics
belt fittings, late Roman 67–8, 72–4, 78, 81–2, 98–9, 103–4, 291–2, 295–6
Benllech, Viking burial, see Traeth Coch
Bernard, bishop of St Davids 352
Beuno, St 272–3, 284, 350–1, 355–6
Biglis, settlement 224–5
  burial in corn-dryer 112–13, 308
bioarchaeology 19
  see also isotope analysis, osteoarchaeology

birds 209–10
  see also hawks
bishop houses of Dyfed 287, 314, 342–3
Board of Celtic Studies (University of Wales) 7–9, 17–18
boars, see pigs
boats 37–8, 41, 223, 425–6
Bodedern, inscribed stone 115–16, 125–6
Bon y Dom, Hiberno-Scandinavian stronghold in Gwynedd 401–3
bone-working, see antler-working
Bordeaux, see France
Borras Quarry 236
  iron furnaces 228–30
Borre style 403
Bowen, E. G. 12–15
bracelets
  Roman 85–6, 98, 103–4, 112–13, 292, 308–10
  see also shale artefacts
Brawdy, inscribed stones 307
bread 192–5, 201–2, 214–15
Brecenanmere, see Llangorse crannog
Brecon Gaer, Roman fort 10, 44, 72, 97
Breiddin, hillfort 38–40, 94–5
  see also New Pieces
Brian Boru, king of Ireland 414
Bridell, ogham stone 117–19, 124–6, 301–2
Brigid, St (Ffraid) 288–9, 351, 363, 405–6
briquetage 10–12, 165
Bristol 256–7, 267–8, 376, 408, 410, 422
Britannia Prima 65, 69–70, 84–5, 111–12, 294–5, 417
British
  Church 290–1, 299–300, 345–8
  identity 114, 127–9, 133, 249–50, 387, 417
  language 117
  names 122–3
Brittany 21–3, 28–9, 34–7, 188–9, 285–8, 315–16, 321, 350–2, 355–6, 362–4, 398–9, 406–7
Brochfael ap Meurig, king of Glywysing 210–11
brooches
  crossbow 67–8, 78, 81–2, 85–6, 93, 98, 103–4
  oval 258–9
  penannular 10–14, 44–6, 85–6, 93, 103–4, 109–10, 152–4, 165, 221–2, 230–3, 235–6, 241–4, 249–50, 261, 266–7, 349, 420

INDEX 493

Type F 86, 106–7, 129
Type G 83, 90, 152, 166–7, 279–80, 292
Roman 113
Brownslade, cemetery 213, 217, 366, 369
Brunanburh, battle 27–8, 405
Brut y Tywysogion ('The History of the Princes')
33, 286–7, 326, 400–1, 422
Brycheiniog 41–2, 120, 123–5, 132, 155,
378–9, 406–7, 417, 422–3
Bryn Eryr, settlement 160
Brynach, St, *Life* of 285
see also Nevern
Bryn Euryn, hillfort 137
Bryn Llithrig, loom weights 224–5
Bryn Maelgwn, hoard 259–60, 403
Brynwgan, settlement 166
corn-dryer 198–200
plant remains 198
Bryn-y-Castell, hillfort 128–9, 306
Buckland Monachorum, inscribed
stone 126
Buellt and Gwerthrynion, early medieval
kingdom 43
buildings 140–1, 147–8, 160–1, 163, 166,
169, 172–9, 222
four-post structures 201
halls 170n.130
roundhouses 170–1
subrectangular 139, 163, 171–2
sunken-floored 158–9
see also church buildings
Builth Wells, sword 226–7, 246
Bullinghope, settlement 170–1
Bulmore, Roman settlement 76–8, 234–5
Abernant cemetery 303–4
Burghead, Moray, promontory fort 150–1
Burgundy, consular dating system 57
burhs, Anglo-Saxon 91–2, 238, 263–5
see also Rhuddlan
burial 302–12, 327–8, 365–9, 376–7, 412
grave types 279–80
of saints 351–6
punishment 154, 377
Roman 126, 302–4
see also cemeteries, commemoration,
shrouds
Burry Holms, island hermitage 16–17,
329, 337–8
Buttington 389, 393, 396
Buttington Cross, corn-dryers 198–200, 308

Byzantium
imports from 90, 152, 251–3
see also coins, silk

Cadfan, king of Gwynedd, *see* Catamanus
Cadog, St 30–2, 107–9
Life of 198, 214, 247–8, 285–7, 315,
358–9, 361
See also charters
Cadwaladr, king of Gwynedd 48
Cadwallon, king of Gwynedd 29, 129
Cae'r Mead, Llantwit Major, Roman villa
76–8, 101–2, 111–12
Cae'r Mynydd, settlement 160–1
Caer Bayvil, cemetery 282–3, 307, 384–5
Caer Dynnaf, hillfort 79–80
Caer Gai, Roman fort
inscribed stone 127–8
Caer Gybi (Holyhead), ecclesiastical site 284,
320–1, 323–4, 345–6
capel-y-bedd 272–3, 355–6
pilgrimage landscape 363
see also Cybi, St
Roman fortlet 87, 97–8
Caer Leb, enclosed settlement 89, 160–1
Caer Lleion, hillfort 137–8
Caerau fields, Caernarfonshire 184–5
Caerau hillfort, Glamorgan 79–80, 102–3,
142–6, 149–50
Caerau, Moylegrove, Pembs., graves 307
Caergwrle Castle 149–50
Caerhun (*Canovium*), Roman fort 87–8, 97–8
Caerleon (*Isca*), legionary fortress 56, 71,
76–8, 80, 97–8, 205–6, 293–4,
303–4, 310–11
martyrdoms of Julius and Aaron 107–9,
294, 350–1
post-Roman activity 107–8, 111–12
Caernarfon 24–5, 88–9, 122–3, 205–6
Christianity 106–7, 111–12
early medieval cemetery 106–7
Hen Waliau 86–7
Roman fort (*Segontium*) 10, 21, 56, 84–7,
91, 97–9, 101, 118–20, 236, 296–7
cereals 193
early medieval artefacts 103–4, 106–7
Mithraeum 86–7, 293–4
road to 44
Seguntienses 66–7, 85–6
Temple of Mithras 86–7

494 INDEX

Caerwent (*Venta Silurum*) 10, 41–2, 56, 68, 72–6, 80, 97, 100–1, 108, 205–7, 294, 374, 415–16
  Christianity in 111–12, 294–6, 310–11
  early medieval activity 103–4, 109–10, 257–8
  early medieval cemeteries 109, 112–13, 246, 248–9, 303–4
  Romano-Celtic temple 293
  rural hinterland 76–8
  Viking burials 409
Caer y Twr (Holyhead Mountain), hillfort and Roman watchtower 87–8, 97–8
Caldey Island (Ynys Bŷr) 22, 286–7, 314–16, 326–7, 329, 420–1
  cross-carved, inscribed stone 60, 277–8, 369–70
  imported pottery 263
Caldicot, settlement 78–9
Caldicot Level, *see* Gwent Levels
Cambrian Archaeological Association 6–7
Cambridge Juvencus 26–7
Camden, William 4–5
Cannington, Somerset, cemetery 302–3
cantref (pl. *cantrefi*) 315, 344–5, 386, 423
Canu Llywarch ('The Song of Llywarch') 27, 41, 54–5, 422–3
Capel Brithdir, inscribed stone 301–2
Capel Colman, cross-carved stone 284
Capel Eithin, cemetery 14–15, 279–80, 304–6, 331, 353
Capel Maelog, settlement and cemetery 17, 170–4, 270–1, 279–80, 282–3, 335–7, 353–5
  Roman artefacts 113–14
capeli-y-bedd ('grave chapels') 272–3, 287–8, 320–1, 324–5, 355–6
Caradog ap Gruffudd, king of south Wales 397–8
Caradog the Hermit 352
Cardiff 408
  Roman fort 71–2, 97
Carew, cross 149–50, 382
  promontory fort 142–51
Carmarthen (*Moridunum*) 80–2, 97, 100–1, 127, 303–4, 415
  see also Llandeulyddog
Carmel Head, Roman watchtower 87–8
Carolingian Europe
  contacts with 370–1
  rulers 380–1
Carrog, settlement 168–9, 176–7

Carthage 251–2
Castell Cadw, Felindre Farchog, settlement 169
Castell Collen, Roman fort
  penannular brooch 103–4
Castell Dwyran, inscribed stone 21–2, 99–100, 122–3, 127–9, 298–9
Castell Henllys 224–5
  hillfort 82–3
Castell Perthi-mawr, hillfort 307
Castell Trefadog, promontory fort 148–9, 165–6, 177
Catamanus (Cadfan), king of Gwynedd 2–3
  see also Llangadwaladr inscribed stone
cattle 205–6, 208, 218, 254, 266, 416–17
  cows as a unit of value 239–41, 245, 248, 261–2, 265, 420
caves
  burial in 309–10, 403–4
  places of ascetic retreat 315–16, 326–8
  Viking hideaways 409
Cefn Cave 309–10
Cefn Cwmwd, settlement 77, 90, 102, 152, 179–80, 234–5, 251–2
Cefn Du, settlement 140–1, 164–5
  corn-dryer 198–200, 215
  penannular brooch 103–4
celestial events 57–8
'Celtic Church' 8–9, 12–13, 15
Cemais, *cantref*
  field systems 184–5, 187
cemeteries 10, 14–18, 44, 61, 112–13, 117, 216–17, 270–1, 273–6, 278–82, 305, 313, 316–21, 324–8, 330–8, 344–8, 382–4, 418, 420–1, 426–7
  see also burial, commemoration
'cemetery settlements' 141
cereals 192–5, 214, 218, 367, 415
Ceredigion, kingdom of 42, 343–4
Cerrig Ceinwen, ecclesiastical site 332–3
Chadwick, Nora 15
Charles-Edwards, Thomas 19–20
charters 137, 180–1, 188–92, 194–5, 205–6, 214, 219, 261, 269, 315–20, 340–3, 375–6, 379, 393–4, 420–1
  Lichfield 25, 52–3
  Llancarfan 26–7
  Llandaf 15, 25, 44–6, 52–3, 107–11, 207–11, 239–41, 245, 248, 250, 286–7, 294, 313, 324, 331, 335, 337, 350–1, 396–7, 423–4

INDEX 495

Chepstow 426
Chester 91–2, 212, 425–6
  battle 376–7
  burh 158–9, 256–7, 346–7
    artefacts 257
    buildings 175
  Hiberno-Scandinavian settlement in 394–5,
    403–6, 410
  legionary fortress (*Deva*) 43, 86–7, 93–4,
    97–8, 293–6, 310–11, 346–7
  St Werburgh's 284
  see also Dublin–Chester trade route
chickens 208, 215–16
children (and infants) 426–7
  burial of 333–5, 366–9, 371–3, 412
Christian
  belief 338, 349–50, 365
  iconography 291–3, 323–4, 340, 349, 365,
    370–1, 373
  identity 120–2, 349–50, 371–3
  landscapes 339–46, 362–4, 421
Christianity 57–60, 111–12, 130–1, 215–16,
  269–89, 412, 417–18, 420–1, 426–7
  afterlife, concepts of 60
  conversion to 14–15, 114, 124–5, 291–2,
    296–303, 309–12, 345–7, 409
  origins of in Wales 75, 294–6, 310–11,
    363–4, 373, 415
  see also monasticism
Chronicle of Ireland 28–9, 318–19
church
  buildings 271–3, 294–5, 328–33, 337–8,
    346–8, 361
  consecration 351–2
  dedications 288–9, 331–3, 335–7, 342–4,
    351–2, 396
  enclosures 282–4, 318–19, 323–5, 335–7,
    420–1
  landholding 341–3
    see also charters, estates
  sites 14–17, 269–71, 313, 325, 347–8,
    426–7
    foundation by saints 350–2
    location 323
    of lesser churches 330–9, 344–5,
      423–4
    of major churches 313–26, 339–41,
      369–73, 378–9, 396
    reuse of prehistoric sites 304
    reuse of Roman sites 87

  see also cemeteries, hermitages, monasteries,
    mother churches
Church, the
  authority of 374–6, 419–20, 423–4
  organization 294–6, 299–300, 302,
    310–11, 313–15, 325, 344–5, 423–4
  see also bishop houses of Dyfed
  role in technological change 219, 420–1
Church Island, Co. Kerry 328–9
Cirencester (*Corinium*) 294–6
Claf Abercuawg 52–3
clas (pl. *clasau*), *see* mother churches
Clearwell Quarry, St Briavels, Glos., iron
  smelting 227–8
Cledemutha, *see* Rhuddlan
climate (of Wales) 46–7, 414
climate change 46–51, 104, 193–4, 200–1,
  203, 205–6, 217–20, 265–8, 414–17,
  419, 424, 426
  see also 'Late Antique Little Ice Age'
Clocaenog, inscribed stone 4–5, 123–4, 127
Clodock, inscription 396–7
Clonfad monastery, Co. Westmeath 195,
  325, 358–9
Clonmacnoise, Co. Offaly 244–5, 271–2,
  355–6
clothing 239–41, 279–80, 359–60, 368–9
  see also textile production
Clydai
  capel-y-bedd 272–3
  inscribed stone 122
Clynnog Fawr, ecclesiastical site 62, 272–3,
  324–5, 355–6
  sundial 58–9
Cnut, king of England, of Denmark, and of
  Norway 259–60
Coelbren, Roman fort 44
Coenwulf, king of Mercia 254–6, 391–3
coins
  early medieval 221–2, 258–65, 267–8,
    424–5
    Byzantine 109–10, 251–2, 361–2
    Carolingian deniers 409
    distribution of in Wales 256
    Kufic 258–9, 261
    pennies 106–7, 109–10, 152–4, 254–6,
      320–1, 327, 368–9, 394–5, 397–8, 403
    Sassanian 402–3
    sceattas (early pennies) 109–10, 254–6
    stycas 106–7

496 INDEX

coins (*cont.*)
    Roman 67–8, 80–2, 84–95, 97–9, 101–2,
        112–13, 266, 291–3, 302–3, 308,
        368–9, 379–80, 415–17
      coin hoards 72–4
      Constantinian 76–8, 82–3, 309
      late bronze *nummi* 72–4
      Theodosian (AD 388–402) 71–6, 78–9,
        97–8, 100–1
      Valentinianic (AD 364–78) 69–72, 75–9
Colchester, Butt Road Roman cemetery 302–3
Cold Knap, Barry, Roman building with later
    settlement 171, 204
Collfryn, enclosed settlement 77, 94–5, 169–70
combs 135–6, 167, 225–7, 237–8, 244–5,
    266, 415–16
commemoration 364–73
    see also burial, inscribed stones
commotes 315, 344–5, 386, 423
Concenn, king of Powys, *see* Cyngen
conflict, *see* violence, warfare
Conkland Hill, settlement 137, 140–1, 162,
    169, 174–5, 424
    plant remains 50, 213
consular dating system 22–3, 57
coracles 41
corn-dryers 61, 112–13
    early medieval 138–43, 163–9, 185–6,
        192–4, 196, 198–201, 203, 218, 308,
        325, 416–17
    Roman 75–6, 94–5
Cornovii 43, 91–2
Cornwall 224–5, 231
    Christianity in 310–11, 346, 356
    early medieval settlements 181–2, 184,
        419–20
    landscape organization 187
    tin 251–4
Corwen, church 287, 340–1
    cross-shaft 28, 395
Cowbridge (*Bovium?*), Roman settlement 76–8
Coygan Camp 82–3, 142–51, 263, 302–3
    artefacts 196–8, 245
craftworkers 238, 266–7, 417, 422–3
craftworking 221–39
crannogs 157–8, 158n.93
    see also Llangorse crannog
Crantock, Cornwall 355–6
Crockysdan Camp, promontory fort 82–3

crop-processing 161–3, 166, 198–203
    see also corn-dryers, malting, mills, quernstones
cross-carved stones 130–1, 333–5, 338, 364,
    393–4, 421
    see also sculpture
crosses, free-standing 4–5, 323–4, 380–2,
    395, 423
    see also sculpture
croziers, *see* relics
crucibles, *see* metalworking
Crugiau Cemais, ancestral site 263–4, 384–5
Cuerdale 258–9, 402–3
Culdees (*Céli Dé*) 314
Culver Hole, cave 409
Cunedda 131–2
currach 37
Cuthbert, St, *see* Lindisfarne
Cwmbrwyn, Roman villa 83–4
Cwrt Llechryd, early medieval settlement 152
Cwyfan, St (Kevin) 288–9, 405–6
Cybi, St, *Life* of 287–8, 320–1, 331
Cyfeiliog, bishop of Archenfield 396–7, 406–7
Cynethryth, queen of Mercia 152–4
Cyngen, king of Powys 361–2
    see also Pillar of Eliseg
Cynog, St, torque of 359–60
cytiau ('r) Gwyddelod ('Irishmen's huts') 129–30

dairying 214–16, 220, *see also* cattle, sheep
Dalkey Island 252
Danegeld 267–8
Danelaw 256–9, 409–11
Daniel ap Sulien of Llanbadarn Fawr 30, 33
Dan-y-Coed, enclosed farmstead, *see* Llawhaden
David, St 2–3, 28–9, 324, 361–2
    cult of 321, 350–2, 359–60, 364
    Rhygyfarch's *Life* of 30–2, 44–6, 52–3,
        58–60, 196–8, 216, 288–9, 314, 325,
        339–40, 342–6, 361–3, 382–4
Davies, Wendy 15, 188–9
De Raris Fabulis 215
De Situ Brecheiniauc 132
Decanti 42–3, 125–6
    see also Degannwy
Deceangli 42–3, 91–2
Dee, River 40–1, 212, 291–2, 340–1, 394–5,
    403–5
deer 208–10
Deer Park Farms, roundhouses 173–4

Degannwy, hillfort 13–14, 95–6, 125–6, 137, 142–51, 226, 263, 378–9, 392–3
Deheubarth 322
Deiniol, St 28–9, 352, 361–2
 see also Bangor
Demetae 42, 80–2, 127
dendrochronology 47–8, 137, 155–7, 418–19
developer-funded excavations 17, 140–1
diet 195–6, 212–17, 412, 414–15, 426–7
Din Lligwy, enclosed hut-group 77, 89, 160–1
 roundel 356–7
Din Sylwy, hillfort 90–1, 402–3
Dinas Brân, hillfort 381–2
Dinas Dinlle, hillfort 62
Dinas Emrys, hillfort 5–6, 10–14, 24–5, 90, 142–51, 179–80, 252, 291–3, 379–80
Dinas Powys, promontory fort 13–14, 16, 144–52, 179–80, 316–18, 374, 378–9, 417
 animal bones 204, 206–9, 212, 218
 artefacts 103–4, 135–6, 142–3, 214–16, 223–7, 245–9, 252–4, 265
 buildings 172–4
 burial 308, 366
 fine metalworking 230–3, 238
 ironworking 227–8, 230
 other crafts 234–6
 Roman artefacts 113–14, 129
 use of internal space 177–8, 196
Dinas Powys Common, Roman-period farmstead 78
Dinas Powys hundred 140, 171
Dinefwr, Roman fort and medieval castle 198–200, 322
Dinorben, hillfort 10–12, 61, 95–6, 101–3, 142–8, 291–2, 379–80
 ploughshare 196–8
Dinorben quarry, Anglesey, Hiberno-Scandinavian broadband arm-rings 8–9, 402–3
display 221–2, 230, 239–50, 266–7, 302–3
dispute settlement 375–6, 379–80, 396–7
dogs 207–10, 261
Dolaucothi, gold mines 80–1, 101
Dolbenmaen
 corn-dryer 193–4, 198–200
 inscribed stone 123–4
 settlement 161, 173–4, 178–9, 201
Dolwyddelan, bell 358–9

Domesday Book 29–30, 34, 134–5, 202–3, 205, 212, 287, 329–30, 347–8, 382, 396–400, 405
Donovan, Edward 5–6
Dorestad 254–6
Drim enclosed farmstead, *see* Llawhaden
Droitwich 254–6
Druid, cemetery 44, 280–1, 305–6
Drwsdangoed, hoard 259–60, 403
Dublin, Hiberno-Scandinavian 33–4, 38, 176–7, 236, 256–7, 261, 267–8, 345–6, 376, 398–9, 401–3, 405–6, 409, 411, 424–5
 artefacts 257–8, 349, 408
Dublin–Chester trade route 256–60, 262–3, 267–8, 399–403, 410, 422
Dudston, Chirbury 389–91
 fields 187–8
Dumbleton, Edgar and Henry 9–10
Dumville, David N. 15
Dunadd, hillfort 233, 245
Dunoding 42–3
Dyfed 42, 123–4, 131–2, 374, 417
 see also Demetae
Dyfrig, St 352
Dysart 4 hoard, Co. Westmeath 258–9
Dyserth, ecclesiastical site 287–9, 329–30, 346–7
 sculpture 237, 277–8, 405–6

Eadred, king of England 262–3
Easter, date of 57–8, 346–7, 373
ecclesiastical sites, *see* church sites
economy 265–8, 415–16, 420, 424–7
 see also farming economy
Edward the Confessor, king of England 375
Edward the Elder, king of the Anglo-Saxons 238–41, 265, 396–7, 406–7
 see also Rhuddlan
Edwin, king of Northumbria 29, 38, 129
Eglwys Gymyn, inscribed stone 117–19, 333
Eglwys Nynnid
 cross-slab 340
 inscribed stone 6–7
Eglwysilan, carved stone 246–7
Eglwyswrw, cemetery 281–2
Elfoddw, 'archbishop' of Gwynedd 57–8, 314, 318–19

498 INDEX

Elgar the Hermit 352
  Life of 326
Elise ap Tewdwr, king of Brycheiniog 157,
    239–41, 396–7, 422–3
Ely, Roman villa 79–80
emotions 350, 363–4, 370–3
enamel 226–7, 231–4, 241–4
England, early medieval 9–10, 13, 424–5
  administrative system 381–2
  cemeteries 250, 278
  church in 346–8
  deer hunting 208–9
  farming economy 195, 202–3, 219
  fishing 211–12
  relations with Wales 387–98
  trackways 44–6
  written sources 29–30
Englynion y Beddau ('Stanzas of the
    Graves') 27–8, 60–2, 380–1
Ergyng (Archenfield) 29, 38–42, 188–9, 206,
    261, 286–7, 393, 396–7
  churches in 335
estate centres 150–1, 154–5, 179–80, 201,
    230, 263–4, 378–9, 419–21, 424
estates 25, 158, 180–1, 183, 188–92,
    203–4, 213, 219–20, 238–9, 266–7,
    286–7, 315, 325, 335, 337–9,
    344–5, 423–4
Etmyg Dinbych ('The Praise of Tenby') 27–8,
    137, 248
Eugenius, Roman usurper 85–6
Expulsion of the Déisi 28–9, 131–2

fairs 381–2, 384–5
farming economy 183, 217–20, 412, 414–15,
    420–1, 424–5
  Roman 193, 196–8, 202–3, 205–7
  see also cattle, cereals, pigs, sheep
farming year 54
farmsteads 138–40, 159–72, 180, 416–17,
    419–21
  see also settlements
Faustus of Riez 315–16
feasting 206–7, 215–16, 218, 220–2, 248–50,
    266, 378–9, 381–2, 417, 422–3
Felindre, corn-dryer 198
Fenton, Richard 5–6
Ffestiniog, inscribed stones 118–20, 122–3,
    128–9, 306, 374

field systems 163–4, 184–8, 219, 419–20, 426
Fishguard 407–8
  cross-carved stone (*Maen Dewy*) 44, 342,
    362–3
fishing 210–13, 220, 397–8, 424–5
Flat Holm (Ynys Echni), hermitage 329
flax 195–6, 223–4, 239–41
fonts 58–60
food
  render 180, 183, 192, 194–5, 201, 203,
    206–7, 213–14, 219–20, 238–9, 244,
    250, 266–7, 325, 378–9, 385, 396–7,
    414–15, 419, 422–3, 425
  security 203, 269, 375–6, 416–17
  see also diet
Ford Farm, Langstone, Roman villa 76–8
Forden Gaer (*Levobrinta?*), Roman fort
    92, 97
Forest of Dean 41–2, 101, 227–8
Four Crosses, Llandysilio, weapon deposit 245
Fox, Cyril 7–8
  Offa's Dyke 9, 389, 391–4
  Personality of Britain 12–13, 35
France, contacts with 35–7, 120, 215–16,
    234–5, 251–6, 258–9, 273–6, 297–8,
    300–1, 310–11, 315–16, 327–8, 344–5,
    351, 364, 417–18
frontier zone between Wales and
    England 387–98, 421
  see also Offa's Dyke, Wat's Dyke, Welsh
    Marches
fruits 195–6, 213, 215–16

games, board 113–14, 248–9
Gangani 42–3
Garn Turne 386
Garranes, ringfort 233
Garryduff, ringfort 233
Gateholm Island 142–6, 148
  Hiberno-Scandinavian artefacts 149–51,
    235–7, 408
  settlement 10–12, 142–3
Gaul, *see* France
Gelli Gaer, Roman fort 228–30
genealogies 22–3, 55–6, 131–2, 380–2
Gerald of Wales 33–4, 40–4, 155, 214, 285–6,
    314, 325, 329, 358–60
Germanus, St 350–1
  Lives of 22, 62, 292–3, 297–8, 315–16

INDEX 499

gift-giving 183, 208–9, 221–2, 239–45,
248, 250, 254, 262–3, 266–7, 374,
378–9, 394–5, 402–3, 417, 422–3
Gildas 300–1, 358–9
De Excidio Britanniae 15, 21–2, 35–7, 40–1,
55–7, 66–7, 107–9, 131–2, 137, 290–1,
294, 299–300, 314, 350–1, 419
'tyrants' in 98, 104, 127–9, 254, 374, 417
penitential 216
Glanfred, promontory fort 138–9, 144, 147–8,
150–1, 179–80, 193–4
Glasbury, bishops of 314
glass, early medieval 152–4, 241–4
Anglo-Saxon glass vessels 254, 265
imported 17–18, 38, 67–8, 94–6, 135–6,
142–3, 149, 215–16, 218, 234–5, 248,
250–4, 264, 266, 316–18, 337–8
Roman 90, 146
see also beads
glass-working 231–5, 238–9
Glywysing 41–2, 397–8, 406–7
goats, *see* sheep
Gododdin, Y 245–7
Gorsedd Arberth (Narberth) 382–4
Gower, kingdom of 42
Graeanog 17, 88–9, 139–40, 185–6
ironworking 228–30
settlements 139, 160–4, 171–2, 175–6,
198–201
graffiti 333–5, 362–3
grazing, rough 184–7, 190–2, 204
Great Orme (Orme's Head) 35–7, 399–401
Cyngreawdr Fynydd ('Hill of Assembly') 384
Gruffudd ap Cynan, king of Gwynedd 315,
318–21, 398–9, 401–3, 422
Latin *Life* of 33–4, 411
Gruffudd ap Llywelyn, king of Gwynedd 1–2,
38, 158–9, 375–6, 378–9, 386, 394–7,
407, 412–13, 425–6
Gwenfrewi, St (Winefride) 330
Lives of 284, 287, 350–1
shrine of 223, 285–6, 357–8
Gwent 41–2, 110, 286–7, 374, 393, 397–8,
406–7
churches in 335
Gwent Levels 17–18, 37, 41–2, 51–2, 78–80,
103, 187–8, 210, 397–8
Gwynedd 42–3, 128–9, 131–3, 180, 314, 374,
400–3, 405–6, 422

Gwynllyw, St 352
Gwytherin
capel-y-bedd 272–3
inscribed stone 123
see also Gwenfrewi, St

hacksilver, Hiberno-Scandinavian 233–4,
258–9, 263–4, 402–3
Hadrian's Wall 391
hagiography 22, 30–2, 52–3, 62, 269, 286–7,
326–31, 344–5, 350–2, 356, 361–2,
364, 421
hair styles 244–5, 299–300
halls, *see* buildings
Haraldsson, Godfrith and Maccus 401–2, 407
hare 209–10, 330
Harleian Chronicle 22–3, 48, 57–8, 137,
149–50, 158–9, 314, 318–19, 321,
392–3, 400–1, 409–10, 422
Harold Godwinson 158–9, 211–12, 394–5,
397–8, 425–6
hawks 207–10
health 216–17
Hen Domen castle 426
earlier settlement 170
open field system 187–8
ridge-and-furrow 196–8
Hen Gastell (Briton Ferry), hillfort 17, 142–4,
146–9, 254
penannular brooch 103–4, 242–3
Roman artefacts 113–14
Hiberno-Scandinavian artefacts 149–51,
235–6, 409
Hen Gastell (Llanwnda), promontory
fort 148–9, 165–6
Hen Waliau, *see* Caernarfon
Henfynyw, ecclesiastical site 343–4
herbs 215–16, 314
Hereford 257, 346–7, 389, 393, 396–8, 425–6
battle 392–3
Herefordshire, hoard 402–3, 406–7
Herewald, bishop of Llandaf 30–2, 335, 337,
344–5, 347–8
hermitages 14–15, 326–30
Heronbridge, Roman industrial settlement 93–4
mass grave 376–7
Hiberno-Scandinavian
artefacts 149–51, 154, 333–5, 349
contacts 332, 422

500 INDEX

Hiberno-Scandinavian (*cont.*)
  identity 154–5
  see also Llanbedrgoch, patronage, Viking
    impact on Wales
High Island, Co. Galway hermitage 327–8
hillforts 10–14, 16–17, 60, 94–6, 102–3,
    137–9, 142–52, 179–80, 266–7,
    415, 417
  afterlives 62, 82–3, 149–50, 292–3, 391
  burials 302–3, 307–8
  enclosures 146–7
  functions 150–1, 263, 266, 290–2, 294,
    374, 378–80, 385, 417–20
  imported pottery and glass found at 252–3
  interior structures 147–8
  location 144–6
  Roman-period occupation of 79–80,
    88–91, 146
Hirfaen Gwyddog, prehistoric standing
    stone 61, 341
Historia Brittonum 15, 23–5, 40–1, 43, 55–8,
    60, 62, 106–7, 125–6, 131–3, 149–50,
    209–10, 231, 292–3, 315–16, 351–2,
    360–1, 387, 412–13, 419
historiography 3–20
Holyhead, *see* Caer Gybi
Holyhead Mountain (Mynydd Cybi),
    see Caer y Twr
holy wells 58–60, 284, 320–1, 421
Holywell 284
  see also Gwenfrewi, St
honey, *see* bees
Honorius, emperor, letter to British towns 64–5
horns, drinking 225–6, 239, 248
horse equipment 43–4, 207–8, 225–7, 230,
    247–8, 349, 409
horses 207–8, 245, 247–8, 254, 261, 266,
    316–18, 391
Hudd, Alfred 10
Hughes, Kathleen 15
hunting 189, 207–9, 220, 239, 246–8, 397–8
hut groups 10–12, 16–17, 88–90
Huxley, hoard 403–4
Hywel ab Edwin, king of Deheubarth 376, 407
Hywel ap Rhys, king of Glywysing 28, 210–11,
    319–20, 369–70
Hywel Dda (Hywel 'the Good') 2–3, 32–3,
    43–4, 361–2, 374–5, 380, 412–13
  penny 262–3, 265, 424–5

Iberia, contacts with 35–7, 251–2, 300–1,
    310–11, 315–16, 344–5, 417–18
identities 221–2, 241–2, 244–5, 248–50,
    256–7, 265–6, 298–9, 361–2, 374,
    377–80, 385, 394–6, 398–9, 403,
    412–14, 422
  see also British identity, Christian identity,
    Hiberno-Scandinavian identity, Roman
    identity
Ieuan ap Sulien of Llanbadarn Fawr 30,
    42, 359–60
Illtud, St 62, 351–2
  Life of 47, 52–3
  see also Llantwit Major
Inchmarnock, hermitage 248–9, 327–8
infield–outfield system 186–8
Ingimund 263–4, 401, 403–4
Inishmurray, Co. Sligo, hermitage 327–8, 367–8
inscribed stones 4, 6–9, 14–15, 19–20, 22–3,
    44, 80–1, 93, 99–100, 114–29, 131–2,
    158, 273, 296–302, 304–8, 310–11,
    315–16, 319–20, 326–7, 331, 338–40,
    346, 351–2, 375–6, 384–5, 412,
    417–18, 420–1
  formulae 120–1
  location 115–17, 123–5, 333
  oghams, *see* ogham
  personal names on 121–2
  Roman titles on 122–3, 128–9
  women commemorated on 54–5, 127–8,
    300–1
inscriptions, Roman 67–8, 81–2
incense 361
Iona 272–3, 355–6
  Adomnán's *Life* of Columba 358–9
Ipswich (*Gippeswic*) 254–6
Irby 170, 405
Ireland, early medieval 13–14, 414, 424–5
  burial 309–10
  change from round to rectangular
    buildings 172–3
  Christianity 282–4, 323–4
  contacts with Wales 158, 225–6, 235, 252,
    254, 276–7, 298–9, 321, 342–6, 370–1
  farming economy 195–8, 200–3, 205–6,
    214, 219
  ferta 115–16, 306–8
  leachta 333–5, 367–8
  relics 356–61

trackways 44–6
written sources 28–9
see also Dublin
Irish
  language 4, 22–3, 26–7, 117, 121–2, 417
  law 32–3
  personal names 4–5, 115–16, 123–6
  place names 130
  raids on Wales 66–7, 71–2, 84–5, 97,
    131–2, 415–16
  settlement in Wales 7, 20–3, 28–9, 98–9,
    104, 114, 117–18, 124–6, 129–32,
    384–5, 417, 422–3
  soldiers in the Roman army 80–1, 98–100
Irish Sea 12–13, 28–9, 33–7, 258–9, 262–3,
  267–8, 398–9, 409–10, 413–14, 417,
  420, 422
iron artefacts 223, 225, 236–7
ironworking 19, 140–1, 183, 185–6, 221,
  226–30, 237–8, 415–16, 420, 425
  furnaces 139–40, 167–9, 267–8
Isle of Man 38, 259–60, 262–3, 273–6, 345–6,
  356, 401–3, 405–6, 409, 422
Isle of May, hermitage 327–8
isotope analysis 38, 43–4, 130, 212–13, 217,
  309–10, 376–7
Italy 414
  see also Rome
Ithel, king of Glywysing 239–41

javelin heads (*plumbatae*) 85–6
Jonathan, *princeps* ('abbot') of Abergele 286–7
Jones, Glanville R. J. 12–13
Jones, Harry Longueville 6–7
Joseph, bishop of Llandaf 322, 375–6
Justinian plague 48–9, 217–18, 251–2,
  418–19

Kenchester (*Magnis*) 296
Kenfig, *Croes y Ddadl* 384
Kildare 351
kingdoms, early medieval 39, 41–3, 344–5,
  417, 419, 422
  formation 127–9, 150–1, 179–80, 374–5,
    378–81, 385–7, 413–14, 419
kingship 374–5, 386
kinship 54–6, 180, 192, 244–5, 301–2, 307–8,
  310–12, 315, 331, 337–8, 344–5, 364,
  385, 418, 420–1, 423–4, 426–7

Knighton 389–91, 396
Knowth, Co. Meath 233

Labbamolaga, Co. Cork 355–6
Lagore, crannog 157–8, 177, 195, 226,
  233, 245
landscape (of Wales) 35–6, 41–3, 413–15,
  420–1
  early medieval 49–53, 184–5, 189–92, 204
  mountains 40
  rivers 40–1
landscapes, archaeological 61, 88–9
  see also Christian landscapes
Last Judgement 60
'Late Antique Little Ice Age' 103, 180, 184,
  418–21, 426–7
  see also climate change
Latin
  language 20–1, 117, 415, 417
  legal texts 32–3
  military loanwords in Old Irish 98–9
  names 122
  poetry 30, 42, 122, 300–1
  see also inscribed stones
Laugharne 424–5
  coins 260–1, 263–4
  cross 408
leather-working 225, 236–7
legumes, cultivation of 195–6
Leland, John 3–4
Lemanaghan, Co. Offaly, wooden staff 359–60
  see also St Manchan's Shrine
Lérins, monastery near Marseilles 315–16,
  327–8
Lesser Garth Cave 309–10
Lhuyd, Edward 4–5, 285–6, 322, 357–60
Liber Commonei 57–8
Liber Landavensis (Book of Llandaf) 30–2
  see also charters
liber vitae ('book of life') 60
Lichfield, diocese of 346–7
Lichfield Gospels 20–1, 26, 322, 359–61
  marginalia 25, 60–1, 188–9, 192, 207–8, 214
  see also charters
life-course 54–5, 244–5
  Christian 58–60, 350
Lifris of Llancarfan 30–2, 107–9
  see also Cadog, St
Lindisfarne 327–8, 351

502 INDEX

linen smoothers 170–1
  see also textile production
Linney Burrows, sand-dune settlement 167
literacy 130–1, 379
liturgical ritual 350–2, 364, 373
llan 287–8, 335–8, 346, 396, 421
Llanaber, inscribed stone 40
  wooden trackway 44–6
Llanarmon bell 358–9
Llanbadarn Fawr 30, 33, 58, 314–15, 343–6,
    423–4
  sculpture 277–8
  see also Ieuan, Rhygyfarch, Sulien
Llanbadrig 288–9
Llanbedrgoch
  churchyard cemetery 331
  early medieval settlement 17–18, 135–6,
    152–5, 177–8, 180, 196, 219, 378–9,
    419–20, 424–5
    animal bones 204
    artefacts 223–7, 235, 237, 242–3,
      245–7, 349
    buildings 168, 172–4, 176–7, 201, 214
    burials 377
    craftworking 230
    Hiberno-Scandinavian activity 38, 230,
      233–4, 236, 238, 254–9, 263–5,
      267–8, 399, 402–3, 422
    molluscs 212
  Roman period settlement 88–9
Llanboidy, inscribed stone 123, 375–6
Llancarfan 30–2, 211–12, 324–5, 407
  scriptorium 26–7
  see also Cadog, St, charters, Lifris of
    Llancarfan, Ynys Echni
Llandaf 286–7, 314, 322, 326, 343–5, 352
  cathedral 271–2, 426
  see also charters
Llandanwg, inscribed stones 122, 273, 320–1
Llanddewi Aber-arth, hogback grave-cover 408
Llanddewibrefi, monastery 343–4
  sculpture 276–7, 324, 369–70
  synod of 382–4
Llandecwyn, cross-inscribed stone 351–2
Llandeilo Fawr 314, 322–4, 341, 343–4
  see also charters, Lichfield Gospels
Llandeilo Llwydarth 287, 342–3
  cross-carved stone 58–60, 284
  inscribed stones 124–5
Llandeilo'r-fân, estate 190–2, 342

Llandeulyddog (Carmarthen), bishop house
    287, 342–3
Llandough, major ecclesiastical site 17,
    111–12, 316–18, 323, 325, 374, 420–1
  cemetery 216, 248–9, 270–1, 279–80,
    285–6, 324–5, 365–9, 376–7
  girdle 223–4, 369
Llandrinio, mother church 323, 346–7, 396
Llandudno, inscribed stone 299–300
Llandudno Junction, whetstone 244–5, 247
Llandwrog, hoard 259–60, 403
Llandybïe, estate 189
Llandyfaelog Fach, carved pillar 239–41,
    244–5
Llandygái
  cemetery 280–1, 306, 353
  multiperiod ritual and settlement
    landscape 161–3, 185–6, 198–200
Llandysilio, ecclesiastical site 284
Llandysul, inscribed stone 123
Llaneilian, mother church 320–1, 324–5
Llanelen, chapel site 337–8
Llaneleu, sculpture 276–7
Llanerfyl, inscribed stone 54–5, 122
Llanfaelog, inscribed stones 115–16
Llan-faes 263–5, 401–3
Llanerfyl, inscribed stone 122, 302
Llanfaelog, inscribed stones 123–6, 299–300,
    331, 351–2
Llanfaglan, church 282–3
  inscribed stone 118–20
Llanfairpwll
  enclosed settlement 165–6
  ringed pin 257–8
Llanfechell, pollen core 50
Llanfair-Mathafarn-Eithaf, church 332–3
Llanfihangel Ysgeifiog, church 332–3
Llanfor, Roman fort
  inscribed stone 127–8
Llangadwaladr, inscribed stone 4–5, 22–3,
    118–20, 123, 129, 298–9, 331, 374
Llangaffo (*Merthyr Caffo*), ecclesiastical
    site 287–8, 320–1
  inscribed stone 123
Llan-gan, cross 239, 244–5, 370–1
Llangefni
  Coed y Meirw cemetery 212–13, 217,
    279–80, 308
    penannular brooch from 103–4, 242–3
  Roman artefacts 113

crop-processing 198, 201–2, 237
Hedd yr Ynys 214
inscribed stones 118–20, 331
see also Trefollwyn
Llangeinwen, ecclesiastical site 332–3
Llangenau, bell 358–9
Llangennith, ecclesiastical site 328–9
Llangernyw, cross-carved stones 276–7
yew trees 285
Llangïan, churchyard boundary 282–3
inscribed stone 122–3
Llan-gors, monastery 158, 356–7, 378–9, 422–3
estates 190–2
Llangorse, crannog 9–11, 17–20, 131–2, 137, 152, 155–8, 177–8, 201, 267–8, 376, 378–9, 396–7, 422–3
animal bones 204, 206–10, 212, 220
artefacts 113–14, 198, 224–6, 231–2, 234–7, 243–9, 285–6, 356–7
craftworking 230, 233, 238
garment 223–4, 239–41
plant remains 50–1, 192–6, 213
woodworking 27, 222–3, 238–9
see also *Canu Llywarch*
Llangorse Lake (Llyn Syfaddon) 41
log-boat 223
Llangwnnadl, bell 358–9
Llangynfelyn
mineral extraction 101
wooden trackway 44–6, 50–1, 222–3
Llangystennin, bell 285–6
Llanhamlach, church 62
Llaniestyn, church and cemetery 332, 353–4
Llanllawer, holy well 284
Llanlleonfel, cross-carved, inscribed stone 60, 365
Llanllŷr, inscription 329–30
Llanmerewig, churchyard enclosure 282–3
Llannor, inscribed stones 115–16, 122–3, 307–8
Llanrhaeadr-ym-Mochant
mother church 315, 323
cross-slab 396
Meusydd cemetery 280–1
Llanrhidian, ecclesiastical site 337–8
Llanrhuddlad, bell 358–9
Llansadwrn, inscribed stone 122–3, 288–9, 298–9, 331, 351–2
Llantrisant, inscribed stone 300–1

Llantwit Major (Llanilltud Fawr) 52–3, 286–7, 314, 319–20, 323, 326, 335
cemetery 47
monastery 22, 315–16, 423–4
Roman villa, *see* Cae'r Mead
scriptorium 26–7
sculpture 5–6, 20, 28, 277–8, 324–5, 369–70
Llanveynoe, sculpture 396–7
Llanwenog, inscribed stone 122, 124–5
Llanwinio, inscribed stone 55, 333
Llanwnda, Pembs., ecclesiastical site 325, 342
Llanwnnws, cross-carved inscribed stone 54–5, 369–70
Llanychlwydog, churchyard 113, 281–2, 333–5
Llanymawddwy, inscribed stone 55, 127–8
Llawhaden, ecclesiastical site 287, 342–3, 362–3
settlements 82–3, 166, 174–5
St Kennox farm, cross-carved stone 276–7, 333–5
Llechgynfarwy, church and cemetery 332
Lloyd, J. E. 7
Llyn Cerrig Bach 291–2
Llyn Fawr, hoard 291–2
Llys Awel
penannular brooches 242–4
votive offerings 291–2, 310–11
Llys Brychan, Roman villa 83–4
Llysfaen Common, ring 394–5
llysoedd ('courts' of Welsh rulers) 158–9, 184–5, 238, 426
Llysworney 247–8, 349
Llywarch Hen, see *Canu Llywarch*
Llywarch Hen's Dyke 190–2
Llywel, inscribed stones 125
Llywelyn ap Seisyll, king of Gwynedd 262–3
Llwynarth, ecclesiastical site 351–2, 360–1
Lodge Hill Camp 79–80
log-boats 41
London (*Lundenwic*) 254–6
Longbury Bank, settlement 17–18, 139–40, 142–4, 146–9, 172–3, 177–8, 190–2
animal bones 204, 208–9, 212
artefacts 214, 224–5, 242, 252, 254, 263, 326–7
metalworking 227–8, 230–3
plant remains 195–6
loom-weights 165, 170–1, 175
see also textile production

504 INDEX

Loughor (*Leucarum*) Roman fort 80–1
  inscribed stone 80–1
Love Lodge Farm, Ffairfach,
    corn-dryers 198–200
Lydney, hillfort and Roman temple 150–1,
    292, 294
Lyminge, barn 201
  plough coulter 196–8, 219

Mabinogi, see *Pedeir Keinc y Mabinogi* ('Four
    Branches of the Mabinogi')
Maelgwn, king of Gwynedd 48, 104,
    128–9, 320–1
Maen Achwyfan cross, Whitford 246,
    382–3, 405–6
Maenclochog, inscribed stone 124–5
  roundhouse 166, 172–4
Maentwrog, inscribed stone 116–17
Maes Osfeilion, see Llan-faes
Maesbury 391–2, 395–6
Maesderwen, Roman villa 76–8
magic 350, 365, 367–9, 371–3
Magnus Barelegs, king of Norway 401–2
Magnus Maximus, Roman usurper 55–6,
    97, 99–100
malting 164–5, 215
Manaw Gododdin 131–2
manuring 196
manuscripts (associated with Wales) 21
Marden, Herefordshire, bell 358–9, 396–7
Maredudd ab Owain, king of Gwynedd 261
Margam, ecclesiastical site 335
  associated landscape 340
  inscribed stones 55–6, 120–1, 298–9
  sculpture 5–6, 207–8, 239, 246–7, 277–8,
    370–2
martyrs 351, 356–7
  British 107–9, 294, 350–1
masculinity 239, 245–7, 249, 376
Mathry, penannular brooch 103–4
Maughold, Isle of Man 345–6
Mawgan Porth, Cornwall, settlement 181–2
Mediterranean, contacts with 35–7, 234–5,
    315–16, 344–5, 417–19
  see also pottery, early medieval imported
meeting places, *see* assembly sites
Meifod, ecclesiastical site 272–3, 284, 323–4
Meirionnydd, early medieval kingdom 42–3
Melangell, St *see* Pennant Melangell

Meliden, cross-shaft 405–6
Melin y Plas, field 186–7
memory 53–4, 60–3, 304
Meols 252, 257–8, 349, 361–2
mercenaries, Hiberno-Scandinavian 246,
    375–6, 407, 422
Mercia, expansion of 254–6, 265–7, 375, 387,
    392–3, 413–14, 421
Merfyn Frych, king of Gwynedd 422
Merlin's Cave 309
merthyr 107–9, 287–8, 294, 350–2
Merthyr, inscribed stone 273, 333
Merthyr Mawr, ecclesiastical site 320–1, 335
  sculpture 277–8, 341–2
metalwork, early medieval ornamental 67–8,
    142–3, 254–6, 265–7
  Anglo-Saxon 95–6, 254–6, 395–8
  Christian 285–6, 337–8, 349, 356–61
metalworking, early medieval 161–3, 222,
    230–4, 333–5, 362–3, 420
  Roman 95–6
  see also ironworking
Meurig ap Tewdrig, king of Morgannwg 375–6
middens 177–9, 196, 212
milestones, Roman 56
Milford Haven 406–8, 410
mills (water) 200–3, 219
Minchin Hole, cave 103–4, 225–6, 260–1, 409
mineral extraction
  early medieval 227–8, 231
  Roman 50–1, 80–1, 89, 93–4, 101, 415
mineral wealth of Wales 414–15
Mithras, *see* Caernarfon
Moel Fenlli, hillfort 24–5, 27–8, 292–3
molluscs 212
monasteries 313–26, 420–1
monasticism 14–15, 269, 299–302, 311–12,
    315–16, 325, 327–8, 338, 346–7, 350,
    423–4, 426
  female monasticism 330
Monmouth (*Blestium*), Roman
    settlement 76–8
  coin hoard 260–1
  early medieval settlement 152, 257, 304–6
Morgannwg 41–2
Morgeneu, bishop of St Davids 321, 407
mortuary enclosures, square-ditched 280–1,
    304–7, 332, 353, 382–5
Mote of Mark, hillfort 233

mother churches 269–70, 315–18, 320–1, 323, 325, 340–1, 344–7, 423–4
   portionary status 287
moulds, *see* metalworking
mountains (of Wales), *see* landscape (of Wales)
Much Wenlock, monastery 346–7, 369
multiple estates 12–13, 188
Muriau Gwyddelod, fields 184–5
music 248, 361
Mynydd Carn, battle 376

Narberth, St Owen's well, inscribed stone 284
Nash-Williams, V. E. 9, 14–15
National Museum of Wales 7–9, 17–18
Neath (*Nidum*), Roman fort 80–1
Nefyn, church, burial 281–2
Nendrum, monastic site, Co. Down 325
   inscribed stones 120–1
   sculpture 4–5, 276–8
   see also Brynach, St
Nevern, ecclesiastical site 263–4, 320–1, 324–5, 352, 384–5
   associated landscape 340
New Pieces, settlement 20, 94–5, 142–4, 252–4
Newport, Mons., church 352
Newton, Llanstadwell, corn-dryers 169
   quernstone 201–2
Newton Moor, penannular brooch 44–6, 235, 242–4
Nobis, 'archbishop' of St Davids 314
Non, St 350–1
Norman invasion 29–30, 401–2, 412, 425–7
Notitia Dignitatum 21, 66–7, 97–9
nuts 213, 215

Octapitae 42
Offa, king of Mercia 55–6, 254–6, 380–1, 387–8, 392–3, 395
Offa's Dyke 3–4, 8–9, 19–20, 254–6, 265, 346–7, 375, 377–8, 386–98, 412–14, 421, 426–7
   see also Dudston
ogham 4, 6–7, 20–3, 80–1, 99–100, 114–21, 123–7, 132, 158, 276–7, 298–9, 301–2, 326–7, 346, 417
Old Oswestry hillfort 391–2
Old Testament names 294, 321–2
Oldbury Flats, Aust, Glos., fish-trap 210–11

Ordinance concerning the Dunsæte 29, 205–8, 261, 396–7
Ordovices 42–3, 91–2, 126, 128–9
origin tales 131–3
osteoarchaeology 54–5, 213, 216–17, 316–18, 332, 365–6, 376–7, 412
Oswald of Northumbria 29, 391–2
Owen, George (of Henllys) 4–5

Padarn, St 30, 58, 352
palaeopathology 19
Pant, Llŷn, settlement 161–3, 230
Pant-y-Saer, hut-group 10–12, 162, 165
   penannular brooch 242–3
Pant-yr-Eglwys, pennies 259–60, 262–3, 384, 403
Parc Cybi, Holyhead 61, 185–6
   corn-dryers 193–4, 198–200
   late Roman cemetery 281–2, 304
parchment 20
Parciau, hillfort 90–1
Partrishow (Merthyr Issau), *capel-y-bedd* 272–3, 287–8, 355–6
Parys Mountain, copper mining 89, 231
pastoral care 22–3, 299–300, 311–12, 323, 325, 337–8, 344–5, 364, 420–1, 423–4
Patrick, St 22, 130–1, 288–9, 299–300, 339–40, 351–2, 362–3
patron–client relationships 374–5, 378–9, 394–5
patronage 230, 233, 237–8, 250, 266–7, 277–8, 286–7, 299–300, 311–12, 315, 318–21, 323–5, 327–8, 330, 340, 343–5, 356–7, 364, 371–3, 405–6, 417, 420–5
   Hiberno-Scandinavian 329–30, 408
Pedeir Keinc y Mabinogi ('Four Branches of the Mabinogi') 32, 62, 382–4
Pembrey, cross-carved stone 276–7
Penally
   estates 190–2
   sculpture 277–8
penannular brooches, *see* brooches
Penbryn, inscribed stone 126, 128–9
Pencadair, battle 376
Penda, king of Mercia 129, 391–2
Penmachno, inscribed stones 22–3, 57, 280–1, 298–9

506 INDEX

Penmon, ecclesiastical site 272–3, 315, 320–1, 323–4, 401–2, 426
   holy well 284
   sculpture 207–10, 237, 277–8
   see also Ynys Seiriol
Pennant, Thomas 5–6
Pennant Melangell, hermitage site 270–1, 329–30, 354–6
Penmynydd, hearth 161–3
Penrice, coin hoard 260–1
Penrhosllugwy, inscribed stone 125–6
Pentre Farm, Pontarddulais, ironworking 230
Pentre Ffwrndan, Roman industrial settlement 66–7
Pen-y-Corddyn-Mawr, hillfort 295–6, 379–80
   see also Llys Awel votive offerings
Phillips, C. W. 10–12
Picts 13
pigs 206–7, 209–10, 214–16, 218, 246–7
pilgrim flasks, Egyptian 251–3, 361–2
pilgrimage 326–8, 361–4, 373
   to Rome 43–4
   see also St Davids
Pillar of Eliseg 5–6, 28, 55–6, 61, 380–2, 385, 392–3, 395, 423
pins, early medieval 110, 225–6, 230, 241–2, 244–5, 349, 365–6
   ringed 109–10, 148, 257–8, 333–5, 403–4, 408
Pistyll, font 403
Pitcarmick, byre house, Perthshire 172–3
place names 34, 130, 140, 205, 287–8, 318–19, 323–4, 327–8, 333, 335–40, 342, 346, 351–2, 379, 382–5, 387–8, 391–2, 394–6, 412
   Scandinavian 399–403, 405–11
plant remains 19, 49–51, 192–6, 367, 412
Plas Coch, Roman villa? 93–4
Plas Gogerddan, cemetery 304–5
ploughing 192
ploughs 186–7, 196–8, 219
plumbatae, see javelin heads
Point of Ayr 405, 410
pollen 19, 49–51, 184, 186–7, 193–4, 198–200, 203–4, 217–19, 222, 412, 416–19, 424, 426–7
population numbers 134–5, 205–6, 265–6, 418–19, 424
Port Talbot, inscribed stone 116–17

Portable Antiquities Scheme (PAS) 18, 72, 76–8, 221, 254–6, 395–7
Porth Clew, chapel and cemetery 281–3
Porth Dafarch, penannular brooch 103–4, 160–1
Porth-y-Rhaw, promontory fort 82–3
Portmahomack, monastery 325
   plough pebbles 196–8
Portskewett 211–12, 397–8
   artefacts 257–8
   Black Rock 69–70
   Hill, possible temple 291–2
   Sudbrook Road grave 308
pottery 122–3, 415–17
   Dyfed gravel-tempered 281–2
   early medieval imported Mediterranean and Continental 13–14, 17–18, 38, 67–8, 82–3, 90, 94–6, 111, 135–6, 142–3, 146–52, 167, 181–2, 215–16, 218, 248, 250–4, 263–4, 292–3, 315–18, 326–7
   lack of in Wales 135–6, 196
   Late Saxon 257
   Roman 67–8, 82–5, 88–9, 94–6, 98, 101–2, 113, 142–3, 146, 148, 150–1, 163–4, 292–3, 308, 379–80, 415
   Samian, recycled 85–6, 113–14
   shell-tempered 67–8, 71–4, 82–5, 89–91, 93–6, 102, 111, 160–1, 171
Poundbury, Dorset 302–3
Powys 22, 55–6, 380–1, 393, 396, 423
prayers for the soul 60, 316–18, 325–7, 369–73, 420–1
prehistoric monuments 60–1, 128–9, 133, 310–12, 415, 418, 421
   burial and ritual monuments reused 62, 115–16, 126, 230, 245, 278, 281, 304–8, 330, 338–40, 355, 363, 366, 380–4, 423
   settlement enclosures reused 282–3, 306–7, 333, 386
   standing stones 189, 341
   trackways 44
Presteigne 389–91
   church 271–2, 347–8
Prittlewell, burial 248
promontory forts, *see* hillforts
Psalter of Rhygyfarch 31, 57–8
Pumsaint, Roman fort 80–1, 101
purgatory 60, 364
   see also prayers for the soul

Quarrington, Lincs., settlement 172–3
quarrying 237, 271–2, 277–8, 327, 391
quartz 363
    pebbles 353–5, 367–8, 371–3
Quentovic 254–6
quernstones 164–5, 167–9, 174–5, 198,
    201–3, 237, 308–9

Radford, C. A. Ralegh 8–9, 13–15
radiocarbon dating 16, 18–19, 68, 137, 149,
    273–6, 278, 281–2, 412, 416–17,
    426–7
Ramsey Island (Ynys Dewi)
    hermitage 314, 328–9
    sundial 58
ransoms 376, 396–7, 401–2, 406–7, 409–10,
    422, 425
Raystown, Co. Meath 200–1
recycling 231–2, 234–5, 238–9, 266, 415–16
    of Roman artefacts/materials 67–8, 74–5,
        80, 89–91, 102–4, 111–14, 117, 224,
        228–30
relics 285, 320–1, 351–3, 355–62,
    409–10, 420
    cult of 130–1, 363–4, 373
    see also shrines
Rendlesham, Suffolk 386–7
Rhodri Mawr, king of Gwynedd 401
Rhos, early medieval kingdom 43
Rhoscrowther, bishop house 287, 342–3
Rhosyr, *llys* 184–5, 426
Rhuddgaer
    field-systems 186–9, 196–8, 204, 219
    lead coffin 99, 296–7, 303–4, 310–11
    settlement 139–40, 163–4, 168, 171–3,
        176, 178–81, 201, 265, 419–20
Rhuddlan (*Cledemutha*) 38, 137, 152, 158–9,
    180, 256–7, 262–4, 267–8, 287, 346–7,
    375, 378–9, 394–5, 422, 424–6
    artefacts 224–5, 247–8, 257, 260–1, 405–6
    buildings 168, 175
    craftworking 225–6, 238
    field boundary 187
    plant remains 195–6
Rhufoniog, early medieval kingdom 43, 392–3
Rhwng Gwy a Hafren 43
Rhydwhyman, ford across the Severn 41, 396
Rhygyfarch ap Sulien of Llanbadarn Fawr 30–2
    see also David, St, Rhygyfarch's *Life of*
Rhys, John 6–7

rings, finger 236, 394–5
ritual deposition 290–4
rivers (of Wales), *see* landscape
    see also Dee, River
    see also Severn, River
Roman
    calendars 56–7, 415
    identity 114, 116–17, 120, 122–3, 127–9,
        215–16, 290, 417
    military 97–8
    roads 44, 116–17, 128–9, 306, 310
    see also beads, belt fittings, bracelets, brooches,
        coins, inscriptions, pottery, recycling
Roman Britain
    chronology of the end of 66–9, 426–7
    forts 111–12
    industrial settlements 93–4
    towns 93–4, 111–12
Roman Wales, later 10, 64, 70, 415–17
    craftworking and industry 61, 234–5
    economy 72–4, 78–9, 84, 91–2, 95–6,
        103–4, 184, 193–4, 205–6, 217–18,
        266, 416–17
    forts 71–2, 80–1, 84–9, 91–2, 97–8, 106–9,
        293–4
    inscriptions 117–20
    milestones 116–17
    military control of 69–71, 84–5, 91
    rural settlements 76–80, 82–4, 88–91, 94–6,
        101–2, 160–1
    towns 72–6, 80–2, 93, 97, 100–1, 111–12,
        124–5, 293, 295–6
    villas 76–80, 83–4, 93–4, 101–2, 111–12,
        179–80, 206–7, 316–18
    watchtowers 87–8, 97–8
    see also cemeteries, coins, farming,
        metalworking, mineral extraction,
        pottery
Romanesque architecture 271–3, 320–1,
    332–3, 355, 426
Romanization 69, 76–8, 84–5
Rome 297–8, 350–1, 356–7, 361–2
Rossett, Roman villa 93–4
Rotherwas, enclosed settlement 170–1
roundhouses, *see* buildings
Rowe Ditch 390, 393–4
Royal Commission on the Ancient and
    Historical Monuments of Wales 7–9
royal inauguration 380–2, 423
runes 28, 395

508 INDEX

saints' cults 344–5, 350–64, 420–1, 423–4
   see also burial of saints
salt trade 254–6, 398, 421
Samson of Dol, St 350–1
   Life of 22, 62, 110, 286–7, 314, 319–20,
      326, 346, 362–3
sanctuary (*noddfa*, *refugium*) 324, 420–1
Sarn-y-bryn-caled, corn-dryers 198–200
Savory, H. N. 13–14
Scandinavia 414
   contacts with 38, 398–9
   see also Hiberno-Scandinavians, Vikings
Scandinavian mythology 382, 405–6
sceattas, *see* coins
Scone, Perthsire, royal inauguration site 381–2
Scotland 414
   early medieval 13–14, 424–5
      caves 309–10
      Christian contacts 273–6
      economy 267–8
      hillforts 10–12
      other settlements 172–3
      relics 356
sculpture, stone 6–9, 16–17, 19–20, 28, 55–6,
      107–9, 237, 246, 269, 273–8, 284, 287,
      318–19, 321–2, 324–7, 329–30, 332–3,
      339–47, 351–2, 362–3, 365, 369–73,
      396–7, 399, 403–6, 408–9, 411,
      420–1, 423–4
   see also cross-carved stones, crosses, fonts,
      inscribed stones
seaweed 196, 213
senses 361, 373
settlements
   early medieval 16, 136, 412, 414–15,
      419–20, 424–7
      coastal 167
      in written sources 137
      problems with identification 134–42
   later medieval 139
   later prehistoric 138–9, 160, 179–80
   see also farmsteads, hillforts, hut groups,
      Roman rural settlements
Severn, River 24–5, 40–1, 60, 69–72, 210–12,
      220, 256–7, 265, 291–2, 315–16, 323,
      326, 389, 393, 397–9, 406–7, 424–5
shale artefacts 236, 238, 244–5
Shavington salt-pan 295–6

sheep (and goats) 207, 214, 223–5, 254
shields 246–7
ships, *see* boats, Vikings
short dykes 9, 390, 393–4, 398
Shrewsbury 257, 425–6
shrines 223, 234, 355–6
   see also relics
shrouds 223–4, 279–80, 303–4, 332, 365–6,
      371–3
Sihtric Anlafsson ('Silkenbeard'), king of
      Dublin 259–60, 262–3, 398–9
Silchester, ogham stone 124–5
Silian, ecclesiastical site 284
silk 223–4, 239–41
Silures 41–2, 72–4
silver bullion 8–9, 154, 221–2, 233–4,
      258–62, 265, 267–8, 318–19, 325, 399,
      402–7, 420, 424–5
silver hoards, late Roman 98–9
Silverdale, hoard 258–9
slaves 25, 192, 254, 256–7, 261, 266, 361–2,
      375–6, 409–10, 412–13, 419–20
Smalls Reef 38
South Cadbury, hillfort 150–1, 174
South Hook, settlement 135–6, 139–41,
      167–9, 171–5, 178–81, 419–20, 424
   cereals 194–5, 198–201, 203
   corn-dryers 196
   flax 195–6
   ironworking 228–30, 238, 267–8, 425
   plough pebbles 196–8
   stone artefacts 201–2, 236–7
Southampton (*Hamwic*) 254–6
spindle whorls 85–6, 113–14, 225–6, 238–9
   see also textile production
Spittal, inscribed stone 54–5
St Albans (*Verulamium*) 294
St Arvans, ecclesiastical site 324, 370–1
   metalwork 285–6, 349
St Asaph (Llanelwy) 314
St Chad Gospels, *see* Lichfield Gospels
St Davids 30, 44–6, 52–3, 219, 286–7,
      314–15, 321–2, 344–5, 407–10,
      423–4
   ecclesiastical landscape associated with
      339–40, 423–4
   increasing influence of 342–4
   inscribed stone near 298–9

pilgrimage to 2–3, 44, 230, 263–4, 325,
    361–3, 367–8, 421
scriptorium 23–4
sculpture 28, 276–7, 324–5
St Non's Chapel 5–6, 58–60
see also *Armes Prydein Fawr* (The Great
    Prophecy of Britain'), Asser,
    Ramsey Island (Ynys Dewi),
    St Patrick's Chapel
St Dogmaels
    inscribed stone 55, 124–5
    raid on 407
St Dogwells, inscribed stone 127
St Edrins, carved stones 342–3
St Harmon, staff of St Curig 359–60
St Ismaels
    bishop house 287, 342–3
    Great Castle Head, Longoar Bay,
        cemetery 273–6, 333–5
St Issels, bishop house 342–3
St Lawrence, sculpture 342–3
St Manchan's Shrine 357–8
St Martin's Haven, cross-carved
    stone 2–3, 362–3
St Mary Hill, stirrups 409
St Molaise's cave, Arran 327–8
St Nicholas, inscribed stone 124–5
St Patrick's Chapel, Traeth Mawr 17, 20, 80–1,
    217, 270–1, 288–9, 333–5, 337, 362–3,
    365–9, 371–3, 421
    artefacts 236, 248–9, 257–8, 263–4,
        285–6
    craftworking 230, 235–6, 256–7
    sculpture 273–6, 280–1
Stafford, *burh*
    cereals 195
    Stafford-type ware pottery 257
Staffordshire, hoard 245
Steepholm Island 406–7
Steynton, plant remains 195–6
Stigand, archbishop of Canterbury 210–11
Strata Florida 33
styli 20
Sulien of Llanbadarn Fawr, bishop of
    St Davids 30, 315, 325, 407
sundials 58–9
Sutton Hoo 247–8
Swansea 408

swords 226–7, 239
    fittings 38, 152–4
    see also weapons

Tai Cochion, Llanidan, Roman settlement 80–1,
    86–7, 99, 198
Talacre (Tan Lan), Viking burial 212–13,
    405, 408
Taliesin 24–5
Tallaght 314
    Martyrology of 318–19, 361–2
Tandderwen, cemetery 17–18, 280–1,
    305–6, 382–4
Tara, Co. Meath 382–4
Tatheus, St 110
    Life of 10
Taxation of Pope Nicholas IV 287
Tegeingl 43, 158–9, 237, 256–7, 346–7, 382,
    386, 394–5, 403–6, 425–6
Teilo, St 286–7, 343–4
    see also Lichfield Gospels, Llandeilo Fawr
Teltown, Co. Meath 384–5
Tenby 243–4
    Byzantine coins 252, 263
    Castle Hill 27–8, 137, 144, 149–50
Tewdwr ab Elise, king of Brycheiniog 157, 379
textile production 183, 223–5, 236–41, 249,
    415–16, 422–3
Thomas, Charles 14–15
Thornwell Farm, settlement 77–9, 102
Tidenham, Glos. 210–11
time, concepts of and ways of
    calculating 53–63, 414–15, 420–1
Tintagel, promontory fort, Cornwall 13–14,
    20, 148, 181–2, 251–4, 263
Tomen-y-Mur, Roman fort 62, 128–9, 306
    inscribed stone 116–17
Torksey, Viking winter camp 233–4
towns, later medieval in Wales 265
trade 215–16, 219, 235–6, 241–2, 244–5,
    250–67, 315–16, 397–8, 407–8,
    410–11, 414–15, 420–2, 424–5
    see also Dublin–Chester trade route
trading settlements 399
Traeth Coch (Benllech), Viking burial 340,
    408–9
Trahaearn ap Caradog, king of Gwynedd 376
transhumance 184–5, 204–5, 220, 424

510 INDEX

Trawsfynydd, inscribed stone 58–60, 298–9
Trearddur Bay
    penannular brooches 243–4
    see also Tywyn-y-Capel
trees, holy 285
tref ('dwelling, farmstead, hamlet, estate')
    180–2, 188–9, 192, 219, 266–7, 419–20
Treflys, inscribed stone 298–9
Trefollwyn, cemetery and inscribed stone 306
Trefwyddog, estate 194–5, 341
Tre'r Ceiri, hillfort 62, 91, 102–3, 291–2
Trethurgy, Cornwall, enclosed settlement 181–2
tribal society 114, 126–7, 374
tribute 183, 220, 261–2, 267–8, 397–8,
    402–3, 411, 422, 425
Troedyrhiw, enclosed farmstead 83
Twlc Point, sand-dune settlement 167
Tŷ Illtud, Neolithic chambered tomb 62
Tŷ Mawr, Holyhead
    cemetery 17, 279–80
    fields 185–6
    settlement 161–2, 173
Tywyn, mother church 320–1, 426
    cross-carved inscribed stone 20–1, 28,
        370–3
    sundial
Tywyn-y-Capel (Capel St Ffraid), cemetery 17,
    217, 244–5, 270–1, 279–80, 332,
    363, 365–8

Uley, Somerset 291–2
Urban, bishop of Llandaf 25, 30–2, 352
Urnes-style 38, 357–8
Usk (*Burrium*), Roman settlement 76–8

vegetables 195–6, 215–16
'Very Coarse Pottery', *see* briquetage
Viking
    burials 212–13, 246–9, 402–3, 405, 408–9
    impact on Wales 385, 400–6, 422
    raids 286–7, 318–21, 323, 356–7, 361–2,
        375–6, 425–7
    settlement 256–7, 261, 263–4, 276–7,
        346–7, 382, 386
    ships 38
    see also Hiberno-Scandinavian, silver bullion
Vikings 35–7
villas, Roman 76–8, 80, 83–4, 93–4, 101–2,
    105–6, 111–12, 206–7, 415

violence 219–20, 261–2, 267–8, 374–7,
    396–7, 425
    see also Irish raids on Wales, Viking impact on
        Wales, Viking raids, warfare
Vortigern, sub-Roman ruler 55–6
Vortipor, ruler of the Demetae 21–2, 104,
    127, 131–2

war bands 230, 378–80, 415–17
Wareham 254–6
warfare 207–8, 245–8, 392–5, 421–2
    see also violence
Wat's Dyke 8–9, 254–6, 265, 346–7, 375–8,
    386–7, 391–6, 398, 412–14,
    421, 426–7
Water Newton (*Durobrivae*), hoard 295–6
Waterford 256–7
weapons 245–8
    see also swords
weights, lead 154, 258–9, 408–9
Wellington Quarry, horizontal watermill 202–3
Welsh
    language 20–1, 25–8, 117, 370–3, 399–400
    legal writing 12–13, 25, 32–3, 184–5,
        187–8, 262–3, 287, 324, 380–1
    poetry 24–5, 27–8, 30, 52–3, 359–60,
        422–3
Welsh March(es) 4–5, 387, 398
Wem, hacksilver hoard 231–2
Wentlooge Level, *see* Gwent Levels
Wessex, expansion of 397–8
West Angle Bay, cemetery and settlement 141,
    193–4, 217, 367–8
Weston under Penyard (*Ariconium*) 38–40, 101
Westwood. J. O. 6–7
Wheeler, Mortimer 7–8, 10, 72, 84–5
Wheeler, Tessa 10
whetstones 236–7, 244–5
Whitford, cross, see *Maen Achwyfan*
Whitford, dyke 389
Whithorn
    monastery, plough pebbles 196–8
    St Ninian's cave 327–8
Whitland 380
Whitley Grange, Roman villa 94, 101–2
Whitton, Roman villa 77–8
Wirral, Hiberno-Scandinavian settlements
    346–7, 394–5, 401, 403–6, 410
    see also Irby, Meols

INDEX 511

Wiston, Roman fort 80–1
women 54–5, 201–2, 205–6, 214, 224, 238–9,
        244–5, 249, 300–1, 330, 350–1,
        365–71, 376, 412, 426–7
wooden trackways 44–6
Woodstown, Viking settlement 233–4
woodworking 183, 223, 237–8, 415–16
Worcester, diocese of 346–7
written sources 20–34, 286–7, 412
writing tablets 20
Wroxeter (*Viroconium*) 43, 65, 91–4, 206–7,
        293–5, 346–7
  cross-shaft 396
  inscribed stone 93, 99–100, 115–16,
        123–4

Wylfa Newydd
  cemeteries 306–7
  shell midden 212

Yeavering, Northumberland 386–7
Ynys Enlli, *see* Bardsey Island
Ynys Ettws, settlement 139
Ynys Seiriol (Priestholm, Puffin Island, Ynys
        Lannog), hermitage 8–9, 35–7, 129,
        314, 329
York 224–5
Ystradfellte, inscribed stone 44–5
Ystrad Tywi, kingdom of 42, 343–4

Zosimus 66–7